INTERNATIONAL SALES

CW00499416

Written for international trade lawyers, practitioners and students from common and civil law countries, this casebook is an excellent starting point for learning about the CISG, providing an article-by-article analysis of the Convention. The commentary on each article is accompanied by extracts from cases and associated comparative materials, as well as references to important trade usages such as the INCOTERMS® 2010. The book features a selection of the most significant cases, each of which has been abridged to enable the reader to focus on its essential features and the relevant questions arising from it. The case extracts are accompanied by a comprehensive overview of parallel provisions in other international instruments, uniform projects and domestic laws.

The analyses, cases, texts and questions are intended to aid readers in their comparative law and international sales law studies. They are designed to draw attention to the particular issues surrounding specific CISG provisions and to provoke careful consideration of possible solutions.

The book is a reference work as well as an introduction to the individual problem areas. In particular, it acts as a preparatory work for the Willem C Vis International Commercial Arbitration Moot. The inclusion of sample questions and answers also makes it particularly helpful for self-study purposes.

International Sales Law

Second Edition

Ingeborg Schwenzer
Christiana Fountoulakis
Mariel Dimsey

·HART·
PUBLISHING
OXFORD AND PORTLAND, OREGON
2012

Published in the United Kingdom by Hart Publishing Ltd
16C Worcester Place, Oxford, OX1 2JW
Telephone: +44 (0)1865 517530
Fax: +44 (0)1865 510710
E-mail: mail@hartpub.co.uk
Website: http://www.hartpub.co.uk

Published in North America (US and Canada) by
Hart Publishing
c/o International Specialized Book Services
920 NE 58th Avenue, Suite 300
Portland, OR 97213-3786
USA
Tel: +1 503 287 3093 or toll-free: (1) 800 944 6190
Fax: +1 503 280 8832
E-mail: orders@isbs.com
Website: http://www.isbs.com

British Library Cataloguing in Publication Data
Data Available

ISBN: 978-1-84946-302-7

Typeset by Compuscript Ltd, Shannon
Printed and bound in Great Britain by
TJ International Ltd, Padstow, Cornwall

Preface

Casebooks have a long tradition as a teaching instrument in law school classes in common law countries and provide cases and other materials on specific topics, which are used by students to guide them through the course in question.

With the CISG itself gaining increasing importance, not only in law faculties, but also in practice amongst young lawyers, a casebook on this very dynamic area of the law has become imperative. The CISG's growing importance is in large part due to the Willem C Vis International Commercial Arbitration Moot Competition, which takes place in the week before Easter every year in Vienna. The Moot presents law students from all around the world with a CISG problem, on the basis of which they formulate a Claimant's and Respondent's Memorandum, respectively, and then present their oral arguments in the final stage of the competition in Vienna. Now in its twentieth year, the Moot has truly gained the significance of a global event, with participants in 2012 numbering 280 universities from 67 countries, and bringing together over 700 of the world's top legal practitioners to adjudicate the students' performances. Its sister moot, the Willem C Vis (East) International Commercial Arbitration Moot, held in Hong Kong, is now in its tenth year and following in the illustrious footsteps of the Vienna Moot. These rapid developments have made the absence of concise learning materials in this area of law all the more apparent.

The CISG, like most other areas of the law, is characterised by an ever-increasing abundance of case law interpreting and discussing its provisions. However, unlike most other areas of the law, this case law has its roots in not one, but several jurisdictions from around the world, both domestic and international. It is thus especially important in this unique area of law that a casebook serves as a 'selection process', whereby those cases of particular interest and significance to the development of international sales law are emphasised and their legal reasoning discussed. It is not only impractical, but also inefficient and laborious to discuss every case ever decided under the CISG. This casebook has chosen a selection of what we consider to be the most significant and relevant cases for inclusion in this book, which have been considerably abridged for the purpose of concentrating on their significance to the particular article at hand. Consequently, a number of cases appear in several places in the book, with only the relevant part of the judgment being included each time. The cases are accompanied by a comprehensive overview of parallel provisions in domestic, regional and other international legal instruments, including the German, French, Austrian, Swiss, and Italian Civil Codes, the Contract Law of the People's Republic of China, the English Sale of Goods Act, the US Uniform Commercial Code and the regional and international law efforts in the form of the 2010 UNIDROIT Principles on International Commercial Contracts, with the consequence that the reader obtains a true comparative perspective on the CISG's place in international legal development. Additionally, the relevant INCOTERMS®[1] 2010 rules are included as reference to relevant trade usages.

This casebook is designed not only for classes on international sales law and comparative law, but also for private study, and is aimed at students from all over the world, not only from common law, but also from civil law countries. It intends to provide a 'reader' which will help students acquire knowledge of the CISG. The cases, texts and questions are intended to aid students in their comparative law and international sales law studies, and are designed to draw attention to the particular issues surrounding specific CISG provisions and to provoke careful consideration from the students of possible solutions. The answers to the sample questions at the end of the book are meant to spur further reflection rather than to suggest definite solutions. In addition to this book's function as a didactical aid, it is also intended as a reference work for leading cases and an introduction into the individual problem areas. In particular, it is also designed as a preparatory and complementary work for the Willem C Vis International Commercial Arbitration Moot.

In general, students are provided with an article-by-article analysis of the CISG. Under each article, cases, associated materials and comparative provisions are included, which are intended to be read before class in order to facilitate in-class discussion on the basis of the questions included in each chapter. Inherent in such a comparative law analysis is the need for translation of foreign provisions. We have indicated in the relevant places where the translation comes from; as you will see, we have often translated the provisions ourselves. As such, these are not 'official' translations, but are merely intended to aid the reader in the ensuing comparison and discussion on the relevant area.

In the same way, many cases have been taken from the website of Pace Law School's CISG Database, which features the Queen Mary Case Translation Programme, a project involving the collection and translation of case law from all over the world. Where so indicated, the cases have been taken from the website without alteration or amendment and, again, are not to be regarded as 'official' translations, but merely aids to understanding.

The CISG-online website, www.cisg-online.ch, should also be mentioned here. This website contains the most concise collection of CISG cases available anywhere, and is administered by Professor Dr Ingeborg Schwenzer, one of the co-authors of this book. This website proved invaluable in the compilation of the cases for this book, and we have included for the reader's ease of reference the CISG-online number in the case heading, to the extent that one was available.

With respect to the cases themselves, with only very few exceptions, the reader will find the facts of the case available in the first instance that the case is referred to. This is indicated in the Table of Cases by bold type. Where no facts have been provided, this was owing to their irrelevance for the law and to space restrictions.

We would like to thank Mareike Schmidt and Bastian Bubel, as well as Adrien Gabellon, Michelle Seiler, Lina Ali and David Tebel for their help in preparing this

---

[1] 'Incoterms®' is a trademark of the International Chamber of Commerce.

book. Not only did they update the book and the various indices, but also assisted in the final stage of editing by correcting texts, compiling the Contents, and ensuring uniformity of reference throughout the book.

We are confident that this casebook will satisfy the current demand for a book of its kind and will make a valuable contribution to the ever-growing jurisprudence of international sales and comparative law. We invite, and indeed welcome, any comments, criticism, and questions to be sent to the authors, Ingeborg Schwenzer, Christiana Fountoulakis and Mariel Dimsey, at their email addresses:

ingeborg.schwenzer@unibas.ch   Ingeborg Schwenzer
christiana.fountoulakis@unifr.ch   Christiana Fountoulakis
mariel.dimsey@web.de   Mariel Dimsey
October 2012

Contents

List of Abbreviations

§/§§	paragraph or section/paragraphs or sections
A *Art-No*	abstract (eg A 1-1)
ABGB	*Allgemeines Bürgerliches Gesetzbuch* (Austrian Civil Code)
AGBG	*Gesetz zur Regelung des Rechts der Allgemeinen Geschäftsbedingungen* (former German Law on the Regulation of General Terms and Conditions)
AG	*Amtsgericht* (German court of first instance)
AR	Arkansas
Art/Arts	article/articles
BezG	*Bezirksgericht* (Swiss District Court)
BGB	*Bürgerliches Gesetzbuch* (German Civil Code)
BGer	*Schweizerisches Bundesgericht* (Swiss Federal Supreme Court)
BGH	*Deutscher Bundesgerichtshof* (German Federal Supreme Court)
Brussels Convention (1968)	Convention of 27 September 1968 on jurisdiction and the enforcement of judgments in civil and commercial matters
Brussels Regulation (2001)	European Council Regulation (EC) No 44/2001 of 22 December 2000 on jurisdiction and the recognition and enforcement of judgments in civil and commercial matters
BW	*Burgerlijk Wetboek* (Dutch Civil Code)
C *Art-No*	case (eg C 1-1)
CA	California
CA	*Cour d'Appel* (French Court of Appeal)/*Corte d'Appello* (Italian Court of Appeal)
CC	*Code Civil* (French Civil Code)
CCI	Chamber of Commerce and Industry
cf	*confer* (compare)
CFR	Cost and Freight (INCOTERMS® 2010)
Ch D	Law Reports, Chancery Division
CIETAC	China International Economic and Trade Arbitration Commission
CIF	Cost Insurance and Freight (INCOTERMS® 2010)
CIM	Uniform Rules Concerning the Contract for International Carriage of Goods by Rail
CIP	Carriage and Insurance Paid To (INCOTERMS® 2010)
Cir	Circuit (US Court of Appeals)
CISG	United Nations Convention on Contracts for the International Sale of Goods
CISG-AC	CISG Advisory Council
CISG-online	Database, includes all relevant CISG case law, the official Secretariat's Commentary and CISG-related legal texts, www.cisg-online.ch
CISG Pace	Database, CISG Pace Law School, www.cisg.law.pace.edu/
Cl	Clause (INCOTERMS® 2010)
CLOUT	Case Law on UNCITRAL Texts (www.uncitral.org/uncitral/en/case_law.html)

CMR	Convention on the Contract for the International Carriage of Goods by Road
Codice Civile	Italian Civil Code
Col	Colorado
CPT	Carriage Paid To (INCOTERMS® 2010)
Ct App	Court of Appeals (USA)
DAT	Delivered At Terminal (INCOTERMS® 2010)
DDP	Delivery Duty Paid (INCOTERMS® 2010)
Del	Delaware
Dist Ct	District Court
Div	Division (US District Courts)
DM	Deutsche Mark (former official currency of Germany)
EC	European Community
eg	*exempli gratia* (for example)
ED	Eastern District (US District Courts)
EGBGB	*Einführungsgesetz zum Bürgerlichen Gesetzbuch* (Introductory Act to the German *BGB*)
EU	European Union
ER	English Reports
et al	*et alii* (and others)
et seq	*et sequens* (and the following)
EXW	Ex Works (INCOTERMS® 2010)
FAS	Free Alongside Ship (INCOTERMS® 2010)
FF	French francs (former official currency of France)
FL	Florida
FOB	Free on Board (INCOTERMS® 2010)
Hfl	Dutch florin (former official currency of the Netherlands)
HGB	*Handelsgesetzbuch* (German Commercial Code)
HGer	*Handelsgericht* (Swiss Commercial Court)
HR	*Hoge Raad der Nederlanden* (Dutch Supreme Court)
ie	*id est* (that is)
ICC	International Chamber of Commerce
ICC eTerms 2004	ICC Terms for Electronic Contracting, 2004 version
IL	Illinois
Int Ct Russian CCI	Tribunal of International Commercial Arbitration at the Russian Federation Chamber of Commerce and Industry
INCOTERMS® 2010	ICC Rules for the Use of Domestic and International Trade Terms, 2010 version
IPRG	*Bundesgesetz über das Internationale Privatrecht* (Swiss Private International Law Act)
KG	*Kantonsgericht* (Swiss Cantonal Court)
LA	Louisiana
LG	*Landgericht* (German Regional Court)
MA	Massachusetts
MD	Middle District
MI	Michigan
Minn	Minnesota
NB	*nota bene*
ND	Northern District (US District Courts)
No	number
NY	New York

OGH	*Oberster Gerichtshof* (Austrian Federal Supreme Court)
OHADA	*Organisation pour l'Harmonisation du Droit des Affaires en Afrique* (Organization for the Harmonisation of Commercial Law in Africa)
OLG	*Oberlandesgericht* (Austrian/German Higher Regional Court)
OR	*Obligationenrecht* (Swiss Code of Obligations)
p/pp	page/pages
PA	Pennsylvania
para/paras	paragraph/paragraphs (text)
PECL	Principles of European Contract Law
PICC 2010	UNIDROIT Principles of International Commercial Contracts, 2010 version
PRC	People's Republic of China
PRC CL	Contract Law of the People's Republic of China
Q *Art-No*	question (eg Q 1-1)
QB	Law Reports, Queen's Bench Division (England)
RMB	Renminbi (official currency of the People's Republic of China)
sA	Austrian schilling (former official currency of Austria)
sec	section
Sf	Swiss franc (official currency of Switzerland)
SD	Southern District (US District Courts)
SGA	Sale of Goods Act 1979 (England)
subs	subsection
Sup Ct	Superior Court
UCC	Uniform Commercial Code (USA)
UCP 600	ICC Uniform Customs and Practice for Documentary Credits (1 July 2007)
UGB	*Unternehmensgesetzbuch* (Austrian Corporate Code)
ULF	Convention relating to a Uniform Law on the Formation of Contracts for the International Sale of Goods (1964)
ULIS	Convention relating to a Uniform Law on the International Sale of Goods
UN	United Nations
UNCITRAL	United Nations Commission on International Trade Law
UNIDROIT	International Institute for the Unification of Private Law
UNILEX	Database of international case law and bibliography on the UNIDROIT Principles of International Commercial Contracts and on the United Nations Convention on Contracts for the International Sale of Goods (CISG), www.unilex.info/
US/USA	United States of America
v	versus
WD	Western District (US District Courts)
ZGB	*Zivilgesetzbuch* (Swiss Civil Code)
ZGer	*Zivilgericht* (Swiss first instance civil court)
ZPO	*Zivilprozessordnung* (Austrian, German or Swiss Code of Civil Procedure)

Table of Cases

Arbitral Tribunals					
Ad hoc Tribunal, Florence		19 April 1994	CISG-online 124	C 6-1	40, 648
American Arbitration Association	Macromex Srl v Globex International Inc	23 October 2007	CISG-online 1645	C 79-2	586–9, 764
Arbitration Court of the Chamber of Commerce and Industry of Budapest (Hungary)		05 December 1995	CISG-online 163	C 3-1	24, 644
Arbitration Court of the Chamber of Commerce and Industry of Budapest (Hungary)		10 December 1996	CISG-online 774	C 66-1	484–5, 737–8
CIETAC		31 July 1997	CISG-online 1072	C 9-1	71–2, 657
CIETAC		27 December 2002	CISG-online 2205	C 71-2	510–12, 743–4
CIETAC		01 January 2007	CISG-online 1974	C 53-1	419–22, 722
Foreign Trade Court of Arbitration at Serbian Chamber of Commerce		23 January 2008	CISG-online 1946	C 78-3	577–8
Hamburg Chamber of Commerce (Germany)	Partial Award	21 March 1996	CISG-online 187	C 79-6	598–9, 766
ICC International Court of Arbitration			Award No 8574; UNILEX	C 75-1	552, 755
ICC International Court of Arbitration			Award No 8740 = CISG-online 1294	C 76-2	560–2
ICC International Court of Arbitration			Award No 8611 = CISG-online 236	C 7-2	49

xxxii   TABLE OF CASES

Introduction

The United Nations Convention on Contracts for the International Sale of Goods, the CISG, has attained the status of a 'world sales law' and is one of the most successful creations of UNCITRAL (United Nations Commission on International Trade Law).

Efforts to unify international sales law began as early as the 1920s, with Ernst Rabel usually being credited with making the first suggestion regarding a potential unification of the law relating to the international sale of goods. These initial attempts were ultimately followed by the Hague conventions on the sale of goods, ULIS and ULF, which were drafted at the Hague Conference in 1964. Although these conventions did not achieve the aim of creating a global unification of international sales law, they paved the way for the CISG, the 'new' uniform sales law drawn up by UNCITRAL.

The CISG is divided into four parts: Part I sets out the rules on its sphere of application and general provisions; Part II deals with the formation of contract; Part III covers the rights and obligations of the parties; and Part IV deals with the public international law provisions. Article 92(1), which allows a Contracting State to implement the Convention without Part II or Part III shows the CISG's flexible approach and its suitability as a global sales convention. A salient feature of the CISG is its 'horizontal' structure, whereby remedies are not 'connected' with particular breaches, but rather with the party entitled to them. In this way, the seller's obligations are followed by the buyer's remedies, and the buyer's obligations are followed by the corresponding remedies of the seller. Indeed, no reference is made to different kinds of breaches, but instead to an all-encompassing notion of 'breach of contract', with the availability of specific remedies dependent on the (further) conduct of the parties and on the circumstances of the individual case.

As an international sales law, uniformity of application lies at the core of the CISG's objectives. Whilst uniform interpretation and application of the CISG is increasing, the number of Contracting States and the volume of case law, as evidenced by this book, highlight the difficulties of reaching international consensus. Concepts such as 'reasonable' undoubtedly give rise to a wide scope of interpretation, which can result in legal uncertainty and inconsistent decisions. Indeed, on particular issues, as is seen by Article 28, international compromise went so far as to reject uniformity, in order to avoid the CISG failing altogether.

The CISG has met with resounding acceptance around the globe. Today, the CISG counts 78 Contracting States among its members, covering more than 80 per cent of global trade and production of goods; nine of the ten leading exporters and importers in world merchandise are Contracting States to the CISG. Of those large industrial nations that are not yet Contracting States to the CISG, notably the UK, both internal and external pressure to ratify is rising.

Until today, courts from 46 jurisdictions and arbitral tribunals have rendered an approximate total of 2,500 decisions involving the CISG, and more than 9,000 academic publications exist in 33 languages. This is in addition to the numerous conferences and other forms of academic discourse dealing with the Convention, most notably the CISG Advisory Council, a global body of CISG and international sales law experts that meets on a regular basis to discuss the significant developments in the field of international sales law and aims at promoting the uniform interpretation of the CISG.

Perhaps the most tangible success of the CISG can be seen in the number of domestic sales laws that have used it as a model. Notably, many Scandinavian countries have used the CISG as the background for the modification of their domestic sales laws, as did Germany in its 2002 *Schuldrechtsreform* (Revision of the Law of Obligations), and the Netherlands in drafting the Law of Obligations in their *Wetboek* (Civil Code). Furthermore, many of the former socialist states in Eastern Europe, including Estonia, the Czech Republic and Croatia, are also basing the redevelopment of their private and domestic sales and commercial laws on CISG concepts. Completing the CISG's global impact is the reform of the Chinese private law. The New Contract Law of the People's Republic of China has adopted many of the legal concepts and institutions promulgated in the CISG and the drafters have acknowledged their use of the CISG as a source of inspiration in this regard.

In addition, the drafting of not only domestic sales laws, but also, increasingly, regional and international principles are guided by CISG principles. The general approach of the Principles for International Commercial Contracts drafted by UNIDROIT (the PICC) and the Principles of European Contract Law, which are intended to pave the way for a European or international law of contract, can be traced back to the CISG. The same is true of the European Directive on Consumer Sales, which mirrors the concepts of conformity and non-conformity set out in the CISG. Furthermore, the OHADA, a union of 16 African states, has adopted a common sales law which follows the CISG almost to the letter.

Efforts at unification of the law are often met with the criticism that the unique peculiarities and historical variety of local laws are 'bulldozed' by an all-consuming 'international' law. This is not the intention of the CISG. It aims to provide a certain, uniform and consistent basis for defining the scope and obligations of international sales contracts for those states that have declared their intention to be bound by it. Moreover, the CISG serves as a stimulus for the development, revision and interpretation of domestic laws under consideration and in awareness of genuine international concepts, which can only be of benefit to the states concerned.

Article 1 CISG

(1) This Convention applies to contracts of sale of goods between parties whose places of business are in different States:
  (a) when the States are Contracting States; or
  (b) when the rules of private international law lead to the application of the law of a Contracting State.
(2) The fact that the parties have their places of business in different States is to be disregarded whenever this fact does not appear either from the contract or from any dealings between, or from information disclosed by, the parties at any time before or at the conclusion of the contract.
(3) Neither the nationality of the parties nor the civil or commercial character of the parties or of the contract is to be taken into consideration in determining the application of this Convention.

I. Overview

Article 1 CISG defines the sphere of application of the Convention. It is a unilateral conflict of laws rule stating that the CISG applies if either the parties to a sales contract have their places of business in different Contracting States (Art 1(1)(a)) and the parties were aware of that at the time of conclusion of the contract (Art 1(2)); or if the rules of private international law of the forum lead to the application of the law of a Contracting State (Art 1(1)(b)). The nationality of the parties and their civil or commercial character are irrelevant to the question of whether the CISG applies (Art 1(3)).

Article 1(1)(a) CISG is said to determine the applicability of the CISG 'autonomously' or 'directly'. The term 'autonomous or direct' indicates that the sphere of application is determined without resorting to the rules of private international law. It is the primary method established in the Convention which applies if the States in which the parties have their relevant place of business are Contracting States. If the requirement of both parties having their place of business in a Contracting State is not fulfilled, the question of whether the CISG applies is governed by Article (1)(1)(b), which acknowledges the application of conflict of laws rules. That is, the CISG will apply if the conflicts rule of the forum points to the application of the law of a Contracting State. Article 1 CISG determines the applicability of the CISG 'objectively', that is, absent a choice of law by the parties. The CISG may apply even if the requirements of Article 1 are not fulfilled but the parties have agreed on its application. Whether such a choice of law is valid is subject to the conflict of laws rules of the forum (see also Article 6 below).

Article 1 CISG is supplemented by Articles 91, 92, 94, 95, 99 and 100 CISG. Article 1 must further be read in conjunction with Articles 2 to 5. Whereas Articles 2 and 3 specify the type of contracts to which the CISG applies, Articles 4 and 5 delimitate the legal issues covered by the CISG.

II. Autonomous Application of the CISG (Arts 1(1)(a), (2) and (3) CISG)

According to Article 1(1)(a), the Convention applies if the parties have their place of business in different Contracting States and if the contract is about the sale of goods. These elements (Contracting States; internationality/place of business; contract of sale of goods) are explained as follows.

A. Contracting States

The CISG applies when, at the time of the conclusion of the contract, the parties have their relevant place of business in different Contracting States. This generally means that, at the time of the conclusion of the contract, the CISG must have been enacted in the corresponding States. Whether a country has become a Contracting State to the CISG can be ascertained by referring to the official website of the United Nations Commission on International Trade Law (UNCITRAL). The website lists all Contracting States and states the date of ratification of the CISG, as well as any reservations made by a Contracting State.[1]

As regards the intertemporal applicability of the CISG, Article 100 draws a distinction between the applicability of Part II and Part III of the Convention: the rules of formation of a contract (Part II) will apply when the offer is made on or after the date the Convention is enacted in accordance with Article 91. In contrast, Part III (Art 25 *et seq.*) only applies if the contract is concluded on or after the date the Convention becomes effective in the Contracting State(s) concerned in accordance with Article 99(2) CISG.

Another reservation referring to Part II and Part III of the Convention can be found in Article 92 CISG: a State may declare that Part II or Part III of the CISG is not binding on it; in that case, it is not to be considered a Contracting State with regard to the Part(s) to which the reservation refers. Unlike Article 100, Article 92 is not concerned with the intertemporal sphere of application of the Convention; rather, it grants Contracting States the opportunity not to be bound by Part II and/or Part III of the CISG and to apply its domestic law instead.

The notion 'Contracting State' can further be limited by way of Article 93: if a State declares that the Convention does not apply to certain of its territorial units, those units do not have the status of a Contracting State (Art 93(3)). So far, Canada is the only Contracting State which has made use of Article 93.

---

[1] www.uncitral.org/uncitral/en/uncitral_texts/sale_goods/1980CISG_status.html.

B. Place of Business in Different States

Article 1(1) CISG requires that the parties have their place of business in different Contracting States. The term 'place of business' has not been defined in the Convention, but it has been addressed in a number of court decisions and arbitral awards. The question is dealt with under Article 10 below.

For the purposes of Article 1 CISG, three elements must be emphasised. First, the parties' place of business must not both be in the same country. Article 1 expressly requires that the parties' place of business be 'in different States'. The requirement is further specified in Article 1(2), according to which the fact that the parties have their places of business in different States must be recognisable from an objective point of view. Article 1(2) lists three sources: the diversity of places should be apparent: (1) from the contract; (2) from any dealings between the parties; or (3) from any information disclosed by the parties that they have their places of business in different States.

Secondly, the reference to the parties' place of business in Article 1 makes it clear that the nationality of the parties is irrelevant to the applicability of the Convention. That is, even if the seller and the buyer have different nationalities, the CISG will not apply if the parties are domiciled in the same country. This is expressly stated in Article 1(3).

Finally, the term 'place of business' implies that the Convention applies to commercial transactions (business-to-business, B2B) only, to the exclusion of consumer contracts. This is expressly stated in Article 2(a) (for details, see below Art 2), but it is also inherent in the term 'place of business'. In this regard, Article 1(3) clarifies that the term 'business' is to be defined autonomously and that any qualification of the parties or the contract as 'civil' or 'commercial' is irrelevant.

C. Case Law

In case law, the applicability of the Convention by way of Article 1(1)(a) is often not expressly discussed. For an example dealing with some of the points mentioned above, see the following case abstract.

C 1-1

La San Giuseppe v Forti Moulding Ltd
Ontario Superior Court of Justice, 31 August 1999,
CISG-online 433[2]

[Facts]

(1) La San Giuseppe ('LSG') brought an action claiming damages for breach of contract against the defendant, Forti Moulding Ltd. LSG is a company situated in Venice, Italy, which

---

[2] Case abstract taken from the Pace database on the CISG and International Commercial Law (references omitted).

manufactures picture frame mouldings. It supplied mouldings to the defendant, a distributor of mouldings and picture frames located in Toronto, from 1989 to 1996.

(2) Generally, Forti Moulding placed orders by fax, specifying whether shipments were to be by sea or air. The mouldings were sold according to code numbers assigned to a particular profile, colour and wood finish. Samples corresponding to the code numbers were kept by the factory to ensure that new orders matched earlier production. Some products had been created to meet Forti's specifications.

(3) Nelson Forti, the principal of Forti Moulding Ltd, first began dealing with LSG in 1989 when he was involved in a company called First Place Mouldings with a partner, Derek Guerini. It was Mr Guerini who facilitated Mr Forti's introduction to the principals of LSG sometime in 1988 or 1989. When that business ceased a short time after dealings began with LSG, Mr Forti continued a similar business under the name of Forti Moulding Ltd.

(4) The parties never had a written agreement. When they began dealing in 1989, there was no commitment as to the volume of product to be supplied by LSG or prices.

(*In 1996, Forti Moulding was behind in payments and soon became unable to pay La San Giuseppe the outstanding amounts that it was owed. Soon afterward, La San Giuseppe brought an action claiming damages for breach of contract against Forti Moulding. Forti Moulding counterclaimed for damages and setoff, claiming that some of the mouldings were defective and that many shipments had varied by more than the 10 per cent originally agreed.*)[3]

(23) Mr Forti, his wife, mother-in-law, and employee, Mr Urrutia, all stated that there were many customer complaints about defective products from LSG, although Mrs Forti, in cross-examination, stated that only a few shipments from LSG were really bad. Mr Forti made a claim for $32,251.38, the value of defective LSG product allegedly in the warehouse, as well as $7,864.50 for storage of the material, which he said had been there for four to five years. He also complained that there had been overshipments in 1994 and 1996 for which he should not have to pay in the amount of $13,906.50.

(24) Finally, Mr Forti also complained about the purchase of a double mitre saw in 1994. Mr Ganss gave evidence that LSG had purchased the saw in Italy at Nelson Forti's request for resale to Forti Moulding. LSG chose the saw in accordance with specifications as to manu-facturer and product code provided by Nelson Forti. There was some evidence that the saw was used at a trade show before the sale. The arrangement was a favour to Forti because of the tax advantages that flowed to the company.

(25) Mr. Forti complained that the saw sent was not the one ordered, because it was not com-puterized. However, the saw was paid for without written complaint. Mr Ganss remembered no complaints about its performance when he was dealing with Forti. Mr Moschini testified that there were no complaints about the performance of the saw until these legal proceedings commenced. [...]

(*Question about whether there were quality problems with regard to the mouldings and the saw. Forti claims for damages.*)

---

[3] Case summary taken from Rajeev Sharma, 'The United Nations Convention on Contracts for the International Sale of Goods: The Canadian Experience', (2005) *Victoria University of Wellington Law Review* 4 849–51, available at CISG Pace.

[Judgment]

(28) Counsel for the plaintiff relies on the *International Sale of Goods Contracts Convention Act*, S.C. 1991, c. 13, which has been in effect in Ontario since 1992 because of the *International Sale of Goods Act*, R.S.O. 1990, c.1.10. These two acts brought into effect in Canada the United Nations *Convention on Contracts for the International Sale of Goods*. While the plaintiff failed to provide documentation that Italy is a signatory, it is a matter of public record that Italy ratified the convention in 1986. Moreover, pursuant to Article 1, the Convention applies both because the contracting parties have places of business in contracting states, and because the rules of private international law lead to the application of the law of a contracting state—namely, Ontario.

(29) The defendant argued that the Convention does not apply because the contract between the parties was made before the Convention came into effect in Ontario—namely, in 1989. Having considered the evidence, I do not find that the parties made a contract in 1989, which continued through to 1996. In their 1989 dealings, the parties began to establish a business relationship that would last several years, but they did not make a contract that set out the terms of their relationship, since they did not set out the key terms of their agreement—for example, price, volume, term, or payment arrangements. In effect, they had an agreement to agree, and each time an order was made by Forti Moulding and accepted by LSG, a contract was created for the shipment of goods. Therefore, the parties had a series of contracts for the supply of goods over the years. The complaints here all arise with respect to shipments in and after 1993, so the Convention does apply.

(30) Moreover, this is a contract for the sale of commercial goods, not a contract for the supply of personal or domestic goods. Therefore, Article 2(a), which provides that the Convention does not apply to goods bought for personal, family or household use, does not exclude these contracts between parties.

[…]

(*In the merits, the court dismissed the counter-claim of the defendant and found in favour of the claimant.*)

D. Contracts for the Sale of Goods

The CISG applies to 'contracts for the sale of goods'. The term has not been defined in the Convention. In case law, it has been circumscribed as a contract pursuant to which the seller is bound to deliver the goods and transfer the property in the goods sold and the buyer is obliged to pay the price and accept the goods.

'Contracts for the sale of goods' require specification in two respects, as both the term 'sales contract' as well as the term 'goods' need to be defined. At this point, the focus is on the concept of 'sales contract', as the definition of 'goods' will be discussed below under Article 3.

Sales contracts involve the delivery of goods in exchange for money. The prevailing opinion adheres to this strict definition. However, according to a minority view, the term 'price' used in Article 14(1), second sentence, and in Articles 53 and 55 CISG is not necessarily restricted to money. A broader understanding of the term 'price' would thus allow for the application of the CISG to countertrade (barter) agreements, whereby the parties would be treated as sellers with regard to the goods delivered by them and as buyers with regard to the goods they receive.

Another controversial question is whether the CISG applies to sales contracts with special financing agreements, such as hire purchase agreements or sale-and-lease-back contracts. In this respect, it has been convincingly argued that, where the parties ultimately aim at an acquisition of the goods by the buyer—as is often the case with hire purchase agreements—the contract should be governed by the CISG, even if it contains special financing conditions.

Finally, it must be determined whether the CISG applies to framework contracts, such as distribution agreements or franchise contracts. The question has been dealt with in a number of cases. See, in this respect, the following cases.

C 1-2

Helen Kaminski v Marketing Australian Products, Pty Ltd Inc, US Dist Ct (SD NY) (USA), 23 July 1997, CISG-online 297

[Facts]

Helen Kaminski is an Australian corporation with its principal place of business in Australia. It manufactures fashion accessories such as hats and bags. MAP is incorporated in Colorado, with its principal place of business in New York, and it distributes fashion accessories. Helen Kaminski and MAP negotiated an agreement in Australia in January 1996 whereby MAP had the exclusive rights to distribute Helen Kaminski goods in North America (the 'Distributor Agreement'). The Distributor Agreement specified the terms on which the parties would do business, including methods of payment, warranty, delivery, etc, and anticipated that MAP would purchase a total of US $2 million worth of products from February 1, 1996 to January 31, 1997. The parties amended the Distributor Agreement in February 1996 to address the sale of specified goods already in the United States. MAP issued purchase orders for additional products and Helen Kaminski sent notice in October and November 1996 to MAP that the products were ready for shipment. Pursuant to the Distributor Agreement, MAP was to open a letter of credit seven days prior to shipment. When MAP failed to do so, on November 1, 1996, Helen Kaminski sent a Notice to Rectify within thirty days. On November 22, 1996, Helen Kaminski sent a notice of default requiring MAP to cure the defects under the Distributor Agreement. When MAP still did not cure, Helen Kaminski sent a notice of termination dated December 2, 1996 and commenced an action in Australia seeking a declaration that the Distributor Agreement was invalid and terminated. [...]

[Judgment]

A. The CISG and the Distributor Agreement [...] Thus, the dispositive issue is whether the CISG applies to the Distributor Agreement. Helen Kaminski maintains that it does, since the agreement, in addition to laying out the terms for the parties' commercial relationship, also governed the disposition of identified goods. Although it does not say so explicitly, it appears that Helen Kaminski is referring to the amendment in February 1996 which addressed specified goods already in the United States. MAP maintains that the Distributor Agreement is merely a 'framework agreement; and that such agreements are not covered by the CISG. The Distributor Agreement requires MAP to purchase a minimum quantity of total goods, but does not identify the goods to be sold by type, date or price. In contrast, the CISG requires an enforceable contract to have definite terms regarding quantity and price.

While both sides cite various secondary sources, there appears to be no judicial authority determining the reach of the CISG and, in particular, whether it applies to distributor agreements. The parties do agree, however, that whether or not the CISG applies turns on whether the Distributor Agreement can be characterised as a contract for the sale of goods—that is, that it contained definite terms for specified goods. In this respect, the only contract for a specified set of goods to which Helen Kaminski points is the February 1996 amendment. As MAP correctly notes, however, these goods were not the subject of the breach. Rather, Helen Kaminski is claiming a breach for goods ordered but not shipped. Helen Kaminski makes no claim that these goods were identified in the Distributor Agreement.

For this reason, although I find that there is little to no case law on the CISG in general, and none determining whether a distributor agreement falls within the ambit of the CISG, Helen Kaminski's rationale for why the CISG applies to the debate about the breach for goods ordered but not shipped is not supported by the facts of the case. The identification in the Distributor Agreement of certain goods—about which there is no claim of breach—is insufficient to bring the Distributor Agreement within coverage of the CISG when the dispute concerns goods not specifically identified in the Distributor Agreement. Thus, while the question does present a controlling issue of law over which there may be substantial disagreement, it does not appear that a determination of the issue would materially advance the litigation as Helen Kaminski does not maintain that the general Distributor Agreement—absent the February amendment which does not concern the goods at issue—is definite enough to constitute a contract for the sale of goods. [...]

C 1-3

ICC International Court of Arbitration, Award No 11849/2003, UNILEX

[Facts]

Claimant and respondent concluded an exclusive distributorship agreement (the Agreement) whereby claimant was granted exclusive distributorship rights to a brand of respondent's fashion products. The Agreement provided that respondent would deliver the products in one or more instalments for the Fall/Winter and Spring/Summer seasons, respectively. Payment was by means of a letter of credit (L/C). Difficulties arose in the course of the Agreement but the parties continued to do business and to negotiate regarding the various problems.

A new dispute arose between the parties when respondent in January sent claimant its price list for that year's Fall/Winter season, indicating that such list was subject to 'little changes'. This list was subsequently substituted by a second one which included higher prices. In June, respondent sent claimant the order confirmations for that year's Fall/Winter season, asking that a letter of credit be opened by claimant 'as soon as possible'. The order confirmation was based on the second price list and claimant requested that it be changed to reflect the first price list. Respondent rejected this request and a dispute arose as to the price of the Fall/Winter season goods. After some attempts to settle this difference, respondent wrote to claimant on 2 August demanding the opening of the letter of credit for the Fall/Winter season within twenty days of receipt and stating that if claimant failed to do so, the Agreement would be terminated. Following a meeting of the parties to attempt to settle their differences, claimant E-mailed respondent on 10 August urging respondent to refrain from terminating the Agreement pending the negotiations. Respondent replied asking claimant to send its proposal for settlement. Claimant replied on 10 August stating that 'we should follow strictly the letter and intent of the distributorship agreement. In this spirit, please send me the particulars necessary to open a letter of credit for the pending shipments'. Claimant sent several requests to respondent asking for information regarding the letter of credit, but did not receive any reply. On 12 September, claimant informed respondent that it had opened a letter of credit. On 19 September, respondent terminated the Agreement.

Claimant initiated ICC arbitration according to the arbitration clause in the Agreement claiming direct losses, lost profits and harm to its reputation. Respondent counterclaimed for payment of overdue invoices and other matters.

[…]

[Judgment]

In the instant case, the parties have agreed that the CISG would apply to the Agreement. As a matter of fact, Art 11.2 of the Agreement provides that: 'The Arbitrator shall apply the 1980 UN Convention on the International Sale of Goods for what is not expressly or implicitly provided for under the contract. Letters of Credit shall be governed by the Uniform Customs and Practices for Documentary Credits (1993 Revision), International Chamber, of Commerce Publication no. 500.'

Claimant's submission that the CISG should be disregarded is based on the assumption that such instrument does not materially regulate the assessment of the correctness of a long-term distribution contract termination. More precisely, claimant's assumption is that the reference to the CISG in the Agreement should be construed as governing only the single sales taking place between the parties (eg possible disputes relating to defaults of the goods), and not to the general framework of the parties' relationship.

The Arbitrator does not share this view. First of all, by submitting the Agreement to the CISG (when such instrument does not, in principle apply to a long term distribution contract), and also by referring to the ICC Uniform Customs and Practices for Documentary Credits, the parties have clearly indicated their intention to avoid their respective internal law rules, and to resort to neutral solutions. Secondly, the way Art 11.2 of the Agreement has been drafted shows that the parties did not intend to limit the application of the CISG to possible disputes related to single sales of products, but did rather submit the whole Agreement to its rules, with the only exception of what 'is not expressly or implicitly provided' by it. The intention of the parties to apply the CISG rules to their possible disputes has therefore been clearly expressed.

This does not mean that the application of other rules of law should necessarily be ruled out. As a matter of fact, the CISG does not regulate all possible questions arising from a sales contract. In case of gaps, Art 7(2) CISG, provides that 'questions concerning matters governed by this convention which are not expressly settled in it are to be settled in conformity with the general principles on which it is based or, in the absence of such principles, in conformity with the law applicable by virtue of the rules of international private law'.

In this case, according to Art 17(1) of the Rules, Art 7(2) of the CISG would in case of gaps lead to the subsidiary application of the appropriate rules of law. The same reasoning should apply whether a given CISG rule could practically not be applied to a particular disputed issue, due to the nature of a contract not falling within the material scope of the uniform law (such as a long-term distribution agreement), but to which it would nonetheless have been submitted by the parties.

The pertinent question is therefore, in the present case, whether it is practically possible to apply the CISG to the assessment of the Agreement's termination by respondent. The answer to that question should be positive, as the CISG provide rules which can easily be applied to the termination of a distribution agreement. Pursuant to Art 17(1) of the Rules, the parties' will to apply the CISG to their dispute should therefore be obeyed. It remains to be seen, still, which of the CISG rules should be applied in the present case. [...]

(The Arbitrator adjudicates the case based on Articles 63, 64, 71, 74, 78 and 80 CISG. He finds that Respondent was not entitled to avoid the distribution agreement and was liable for damages under Article 74 CISG, including interest under Article 78 CISG.)

Questions

Q 1-1

When does the CISG apply according to Article 1(1) CISG?

Q 1-2

Which other provisions of the CISG complement Article 1(1) CISG?

Q 1-3

What is meant by an 'autonomous' or 'direct' definition of the Convention's sphere of application (Art 1(1)(a))?

Q 1-4

Why are Articles 92, 93, 99 and 100 CISG relevant in connection with Article 1(1)(a) CISG?

Q 1-5

(a) What is meant by the requirement that the fact that the parties have their place of business in different States be 'objectively recognisable'?
(b) Which other provision is to be taken into account when assessing a party's place of business?

Q 1-6

What is the purpose of Article 1(3) CISG?

Q 1-7

(a) Why did the CISG apply in C 1-1?
(b) Why was it important to decide at what point in time the contract was concluded?

Q 1-8

(a) Did the CISG apply to the distribution agreement in C 1-2? Why or why not?
(b) Why did the CISG govern the distribution agreement in C 1-3?
(c) Considering C 1-2 and C 1-3, can you develop a rule as to when the Convention could apply to a distribution agreement?

III. Applicability of the CISG in Private International Law (Article 1(1)(b) CISG)

A. Operation

By virtue of Article 1(1)(b) CISG, the Convention also applies where only one party, or neither party, has its relevant place of business in a Contracting State but the rules of private international law lead to the law of a Contracting State. This mechanism is called the 'indirect applicability' of the CISG. Thus, the CISG will, for example, apply if the choice-of-law rules of the forum state that the law governing the sales contract is the law of the state in which the seller (the party performing the characteristic performance) is domiciled and if that state has implemented the CISG. According to prevailing opinion, Article 1(1)(b) CISG points to the substantive law of the Contracting State and not to the choice-of-law rules of that State. This means that, even if the conflict of laws rules of the Contracting State referred back to the law of the forum state, or to the law of a third state, such *renvoi* will be ignored. Finally, if, in application of Article 1(1)(b), the law of a Contracting State has been found to govern the contract in question, the CISG must be applied as part of the law of that Contracting State. In other words, the court cannot apply the domestic law instead of the CISG.

B. The Reservation in Article 95 CISG

Article 1(1)(b) CISG extends the sphere of application of the Convention considerably. Reservations expressed against Article 1(1)(b) at the Drafting Conference are the reason why Article 95 allows for the possibility of becoming a Contracting State to the Convention without adopting Article 1(1)(b). Article 95 reads:

> **Article 95.** Any State may declare at the time of the deposit of its instrument of ratification, acceptance, approval or accession that it will not be bound by subparagraph (1)(b) of article 1 of this Convention.

Currently, there are six Contracting States which have made a reservation under Article 95 CISG: Armenia, China, the Czech Republic, Slovakia, Singapore and the USA.

Article 95 CISG certainly comes into play where the claim is brought before a court in a reservation State. It is virtually undisputed that, in this case, the CISG will (only) apply if the requirements of Article 1(1)(a) are met or if the conflicts rule of the forum leads to the application of the law of a Contracting State which has not made any reservation under Article 95. Case C 1-4 is such an example; it further illustrates how the question of the applicability is examined through Article 1(1)(a), (b) while also taking into account Articles 1(2) and 95 CISG.

C 1-4

Impuls ID International, SL et al v Psion Teklogix Inc, US Dist Ct (SD FL), 22 November 2002, CISG-online 783

[Facts]

[...] The parties in the above-styled cause are as follows. Plaintiff Impuls I.D. Internacional, S.L. (hereinafter 'Impuls-Spain') is a Spanish corporation that develops, markets and sells computer products throughout Europe and Latin America. Plaintiff Psiar, S.A. (hereinafter "Psiar") is an Argentine corporation that distributes computer products in Argentina. Plaintiff Impuls I.D. Systems, Inc (hereinafter 'Impuls-US') is a Florida corporation that is responsible for distributing products for Impuls-Spain throughout Latin America. The Court will refer to the Plaintiffs collectively as 'the Plaintiffs,' or individually as necessary.

The Defendant, Psion-Teklogix, Inc (hereinafter 'the Defendant') is an Ontario-based Canadian corporation. The Plaintiffs' Complaint alleges that the Defendant is a Delaware corporation with its principle place of business in Kentucky. However, the Kentucky-based corporation is a subsidiary of the Defendant, not the Defendant.

The above-styled cause arises out of an alleged oral contract (hereinafter the 'contract') entered into by Impuls-Spain and Psiar, on the one hand, and Psion PLC and Psion Enterprise Computing, Ltd, on the other hand, on June 21, 2000. Psion PLC is the British parent company of Psion Enterprise Computing, Ltd, also a British company. Neither Psion PLC nor Psion Enterprise Computing, Ltd is a defendant in the above-styled cause.

Prior to June 21, 2000 Impuls-Spain developed, marketed and sold computer products in Latin America. Due to its desire to expand its business, Impuls-Spain became interested in purchasing the assets of Psiar. Impuls-Spain's business plan was to merge with Psiar to distribute certain computer products manufactured by Psion PLC and Psion Enterprising Computing, Ltd throughout Latin America. To this end, the President of Psiar and the Executive Vice-President of Impuls-Spain met with representatives of Psion PLC and Psion Enterprise Computing, Ltd in London, England on June 21, 2000. The Plaintiffs allege that they proposed their business plan to Psion PLC and Psion Enterprising Computing, Ltd, wherein the Plaintiffs would purchase computer merchandise from Psion Enterprising Computing, Ltd to be distributed throughout Latin America. Central to the Plaintiffs' business plan was the arrangement that all merchandise bought by the Plaintiffs would be delivered to Impuls-US in Fort Lauderdale. Under the contract, Psiar would place orders with Psion Enterprising Computing, Ltd, and then the computer products would be shipped to Impuls-US in Florida. From Florida, the computer products would be distributed throughout Latin America. The Plaintiffs further allege that from July 2000 until December 2000, Psion Enterprising Computing, Ltd followed the provisions of the contract and merchandise was shipped to Impuls-US in Florida.

In September 2000, Psion PLC acquired Teklogix, Inc, a Canadian company, which became the Defendant, Psion Teklogix, Inc. In December 2000, the Plaintiffs received an e-mail communication from Mr Mike Rose, President of the Defendant informing them that all contracts would be terminated in ninety (90) days and that the Defendant was reorganizing its distribution plan. The Plaintiffs explained that this strategy was unacceptable because it would destroy their business plan. The Defendant offered the Plaintiffs the option of continuing as a reseller, which the Plaintiffs refused. Believing that the actions of the Defendant constituted a breach of the contract reached on June 21, 2000, the Plaintiffs filed suit in the United States District Court for the Southern District of Florida.

[Judgment]

Specifically, the Plaintiffs allege that the above-styled cause arises under the United Nations Convention on Contracts for the International Sale of Goods because all the parties to the contract have their places of business in Contracting States. United Nations Convention on Contracts for the International Sale of Goods, opened for signature April 11, 1980 (CISG). A 'Contracting State' is a country that has become a party to the CISG. The United States, Spain, Argentina, and Canada are all Contracting States. The United Kingdom, however, is not a Contracting State. The Defendant contends that the CISG does not apply ... because the contract was entered into by Psion PLC and Psion Enterprise Computing, Ltd, both of which have their places of business in the United Kingdom, a non-Contracting State. The Defendant further contends that subsequent changes of parties to the contract cannot render the CISG applicable.

The Court notes that 'in construing a treaty, as in construing a statute, [courts] first look to its terms to determine its meaning.' Article 100 of the CISG states that 'This Convention applies to the formation of a contract only when the proposal for concluding the contract is made on or after the date when the Convention enters into force in respect of the Contracting States referred to in subparagraph (1)(a) or the Contracting State referred to in subparagraph (1)(b) of article 1.' CISG, art 100(1). As noted above, the 'proposal for concluding' the contract was made on June 21, 2000 in London, England between Impuls-Spain, a Spanish corporation, Psiar, an Argentine corporation, and both Psion PLC and Psion Enterprise Computing, Ltd, each of which are corporations of the United Kingdom. The United Kingdom was not a signatory to the CISG at the time 'when the proposal for concluding the contract' was formulated. Therefore, the language of Article 100 supports the Defendant's contention that the contract in question here is not governed by the CISG.

The Court finds further support for the contention that the CISG does not apply from Article 1(2) of the CISG. Article 1(2) states that 'the fact that the parties have their places of business in different States is to be disregarded whenever this fact does not appear either from the contract or from any dealings between, or from information disclosed by, the parties at any time before or at the conclusion of the contract.' CISG, Art 1(2). Therefore, to the extent that the Defendant, a Canadian corporation located in a Contracting State, is now a party to the contract is a fact that 'is to be disregarded' because it was not known to the parties 'at any time before or at the conclusion of the contract.' In other words, what the parties knew when they concluded the contract of June 21, 2000 was that the United Kingdom was not a signatory to the CISG and that the CISG would not apply. [...] Based upon a careful reading of the terms of the CISG, the Court finds that it does not govern the contract.

Next, the Court notes that it may also look at the 'history of negotiation and practice' under the CISG to determine whether it governs the contract. Here, the Court notes that the development of the CISG can be traced back to the 1964 Hague Conventions. The 1964 Hague Conventions adopted a 'universalist' approach which sought to apply the rules of the Convention to international sales regardless of whether the parties had contact with a Contracting State. This 'universalist' approach was specifically rejected by the CISG, however, in favor of Article 1, which states that the CISG will apply only to contracts between parties whose places of business are in Contracting States. Therefore, the Court finds no support for the proposition that the contract at issue here should be governed by the CISG when the negotiations leading up to the CISG specifically rejected a "universalist" approach to its application.

Moreover, the Court notes that the United States, pursuant to Article 95 of the CISG, ratified the CISG with the following declaration: "Pursuant to article 95 the United States will not be bound by subparagraph (1)(b) of Article 1." CISG, app. B. Subparagraph (1)(b) allows for the application of the CISG when a party is not from a Contracting State. The United States specifically rejected being bound by subparagraph (1)(b). Therefore, the only circumstance in which the CISG could apply is if all the parties to the contract were from Contracting States. But as noted above, both Psion PLC and Psion Enterprise Computing, Ltd were from the United Kingdom, a non-Contracting State.

Finally, the Court notes that it has found no case law supporting the proposition that a contract entered into by a party in a non-Contracting State is governed by the CISG when a subsequent party to the contract located in a Contracting State allegedly breaches the contract. Rather, the cases found by this Court all show that the CISG applied because the original parties to the contract had their places of business in Contracting States.

Based upon a reading of the CISG, the history of negotiation and practice under the CISG, as well as oral argument of counsel and the papers submitted by the parties, the Court finds that the CISG does not govern the contract at issue here and that there is no federal question present in the above-styled cause. [...]

(The Court discusses the question of jurisdiction and finds that it that complete diversity is lacking. It thus dismisses the cause without prejudice for lack of jurisdiction over the subject matter.)

C 1-5 and A 1-1 refer to the interplay of Article 1(1)(b) and Article 95 CISG in a setting different from that in C 1-4. In C 1-5, the claim is not brought before the court of a reservation State but rather before the court of a (then) non-Contracting State.

C 1-5

Oberlandesgericht Düsseldorf (Germany),
2 July 1993,
CISG-online 74[4]

[Facts]

[...] Plaintiff buyer had its place of business in Krefeld, Germany. Buyer purchased a cutting machine from defendant seller, whose place of business was located in Indiana, USA. The cutting machine was to be installed in the veneer processing unit of a Russian furniture combine. After the machine had been put into operation, an accident occurred which led to the death of a worker and caused injuries to another. Subsequently the Russian sub-purchaser demanded repair of the defective machine from buyer, whereupon buyer sued to recover the costs of repair from seller. In its complaint, buyer also moved for a declaratory judgment from the court

---

[4] Translation taken from CISG Pace (citations omitted).

establishing that seller was required to indemnify buyer against all damage claims raised by the Russian sub-purchaser and furniture combine with respect to the accident in dispute.

Seller contested the local jurisdiction of the Krefeld District Court which, in an interlocutory decision, held that it had local and international jurisdiction over the matter. The court based its findings on § 23 Code of Civil Procedure, stating that the defendant seller had assets in the local forum. In its appeal from the interlocutory judgement, seller claims that § 23 ZPO is not applicable to the jurisdictional issue. The appeal is not meritorious.

[Judgment]

The District Court was correct in asserting international jurisdiction over the issue in dispute. [...]

II. Pursuant to § 29 Par 1 ZPO, jurisdiction over contractual disputes shall be in the forum where the performance at issue is to be tendered. In this case, the forum is in Krefeld.

1. Indiana law determines the place of performance for the claims raised in the complaint. This follows from Art 28 EGBGB (Conflict of Law provision in the Introductory Law of the German Civil Code). This provision provides that the law of the place where the contractor's headquarters is located shall be applied to contracts for work and materials [...]. The parties entered into a contract for work and materials with respect to the cutting machine. The seller contractor maintains its business headquarters in Indiana. Therefore, the laws of this state are applicable.

The UN Convention on the International Sale of Goods from April 11, 1980 ('the CISG') has been in force in Indiana since January 1, 1988—hence, effective at the time the contract was concluded by the parties in dispute. Consequently, the provisions of the CISG govern the contract between the parties pursuant to Art 1 Par 1(b) and Art 3 Par. 1 of the CISG.

By contrast, German law would apply had the parties agreed to its applicability in accordance with Art 6 of the CISG, 27 EGBGB. In this event, the CISG would not have been relevant because in Germany it entered into force on January 1, 1991 which was after the formation of the contract (BGBI.II, 1477). Nonetheless, the parties never agreed to the applicability of German law [...]

(*The court ruled that performance was to be tendered at the seller's principal place of business.*)

A 1-1

Peter Schlechtriem, *Commentary on Oberlandesgericht Düsseldorf*, 2 July 1993[5]

[...] Applicability of the CISG: effect of an Article 95 reservation

At issue was the jurisdiction and venue of the German courts. Under the German Code of Civil Procedure § 29 (as under Art 5, No. 1 of the European Convention on Jurisdiction and Enforcement of Judgments in Civil and Commercial Matters), jurisdiction and venue are

---

[5] Taken from CISG Pace (citations omitted).

'docked' onto the place of performance. Therefore, the applicable sales law and its provision regulating the place of performance for the German buyer's claims had to be determined. Since at the time of the formation of the sales contract Germany had not yet enacted the Convention, although the USA had already been a Contracting State, the CISG could not be applied pursuant to Art 1(1)(a). Following the German conflict of law rules, the court held that Indiana law (as the law of the seller's place of business) was applicable and erroneously found this to be the CISG since the USA had enacted the Convention. The court ignored, however, that the USA was one of the few Contracting States which had invoked the reservation under Art 95 of the CISG, thereby not enacting Art 1(1)(b), the only the CISG provision making the Convention applicable, in the event of one or both parties not having their place of business in Contracting States [...]

IV. Applicability of the CISG through the Parties' Choice of Law

Article 1 CISG determines the applicability of the Convention where the parties have not made a choice of law. Of course, the CISG may also apply by effect of party autonomy, because the parties have chosen it as the law governing their contract, and regardless of whether or not they have their places of business in a Contracting State. However, the question of whether the CISG can be chosen as the law applicable to their contract is not governed by the CISG but by the conflict of laws rules of the forum. It depends on the degree of party autonomy granted by the applicable private international law regarding the choice of the substantive law.

V. Comparison with Other Legal Provisions

A. UNIDROIT Principles

The UNIDROIT Principles (PICC 2010) state general principles for International Commercial Contracts. Their preamble reads:

These Principles set forth general rules for international commercial contracts.

They shall be applied when the parties have agreed that their contract be governed by them.

They may be applied when the parties have agreed that their contract be governed by 'general principles of law', the *lex mercatoria* or the like.

They may be applied when the parties have not chosen any law to govern their contract.

They may be used to interpret or supplement international uniform law instruments.

They may be used to interpret or supplement domestic law.

They may serve as a model for national and international legislators.

A 1-2

UNIDROIT Principles, Official Comment, p 1 *et seq.*

[...] The international character of a contract may be defined in a great variety of ways. The solutions adopted in both national and international legislation range from a reference to the place of business or habitual residence of the parties in different countries to the adoption of more general criteria such as the contract having 'significant connections with more than one State', 'involving a choice between the laws of different States', or 'affecting the interests of international trade'. The Principles do not expressly lay down any of these criteria. The assumption, however, that the concept of 'international' contracts should be given the broadest possible interpretation, so as ultimately to exclude only those situations where no international element at all is involved, ie where the relevant elements of the contract in question are connected with one country only. [...]

B. Principles of European Contract Law (PECL)

Article 1:101 PECL:

(1)   These Principles are intended to be applied as general rules of contract law in the European Communities.
(2)   These Principles will apply when the parties have agreed to incorporate them into their contract or that their contract is to be governed by them.
(3)   These Principles may be applied when the parties:
     (a)   have agreed that their contract is to be governed by 'general principles of law', the '*lex mercatoria*' or the like; or
     (b)   have not chosen any system or rules of law to govern their contract.
(4)   These Principles may provide a solution to the issue raised where the system or rules of law applicable do not do so.

Questions

Q 1-9

Why is the application rule in Article 1(1)(b) CISG called an 'indirect application mechanism'?

Q 1-10

Why does Article 95 CISG provide for the possibility of a reservation?

Q 1-11

(a)   In C 1-4, why did the CISG not apply through Article 1(1)(a)?
(b)   Why did the CISG not apply through Article 1(1)(b)?

Q 1-12

(a) In C 1-5, did the parties litigate before the court of a State which had made a reservation under Article 95 CISG?
(b) In this case, why was the CISG not applicable through Article 1(1)(a)?
(c) The decision of the court to apply the CISG was criticised in A 1-1. Do you agree that Article 95 should be respected not only by the courts of the State which has made such a reservation, but rather every time the conflicts rule of the forum leads to the application of the law of a reservation State?
(d) Could the court have found out that the USA had made a reservation under Article 95 CISG? Where could it have looked it up?

Q 1-13[6]

Look at the following examples and decide whether the CISG is the applicable law, assuming that the parties have not made a choice of law:

(a) A Czech and a Brazilian party litigate before a Czech court; the *lex fori* leads to the application of Czech law.
(b) A claim arising from a sales contract between a US and an Italian enterprise has been brought before a US court.
(c) An English and a Chinese party litigate before a Swiss court; the *lex fori* leads to the application of the law of China.
(d) A US buyer sues a Slovakian seller in a US court.

Q 1-14

Describe the significant differences between the applicability of the PICC 2010, the PECL and the CISG. Consider the legal status of the PICC 2010 and the PECL.

Q 1-15

Compare the way in which 'international' is defined in the PICC 2010 and the CISG.

Q 1-16

Are the parties to an international sales contract able to choose the PICC 2010 or the PECL as the law applicable to their contract?

---

[6] For this question you need an updated list of all Contracting States and any reservations they have made, see http://www.uncitral.org/uncitral/en/uncitral_texts/sale_goods/1980CISG_status.html.

Article 2 CISG

This Convention does not apply to sales:

(a) of goods bought for personal, family or household use, unless the seller, at any time before or at the conclusion of the contract, neither knew nor ought to have known that the goods were bought for any such use;

(b) by auction;

(c) on execution or otherwise by authority of law;

(d) of stocks, shares, investment securities, negotiable instruments or money;

(e) of ships, vessels, hovercraft or aircraft;

(f) of electricity.

I. Overview

Article 2 CISG excludes certain types of sales contracts from the application of the CISG, based either on the purpose for which the goods were purchased (Art 2(a)), on the type of transaction (Art 2(b)–(d)), or on the kinds of goods sold (Art 2(e), (f)). The exceptions enumerated in this article are exhaustive and may not be applied by way of analogy to other cases.

II. Article 2(a) CISG

A. Purpose of Excluding Consumer Contracts

Consumer contracts have been excluded from the CISG in order to avoid an overlap or rivalry between the CISG and domestic consumer law. The CISG defines consumer contracts by reference to the private purpose for which the goods are bought.

B. Exception to the General Rule in Article 2(a) CISG

The exclusion of the applicability of the CISG to consumer sales contracts is narrowed by the second half-sentence in Article 2(a). Where, at any time before or at the conclusion of the contract, the seller neither knew nor ought to have known of the fact that the buyer is a consumer the CISG applies to the contract, if all other requirements for its applicability are met. Therefore, where the buyer does not make it clear that it is purchasing the goods for personal, family or household use, it must accept the consequence of being treated as a commercial buyer.

Article 2(a) CISG may create a conflict with domestic consumer protection laws which claim applicability regardless of whether or not the seller knows or ought to know of the personal or family use the goods are bought for. The question has been discussed particularly in relation to EC consumer law. Problems arise if a mandatory consumer law provision settles a question which is dealt with by the Convention in a different manner, for example, if domestic consumer law requires specific form requirements, whereas Article 11 CISG states the principle of freedom from form requirements. While the question is disputed, it seems preferable to assume that, in such cases, the CISG prevails in cases where both parties are located in a CISG Contracting State. This may be explained by the fact that Contracting States, by signing and implementing the CISG, are bound to the Convention by public international law and cannot enact contradictory mandatory consumer law with regard to questions dealt with in the CISG without breaching their public international law duties.

C. Comparison with Other Legal Provisions

§ 2-104(1) UCC

'Merchant' means a person who deals in goods of the kind or otherwise by his occupation holds himself out as having knowledge or skill peculiar to the practices or goods involved in the transaction or to whom the knowledge or skill may be attributed by his employment of an agent or broker or other intermediary who by his occupation holds himself out as having such knowledge or skill.

PICC 2010

Preamble (Purpose of the Principles)
These Principles set forth general rules for international commercial contracts. [...]

A 2-1

UNIDROIT Principles, Official Comment (Preamble)

[...] The restriction to 'commercial' contracts is in no way intended to take over the distinction traditionally made in some legal systems between 'civil' and 'commercial' parties and/or transactions, i.e. to make the application of the Principles dependent on whether the parties have the formal status of 'merchants' [...] and/or the transaction is commercial in nature. The idea is rather that of excluding from the scope of the Principles so-called 'consumer transactions' which are within the various legal systems being increasingly subjected to special rules, i.e. a party who enters into the contract otherwise than in the course of its trade or profession.

The criteria adopted at both national and international level also vary with respect to the distinction between consumer and non-consumer contracts. The Principles do not provide any express definition, but the assumption is that the concept of 'commercial' contracts should be understood in the broadest possible sense, so as to include not only trade transactions for the supply or exchange of goods or services, but also other types of economic transactions, such as investment and/or concession agreements, contract for professional services, etc. [...]

§ 13 BGB:[7]

Consumer means every physical person who enters into a legal transaction for a purpose that can be attributed neither to her commercial nor to her independent professional activity.

Questions

Q 2-1

(a)   Why have consumer contracts been excluded from the CISG?
(b)   Why are consumer contracts sometimes treated differently from commercial contracts? See also section 2-104(1) UCC, and § 13 BGB.

Q 2-2

(a)   Do the PICC 2010 apply to consumer contracts?
(b)   Do the PICC 2010 provide for a reservation similar to Article 2(a) CISG, second half-sentence?

III. Article 2(b) to (f) CISG

The exclusions from the CISG stated in Article 2(b) to (f) are miscellaneous and there are different reasons for them. The exclusion of the CISG in sales contracts concluded by auction (subparagraph b) or on execution or otherwise by authority of law (subparagraph c) can be traced back to the drafters' respect for specific domestic rules governing these kinds of sales contracts; these rules are often mandatory. The same reason led the drafters of the CISG to exclude its application from sales of stocks, shares, investment securities, negotiable instruments or money (subparagraph d). There are also many mandatory provisions in this field.

The exclusion of ships, vessels, hovercraft or aircraft (subparagraph e) as well as the sale of electricity (subparagraph f) had already been stated in the ULIS. Article 2(f) can be explained by the fact that many states still have a monopoly on electricity, with the consequence that contracts for the supply of electricity are often subject to special provisions rooted in public law. It should be noted that the exclusion stated in Article 2(f) CISG cannot be extended to contracts for gas or oil.

---

[7] Author's translation.

The exclusion of ships and other vessels set out in Article 2(e) CISG is based on the idea that these vehicles are usually registered and are thus considered to be immovable goods. Even though not all domestic laws require registration of a ship, the CISG opted for a global solution, without distinguishing between vessels subject to registration and vessels not subject to registration. Thus, all vehicles potentially subject to registration are excluded from the scope of the CISG. However, from the rationale of Article 2(e) CISG, according to which the sale of water crafts is excluded because of its potential similarity to a sale of an immovable good, it can be deduced that the exclusion from the scope of application of the CISG refers only to watercrafts intended for continual movement, whereas the sale of boats and other water vehicles intended for merely local use does fall under the Convention.

Questions

Q 2-3

Why were sales by auction excluded from the Convention's sphere of application (Art 2(b) CISG)?

Q 2-4

(a) Why have sales of stocks, investment securities and negotiable instruments been excluded (Art 2(d) CISG)?
(b) Documentary sales are types of contract for the sale of goods in which possession of the goods is transferred from the seller to the buyer through delivery of a negotiable document of title issued by the carrier. They are governed by the CISG (see below, Art 57 *et seq*). Explain the difference between a documentary sale and a sale of stocks, negotiable instruments etc excluded under Article 2(d) CISG.

Q 2-5

(a) Why is the sale of ships, vessels, aircrafts and hovercrafts not governed by the CISG (Art 2(e))?
(b) The sale of parts of those goods (motor, railing, furniture, etc) is governed by the Convention. Explain why.

Article 3 CISG

(1) Contracts for the supply of goods to be manufactured or produced are to be considered sales unless the party who orders the goods undertakes to supply a substantial part of the materials necessary for such manufacture or production.

(2) This Convention does not apply to contracts in which the preponderant part of the obligations of the party who furnishes the goods consists in the supply of labour or other services.

I. Overview

Article 3 CISG defines how 'sales contract' is to be understood for the purposes of the Convention. It deals with two different situations in which the contract includes something in addition to the supply of goods. There are a large number of cases where the contract is not only for the sale of 'ready-made' goods but for the sale of goods to be manufactured or produced. Thus it is important to understand what sort of 'mixed contract' is governed by the CISG.

Many domestic sales laws provide for a rule similar to Article 3 CISG, according to which the applicability of sales law rules is extended to certain contracts providing for more than simply delivery and transfer of ownership of goods. However, the criteria among the various laws may differ.

II. The Definition of 'Goods'

First of all, the term 'goods' needs to be explained. Not having been defined in the Convention, it has been left to the judiciary and legal commentary to determine what is meant by 'goods'. In this regard, Article 7(1) CISG must be taken into consideration, which states that the Convention and, consequently, any of its terms, are to be interpreted autonomously.

Based on these guidelines, it has been stated that, for the purposes of the CISG, the term 'goods' includes moveable and tangible objects. They can be new or old, natural or artificial. They can be an end product or just a part of the whole. The term includes animals as well as liquid or gaseous goods (but see the exclusion of electricity from the scope of application in Article 2(f)). What is decisive is that the goods are moveable and tangible at the moment of delivery: growing crops are 'goods' within the meaning of the CISG, even if, prior to delivery, they were literally rooted to the ground.

A number of questions have been left open. The CISG has principally been drafted for the sale of tangible goods, which is evidenced by the terms 'delivery', 'taking over', 'passing of risk *in transitu*' and so on. However, in view of technological developments, more and more non-tangible products, such as computer software, are sold. It is thus important to decide whether those contracts fall within the scope of the CISG.

Case law has been rather restrictive on this point, with the argument that software are non-tangible goods and thus governed by the law for service contracts, at least for individualised software. Most legal writing does not make a distinction between individualised and standardised software but tends to consider every supply of software as the supply of goods. In this respect, see the following excerpt.

A 3-1

Schwenzer/Hachem, in Schwenzer (ed), Schlechtriem & Schwenzer, *Commentary on the Convention on the International Sale of Goods (CISG)*, (3rd edn) (2010) Art 1 CISG para 18

[...] If software is permanently transferred to the other party in all respects except for the copyright and restrictions to its use by third parties and becoming part of the other party's property—as opposed to mere agreements on temporary use against payment of royalties—it can be the object of a sales contract governed by the CISG. In this case, the situation is comparable to the sale of a machine, where the seller retains the intellectual property rights necessary for the operation of the machine (patents etc). It does not matter whether the software is standard software, software adjusted to the customer's needs, or fully customised software, since Article 3(1) makes clear that this distinction does not matter in determining the sphere of application of the Convention. As in the case of other goods to be manufactured, the 'services' (work etc) necessary to the manufacture of goods are to be disregarded. [...]

In many cases, the seller may be contractually obliged to render further services, eg instructing the buyer or its employees. The CISG remains applicable also in these cases unless the services to be rendered from the 'preponderant part' (Article 3(2)) of the seller's obligations. [...]

III. Goods to be Manufactured or Produced (Article 3(1) CISG)

Article 3(1) CISG states the general rule that the contract concerning goods that must first be produced or manufactured falls within the scope of the CISG. An exception to that rule is made for cases in which the buyer supplies a 'substantial part of the materials'; in this situation, the contract is not governed by the CISG. There used to be two difficulties in interpreting this paragraph. First, what is meant by 'materials';

do only raw or half-processed materials fall under this provision, or does it also cover plans, know-how, licenses and so on ? The question seems to have been settled to the effect that such immaterial contributions on behalf of the buyer do not prevent the application of the CISG (see C 3-2, point 5). However, they may have an influence on the question of whether the buyer supplied 'a substantial part of the materials': for instance, where the buyer provides part of the material which is valuable because of the know-how or the license on which it is based, the CISG will not apply if that part of the material(s) is 'substantial'.

This leads us to the second difficulty underlying Article 3(1), that is, the interpretation of the term 'substantial part'. The CISG does not provide any specific criteria. As to how the term has been applied and understood, see the following abstracts.

C 3-1

Arbitration Court of the Chamber of Commerce and Industry of Budapest (Hungary),
5 December 1995,
CISG-online 163[8]

[...] The sole arbitrator found that the contract was an international sales contract governed by CISG as the materials supplied by the buyer did not amount to a substantial part of the materials necessary for the production of the goods (Art 3(1) CISG). In the case at hand, the value of the materials supplied by the buyer amounted to approximately 10% of the total value of the containers to be produced. [...]

C 3-2

Oberlandesgericht München (Germany),
3 December 1999,
CISG-online 585[9]

[Facts][10]

An Italian seller and a German buyer concluded a contract for the sale of machinery for the manufacturing of windows. The machinery had to be produced by the seller according to the buyer's specifications and design and the buyer had to supply a part of the materials necessary for such production. The seller also had to install the machinery and put it into operation. A dispute arose when the buyer, faced with delays in delivery, declared the contract avoided.

---

[8] English summary taken from UNILEX.
[9] Translation taken from CISG Pace (citations omitted).
[10] Summary of facts taken from UNILEX.

[Judgment]

[...] Contracts for the supply of goods to be manufactured or produced are according to Article 3(1) CISG to be considered sales unless the party who orders the goods undertakes to supply a substantial part of the materials necessary for such manufacture or production. Accordingly, the Convention is also applicable to the contract calling for the delivery of a window production plant concluded between the [buyer] and the [seller] [...]. The few tools which were to be supplied by the [buyer] are neither with respect to their value nor their function essential ones—the French text of the Convention speaks of 'part essentielle'—nor 'substantial parts'—as stated in the English text of the plant to be delivered [...]. This is particularly true as the plant ordered is, as has been argued by both parties, a standard model. [...]

C 3-3

Oberlandesgericht Innsbruck (Austria), 18 December 2007, CISG-online 1735[11]

[Facts]

The [Buyer] concluded a contract for the delivery and laying of steel bars with the [Seller] in autumn 2004 in respect to the aforementioned project. A fixed price was guaranteed until 30 April 2005. Subsequent to that date, a new price was to be set. In fact, on 29 March 2005 the parties agreed on a new (reduced) fixed price, which should be valid between 1 April 2005 and 31 March 2006.

The wholesale price index declined considerably in the aftermath. Therefore, the [Buyer] claimed that this should entail a decline of the agreed price. The [Buyer] thus unilaterally reduced the price of the invoices issued in respect to the delivery and laying of steel bars.

[Judgment]

[...] [I]t cannot be decided conclusively on the basis of the current state of the procedure whether the CISG actually can be applied to the present case. The parties have at least not concluded a pure contract of sale. It is true that according to Article 3(1) CISG contracts for the supply of goods to be manufactured or produced are to be considered sales unless the party who orders the goods undertakes to supply a substantial part of the materials necessary for such manufacture or production. Mixed-type contracts are not governed by the United Nations Convention on Contracts for the International Sale of Goods if the part which does not relate to the sale is crucially predominant. The individual circumstances of the relation between the part which relates to the sale and the part which does not relate to the sale are decisive [...]. The quantitative balance does not constitute the sole requirement in respect to the question whether the supply of services is predominant. In addition, further components have to be taken into account in each case such as in particular the interest of the parties as regards the remaining performances. It is true that it has been established in the present case that the price for the delivery of the steel is considerably higher than the price for the laying. This, however, does not suffice to decide whether the element relating to the sale was predominant in the present case—as can be seen from the aforementioned legal position. Nevertheless, it does not have to be decided whether the United Nations Convention on

---

[11] Case abstract taken from CISG Pace (references omitted).

Contracts for the International Sale of Goods is applicable to the present case as—as can be seen from the following assessment—the legal outcome is similar irrespective whether the United Nations Convention on Contracts for the International Sale of Goods or other Austrian law is applied. [...]

CISG Advisory Council Opinion No 4: Contracts for the Sale of Goods to Be Manufactured or Produced and Mixed Contracts (Article 3 CISG):[12]

1. Paragraphs (1) and (2) of Article 3 CISG govern different matters, though in complex trans-actions there may be some reciprocal influence in their interpretation and application.
2. In interpreting the words 'substantial part' under Article 3(1) CISG, primarily an 'economic value' criterion should be used. An 'essential' criterion should only be considered where the 'economic value' is impossible or inappropriate to apply taking into account the circumstances of the case.
3. 'Substantial' should not be quantified by predetermined percentages of value; it should be determined on the basis of an overall assessment.
4. The supply of labour or other services necessary for the manufacture or production of the goods is covered by the words 'manufactured or produced' of Article 3(1) CISG and is not governed by Article 3(2) CISG.
5. The words 'materials necessary for such manufacture' in Article 3(1) CISG do not cover drawings, technical specifications, technology or formulas, unless they enhance the value of the materials supplied by the parties.
6. In the interpretation of Article 3(1) CISG, it is irrelevant whether the goods are fungible or non-fungible, standard or custom-made. [...]

Questions

Q 3-1

Which terms used in the CISG indicate that it was originally drafted for the sale of tangible goods?

Q 3-2

Why should the distinction between contracts for standard software and contracts for cus-tomised software be irrelevant to the question of whether the CISG applies? See A 3-1.

Q 3-3

(a) How did the court in C 3-1 interpret the term 'substantial part' mentioned in Article 3(1) CISG?
(b) What were the criteria applied in C 3-2 and C 3-3 with regard to the interpretation of 'a substantial part'?
(c) Compare the results with CISG Advisory Council Opinion No 4: in which ways can 'substantial part' be understood? Which interpretation seems better to you? Give your reasons.

---

[12] Taken from www.cisgac.com.

Q 3-4

Could the parties agree on the applicability of the CISG to contracts which would normally be excluded pursuant to Article 3(1) CISG? Remember what has been stated above, Article 1 CISG, section I.

IV. Supply of Labour or Other Services (Article 3(2) CISG)

Article 3(2) CISG deals with situations where the seller's obligations include not only the delivery of goods, but also some kind of service. As a rule, the CISG also applies to those mixed contracts. An exception is made for cases in which the service constitutes the 'preponderant part' of the contract.

In order to determine the CISG's applicability, it must first be decided whether the parties agreed on a single 'mixed contract' or whether they concluded two separate contracts. For that purpose, the criteria enumerated in CISG Advisory Council Opinion No 4 provide some guidance.

The second question concerns the term 'preponderant part': as with paragraph 1 of Article 3 CISG, paragraph 2 does not apply where the non-sales part forms the 'preponderant part' of the seller's contractual duties. The following abstracts deal with that question.

CISG Advisory Council Opinion No 4: Contracts for the Sale of Goods to be Manufactured or Produced and Mixed Contracts (Article 3 CISG):[13]

[...]

7. Article 3(2) CISG governs mixed contracts. Whether the different obligations as to goods and services are agreed upon in one mixed contract or in several contracts is a matter of contract interpretation.

8. In the interpretation of the parties' agreements relevant factors include, inter alia, the denomination and entire content of the contract, the structure of the price, and the weight given by the parties to the different obligations under the contract.

9. In interpreting the words 'preponderant part' under Article 3(2) CISG, primarily an 'economic value' criterion should be used. An 'essential' criterion should only be considered where the 'economic value' is impossible or inappropriate to apply taking into account the circumstances of the case.

10. 'Preponderant' should not be quantified by predetermined percentages of value; it should be determined on the basis of an overall assessment.

---

[13] Taken from www.cisgac.com.

C 3-4

Oberlandesgericht München (Germany),
3 December 1999,
CISG-online 585[14]

For a summary of the facts see C 3-2 above.

[Judgment]

[...] The supply agreement between the [buyer] and the [seller] is furthermore not excluded from the scope of the Convention by virtue of Article 3(2) CISG. The [seller]'s 'inclusive' obligation to assemble the plant and put it into operation at the [buyer]'s place of business does not constitute the preponderant part of the [seller]'s obligations under the contract. Whether certain obligations constitute the preponderant part of obligations depends primarily on the relative value of each element. Additionally, the particular interest that the purchasing party places on an obligation, i.e., the characteristic obligation can be decisive. An approximately identical value of the different obligations is sufficient to render the Convention applicable. In the present case, the value of the agreed services of several mechanics for the period of six weeks merely constitutes a small part of the total costs for the plant of DM 1,245,000.00. Additionally, the characteristic obligation to manufacture the plant does not carry less weight than its assembly and putting into operation. [...]

C 3-5

International Court of Commercial Arbitration Chamber
of Commerce and Industry of the Russian Federation,
Award No 356/1999, 30 May 2000,
CISG-online 1077[15]

[Facts]

A German seller and a Russian buyer entered into a contract for the supply [of] certain equipment as well as performance of some specific services (construction work, balancing and commissioning, geodetic work and so on). According to a subsequent agreement, the entire contract price had to be split into two parts, one for shipment of equipment (which amounted to more than 50% of the whole price) and the other for services. Following the buyer's refusal to pay the price, the seller commenced arbitral proceedings, claiming payment of the price.

[Judgment]

The Tribunal held that the contract was governed by CISG pursuant to Art 3(2), since the price of the goods (i.e. equipment) amounted to more than 50% of the entire contract price. [...]

---

[14] Translation taken from CISG Pace (citations omitted).
[15] English abstract taken from UNILEX.

Questions

Q 3-5

What factors are taken into account when determining whether the seller fulfils mere ancillary obligations of a sales contract or whether its duty is to perform a mixed contract which does not fall within the scope of the CISG in its entirety?

Q 3-6

(a)   How does the *Oberlandesgericht München* in C 3-4 quantify the 'preponderant part'?
(b)   Should such an approach, which is based on the economic value of the various performances, be followed?
(c)   The Russian Tribunal in C 3-5 adopts a 'percentage' view to determine the 'preponderant part'. Is this approach any different from that adopted in C 3-4?

Article 4 CISG

This Convention governs only the formation of the contract of sale and the rights and obligations of the seller and the buyer arising from such a contract. In particular, except as otherwise expressly provided in this Convention, it is not concerned with:

(a) the validity of the contract or any of its provisions or of any usage;
(b) the effect which the contract may have on the property in the goods sold.

I. Overview

Whereas Articles 1 to 3 and 6 CISG define the sphere of application in general, Article 4, together with Article 5 CISG, defines the legal issues to which the CISG applies. Sentence 1 of Article 4 lists the matters governed by the CISG, whereas sentence 2 contains a non-exhaustive list of issues not dealt with in the CISG.

Article 4(a) clarifies that the CISG does not govern questions concerning the validity of the contract or any of its terms. Thus, the Convention is not concerned, for example, with the requirements of capacity to contract, unconscionability (*Sittenwidrigkeit, contrats illicites*), illegality, vitiated consent (*Irrtum, erreur,* mistake, duress, fraud), and so on. The purpose of the 'validity' exception in Article 4(a) CISG was to preserve national rules that embodied important social values and could not be waived by mutual agreement.

Furthermore, the CISG does not deal with agency, the validity of usages, standard terms, penalties, settlements, choice of law or forum selection clauses, the issue of assignment, assumption of debts, or promissory letters. These questions have to be resolved by having recourse to the applicable national law. Whether some questions, though not expressly addressed in the CISG, are now accepted as being uniformly settled thereunder, without having recourse to the rules of private international law, remains open to debate. The issues of set-off, burden of proof, or the applicable interest rate may serve as examples (see below Art 7 CISG).

Article 4(b) CISG states that the CISG provides no rule as to the transfer of title. This means that it does not answer the question of when and under which requirements the buyer becomes the legal owner of the goods. Furthermore, it does not govern the question of how good title is acquired which emerges if the seller is not the owner or if he has only a voidable title in the goods.

II. Matters of Validity (Article 4(a) CISG)

A. Operation of Article 4(a) CISG

The fact that the CISG only governs the formation of the sales contract and the rights and obligations of the seller and the buyer created under the contract has often been stated in case law. For the legal aspects that are not governed by the CISG, reference is to be made to the law determined by the private international law of the *lex fori* and *lex fori arbitri*, respectively.

B. Comparison with Other Legal Provisions

PICC 2010:

Article 3.1.4 (Mandatory character of the provisions)

> The provisions on fraud, threat, gross disparity and illegality contained in this Chapter are mandatory.

Article 3.2.5 (Fraud)

> A party may avoid the contract when it has been led to conclude the contract by the other party's fraudulent representation, including language or practices, or fraudulent non-disclosure of circumstances which, according to reasonable commercial standards of fair dealing, the latter party should have disclosed.

Article 3.2.6 (Threat)

> A party may avoid the contract when it has been led to conclude the contract by the other party's unjustified threat which, having regard to the circumstances, is so imminent and serious as to leave the first party no reasonable alternative. [...]

Article 3.2.7 (Gross Disparity)

> (1)(1) A party may avoid the contract or an individual term of it if, at the time of the conclusion of the contract, the contract or term unjustifiably gave the other party an excessive advantage. [...]

III. Matters of Property (Article 4(b) CISG)

The CISG does not contain any rules on the transfer of property in the goods sold under the contract. To this extent, it is the applicable domestic law that determines when property in the goods is transferred to the buyer and under which requirements property is acquired in good faith. Where the parties have agreed that the seller shall hold retention of title over the goods, a distinction must be drawn between the contractual effect of such a clause and the effect it has on the buyer's rights over the goods. The contractual effect of retention of title is a matter that generally affects the CISG; the parties, by agreeing on a retention of title, modify the seller's duties to the effect that the seller is not obliged to transfer the property in the goods immediately, but only after the buyer has fulfilled all of its own duties, for example, paid the total purchase price. As long as the buyer does not comply with its contractual obligations, the seller is not bound to transfer property in the goods. A general expression of the right of retention can be found in Article 71 CISG. We must thus draw a distinction between the contractual right of retention and the buyer's rights in the goods during the period in which the seller still has title. It is the applicable domestic law which states whether, during that period, the buyer is in any way entitled in the goods or what the requirements for passing of title in the goods are once the buyer has complied with all of its duties.

A question that several cases have dealt with concerns the interaction between the buyer's rights relating to the goods not yet received on the one hand, and the rights of a third party over those goods on the other hand. Where, for example, a third party has a security right over the goods sold by the seller to the buyer, the question arises as to which right prevails: the buyer's contractual right to receive the goods or the third party's security right over those goods? Read the following case in this regard.

C 4-1

Usinor Industeel v Leeco Steel Products, Inc,
US Dist Ct (ND IL), 28 March 2002,
CISG-online 696

[Facts]

[...] Leeco is a corporation incorporated under the laws of the State of Illinois with its principal place of business in Illinois. Leeco has operations in Chicago, St. Louis, Pittsburgh, Wisconsin, South Carolina and Tennessee. Leeco is an independent steel center, specializing, securing, processing and delivering sheet and plate grades of steel. [...]

In early February 2000, Leeco began placing orders with Usinor for the purchase and shipment of certain tonnage of Creusabro 8000. Leeco ordered the steel in order to participate in a proposed new project of Caterpillar relating to large mining vehicles. [...]

Under Paragraph 7 of the sales agreement between Usinor and Leeco for the Steel Shipments (the 'Agreement') Usinor 'remain[s] the owner of the goods up to the complete and total payment of all sums due.' Also, pursuant to the terms of the Agreement, Leeco was obligated to pay Usinor within 60 days following receipt of the steel. In addition, Leeco agreed that any dispute regarding the Steel Shipments would be resolved in the French court system.

Usinor states that Leeco's early enthusiasm for the Caterpillar project resulted in extraordinary demands on Usinor to deliver substantial quantities of Creusabro 8000 steel plate. Therefore, beginning in December 2000 and continuing until April 20 2001, Usinor produced and exported multiple shipments of the steel, valued at $1,188,817.30, from France to Leeco's designated locations in accordance with Leeco's delivery schedule. At some time in the year

2000, Caterpillar notified its own suppliers, as well as Leeco and Usinor, that it was halting or considering halting, the fabrication of truck beds in the mining vehicle program. Leeco now has possession of Creusabro 8000 steel that Leeco was unable to sell to Caterpillar, although Usinor asserts it has many alternate uses. Leeco took delivery of the Steel Shipments, and Usinor asserts on information and belief, has used portions of the Steel Shipments in its operations and/or sold portions to others. Leeco has made a partial payment on the total value of only one of the Steel Shipments for the portions that it has used in its operations or sold to others. Leeco has not made a complete and total payment for the Steel Shipments, and has not returned the Steel Shipments, after demand by Usinor to do so. Currently, Leeco still owes Usinor at least $988,817.36 of the total value of the Steel Shipments. Usinor asserts on information and belief that the value of the remaining steel from the Steel Shipment in the possession of Leeco is worth substantially less than the amount of money that Leeco owes Usinor. Instead of making complete and total payment for the Steel Shipments, Usinor asserts that Leeco has instead sought to use its control over the improved steel to force Usinor to provide Leeco a refund on the steel it had purchased, but not used.

Leeco purchased the Steel Shipment using a line of credit (the 'Loan') from LaSalle Bank. Usinor asserts that Leeco is in default on the Loan and has been urged by LaSalle Bank to sell the Steel Shipments to pay off any remaining debt owed by Leeco to that lender under the Loan. Usinor asserts on information and belief that Leeco may be facing insolvency through its default on the Loan and would not be able to pay any damages that Usinor might recover from Leeco for breach of the sales agreement.

[Judgment]

[...] The conflict that the Court must face in its determination is one between maintaining the purpose of the CISG and the purpose of the UCC. [...] The issue of first impression facing the Court is whether the CISG applies to a transaction between a buyer and seller when a third party has an interest in the goods. The Court needs to determine whether or not when a third party is involved, if local law, the UCC, preempts the interest given to the seller by the CISG.

[...] Here the buyer and seller are parties whose place of business are France and the US, both signatories to the CISG. [...] While there are few cases in the US dealing with the CISG, it is clear that the CISG governs the transaction between Usinor and Leeco such that if LaSalle were not a party to this controversy, the resolution would be clear: under the Supremacy Clause of the United States Constitution, the Convention would displace any contrary state sales law such as the UCC. [...]

However, the text of the CISG and analysis by commentators suggest that the CISG applies only to buyer and seller, not to third parties. Therefore, application of the CISG here requires a court to resolve an issue for first impression. To wit, the court must determine whether the CISG governs a controversy if a third party has a security interest in the goods. [...]

The key provision of the CISG which is at issue here is Article 4, which states that the CISG 'governs only the formation of the contract of sale and the rights and obligations of the seller and the buyer arising from such a contract. In particular, except as otherwise expressly provided in this Convention, it is not concerned with: (a) the validity of the contract or of any of its provisions or of any usage; (b) the effect which the contract may have on the property in the goods sold.'

Leeco's argument is that section (b) of Article 4 excludes the application of the CISG to the case at hand. Usinor's position is that Article 4(b) means that those property interests placed outside CISG's scope are property interests arising prior to sale, and that here, LaSalle does not have property interests in the Steel Shipments prior to the sale.

The State Department states of Article 4(b) that '[w]hether the sale to the buyer cuts off outstanding property interests of third persons is not dealt with by the Convention. This specific provision illustrates the general rule of Article 4 that the Convention is concerned only with the "rights and obligations of the seller and the buyer" arising from the sales contract.' Usinor asserts that the State Department is referring only to property interests that exist at the time of sale. However, other commentators support a different reading, simply that the CISG does not govern the rights of third persons who are not parties to the contract. [...]

Similarly, John Honnold writes in Uniform Law for International Sales § 444 (3d ed 1999) that '[t]he seller's right under the Convention to recover the goods is subject to practical limitations. This remedy is of special importance when the buyer is insolvent; in this setting the rights of creditors are likely to intervene by levy of execution or by the designation of a receiver or trustee in bankruptcy. The Convention will not override the rights of creditors, purchasers and other third persons granted by domestic law; under Article 4, the Convention "governs only . . . the rights . . . of the seller and the buyer . . .". As Honnold goes on to state, "One question remains: Does applicable domestic law invalidate (Art 44(a)) a contractual provision allowing reclamation of the goods on non-payment? Such a rule of invalidity is conceivable but seems unlikely. (He cites to UCC 9-503 and UCC 1-201(37)). However, as we have seen, the Convention's rules are limited (Art 4) to the rights "of the seller and the buyer" and yield to the rights of third persons such as creditors and purchasers.' [...]

The 'conceivable' but 'unlikely' that Honnold notes is what occurred in the transaction at hand. The remedy of avoidance under the CISG is not available to Usinor if LaSalle has a right to the Steel Shipments under domestic law. The remedy of replevin is not available if Usinor does not have title to the Steel Shipments under domestic law. Therefore, the question the Court next needs to determine is whether domestic law grants LaSalle such a right, a right to the Steel Shipments that supersedes that of Usinor's. [...]

[...] First, the Court needs to determine which domestic law applies, that of France or Illinois. Under French law, the seller of goods has an absolute right to contract for title until payment, and therefore the retention of title clause in the Agreement would be determinative. However, under the UCC, Usinor would only have a reservation of a security interest.

Under the 'most significant contacts rule' of the Restatement (Second) which Usinor asks the Court to apply, and the UCC choice of law provision which Leeco argues should be the governing test, the Court finds the same result: Illinois law applies. [...] Therefore, the Court finds that the UCC governs the determination of whether LaSalle has title in the Steel Shipments, or, to phrase it in a different way, application of the UCC determines the validity of the retention of title provision in the contract.

[...] Under UCC Section 2-401(a), Usinor has a reservation of a security interest only. [...] Therefore, under domestic law, Usinor's retention of title in the contract did not effectively retain title in Usinor. Rather, transfer of title was effected upon delivery to Leeco. [...]

At the date of the sale of the Steel Shipments to Leeco, LaSalle did not have a perfected security interest in the Steel Shipments; its perfected interest arose only on November 15, 2001, after the sale of the Steel Shipments, once it was in the possession of Leeco, and LaSalle filed the continuing financing statement. Usinor's Complaint was filed on January 23, 2002, after LaSalle's security interest was perfected.

[...] Usinor does not have title in the Steel Shipments, only a reservation of a security interest. Therefore, the remedy of replevin is unavailable to Usinor. [...] ('Replevin' is a possessory action and the plaintiff must recover, if at all, on the strength of his own title or his right to immediate possession.)

Usinor has a security interest in the Steel Shipments, but it is not perfected. A perfected security interest prevails over the retained interest of an unpaid seller who did not perfect a security interest. Therefore, LaSalle's perfected security interest prevails over the retained interest of Usinor in the Steel.

ORDERED: Usinor's motion for replevin is denied. Usinor's motion to avoid the sales agreement between Usinor and Leeco under the CISG is denied. [...]

Questions

Q 4-1

Which law governs the issues which do not fall within the CISG's scope of application?

Q 4-2

Are remedies for vitiated consent based on domestic law applicable in addition to the CISG?

Q 4-3

Other uniform law does not show the same restriction in the scope of application. The PICC 2010, for example, also deal with the validity of contract, including mistake, fraud, threat and gross disparity.

(a) Why did the drafters of the CISG refrain from settling issues affecting the validity of the contract?
(b) Why are there no particular difficulties when dealing with those issues in the PICC 2010?

Q 4-4

What might have been the reason for excluding the issue of ownership from the Convention's scope of application?

Q 4-5

When will domestic law pre-empt a right granted to a party to the contract by the CISG? See C 4-1.

Article 5 CISG

This Convention does not apply to the liability of the seller for death or personal injury caused by the goods to any person.

Pursuant to Article 5 CISG, losses arising from death or personal injury are excluded from the CISG's scope of application. This is an exception to the general rule that all direct losses are remunerable under the Convention (see below, Article 74 CISG). The reason is that the CISG should not compete with domestic rules on product liability. The following abstract deals with the question of whether the CISG is superseded by domestic non-contractual products liability law only or whether domestic law takes precedence also if it resolves product liability in contract law.

A 5-1

Peter Schlechtriem, Uniform Sales Law: The UN Convention on Contracts for the International Sale of Goods, (Vienna, Springer Verlag, 1986) pp 34–35

A proposal sponsored by Finland, France, and the United States to exclude from the Convention claims based on death or personal injury caused by the goods was accepted in Vienna and embodied in Article 5. The basic idea is simple: the Convention does not govern products liability. Domestic law, therefore, remains in force. To the extent products liability is characterised as non-contractual under domestic law, Article 5 merely states the obvious. [...] However, since some legal systems resolve problems of product liability in contract, this Article was needed to ensure that these domestic rules would still apply when the Convention is enacted. Therefore the contractual remedies of *'positive Vertragsverletzung'* or § 463 BGB under German law or the responsibility of the *'vendeur professionel'* under Articles 1645 and 1646 of the French Civil Code are applicable in case of death or personal injury. [...]

Liability for death or personal injury is only one—although probably the most important— field of products liability. Liability for damage caused to property is not excluded by Article 5. The Conference considered whether a broader term, such as 'claims based on product liability,' could be used, but no agreement could be reached as to the extent to which the Convention should apply to property damage caused by defective goods which are used as foreseen by the contract. Semi-finished products ruined by a defective machine and raw materials wasted because they were combined with unsuitable materials are typical cases where the buyer's contract expectations are frustrated and which therefore belong to the core of the matter to be regulated by sales law. In my opinion, damages in those circumstances should be governed by the Convention and compensated in conformity to the provisions set forth in Article 74. The question of whether a concurrent action in tort would lie must be decided by domestic law.

A 5-1 also clarifies that, with regard to property damage (as opposed to liability for death or personal injury), the buyer's claim for damages will be governed by the CISG. However, the question then arises of whether, in such a case, Article 5 CISG excludes the concurrent application of domestic tort law. The view expressed in A 5-1 appears to be the view prevailing in scholarly writing: it is in the hands of the applicable domestic law to determine whether a claim available under domestic law in the case at hand is a tort claim. If it is a tort claim, it should be available as a concurrent remedy. A more clear-cut and more predictable approach which has recently been suggested in the literature would be to hold that the CISG always pre-empts domestic law.

Another question is whether Article 5 CISG also excludes the application of the CISG in the case where it is not the buyer who suffered personal injury but third parties who died or were injured as a consequence of the seller's breach of contract; will the buyer who is faced with liability claims from its customers and who seeks indemnification from the seller, base its claims on the CISG or—because of Article 5 CISG—on domestic law? The question is discussed in the following excerpt.

A 5-2

Loukas Mistelis and John Ribeiro, in Kröll, Mistelis, and Perales Viscasillas (eds), *UN Convention on Contracts for the International Sale of Goods (CISG), Commentary*, 2011, Art 5 n 11 *et seq.*[16]

One view is that the text of Art. 5 ('to any person') should be given an all-inclusive interpretation to the effect that, as a third party is 'any person', the buyer's claims for indemnification should also be excluded from the scope of the Convention and be governed by the applicable domestic law. In other words, this view excludes outright all claims arising from personal injury before considering the kind of loss the buyer is claiming damages for. This all-inclusive interpretation appears to be in accord with the legislative intent of the Convention and has received support from the majority of commentators. [...] The alternative view is that the buyer is merely seeking to recover the economic loss of having to compensate his customers rather than trying to hold the seller liable for death or personal injury. In this sense, the buyer's claim should be understood as one of consequential loss covered by Art 74 and not excluded by Art. 5. [...] In this authors' opinion, the alternative view is preferred. Although the legislative history suggests a literal interpretation of Art 5, too much emphasis on this should be avoided. It is suggested that adopting a literal interpretation of Art. 5 runs contrary to the observance of the international character of the CISG and promotion of uniformity that the Convention seeks to attain in international trade (Art. 7(1)). Fawcett/Harris/Bridge elucidate this contravention by noting that treating a buyer's claim to be indemnified for the death or personal injury of his customers caused by defective goods as a matter of domestic law and dealing with claims for recovery or price reduction that arise from the same

---

[16] References omitted.

defective goods separately under the CISG 'would lead to an untidy dépeçage' in respect of the buyer's claims against the seller.

Questions

Q 5-1

(a)   Why does the CISG not apply to damages for death or personal injury?
(b)   In this respect, is it relevant whether the claims available under the applicable domestic law are non-contractual or contractual damages? In other words, is the CISG always pre-empted in case of damages claims for death or personal injury or only if the respective claim under the domestic law would be tort claim? See A 5-1.

Q 5-2

(a)   Which law governs a claim for damages to property other than the goods sold which are due to the seller's breach of contract? See A 5-1.
(b)   Can extra-contractual claims for which the applicable domestic law would provide in such a case be concurrently relied on? See A 5-2.

Q 5-3

If, because of the seller's breach of contract, the buyer is sued for personal injury caused to its customers by the defective product, does the buyer's claim for indemnity against the seller fall under the CISG?

Article 6 CISG

The parties may exclude the application of this Convention or, subject to Article 12, derogate from or vary the effect of any of its provisions.

I. Overview

Pursuant to Article 6 CISG, the parties may exclude the CISG partially or entirely. A total exclusion of the CISG may also be referred to as 'opting-out'; a partial exclusion is usually referred to as 'derogation from' or 'modification of' the CISG. The first principle embodied in Article 6 is the principle of party autonomy: the parties are free to choose the law applicable to their contract. Most legal systems recognise this principle.

The second principle which can be found in Article 6 CISG is the non-mandatory character of the CISG. All provisions are non-mandatory; the only exception is Article 12 CISG, which deals with reservations a Contracting State may have concerning the freedom from form requirements and which expressly states that the parties may neither derogate from Article 12 CISG nor vary its effect.

II. Opting-out of the CISG

The question of whether the parties have excluded the application of the CISG—which would otherwise apply by way of Article 1—is governed by the CISG. In this respect, it is now virtually undisputed that an opting-out of the CISG can be explicit or implicit. An explicit exclusion of the CISG is where the parties clearly state in their contract that the CISG does not apply. An implicit exclusion of the CISG is, for example, the choice of law of a non-Contracting State, such as English or Irish law.

The greatest controversy arises from a choice of law clause in which the parties agree on the application of the law of a Contracting State. If the parties agree, for example, on 'French law', did they mean that they want the *Code Civil*, *Code de Commerce* and so on to apply to their contract, thereby excluding the CISG? Or was such a clause rather a reference to the entire French Commercial Sales Law, to the effect that, with regard to *international* commercial sales, the CISG, as the law governing such contracts in France, will apply? See the following cases in this regard.

C 6-1

Ad hoc Tribunal, Florence
19 April 1994,
CISG-online 124[17]

[Facts]

On 1 June 1989, company X, [seller], having its registered office in Florence [Italy] and company Y, [buyer], having its registered office in Tokyo [Japan] entered into a contract for the supply of leather and/or textile wear, manufactured by [seller] and bearing the trademark [HM]; the contract granted [buyer] exclusivity rights for Japan and required [buyer] to purchase a minimum amount of goods for a period of five years, from 1 July 1989 to 30 June 1994.

[Judgment]

2. Applicability of Vienna Convention (CISG)

Since counsel for [buyer] in several occasions referred to the principles of the Vienna Convention of 11 April 1980 on Contracts for the International Sale of Goods [CISG] (ratified in Italy by Law 11 December 1985 n. 765 and in force since 1 January 1988), the majority of the Tribunal holds, without ascertaining whether the Convention is relevant to the merits of the dispute, that the applicability of the Convention must be excluded. This is because the Convention has not yet been ratified in Japan and also because clause 39 of the supply contract specifies that the contract is governed exclusively by Italian law.

[...]

One of the arbitrators, dissenting from the majority of the Tribunal, summarized his position as follows:

'The Arbitrator does not agree with the decision of the majority of the Tribunal, in particular for the following reasons:

(a)   because the majority has decided that the Vienna Convention does not apply to the contract between the parties; on the contrary, the Convention is applicable pursuant to Art. 1(1)(b) CISG, since the choice of Italian law as the governing law confirms the applicability of the Convention, rather than excluding it pursuant to article 6 CISG;

(b)   ...'

It must be noted that the view expressed by the majority of the Arbitral Tribunal has remained the exception. Most court decisions and arbitral awards have adopted the position depicted in C 6-2 and C 6-3.

---

[17]   Case abstract taken from CISG Pace (references omitted).

C 6-2

Oberlandesgericht Stuttgart (Germany),
31 March 2008,
CISG-online 1658

[Facts]

[...] The [Buyer], a Latvian corporation, claims the reverse transaction of a contract for the sale of a car concluded with the [Seller], a German professional car dealer, in the form of a repayment of the purchase price conditional upon the handing over of the car. [...] The contract refers for the remainder to standard terms of the [Seller] which provided for the jurisdiction of the court at the place where the [Seller] was domiciled. [...]

[Judgment]

[...] The CISG is applicable to the present contract. Both Germany and Latvia are Contracting States of the Convention on Contracts for the International Sale of Goods. Hence, it is irrelevant whether the German International Private Law provides for German or Latvian law. The subject matter and personal requirements for the application of the CISG are met as well. [...] The parties did not exclude the application of the CISG. It is true that the CISG provides for freedom of contract and thus for the possibility to exclude its application (Article 6 CISG), which leads to the application of the respective national law as provided for by the IPR. However, there is no such exclusion in the present case—neither at the time of the conclusion of the contract nor after this point in time. The parties have neither explicitly agreed on the application of specific provisions nor do the standard terms—the inclusion of which is disputed in any case—contain any clause in this respect. It has to be taken into account that the CISG is incorporated into German law. Hence, the assumption that 'German law would naturally apply' does not mean that solely the BGB and the HGB are applicable. A clause such as 'the provisions of the BGB are applicable' would have been necessary in this case. An exclusion of the application of the CISG cannot be inferred from the fact that the standard terms of the [Seller] provided for German jurisdiction. It is true that the denomination of the jurisdiction of a certain State can often be interpreted as a hint that the law of this very State should apply. This is based on the assumption that the application of foreign law by a court is time-consuming and expensive. However, this does not apply to the CISG which is a uniform law that can easily be applied by its Member States. Therefore the choice of German law automatically implies the application of the CISG. Thus, more precise hints would have been necessary in order to exclude the application of the CISG. [...]

C 6-3

Asante Techs, Inc v PMC- Sierra, Inc,
US Dist Ct (ND CA), 27 July 2001,
CISG-online 616

[Facts]

[...] [Buyer] is a Delaware corporation having its primary place of business in Santa Clara County, California. The Court concludes that [seller's] place of business for the purposes of the contract at issue and its performance is Burnaby, British Columbia, Canada.

[Judgment]

C. The effect of the choice of law clauses

[Buyer] next argues that, even if the Parties are from two nations that have adopted the CISG, the choice of law provisions in the 'Terms and Conditions' set forth by both Parties reflect the Parties' intent to 'opt out' of application of the treaty. Article 6 of the CISG provides that 'the parties may exclude the application of the Convention or, subject to Article 12, derogate from or vary the effect of any of its provisions.' [...] [Seller] asserts that merely choosing the law of a jurisdiction is insufficient to opt out of the CISG, absent express exclusion of the CISG. The Court finds that the particular choice of law provisions in the 'Terms and Conditions' of both parties are inadequate to effectuate an opt out of the CISG.

Although selection of a particular choice of law, such as 'the California Commercial Code' or the 'Uniform Commercial Code' could amount to implied exclusion of the CISG, the choice of law clauses at issue here do not evince a clear intent to opt out of the CISG. For example, [seller's] choice of applicable law adopts the law of British Columbia, and it is undisputed that the CISG is the law of British Columbia. (International Sale of Goods Act ch. 236, 1996 S.B.C. 1 et seq. (B.C.).) Furthermore, even [buyer's] choice of applicable law generally adopts the 'laws of' the State of California, and California is bound by the Supremacy Clause to the treaties of the United States. [...] Thus, under general California law, the CISG is applicable to contracts where the contracting parties are from different countries that have adopted the CISG. In the absence of clear language indicating that both contracting parties intended to opt out of the CISG, and in view of [seller's] Terms and Conditions which would apply the CISG, the Court rejects [buyer's] contention that the choice of law provisions preclude the applicability of the CISG. [...]

III. Derogation from or Modification of the CISG

The question as to whether the parties have derogated from or modified the CISG is governed by the CISG. A derogation from or modification of the CISG may assume different shapes. The parties may, for example, refer to a domestic law as the law applicable to their contract and thus modify Article 7(2) CISG (see also section II above). They may also, for example, agree on additional contract clauses or on trade usages such as INCOTERMS®. Or they may replace certain CISG provisions by the provisions of another set of rules. They may also simply strike certain provisions out; for example, they can delete Article 72 (right to avoid the contract for anticipatory breach) without agreeing on any other law or provisions, thereby leaving it to the applicable rules of private international law to determine the applicable law.

IV. Opting-in to the CISG

The possibility of opting-in to the CISG is not explicitly mentioned in the text of the Convention. Whether the CISG may be chosen as the applicable law in contracts which would otherwise not be governed by it—be it because neither Article 1(1)(a) nor 1(1)(b) leads to the application of the CISG, or because the Convention is inapplicable because of its Articles 2 and 3—is a question governed by the conflict of laws rules of the forum (see above Art 1 CISG).

V. Comparison with the PICC 2010

Art 1.5 PICC 2010:

> The parties may exclude the application of these Principles or derogate from or vary the effect of any of their provisions, except as otherwise provided in the Principles.

Questions

Q 6-1

What options are available to the parties under Article 6 CISG?

Q 6-2

(a) Can you explain why the greatest controversy arises from a choice of law clause in which the parties agree on the application of the law of a Contracting State?
(b) How has the issue been decided in C 6-1 to C 6-3? Is it reasonable to assume that, in these cases, the parties opted out of the CISG?
(c) Draft a clause under which there is an effective opting-out of the CISG.

Q 6-3

On what does it depend whether the parties are allowed to opt into the CISG?

Q 6-4

(a) If the parties have excluded the CISG, which law will apply instead of the CISG:
  —   if the parties have chosen a particular law;
  —   if the parties have not settled that question?
(b) Which law governs the question of whether the parties have effectively agreed on modifying a provision of the CISG?

Q 6-5

(a) Why is the reservation in Article 1.5 PICC 2010 extraordinary? Compare the legal status of the PICC.
(b) Are there any provisions in the PICC 2010 which are of such a mandatory character?

Article 7 CISG

(1) In the interpretation of this Convention, regard is to be had to its international character and to the need to promote uniformity in its application and the observance of good faith in international trade.
(2) Questions concerning matters governed by this Convention which are not expressly settled in it are to be settled in conformity with the general principles on which it is based or, in the absence of such principles, in conformity with the law applicable by virtue of the rules of private international law.

I. Overview

Article 7 CISG contains rules for the interpretation (Art 7(1)) and gap-filling of the CISG (Art 7(2)). Its goal is to ensure an internationally uniform interpretation and application. This means that its interpretation and application should not be influenced by the principles of the particular legal system of the forum state. Article 7 CISG is a provision of great importance, since the various national sales laws differ in both approach and concept.

II. Article 7(1) CISG

A. International Character and Uniform Application

(a) Autonomous Interpretation

Article 7(1) CISG states that, in its interpretation, regard must be had to the international character and the uniform application of the Convention. It establishes a rule for the interpretation, application and gap-filling of the CISG which can be found in most of UNCITRAL's uniform law instruments. In case law, one often finds the expression that the Convention ought to be interpreted 'autonomously'.

Sometimes courts have stated that, when interpreting the CISG, one should also consider decisions based on national law where the wording of the CISG corresponds to provisions of the national sales law, even if the national law does not apply to the case at hand. However, the case law and other legal materials relating to another legal system may only be consulted to the extent that certain terms or solutions have clearly been influenced by this legal system (for example, Art 74, sentence 2 CISG contains the 'foreseeability doctrine' to reasonably narrow down damages; the 'foreseeability test' can be traced back to the common law doctrine established in *Hadley v Baxendale* (discussed below under Art 74)).

(b) Persuasive Precedents

Unlike, for instance, in the EU, there is no 'final instance CISG court', no court of ultimate resort to promote uniformity in interpretation of the law. Another method must, therefore, be found to ensure the uniform interpretation of the CISG. It seems clear that foreign decisions or awards, as well as foreign literature, must be considered. If there is consensus in literature and case law as to how a specific question should be handled, later decisions should follow this. In particular, where a court of last resort of a Contracting State has decided a question in a particular way, the ratio of this decision has persuasive authority for other courts. With respect to the consultation of foreign CISG case law, there are considerable differences. Some Italian court decisions have recently taken an almost excessive comparative law approach, whereas, for example, US courts have traditionally been hesitant to consider foreign CISG case law.[18] However, courts and tribunals now quote foreign CISG decisions quite regularly. See, for example, the following US decision.

C 7-1

Chicago Prime Packers, Inc v Northam Food Trading Co et al, US Dist Ct (ND IL), 21 May 2004, CISG-online 851[19]

[Facts][20]

An U.S. company ('Seller') purchased from another U.S. company 40 500 pounds of frozen pork ribs which it immediately afterwards resold to a Canadian meat wholesaler ('Buyer'). Buyer, which had picked up the goods at the first supplier's factory, entrusted a U.S. meat processor with the task of processing them. When receiving the goods the U.S. processor stated that they were in good condition with the exception of 21 boxes that had holes gouged in them. However, soon after it had begun processing the ribs, a United States Department of Agriculture inspector ordered it first to stop processing the ribs and finally to destroy them altogether due to their poor condition. As a consequence Buyer informed Seller that it was not willing to pay the price for the goods. At this point Seller, which had already paid its own

---

[18]   *Cf* the list of US court decisions applying the CISG in *Usinor Industeel v Leeco Steel Products Inc.*, US Dist Ct (ND IL), 28 March 2002, CISG-online 696, pointing only to US case law.
[19]   1st instance US Dist Ct, 29 May 2003, CISG-online 796 (cited below Art 7 CISG, C 7-1).
[20]   Summary of facts taken from UNILEX.

supplier for the same goods, moved for summary judgment against Buyer for the payment of the price, arguing that Buyer had not given timely notice of the defects.

[Judgment]

[...] A number of foreign courts have also addressed the question of how much time a buyer has to examine goods or discover defects under the CISG. [...] In one German case, for example, a buyer lost the right to rely on lack of conformity by failing to promptly inspect ham delivered by the seller or give notice of the ham's nonconformity within a reasonable time. [...] The court found that because the alleged defect (inadequate seasoning) was easily recognizable, the buyer should have examined the goods within three days of delivery. See also [...] Oberlandesgericht Karlsruhe Decision of 25-06-1997 [...].

In a case dealing with insufficient quantity as a defect, another German court held that under Article 38, examination of the quantity of items delivered must be done immediately at the place of performance of the obligation or at the agreed destination. [...] See also [...] Decision of the Tribunal of Vigevano, Italy, July 12, 2000, [...].

[...] A buyer bears the burden of showing that notice of nonconformity has been given within a reasonable time. [...] Landgericht Frankfurt am Main, Germany (July 13, 1994) [...] The evidence shows that, shortly after Beacon discovered the ribs were 'off condition' and did not 'look good,' both Northam and Chicago Prime were notified of a potential problem.

Chicago Prime therefore received notice within a reasonable time after Northam discovered the problem; however, the question here is whether Chicago Prime was notified within a reasonable time after Northam should have discovered the problem.

A court in Italy found that the reasonableness of the time for a notice of non-conformity provided in Article 39 is strictly related to the duty to examine the goods within as short a period as is practicable in the circumstances set forth in Article 38. See [...] Tribunale Civile di Cuneo, Sez. I, Italy (Jan 31, 1996) [...]. The court further noted that when defects are easy to discover by a prompt examination of the goods, the time of notice must be reduced. [...]

(c) The CISG Advisory Council and the UNCITRAL Digest

The difficulties arising from the absence of a CISG court of final appeal are mitigated by two factors. The first is the publication of a Digest by UNCITRAL, which is regularly updated (latest edition: 2012). The Digest provides for a synopsis of the relevant case law on each article of the CISG. By highlighting common views and reporting any divergent approaches, the Digest is intended to portray the evolution of case law.

The second factor is the creation of the Advisory Council of the CISG (CISG-Advisory Council). This Council was established in 2001 to respond to the need to address some controversial, unresolved issues relating to the CISG. The primary purpose of the CISG Advisory Council is to issue Opinions relating to the interpretation and application of the Convention. Nine CISG Advisory Council Opinions have been published as at March 2012, relating to issues including whether electronic communications are to be considered as 'writing', and how the periods relating to the examination of the goods and the notice of any non-conformity should be calculated.[21] Seven new Opinions are in preparation. The members of the CISG Advisory Council are

---

[21] CISG Advisory Council Opinions Nos 1–9, available at www.cisgac.com.

scholars from all over the world who are not bound to any mandate of UNCITRAL but take an independent, critical, and innovative approach and address issues not previously dealt with by judicial or arbitral decisions.

(d) Towards a Uniform Interpretative Approach

It is sometimes said that the various language versions of the CISG cause diffculties in interpreting and applying the CISG in a uniform way. There are, in fact, six authentic texts of the CISG in Arabic, Chinese, English, French, Russian and Spanish, which inevitably produces some textual non-uniformity. However, the difficulties should not be overrated. Although a definitive interpretative approach under the CISG is yet to be developed, it is often emphasised in the literature and in the case law that a literal interpretation of the CISG is just one interpretative approach out of several. Interpretation of the CISG often starts with a consideration of the words of the Convention, but it is undisputed that the broader context must be taken into account, that is, in the first line, the purpose (rationale) of the respective provision, but also the *travaux préparatoires* and comparative material. This approach may also be found in Article 31(1) of the Vienna Convention on the Law of Treaties of 1969, according to which: 'A treaty shall be interpreted in good faith in accordance with the ordinary meaning to be given to the terms of the treaty in their context and in the light of its object and purpose', including 'recourse ... to supplementary means of interpretation, including the preparatory work of the treaty and the circumstances of its conclusion' (Art 32 Vienna Treaties Convention). Even if the Vienna Treaties Convention has not been adopted by all CISG Contracting States, it is widely regarded as a source of general principles of international law that should be relied on even by non-contracting states.

   In fact, the various official CISG texts are actually averting too literal (and too technical) an interpretation and are instead promoting an integrated purposive approach with reference to the CISG's international character, its underlying principles and its drafting history.

B. The Principle of Good Faith

(a) 'Good Faith' under the CISG

When interpreting the CISG, not only do its international character and the need to promote uniformity have to be observed, but also the principle of 'good faith in international trade'. As a principle for interpreting the CISG itself, it is embodied in numerous provisions. For example, Article 16(2)(b) CISG states that an offer is irrevocable where it was reasonable for the offeree to rely upon the offer being held open and the offeree acted in reliance on the offer; another illustration is Article 21(2) CISG, which regulates the status of a late acceptance, which was sent in such circumstances that if its transmission had been normal it would have reached the offeror in due time (for details see below, Art 7(2) CISG). In this respect, it has often been stated that 'good faith' only governs the interpretation of the Convention and does not create a duty to act in good faith between the parties. See the following case abstract.

C 7-2

ICC International Court of Arbitration, Award No 8611/1997, CISG-online 236[22]

[Facts]

A German seller and a Spanish buyer concluded an agreement pursuant to which the buyer was to be the exclusive distributor in Spain of industrial equipment produced in Germany. Several individual sales contracts were then concluded between the parties. Four years later the German company informed the Spanish buyer that due to the insufficiency of the latter's sales it would sell its products in Spain through another company with whose parent it had recently merged. Thereafter, upon the buyer's refusal to pay for some of the deliveries, the seller filed arbitral proceedings. The buyer counterclaimed damages arising from breach of the exclusive distributorship agreement as well as from lack of conformity of certain products and failure to deliver spare parts.

[Judgment]

[...] Finally, the sole arbitrator observed that the principle of good faith mentioned in Art. 7(1) CISG was applicable in the interpretation of CISG only, and was not to be referred to as a source of the parties' rights and duties as concerns the performance of the contract. Therefore, while under German law the mass producer of technical equipment is generally expected to provide spare parts according to the principle of good faith, no implied secondary obligation of the parties derives from the principle of good faith when CISG is applicable. ...

Nevertheless, in the case at hand, the delivery of spare parts was considered to be a practice established between the parties under Article 9 CISG. The seller was thus obliged to deliver them within a reasonable time. As it had not done so, the buyer was entitled to set its damages claim off against the seller's claim.

(b) 'Good Faith' in Other Legal Systems

Art 1.6 PICC 2010:

(1) In the interpretation of these Principles, regard is to be had to their international character and to their purposes including the need to promote uniformity in their application.
(2) Issues within the scope of these Principles but not expressly settled by them are as far as possible to be settled in accordance with their underlying general principles.

---

[22] English abstract taken from UNILEX.

Art 1.7 PICC 2010:

(1)   Each party must act in accordance with good faith and fair dealing in international trade.
(2)   The parties may not exclude or limit this duty.

§ 242 BGB:[23]

The obligor must perform in a manner consistent with good faith, taking into account accepted practice.

§ 157 BGB:[24]

Contracts must be interpreted according to good faith as required by common usage.

Art 2(1) ZGB:[25]

Everyone must act in good faith when exercising his rights and performing his duties.

Art 1135 CC:[26]

Agreements are binding not only as to what is therein expressed, but also as to all the consequences which equity, usage or statute give to the obligation according to its nature.

Art 1160 CC:[27]

Terms which are customary shall be supplemented in the contract, even though they are not expressed there.

§ 2-103(j) UCC:

'Good faith', except as otherwise provided in Article 5, means honesty in fact and the observance of reasonable commercial standards of fair dealing.

---

[23] Author's translation.
[24] Author's translation.
[25] Author's translation.
[26] Translation taken from www.legifrance.gouv.fr.
[27] Translation taken from www.legifrance.gouv.fr.

Questions

Q 7-1

(a) How do major states, such as the USA, or state-like organisations, such as the EU, ensure that the common nucleus of their law is applied and interpreted uniformly?
(b) Is this possible in relation to the CISG?

Q 7-2

Are CISG precedents binding?

Q 7-3

When should case law and literature relating to law other than the CISG be considered?

Q 7-4

(a) What might cause difficulties when consulting foreign decisions? Consider language, accessibility etc.
(b) Can you explain what prompted the 'turn-around' with respect to quoting foreign CISG decisions?

Q 7-5

Compare the UNCITRAL Digest to the Opinions of the Advisory Council. What are their similarities and differences?

Q 7-6

(a) In which countries are legal texts published in more than one offcial language?
(b) Does the fact that there are six authentic texts of the CISG really cause major difficulties in the interpretation of the CISG?

Q 7-7

(a) Explain the principle of good faith embodied in Article 7(1) CISG. Does this rule apply only to the interpretation of the provisions of the CISG , or should it also be applied in interpreting the contract and behaviour of the parties? See also C 7-1.
(b) What is the consequence of holding 'good faith' to be a rule for the interpretation of the CISG?
(c) Can you find provisions in the CISG which reflect the principle of good faith?

(d) Compare Article 7(1) CISG with similar provisions from other sets of rules. Which ones provide for a solution similar to that under the CISG; which ones are different?
(e) Why did the drafters of the CISG refrain from establishing a 'good faith' principle for interpreting the parties' contract or any of their statements?

III. Article 7(2) CISG

A. Primacy of 'General Principles' when Filling Gaps under the CISG

Article 7(2) CISG addresses the question of how matters governed but not expressly settled in the CISG must be resolved. First, those matters are to be settled in conformity with the general principles on which the CISG is based. Thus, each time an issue arises for which no explicit rule exists, it must be decided whether a general principle can be derived from one (or several) CISG provision(s) with the aid of which the issue can be settled without having recourse to domestic law (so-called internal gap). If no such general principle can be found, the matter is governed by the law determined by the private international law of the forum.

B. Important General Principles

It is sometimes difficult to determine whether or not a matter has been deliberately left open, assuming that it should be settled in conformity with the applicable domestic law. The difficulty in deciding whether a gap should be filled uniformly or by the applicable domestic law is increased by the fact that the CISG contains almost no general principles which are explicitly described as such. Notwithstanding this lack of clarity, some principles are not difficult to identify, such as the principle of reasonableness (Arts 8, 16, 18, 25, 33 etc); the principle of freedom from form requirements (Art 11); the principle of party autonomy (Art 6); the principle of full compensation (Art 74); the principle of concurrent exchange of performances (Art 81(2)); and the principle of avoiding economic waste (Arts 25, 77).

Whether further general principles can be derived from the CISG is controversial. Court decisions and arbitration awards have taken differing views at different times. The following case abstracts illustrate the differing positions and arguments with regard to specific questions. C 7-3 and 7-4 refer to the question of the interest rate; C 7-5 deals with the question of burden of proof; and C 7-6 and C 7-7 refer to the problem of set-off.

C 7-3

Chicago Prime Packers, Inc v Northam Food Trading Co et al,
US Dist Ct (ND IL), 21 May 2004,
CISG-online 851

For a summary of the facts see C 7-1 above.

[Judgment]

[...] The CISG further provides that '[i]f a party fails to pay the price or any other sum that is in arrears, the other party is entitled to interest on it, without prejudice to any claim for damages recoverable under article 74.' CISG, Art. 78. Thus, Chicago Prime is clearly entitled to prejudgment interest. However, Article 78 does not specify the rate of interest to be applied or how the rate should be determined; and the parties have not addressed the issue. The court's research has revealed that the interest issue under the CISG has been the subject of great controversy. In fact, '[t]he interest issue, while relatively mundane-sounding, has been the subject of up to 30 percent of total CISG cases worldwide.' [...] One author outlined nine different approaches that courts have used (or authors have suggested) in determining the rate of interest under the CISG, including using the law applicable to the contract in the absence of the CISG, the law of the creditor's place of business, the law of payment currency, trade usages observed in international sale, general principles of full compensation and the law of the forum. [...] Another author, finding that the current approaches do not fully satisfy the objectives of a default rule (such as international uniformity), suggests that adjudicators should 'customise' the rate by awarding the actual borrowing or savings rate or the lending rate in the absence of evidence of borrowing costs.

[...] However, because there is no single approach used by all courts and the parties have failed to address the interest issue or provide information necessary to 'customise' a rate, this court will award interest according to the principles used by federal courts in determining choice of law issues. It is well-settled that '[a] federal court sitting in diversity jurisdiction must apply the substantive law of the state in which it sits,' including its choice of law.

[...] In contract disputes, Illinois follows the Restatement (Second) of Conflict of Laws, which refers courts either to a choice of law provision in the contract at issue, or to the place of performance. [...] In this case, there is no choice of law provision found in the contract but performance undoubtedly took place in Illinois. The contract was one for the purchase of ribs and the ribs were delivered to Northam's agent in Illinois. 'In Illinois, prejudgment interest, whether grounded in a statute or equity, is based on the concept of fairness and is awarded to make the plaintiff whole for the loss of use of money wrongfully withheld.' [...] The Illinois Interest Act, 815 ILCS § 205, provides a statutory rate of 5% per annum, calculated from the time the money was due under the contract: 'Creditors shall be allowed to receive at the rate of a five (5) per centum per annum for all moneys after they become due on any bond, bill, promissory note, or other instrument of writing; on money lent or advanced for the use of another; on money due on the settlement of account from the day of liquidating accounts between the parties and ascertaining the balance…' [...]. Coincidently, the result of applying

Illinois choice of law rules in this case is to apply the law of Illinois, the forum state. Using the forum's interest rate is a common choice in CISG cases, notwithstanding its tension with the CISG's goal of promoting international uniformity. [...]

The same ruling can be found in a number of other cases, see, for example, *Rechtbank Breda* (*Watermelon* case) 16 January 2009, CISG-online 1789; District Court Michalovce, 11 October 2010, CISG-online 2211.

C 7-4

Internationales Schiedsgericht der Bundeskammer der gewerblichen Wirtschaft in Österreich,
SCH-4366, 15 June 1994,
CISG-online 121/691[28]

[Facts]

1. By the request of arbitration of 30 March 1993, the [seller] [a company with place of business in Austria] applied for an award against the [buyer] [a company with place of business in Germany] for payment of a total of US$ ... DM ... . It submitted that the [buyer] had not fulfilled its obligations on the basis of two contracts for the delivery of cold-rolled sheet concluded with the claimant, since it had either not taken delivery of or had not paid for part of the goods purchased.

[Judgment]

[...] 5.2. In accordance with Art. 78 of the CISG, the seller is entitled to interest in the event of arrears in payment of the price by the buyer.

5.2.1. The interest is payable from the effective date of the obligation for payment of the purchase price. According to Art. 58(1) of the CISG, this time is primarily determined by the agreements between the parties themselves; only in the absence of such a special agreement is it the time when the seller places the goods at the buyer's disposal in accordance with the contract. In the present case, the parties had derogated from the payment modalities and time-limits originally laid down in the contract by subsequently agreeing that the [buyer] could take delivery of and pay for the goods in partial consignments according to its possibilities of resale, provides that it bore the storage costs incurred thereby[...]... Accordingly, the invoices in question here stipulate 'Payment: immediately upon receipt of the invoice'. It was therefore at that time, and not earlier, that the [buyer] was under the obligation to pay the amount invoiced at the time, and it is only from that time that the [seller] was entitled to interest [...].

5.2.2. Article 78 of the CISG, while granting the right to interest, says nothing about the level of the interest rate payable. In international legal writings and case law to date it is disputed whether the question is outside the scope of the Convention—with the result that the interest rate is to be determined according to the domestic law applicable on the basis of the relevant conflict-of-laws rules—or whether there is a true gap in the Convention within the meaning of Article 7(2) so that the applicable interest rate should possibly be determined autono-

---

[28] Translation taken from UNILEX.

mously in conformity with the general principles underlying the Convention. This second view is to be preferred, not least because the immediate recourse to a particular domestic law may lead to results which are incompatible with the principle embodied in Art. 78 of the CISG, at least in the cases where the law in question expressly prohibits the payment of interest. One of the general legal principles underlying the CISG is the requirement of 'full compensation' of the loss caused (cf. Art. 74 of the CISG). It follows that, in the event of failure to pay a monetary debt, the creditor, who as a business person must be expected to resort to bank credit as a result of the delay in payment, should therefore be entitled to interest at the rate commonly practiced in its country with respect to the currency of payment, i.e. the currency of the creditor's country or any other foreign currency agreed upon by the parties (cf. Art. 7.4.9 of the Principles of International Commercial Contracts prepared by the International Institute for the Unification of Private Law (UNIDROIT)). The information received from the leading Austrian banks is that the average 'prime borrowing rates' for US dollars and DM in Austria in the period in question were 4.5% and 8%, respectively. The interest due from the [buyer] should be calculated at those rates. ...

It should be noted that an Opinion by the CISG Advisory Council on the question of how the interest rate under Article 78 is to be determined is in preparation.

C 7-5

Bundesgericht (Switzerland),
15 September 2000,
CISG-online 770[29]

[Facts][30]

In March 1994, an Italian seller and a Swiss buyer entered into a contract for the sale of Egyptian cotton, to be delivered by 5 June in four deliveries of five tons each. Since the seller did not inform the buyer in good time that the delay indicated in the first contract would not be respected, the buyer was forced to purchase substitute goods from other suppliers at a higher price. The buyer commenced a legal action, asking for damages. The First Instance Court held that the seller was liable for non-performance and ordered the seller to compensate the buyer for the loss it had suffered. The seller appealed.

[Judgment]

[...]

The [seller] invokes breaches of many rules to contest the principle and the amount of the damages held by the cantonal Appellate Court.

(a) [Burden of proof of damages]

The [seller] argues that, especially, the Appellate Court violated Article 8 of the Civil Code of Switzerland concerning the burden of proof by considering that the claimant [buyer] had proven its damages concerning the replacement goods.

---

[29] Translation taken from CISG Pace (citations omitted).
[30] Summary of facts taken from UNILEX.

That legal rule is not applicable even though CISG does not contain direct rules on the burden of proof and all procedural questions are outside its scope of application. When the judge examines this question, he should keep in mind the content of the material law applicable, the *lex causae*, which, in this case, is the CISG. The competent tribunal should not found its solution on the domestic law. Indeed, in an indirect way, CISG contributes to the repartition of the burden of proof, and the reason for this is the meaning of the wording used in the provisions of the CISG. There is the establishment of a relationship between a rule and its exception. That is why, in general, we can use the maxim 'actori incumbit probatio'. The result is that the party who invokes a right bears the burden of proof to its establishment of that right and, on the other hand, the other party must prove any facts that exclude the invoked claim [...].

The court goes on to examine the seller's appeal from the Appellate Court concerning the damages and finally dismisses it.

Similar views have been taken in numerous other cases. For a recent example, see District Court Trnava (Slovak Republic), 9 March 2011, CISG-online 2210.

C 7-6

Oberster Gerichtshof (Austria),
22 October 2001,
CISG-online 614[31]

[Facts]

[...] On 4 February 1994 a Hungarian seller and the Austrian buyer concluded a supply contract over the delivery of gasoline and gas oil from 1 February 1994 to 31 January 1995. The contract contained a choice of law clause in favor of Austrian law. After this supply contract had ended, the seller on 28 February 1995 sent the buyer a draft of an annual contract for the delivery of gasoline and gas oil for the period 1 March 1995 to 29 February 1996. The proposal was already signed by the seller and provided inter alia, that payment would be made in U.S. Dollars [US $], provisions of Incoterms® [last edition] would apply to matters not settled in the contract, and that the contract was governed by Austrian law. While the buyer did not sign the seller's proposal, the buyer placed numerous orders with the seller. The seller makes a claim in the amount of US $4,948,668.43 for the outstanding invoices pertaining to the deliveries. Additionally, a Hungarian joint-stock corporation [the assignor] maintained a business relationship with the seller predecessor in title. The assignor allegedly possessed a claim for 609,810,397 Ft [Hungarian Forint] against the seller. On 14 June 1995, the assignor transferred his claim to the buyer. The seller makes a claim for payment for the purchase price of the delivered gas oil and gasoline, in the amount of US $4,949,668.43. The buyer objects that the claim was redeemed due to buyer's set-off with a counterclaim of 609,810,397 Ft. On 21 June 2000, the Commercial Court Vienna [Court of First Instance] granted the seller's claim [...]. Upon the buyer's appeal, the Vienna Court of Appeals affirmed the decision of the Court of First Instance on 23 November 2000 [...]. The Supreme Court, acting as the final appellate court, denied the buyer's appeal.

---

[31] Translation taken from CISG Pace (citations omitted).

Issue: In a contract governed by the CISG, may a party apply a set-off to a debt? Holding: No. Among other matters, this is the case for the set-off of a claim that does not result from a contract governed by the Convention, in the present dispute the claim of unjustified enrichment was assigned to the buyer. As the CISG does not provide for a set-off of such claims, the effects of the set-off, its validity, and possible impediments to the set-off need to [be] settled under the domestic law applicable by virtue of the rules of private international law. Therefore, the relevant question in the present case, i.e., whether there is an impediment to the set-off, is to be assessed under Austrian law. This leads to the application of Austrian Civil Code [ABGB] § 1440 and raises the question whether the buyer's counterclaim possesses the prerequisite of similarity which is necessary for the settlement by set-off. [...]

C 7-7

Oberlandesgericht Hamburg (Hanseatisches Oberlandesgericht)
(Germany),
26 November 1999,
CISG-online 515[32]

[Facts]

The Brazilian plaintiff [seller] claims payment from defendant [buyer], a textile trader in Hamburg, for two deliveries of jeans trousers, alternatively payment of the surplus gained by [buyer] from the sale of the goods, by which sale [buyer] took justice into its own hands. [Buyer], on the other hand, claims avoidance of the contract on the ground of breach of contract by [seller] and sets off [seller]'s claim for payment against a claim for damages for defective delivery, i.e., delivery of poor quality. [...]

[Judgment]

[Buyer] is not only entitled to set-off the claim for damages for breach of contract against the purchase price, but also against the claim for payment of the profits from the sale (by taking the law in its own hands) under article 88(3), second sentence, CISG. The set-off is considered a general principle in the meaning of article 7(2) CISG in any case in so far as two reciprocal claims arising from the Convention are facing each other. It remains to be seen whether [buyer]'s right to retain the profits of the sale for reasons of having a claim for damages against [seller] can be derived directly from the Convention or whether the set-off is dealt with by the applicable national law. Also on the grounds of the applicable national law, [buyer] has maintained its right by way of timely notification of defect under § 479 German Civil Code to set-off its claim for damages for breach of contract against the claim for payment of the exceeding profits from the sale. [...]

The Court finds that the buyer's appeal is fully founded.

---

[32] Translation taken from CISG Pace (references omitted).

Questions

Q 7-8

What is the rule established in Article 7(2) CISG?

Q 7-9

The issue of burden of proof was highly disputed at the Drafting Conference. The drafters feared an overlap with procedural matters, for which UNCITRAL had no mandate, and were thus reluctant to settle the burden of proof in a general way.

(a)   Does the court in C 7-5 consider the burden of proof to be a procedural question or a substantive law issue?
(b)   Why does the court come to the conclusion that the CISG contains rules on the burden of proof?
(c)   Is there a provision in the CISG which, through its wording, makes it clear who has to prove a certain fact?

Q 7-10

(a)   What was the question to be decided in C 7-6 and C 7-7?
(b)   What was the holding of the respective courts?
(c)   What was different in C 7-6 and C 7-7 with regard to the legal question at issue? Might this explain the difference in the verdicts?
(d)   Which provision might constitute the basis for deriving a general principle of set-off?

Q 7-11

(a)   Are there any questions which cannot be settled in accordance with the general principles underlying the Convention but must rather be answered under the applicable domestic law?
(b)   Which provision of the CISG would help answer this question?

Q 7-12

What diffculties do we encounter when deciding whether we can develop a general principle from a particular provision of the CISG?

Article 8 CISG

(1) For the purposes of this Convention statements made by and other conduct of a party are to be interpreted according to his intent where the other party knew or could not have been unaware what that intent was.
(2) If the preceding paragraph is not applicable, statements made by and other conduct of a party are to be interpreted according to the understanding that a reasonable person of the same kind as the other party would have had in the same circumstances.
(3) In determining the intent of a party or the understanding a reasonable person would have had, due consideration is to be given to all relevant circumstances of the case including the negotiations, any practices which the parties have established between themselves, usages and any subsequent conduct of the parties.

I. Overview

Article 8 CISG deals with the interpretation of statements and declarations exchanged between the parties, as well as with the interpretation of a party's conduct. Although Article 8 CISG appears to be applicable merely to the interpretation of unilateral acts of each party, it is 'equally applicable to the interpretation of the contract, when the document is embodied in a single document'.[33]

The statements and conduct mentioned in Article 8 CISG must relate to a matter governed by the Convention. Topics which are excluded from its scope (see in particular Art 4 CISG) must be interpreted according to the law governing the matter. Article 8 is distinct from Article 7 CISG in that it relates to the statements and conduct of the *parties*, whereas Article 7 concerns the interpretation and gap-filling of the *Convention*. Therefore, the principle of 'good faith' mentioned in Article 7(1) CISG relates only to the Convention itself and does not constitute an interpretation maxim under Article 8 CISG (see above Art 7 CISG).

---

[33] UN Conference on the CISG, 10 March–11 April 1980, OR, Doc 1981, 18.

II. Article 8(1) CISG

First, the statement of a party must be interpreted 'subjectively', that is, according to the party's intent. Article 8(1) applies not only to unilateral statements, but also to the interpretation of the contract in general. Thus, as a first step, a contract must be interpreted according to the parties' 'actual' intention. What the parties specifically meant, wanted or envisaged with regard to a particular statement or conduct or when drawing up the contract is decisive. However, as Article 8(1) states, this subjective intention is only relevant if the addressee knew or could not have been unaware of the intention of the statement-maker. The fact that the addressee knew or could not have been unaware of that intent must be proven by the statement-maker. Such evidence may be difficult to provide, which is why Article 8(2) with its 'objective intent theory' is, in general, the more important rule of interpretation under the Convention.

III. Article 8(2) and (3) CISG

Article 8(2) CISG reflects the general principle of reasonableness governing the Convention. When interpreting a statement or conduct of one or both parties, and if the real intent behind that statement cannot be proven, one has to ask how a reasonable person in the shoes of the other party would have understood the statement or conduct. Article 8(2) CISG applies to any kind of statement (French 'indications', Spanish 'declaraciones') or conduct (French 'autres comportements', Spanish 'otros actos'). It provides, for instance, the basis of determining—from a 'reasonable point of view'—whether a statement constitutes an offer, whether a statement or conduct are to be considered as an acceptance, a declaration of avoidance, a notice of non-conformity, a fixing of an additional period of time, and so on.

   Article 8(3) CISG provides several criteria which are to be considered when interpreting statements and other conduct of a party. For an illustration of how Article 8(2), (3) CISG may apply to a case, see below, C 8-1.

IV. Interpretation of One Party's General Conditions

A frequently discussed question is whether standard terms have been included in the contract. Various courts have stated that, to solve the problem of whether the standard terms of one of the parties were validly included in the contract, regard must be had to how a 'reasonable person of the same kind as the other party' would have understood the statement. Reference is thus made to Article 8(2), (3) CISG. The issue is dealt with in more detail below at Article 14 *et seq.*

V. Comparison with Other Legal Provisions

Art 4.1 PICC 2010:

(1) A contract shall be interpreted according to the common intention of the parties.
(2) If such intention cannot be established, the contract shall be interpreted according to the meaning that reasonable persons of the same kind as the parties would give to it in the same circumstances.

Art 4.2 PICC 2010:

(1) The statements and other conduct of a party shall be interpreted according to that party's intention if the other party knew or could not have been unaware of that intention.
(2) If the preceding paragraph is not applicable, such statements and other conduct shall be interpreted according to the meaning that a reasonable person of the same kind as the other party would give to it in the circumstances.

Art 4.3 PICC 2010:

In applying Articles 4.1 and 4.2, regard shall be had to all the circumstances, including

(a) preliminary negotiations between the parties;
(b) practices which the parties have established between themselves;
(c) the conduct of the parties subsequent to the conclusion of the contract;
(d) the nature and purpose of the contract;
(e) the meaning commonly given to terms and expressions in the trade concerned;
(f) usages.

Art 4.7 PICC 2010:

Where a contract is drawn up in two or more language versions which are equally authoritative there is, in case of discrepancy between the versions, a preference for the interpretation to a version in which the contract was originally drawn up.

Questions

Q 8-1

(a) What is the purpose of Article 8 CISG?
(b) Explain the difference in scope between Articles 7 and 8 CISG.

Q 8-2

(a) How can Article 8(1) and (2) CISG be distinguished?
(b) Do the PICC 2010 make the same differentiation? See Articles 4.1 and 4.2 PICC 2010.

VI. Applicability of Other Rules of Interpretation and Evidence

A. Introduction

Article 8 CISG deals with the issue of interpretation in an exhaustive manner, thereby excluding the applicability of domestic interpretative rules. Case law under Article 8 CISG has dealt with three questions in particular, namely whether the Plain Meaning Rule, the Parol Evidence Rule and the Merger Clause Rule, respectively, should apply under the CISG. These questions will be discussed below.

B. Plain Meaning Rule

(a) Operation of the Plain Meaning Rule

The Plain Meaning Rule is an interpretation maxim known to some common law jurisdictions. It prevents a court from considering evidence external to an unambiguous piece of writing. It is based on the premise that, when language is sufficiently clear, its meaning can be determined without resorting to extrinsic evidence. In 2005, the CISG Advisory Council issued the following Opinion with regard to the Plain Meaning Rule under the Convention:

CISG Advisory Council, Opinion No 3: Parol Evidence Rule, Plain Meaning Rule, Contractual Merger Clause and the CISG[34]

> [...]
> 2. In some common law jurisdictions, the Plain Meaning Rule prevents a court from considering evidence outside a seemingly unambiguous writing for purposes of contractual interpretation. The Plain Meaning Rule does not apply under the CISG.
>
> [...]

(b) Comparison with PICC 2010

Art 4.4 PICC 2010:

> Terms and expressions shall be interpreted in the light of the whole contract or statement in which they appear.

---

[34] Taken from www.cisgac.com.

C. Parol Evidence Rule

Several US court decisions have dealt with the question of whether the Parol Evidence Rule applies to contracts subject to the CISG. The Parol Evidence Rule has been developed by common law courts to determine the role to be ascribed to written contractual documents. Its purpose is to guarantee the integrity of written contracts by preventing courts from admitting oral statements or previous correspondence which contradict the written agreement. The Parol Evidence Rule applies if the agreement has been reduced to writing and was designed to protect a written contract against unreliable testimony regarding oral terms. It is largely unknown in civil law systems, at least as far as commercial law is concerned. Although the Parol Evidence Rule differs within the various common law legal systems, section 2-202 UCC may serve as an illustration:

§ 2-202 UCC:

> Terms with respect to which the confirmatory memoranda of the parties agree or which are otherwise set forth in a writing intended by the parties as a final expression of their agreement with respect to such terms as are included therein may not be contradicted by evidence of any prior agreement or of a contemporaneous oral agreement but may be explained or supplemented
>
> (a) by course of performance, course of dealing, or usage of trade (Section 1–303); and
> (b) by evidence of consistent additional terms unless the court finds the writing to have been intended also as a complete and exclusive statement of the terms of the agreement.

The following case deals with the question of whether the Parol Evidence Rule may be applied in a sales contract which is governed by the CISG. The holding has recently been upheld in *ECEM European Chemical Marketing BV v The Purolite Company*, US Dist Ct for the Eastern District of Pennsylvania, 29 January 2010, CISG-online 2090.

C 8-1

MCC-Marble Ceramic Center, Inc v Ceramica Nuova D'Agostino SpA, US Ct App (11th Cir), 29 June 1998, CISG-online 342

[Facts]

[...] The plaintiff–appellant, MCC-Marble Ceramic, Inc. [buyer], is a Florida corporation engaged in the retail sale of tiles, and the defendant-appellee, Ceramica Nuova SpA [seller] is an Italian corporation engaged in the manufacture of ceramic tiles. In October 1990, [buyer's] president, Juan Carlos Mo[n]zon, met representatives of [seller] at a trade fair in Bologna, Italy and negotiated an agreement to purchase ceramic tiles from [seller] based on samples he examined at the trade fair. Monzon, who spoke no Italian, communicated with Gianni Silingardi, then [seller's] commercial director, through a translator, Gianfranco Copelli, who was himself an agent of [seller]. The parties apparently arrived at an oral agreement on the crucial terms of price, quality, quantity, delivery and payment. The parties then recorded these terms on one of [seller's] standard, pre-printed order forms and Monzon signed the contract on [buyer's] behalf. According to [buyer], the parties also entered into a require-ments contract in February 1991, subject to which [seller] agreed to supply [buyer] with high grade ceramic tile at specific discounts as long as [buyer] purchased sufficient quantities of tile. [Buyer] completed a number of additional order forms requesting tile deliveries pursuant to that agreement.

[Buyer] brought suit against [seller] claiming a breach of the February 1991 requirements contract when [seller] failed to satisfy orders in April, May, and August of 1991. In addition to other defenses, D'Agostino responded that it was under no obligation to fill MCC's orders because MCC had defaulted on payment for previous shipments. In support of its position, D'Agostino relied on the pre-printed terms of the contracts that MCC had executed. The executed forms were printed in Italian and contained terms and conditions on both the front and reverse. According to an English translation of the October 1990 contract, the front of the order form contained the following language directly beneath Monzon's signature:

[T]he buyer hereby states that he is aware of the sales conditions stated on the reverse and that he expressly approves of them with special reference to those numbered 1 2 3 4 5 6 7 8. Clause 6(b), printed on the back of the form states: '[D]efault or delay in payment within the time agreed upon gives D'Agostino the right to … suspend or cancel the contract itself and to cancel possible other pending contracts and the buyer does not have the right to indem-nification or damages.'

D'Agostino also brought a number of counterclaims against MCC, seeking damages for MCC's alleged nonpayment for deliveries of tile that D'Agostino had made between February 28, 1991 and July 4, 1991. MCC responded that the tile it had received was of a lower quality than contracted for, and that, pursuant to the CISG, MCC was entitled to reduce payment in proportion to the defects. [Art 50] D'Agostino, however, noted that clause 4 on the reverse of the contract states, in pertinent part: 'Possible complaints for defects of the merchandise must be made in writing by means of a certified letter within and not later than 10 days after receipt of the merchandise ….'

Although there is evidence to support MCC's claims that it complained about the quality of the deliveries it received, MCC never submitted any written complaints.

MCC did not dispute these underlying facts before the district court, but argued that the parties never intended the terms and conditions printed on the reverse of the order form to apply to their agreements. As evidence for this assertion, MCC submitted Monzon's affida-vit, which claims that MCC had no subjective intent to be bound by those terms and that D'Agostino was aware of this intent. MCC also filed affidavits from Silingardi and Copelli, D'Agostino's representatives at the trade fair, which support Monzon's claim that the parties subjectively intended not to be bound by the terms on the reverse of the order form. The magistrate judge held that the affidavits, even if true, did not raise an issue of material fact regarding the interpretation or applicability of the terms of the written contracts and the district court accepted his recommendation to award summary judgment in D'Agostino's favor. MCC then filed this timely appeal.

[Judgment]

[...] The parties to this case agree that the CISG governs their dispute because the United States, where [buyer] has its place of business, and Italy, where [seller] has its place of business, are both States Party to the Convention. See CISG, Art. 1. Article 8 of the CISG governs the interpretation of international contracts for the sale of goods and forms the basis of [buyer's] appeal from the district court's grant of summary judgment in [seller's] favor. [Buyer] argues that the magistrate judge and the district court improperly ignored evidence that [buyer] submitted regarding the parties' subjective intent when they memorialised the terms of their agreement on [seller's] pre-printed form contract, and that the magistrate judge erred by applying the parol evidence rule in derogation of the CISG.

I. Subjective Intent under the CISG

Contrary to what is familiar practice in United States courts, the CISG appears to permit a substantial inquiry into the parties' subjective intent, even if the parties did not engage in any objectively ascertainable means of registering this intent. Article 8(1) of the CISG instructs courts to interpret the 'statements ... and other conduct of a party ... according to his intent' as long as the other party 'knew or could not have been unaware' of that intent. The plain language of the Convention, therefore, requires an inquiry into a party's subjective intent as long as the other party to the contract was aware of that intent. ...

II. Parol Evidence and the CISG

Given our determination that the magistrate judge and the district court should have considered [buyer's] affidavits regarding the parties' subjective intentions, we must address a question of first impression in this circuit: whether the parol evidence rule, which bars evidence of an earlier oral contract that contradicts or varies the terms of a subsequent or contemporaneous written contract, plays any role in cases involving the CISG. We begin by observing that the parol evidence rule, contrary to its title, is a substantive rule of law, not a rule of evidence. [...] The rule does not purport to exclude a particular type of evidence as an 'untrustworthy or undesirable' way of proving a fact, but prevents a litigant from attempting to show 'the fact itself—the fact that the terms of the agreement are other than those in the writing.' [...] As such, a federal district court cannot simply apply the parol evidence rule as a procedural matter—as it might if excluding a particular type of evidence under the Federal Rules of Evidence, which apply in federal court regardless of the source of the substantive rule of decision.

[...] The CISG itself contains no express statement on the role of parol evidence. [...] It is clear, however, that the drafters of the CISG were comfortable with the concept of permitting parties to rely on oral contracts because they eschewed any statutes of fraud provision and expressly provided for the enforcement of oral contracts. Compare CISG, Art. 11 (a contract of sale need not be concluded or evidenced in writing) with U.C.C. § 2–201 (precluding the enforcement of oral contracts for the sale of goods involving more than $500). Moreover, article 8(3) of the CISG expressly directs courts to give 'due consideration ... to all relevant circumstances of the case including the negotiations ... ' to determine the intent of the parties. Given article 8(1)'s directive to use the intent of the parties to interpret their statements and conduct, article 8(3) is a clear instruction to admit and consider parol evidence regarding the negotiations to the extent they reveal the parties' subjective intent. [...]

(Court discusses the US cases Filanto SpA v Chilewich International Corp, US Dist Ct, SD NY, 14 April 1992, CISG-online 45 (Parol Evidence Rule rejected) and Beijing Metals & Minerals Import/Export Corp v American Bus Ctr, Inc, 993 F.2d 1178 (5th Cir 1993) (Parol Evidence Rule applied).)

Our reading of article 8(3) as a rejection of the parol evidence rule, however, is in accordance with the great weight of academic commentary on the issue. ... [A]lthough jurisdictions in the United States have found the parol evidence rule helpful to promote good faith and uniformity in contract, as well as an appropriate answer to the question of how much consideration to give parol evidence, a wide number of other States Party to the CISG have rejected the rule in their domestic jurisdictions. One of the primary factors motivating the negotiation and adoption of the CISG was to provide parties to international contracts for the sale of goods with some degree of certainty as to the principles of law that would govern potential disputes and remove the previous doubt regarding which party's legal system might otherwise apply. [...] Courts applying the CISG cannot, therefore, upset the parties' reliance on the Convention by substituting familiar principles of domestic law when the Convention requires a different result. We may only achieve the directives of good faith and uniformity in contracts under the CISG by interpreting and applying the plain language of article 8(3) as written and obeying its directive to consider this type of parol evidence.

This is not to say that parties to an international contract for the sale of goods cannot depend on written contracts or that parol evidence regarding subjective contractual intent need always prevent a party relying on a written agreement from securing summary judgment. To the contrary, most cases will not present a situation (as exists in this case) in which both parties to the contract acknowledge a subjective intent not to be bound by the terms of a pre-printed writing. In most cases, therefore, article 8(2) of the CISG will apply, and objective evidence will provide the basis for the court's decision. [...] Consequently, a party to a contract governed by the CISG will not be able to avoid the terms of a contract and force a jury trial simply by submitting an affidavit which states that he or she did not have the subjective intent to be bound by the contract's terms. [...] Moreover, to the extent parties wish to avoid parol evidence problems they can do so by including a merger clause in their agreement that extinguishes any and all prior agreements and understandings not expressed in the writing.

Considering [buyer's] affidavits in this case, however, we conclude that the magistrate judge and the district court improperly granted summary judgment in favor of [seller]. Although the affidavits are, as [seller] observes, relatively conclusory and unsupported by facts that would objectively establish [buyer's] intent not to be bound by the conditions on the reverse of the form, article 8(1) requires a court to consider evidence of a party's subjective intent when the other party was aware of it, and the Silingardi and Copelli affidavits provide that evidence. [...] [B]ecause article 8 requires a court to consider any 'practices which the parties have established between themselves, usages and any subsequent conduct of the parties' in interpreting contracts, CISG, Art. 8(3), whether the parties intended to adhere to the ten day limit for complaints, as stated on the reverse of the initial contract, will have an impact on whether [buyer] was bound to adhere to the limit on subsequent deliveries. [...]

[W]e conclude that the CISG, which governs international contracts for the sale of goods, precludes summary judgment in this case because [buyer] has raised an issue of material fact concerning the parties' subjective intent to be bound by the terms on the reverse of the pre-printed contract. The CISG also precludes the application of the parol evidence rule, which would otherwise bar the consideration of evidence concerning a prior or contemporaneously negotiated oral agreement. Accordingly, we REVERSE the district court's grant of summary judgment and REMAND this case for further proceedings consistent with this opinion. [...]

D. Merger Clauses

(a) Under the CISG

Many international commercial contracts provide for a Merger or Entire Agreement Clause. Its purpose is to prevent a party from relying on statements or agreements not contained in the written document. For the question of whether Merger Clauses apply under the CISG, see C 8-2.

C 8-2

Ajax Tool Works, Inc v Can-Eng Manufacturing Ltd,
US Dist Ct (ND IL), 29 January 2003,
CISG-online 772

[Facts]

Plaintiff [buyer], an Illinois corporation, is a manufacturer of chisels, hammers, and other tools. Defendant [seller], an Ontario, Canada corporation, manufactures industrial furnaces, including a fluidized bed furnace, which is at issue in this case. In January 1996, at the request of Lindberg Technical and Management Services, a consulting firm retained by [buyer], [seller] submitted a proposal in which it offered to supply a fluidized bed furnace to [buyer]. [Buyer] did not accept this offer. Over the course of 1996, [seller] submitted two follow-up proposals to [buyer], neither of which was accepted. On January 27, 1997, [seller] sent [buyer] a fourth proposal to sell a fluidized bed furnace to [buyer] for $ 90,000. After issuance of the proposal, the parties entered into an agreement whereby [buyer] purchased the furnace from [seller]. The terms of the January 27, 1997, proposal formed the parties' contract. Page 4 of [seller]'s fourteen-page proposal contained the following relevant terms and conditions:

'WARRANTY—[Seller] in connection with apparatus sold will repair or replace, at the option of [seller], f.o.b. our factory, any defects in workmanship or material which may develop under proper and normal use during a period of ninety days from date of shipment or completion of installation if installation is undertaken by [seller]. Such repair or replacement shall constitute a fulfillment of all [seller] liabilities with respect to such apparatus. [Seller] shall not be liable for consequential damages. This warranty shall not apply if alterations or modifications of any nature are made by the Purchaser or if erection, installation or stating up is not performed under [seller] supervision or under [seller] approved methods.

'[Seller]'s liability for the service of any refractories, alloy or other component parts manufactured by other than [seller] but incorporated in the equipment furnished to Purchaser, shall be limited to the guarantee or liability to [seller] of the manufacturer or supplier of such components. [Seller] is not responsible in any manner for operation of the equipment in Purchaser's plant.

'[Seller]'s warranties or guarantees do not cover the process of manufacture or the quality of the product on which this equipment may be used. ....

'OTHER UNDERSTANDINGS—All previous oral or written agreements between the parties hereto which are contrary to or inconsistent with this proposal are hereby abrogated, it being understood that there are no agreements, guarantees or understandings which are in conflict with or inconsistent with this proposal. A purchase order covering the materials, apparatus or equipment specified herein shall be considered by both the Purchaser and [seller] to be merely an acceptance of this Proposal and the Terms and Conditions set forth herein, and any other terms or conditions which may be printed or contained on such purchase order which are in conflict with or inconsistent with this proposal shall be not applicable. This agreement shall be governed by the laws of the Province of Ontario, Canada. Any terms and conditions herein, which may be in conflict with Ontario Law, shall be deleted, however, all other terms and conditions shall remain in force and effect.'

[Seller] shipped the furnace to [buyer] on June 26, 1997, and it arrived at [buyer]'s plant on June 27, 1997. [Buyer] installed and started the furnace itself. Over the course of the next four years, [buyer] experienced problems with the furnace, particularly that the furnace would not attain and hold the selected temperature, used an excessive amount of sand, and did not function properly with compressed air as the atmosphere. The parties dispute exactly when and how often [buyer] reported these problems to [seller], but viewing the evidence in the light most favorable to [buyer], the non-moving party, as this court must, this court finds that [buyer] lodged a considerable number of complaints with [seller]. It appears that all of these complaints were made more than ninety days after installation. In response to many of these complaints, [seller] attempted to repair or in some way remedy the problem, some, at least, at no cost to [buyer].

[Judgment]

[...] In this case, it is undisputed that [buyer], an Illinois corporation, and [seller], an Ontario corporation, are parties whose places of business are in different States and that these states are Contracting States. Thus, unless the parties have opted-out, the CISG applies here. The parties' contract states that the 'agreement shall be governed by the laws of the Province of Ontario, Canada.' Obviously, this clause does not exclude the CISG. Further, although the parties have designated Ontario law as controlling, it is not the provincial law of Ontario that applies; rather, because the CISG is the law of Ontario, the CISG governs the parties' agreement.

[...] The CISG does not preempt a private contract between parties; instead, it provides a statutory authority from which contract provisions are interpreted, fills gaps in contract language, and governs issues not addressed by the contract. In fact, Article 6 states that parties may, by contract, 'derogate from or vary the effect of any of [the CISG's] provisions.' Accordingly, under the CISG, the terms of the parties' agreement control. In this case, the limited warranty, as part of the contract executed by the parties, lawfully limits [buyer]'s remedies. As will be discussed below, however, there are material facts in dispute as to whether [seller] has waived this limited warranty.

(The Court adjudicates all of buyer's claims based on the explicit written terms of the contract, considering that the parties had derogated from Articles 35 et seq and Articles 45 et seq. of the Convention. As genuine issues of material fact exist with regard to the breach of contract, the Court denies summary judgment in this respect.)

The effects of a merger clause can be twofold: first, it can bar extrinsic evidence which could supplement or contradict the written terms. Secondly, it may bar extrinsic evidence for the purpose of contract interpretation. The latter constitutes a derogation from the interpretation rules of Article 8 CISG. The extent to which a merger clause accomplishes one or both of these purposes is a question of interpretation of the clause.

Since the CISG does not deal with merger clauses, the question of whether a merger clause bars the consideration of extrinsic evidence must be answered by reference to the criteria set out in Article 8 CISG, without reference to domestic law. Therefore, all relevant facts and circumstances have to be taken into consideration in order to determine the effect that the parties intended the merger clause to have.

(b) Comparison with Other Legal Provisions

Art 2.1.17 PICC 2010:

A contract in writing which contains a clause indicating that the writing completely embodies the terms on which the parties have agreed cannot be contradicted or supplemented by evidence of prior statements or agreements. However, such statements or agreements may be used to interpret the writing.

Questions

Q 8-3

(a) In which legal systems are the Parol Evidence Rule and the Plain Meaning Rule rooted?
(b) What is the difference between the Parol Evidence Rule and the Plain Meaning Rule?

Q 8-4

(a) What was the legal question at issue in C 8-1?
(b) What does the court state with regard to whether the Parol Evidence Rule applies under the CISG? On what considerations does it base its decision?

Q 8-5

Explain the effect of a merger clause. See also C 8-2.

Q 8-6

How will a merger clause be interpreted under the CISG?

Q 8-7

The PICC 2010 specifically address merger clauses.

(a) Can you explain why they deal with merger clauses, while the CISG does not?
(b) How should a merger clause be interpreted under Article 2.1.17 PICC 2010? Compare this answer to the respective rule under the CISG.

Article 9 CISG

(1) The parties are bound by any usage to which they have agreed and by any practices which they have established between themselves.
(2) The parties are considered, unless otherwise agreed, to have impliedly made applicable to their contract or its formation a usage of which the parties knew or ought to have known and which in international trade is widely known to, and regularly observed by, parties to contracts of the type involved in the particular trade concerned.

I. Overview

Article 9 CISG differentiates between usages to which the parties have agreed, or practices which they have established between themselves, on the one hand (Art 9(1)), and usages which apply by virtue of their prevalence and their recognition, regardless of whether the parties have agreed on them or not, on the other hand (Art 9(2)).

II. Article 9(1) CISG

A. Usages to which the Parties have Agreed

Usages are sets of rules in commercial trade which are regularly observed by the respective branches. Pursuant to Article 9(1) CISG, the parties are bound by any usage to which they have agreed. Such usages may be international, regional or local, and they may also be usages of other trade sectors. What is decisive is that the parties, by agreement, have made a usage part of their contract. The agreement on such usage may be explicit or implicit. Whether the parties have actually agreed on any usages is to be decided by applying the rules of the CISG governing the formation of a contract (Arts 8, 14 *et seq.* CISG). If the parties have agreed on a usage, the provisions of the CISG dealing with the respective issue are derogated from. For an illustration, see C 9-1.

C 9-1

CIETAC Arbitration Award,
31 July 1997,
CISG-online 1072[35]

[Facts]

According to the documents submitted by the parties and the investigation through court session, the Arbitration Tribunal finds the following facts: 1. On 12 September 1994, the [Buyer] and the [Seller] concluded Contracts No. 94CQJ3-13838A1 and No. 94CQJ3-1838A2. Later, the parties signed five other contracts numbered 95CQJ3-1838001, 95CQJ3-183804, 95CQJ3-183804A, 95CQJ3-183804B, and 95CQJ3-183804C on 15 February, 5 May, 8 June, 20 July, and 28 September of 1995 (hereafter 'the contract').

According to the contract, the [Seller] will manufacture and sell different sizes of hubs and axle sleeves in accordance with the blueprint provided by the [Buyer]. The delivery date was from September 1994 to October 1995, and the destination ports included Memphis, San Francisco, Chicago, and Dallas. The first two contracts listed the payment terms as D/A 120 days, and others were D/A 90 days. On the reverse side of the contract, it was stated in Section 1 that:

'Any claim arising out of the quality of the goods must be raised within thirty days after the goods arrive at the destination port, and the claims relating to the quantity of the goods must be raised within fifteen days after the goods arrive at the destination port. The inspection report issued by the [Seller]'s authorized agency must be presented. If the [Seller] is liable, the [Seller] must respond to the [Buyer] within twenty days after knowing the claim, and must give opinions of solution.'

2. After the contract was concluded, the [Seller] made seventeen deliveries of the goods from November 1994 to October 1995 with a total price of US $286,378.14. The [Buyer] has received all seventeen deliveries. The [Buyer] has paid US $159,668.57 for the first to the eighth delivery, however, it has not paid the price for the ninth to seventeenth delivery, which is US $126,709.57. Both parties have no objection to the above amount. [...]

4. Before manufacturing and shipping the goods to the [Buyer], the [Seller] asked the [Buyer] to examine the sample goods. The [Buyer] had pointed out certain quality problem for the [Seller] to improve before manufacturing. On 28 February 1994, the [Buyer] sent a fax to the [Seller], which stated: 'After telephone conversation, our customers complained that "the upper range was too big, which caused it to be difficult to put on to the shaft. It is a waste of time and employee's salary". I have told the customers that it was a small problem, and it could be fixed by scrubbing more during manufacturing. In addition, the axle sleeves have been heated, therefore, there should be no problem. Our customers are scrubbing the axle sleeves. They may test it. If they accept, they may order thirty-forty thousands next time.'

---

[35] Translation taken from CISG Pace (citations omitted).

5. In the fax sent by the [Buyer] to the [Seller] on 27 October 1994, the [Buyer] said that 'if the eccentric and angle problems have been improved, continue to manufacture'. It also asked, 'Is there a sample for the Chengdu axle sleeve? When can you manufacture one container?'

6. After the first delivery of the goods in November 1994, the [Buyer] sent a fax to the [Seller] and notified that there were problems with the quality of the goods after the customers have used the goods for the first time. Later, the [Buyer] sent faxes on 3 October, 10 October, and 10 November mentioning that there were problems with the goods complained about by customers, but the [Buyer] never mentioned seeking compensation from the [Seller]. Nor did [Buyer] demand to have the goods inspected. In response to the problem on the No. 825, 826 axle sleeves and 01#, 02# hubs mentioned by the [Buyer] in its faxes sent on 3 October 1995 and 9 October 1995, the [Seller] stated, 'it is possible that the screw thread has been damaged'. In the fax sent on 11 October, it said, 'No. 825, 826 screw thread, I think it is possible.'

[Judgment]

1. The parties did not stipulate the applicable law in the contract. However, the parties did mention the United Nations Convention on Contracts for the International Sales of Goods (hereafter the 'CISG') during their statements and arguments. China and the United States are both Contracting States of the CISG, and the places of business of the parties are in the United States and China, therefore, the CISG should be applied here.

2. The inspection and compensation clause is very important for international sales contracts. The clause determines that the goods should be handed over to the inspection agency agreed by both parties within a certain period of time after the goods arrive at the destination port. If there is a quality or quantity problem, the [Buyer] should demand compensation from the [Seller] within a certain period of time. This is a common clause in international sales contracts, and it is also a trade usage. The quality clause in the instant case, which is also the inspection and compensation clause, follows the trade usage and it was agreed to by both parties.

Article 9(1) CISG states: 'The parties are bound by any usage to which they have agreed and by any practices which they have established between themselves.'

Therefore, the inspection and compensation clause in the instant case is valid, and the parties should be bound by the clause. The [Buyer] should have the goods inspected by the agreed inspection agency within thirty days after the goods arrive at the destination port, and questions about the quantity of the goods should be raised within fifteen days after the arrival of the goods. If the [Buyer] finds any non-conformity of the goods, it must give notice and claim for compensation within the aforesaid time limit. The inspection report should be presented together.

3. According to the inspection and compensation clause in the contract and Articles 38, 39 CISG, the [Buyer] should have inspected the goods within the time stipulated in the contract, and given notice of the problem to the [Seller], otherwise, the [Buyer] loses the right to rely on a lack of conformity of the goods.

The Arbitral Tribunal found that the buyer did not inspect the goods as determined in the contract and it should pay the price and interest for late payment. However, since the buyer did mention quality problems to the seller and the seller admitted that there might be problems with some of the goods, 'the seller should take responsibility for the quality problem admitted'.

B. Practices established between the Parties

The parties are also bound by practices established between them. The Convention does not define the length or intensity that a particular practice must satisfy in order to fall within the definition of a 'practice established between the parties'. However, it is generally acknowledged that the parties' relationship must have lasted for some time and must have led to the conclusion of various contracts. See, in this respect, C 9-2.

C 9-2

Zivilgericht Baselstadt (Switzerland),
3 December 1997,
CISG-online 346[36]

[Facts]

A Swiss seller and an Italian buyer concluded a contract for the sale of two ship cargoes of urea. The parties agreed upon payment within 30 days after the issue of the bill of lading. The seller issued an invoice containing the note that payment had to be made by bank transfer to the seller's bank account which it held with a Swiss bank in a certain region. Since the purchase price remained unpaid, the seller commenced an action to recover the price before the Court of the region where the seller's bank was located, whereas the seller's place of business was in a different region. [...]

[Judgment]

[...] The Court also dismissed the seller's allegation that the indication on the invoice of the seller's bank account established a practice between the parties under which the buyer was bound to pay at the seller's bank, therefore the bank's place being the place of performance. In the Court's opinion, although it left open the issue of whether the parties concluded one or two different contracts for the delivery of two ship cargoes, it held that under Art. 9(1) CISG two contractual relationships were anyway not sufficient to establish a practice between the parties. According to the Court, in order for a practice between the parties to be established, long lasting contractual relationships involving more sale contracts between the parties is required. [...]

If the parties have established a practice between themselves, that practice supersedes the provisions of the Convention relating to the relevant issue. In case law, an established practice between the parties may refer to the way in which a contract is concluded, the remedies available, the means and/or procedure of payment, the quality of the goods, or the use of certain means of communication to order the goods. A recurrent issue is whether standard terms and general conditions have been included in the contract by way of an established practice between the parties. C 9-3 illustrates this.

---

[36] English abstract taken from UNILEX.

C 9-3

Oberster Gerichtshof (Austria),
6 February 1996,
CISG-online 224[37]

[Facts][38]

The plaintiff, a German buyer, and the defendant, an Austrian seller, entered into an agreement for the FOB delivery of a certain quantity of propane gas. The parties exchanged communications by facsimile and telephone on the terms of their agreement, including the method of payment (letter of credit). The buyer, however, did not obtain a letter of credit since an essential element was missing, i.e. the seller failed to name the port of origin. In addition, the seller made the delivery of the gas subject to the conditions that it was not to be resold in the Benelux countries.

The parties had initially intended to enter into a 'basic agreement', which would contain the general conditions of the seller and would constitute the trade usages that would govern the transactions between the parties, but could not reach an agreement. The draft of the 'basic agreement' stated that all orders should be in writing. However, the seller could not prove that the 'basic agreement' nor the general conditions had been made known to the buyer.

[Judgment]

[...] The CISG does not contain specific requirements for the incorporation of standard business conditions, such as the [sellers'] general conditions of sale, into a contract. Therefore, the necessary requirements for such an inclusion are to be developed from Art. 14 et seq. CISG, which contain the exclusive requirements for the conclusion of a contract [...]. Consequently, the general conditions of sale have to be part of the offer according to the offeror's intent, where the offeree could not have been unaware of that intent, in order to become a part of the contract (Art. 8(1) and (2) CISG). This inclusion into the offer can also be done implicitly or can be inferred from the negotiations between the parties or a practice which has developed between them.

The fundamental question at issue is whether the parties concluded a contract of sale regarding 3,000 mt propane gas, which the lower courts decided in the affirmative. In denial of the existence of a contract of sale, the [sellers] argue that it can be inferred from the general conditions of sale, the draft of the framework agreement, and the correspondence between the parties that the [sellers] generally only conclude contracts in writing and only when the payment is guaranteed by letter of credit or some other means of securing payment; in addition, in the preliminary correspondence, the [buyer] explicitly referred to the 'usual conditions' and 'delivery on a contractual basis'. The [sellers] admit that no prior contract has been concluded between the parties and that this, therefore, would constitute their first contract—if a contract was ever concluded, which is still denied by the [sellers]—with the consequence that practices in the meaning of Art. 9 CISG could not have been developed between the parties. The [sellers] claim, however, that prior business conversations between the parties (the general conditions of sale, the prior correspondence and the draft of the framework agree-

---

[37] Translation taken from CISG Pace (citations omitted).
[38] Summary of facts taken from UNILEX.

ment) show the [sellers'] usual approach when concluding contracts, i.e., their principle of concluding contracts in writing only. According to the [sellers], this prior conduct can qualify as 'practices' in the sense of Art. 9 CISG, which means that a contract has not been agreed upon, because the written form requirement was not observed.

The argument of the [sellers] is without merit: It is generally possible that intentions of one party, which are expressed in preliminary business conversations only and which are not expressly agreed upon by the parties, can become 'practices' in the sense of Art. 9 CISG already at the beginning of a business relationship and thereby become part of the first contract between the parties. This, however, requires at least (Art. 8, especially paragraph (1) of Art. 8 CISG) that the business partner realises from these circumstances that the other party is only willing to enter into a contract under certain conditions or in a certain form. In the present case, it cannot be determined whether the [sellers'] general conditions of sale were given to the [buyer], whether agreement was reached about their application, or whether the [buyer] got to know them at all. The lower courts could not determine that the [buyer's] general contract manager had ever received the brochure containing the general conditions of sale; and the findings of the lower courts do not support the conclusion that the [buyer] was informed of the contents of the general conditions of sale in the aftermath (i.e., following the first informational conversations). As it cannot be determined that the [buyer] had knowledge of the general conditions of sale of the [sellers], the Court cannot draw the conclusion that they formed the basis of the contractual agreement between the parties in the meaning of Art. 9 CISG.

[…]

The correspondence of the parties does not support the [sellers'] point of view either. The mere allusion to 'usual conditions' or to 'on a contractual basis' does not mean that the [buyer] was referring to the [sellers'] general conditions of sale or to general contractual conditions, which were discussed in connection with the completely different framework agreement, which ultimately was not agreed upon and which did not even cover the kind of contract at issue here.

As the [sellers'] general conditions of sale did not become part of the contract, their content is of no relevance here and no determinations regarding their content had to be made by the courts. It was equally unnecessary to determine the content of the parties' correspondence (as the [sellers] demanded), because even if the [sellers'] claims regarding those facts could be substantiated, this would not lead to a different result.

As a specific form for the conclusion of a contract was not agreed upon during the negotiations of 19 December 1990 and the facts do not establish that it was self-evident for the parties (Art. 9(1) CISG) that contracts could only be agreed upon in writing as a condition for the conclusion of a contract, the observance of the form requirement, i.e., the written form, was not a condition for the formation of a valid contract (Art. 11 CISG). When deciding this question, oral declarations of the parties have to be equally taken into consideration.

Therefore, the Court of Appeal correctly decided that neither the contractual negotiations nor the practices having developed between the parties could have made the general conditions of sale of the [sellers] part of their offer. It is true that the usual requirements for the formation of a contract can be modified by industry usages [...], if the parties refer to such usages upon conclusion of the contract (Art. 9(2) CISG); however, a custom in the oil industry to conclude contracts of sale in writing only was neither found nor claimed by the [sellers] in this case. [...]

Questions

Q 9-1

Which rules govern the question of whether a usage has been agreed on or a practice established?

Q 9-2

What is the hierarchy of legal norms applicable to a CISG contract? Rank the following legal sources:
— provisions of the CISG;
— individually negotiated contract clauses;
— usages agreed upon by the parties or practices established between themselves (Art 9(1) CISG);
— widely known and regularly observed international trade usages (Art 9(2) CISG).

Q 9-3

(a) Is it necessary for the usages agreed upon to be internationally accepted?
(b) Why was the buyer in C 9-1 held to not have inspected the goods on time?
(c) According to C 9-2, how many times must a particular practice have taken place in order to satisfy the requirement of an 'established practice' in Article 9(1) CISG?
(d) How does the decision of the *Oberster Gerichtshof* in C 9-3 extend that rule?

Q 9-4

Why did the Court in C 9-3 find that the parties had effectively concluded a contract?

III. Article 9(2) CISG

A. International Usages Regularly Observed in the Trade Concerned

According to Article 9(2) CISG, the parties are considered to have impliedly made a usage applicable of which the parties knew or ought to have known and which is widely known to, and regularly observed by, parties to contracts of the type involved in the particular trade concerned. The character of such usages has been controversially discussed. Whereas some consider them as implied terms, others hold that they are objective 'sources of the law'. The difference between the two positions is that, under the first view, those usages will be interpreted according to Article 8, whereas, under the second view, the usages would be interpreted according to Article 7(1).

Despite the seeming differences, the dispute does not seem to have had a practical impact to date.

Case law in which the courts or tribunals have acknowledged an 'international usage' under Article 9(2) is quite rare. An interesting case is C 9-4, in which the question of whether local or regional usages can be considered 'a usage which in international trade is widely known to, and regularly observed by, parties to contracts of the type involved in the particular trade concerned' is discussed.

C 9-4

Oberster Gerichtshof (Austria), 21 March 2000, CISG-online 641[39]

[Facts]

Plaintiff [Seller], seated in Germany, sold wood to Defendant [Buyer] whose domicile was in Austria. [...] According to Art. 1(1) CISG the case is governed by the Convention.

[Judgment]

In a former judgment [...], the Supreme Court stated that Austrian wood trade usages, which fall among commercial customs under § 346 of the Austrian Commercial Code [...], do not only apply if expressly or impliedly underlied by the parties of the trade contract. As far as they were referred to by legal provisions, trade usages had been adopted as part of these legal provisions themselves. Thus being a part of the governing law, they had to be applied irrespective of whether agreed upon by the parties or not—even in case they had been totally unknown to the parties.

[...] Art. 9(1) CISG states that the parties to a contract are bound by any usage to which they have agreed and by any practices which they have established between themselves. According to Art. 9(2) CISG the parties are considered, unless otherwise agreed, to have impliedly made applicable to their contract or its formation a usage of which they knew or ought to have known and which in international trade is widely known to, and regularly observed by, parties to contracts of the type involved in the particular trade concerned. Yet, usages which are expressly or impliedly agreed upon by the parties (Art. 9(1) CISG) do not need to be widely applied in international trade. [...] [T]o be applicable these usages must be known or ought to be known to parties which either have their place of business within the area of these usages, or which continuously do business in this area for a considerable period of time. Thus adopted, agreed usages, established practices and—widely known and—regularly observed usages prevail over other deviant CISG provisions. The question whether Austrian wood trade usages constitute commercial customs acknowledged by Austrian commercial law is a question of fact rather than of law, and therefore is not to be decided within appellate proceedings before the Supreme Court. The same applies to the question whether these trade usages can be considered as widely known and regularly observed usages of international trade under Art. 9(2) CISG [...].

---

[39] Translation taken from CISG Pace (citations omitted).

The Court of First Instance followed [Seller]'s submission, which has not been disputed by [Buyer], that the '*Tegernseer Gebräuche*' are commercial customs for sales contracts on wood and fall under Art. 9(2) CISG. They were widely known and regularly observed in wood trade contracts between German and Austrian parties. As the parties had entered into business relations before and as [Seller] in his confirmation of [Buyer]'s order expressly assumed these usages to be applicable, the Court of First Instance's contention that [Buyer] ought to have known these usages does not result from a gross misinterpretation of the law.

As acknowledged customs, the '*Tegernseer Gebräuche*' have priority over other CISG provisions. [...]

B. Particular Aspects

(a) Letter of confirmation

(i) Under the CISG

In various legal systems, such as Germany, Denmark, and Switzerland, a letter of confirmation is held to have a 'constitutive effect'. If one party sends a confirmation letter to which the other party does not respond, the parties will be considered to have concluded a contract on the terms stipulated in the confirmation letter. In other countries, for example in France or Italy, such an effect of a confirmation letter is unknown. There is some case law in this respect, mostly from Germany. The case chosen as an illustration (C 9-5) is from Switzerland.

C 9-5

Zivilgericht Basel-Stadt (Switzerland),
21 December 1992,
CISG-online 55[40]

[...] The plaintiff [seller] is a company with limited liability under Austrian law established in [...] Austria. The defendant is a joint stock company established in Basel. [...]

(*Applicability of the CISG approved.*)

The [seller] alleges that in 1989 the defendant ordered 187,000 meters of material. The order was confirmed by a letter of 24 February 1989. Later the quantities were specified as 176,000 meters. Then invoices were made and credit notes were issued for a faulty partial delivery. The last invoice of 15 January 1990 for 433,755 Ffr [French francs] (Annex 6e to Statement of Claim) was not paid. Payment of this is claimed.

---

[40] Translation taken from CISG Pace (citations omitted).

The defendant [...] alleges that the contract on which the [seller] bases his claim was not between the [seller] and herself, but was concluded between the [seller] and a third company, firm [...], resident in France. In the development of the contract, the defendant claims that she merely had the function of an agent.

3. 3.1. In the case at hand, there is no written contract. Under Article 11 CISG, a contract of sale can be concluded informally, it need neither be concluded in writing nor evidenced in writing.

It is not contested that in February 1989 negotiations took place in [...] (France), in which [...] as representative of the [seller], as well as Mrs. [...] the CEO of firm [...] took part, [nor is it contested that] the contract upon which the [seller] bases his claim was the subject of the talks.

Only the telex drawn up by [...] of 14 February 1989 [...] confirms the position of the defendant that there was only one contract concluded with [...]. This telex is addressed to Mrs [...]. In this telex, reference is made to "OUR VISIT WITH [...], ON 10/02/89 AT [...]. PRODUCTION [...] AND [...]"

The telex contains, inter alia, the acknowledgement concerning the article [...] "3. Confirmation of your new order in Article [...]" for 252,000 meters, to be delivered from May to December 1989. The communication states further that the defendant had received a copy of the telex of 14 February 1989. This communication standing alone would allow the conclusion that the contract was verbally concluded between the [seller] and firm [...], and not between the [seller] and the defendant.

However, on 24 February 1989, the [seller] drew up a confirmation of order addressed to the defendant. It confirmed the order [...].

Moreover, in the future, invoices and correspondence were delivered to the defendant without ever having made clear that she was acting only as a representative of firm [...]:

- By a communication of 19 July 1989 the quantity to be delivered was changed to 176,000 meters [...].
- The [seller] invoiced the defendant for the delivered material on 5 September (No. 891804), 15 September (No. 892196), 11 October (892406) and 4 December 1989 (No. 892868) as well as 15 January 1990 (No. 905093) (Annex 6a to e to Statement of Claim).
- The [seller] reminded the [buyer] about, inter alia, the last-named invoice for 433,755 Ffr with a communication of 28 March 1990 [...].

In addition, for "wrongly delivered goods" with article number [...], the defendant was given a credit note with the letter of 31 December 1989 for invoice No. 890352 for the amount of 17,188.92 Ffr (Annex 7 to defendant's plea). Another credit note to the defendant for the amount of 56,250.—Ffr was issued on 27 June 1990 (Annex 8 to defendant's plea). The defendant recognised that form of compensation. She announced by telex: 'We have given directions to our bank to transfer to the account (of the claimant) with [...] in [...] account [...] the amount of 354,421 Ffr: (According to the list contained in the telex the defendant deducted the credited sums mentioned above from the total sum of 427,850.10 Ffr. (see Annex 9 to defendant's plea).

3.2. The question arises now, whether the confirmation of order of 24 February 1989 and the subsequent communications, insofar as the recipient does not object, is to be considered binding in the sense of business relations.

With regard to the coming into existence of the contract, the CISG basically has regard only to the express consent that results from offer and acceptance.

According to the prevailing opinion, a confirmation of order only has contractual effect in the meaning of the CISG, if this form of contract formation can be qualified as commercial practice under Article 9 of the CISG [...].

Article 9(1) CISG provides that the parties are bound by any usage to which they have agreed and by any practices which they have established between themselves. Under Article 9(2), the parties are considered, unless it has been otherwise agreed, to have impliedly made applicable to their contract or its formation a usage of which the parties knew or ought to have known and which in international trade is widely known to, and regularly observed by, parties to contracts of the type involved in the particular trade concerned.

At the outset, it is to be noted that in both Austria and Switzerland the contractual effect of commercial communications of confirmation (in domestic contractual relations) is not denied and thus that both parties recognised the legal effects of such a communication and also had to take into account that they might be held to those legal effects. For Swiss Law, the contractual effect of a letter of confirmation is based on Article 6 of the Code of Obligations. According to the prevailing opinion, a letter of confirmation constitutes an 'indication for the formation and the content of the concluded contract'. [...] As the legal systems of both States generally agree on this issue for domestic contractual relationships, it is not to be assumed that other rules are applicable to contracts for the supply of textiles in international relationships between contractual partners established in Switzerland and Austria.

A corresponding commercial usage, at least in the sense of Article 9(2) CISG, is thus confirmed.

Moreover, the [seller] had not only drawn up a confirmation letter in connection with the contested invoice for 433,755 Ffr [...], but also another concerning an order for 6,500 meters of articles 26166 [...] on 24 February 1989.

The defendant likewise does not argue that the first mentioned confirmation letter had represented an innovation with relation to the business relations between the parties. This allows the conclusion that the letters of confirmation must have constituted a practice that the parties had established between themselves in the sense of Article 9(1) CISG.

The parties, in this case namely the defendant, are bound by the effects of this usage. Had the defendant, after receipt of the confirmation letter of 24 February 1989, wished to have been understood by the [seller] to be in fact not a contractual partner but rather an agent, she would have had to inform the [seller] of this at that moment. [...]

(The argument that defendant was only an agent was also dismissed based on the fact that defendant's purpose registered in the commercial register read 'Purchase, sale and supply of textiles of all kinds' and defendant had made no attempt to correct the inaccuracy of this entry, so that defendant was held as a party to the contract.)

(ii) Under the PICC 2010

Art 2.1.12 PICC 2010:

If a writing is sent within a reasonable time after the conclusion of the contract and which purports to be a confirmation of the contract contains additional or different terms, such terms become part of the contract, unless they materially alter the contract or the recipient, without undue delay, objects to the discrepancy.

(b) Trade Terms and Other Sets of Rules

Isolated cases have dealt with the issue of whether trade terms, such as the INCOTERMS®[41] or the UCP 600, constitute international trade usages within the meaning of Article 9(2) CISG. In recent years, another recurrent question in arbitral awards has been whether uniform sets of rules, such as the PICC and the PECL, may be considered usages within the meaning of Article 9(2) CISG. This last-mentioned question has usually arisen with regard to an issue not explicitly dealt with in the Convention.

With regard to that issue, the preferable view is the following: where the CISG provides clear guidance, uniform sets of rules cannot supersede the provisions of the Convention with the argument that they constitute trade usages which would take precedence over the CISG. The only way to derogate from the CISG in favour of uniform sets of rules is a contractual derogation in the sense of Article 6 CISG. In other words, uniform sets of rules can only have a gap-filling function within the Convention. In this respect, the correct approach should be the detour via Article 7(2) CISG: it must be examined whether the issue can be solved based on one or more general principles of the Convention. When determining whether such general principles under the CISG exist, regard may be also had to the PICC (and, in a European context, to the PECL). Those sets of rules might be relied on if they reflect principles inherent to the CISG; but then, the found solution is one found under the CISG, that is, a CISG-internal solution based on Article 7(2) CISG.

The gap-filling approach just described does not completely rule out the application of uniform sets of rules by way of Article 9(2) CISG. Thus, if a trade usage is widely known in international trade and regularly observed by parties in the trade branch concerned, and if such usage is settled in the PICC or other bodies of rules, the latter can be regarded as applying to the contract to the extent that they actually reflect the trade usage.

IV. Comparison with Other Legal Provisions

Art 1.9 PICC 2010:

(1) The parties are bound by any usage to which they have agreed and by any practices which they have established between themselves.
(2) The parties are bound by a usage that is widely known to and regularly observed in international trade by parties in the particular trade concerned except where the application of such a usage would be unreasonable.

---

[41] The INCOTERMS® (International Commercial Terms) are a universally recognised set of definitions of international trade terms, such as FOB, CFR and CIF, developed by the International Chamber of Commerce (ICC) in Paris, France. They define the trade contract responsibilities and liabilities between buyer and seller and is a highly cost-saving tool. The exporter and the importer need not undergo lengthy negotiations about the conditions of each transaction. Once they have agreed on a commercial term like FOB, they can sell and buy at FOB without discussing who will be responsible for the freight, cargo insurance, and other costs and risks. The INCOTERMS® were first published in 1936 (INCOTERMS® 1936) and are revised periodically to keep up with changes in international trade needs. The complete definition of each term is available from the current publication (INCOTERMS® 2010).

Questions

Q 9-5

(a)   Under Article 9(2) CISG, must there be evidence that the parties positively agreed on a usage?
(b)   Compare Article 9(2) CISG with Article 1.9(2) PICC 2010. Do you see any differences?

Q 9-6

Can you find any examples of usages that, in cross-border sales, are widely known and regularly observed by parties in the trade concerned?

Q 9-7

(a)   In C 9-4, it was held that even merely local usages may be usages in the meaning of Article 9(2) CISG. According to that decision, when will that be the case?
(b)   Does the fact that domestic and even local usages may constitute usages within the meaning of Article 9(2) CISG comply with the wording of Article 9(2) CISG?

Q 9-8

(a)   Why did the court in C 9-5 affirm that there was a usage within the meaning of Article 9(2) CISG with regard to the effects of a letter of confirmation?
(b)   Would the court have come to the same conclusion if the letter of confirmation had been sent from a German party to a party located in a country whose law does not provide for the same effect of such confirmation letter?
(c)   In light of this, can we ignore the parties' domestic law with respect to whether a merely local or regional usage is considered a usage within the meaning of Article 9(2) CISG?

Article 10 CISG

For the purposes of this Convention:

(a) if a party has more than one place of business, the place of business is that which has the closest relationship to the contract and its performance, having regard to the circumstances known to or contemplated by the parties at any time before or at the conclusion of the contract;

(b) if a party does not have a place of business, reference is to be made to his habitual residence.

I. Overview

Article 10 CISG sets up a twofold rule: Article 10(a) CISG indicates which place of business, out of several, is decisive for answering questions such as whether the Convention applies (Art 1(1)(a)); whether any reservations made under the Convention apply (Art 12); whether holiday or non-business days must be observed (Art 20(2)); whether delivery or payment was made (Art 31(c), 57(1)(a)); or whether risk has passed (Art 69(2)). There are a few more references to the 'place of business' in the Convention (Art 42(1)(b), Art 90, Art 93(3), Art 94(1), (2) and Art 96). Article 10(b) CISG states a default rule in that, where a party does not have a place of business, its habitual residence is to be taken into account.

II. Article 10(a) CISG

The CISG does not define the term 'place of business', which must therefore be interpreted autonomously. In this respect, it is widely accepted that 'place of business' implies a certain permanence or stability; that is, the location from which business is conducted must be more than a mere temporary place, such as a market stand or a store-room. 'Place of business' further implies a certain autonomy; that is, the ability to conduct a minimum of actual, non-ancillary functions within the business of the company or enterprise.

Article 10(a) CISG raises a major difficulty: it focuses on the closeness of the place of business to the contract *as well as* to its performance. Those places may, in fact, be two different ones: in practice, it is not unusual to conclude the contract through one of several branch offices and to agree on performance through or at another branch office. It must then be decided which of the places is the relevant one for the purposes of the Convention. In this respect, what the parties agreed upon, or whether there was a practice established or a usage to which the parties were bound, will be decisive. If the contract, practices or usages do not provide for a specific agreement as to which place of business is decisive, the relevant place of business must be determined from an objective point of view. In practice, the determination of the relevant place of business is based on a number of factors, such as where the contract representations came from, or where the price quotations came from (where the purchase orders were submitted), the language of the contract, or the place the correspondence came from.

For an illustration, see C 10-1.

C 10-1

Vision Systems, Inc et al, Vision Fire & Security Pty, Ltd v EMC Corporation,
Sup Ct MA, 28 February 2005,
CISG-online 1005

[Facts][42]

EMC, a US buyer (defendant) purchased smoke detection units ('SDUs') from Vision, a seller (plaintiff) whose principal place of business was located in Australia (VFS) and whose subsidiary (VSI) was located in the United States. The seller filed a complaint alleging that, although under the contract the buyer was bound to purchase some SDUs per year for three years, after the initial deliveries the buyer refused to perform the contract before hand, by notifying the seller that it intended to discontinue all further purchases of SDUs. The buyer filed a motion for summary judgment at the Superior Court of Massachusetts to dismiss the seller's claims.

[Judgment]

... [The second complaint] is grounded upon the CISG. CISG is an international version of the Uniform Commercial Code.... Vision points to CISG because, unlike the UCC, it has no Statute of Frauds provision. CISG, however, applies to contracts for the sale of goods made between buyers and sellers in different countries. 'This Convention applies to contracts of sale of goods between parties whose places of business are in different States: (a) when the States are Contracting States ... CISG, Art. 1(1)(a) "Contracting State" is a country which is a signatory to CISG.' The international component is a jurisdictional prerequisite to the application of CISG. ...

Contracts between a United States company, like EMC here, and the United States subsidiary of a foreign company, like VSI here, 'do not fall within the ambit of the CISG.' ...

---

[42] Summary of facts taken from UNILEX.

Similarly, CISG does not apply to the sale of goods between parties if one party has 'multiple business locations' unless it is shown that that party's international location 'has the closest relationship to the contract and its performance.' ...

Here, EMC is an American corporation, based in Hopkinton, Massachusetts. Vision, with which EMC was dealing, is multi-national, with entities such as VFS within its corporate family in Australia and entities like VSI, also an American corporation, located in Massachusetts. The center of gravity of the transaction, however, seems clearly in Massachusetts. As noted above, EMC's first contact with Vision was with Ronald Ouimette, a business development executive employed by VSI. Ouimette was directly responsible for developing the business relationship between Vision and EMC. Ouimette remained Vision's principal contact with EMC. He was the 'Account Manager for EMC,' and was EMC's main contact person for 'orders, deliveries, etc.'

Additionally, James Rose, another VSI employee, was principally responsible for various engineering issues relating to the integration of Vision's products into EMC's data storage systems. He was the only other Vision employee in regular contact with EMC. The June 10, 2002, e-mail from Ouimette came from 'Vision Systems, Inc., 35 Pond Park Road, Hingham, MA.' And, most tellingly, all price quotations to EMC were provided by VSI; all sales to EMC were F.O.B. Hingham, Massachusetts; and all orders from EMC were submitted to VSI at its Hingham office.

As a matter of law, the jurisdictional prerequisites to applicability of CISG are not met. [The second submission] must be dismissed.

III. Article 10(b) CISG

If a party has no place of business, reference is to be made to its habitual residence. By stating this, Article 10(b) CISG refers to where the party is actually located. This rule is in accordance with most domestic rules of private international law, but has only rarely been referred to. It is generally acknowledged that a short time at a particular location will not be sufficient; for example, a temporarily rented hotel room will not generally constitute a habitual residence within the meaning of Article 10(b) CISG.

   The practical importance of Article 10(b) CISG is to physical persons and non-incorporated enterprises; it cannot be applied to corporations, as corporations must be incorporated somewhere and are thus, by necessity, related to a country.

Questions

Q 10-1

What is the significance of the 'place of business'?

Q 10-2

(a)   What difficulty arises from the fact that Article 10(a) CISG simultaneously relies on the closeness to the contract and its performance?

(b)   In case law, what have been the indicating factors for deciding which out of several places of business has the closest connection to the contract and its performance? See C 10-1.

Q 10-3

Is the parties' nationality significant in answering the question of where their place of business is?

Article 11 CISG

A contract of sale need not be concluded in or evidenced by writing and is not subject to any other requirement as to form. It may be proved by any means, including witnesses.

I. Overview

Article 11 CISG lays down the principle of freedom from form requirements. A contract may be concluded orally or implicitly through the parties' conduct. The parties are, however, free to agree on a writing requirement. They may also provide for another requirement indicating intention to be bound, for instance, *consideration* as it is generally required in legal systems of the common law.

II. Principle of Freedom from Form Requirements

Article 11 CISG governs only the matters which are not excluded from the scope of application of the Convention (see above, Art 4). For example, form requirements for jurisdiction or arbitration clauses are not governed by Article 11 CISG but are subject to the applicable procedural rules of law. It must, however, be noted that this last-mentioned point is controversial.

For matters governed by the CISG, form requirements of domestic laws do not apply, except for those cases that fall within the scope of Articles 12 and 96 CISG (see below, Art 12).

In order to prevent domestic procedural rules from undermining the principle of freedom from form requirements under Article 11 CISG, its second sentence makes it clear that the existence of a contract (and the parties' contractual statements) may be proven by any means. Therefore, in a CISG case, it is up to the judge to evaluate the evidence presented by the parties. When taking evidence, it may very well be that a contractual document receives special consideration, since it is an exception to the general rule of freedom from form requirements; however, domestic rules, for example, the Plain Meaning Rule, which globally bars extrinsic evidence external to a seemingly unambiguous piece of writing, are inapplicable under the CISG (see above, Art 8).

III. Comparison with Other Legal Provisions

Art 1.2 PICC 2010:

> Nothing in these Principles requires a contract, statement or any other act to be made in or evidenced by writing. It may be proved by any means, including witnesses.

§ 2-201 UCC:

> (1) Except as otherwise provided in this section a contract for the sale of goods for the price of $500 or more is not enforceable by way of action or defense unless there is some writing sufficient to indicate that a contract for sale has been made between the parties and signed by the party against whom enforcement is sought or by his authorized agent or broker. A writing is not insufficient because it omits or incorrectly states a term agreed upon but the contract is not enforceable under this paragraph beyond the quantity of goods shown in such writing.
>
> (2)   ...
>
> (3) A contract which does not satisfy the requirements of subsection (1) but which is valid in other respects is enforceable
>
>   (a) if the goods are to be specially manufactured for the buyer and are not suitable for sale to others in the ordinary course of the seller's business and the seller, before notice of repudiation is received and under circumstances which reasonably indicate that the goods are for the buyer, has made either a substantial beginning of their manufacture or commitments for their procurement; or
>
>   (b) if the party against whom enforcement is sought admits in his pleading, testimony or otherwise in court that a contract for sale was made, but the contract is not enforceable under this provision beyond the quantity of goods admitted; or
>
>   (c) with respect to goods for which payment has been made and accepted or which have been received and accepted (Sec 2-606).

Art 1341 CC:[43]

> (1) An instrument before notaires or under private signature must be executed in all matters exceeding a sum or value fixed by decree,[*] even for voluntary deposits, and no proof by witness is allowed against or beyond the contents of instruments, or as to what is alleged to have been said before, at the time of, or after the instruments, although it is a question of a lesser sum or value.
>
> (2) All of which without prejudice to what is prescribed in the statutes relating to commerce.

Questions

Q 11-1

(a)   Which principle is stated in Article 11 CISG?
(b)   Compare Article 11 CISG with Article 1.2 PICC 2010.

---

[43] Translation taken from www.legifrance.gouv.fr.
[*] 1500 € (Art 56 of the Decree no 2004–836 of 20 August 2004, in force since 1 January 2005).

(c)   Compare the result with Section 2-201 UCC, Article 1341 CC. What are the differences?

(d)   What is the effect of an unwritten contract that exceeds the indicated sum under the UCC? Is it invalid?

Q 11-2

(a)   Can the parties to a CISG contract still agree that a certain form must be complied with?

(b)   Is an implied modification or termination of the contract possible pursuant to Article 11 CISG? See also Article 29 CISG.

Q 11-3

According to Article 11, sentence 2 CISG, the existence of a contract may be proven by any means. Why was Article 11, sentence 2 CISG incorporated into the CISG?

Article 12 CISG

Any provision of article 11, article 29 or Part II of this Convention that allows a contract of sale or its modification or termination by agreement or any offer, acceptance or other indication of intention to be made in any form other than in writing does not apply where any party has his place of business in a Contracting State which has made a declaration under article 96 of this Convention. The parties may not derogate from or vary the effect of this article.

I. Overview

According to Article 12 CISG, Contracting States may derogate from the principle of freedom from form requirements, as stated in Articles 11, 29 and 14 to 24, by making a declaration under Article 96 CISG. Article 12 CISG was incorporated at the insistence of the former Soviet Union and recognises that, for some Contracting States, it is important that the conclusion of a contract, its modification or termination by agreement be only in writing. Article 12 is the only provision in the Convention that is mandatory and from which the parties cannot derogate.

II. Operation of Article 12 CISG

Whether or not a State has made a declaration within the meaning of Article 96 CISG can be ascertained from the website of UNCITRAL[44] (see also above Art 1 CISG). Article 96 reads as follows:

Art 96 CISG:

A Contracting State whose legislation requires contracts of sale to be concluded in or evidenced by writing may at any time make a declaration in accordance with Article 12 that any provision of Article 11, Article 29, or Part II of this Convention, that allows a contract of sale or its modification or termination by agreement or any offer, acceptance, or other

---

[44] www.uncitral.org/uncitral/en/uncitral_texts/sale_goods/1980CISG_status.html.

indication of intention to be made in any form other than in writing, does not apply where any party has his place of business in that State.

From the text of Article 96 CISG, it is clear that only those states whose national law requires contracts of sale to be concluded in or evidenced by writing may make a declaration under this article. For the rest, the situations in which Articles 12 and 96 CISG apply are disputed. There is some authority suggesting that the principle of freedom from form requirements of Article 11 CISG is derogated from whenever one party has its place of business in a Reservation State. This view is prima facie supported by the wording of Articles 12 and 96 CISG. However, it would have the effect that the law of the Reservation State would always prevail, regardless of whether, from a conflict of laws point of view, the law of the Reservation State would actually be the law governing the contract. Thus, from the system of rules that govern the application of the Convention, another view seems preferable: the principle of freedom from form requirements is only derogated from if the applicable choice-of-law rules point to the law of the state which has made a reservation under Article 96 CISG. In other words, a court must apply its international private law and determine whether the law that would govern the question of form of the declaration that is at issue in the absence of the CISG provides for a reservation under Article 96 CISG or not. If the law applicable in default of the CISG were the law of a Reservation State, the domestic writing requirements of that State will be applicable in the case in question. If the law applicable in default of the CISG were the law of a Non-reservation State, the question of form requirements will be governed by the CISG (which, failing another agreement, practice or usage, will be the principles of freedom from form requirements).

Similarly, the form requirements of a state that has made a reservation within the meaning of Article 96 CISG should not apply where the parties have chosen the law of a Contracting State that has not made a declaration under Article 96 CISG: since the choice of law of a Contracting State leads to the application of the CISG (see above Art 6 CISG), such cases are then governed by Article 11 CISG. For an illustration of the view adopted here, see C 12-1.

C 12-1

Forestal Guarani SA v Daros International, Inc,
US Ct App (3rd Cir), 21 July 2010
CISG-online 2112[45]

[Facts]

Forestal Guarani is an Argentina-based manufacturer of various lumber products, including wooden finger-joints. Daros International, Inc, is a New Jersey-based import-export corporation. In 1999, Forestal and Daros entered into an oral agreement whereby Daros agreed to sell Forestal's wooden finger-joints to third parties in the United States. Pursuant to that agreement, Forestal sent Daros finger-joints worth $1,857,766.06. Daros paid Forestal

---

[45] Case taken from CISG Pace (references omitted).

a total of $1,458,212.35. Forestal demanded the balance due but Daros declined to pay. In April 2002, Forestal sued Daros in the Superior Court of New Jersey, asserting a breach-of-contract claim based on Daros' refusal to pay. Daros thereafter removed the case to the United States District Court for the District of New Jersey. In its answer, Daros admitted that it had paid Forestal $1,458,212.35 in exchange for the finger-joints but denied that it owed Forestal any additional money. Discovery ensued.

In June 2005, Daros moved for summary judgment, arguing that the parties lacked a written agreement in violation of the [CISG], and that Forestal could not otherwise substantiate its damages claim with credible evidence. The District Court summarily denied the motion, concluding that genuine questions of material fact existed. The Court later held a conference with the parties and ordered briefing on several specific questions regarding the applicability of the CISG. Both parties complied and agreed that the CISG governed Forestal's claim. In October 2008, the District Court granted Daros' summary judgment motion, concluding that the CISG governed the parties' dispute and barred Forestal's claim because the parties' agreement was not in writing. The Court also found that Forestal had not adduced any other evidence of its alleged agreement with Daros. Forestal has timely appealed the District Court's ruling.

[Judgment]

... The parties do not dispute that the CISG governs their dispute. While Daros does not deny that it had a contract with Forestal, the thrust of Daros' argument is that the parties do not have a written contract and that, under the CISG, the absence of a writing precludes Forestal's claim. While conceding that the CISG applies generally, Forestal contests the District Court's ruling on the ground that the lack of a writing, in its view, is inconsequential in light of the parties' course of dealing, as evidenced by Forestal's delivery of finger-joints to Daros and Daros' remittance of payments to Forestal, as well as an accountant's report and invoices Forestal claims show that Daros owes it money.

... Because both the United States, where Daros is based, and Argentina, where Forestal is based, are signatories to the CISG and the alleged contract at issue involves the sale of goods, we agree with the parties that the CISG governs Forestal's claim. ...

... The United States has not made an Article 96 declaration, so Article 11 governs contract formation in cases involving a United States-based litigant and a litigant based in another non-declaring signatory state. Argentina, however, has made a declaration under Article 96, thereby opting out of Article 11, Article 29 and Part II. Our research has turned up almost no case law from courts in the United States informing how to address a case, such as this one, in which one state has made an Article 96 declaration and the other has not. Courts in foreign jurisdictions and commentators alike are divided over how to proceed in such a scenario. According to one school of thought, a court must at the outset conduct a choice-of-law analysis based on private international law principles to determine which state's law governs contract formation, and then apply that law to a party's claim. Our study of the available sources on the subject establishes this position as the clear majority view. In contrast, under what appears to be the minority view, a court should simply require the existence of a writing without reference to either state's law, though it is unclear what form such a writing would have to take to be considered sufficient.

Although none of the supporters of what we perceive as the majority view have explained their reasoning in any detail, we conclude that the majority has it right. Our conclusion is compelled by the CISG's plain language. The CISG says [in Art 7(2)] that '[q]uestions concerning matters governed by this Convention which are not expressly settled in it are to be settled in conformity with the general principles on which it is based or, in the absence of such principles, in conformity with the law applicable by virtue of the rules of private international law [i.e. choice of law].'. Because Argentina has opted out of Articles 11 and 29 as well as Part II of the CISG, the CISG does not 'expressly settle' the question whether a breach-of-contract claim is sustainable in the absence of a written contract. So Article 7(2) tells us to consider the CISG's 'general principles' to fill in the gap. We have already outlined some of the general principles undergirding the CISG, but we fail to see how they inform the question whether Forestal's contract claim may proceed. Indeed, given the inapplicability in this case of any of the CISG's provisions relaxing or eliminating writing requirements, we do not believe that we can answer the question presented here based on a pure application of those principles alone. Given that neither the CISG nor its founding principles explicitly or implicitly settle our inquiry, Article 7(2)'s reference to 'the rules of private international law' is triggered. In other words, we have to consider the choice-of-law rules of the forum state, in this case New Jersey, to determine whether New Jersey or Argentine form requirements govern Forestal's claim.

(The Court explains the choice-of-law rules of New Jersey and concludes:)

In the end, we think it unwise either to venture into this choice-of-law thicket—the outcome of which is determinative of this case—or to engage in a largely speculative exercise about the viability of Forestal's claim under either jurisdiction's law without the benefit of either any briefing whatsoever by the parties or any analysis by the District Court on this point. Because these issues deserve a full airing, we conclude that remand is a better course of action. [...]

Questions

Q 12-1

What was the reason for incorporating Articles 12 and 96 CISG into the CISG? See also above Article 1 CISG.

Q 12-2

Why did the court in C 12-1 adopt the view that domestic form requirements must only be observed if the international private law of the forum leads to the application of the law of the Reservation State?

Article 13 CISG

For the purposes of this Convention 'writing' includes telegram and telex.

I. Overview

Article 13 CISG refers to situations in which the contract or other contractual statements must be in writing. Such writing requirement may exist because the parties have
agreed on a writing requirement or are bound to it by established practice between
them or by a trade usage (see above Art 11 CISG). Apart from those situations, a
writing requirement may exist if a party has its place of business in a State that has
made a declaration within the meaning of Article 12 CISG.

   The goal of Article 13 CISG is to ensure that 'writing' does not only refer to the
traditional written form but that it also includes more modern means of communication.
Article 13 CISG is thus an interpretative provision.

   In case law, this provision has been referred to very rarely.

II. Modern Interpretation of Article 13 CISG

It is widely recognised that Article 13 CISG contains a gap in that it only refers to older
forms of technology and does not provide for more recent forms of communication,
such as fax, e-mail, internet or other electronic communication. See, in this regard,
the following statement.

**CISG Advisory Council Opinion No 1: Electronic Communications under CISG,
Opinion, and Comment (on Art 13 CISG):[46]**

OPINION[:] The term 'writing' in CISG also includes any electronic communication
retrievable in perceivable form.

COMMENT[:] 13.1. CISG Arts 11, 12, 13, 21, 29 and 96 contain the term 'writing'. In the
traditional paper world this term was uncomplicated and referred to documents written on
paper [or other durable medium] by pencil, pen, etc. The problem is now whether electronic

---

[46] Taken from www.cisgac.com.

documents other than telegram and telex may also constitute 'writing'. The prerequisite of 'writing' is fulfilled as long as the electronic communication is able to fulfil the same functions as a paper message. These functions are the possibility to save (retrieve) the message and to understand (perceive) it.

13.2. The parties may agree on what type of written form they intend to use (CISG Art 6). They may, for instance, agree that they only accept paper letters sent by a particular courier service. Unless the parties have limited the notion of writing, there should be a presumption that electronic communications are included in the term 'writing'. This presumption could be strengthened or weakened in accordance to the parties' prior conduct or common usages (CISG Art 9(1) and (2)).

13.3. This Opinion does not deal with reservations made by States in accordance with CISG Art 96 nor does it impose any restrictions on States that have made such a reservation.

III. Impact on Article 12 CISG

Article 13 CISG refers not only to writing requirements agreed on by the parties under the Convention, but also to domestic writing requirements which remain applicable by virtue of Article 12 CISG. This is shown by the Drafting History of Article 13 CISG as well as by the way in which the provision is positioned within the CISG. Article 13 CISG should in some way limit the consequences of Article 12 CISG, that is, the fact that the Contracting States may make a reservation concerning the principle of freedom of contract of Article 11 CISG. Accordingly, Article 13 CISG broadens the term 'writing' to include documents produced through other means of communication, regardless of whether the writing requirement comes from the parties' agreement or from domestic law.

IV. Comparison with Other Legal Provisions

UNCITRAL Model Law on Electronic Commerce 1996:

Art 1

This Law applies to any kind of information in the form of a data message used in the context of commercial activities.

Art 2

For the purposes of this Law: (a) 'Data message' means information generated, sent, received or stored by electronic, optical or similar means including, but not limited to, electronic data interchange (EDI), electronic mail, telegram, telex or telecopy; ...

Art 6

(1) Where the law requires information to be in writing, that requirement is met by a data message if the information contained therein is accessible so as to be usable for subsequent reference.

(2)   Paragraph (1) applies whether the requirement therein is in the form of an obligation or whether the law simply provides consequences for the information not being in writing.

(3)   The provisions of this article do not apply to the following: ….

Art 1.11 PICC 2010:

In these Principles …

'writing' means any mode of communication that preserves a record of the information contained therein and is capable of being reproduced in tangible form.

Art 8 UN Convention on the Use of Electronic Communications in International Contracts:

(1)   A communication or a contract shall not be denied validity or enforceability on the sole ground that it is in the form of an electronic communication.

(2)   Nothing in this Convention requires a party to use or accept electronic communications, but a party's agreement to do so may be inferred from the party's conduct.

Questions

Q 13-1

To which situations does Article 13 CISG refer?

Q 13-2

What might be the reasons for subjecting a contract to written form?

Q 13-3

(a)   How could Article 13 CISG be extended to include electronic communication data? In this respect, can the UNCITRAL Model Law on Electronic Commerce, the PICC 2010 and the UN Convention on the Use of Electronic Communications in International Contracts be of interpretive help?

(b)   In the light of the purpose of writing requirements, should, for example, short text messages made by mobile telephones be on par with 'writing'?

Article 14 CISG

(1) A proposal for concluding a contract addressed to one or more specific persons constitutes an offer if it is sufficiently definite and indicates the intention of the offeror to be bound in case of acceptance. A proposal is sufficiently definite if it indicates the goods and expressly or implicitly fixes or makes provision for determining the quantity and the price.

(2) A proposal other than one addressed to one or more specific persons is to be considered merely as an invitation to make offers, unless the contrary is clearly indicated by the person making the proposal.

I. Overview

A. Content and Purpose of Article 14 CISG

The CISG relies on the mechanism of offer and acceptance for the conclusion of a contract. Article 14(1) CISG sets out the prerequisites for holding a proposal to conclude a contract to be an offer under the CISG. The two central prerequisites are a certain minimum content, and an intention by the party making the offer to be bound. Article 14(2) CISG clarifies how offers made to more than one person are to be construed.

B. Drafting History

Terms defining the offer were already present in Article 4 ULF and in the associated drafts. In the preparatory work of UNCITRAL and in the working group, the inclusion of a provision dealing with this issue was never questioned. Initially, difficulties arose with respect to general offers to the public, but also, in particular, with the requirement of an express or implicit determination of the price. Whether a contract could be concluded despite a lack of means for determining the price was debated in the drafting of the CISG. Although the first working group found the inclusion of the phrase 'that a price is to be paid' sufficient, the second sentence of Article 12(1) New York Draft 1978 contained a provision comparable with the second sentence of Article 14(1) CISG.

At the Vienna Conference, these two positions were again disputed. Whilst one group of countries made various proposals and applications which aimed at allowing an offer, and thereby a contract, without a means for expressly or implicitly determining the price, other countries wished to strictly enforce the requirement of a price that was determined or at least determinable. The result was that the current provision was included because a number of participants assumed that their national law, which did not contain such a requirement of a definite or determinable price at the time of conclusion of the contract, would apply by means of the opting-out mechanism under Article 92(1) CISG.

II. Article 14(1) CISG

A. Definite Proposal

The first element giving rise to a valid offer under the CISG is that a proposal must be sufficiently definite. The second sentence of paragraph (1) provides that a proposal is sufficiently definite if it indicates the goods and expressly or implicitly fixes or makes provision for determining the quantity and the price. Existing practices between the parties or in the trade branch concerned may provide details as to any of these criteria.

C 14-1

Geneva Pharmaceuticals Tech Corp v Barr Labs, Inc,
US Dist Ct (SD NY), 10 May 2002,
CISG-online 653[47]

... Plaintiff Geneva Pharmaceuticals Technology Corp. ('GPTC') is a New Jersey corporation with its principal place of business in New Jersey. GPTC is in the business of developing, manufacturing and marketing generic pharmaceuticals. GPTC is a wholly owned subsidiary of Geneva Pharmaceuticals, Inc ('Geneva'), which itself is a member of the generics Sector of Novartis AG, the Austrian pharmaceutical company. Until its purchase by Geneva in December 1999, GPTC was known as Invamed, Inc ('Invamed').

... Defendant Barr Laboratories, Inc ('Barr') is a New York corporation with its principal place of business in New York. Barr is engaged in the business of developing, manufacturing and marketing generic pharmaceuticals.

... Defendant Dr Bernard C Sherman ('Sherman') is an individual residing in Canada. Sherman founded Apotex in 1974 and is the chairman of its board of directors. Sherman is also a member of the board of directors of Barr and the president of Apotex Holdings.

---

[47] Footnotes omitted.

[Facts]

... The Supply and Confidentiality Agreements

In the summer of 1995, Barr and ACIC began discussions regarding a supply agreement for commercial quantities of clathrate. ACIC demanded an arrangement in which a pharmaceutical company would pay for a substantial amount of clathrate prior to receiving FDA approval. Calenti told Barr that if Barr did not strike an agreement with ACIC, Calenti would try to make one with another company.

1. The Supply Agreement

By letter agreement dated September 19, 1995 (the 'Supply Agreement'), Barr and ACIC contracted for ACIC to supply Barr with clathrate. The Agreement obligated Barr to purchase 900 kilograms of clathrate from ACIC for $1.8 million regardless of whether it could use the product or not. The Supply Agreement was negotiated as an arm's length transaction, and at the time it was signed, Barr's President, Bruce Downey, was unaware of any relationship between ACIC/Brantford and Apotex or Sherman. The Supply Agreement provided that ACIC would exclusively supply Barr with commercial quantities of clathrate in the US until another manufacturer began selling generic warfarin sodium. Barr agreed to purchase 100% of its commercial requirements from ACIC during the exclusivity period. As to delivery requirements, the Supply Agreement provided that 'ACIC will supply the [clathrate] in quantities requested by Barr, provided that Barr provides ACIC with lead times consistent with its normal operations.' ...

2. Clathrate

On September 20, 1994, Dave discussed the availability of clathrate with Getrajdman, who told him there was no exclusive on the material and that ACIC could provide it to Invamed. The next day, Dave telephoned ACIC for a price on 5–10 kilograms of clathrate and was quoted an approximate price of $2,500 per kilogram. On September 26, 1994, ACIC sent Invamed clathrate samples of 1g and 10g, and technical information, free of charge. Invamed also received research and development quantities of clathrate in February 1995 and March 1995, free of charge. ACIC/Brantford provided the samples free of charge in anticipation of selling Invamed substantial quantities of clathrate if Invamed successfully developed warfarin sodium. Invamed also purchased 15 kilograms of clathrate from ACIC/Brantford in February 1995 and an additional 5 kilograms in July 1995, at a price of $2500 per kilogram. The February 1995 purchase order contained an attachment requesting a variety of other information and materials in addition to the requested quantity of clathrate. On March 7, ACIC shipped the 15 kg clathrate order, and on March 21 it shipped the three additional 50-gram samples with requested information. On April 3, 1995, ACIC sent the FDA a DMF reference letter as requested in the purchase order and attachment. The same day, ACIC sent a copy of the letter to Invamed. ... On July 21, 1995, Dave submitted a Second standard purchase order and attachment to Getrajdman for 5 kg of clathrate, and requested ACIC's safety and handling procedures for the product. ACIC faxed the requested information to Invamed on July 24, and Invamed received the shipment early in August. ... In January 1996, Dave placed an order for an additional 12 to 14 kilograms of clathrate from ACIC/Brantford to perform tests on a particular machine. Getrajdman advised Invamed that he did not know when availability would allow ACIC to accept an order for clathrate, and that he would have to check with Calenti. In a fax sent the next week, Dave asked Getrajdman to 'let him know' so he could submit a confirming purchase order.

The January 1996 order was never fulfilled, and Invamed concluded that the failure to deliver was a result of 'poor communication' between the two companies or that ACIC/Brantford was 'too busy' to fill a small order. The principals of Invamed did not consider the failure to be serious. In place of ACIC/Brantford's clathrate, Invamed used non-FDA approved material it received from Hoechst. Before 1996 and in 1996, Patel told Getrajdman that Invamed was working with ACIC/Brantford's material and would be filing its ANDA with it. Plaintiffs claim that Invamed also specifically advised ACIC/Brantford that it would be obligated to supply commercial quantities of clathrate when Invamed's ANDA was approved. Sometime in 1995, Getrajdman told Patel that ACIC/Brantford was one of the suppliers that had clathrate available and that when Invamed placed its order ACIC/Brantford would provide the material. Plaintiffs also claim that ACIC/Brantford 'repeatedly assured' Invamed that it would supply commercial quantities of clathrate to it on numerous occasions in 1996. Plaintiffs claim that as part of this implied-in-fact contract, Invamed and ACIC agreed on the price and on a 'commercial quantity.' Further, Patel testified that as part of the agreement, Invamed had to give commercially reasonable notice of its orders. They did not agree on delivery dates. By January 1996, ACIC/Brantford advised Invamed that it was looking to other API suppliers as possible replacement sources of clathrate for Invamed. At that time, Getrajdman told Dave about a possible switching of the manufacturing to Signa in Mexico to obtain clathrate for Invamed. On May 29, 1997, Getrajdman also advised Patel about a possible clathrate source in Italy, but Patel did not want to pursue that option. On February 14, 1996, Dave sent a fax to Antoniette Walkom, ACIC's manager of regulatory affairs ('Walkom'), requesting that she provide 'information with reference to Warfarin Sodium as requested by the FDA.' Later the same day, Dave sent another fax to Walkom stating: 'I feel that we have not been treated right and it seems to me that you are not dealing in good faith. I have some important questions regarding WARFARIN SODIUM BULK DRUG SUBSTANCE.' Walkom forwarded the technical information to Dave on February 16 and 27, noting her displeasure with the tone and content of his fax. ...

[Judgment]

... VI. Invamed's State Law Claims against ACIC/Brantford Invamed alleges claims against ACIC/Brantford based on breach of contract, promissory estoppel, negligence and negligent misrepresentation. Each is addressed in turn.

A. Breach of Contract

[24] Invamed alleges that an 'implied-in-fact contract' was created for Brantford to supply Invamed with clathrate under the Convention for the International Sale of Goods ('CISG'), 15 U.S.C.App. 52, and that ACIC/Brantford breached the contract by failing to supply clathrate in response to a specific purchase order. Invamed alleges that an implied-in-fact contract existed because it (1) purchased research and development quantities of clathrate from ACIC/Brantford (at $2,500 per kilogram); (2) invested a substantial amount of money in developing its warfarin sodium product based on ACIC/Brantford's raw material; and (3) relied on the reference letter provided by ACIC/Brantford in connection with the ANDA for warfarin sodium that it submitted to the FDA.

[25] The CISG, intended to ensure the observance of good faith in international trade, CISG Art 7(1), embodies a liberal approach to contract formation and interpretation, and a strong preference for enforcing obligations and representations customarily relied upon by others in the industry. E.g., MCC-Marble Ceramic Center, Inc v Ceramica Nuova d'Agostino, S.p.A., 144 F.3d 1384, 1387 (11th Cir.1998) (CISG abandons parol evidence rule); Delchi Carrier S.p.A v Rotorex Corp., 71 F.3d 1024, 1028 (2d Cir. 1995) (UCC case law is not per se

applicable to cases governed by the CISG). A contract may be proven by a document, oral representations, conduct, or some combination of the three. CISG Art 11. The usages and practices of the parties or the industry are automatically incorporated into any agreement governed by the Convention, unless expressly excluded by the parties. CISG Art 9. While embodying a liberal approach, the CISG does not vitiate the need to prove concepts familiar to the common law, including offer, acceptance, validity and performance. ACIC/ Brantford challenges all of these elements.

1. Offer Article 14 of the CISG states two requirements for the creation of an offer: it must (1) be 'sufficiently definite,' meaning that it indicates the goods and expressly or implicitly fixes or makes provision for determining the quantity and price; and (2) indicate the intention of the offeror to be bound in case of acceptance. CISG Art 14(1). [Claimant] claims that a well-established custom in the industry was to rely on implied, unwritten supply commitments. Defendant Sherman affirmed under oath that 'the predominant practice is for these commitments not to be embodied in formal legal documents.' Further, he stated, 'When a supplier provides access to a manufacturer to its Drug Master File and the manufacturer relies upon such access as the basis of its New Drug Submission, it is the custom and the understanding of both the manufacturer and the supplier that, upon the issuance of the Notice of Compliance, the supplier will supply the product.' The alleged contract clearly identifies the goods at issue, clathrate. [Claimant] alleges that the parties had already agreed to a price and to the production of 'commercial quantities' of clathrate and admits no discussion took place regarding a delivery schedule. However, accepting as true Invamed's allegations of an industry custom, the contract was sufficiently definite. Further, the alleged contract indicated Invamed's intention to be bound; it would only send in a purchase order if it in fact needed a commercial quantity of clathrate.

§ 2-204 UCC:

(1) A contract for sale of goods may be made in any manner sufficient to show agreement, including conduct by both parties which recognises the existence of such a contract.
(2) An agreement sufficient to constitute a contract for sale may be found even though the moment of its making is undetermined.
(3) Even though one or more terms are left open a contract for sale does not fail for indefiniteness if the parties have intended to make a contract and there is a reasonably certain basis for giving an appropriate remedy.

Questions

Q 14-1

On what basis did the court in the *Geneva Pharmaceuticals* case (C 14-1) hold that the offer was 'sufficiently definite'?

Q 14-2

(a) What other instances can be held as being 'sufficiently definite' to constitute an offer under the CISG?
(b) What about under Section 2-204 UCC?

Q 14-3

An offer will not be valid by virtue of Article 14 CISG alone. What matters under domestic law will also need to be taken into consideration in determining whether or not a valid offer has been made?

C 14-2

Magellan International Corp v Salzgitter Handel GmbH, US Dist Ct (ND IL), 7 December 1999, CISG-online 439[48]

[Facts]

... Magellan is an Illinois-based distributor of steel products. Salzgitter is a steel trader that is headquartered in Düsseldorf, Germany and maintains an Illinois sales office. In January 1999 Magellan's Robert Arthur ('Arthur') and Salzgitter's Thomas Riess ('Riess') commenced negotiations on a potential deal under which Salzgitter would begin to act as middleman in Magellan's purchase of steel bars—manufactured according to Magellan's specifications— from a Ukrainian steel mill, Dneprospetsstal of Ukraine ('DSS'). By letter dated January 28, Magellan provided Salzgitter with written specifications for 5,585 metric tons of steel bars, with proposed pricing, and with an agreement to issue a letter of credit ('LC') to Salzgitter as Magellan's method of payment. Salzgitter responded two weeks later (on February 12 and 13) by proposing prices $5 to $20 per ton higher than those Magellan had specified. On February 15 Magellan accepted Salzgitter's price increases, agreed on 4,000 tons as the quantity being purchased, and added $5 per ton over Salzgitter's numbers to effect shipping from Magellan's preferred port (Ventspills, Latvia). Magellan memorialised those terms, as well as the other material terms previously discussed by the parties, in two February 15 purchase orders. Salzgitter then responded on February 17, apparently accepting Magellan's memorialised terms except for two 'amendments' as to prices. Riess asked for Magellan's 'acceptance' of those two price increases by return fax and promised to send its already drawn-up order confirmations as soon as they were countersigned by DSS. Arthur consented, signing and returning the approved price amendments to Riess the same day.

On February 19 Salzgitter sent its pro forma order confirmations to Magellan. But the general terms and conditions that were attached to those confirmations differed in some respects from those that had been attached to Magellan's purchase orders, mainly with respect to vessel loading conditions, dispute resolution and choice of law. Contemplating an ongoing business relationship, Magellan and Salzgitter continued to negotiate in an effort to resolve the remaining conflicts between their respective forms. While those fine-tuning negotiations were under way, Salzgitter began to press Magellan to open its LC for the transaction in Salzgitter's favor. On March 4 Magellan sent Salzgitter a draft LC for review. Salzgitter wrote back on March 8 proposing minor amendments to the LC and stating that 'all other terms are acceptable.' Although Magellan preferred to wait until all of the minor details (the remaining conflicting terms) were ironed out before issuing the LC, Salzgitter continued to press for its immediate

---

[48] Footnotes omitted.

issuance. On March 22 Salzgitter sent amended order confirmations to Magellan. Riess visited Arthur four days later on March 26 and threatened to cancel the steel orders if Magellan did not open the LC in Salzgitter's favor that day. They then came to agreement as to the remaining contractual issues. Accordingly, relying on Riess's assurances that all remaining details of the deal were settled, Arthur had the $1.2 million LC issued later that same day.

[Judgment]

Under Convention Art 14(1) a 'proposal for concluding a contract addressed to one or more specific persons constitutes an offer if it is sufficiently definite and indicates the intention of the offeror to be bound in case of acceptance.' So, if the indications of the proposer are sufficiently definite and justify the addressee in understanding that its acceptance will form a contract, the proposal constitutes an offer (id. Art 8(2)). For that purpose '[a] proposal is sufficiently definite if it indicates the goods and expressly or implicitly makes provision for determining the quantity and the price' (id. Art 14(1)). In this instance Magellan alleges that it sent purchase orders to Salzgitter on February 15 that contained the material terms upon which the parties had agreed. Those terms included identification of the goods, quantity and price. Certainly an offer could be found consistently with those facts.

C 14-3

Oberster Gerichtshof (Austria), 20 March 1997, CISG-online 269[49]

[Facts]

An Austrian company ('the buyer') and a Russian company ('the seller') entered into negotiations for the supply of chemical products, during which the quality of the goods to supply was subject to controversy. Finally the seller sent an offer to the buyer indicating the quantity of the goods, the possible variation in quantity within a specified range (depending on the capacity of the chosen cargo) and the price, as well as the quality which the seller erroneously thought to be the one requested by the buyer. The buyer, in its reply, stated that the possible variation in quantity should be broader than the one contained in the seller's offer. However, the buyer did not object to the specification of the quality of the products. Later on, the buyer sent a Second fax indicating a different price and a different quality. Since the parties could not reach an agreement with respect to the quality of the products, the buyer brought an action against the seller claiming inter alia damages. The issues raised in this case related to whether a contract had been validly concluded under CISG, applicable according to Art 1(1)(a) CISG.

[Judgment]

Firstly, the Court examined the existence of an offer according to Art 14(1) CISG. The Court held that, in order to determine if the seller's offer was sufficiently definite (Art 14(1) CISG), the offer had to be interpreted according to the understanding that a reasonable person of the same kind as the receiver would have had in the same circumstances (Art 8(2) CISG).

---

[49] English abstract taken from UNILEX.

The court held that the question of whether the offer was sufficiently definite within the meaning of Article 14 CISG was to be remanded to the lower court for determination.

Question

Q 14-4

(a)   Upon whose understanding do you think the court placed emphasis in C 14-2 and C 14-3, respectively—that of the buyer or that of the seller?
(b)   What was the reasoning behind this?
(c)   Which principle, present in both civil and common law domestic systems, does this approach reflect?

B. Intention to be Bound

For a proposal to constitute an offer for the purposes of the CISG, it must not only be sufficiently definite, but also exhibit an intention on behalf of the offeror to be bound. Whether an intention to be bound exists is to be interpreted on the facts of the individual cases by recourse to the provisions of Article 8 CISG.

C 14-4

Hanwha Corp v Cedar Petrochemicals Inc,
US Dist Ct (SD NY), 18 January 2011,
CISG-online 2178[50]

...

I. Background

From January 2003 to April 2009, Cedar, a New York corporation, and Hanwha, a Korean corporation, entered into twenty discrete transactions for the purchase and sale of various petrochemicals. In each of the twenty transactions, the parties formed contracts under the same procedure. First, Hanwha would submit a bid to Cedar for a given petrochemical at a given quantity and at a given price. Cedar would accept Hanwha's bid, forming what the parties describe as a 'firm bid,' or an agreement regarding product, quantity, and price. Following formation of the firm bid, Cedar would transmit a package of contract documents to Hanwha, meant to incorporate and finalize all the terms of the contract. The package of documents contained two items: (i) a 'contract sheet' that embodied the terms of the firm bid and a choice of law to govern the contract, and (ii) a set of 'standard' terms and conditions incorporated by reference in the contract sheet. Cedar always signed the contract sheet when submitting these documents to Hanwha.

---

[50] Taken from CISG Pace database (footnotes omitted).

The contract sheets drafted by Cedar for the twenty contracts provide the same substantive information, which can be described in three parts. First, at the top, Cedar provided a provision stating, 'We hereby confirm the following transaction between Hanwha Corp. and ... Cedar Petrochemicals. [The] [f]ollowing sets forth the entire agreement of the parties.' Declaration of William H. Sparke III in Support of Cedar Petrochemical's Summary Judgment Motion ('Spark Decl.'), Exs. 1-20. Second, in the body of the contract sheets, Cedar would identify the product, quantity, and price contemplated by the firm bid. Third, at the bottom, Cedar would provide a provision incorporating the standard terms and conditions by reference. This final provision also identified the laws Cedar chose to govern the contracts, and typically provided that New York law, the Uniform Commercial Code ('UCC'), and Incoterms® 2000 governed the contract. This choice of law was reinforced by a provision in Cedar's standard terms and conditions, which also provided that New York law was to govern.

After Cedar would send these signed contract documents to Hanwha, Hanwha would do one of three things: it would countersign and return the contract sheet, accepting Cedar's terms; or modify the contract sheet, and then sign and return it for Cedar's consideration; or not sign at all. On three occasions, Hanwha modified the contract sheets by providing its own choice of law to govern the contracts. Whenever Hanwha modified the contract sheets and sent them back to Cedar, Cedar did not object to the changes—including Hanwha's choices of law—but did not countersign Hanwha's version. On all twenty occasions, upon completion of this process, Cedar and Hanwha both performed their obligations under their contracts.

The present case concerns the parties' efforts to form a twenty-first contract. On May 27, 2009, Hanwha submitted a bid for the purchase of 1,000 metric tons of the petro-chemical Toluene at $640 per metric ton, the market rate at the time. Cedar accepted the bid, thus creating a firm bid for the purchase and sale of the Toluene. Cedar followed up its acceptance of the bid by sending Hanwha, via email, a signed contract sheet and a document setting forth Cedar's usual standard terms and conditions. As per usual, Cedar provided in the contract sheet that New York law, the UCC, and Incoterms® 2000 would govern the contract, and also provided in the standard terms and conditions that New York law would govern. Hanwha did not immediately respond to the contract docu-ments, but engaged with Cedar in preparing a bill of lading and nominating a vessel for the ocean carriage.

Approximately a week after Cedar had sent Hanwha the contract documents for the Toluene sale, Hanwha returned them in modified form. On the contract sheet, Hanwha had modified the provision providing for governing law, crossing out New York law and the UCC, leaving only the provision that Incoterms® 2000 was to govern the contract. Hanwha also provided a new set of 'standard' terms and conditions; in relevant part, Hanwha's new set of conditions provided that Singapore law would govern the contract, rather than New York law. In sum-mary, Hanwha struck Cedar's nomination of New York law, the UCC, and Incoterms® 2000 to govern the contract, substituting instead Singapore law and Incoterms® 2000.

When Hanwha returned the amended contract documents, it added an additional term, stated in the body of the email transmitting the amended documents. In the email, Hanwha provided that no contract would 'enter into force' unless Cedar countersigned Hanwha's proposed version of the contract documents. Declaration of Cho Yong in Support of Cedar Petrochemical's Motion to Dismiss ('Cho Yong Decl.'), Ex. 6. Cedar refused to accept Hanwha's terms, and sent Hanwha an email explaining that the contract would be finalized only if Hanwha accepted Cedar's original terms. The email asked Hanwha to sign and return an unaltered version of the contract documents.

While Cedar waited for a response to this last request, the parties worked out the necessary letter of credit for the transaction. Hanwha submitted a letter of credit unsatisfactory to Cedar on June 8, 2009, and an acceptable letter of credit on June 10, 2009. However, the next day, June 11, 2009, Cedar advised Hanwha that because of its failure to sign the version of the contract tendered by Cedar, there was no contract between the parties, and Cedar had the right to sell the Toluene to another party. The price of Toluene as of that date, June 11, 2009, had risen from $640 per metric ton to $790.50.

…

III. Discussion

…

b. The Merits

The issue in this case is whether Hanwha made a binding offer within the meaning of the CISG when it bid on the 1,000 metric tons of Toluene. Several articles of the CISG bear upon this issue. First, Article 14 of the CISG states, '[a] proposal for concluding a contract addressed to one or more specific persons constitutes an offer if it is sufficiently definite and indicates the intention of the offeror to be bound in case of acceptance'. CISG Art 14(1) (emphasis added). Second, in complementary fashion, Article 8 of the CISG sets out the relevant considerations for finding an offeror's intent.

…

Finally, Article 19(1) modifies the analysis by providing that '[a] reply to an offer which purports to be an acceptance, but contains additions, limitations or other modifications is a rejection of the offer and constitutes a counter-offer.' Even if the additional or altered terms are not 'material' to the contract, the offeree's amendments constitute a counter-offer if the offeror objects to them 'without undue delay.' Id. Art 19(2).

In this case, it is clear that Hanwha made, and Cedar accepted, a 'sufficiently definite' offer within the meaning of Article 14(1), for Hanwha's bid was for a specific product, at a specific price, and for a specific quantity. Beyond this, however, Article 14 requires that Hanwha must also have intended to be bound when it made the bid. Id. On this latter point, the undisputed facts make clear Hanwha did not possess this intent. Rather, the course of dealing between the parties makes clear that neither party was to be bound until they agreed on other material terms and conditions, namely the choice of law and forum-disputes provisions.

As a threshold point, although the CISG expresses a preference that the offeror's intent be considered subjectively, that consideration is not possible in this case since neither party submitted any competent evidence of their subjective intentions. See id. Art 8(1). The parties have submitted only self-serving declarations of how they respectively viewed the other side's offers and counter-offers, from the hindsight of their dispute. Such declarations do nothing more than make out 'the mere possibility of a factual dispute,' Quinn, 613 F.2d at 445, and can be neither a basis to grant or deny either party's motion, see Jeffreys, 426 F.3d at 554.

Turning to the objective analysis called for by Article 8(2), it is clear from all the relevant circumstances that Hanwha did not intend to be bound by making its bid for the 1,000 metric tons of Toluene. Id. Art 8(3). In the twenty prior transactions, these parties had engaged in a familiar two-step process, whereby they first formed their firm bid and then negotiated the final terms and conditions of the contracts. On each of these twenty prior occasions, the parties did not perform until after they had achieved agreement, explicit or implicit, on all the final terms of the contract. The contract sheets reflect this, for each bears a provision stating, '[The] [f]ollowing sets forth the entire agreement of the parties.' Spark Decl., Exs. 1-20. From this, it is clear that these parties did not enter into a final contract until they agreed to the final terms embodied in the contract documents, and not when they agreed Hanwha's bids on product, quantity, and price.

On this occasion, the undisputed facts show that the parties never worked out the final terms of the contract because they never formed an agreement on a term they deemed material, a choice of governing law. Previously, Hanwha had on several occasions proposed a different choice of law and Cedar had accepted the proposal, either implicitly or explicitly. The parties thereafter performed under the various contracts. But here, after Hanwha modified Cedar's contract documents and proposed a different choice of law, Cedar rejected the change. These activities constitute a counter-offer, and a rejection of the counter-offer, within the meaning of Article 19(1).

Further evidence that the parties failed to contract can be seen by the way they treated Hanwha's modification of Cedar's choice of law. Beyond simply modifying Cedar's choice of law, Hanwha insisted that Cedar accept the modification explicitly, by advising Cedar that the contract could 'enter into force' only if Cedar explicitly countersigned Hanwha's version of the contract documents. Cho Yong Decl., Ex. 6. By objecting immediately and insisting on its own nomination, Cedar made clear that it regarded the change as material, thus rendering the different choice of law a material term under Article 19(2). As the parties thereafter failed to reconcile their views, it is apparent that they never formed a final contract.

...

IV. Conclusion

For the foregoing reasons, Cedar's motion for summary judgment is granted, and the case is dismissed. Hanwha's cross-motion for summary judgment is denied. The Clerk shall terminate the motions (Doc. Nos 17 and 21) and close the case.

Question

Q 14-5

Why was a contract not concluded in the above case?

C. Relationship between Article 14(1) and Article 55 CISG

Article 14(1) CISG provides that a proposal to conclude a contract is sufficiently definite if it 'fixes or makes provision for determining' the price. Therefore, on a proper reading of this provision, without the determinability of the price, a valid offer cannot be made. However, the contrary is asserted in Article 55 CISG, which sets out a price formula for situations 'where a contract has been validly concluded but does not expressly or implicitly fix or make provision for determining the price'. Such price is determined by reference to the 'price generally charged ... under comparable circumstances in the trade concerned'. Article 55 CISG, therefore, is particularly important where the CISG is to be applied without Part II (owing to a reservation made by the Contracting State concerned) and the domestic law applicable permits a contract to be concluded without a price being determined. However, where Part II of the Convention has not been excluded, the legal position must be examined (see further discussion on Art 55 CISG below).

C 14-5

International Court of Commercial Arbitration Chamber of Commerce and Industry of the Russian Federation, 3 March 1995, CISG-online 204[51]

[Facts]

The relationships as between the parties, wherefrom the dispute has arisen, were set forth in three documents: (1) a supplement to the contract concluded by th[e] parties two years prior to it, with the supplement stating the name, quantity, price and time of delivery of the goods and also giving the [buyer] a one-month option to purchase an additional lot of the same goods; (2) the [seller]'s telex sent to the [buyer] five months later and providing for a cut in the price of the goods, stated in the supplement, and containing an offer to deliver the additional quantity of the goods in the first quarter of the following year at prices to be agreed upon by the parties ten days before the new year began; (3) the [buyer's] telex confirming the acceptance of the [seller's] offer (sent four days after receipt of the [seller's] telex). The delivery of the goods, provided for in the supplement, was effected, in the main, at the appointed time. The non-delivered part of the goods was made up in the first quarter of the following year. The price of the additional lot of the goods offered to be delivered by the [seller] in the first quarter of the following year had not been agreed upon by the parties: the [seller] omitted to quote it and subsequently (in January of the following year) advised the [buyer] of the impossibility of the delivery of this additional Part Settlement for the delivered goods was made in accordance with changed prices agreed upon by the parties. The [buyer] failed, however, to pay the [seller] for a part of the price of the delivered goods demanding that obligations relating to the additional lot of the goods be fulfilled. The [seller's] demands in the statement of the claim contained the price of the unpaid part of the delivered goods and interest on the delayed amount of payment. In the [seller's] view the contract for the delivery of the additional lot of the goods in the first quarter of the following year was not concluded by the parties since they had not agreed on the price. As far as the option is concerned, as was given to the [buyer] in the supplement, the [buyer] failed to avail himself thereof either within the time appointed in the supplement or within the extra time granted [to] him by the [seller]. Considering the [seller's] demand that the delivered goods be paid for in full to be justified, the [buyer] set up the following defense: (1) the [seller] agreed to defer the payment; (2) the contract for the delivery of the additional lot of goods was concluded by the parties and the [seller's] failure to perform it caused the [buyer] losses substantially exceeding the amount of claim; (3) the price of the goods was set in the telexes exchanged by the parties for the definite

---

[51] English abstract taken from CISG Pace (citations omitted).

period of delivery. Presenting in the following year bills for the goods delivered in January at prices provided for in his telex the [seller] thus confirmed his consent to the retention of these prices in the first quarter of the following year, too, and accordingly, to their application to the additional lot of the goods to be delivered. The [buyer] filed a counterclaim including the following demands: (1) compensation to him of damages, caused by the non-delivery of the additional lot of the goods, calculated as the difference between the current market prices, applied in the first quarter of the following year, and the prices set by the exchange of telexes; (2) compensation of moral harm; (3) indemnification of expenses incurred in making attempts to attain an amicable settlement of the dispute. Objecting to the counterclaim, the [seller] asserted in this principal claim that the contract for the delivery of the additional lot of the goods had not been concluded by the parties and, accordingly the claim of damages caused by its non-performance was unjustified. He also challenged the ICCA competence to consider the demands contained in the counterclaim.

[Judgment]

...

(f) When filing a counterclaim as follows from the materials of the case and the explanations of the [buyer's] counsel, the [buyer] proceeded from the fact that a contract for the delivery of the additional lot of the goods in the first quarter of the following year had been concluded by the parties. The analysis of the materials of the case led the Arbitration Court to a conclusion that such a contract had not been concluded by the parties.

Under the Vienna Convention (Art 14) a proposal to conclude a contract must be fairly definitive. It is to be deemed as such if goods are indicated therein, and the quantity and the price, or the mode of their determination, are directly or indirectly provided for in it. The [seller's] telex relating to the deliveries in the first quarter of the following year indicated the goods and their quantity. But it failed to provide for either the price of the goods, or the mode of its determination. The statement in the telex that the prices of these goods would be agreed upon (revised) ten days before the new year began could not be construed as signifying the mode of the determination of the price. It was only the expression of consent to determine the price of goods in future by agreement of the parties. Having confirmed this proposal by his telex, the [seller] thus agreed to the price of these goods being subject to an additional agreement of the parties. Taking into account the above-said, to this case was inapplicable Article 55 of the Vienna Convention enabling the price of goods to be determined when it had not directly or indirectly been set in the contract, or the mode of its determination had not been provided for therein. It followed from the [buyer's] confirmation ... of the [seller's] proposal, as noted above, that the parties implied the necessity to reach an agreement on the price in the future. It followed from the materials of the case and the explanation by the parties that subsequently (following the exchange of telexes) they had not agreed on the price of this lot of the goods. The [buyer's] assertion ... that, having presented bills for the goods delivered in January at the price set for the principal lot of the goods, the [seller] thus agreed to the retention in the first quarter of the following year of the price set by the parties in respect of the goods to be delivered in the preceding year could not be held justified. Firstly, when construing, under the provisions of Article 8 of the Vienna Convention, the contents of the proposal of the [seller], confirmed by the [buyer], a conclusion should be drawn that the price had been agreed upon by the parties only in respect of the goods to be delivered in the preceding year as the main lot of the goods. Accordingly, it was at this price that the goods, delivered in January of the following year to make up the non-delivery of this quantity in the preceding year, were to be paid for. Therefore, the presentation for payment of bills for these goods at the price agreed upon regarding the main lot of the goods conformed to the parties' agreement.

Secondly, the delay in the delivery of the goods could not by itself entitle the delaying party to demand that the goods be paid for at higher prices. If an approach suggested by the [buyer] were to be taken, then a conclusion should have been drawn that the [seller] would have been entitled to present bills for the delayed goods at prices set for the deliveries in the first quarter of the following year, if such prices had been agreed upon by the parties. The level of these prices, judging from the materials, filed by the [buyer], would have been substantially higher.

The Tribunal found that a contract had not been concluded between the parties.

Questions

Q 14-6

(a)   Did the Tribunal rely on Article 55 CISG in C 14-5?
(b)   Why or why not?

Q 14-7

Would a clause whereby price will be determined at an agreed point of time in the future be sufficient to satisfy the requirements of Article 14 CISG?

C 14-6

Oberster Gerichtshof (Austria),
10 November 1994,
CISG-online 117[52]

[Facts]

In April 1991, the seller, resident in Germany, sent to the buyer, resident in Austria, 249 Chinchilla furs. The buyer sold them to an Italian fur trader and paid to the seller an (converted) amount of DM 2,400 [German marks]. The seller demands further payment of sA 66,740 on the grounds that he had sold to the buyer furs of constantly good quality at a price between DM 35 and DM 65 per fur. The buyer seeks rejection of the claim on the grounds that she had on-sold the furs on account of the seller and could not get a higher purchase price than DM 2,400. The Court of First Instance sustained the claim relying on the following facts: In March 1991 the buyer ordered from the seller, who breeds Chinchilla in Germany, a large number of Chinchilla furs at an exhibition in Fuerstenstein [Germany]. The parties stipulated that the furs should be of medium or superior quality at a price range between DM 35 and DM 65 per item. At the beginning of April, the seller packaged a total of 249 furs 236 of which were of average (medium) and 13 of which were of inferior quality,

---

[52] Translation taken from CISG Pace (citations omitted).

and sent them to the buyer. On 6 April 1991, the buyer delivered these packaged furs to an Italian fur trader where the packages were opened for the first time. The Italian fur trader purchased a total of 236 furs. The buyer sent to the seller a (collective) fur-list in which she complained of and listed by item numbering the 13 furs that had been excluded. Apart from that she did not raise any other complaints with the seller. Chinchilla furs of medium quality are traded at a price of up to DM 60 per item.

[Judgment]

...

The Court of Appeal was right to consider the CISG applicable. It was also correct in taking the view that by ordering a larger amount of Chinchilla furs, the buyer had made an offer to the seller for the conclusion of a sales contract. According to Article 14 CISG, a proposal to conclude a contract addressed towards one or more specific persons constitutes an offer if it is sufficiently definite and indicates the intention of the offeror to be bound in case of acceptance. A proposal is sufficiently definite if it indicates the goods and expressly or implicitly fixes or makes provision for determining the quantity and the price. Therefore, the content of the proposal must be sufficiently definite. This is the case where a proposal indicates the goods and expressly or implicitly fixes or makes provision for determining the quantity and the price. The condition is fulfilled where the essentialia negotii are expressly fixed in the offer; however, the Second sentence of Article 14(1) CISG also allows for an 'implicit determination', i.e., [giving] criterions which allow for an interpretation that results in a definite price, definite goods or (and) their quantity. For the validity of the offer [i.e., whether it can be validly accepted], it also suffices that the required minimum content can be understood as being sufficiently definite by 'a reasonable person of the same kind' as the other party (offeree) would have 'in the same circumstances' (Art 8(2) CISG). According to Article 8(3) CISG, in determining the intent of a party or the understanding a reasonable person would have had, due consideration is to be given to all relevant circumstances of the case including the negotiations, any practices which the parties have established between themselves, usages and any subsequent conduct of the parties. In summary, therefore, an implicit determination suffices as well as a provision enabling the determination by circumscribing the quantity and the price of goods. Applying these principles, the buyer's view that the 'order of a larger amount of Chinchilla furs' lacked the necessary definiteness of the quantity of the goods must be rejected. The primary point to be taken into consideration is the buyer's later conduct of on-selling the delivered furs apart from a small number, without raising any objection as to the quantity of the goods delivered. Based on the later conduct of the parties, it must be assumed that the order of 'a larger number of furs' is to be seen as sufficiently definite. According to the principles outlined above, the requirement of definiteness of the agreed price under Article 14 CISG has also been met in this case. This condition is already fulfilled where the parties have implicitly referred to an at least determinable price without expressly indicating the relevant factors for its determination, i.e., providing criteria which allow for the determination of a definite price. By agreeing upon a price range between DM 35 and DM 65 for furs of medium and superior quality the parties have provided sufficient criteria from which a definite price can be drawn depending on the quality of the delivered furs. This price agreement must be viewed as sufficient in the sense of Article 14 CISG. The contract has thus been concluded with an at least determinable quantity and an at least determinable price. In this case, the question can remain open whether, at the relevant point of conclusion and in absence of an express or implicit determination of the price, a contract can be validly concluded through the fiction of an agreement on the usual price (Art 55 CISG).

C 14-7

Legfelsobb Bíróság (Hungary),
25 September 1992,
CISG-online 635[53]

[Facts and Judgment]

The appeal was well founded. The Court of Appeals modifies and amends the bearing of the case, established by the court of the first instance, on the basis of all the accumulated data of the lawsuit, with special attention to those contained in the letter of intention, dated on December 4, 1990, the proposal, dated on December 14, 1990 and Defendant's letter, dated December 21, 1990, and also based on the Plaintiff's declaration during the appeal proceedings, as follows below. The parties to the suit had been conducting negotiations since the fall of 1990, on the one hand, about Plaintiff replacing the engines on the Soviet built TUPOLYEV TU-154 aircrafts, on the other hand, about Defendant purchasing engines from Plaintiff for its wide bodied aircrafts, that were to be bought. On November 9, 1990 Plaintiff sent a support offer to Defendant about assembling the wide bodied aircrafts with engines manufactured by the Plaintiff. On December 4, 1990 they signed a letter of intention (memorandum) about their negotiations concerning the replacement of the engines. In this document, the Parties stated (Point 8.b) that, among other things, the contract depends on whether Defendant accepts one of the Plaintiff's two support offers, dated November 9, 1990, i.e. whether Defendant selects the PW 4000 series engine for the new wide bodied aircrafts. In case Defendant would not accept this offer, Plaintiff reserved the right to revise its declaration of intention in respect of the TUPOLYEV engine replacement program, which—by the way—was signed without undertaking any sort of obligations. Apart from the above, the strong connection between the replacement program and the sale of aircraft engines is also proven by Defendant's December 21, 1990 declaration and Plaintiff's letter, dated on January 11, 1991. On December 14, 1990 Plaintiff made two different offers in case Defendant selects Boeing or in case it selects Airbus. These offers annulled the November 9, 1990 offers and replaced them. In the December 14, 1990 purchase-support offer for the Boeing scenario Plaintiff indicated two engines, taking the modification also into consideration, the PW 4056 and the PW 4060, from which, according to Point Y.1 of the offer Defendant was to choose and to notify the aircraft manufacturer about its choice. In Point Y.2 Plaintiff undertook to sell the engines to Defendant on the basis of a separate agreement with the manufacturer. In this offer Plaintiff indicated the price of the new PW 4056 engine to be USD 5,847,675, which could increase according to the stability of value calculations from December, 1989. The modified offer does not contain the base price of the PW 4060 engine and spare engine. The other offer, dated on the same day and intended for the Airbus scenario, among the PW 4000 series engines indicated two engines, PW 4152 or PW 4156, a jet engine system and a spare engine, from which Defendant was to make its selection according to Point Y.1 and Y.2 of the offer, and upon acceptance of the offer to notify the aircraft manufacturer immediately. According to Point Y.2 Plaintiff undertook to sell the jet engine systems, the number of which was indicated, on the basis of a separate contract made with the aircraft manufacturer. In this offer Plaintiff indicated the price of

---

[53] Translation taken from CISG Pace (citations omitted).

the new PW 4152 spare engine base unit to be USD 5,552,675, and the price of the new PW 4156/A spare engine to be USD 5,847,675, with stabilizing their values starting from) December, 1989.

According to Point Y.4 of both offers, with the acceptance of the offer Defendant was to send a finalised and unconditional order for the spare engines indicated in the offers. In case of the offer for the Airbus scenario, the indicated jet engine system includes the engine, other parts and the gondola as well, while 'engine' means the motor only, therefore the price of the jet engine system is not identical with the price of the engine (motor). The offer contained the price of neither jet engine system. In the appeal proceedings, based on the Defendant's appeal, a declaration was to be made also about whether, interpreting the Parties' declarations on the basis of Paragraph 1, Section 8 of the Agreement, Plaintiff's December 14, 1990 offers comply with the conditions stipulated in Paragraph 1, Section 14 of the Agreement and whether Defendant's December 21, 1990 declaration qualifies as an acceptance. According to Paragraph 1, Section 14 of the Agreement a proposal to enter into a contract, addressed to one or more persons, qualifies as a bid if it is properly defined and indicates the bidder's intention to regard itself to be under obligation in case of acceptance. A bid is properly defined if it indicates the product, expressly or in essence defines the quantity and the price, or contains directions as to how they can be defined. This means that the Agreement regards the definition of the subject of the service (product), its quantity and its price to be an essential element of a bid. It can be determined on the basis of the given evidence and the Parties' declarations, that Plaintiff made two parallel offers for the same deal on December 14, 1990, depending on Defendant's choice of the Boeing or the Airbus aircraft. In case Boeing was selected, within the respective offer two separate engines (PW 4056 and PW 4060) were indicated. This offer did not contain the base price of the PW 4060 engine. In case Airbus was selected, within the respective offer two different jet engine systems (PW 4152 and PW 4156), belonging to the same series, and two different spare engines (PW 4152 and PW 4156/A) were indicated. The base price of the jet engine system is not included in the offer, only that of the spare engines, in spite of the fact that these two elements are not identical either technically or in respect of price. In case there is no base price, value stability calculations have no importance. The price cannot be determined according to Section 55 of the Agreement either, as jet engine systems have no market prices. The Court of Appeals did not accept Plaintiff's position, according to which it did not have to make an offer in respect of the jet engine systems' price, for these would have been billed to the aircraft manufacturer, who includes it in the price of the airplane. For according to the offers (Point Y.2) the engines, the jet engine systems and the spare engines would have been purchased by Defendant from Plaintiff, therefore Plaintiff would have established a contractual relationship with Defendant, as the buyer. That is, the two offers, involved in the suit, related not only to the sales of the spare engines, but also to the engines to be built in and the jet engine systems. Therefore, according to Section 14 of the Agreement, Plaintiff would have had to provide the price of all the products, engines and jet engine systems in its parallel or alternative offer involved in the suit, or the directions for the determination of the price thereof, to the Defendant. It clearly follows from the above, that none of Plaintiff's offer, neither the one for the Boeing aircraft's engines, nor the one for the Airbus aircraft's jet engine systems, complied with the requirements stipulated in Paragraph 1, Section 14 of the Agreement, for it did not indicate the price of the services or it could not have been determined. Plaintiff's parallel and alternative contractual offers should be interpreted, according to the noticeable intention of the offer's wording and following common sense, so, that Plaintiff wished to provide an opportunity to Defendant to select one of the engine types defined in the offer at the time of the acceptance of the offer.

For according to the wording of Section Y of the offers:

— Defendant, following the acceptance of the proposal, immediately notifies the aircraft manufacturer about the selection of one of the numerically defined engines (jet engine systems) for use on the wide bodied aircrafts;
— Plaintiff sells the selected engine (jet engine system) to Defendant according to a separate agreement made with the aircraft manufacturer;
— Thereby (that is, with the acceptance of the proposal) Defendant sends a final and unconditional purchase order to Plaintiff for the delivery of the spare engines of the determined type.

In addition to grammatical interpretation, the assumption of Plaintiff granting 'power' to Defendant, made by the Court of First Instance, essentially entitling Defendant to make its selection until some undetermined point of time or even during performance from the services offered alternatively, goes against economic reasoning as well. For the legal consequences of this would be that Plaintiff should manufacture the quantity, stipulated in the contract, of all four types—two engines and two jet engine systems—and prepared with its services wait for Defendant to exercise its right to make its selection with no deadline. It follows from all this that Plaintiff provided an opportunity to choose a certain type of engine or jet engine system at the time of the acceptance of its offer. Plaintiff's offers were alternative, therefore Defendant should have determined which engine or jet engine system, listed in the offers, it chose. There was no declaration made, on behalf of Defendant, in which Defendant would have indicated the subject of the service, the concrete type of the engine or jet engine system, listed in the offers, as an essential condition of the contract. Defendant's declaration, that it had chosen the PW 4000 series engine, expresses merely Defendant's intention to close the contract, which is insufficient for the establishment of the contract. Therefore, the court of first instance was mistaken when it found that with Defendant's December 21, 1990 declaration the contract was established with the 'power'—or, more precisely stipulation—according to which Defendant was entitled to select from the indicated four types (PW 4056 orPW 4060 engine and spare engine, PW 4152 or PW 4156 jet engine system and spare engine) with a unilateral declaration later, after the contract had been closed. The opportunity to choose after closing the contract does not follow from the offer. If perhaps such a further condition would have been intended by Defendant, then this should have been regarded as a new offer on its behalf. Lacking an appropriately explicit offer from Plaintiff and not having a clear indication as to the subject of the service in Defendant's declaration of acceptance, no sales contract has been established between the Parties. It is a different issue, whether the series of discussions and Defendant's declaration of acceptance created such a special atmosphere of confidence, where Plaintiff could seriously count on closing the contract and failing that Plaintiff suffered economic and other disadvantages. With this question and with its legal grounds, no suit being initiated, the Court of Appeals was not entitled to deal with. The stipulation of the contract, that the validity of the offer's acceptance dependent [sic] on the approval of the United States or of the Hungarian Government, could bear with any significance only if the acceptance of the offer would have resulted in a contract, however, since a contract was not established, the above-mentioned uncertain future circumstances bear with no significance in relation to the judgment passed in this present suit. The degree to which the discussions between the Parties about the replacement of the TU-154 aircrafts' engines were related to the acceptance of the offers involved in the suit also had no significance, although Defendant's letter of December 21, 1990 and Plaintiff's letter of February 11, 1991 clearly proves that the Parties, besides the present offers, were continuously negotiating and that Defendant's understanding of the cooperation with Plaintiff included the replacement of the engines.

Questions

Q 14-8

(a) Which phrase did the court cite as being 'sufficiently certain' in C 14-6 in holding that a valid offer had been made?
(b) What does this case say about the relationship between Articles 14 and 55 CISG?

Q 14-9

(a) Do you think the court made the correct judgment in C 14-7 with respect to the existence of an offer under Article 14(1) CISG?
(b) What limitation did it place on the interpretation of Article 55 CISG?

III. Article 14(2) CISG

Article 14(2) CISG deals with the controversial question of 'offers' made to the public.

Question

Q 14-10

(a) What principle, present in both civil and common law systems, is reflected in Article 14(2) CISG?
(b) Does the wording of Article 14(2) CISG reflect more the common law or the civil law approach?

IV. Incorporation of Standard Terms

The content of the contract may not only be set out in the offer itself, but also by means of a reference to general business terms.

C 14-8

Bundesgerichtshof (Germany), 31 October 2001, CISG-online 617[54]

[Facts]

Defendant No. 1 [seller] sold to the plaintiff [buyer], a company located in Spain, pursuant to an order confirmation of June 25, 1998, 'based' on [seller's] Sales and Delivery Terms, a used computer-controlled CNC rolling-milling machine of the make L., model L 1202, year of manufacture 1981, 'incl. the provision of an L. mechanic at your plant for the duration of one business day' for the price of DM [Deutsche Mark] 370,000; the Sales and Delivery Terms of the [seller], according to which used machines are sold and delivered 'without any warranty against defects,' were not attached to the order confirmation of June 25, 1998. After the machine was transported to Spain by a moving company hired by the [buyer], the [buyer] had the machine installed and connected by a Spanish company. Mechanic A., who was dispatched by company L., was unable to put the machine into operation during his visits of July 15–18, 1998 and July 21–27, 1998. With the assistance of an electronics specialist from company L., only during a third visit of September 28 to October 1, 1998, were the problems resolved; since then, the machine has been working without problems. The Plaintiff [buyer] demands from the Defendant No. 1 [seller], and from Defendant No. 2, the personally liable shareholder, the damages that arose in connection with this work. The Landgericht [Regional Court, Court of First Instance] granted the [buyer's] claim in the amount of DM 46,519.18 plus interest and dismissed [buyer's] claim with respect to an amount of DM 3,449.57. The Court viewed the order confirmation of June 25, 1998 as providing that the [seller], by promising to provide a mechanic for the duration of one business day, wanted to be responsible for the successful putting into operation of the machine, so that the [seller] was responsible for dispatching a sufficiently qualified technician and is liable for the costs of the technically under-qualified mechanic A. The Oberlandesgericht [Court of Appeals, Court of Second Instance] vacated the judgment of the Court of First Instance insofar as the Defendants were found liable to pay and remanded the matter to the Lower Court. With their—permissible—appeal, the Defendants further pursue their motion to dismiss.

[Judgment]

I. The Court of Appeals explained that the proceeding in the Lower Court suffers from a material defect because the Court of First Instance did not completely understand and take into consideration the statements of the [seller] concerning the 'provision of an L. mechanic,' thus incorrectly interpreted the agreement of the parties and, on this basis, omitted the necessary further clarification. The duty to 'provide an L. mechanic for the duration of one business day' is already 'per se,' according to its wording, unambiguous and not to be interpreted the way the appealed decision did. The undisputed statements of the [seller] that the agreement was reached within the framework of the price negotiations after the [seller] was not prepared to agree to further price reductions and the [buyer] pointed to its costs for the installation and instruction, squarely contradicts the interpretation of the Court of First

---

[54] Translation taken from CISG Pace (citations omitted).

Instance. Against this background, the Court of Appeals held that the temporally clearly-defined promise to 'provide an L. mechanic' must be deemed a financial accommodation alone. The Court of Appeals held that the lawsuit is also not ripe for decision for any other reason. The [buyer] has properly pleaded a claim for damages under arts 45(1)(b), 35(1), 74 CISG against the [seller], for which Defendant No. 2 is liable under §§ 162(2), 128 HGB. The [seller] has not effectively precluded its liability for any breach of contract. Because the [seller's] Sales and Delivery Terms were not made applicable to the contractual relationship pursuant to the CISG, the warranty exclusion in that body of law does not apply. The decision of the lawsuit, thus depends on whether the rolling-milling machine was afflicted with a defect that was covered by a warranty at the time of the transfer to a freight carrier and what costs arose from its removal. The Court of First Instance must evaluate the evidence relating to this issue.

II. These arguments do not withstand legal scrutiny in all respects. ...

1. According to the general view, the inclusion of general terms and conditions into a contract that is governed by the CISG is subject to the provisions regarding the conclusion of a contract (Arts 14, 18 CISG); recourse to the national law that is applicable based on a conflict of laws analysis is generally not available ... . The CISG does not, however, contain special rules regarding the inclusion of standard terms and conditions into a contract. This was not deemed necessary because the Convention already contains rules regarding the interpretation of contracts. ...

2. Thus, through an interpretation according to Art 8 CISG, it must be determined whether the general terms and conditions are part of the offer, which can already follow from the negotiations between the parties, the existing practices between the parties, or international customs (Art 8(3) CISG). As for the rest, it must be analysed how a 'reasonable person of the same kind as the other party' would have understood the offer (Art 8(2) CISG). It is unanimously required that the recipient of a contract offer that is supposed to be based on general terms and conditions have the possibility to become aware of them in a reasonable manner ... An effective inclusion of general terms and conditions thus first requires that the intention of the offeror that he wants to include his terms and conditions into the contract be apparent to the recipient of the offer. In addition, as the Court of Appeals correctly assumed, the Uniform Sales Law requires the user of general terms and conditions to transmit the text or make it available in another way ... . The opponent [other party] of the user of the clause can often not foresee to what clause text he agrees in a specific case because significant differences exist between the particular national clauses in view of the different national legal systems and customs; also, a control of the content of general terms and conditions under national law (Art 4 (Second sentence)(a) CISG) is not always guaranteed ... . It is true that, in many cases, there will be the possibility to make inquiries into the content of the general terms and conditions. This can, however, lead to delays in the conclusion of the contract, in which neither party can have an interest. For the user of the clauses, however, it is easily possible to attach to his offer the general terms and conditions, which generally favor him. It would, therefore, contradict the principle of good faith in international trade (Art 7(1) CISG) as well as the general obligations of cooperation and information of the parties ... to impose on the other party an obligation to inquire concerning the clauses that have not been transmitted and to burden him with the risks and disadvantages of the unknown general terms and conditions of the other party

...

3. Insofar as the general terms and conditions at issue become a part of the contract under German non-CISG law and/or in commercial relations between merchants where the

customer does not know them but has the possibility of reasonable notice—e.g., by requesting them from the user ..., this does not lead to a different result. In the national legal system, the clauses within one industry Sector are often similar and usually known to the participating merchants. To the extent that this does not apply to a commercially-active contract party, it can be expected of him, in good faith, that he make the clauses available to the other party, if he wants to close the deal—as offered by the user based on the general terms and conditions. These requirements do not, however, apply to the same extent to international commercial relations, so that, under the principles of good faith of the other party, a duty to inquire cannot be expected of him.

...

5. If, therefore, the effective inclusion of the Sales and Delivery Terms of the [seller] into its contract with the [buyer] is missing, the objections raised—in the alternative—by the [buyer] against the effectiveness of a complete exclusion of warranties in the sale of used machines, is irrelevant.

IV. The appealed judgment is thus vacated, and the matter remanded to the Court of Appeals for further clarification concerning the defects in the delivered rolling-milling machine alleged by the [buyer] and, if appropriate, concerning the extent of the necessary expenses for removal.

C 14-9

Oberster Gerichtshof (Austria),
17 December 2003,
CISG-online 828[55]

[Facts]

Plaintiff [Seller], a registered company seated in Hong Kong, sued Defendant [Buyer], who is domiciled in Austria, for payment for delivered Tantalum powder. The transaction had been mediated by N.G. Ltd., which was represented by Chris H. [Seller]'s director, Alan C., who together with his son John C. represented [Buyer] in the transaction, is also owner and director of N. Ltd. which functions as logistics provider and also liquidates open claims for [Seller]. His son's company, P. Inc., registered in California U.S., sells metal products on the U.S. market. Both companies, N. Ltd. and P. Inc. served as trade agents in [Seller]'s transaction. [Buyer] produces Tantalum wire to be used in mobile phones, computers and cars. ... Chris H.'s N.G. Ltd. had been supplying [Buyer] with Tantalum products for years. Harald M., one of [Buyer]'s representatives, asked Chris H. for delivery of Tantalum powder, which he specified in a letter, written in English, on 19 August 1999. Among other physical quality standards, the specification required a maximum oxygen content of 1100 µg/g. As Chris H. was not able to deliver this Tantalum powder himself, he contacted [Seller]'s representatives, Alan and John C., forwarding them [Buyer]'s quality requirements. In an e-mail of 15 November 1999, Chris H. informed [Buyer] that he found a Tantalum producer in China, who could provide Tantalum with an oxygen content of 1300 µg/g and asked if that was acceptable for [Buyer]. Correspondingly, [Buyer]'s representative, Harald M., asked for a sample of 1 kg Tantalum. The sample powder contained the promised oxygen content of 1300 µg/g and met [Buyer]'s other requirements. On 16 January 2000, [Buyer] ordered another 41 kg sample from Chris H.'s N.G. Ltd. The order itself was written in English, but referred to [Buyer]'s standard purchase conditions which were printed in German on the backside of the document. This Second sample, delivered to [Buyer] on 15 February 2000, neither met the required quality standards, nor was it identical with the first 1 kg sample. Yet, it could be used for [Buyer]'s purposes. On 19 July 2000, [Buyer] ordered directly from [Seller] 500 kg Tantalum powder, 'sinter quality (Sinterqualität) for test purposes'. In the English written order, [Buyer] again referred to his German standard terms on the back of the document. … On 4 January 2001, referring to the offer in the telephone conversation two days before, [Buyer] sent an order to [Seller], in which he confirmed the purchase of 9,000 kg Tantalum powder, sinter quality, of about 180 mesh, ex China, according to sample #0001T2-1 and ZCCW, lot 2000–3 for the price of US $1,049.40 per unit, in total US $9,444,600.00. Delivery was due on 2 August 2001. The English written document referred to [Buyer]'s standard purchase conditions, which were printed in German at the backside. As had become established practice, [Seller] did not sign and return the order to [Buyer], but accepted it implicitly by delivering the installments. On the other hand, the order was not signed by either Alan or John C., as they were assuming that the actual contract had already been concluded in the telephone conversation of 2 January 2001. […] On 30 October 2001, [Seller] delivered another installment of 1,500 kg Tantalum powder. The goods were certified to contain 968 µg oxygen per g. In a letter of 30 October 2001, [Buyer] refused to accept delivery. As after delivery and payment for a total amount of 3,017.10 kg Tantalum, [Buyer] had declared the contract terminated, he asked [Seller] to take back this further delivery. [Seller] did not comply. [Buyer] did not pay the purchase price of US $1,574,100.00 for this further delivery. … [Seller] further argued that [Buyer]'s standard terms, printed in German at the backside of his order, have not been validly incorporated in the English written contract between the parties.

[Judgment]

[…]

Therefore, the vital question as regards this appeal is whether [Buyer] was entitled to avoid the contract for the future. This depends on whether [Buyer]'s standard terms have been validly incorporated in the contract. […]

In his appeal, [Buyer] argues that, as all of his English written orders refer to his standard terms printed in German on the backside of the document, [Seller], by impliedly accepting this routine, established a practice in the sense of Art 9(1) CISG according to which he is bound to the thus incorporated standard terms. The fact that the conditions were formulated in a foreign language would not hinder their applicability to the contract, because they had been expressly referred to in English on the order document. Although the CISG does not specifically provide for standard terms, their incorporation is governed by Art 8 CISG and Art 14 CISG et seq., which provide for the formation of a contract under the Convention in general. Following Art 8(1) and (2) CISG, standard terms, in order to be applicable to a contract, must be included in the proposal of the party relying on them as intended to govern the contract in a way that the other party under the given circumstances knew or could not have been reasonably unaware of this intent. This might be done through express or implied reference to them in the statement. This intent might also be expressed within the negotiations to the contract, or through an established practice as provided for in Art 9(1) CISG. The Court of First Appeal did not investigate further as to whether [Buyer]'s standard terms could have been validly incorporated through established practice in the sense of Art 9(1)

CISG, as it held that, in any event, standard terms written in German language were not applicable to a contract written in English. This undifferentiated view cannot be upheld by the Supreme Court. The incorporation of standard terms depends on whether the intent to apply the standard conditions to the contract is known or ought to have been known to the other party. Whether this is the case depends on the circumstances of the particular case. It requires an unambiguous declaration of the provider's intent. Hence, a reference to standard terms given in the actual proposal must be specified and clear enough so that a reasonable person 'standing in the shoes of the other party' would understand it. In determining the intent of a party, or the understanding a reasonable person would have had, due consideration is to be given to all relevant circumstances of the case, including negotiations and practices established between the parties (Art 8(3) CISG). In any event, the addressee must be referred to the standard terms in a way that he could not be reasonably unaware of them: He must have knowledge to be able to understand them. This also depends on the language the conditions are formulated in, and on the language they are referred to in the contract: According to German doctrine, standard terms written in a foreign language might still be validly incorporated in a contract if they are referred to in the language the negotiations have been conducted in and in which the contract has been concluded. In an obiter dictum to the ruling of 7 Ob176/98b, the Austrian Supreme Court joined this opinion. Criteria for cases in which the addressee might be expected to have knowledge and understanding of standard terms written in a foreign language are: length, intensity and economic importance of the business relations between the parties, as well as the spreading and use of the language within their society: The more intense and economically important the business relation becomes, the more can it be expected that the addressee of long and frequently referenced standard terms written in a foreign language will take measures to understand them, i.e., will ask for a translation to be provided by the other party or will attend to such a translation himself. According to widespread opinion among German and Austrian scholars, it suffices that standard terms were formulated in a language the addressee is familiar with, respectively, in one of the few internationally common languages, such as English, French and German. In case an international enterprise thus provides standard terms in one internationally common language, it is for the addressee to notify the other party of his lack of understanding, otherwise his knowledge can be reasonably presumed. During the business relationship with [Seller], [Buyer] on several occasions referred in English to his German written standard terms printed on the backside of his documents. As the parties entered into a deal of roughly about 7 million Euro, an economic importance in the sense mentioned above can be concluded. Further, it must be taken into account that Chris H., who mediated the deal between the parties and functioned as a representative of N. G. Ltd., a sales agent of [Seller], had a good command of the German language—a fact that due to their long term business relations must have been known to [Seller]'s representatives John and Alan C.

Questions

Q 14-11

According to the *Bundesgerichtshof* (C 14-8) and the *Oberster Gerichtshof* (C 14-9), what other provisions of the CISG should a court have reference to in determining whether standard terms have been incorporated into the contract?

Q 14-12

(a) What is required of a party seeking to rely on standard terms to incorporate them into the contract?
(b) How is this achieved?

Q 14-13

(a) What role does the language of the standard terms play in determining whether or not they will be held to have been validly incorporated into the contract?
(b) Do you think this is the correct approach? Why or why not?

Article 15 CISG

(1) An offer becomes effective when it reaches the offeree.
(2) An offer, even if it is irrevocable, may be withdrawn if the withdrawal reaches the offeree before or at the same time as the offer.

I. Overview

A. Content and Purpose of Article 15 CISG

Article 15(1) CISG lays down the rule as to when an offer becomes effective under the CISG. Article 15(2) CISG is self-explanatory. It draws a distinction between 'withdrawal' before an offer becomes effective, and 'revocation' (Art 16 CISG) after the offer has reached the offeree.

B. Domestic Laws

Article 15 CISG generally reflects the position held under domestic legal systems. For example, Article 15(1) CISG corresponds to the first sentence of § 130(1) BGB.

§ 130(1) BGB:[56]

A declaration of intention, which is to be executed vis-à-vis another party, becomes effective, to the extent that it is executed in that party's absence, at the point in time in which it is received by that other party. [...]

Article 15(2) CISG also shows considerable similarities with the second sentence of § 130(1) BGB.

---

[56] Author's translation.

§ 130(1) BGB:[57]

> [...] It [the declaration of intention] does not become effective if the other party receives a revocation earlier or simultaneously.

C. Drafting History

Article 15 CISG can be traced back to Article 5(1) ULF, but uses clearer terminology than the earlier provision, making a distinction between 'withdrawal' (up until receipt) and 'revocation' (after receipt), the latter of which is regulated in Article 16 CISG. Together, these two provisions serve to clarify the distinction between when an offer becomes effective, and when it becomes binding.

II. Operation of Article 15 CISG

An offer and its content do not become effective until they have 'reached' the offeree. The concept of when an offer 'reaches' the offeree has important consequences for the notion of revocability in certain cases; for the concept of 'reaching', please refer to Article 24 CISG below.

There are, as yet, no reported cases dealing directly with either Article 15(1) or 15(2) CISG, however, the CISG Advisory Council has discussed the Article in light of electronic communications implications.

CISG Advisory Council Opinion No 1: Electronic Communications under CISG:[58]

[...]

CISG Art 15

[...]

OPINION The term 'reaches' corresponds to the point in time when an electronic communication has entered the offeree's server. An offer, even if it is irrevocable, can be withdrawn if the withdrawal enters the offeree's server before or at the same time as the offer reaches the offeree. A prerequisite for withdrawal by electronic communication is that the offeree has consented, expressly or impliedly, to receive electronic communications of that type, in that format and to that address.

---

[57] Author's translation.
[58] Taken from cisgac.com.

Chinese law also discusses the position with respect to electronic communications:

Art 16 PRC CL:[59]

> An offer becomes effective when it reaches the offeree.
>
> When a contract is concluded by the exchange of electronic messages, if the recipient of an electronic message has designated a specific system to receive it, the time when the electronic message enters into such specific system is deemed its time of arrival; if no specific system has been designated, the time when the electronic message first enters into any of the recipient's systems is deemed its time of arrival.

Questions

Q 15-1

In what way is the operation of Article 15 CISG relevant in light of modern forms of communication?

Q 15-2

What problems can you perceive associated with the 'receipt' of messages by electronic communication?

Q 15-3

(a)   More specifically, do you think the approach of the CISG Advisory Council to the term 'reaches' is appropriate in light of the modern problems associated with spam filters?

(b)   Do you think the approach under Article 16 PRC CL is appropriate?

---

[59] Translation taken from www.novexcn.com/contract_law_99.html.

Article 16 CISG

(1) Until a contract is concluded an offer may be revoked if the revocation reaches the offeree before he has dispatched an acceptance.
(2) However, an offer cannot be revoked:
    (a) if it indicates, whether by stating a fixed time for acceptance or otherwise, that it is irrevocable; or
    (b) if it was reasonable for the offeree to rely on the offer as being irrevocable and the offeree has acted in reliance on the offer.

I. Overview

A. Content and Purpose of Article 16 CISG

Article 16(1) CISG regulates the point in time until which an offer to conclude a contract remains non-binding. Once an offer has been received by the offeree, it can no longer be 'withdrawn' under Article 15 CISG (see discussion on previous article), but can only be revoked. The offeror's right to revoke is lost once the offeree has dispatched an acceptance, even though the contract has not yet been concluded at that point in time. Article 16(2) CISG sets out some limitations to the generally wide revocability under Article 16(1).

B. Domestic Laws

The issue as to whether an offeror is bound by its offer is subject to widely differing approaches under different national legal systems.

(a) Anglo-American Law

The basic position in Anglo-American law is that an offer is not binding and can be revoked at any time before acceptance, even if the offeror has promised not to revoke the offer.

Dickinson v Dodds [1876] 2 Ch D 463 (English law):

> [I]t is clear settled law, on one of the clearest principles of law, that [a] promise, being a mere nudum pactum was not binding, and that at any moment before a complete acceptance by [the offeree], [the offeror] was as free as [the offeree]. ... It must, to constitute a contract, appear that the two minds were at one, at the same moment of time, that is, that there was an offer continuing up to the time of acceptance.

> However, this rule is subject to certain exceptions, under which the offeror can be held bound to its offer for a certain period of time before such offer lapses.

> In the US legal system, special types of contracts that are promoted as remaining open for a certain period of time, known as option contracts, cannot be revoked within that period.

§ 2-205 UCC:

> An offer by a merchant to buy or sell goods in a signed writing which by its terms gives assurance that it will be held open is not revocable, for lack of consideration, during the time stated or if no time is stated for a reasonable time, but in no event may such period of irrevocability exceed three months; but any such term of assurance on a form supplied by the offeree must be separately signed by the offeror.

Restatement Second, Contracts 2d, § 87:

> (1) An offer is binding as an option contract if it
>   (a) is in writing and signed by the offeror, recites a purported consideration for the making of the offer, and proposes an exchange on fair terms within a reasonable time; or
>   (b) is made irrevocable by statute.
> (2) An offer which the offeror should reasonably expect to induce action or forbearance of a substantial character on the part of the offeree before acceptance and which does induce such action or forbearance is binding as an option contract to the extent necessary to avoid injustice.

Under English law, the only exception to the offeror's generally unrestricted ability to revoke the offer is where the offeree has purchased an option to keep the offer open.[60] However, the mailbox rule under English law provides an indirect limitation similar to that in Article 16 CISG, according to which an acceptance becomes effective as soon as it is dispatched, thereby precluding the revocation of an offer during the time that the acceptance is 'on its way' to the offeror.

(b) Civil Legal Systems

In contrast thereto, the position that an offeror is bound to its offer is established under many civil law systems, most notably the Germanic (for example in § 145 BGB) and Scandinavian legal systems.

---

[60] Michael Bridge, *The International Sale of Goods: Law and Practice* (Oxford, Oxford University Press, 1999) para 3.03.

§ 145 BGB:[61]

> A person who makes an offer to another to conclude a contract is bound by this offer unless she excludes it from being binding.

Art 19 PRC CL:[62]

> An offer many not be revoked:
>
> (i)   if it expressly indicates, whether by stating a fixed time for acceptance or otherwise, that it is irrevocable;
> (ii) if the offeree has reason to regard the offer as irrevocable, and has undertaken preparation for performance.

Question

Q 16-1

Based on the above, do you think it is accurate to say that Article 16 CISG represents a compromise between the different legal systems? Why or why not?

C. Drafting History

The problem addressed under Article 16 CISG as to when an offer becomes binding was one of the most difficult questions in the unification of the sales law. Reconciling the various national preconceptions (mentioned above) proved to be a difficult task. In the final version, a compromise was reached, albeit at the cost of clarity. The common law theory that a mere offer is not binding is reflected in Article 16(1) CISG. Germanic legal systems, in particular, were duly considered by the inclusion of Article 16(2) CISG, which provides for certain exceptions to the right to revoke.

II. Article 16(1) CISG

According to Article 16(1) CISG, the right to revoke an offer terminates when the offeree has dispatched an acceptance.

---

[61] Author's translation.
[62] Translation taken from www.novexcn.com/contract_law_99.html.

CISG Advisory Council Opinion No 1: Electronic Communications under CISG:[63]

...

CISG Art 16(1)

...

OPINION In case of electronic communications the term 'reaches' corresponds to the point in time when an electronic communication has entered the offeree's server. An offer may be revoked if the revocation enters the offeree's server before the offeree has dispatched an acceptance. A prerequisite is that the offeree has consented, expressly or impliedly, to receiving electronic communications of that type, in that format, and to that address. In electronic communications the term 'dispatch' corresponds to the point in time when the acceptance has left the offeree's server. The offeror may revoke the offer by sending a revocation that enters the offeree's server before the offeree's acceptance leaves the offeree's server. A prerequisite is that the offeror has consented, expressly or impliedly, to receiving electronic communications of that type, in that format and to that address.

Questions

Q 16-2

(a)   Why is it sufficient to dispatch acceptance?
(b)   When does acceptance become effective?

Q 16-3

In what way does Article 16(1) CISG apply to electronic communications? See CISG Advisory Council Opinion No 1 above. Consider also the problems associated with spam filters addressed in Q 15-3 above.

III. Article 16(2)(a) CISG

Article 16(2)(a) CISG provides that an intention to be bound may be particularly expressed where the offer states a fixed time for acceptance. That stating a fixed time led to irrevocability during that time was a point of contention at the Vienna Conference, as common law countries merely view the statement of a period of time for acceptance as meaning that the offer lapses after the expiry of such period. Although some authors still express the view that the effect of Article 16(2)(a) CISG is to make the offer irrevocable until the expiry of any fixed period, the history of the provision indicates that the fixing of a period for acceptance merely gives rise to a rebuttable presumption of an intention to be bound for that period.

---

[63] Taken from www.cisgac.com.

C 16-1

Audiencia Provincial de Murcia (Spain), 15 July 2010, CISG-online 2130[64]

[…]

LEGAL REASONING

[…]

An examination of the evidence attached to the briefs (on page 66) leads us to the conclusion that by means of an e-mail dated June 19th, 2008, the company Grúas Andaluza, SA, informed the plaintiff, KranE MASCHINEN SERVICE GMBH & CO. HANDELS KG (hereinafter KRANE), the amendment of the invoice of sale, setting 512,000 Euros as the price of the crane, with delivery in the Port of Bilbao. Grúas Andaluza, S.A. offered the possibility to KRANE to perform the transaction in advance, provided that it would be made prior to 25th June 2008, delivering an up-front payment of 60,000 Euros as proof of reserve.

The invoice corresponding to the abovementioned transaction, issued by GRÚAS ANDALUZA, S.A., is attached to the claim on page 68, document number 16. The claimant KRANE, on 20th June 2008, made a 60,000 Euros bank deposit in favor of the defendant, page 70. It is recorded that the bank deposit was rejected by GRÚAS ANDALUZA, S.A. On 20th June 2008, GRÚAS ANDALUZA, S.A. notified by phone to KRANE that another purchaser had contacted the former to inform that the whole crane price would be paid by means of a bank deposit. GRÚAS ANDALUZA, S.A. also informed KRANE about their intention to terminate the contract, and as a result of this decision, GRÚAS ANDALUZA, S.A. ordered the bank not to accept any bank deposit.

Article 14 of Vienna Convention establishes: '1) A proposal for concluding a contract addressed to one or more specific persons constitutes an offer if it is sufficiently definite and indicates the intention of the offeror to be bound in case of acceptance. A proposal is sufficiently definite if it indicates the goods and expressly or implicitly fixes or makes provision for determining the quantity and the price'.

Article 15 states that: '1) An offer becomes effective when it reaches the offeree. 2) An offer, even if it is irrevocable, may be withdrawn if the withdrawal reaches the offeree before or at the same time as the offer'.

Article 16 establishes that: '1) Until a contract is concluded an offer may be revoked if the revocation reaches the offeree before he has dispatched an acceptance. 2) However, an offer cannot be revoked: a) if it indicates, whether by stating a fixed time for acceptance or otherwise, that it is irrevocable; or b) if it was reasonable for the offeree to rely on the offer as being irrevocable and the offeree has acted in reliance on the offer.

---

[64] Translation taken from Universidad Carlos III de Madrid www.globalsaleslaw.org/content/api/cisg/translations/2130.pdf

Taking into consideration the abovementioned, it is clear that a binding offer existed prior to the one from KRANE, whereby payment of 60,000 Euros was requested on 20th June 2008, as up-front payment and reservation proof, and granting till the 25th of June 2008 as a period to pay the remaining amount of the transaction. It is proved that the claimant accepted the abovementioned offer, as it results from the wire transfer amounting to 60,000 Euros made on the appointed day. Nevertheless, the defendant company, GRÚAS ANDALUZA, S.A. unjustifiably breached the offer, without waiting to the deadline granted to satisfy the transaction amount. We can state therefore, that an offer and an accepted offer existed and as a result, the sale contract was concluded. Consequently, noncompliance of the offer is attributable to the defendant company. In this regard, articles 1114 and 1454 of the Spanish Civil Code are not applicable to the case at hand and the Vienna Convention shall come to application, as well as in any event, the terms and conditions of the final offer to sell, set forth in the e-mail dated 19 June 2008. According to this e-mail, there are no further conditions other than payment of a bond of the offer as proof of reserve) and the granting of a period of time until the 25 June 2008. The defendant breached such conditions of the offer by selling the crane to a third party and ignoring the terms of the offer, which had been accepted by the claimant. Neither can it be implied from the said e-mail that the defendant company and the offeror were entitled to cancel the offer and the conclusion of the contract in the event the bond amount was returned in accordance with the provisions of article 1.454 of the Civil Code. Furthermore, the said amount, in the case at hand, was never received by the defendant company, for reasons attributable to its own acts.

[…]

Questions

Q 16-4

How did the conclusion of the contract arise in the above case (C 16-1)? See also the discussion of Article 18(3) CISG below.

Q 16-5

Why was the seller not entitled to cancel its offer?

IV. Article 16(2)(b) CISG and Promissory Estoppel

In the context of Article 16(2)(b) CISG, the interaction between 'act[ing] in reliance' and the equitable doctrine of promissory estoppel—or, under US law, detrimental reliance—becomes relevant.

C 16-2

Geneva Pharmaceuticals Tech Corp v Barr Labs, Inc,
US Dist Ct (SD NY), 10 May 2002,
CISG-online 653

For a summary of the facts see C 14-1 above.

[Judgment]

[...]

Invamed's other claims [see Art 14 CISG above] include promissory estoppel, negligence, negligent misrepresentation and tortious interference. The CISG clearly does not preempt the claims sounding in tort. *Viva Vino Import Corp. v Farnese Vini S.r.l*, 2000 WL 1224903 (E.D.Pa. Aug.29, 2000) ('The CISG does not apply to tort claims.'). The question of whether it preempts a separate claim for promissory estoppel presents a closer question. Breach of contract and promissory estoppel 'are two sides of the same coin, and that coin is a cause of action for breach of contract.' Commentary on the CISG has not specifically addressed the issue of whether it should preclude a claim for promissory estoppel. However, one commentator's discussion of the provision for 'firm offers' under the CISG provides insight into the issue. Article 16(2)(b) provides that an offer is irrevocable 'if it was reasonable for the offeree to rely on the offer as being irrevocable and the offeree has acted in reliance on the offer.' CISG, Art 16(2)(b). The commentator writes: 'Paragraph 2(b) looks very much like American promissory estoppel doctrines, although it does not expressly require that the offeree's reliance must have been foreseeable to the offeror and does not expressly require that the offeree's reliance be detrimental. Despite these omissions, we can expect that many tribunals will apply paragraph 2(b) in much the same fashion as American courts have used promissory estoppel.' Henry Mather, Firm Offers Under the UCC and the CISG, 105 Dick. L.Rev. 31, 48 (Fall 2000). The fact that Article 16(2)(b) appears to employ a modified version of promissory estoppel suggests that if a plaintiff were to bring a promissory estoppel claim to avoid the need to prove the existence of a 'firm offer,' that claim would be preempted by the CISG. The CISG establishes a modified version of promissory estoppel that does not appear to require foreseeability or detriment, and to apply an American or other version of promissory estoppel that does require those elements would contradict the CISG and stymie its goal of uniformity.

Question

Q 16-6

(a) Can you reiterate the difference between Article 16(2)(b) CISG and the doctrine of promissory estoppel/detrimental reliance?
(b) What would be the consequences of allowing the doctrine of promissory estoppel to pre-empt the CISG?

Article 17 CISG

An offer, even if it is irrevocable, is terminated when a rejection reaches the offeror.

There are no reported cases interpreting the operation of Article 17 CISG. However, one can refer to other international contractual law principles for examples of similar approaches to this issue.

Art 2.1.5 PICC 2010:

An offer is terminated when a rejection reaches the offeror.

CISG Advisory Council Opinion No 1: Electronic Communications under CISG:[65]

[…]

CISG Art 17

[…]

OPINION The term 'reaches' corresponds to the point in time when an electronic message has entered the offeror's server. An offer is terminated when a rejection enters the offeror's server. A prerequisite is that the offeror has consented expressly or impliedly to receiving electronic communications of that type, in that format, and to that address.

Questions

Q 17-1

(a)   What might be the cases in which Article 17 CISG may play a practical role?
(b)   Explain the interplay between Article 19(1) (see Article 19 section II below) and Article 17 CISG.

Q 17-2

How could Article 17 CISG play a role in cases in which the offeree dispatches a rejection of the offer, but then decides that it does, in fact, want to accept?

Q 17-3

Consider the approach of the CISG Advisory Council in light of the modern problems associated with spam filters addressed in Q 15-3 above.

---

[65] Taken from www.cisgac.com.

Article 18 CISG

(1) A statement made by or other conduct of the offeree indicating assent to an offer is an acceptance. Silence or inactivity does not in itself amount to acceptance.

(2) An acceptance of an offer becomes effective at the moment the indication of assent reaches the offeror. An acceptance is not effective if the indication of assent does not reach the offeror within the time he has fixed or, if no time is fixed, within a reasonable time, due account being taken of the circumstances of the transaction, including the rapidity of the means of communication employed by the offeror. An oral offer must be accepted immediately unless the circumstances indicate otherwise.

(3) However, if, by virtue of the offer or as a result of practices which the parties have established between themselves or of usage, the offeree may indicate assent by performing an act, such as one relating to the dispatch of the goods or payment of the price, without notice to the offeror, the acceptance is effective at the moment the act is performed, provided that the act is performed within the period of time laid down in the preceding paragraph.

I. Overview

A. Content and Purpose of Article 18 CISG

Article 18 CISG deals with the concept of acceptance and brings together a number of provisions from ULF, its predecessor. Paragraph (1) of Article 18 addresses what constitutes acceptance of an offer under the CISG, while paragraphs (2) and (3) set out when acceptance will be regarded as having taken place. Generally, to constitute an effective acceptance, the offeree's assent to an offer must 'reach' the offeror in due time (Art 18(2) CISG). It thus mirrors Article 15(1) CISG. Just as the requirements of Article 14 CISG can be applied to interpret counter-offers, so can the requirements of Article 18 CISG be applied to interpret the acceptance of counter-offers.

B. Domestic Laws

Acceptance by conduct is permitted under most domestic legal systems. Not only common law countries, such as England,[66] but also continental systems, such as that in Germany, allow acceptance of an offer to be made implicitly.

---

[66] *Cf Felthouse v Bindley* (1862) 11 CBNS 869, 142 ER 1037.

§ 151 BGB:[67]

> The contract is concluded by acceptance of the offer, without the need for acceptance to be declared to the offeror, if such a declaration, in accordance with the common usage, is not to be expected or the offeror has waived its right thereto.

With respect to when an acceptance becomes 'effective', national laws adopt a variety of different approaches. Under German law, for example, § 130 BGB provides that declarations become effective only when received by their intended recipient. Although the predominant rule in England also provides for receipt as a requirement of validity, the mailbox rule still constitutes an important exception, whereby an acceptance sent by post becomes effective upon its dispatch (however, in practice, this really only has significance with respect to the issue of revocability of the offer, cf the discussion under Arts 15 and 16 CISG above). Similarly, in the Restatement of the Law, Second: Contracts 2d, § 63, the US position is that 'the manifestation of mutual consent [is completed] as soon as put out of the offeree's possession, without regard to whether it ever reaches the offeror.'

II. Article 18(1) CISG: Acceptance by Conduct/Silence

Whether or not conduct is to be understood as indicating assent to an offer is to be determined by reference to Article 8 CISG. Silence will not be deemed to constitute acceptance.

A. Acceptance by Conduct

C 18-1

Oberlandesgericht Frankfurt am Main (Germany),
23 May 1995,
CISG-online 185[68]

[Facts]

The [seller], a company under Italian law, is suing the [buyer] for payment of the purchase price for two deliveries of shoes at an overall price of Italian Lira [It£] 144,148,790. In the proceedings before the Court of First Instance, the [buyer] argued that the delivered shoes were defective. The [buyer] further pleaded that the [seller]'s delivery was 540 pairs of shoes short, and that the [buyer] had suffered a loss of profit in the (converted) amount of It£ 8,100,000 for that reason. Moreover, Mr. […], who in the meantime was appointed

---

[67] Author's translation.
[68] Translation taken from CISG Pace (citations omitted).

as the [buyer]'s manager, allegedly assigned to the [buyer] a claim against the [seller] for compensation arising out of a commercial agency. The [buyer] declared a set-off with this claim.

For the details of the pleadings before the Court of First Instance, the Appellate Court refers to the statements of facts in the appealed decision.

[Judgment]

The [buyer]'s appeal is admissible, but unsuccessful.

[...]

2. [Buyer's claim for damages is dismissed]

The [buyer] is further unable to set-off against the [seller]'s claims a claim for damages in the amount of It£ 8,100,000. This amount constitutes the alleged loss of profit—converted into It£—which the [buyer] supposedly would have been able to make from 540 pairs of shoes not delivered. The prerequisites of Art 74 CISG are not met. The [buyer] alleges that she ordered 3,240 pairs of the shoes (item no. 643). It is undisputed that [buyer] received 2,700 pairs. The [seller] denies that the [buyer] made an order for the alleged quantity. During the proceedings before the Court of First Instance, the [buyer] initially relied on the 'presentation of the sales contract' and subsequently on a submission of the written order. The Court of First Instance considered the [buyer]'s contention as unfounded as the [buyer] produced neither of those two documents. During the appellate proceedings, the [buyer] relies for proof of the order on the testimony of her manager as well as the written order, which—while described as attachment B1 to [buyer]'s brief—has not been submitted. The [buyer] has failed to make sufficient submissions regarding her alleged claim in a way that would lead the Appellate Court to conclude that the [seller] was obliged to deliver more than 2,700 pair of shoes. It can only be gathered from the [buyer]'s pleadings that she allegedly placed an order for 3,240 pairs of shoes. It does not follow from [buyer]'s submissions how the [seller] is supposed to have accepted this order. The [buyer]'s alleged order would constitute an offer in the meaning of Arts 14 and 15 CISG. The [seller]'s delivery of 2,700 pairs of shoes would then indicate an assent to the offer in the meaning of Art 18(3) CISG. As the delivery did not relate to the entire quantity allegedly ordered, it would have constituted a material modification of the offer. Therefore, the [buyer]'s offer would have to be considered rejected and the [seller]'s delivery seen as a counter-offer. Even if the [buyer] had then complained about the missing 540 pairs of shoes—a fact that is disputed between the parties—a sales contract was not formed and an obligation of the [seller] to deliver more shoes did not exist. After all, the [seller]'s acceptance regarding the disputed quantity was still missing. Independent of this matter, the [buyer]'s claim for damages also fails because the [seller] denies that a loss of profit in the amount of 8,100 DM, (respectively, It£ 8,100,000) was incurred. Again, the [buyer]'s manager cannot be heard as a witness for the amount of damage incurred.

C 18-2

Oberlandesgericht Saarbrücken (Germany),
13 January 1993,
CISG-online 83[69]

[Facts]

A German buyer, who had established a business relationship with a French seller, ordered doors to be produced by the seller in order to resell them to its customers. The seller sent to the buyer a letter of confirmation containing (printed on the back page) its standard terms according to which 'Notice of defects is valid only if made within 8 days after the date of delivery'. The buyer refused to pay alleging, inter alia, non conformity of the goods. The seller commenced an action requiring full payment of the price. It assumed that the buyer did not have the right to rely on a lack of conformity of the goods since it had not examined them and given notice of their non-conformity in compliance with Arts 38(1) and 39(1) CISG.

[Judgment]

In the Court's opinion, a sales contract had been validly concluded between the parties. The Court noted that the buyer's taking delivery of the goods constituted conduct indicating assent to the offer and amounted therefore to an implied acceptance of the standard terms contained in the letter of confirmation sent by the seller (Art 18(1) CISG).

C 18-3

Golden Valley Grape Juice and Wine, LLC, Plaintiff, v
Centrisys Corporation, Defendants, Centrisys Corporation,
Third-Party Plaintiff, v Separator Technology Solutions Pty Ltd,
Third-Party Defendants,
US Dist Ct (ED CA), 21 January 2010,
CISG-online 2089

[...]

FACTUAL OVERVIEW

This dispute arises from a contractual agreement between plaintiff Golden Valley Grape Juice and Wine, LLC ('Golden Valley') and defendant Centrisys Corporation ('Centrisys'). On April 2, 2008, Golden Valley (a California LLC) purchased a STS200 centrifuge (the 'centrifuge') from Centrisys, a Wisconsin Corporation, for use in Golden Valley's grape juice applications. (Doc. 1, Amended Complaint P5.) STS (an Australian business entity) manufactured the centrifuge and sold it under a separate agreement to its then distributor,

---

[69] English abstract taken from UNILEX.

Centrisys. STS, generally, builds centrifuges and then sells the centrifuges to other businesses for eventual sale in the stream of commerce to end users. (Doc. 16, Whittington Decl. P2.)

After installation of the centrifuge and startup in September 2008, the centrifuge did not perform to specifications. (Doc. 1, Amended Complaint P7.) Golden Valley notified Centrisys of the non-conformity. According to the amended complaint, '[d]efendant and the manufacturer repeatedly assured Plaintiff that the problems would be cured.' (Doc. 1-2, Amended Complaint P8.) Golden Valley eventually filed this action against Centrisys. Centrisys then filed a third party complaint against STS. Centrisys alleges claims against STS for: (1) indemnity, (2) contribution, and (3) declaratory relief.

STS argues that pursuant to the parties' contract, STS and Centrisys agreed to resolve any disputes in Australia. STS submits the 'General Conditions' to the STS/Centrisys contract. STS argues that when STS and Centrisys entered into their contract, the 'General Conditions' were part of the contract. In pertinent part, the 'General Conditions' provide for forum selection in Victoria, Australia. The forum selection clause states in its entirety: 'Any dispute between the parties shall be finally settled in accordance with laws of Victoria (the jurisdiction shall be the State of Victoria) or through arbitration at STS P/L's option.' (Doc. 23, Whittington Decl. Exh. 1, P14.) Centrisys, however, disputes that the 'General Conditions' was part of the parties' contract.[1] Centrisys offers evidence that the 'General Conditions' was neither attached to any correspondence nor agreed to be part of the contract. Thus, Centrisys' position is that it never agreed to the General Conditions and thereby never agreed to the forum selection clause. In short, Centrisys disputes the validity of the contract's clause naming Australia as the forum.

ANALYSIS AND DISCUSSION

…

B. United Nations Convention on Contracts for the International Sale of Goods

The disputes in this case arise out of an agreement for a sale of goods from an Australian party to a United States party. Such international sales contracts are ordinarily governed by a multilateral treaty, the United Nations Convention on Contracts for the International Sale of Goods ('CISG'). …

The CISG also addresses contract offer and acceptance. A proposal is an offer if it is sufficiently definite to 'indicate[ ] the goods and expressly or implicitly fix[ ] or make[ ] provision for determining the quantity and the price,' CISG, Art 14. An offer is accepted if the offeree makes a 'statement … or other conduct … indicating assent to an offer.' CISG, Art 18.'A contract is concluded at the moment when an acceptance of an offer becomes effective.' CISG, Art 23.

Here, STS and Centrisys acknowledge that the United States and Australia are signatories to the CISG. They agree that their contract is governed by the CISG. Thus, the CISG governs the substantive question of contract formation, including whether the forum selection clause was part of the parties' agreement.

C. The Forum Selection Clause is Part of the Parties' Agreement

The Court must first determine whether the forum selection clause was part of the contract, pursuant to the CISG, taking into account its articles and any pertinent precedent.

Centrisys does not dispute that the parties had a contract for the sale of the centrifuge to Centrisys. Centrisys argues that the General Conditions to the contract was not part of the contract because Centrisys never consented to or approved the General Conditions of Sale. (Doc. 35, Supplemental Brief; Doc. 30, Mahoney Decl. P2.)

1. The Offer

STS' offer was contained in the February 29, 2008 sales quote to Thomas Junod, of Centrisys. In an e-mail dated February 29, 2008, STS sent, and Centrisys received, a sales quote for the sale of the STS200 centrifuge to Centrisys. (Doc. 22, Mahoney Decl. P5, Exh. 'A'.) Under the CISG, this sales quote was sufficient to constitute an offer. A proposal is an offer if it is sufficiently definite to 'indicate[ ] the goods and expressly or implicitly fix[ ] or make[ ] provision for determining the quantity and the price,' CISG, Art 14. The sales quote identified the goods for sale, the quantity of goods and the price. Thus, the offer for the sale of the centrifuge was contained in the February 29, 2008 e-mailed sales quote. Under the CISG, an adequate offer was made.

The same e-mail to Centrisys included the General Conditions. According to Mr. Whittington, this e-mail 'attached' the General Conditions. The February 29, 2008 e-mail consisted of the sales quote, with an attachment for the General Conditions, another attachment for the Warranty and another attachment for banking information. (See Doc. 33, Whittington Decl. Exh. 2.) The e-mail to Thomas Junod contained four attachments. Thus, the e-mail to Tom Junod not only included the sales quote to Tom Junod, but also attached the General Conditions in the same e-mail. STS' offer included, not just the sales quote, but also the attachments to the e-mail because all of the terms were offered at the same time. The General Conditions were part of STS' offer.

2. The Acceptance

Under the CISG, conduct is adequate acceptance. 'Conduct of the offeree indicating assent to an offer is an acceptance.' CISG, Art 18(1). After receiving the sales quote, Centrisys then incorporated the STS quote into its presentation to Golden Valley. (Doc. 33, Whittington Decl. Exh. 5.) In a March 6, 2008 e-mail correspondence between Tom Junod of Centrisys and Gerald Homolka, of Golden Valley, Centrisys proposed the purchase of the centrifuge. Golden Valley ultimately entered into a contract on April 2, 2008 with Centrisys to purchase the centrifuge. (Doc. 1, Complaint P5.) Centrisys ordered the centrifuge and it was delivered to Golden Valley. Thus, the terms of STS' offer were accepted because Centrisys sold the centrifuge to Golden Valley. See CISG, Art 19 [sic—this should be a reference to Art 18(3)] ('the offeree may indicate assent by performing an act, such as one relating to the dispatch of the goods or payment of the price, without notice to the offeror, the acceptance is effective at the moment the act is performed.')

Centrisys argues that the mere receipt of the General Conditions is not enough to accept the conditions. Centrisys argues that it did not 'accept' the terms of the General Conditions because it did not affirmatively agree to the General Conditions. (Doc. 35 Supplemental Brief p.3.) Centrisys argues that a unilateral attempt to impose the conditions is insufficient, citing Chateau Des Charmes Wines, Ltd v Whitehall Specialties, Inc., 328 F.3d 528 (9th Cir. 2003).[2]

Chateau Des Charmes Wines, however, is distinguishable on its facts. ...

Here, however, the General Conditions accompanied the sales quote. The General Conditions were attached, contemporaneously, with the sales quote and with other sale information, such as warranty information and banking information, which were included in the e-mail. Unlike Chateau and Solae, the General Conditions were not sought to be imposed after the contract had been formed. The General Conditions were part of the offer. Indeed, it is without dispute that Centrisys reviewed at least one other attachment in the same e-mail—the warranty. (See e.g., Doc. 33, Whittington Decl. P16 and Exh. 2.) Throughout the proceedings in this Court, Centrisys has alerted the Court to the warranty provided by STS as a means of establishing STS' 'minimum contacts' with California. (See Doc. 20, Centrisys opposition to Motion to Dismiss p. 9.) Thus, some of the attachments to the February 29, 2008 e-mail were reviewed by Centrisys. See CFMOTO Powersports Inc v NNR Global Logistics USA, Inc., 2009 US Dist LEXIS 113058, 2009 WL 4730330, 3 (D.Minn. 2009) (Although Mirman now asserts that he did not receive any terms and conditions when he signed the Customs POA, that after-the-fact assertion directly contradicts the evidence in the record.)

Pursuant to the CISG, acceptance does not require a signature or formalistic adoption of the offered terms. Pursuant to Art 18(3), 'the offeree may indicate assent by performing an act, such as one relating to the dispatch of the goods or payment of the price, without notice to the offeror, the acceptance is effective at the moment the act is performed.' The evidence establishes that at the time STS sent its sales quote to Centrisys, it contemporaneously sent its General Conditions as part of the attachments. By adopting the terms of the sales quote, Centrisys accepted the terms upon which the centrifuge had been offered, including the General Conditions. Thus, Centrisys accepted the General Conditions.

Art 13 UN Convention on the Use of Electronic Communications in International Contracts 2005:

Availability of contract terms

Nothing in this Convention affects the application of any rule of law that may require a party that negotiates some or all of the terms of a contract through the exchange of electronic communications to make available to the other party those electronic communications which contain the contractual terms in a particular manner, or relieves a party from the legal consequences of its failure to do so.

Questions

Q 18-1

(a)   Was acceptance found to have been made in the *Frankfurt am Main* case (C 18-1)?
(b)   On which factors did the court base its decision?
(c)   How does this compare with the position under your domestic legal system?

Q 18-2

(a)   Was there acceptance in the *Saarbrücken* case (C 18-2)?
(b)   If so, how was it given?

Q 18-3

(a)   Does the decision in the US Federal District Court case have implications for electronic commerce?
(b)   What kind of implications?
(c)   Is the position taken in this case in accordance with Article 13 UN Convention on the Use of Electronic Communications in International Contracts?

C 18-4

Pasta Zara SpA, Plaintiff, v United States, Defendant, and American Italian Pasta Company, Dakota Growers Pasta Company, and New World Pasta Company, Defendant-Intervenors, US Court of International Trade, 7 April 2010, CISG-online 2094[70]

[...]

OPINION AND ORDER

Timothy C. Stanceu, Judge: Plaintiff Pasta Zara S.p.A. ('Zara S.p.A.' or 'Zara'), an Italian producer and exporter of pasta products, contests the final determination ('Final Results') that the International Trade Administration, United States Department of Commerce ('Commerce' or the 'Department'), issued to conclude the eleventh administrative review of an antidumping duty order on certain pasta from Italy (the 'subject merchandise'). Certain Pasta From Italy: Notice of Final Results of the Eleventh Admin. Review & Partial Rescission of Review, 73 Fed. Reg. 75,400, 75,400 (Dec. 11, 2008) ('Final Results'). Zara S.p.A. advances three claims. It claims, first, that Commerce erred in deeming Zara S.p.A.'s sales of subject merchandise to be constructed export price ('CEP') sales rather than export price ('EP') sales.

[...]

II. DISCUSSION

[...]

A. The Court Must Sustain Commerce's Determination that Zara's Sales of Subject Merchandise Were Constructed Export Price Sales

Zara S.p.A. contests as unsupported by substantial record evidence Commerce's determination that its sales of subject merchandise were constructed export price sales as defined by 19

---

[70] Taken from CISG Pace.

U.S.C. § 1677a(b) rather than export price sales as defined by § 1677a(a). Compl. PP 10-13; 19 U.S.C. § 1677a(a)-(b) (2006). Based on the administrative record, the court must sustain Commerce's determination.

[…]

Plaintiff argues that the placement of the purchase orders and Zara S.p.A.'s 'acceptance-in-fact,' Pl. Br. 9, by beginning production in response to the purchase orders created a binding agreement under the UN Convention, i.e., the CISG, to which the United States is a party. Id. at 9, 17 (citing CISG, arts. 14, 18, S. Treaty Doc. 98-9, at 25, 19 I.L.M. at 674-75). The CISG recognizes that

'if, by virtue of the offer or as a result of practices which the parties have established between themselves or of usage, the offeree may indicate assent by performing an act, such as one relating to the dispatch of the goods or payment of the price, without notice to the offeror, the acceptance is effective at the moment the act is performed, provided the act is performed within the period of time laid down in the preceding paragraph.'

CISG, Art 18.3, S. Treaty Doc. 98-9, at 25, 19 I.L.M. at 675. The preceding paragraph states that '[a]n acceptance is not effective if the indication of assent does not reach the offeror within the time he has fixed or, if no time is fixed, within a reasonable time . …' Id., Art 18.2, S. Treaty Doc. 98-9, at 25, 19 I.L.M. at 675. The court does not agree that the CISG required Commerce to conclude, on the record before it, that binding agreements to sell the subject merchandise necessarily were formed when Zara S.p.A. began production of merchandise in response to the purchase orders. Commerce was not required to view the course of dealing between Zara S.p.A., Zara-USA, and the single unaffiliated U.S. purchaser, on which plaintiff relies for its claim, in isolation and without also considering the evidence revealing the entire circumstances in which the three parties, in practice, arranged the transactions. Those circumstances include the practices involving invoicing. Zara S.p.A. admits that it did not provide the unaffiliated customer a written acknowledgment of its acceptance of the purchase, see Pl. Br. 7-9, and it does not identify specific record evidence from which Commerce was required to conclude, contrary to other evidence on the record, that the parties unequivocally intended production against the purchase orders to constitute acceptance of the offers made by those purchase orders. In summary, plaintiff's argument would require the court to ignore the significance of the substantial record evidence supporting Commerce's factual findings. Those findings were more than adequate to support the conclusion that the sales of the subject merchandise were made by Zara-USA, after importation. The CISG did not require Commerce to ignore this substantial evidence or make findings contrary to it.

Question

Q 18-4

(a) Was there acceptance by conduct in the US Court of International Trade case (C 18-4)?
(b) What factors did the court take into account in reaching its decision?

For further information in this regard, please refer to the discussion on the battle of the forms in Article 19 V. below.

B. Silence or Inactivity as Acceptance

Where there is no other indication of assent to an offer, silence or inactivity will not constitute assent for the purposes of the CISG. However, under Article 9(1) and (2) CISG, the parties are bound by any trade usages and any practices established between them. To the extent that such a practice was accepting through silence or inactivity, this will lead to a binding agreement.

C 18-5

Rechtbank Arnhem (The Netherlands),
17 January 2007,
CISG-online 1455/1476[71]

[...]

2.1. In the main issue, [Buyer's successor] requested the Court to order [Buyer] to pay compensation for the damages [Buyer's successor] suffered due to the fact that the two Teguflex compensators [Buyer] delivered were defective because of a production fault. [Buyer] challenged this claim and requested to be allowed to demand warranty compensation from [Seller], the party that had supplied the compensators. This request was approved by judgment of 26 July 2006. By summons of 25 August 2006, [Buyer] demanded warranty compensation from [Seller].

2.2. [Seller] filed an incidental plea requesting the Court to declare itself not competent to rule on the claim filed by [Buyer]. To support its position, it alleged that [Seller]'s General Terms and Conditions were applicable to the contract between [Buyer] and [Seller].

[...]

2.5. However, there is a threshold question to be decided whether the parties had agreed upon an arbitration clause that would bar this Court from ruling on [Buyer]'s claim. The question has to be answered on the basis of the substantive law which, pursuant to the Private International Law of the Court invoked, is applicable to the contract. In this case, no choice of any national body of laws has to be made, since the Netherlands and Sweden are both parties to the CISG. The CISG is applicable. The CISG is the substantive law that governs this sale of compensators. The formal and temporal applicability of this Convention is present.

2.6. The question whether the parties agreed to include the [Seller]'s general terms in their contract has thus to be judged by the provisions of the CISG. To determine whether the parties had agreed upon the Arbitration Clause in the instant case, the general principles on which the CISG is based have to be taken into account, pursuant to Art 7(2) CISG (HR 28 January 2005, NJ 2006/517).

General principles are to be found:

— First: in Art 8 CISG, concerning the interpretation of declarations of the parties;
— Second: in Art 11 CISG, which provides that agreements between parties may be established without formal requirements (from which it follows that there is no need for formal requirement to agree upon general terms or an arbitration clause); and

---

[71] Translation taken from CISG Pace database.

— Third: in the general provisions regarding formation of the contract (Part II, Arts. 14-24 CISG).

2.7. It is neither alleged nor has it been proven that [Buyer] explicitly accepted [Seller]'s general terms, which contained the Arbitration Clause. Pursuant to Art 18(1) CISG, silence in itself cannot be considered as an acceptance.

— Only if the parties act in their field of business and have frequent commercial relations with one another and under further prerequisites, can it be taken into account that the parties established a practice between themselves, by virtue of which the other party tacitly accepted the general terms.
— At hand, it is neither alleged nor proven that there was a steady business relationship between the parties, even though they deal or dealt with each other. Consequently, it cannot be assumed that [Buyer] accepted [Seller]'s general terms tacitly or expressly. That is why [Seller]'s invocation of the arbitration clause, contained in its general terms, fails.

The [Seller]'s claim that the Court does not have competence thus has to be rejected. For these reasons, it is also not decisive if [Buyer] received [Seller]'s general terms, whether by fax or by letter, or if the use of general terms is typical in the field of business in which the parties operate.

Question

Q 18-5

(a)   In the *Arnhem* case why did the court find that the seller's terms had not been incorporated into the contract?
(b)   What factors did the court indicate were relevant in making this determination?

III. Article 18(2) CISG

Article 18(2) CISG addresses the issue of when an acceptance of an offer becomes effective. Again, this subsection must now receive new consideration in light of advances in electronic communication.

CISG Advisory Council Opinion No 1: Electronic Communications under CISG:[72]

[...]

CISG Art 18(2) [...]

OPINION An acceptance becomes effective when an electronic indication of assent has entered the offeror's server, provided that the offeror has consented, expressly or impliedly, to receiving electronic communications of that type, in that format, and to that address. The term 'oral' includes electronically transmitted sound in real time and electronic communications in real time. An offer that is transmitted electronically in real time communication must be accepted immediately unless the circumstances indicate otherwise provided that the

---

[72] Taken from www.cisgac.com.

addressee consented expressly or impliedly to receiving communications of that type, in that format, and to that address.

Questions

Q 18-6

(a) Is there a requirement in the electronic communications world that the offeror actually read the acceptance?
(b) Why or why not?
(c) What are the problems associated with this approach? Refer to Q 15-3 above.

Q 18-7

Explain how the 'oral offers' requirements for acceptance apply to electronic communications.

Article 19 CISG

(1) A reply to an offer which purports to be an acceptance but contains additions, limitations or other modifications is a rejection of the offer and constitutes a counter-offer.
(2) However, a reply to an offer which purports to be an acceptance but contains additional or different terms which do not materially alter the terms of the offer constitutes an acceptance, unless the offeror, without undue delay, objects orally to the discrepancy or dispatches a notice to that effect. If he does not so object, the terms of the contract are the terms of the offer with the modifications contained in the acceptance.
(3) Additional or different terms relating, among other things, to the price, payment, quality and quantity of the goods, place and time of delivery, extent of one party's liability to the other or the settlement of disputes are considered to alter the terms of the offer materially.

I. Overview

A. Content and Purpose of Article 19 CISG

Article 19 CISG is a consequence of the offer-acceptance mechanism for concluding a contract under the CISG. The general principle embodied in Article 19 CISG is that of the mirror-image rule, whereby any acceptance that does not 'mirror' the offer is no longer regarded as such and is deemed a counter-offer. The exception to this principle is found in Article 19(2) CISG with respect to immaterial alterations. Article 19(3) CISG, in turn, sets out a non-exhaustive list of terms that are deemed to operate as material changes.

B. Domestic Laws

Article 19 CISG was originally modeled against the background of Section 2-207 UCC.

§ 2-207 UCC:

(1) A definite and seasonable expression of acceptance or a written confirmation which is sent within a reasonable period of time operates as an acceptance even though it states terms additional to or different from those offered or agreed upon, unless acceptance is expressly made conditional on assent to the additional or different terms.

(2) The additional terms are to be construed as proposals for addition to the contract. Between merchants such terms become part of the contract unless:
(a) the offer expressly limits acceptance to the terms of the offer;
(b) they materially alter it; or
(c) notification of objection to them has already been given or is given within a reasonable time after notice of them is received.

Under German law, the position is similar to that under Article 19(1) CISG. According to § 150(2) BGB, an acceptance made with additions, limitations or other changes is deemed a refusal combined with a new offer. The English legal position on this point is similar; however, it goes one step further: 'immaterial' modifications still operate as a counter-offer; under the 'last shot' rule, failure to respond to such altered terms could indicate an intention on behalf of the offeror to contract on the altered terms.

C. Drafting History

The distinction between an 'immaterially different' and 'materially different' acceptance was first introduced at the Hague Conference. The reason behind this provision was, in the case of immaterial changes, to allow the offeror to accept such changes 'by acquiescence'; failing objection by the offeror, the new—immaterial—terms were incorporated into the contract. There were lengthy debates at the Vienna Conference concerning criticism that this arguably arbitrary distinction was too uncertain and difficult in practice. The solution to this problem is now found in Article 19(3) CISG, which provides non-exhaustive, illustrative examples of alterations that are to be regarded as material.

II. Article 19(1) CISG

Article 19(1) CISG corresponds to the mirror-image rule widely accepted in domestic legal systems.

C 19-1

Oberlandesgericht Frankfurt am Main (Germany),
4 March 1994,
CISG-online 110[73]

[Facts]

Subsequent to making a basic inquiry about [seller's] products, the [buyer], located in Sweden, invited by letter the [seller] to make an offer for specified screws of a certain quality [W]. The

---

[73] Translation taken from CISG Pace (citations omitted).

[seller] answered by filling in the prices and the delivery periods. By fax dated 5 March 1992, [buyer] ordered 3,400 pieces of the named screws, stated by price, as well as 290 pieces of six other items not previously mentioned. On 10 March 1992, the [seller] thanked the [buyer] for the order and informed the [buyer] of [seller's] request for payment in advance or a letter of credit. In the pro-forma invoice that was requested by the [buyer], the [seller] listed all ordered items of a [lower quality] with their respective prices. The [buyer] immediately objected and requested delivery in the 'ordered' quality. The [seller] replied that, according to the catalogue, only items in the [lower quality] could be delivered; for items in the higher quality there would be longer delivery periods and higher prices applied. The [buyer], through its lawyer's letter, dated 16 March 1992, rejected [seller's] reply and insisted on delivery of goods in the [higher quality] for the prices stated in the pro-forma invoice and threatened to file a claim for damages for breach of contract. [...]

[Judgment]

[...] [T]he Court of First Instance dismissed the [buyer's] claim with appropriate reasoning. The [buyer] does not have a claim for damages against the [seller] ... since no contract has come into existence. The fax dated 12 February 1992 constituted—and the [buyer] does not dispute this—merely a production inquiry, the response to which did not constitute a contractual obligation. The inquiry the [buyer] made on 17 February 1992, with which it requested an offer, is to be assessed as an invitation to make an offer (invitatio ad offerendum), so that the return fax containing the pricing constitutes an offer by the [seller]. The [seller's] fax contains all the essential elements of a contract for the sale of goods: namely, description of the goods, quantity, price, and time of delivery. However, the [buyer] did not accept this offer, certainly not by placing its 'order' dated 5 March 1992. With this order the [buyer] deviates from the [seller's] offer insofar as the [buyer] ordered quantities different than the offered terms and, furthermore, additional items which had not yet been offered as deliverable and for which the price was not yet determined. ... An acceptance containing a modification is classified as a rejection according to ... Art 19(1) [CISG]. The Court of First Instance held that the [buyer's] order constitutes a counter-offer according to ... Art 19(1) CISG; however, this new offer could not lead to an effective conclusion of a contract due to lack of sufficient certainty. An offer is sufficiently definite within the meaning of ... Art 14(1) CISG, only if it provides the basis for determining the price upon acceptance. This was not possible in the present case, since the price of some ordered items was neither fixed nor determinable. Though it could be conceivable to presume a contractual agreement pertaining to the matching items in the [seller's] offer, this presumes a divisibility of the complete order. However, that would be something that the [buyer] explicitly did not want: in its written order dated 5 March 1992, the [buyer] expressly insisted on the delivery of the total order of all items. Therefore, only the pro-forma invoice sent by [seller] at [buyer's] request contained the essential elements of an offer that is sufficiently definite and which could be accepted by a simple 'yes'. However, this offer was not accepted by the [buyer], who rejected it due to the different quality offered, whereby the contractual efforts of the parties finally failed.

Question

Q 19-1

(a) Explain the mechanism of Article 19 CISG in the above case (C 19-1).
(b) How would this case have been decided under your domestic legal system?
(c) What are the similarities and differences between that system and the CISG?

III. Article 19(2) CISG

Article 19(2) CISG addresses immaterial changes contained in an acceptance of an offer. Whether alterations to an offer are to be regarded as material or immaterial is to be interpreted under Article 8 CISG. If the parties substantially agree on the terms of their contract, a consensus exists; mere discrepancies in wording or different forms of expression will not materially alter the terms of the offer. However, the offeror still retains the right to object to a contract coming into existence on immaterially different terms.

C 19-2

Landgericht Baden-Baden (Germany),
14 August 1991,
CISG-online 24[74]

[Facts]

[…] The Italian [seller] brings a claim against the German [buyer] for the amount still owing for two deliveries of wall tiles. The parties have been in an ongoing business relationship since 1982. The [buyer] ordered tiles from the [seller]. Under 'Terms of Payment' in Order No. 1853 is written: '14 Days 3%–30 Days net.' And in Order No. 1856: 'as in the past.' These represent written confirmations sent to the [buyer] of orders which were previously communicated orally. Underneath, on the right side, is written: 'We thank you for this order, which was accepted under reservation of confirmation according to our delivery and payment conditions; respectively, delivery and payment conditions of the shop for which this order is destined.' The [seller] debited the [buyer's] account on February 22, 1990 in the amount of 8436.92 DM and, on June 7, 1990, in the amount of 8466.30 DM. The invoice of the [seller] contained the following printing: 'complaints will be acknowledged only before the installation of the goods; in any case the goods may be rejected only up to 30 days from the date of the invoice.' The [buyer] paid only an installment payment. She gave notice of lack of conformity of the 'Anna' tiles which were invoiced on February 22, 1990, and were already installed. Based on the foregoing, the [seller], the [buyer] and the layer of the tiles agreed that the delivery of replacement tiles be without charge and that the [buyer] be credited. The replacement delivery of tiles was never installed due to reported defects. The [buyer] maintains that the Second shipment of tiles displayed an even higher number of defects than the original one. She therefore asserts a set-off claim for damages.

[Judgment]

[…] 2. The set-off claim, set off against the sales price, pursuant to the invoice of February 22, 1990 and of June 7, 1990, with further claims for damages for the delivery of defective tiles, which were sold to customers, is invalid. The [buyer] cannot recover damages because she did not complain in a timely fashion to the [seller] about the defects. The [seller] made

---

[74] Translation taken from CISG Pace (citations omitted).

the acknowledgment of rejections depend on their being declared before the installation of the goods, but in any case no later than 30 days after the invoice date. This statement, which appeared on the invoices of the [seller], became a part of the contract. The [seller's] agent referred to this statement in his confirmations of the orders. Pursuant to Article 19(2), CISG, a modified acceptance, modified by comparison with the original order of the [seller], would be effective, because such a modification would not fundamentally change the terms of the offer and the [buyer] did not object to it.

Question

Q 19-2

(a) What factor did the court rely on in applying Article 19 CISG in the *Baden-Baden* case (C 19-2)?
(b) How could a term appearing on an invoice become part of the bargain?
(c) Did the court decide that this term was a material or an immaterial deviation?

C 19-3

Oberlandesgericht Hamm (Germany),
22 September 1992,
CISG-online 57[75]

[Facts]

A German buyer, defendant, offered to purchase ten lots of wrapped bacon from an Italian seller, plaintiff. The seller's reply to the buyer's offer referred instead to unwrapped bacon. However, in its reply to the seller, the buyer did not object to the change in terms. After four lots had been delivered, the buyer refused to accept further deliveries. Therefore, the seller declared the contract avoided and sold the remaining six lots at a price much lower than both the market—and the agreed purchase—price. The seller claimed damages, the outstanding purchase price and interest.

[Judgment]

The court held that the seller's reply to the buyer's offer was a counter-offer (Article 19(1) CISG) and not an acceptance (Article 18(1) CISG), and that the buyer's reply to the counter-offer, in as much as it did not contain any objections to the change in terms, should be considered an unconditional acceptance (Article 8(2) CISG). Consequently, the seller was entitled to declare the contract avoided because the buyer's failure to take delivery of more than half of the goods constituted a fundamental breach of contract (Article 64(1)(a) CISG).

The court also held that the seller was entitled to claim damages (Articles 61(1)(b) and 74 CISG).

---

[75] English abstract taken from UNILEX.

Question

Q 19-3

(a) What was the offer, and what was the acceptance, according to the court?
(b) Do you agree with the finding of the court?
(c) How would this have been decided under your national legal system?

IV. Article 19(3) CISG

The most obvious potential problem that could arise in respect of the interpretation of Article 19 CISG has already been dealt with in the Article itself—that of the
materiality of the proposed amendments. Although the matters listed in Article 19(3)
CISG should not be regarded as exhaustive, they do provide some useful guidelines
for the determination of other material matters which would change an acceptance
into a new offer.

C 19-4

Cour de Cassation (France),
16 July 1998,
CISG-online 344[76]

...

On [buyer's] first argument

The appeal is of a ruling that set aside the competence of the Commercial Tribunal of
Orléans as stipulated in the order form the French [buyer] addressed to its German supplier
through [seller's] intermediary, the French company Lonza. The Court of Appeals ruled that
the French tribunal is not competent to rule on the argument relative to the delivered goods.
[Buyer] alleges that the Court's ruling against [buyer's] jurisdiction clause did not take into
consideration the role of [seller's] subsidiary company, Lonza France; and that the Court
erred by relying on a contradictory jurisdiction clause stipulated by the [seller].

However, considering that [seller's] terms and conditions contained a clause, conferring
jurisdiction upon the courts at [seller's] principal place of business [in Germany], the Court
of Appeals came to the justified conclusion that the different jurisdiction clause stipulated in
[buyer's] forms could not be found applicable. Indeed, considering articles 18 and 19 of the
Vienna Convention of 11 April 1980 on International Sales Contracts, an answer which leans
towards the acceptance of an offer, but contains different elements substantially altering the
terms of the offer, such that, according to article 19(3), there is a different stipulation on the
settlement of disputes, does not lead to the application of the clause contained in [buyer's] form.

---

[76] Translation taken from CISG Pace database.

The ruling of the Court of Appeals is, on this point, legally justified.

[…]

Reasons given by counsel for [buyer]

[…]

[Buyer's] first reasons for reversal

[…]

[Buyer] bases its claim on the clause contained in its purchase order form specifying that the Commercial Tribunal of Orléans shall have jurisdiction in the event of dispute.

[Buyer] emphasizes that on this form it is stated that 'the acceptance of our orders implies the acceptance of the general conditions of purchase stipulated in the front and the back of this form.'

[…]

[Seller] cannot take advantage of the different jurisdiction clause contained in its general sales conditions which, obviously, were not accepted by the buyer.

[…]

Article 8 of [buyer's] general purchase conditions provides that the sending of an acknowledgment of receipt joined with the order 'will mark' the acceptance of the provider of both the order and the general purchase conditions and its particularities. By focusing only on the fact that such an acknowledgment of receipt was not sent by [seller], the Court of Appeals erred in deducing that [seller] did not accept [buyer's] jurisdiction clause, without removing any other element that would result for this company—without any explanation for why, once the litigation began, [seller] can take advantage of solely the jurisdictional clause. …

Ignoring the actions of [seller] and of its subsidiary Lonza France, which received [buyer's] order as well as the general purchase conditions that were attached to it and performed the contract without discussing or asking for any modification, the Court of Appeals contented itself with the fact that [seller] has not signed any document containing the jurisdictional clause; notably, that [seller] did not send an acknowledgement of receipt from which one could deduce that it accepted [buyer's] clause. This does not pay proper attention to the principle of consensus; it violates article 1134 of the Civil Code.

[…]

In conformity with article 18 of the Vienna Convention of 11 April 1980, declared applicable in this case, the performance by [seller] of the sales contract, without discussing any clause of the offer that had been proposed to it by [buyer], constitutes acceptance of [buyer's] offer.

By supposing that the confirmations of the order sent by [seller] contained a jurisdictional clause different from that in [buyer's] general purchase conditions, such clause alters substantially the terms of the offer according to article 19 CISG, so that the terms of the contract can only be those contained in [buyer's] offer.

By excluding the acceptance of the clause contained in [buyer's] offer under the pretext that [seller's] confirmations of the order contain a different jurisdiction clause, the Court of Appeals violated articles 18 and 19 CISG.

…

Question

Q 19-4

Why were the terms of the seller's confirmations of order not part of the contract between the parties in the above case?

C 19-5

Belcher-Robinson, LLC v Linamar Corporation, et al,
US Dist Ct (MD), AL ED 31 March 2010,
CISG-online 2092[77]

[...]

I. INTRODUCTION

[...]

The case is presently before the Court on a motion to dismiss for improper venue, which defendant Linamar Holdings, Inc., doing business as Roctel Manufacturing, ('Roctel') filed on July 14, 2009. Roctel argues by this motion that a forum-selection clause is binding on the parties and requires that this litigation take place in the courts of Ontario, Canada. Alternately, Roctel argues that the court should dismiss this case pursuant to the doctrine of forum non conveniens.

...

III. FACTUAL AND PROCEDURAL BACKGROUND

A. Facts in the Complaint

According to the allegations in the complaint, this case arises from a dispute between Belcher-Robinson, a Delaware limited liability company with its principal place of business in Tallapoosa County, Alabama, and defendants Linamar Corporation ('Linamar'), a Canadian corporation doing business in the State of Alabama; Roctel, a Canadian corporation doing business in the State of Alabama; Linamar de Mexico S.A. de C.V., a Mexican corporation doing business in the State of Alabama; and five fictitious defendants.

Between January 1, 2007 and September 30, 2008, Belcher-Robinson manufactured malleable iron stator shafts which Linamar and Roctel ordered. Belcher-Robinson delivered the shafts to Linamar and Roctel, but the defendants failed to pay for them as agreed.

[...]

B. Defendant's Evidence

Roctel submitted with its motion to dismiss several exhibits. Principal among them is a purchase order. Roctel claims that the terms of this purchase order govern this dispute between

---

[77] Taken from CISG Pace; footnotes and citations omitted.

the parties. This 'Blanket Purchasing Agreement,' blanket order number fifty-five ('purchase order 55'), dated November 28, 2005, states that all shipping documentation should reference 'PO # 22533,' and was signed by Mario Martini, an employee of Roctel. The location on the purchase order specified for 'Supplier Acknowledgment' is blank, as is the associated place for the date of any such acknowledgment.

The Second page of the purchase order is headlined 'Terms and Conditions' and contains a full page of small-font boilerplate. The final term and condition ('paragraph 25') governs choice of law and jurisdiction:

'25. CHOICE OF LAW AND JURISDICTION: The Buyer and Seller Agree that the courts of Ontario shall have jurisdiction for all purposes. The International Sales of Goods Act shall not apply.

[...]

IV. DISCUSSION

Roctel's extensive briefing in support of its motion to dismiss contains two principal arguments. First, Roctel argues that the forum-selection clause in its purchase order 55 binds the parties to this action and requires dismissal of the claims against Roctel. ...

A. Forum-selection Clause

[...]

The resolution of the motion to dismiss turns largely on the fact-finding standards applicable to motions to dismiss for improper venue. Applying these standards to the case at bar, the Court finds that Belcher-Robinson is not bound by paragraph 25 of purchase order 55—neither the forum-selection clause nor the exclusion of the CISG—because paragraph 25 is not part of a contract between the parties. The Court stresses that this conclusion is not an adjudication on the merits of this question—at a later stage, the evidence might show that Belcher-Robinson is bound by those terms—but is the result of an analysis of the evidence currently in the record, viewed in the light most favorable to the plaintiff, and with all factual disputes resolved in the plaintiff's favor.

As Roctel points out, the contract between the parties could have been formed in two ways. First—and this is the way Roctel thinks it happened—purchase order 55 might have been an acceptance of an offer that took the form of Belcher-Robinson's price quote. Second, purchase order 55 could have been the offer, which was accepted in Massachusetts by Belcher-Robinson.

The crux of the venue question, at least initially, is whether the parties agreed to the choice of law and jurisdiction provision such that the provision is binding on them, provided the plaintiff is not excused from enforcement for some other reason. As evidence that the parties assented to this term, Roctel offers the original and revised blanket purchase order 55, which contains the subject term. That purchase order contains instructions to reference PO# 22533 on all shipping documentation. To prove that Belcher-Robinson assented to the terms on the Second page of the purchase order, Roctel offers the numerous invoices and packing lists that reference 'Purchase Order 22533-Blank 55.'

If the contract was formed in Ontario by the issuance of purchase order 55, which is what Roctel contends happened, it is an acceptance that contains an additional term (i.e., the forum-selection clause). The CISG treats additional terms differently depending on whether they materially alter the offer, but it does not clearly identify whether a forum-selection clause materially alters the offer. Terms 'relating ... to' the 'extent of one party's liability to the other or the settlement of disputes' do materially alter the terms of the offer. CISG, Art 19(3). The list of materially-altering terms given in the CISG is non-exclusive. See Id. (noting that, 'among other things,' the listed types of terms materially alter the offer). The non-exclusive nature of the list and the reasonable argument that forum-selection clauses relate to the settlement of disputes indicate that a forum-selection clause would materially alter the offer under the CISG. At least two United States federal courts have reached this conclusion. See *Chateau Des Charmes Wines Ltd. v Sabate USA Inc.*, 328 F.3d 528, 531 (9th Cir.2003) (classifying a forum-selection clause as relating to the settlement of disputes within the meaning of CISG Art 19(3)); *Solae, LLC v Hershey Canada, Inc.*, 557 F.Supp.2d 452, 457-58 (D.Del.2008) (agreeing with *Chateau Des Charmes Wines*). However, because the Eleventh Circuit has yet to discuss this issue, the forum-selection clause will be evaluated as both a materially-altering and non-materially-altering term for the purpose of deciding the motion to dismiss.

A reply to an offer which contains additional terms that materially alter the offer constitutes a rejection and counter-offer rather than an acceptance. Id., Art 19. In this scenario, the inclusion of the forum-selection clause in purchase order 55 materially altered the offer made by Belcher-Robinson. Therefore, it constituted a rejection and a counter-offer, which Belcher-Robinson could either accept or reject. In the affidavit of Richard Porter, president of Belcher-Robinson at the relevant times, Porter expressly declares that Belcher-Robinson did not agree to, consent to, or acquiesce in the terms and conditions printed on purchase order 55 and did not enter into any forum-selection agreement. The Court is compelled by the law of this Circuit to credit these assertions for purposes of this motion. Moreover, Porter claims to have actively objected to the forum-selection clause and to have communicated this objection to Roctel. Again, for purposes of this motion, the Court must believe this testimony. Additionally, Roctel has failed to produce conclusive evidence contrary to Porter's assertions. Neither the original purchase order 55 nor the final revision provided to the Court contain a signature in the place appointed for 'Supplier Acknowledgment,' as one would expect if these purchase orders are to support an inference that Belcher-Robinson assented to their terms. When viewed in the light most favorable to Belcher-Robinson, these documents do not support the conclusion that Belcher-Robinson agreed to the forum-selection clause. Therefore, under the standard for this motion to dismiss, Belcher-Robinson never agreed to Roctel's counter-offer, which included the forum-selection clause.

The other possibility is that a forum-selection clause does not materially alter the offer. When a reply to an offer contains additions or modifications that do not materially alter the offer, the reply constitutes an acceptance, 'unless the offeror, without undue delay, objects orally to the discrepancy or dispatches a notice to that effect.' CISG, Art 19 (emphasis added). If the offeror does make timely objections, 'the reply of the offeree is to be considered as a rejection of the offer rather than as an acceptance.' Secretariat Commentary, Aug. 29, 2006,. <http://cisgw3.law.pace.edu/cisg/text/Secomm/Secomm-19.html>. As noted above, under the standard for evaluating this motion to dismiss, the Court must find that Belcher-Robinson timely objected to the forum-selection clause in the reply of the offeree. Therefore, under the CISG purchase order 55 is to be considered a rejection of the offer rather than an acceptance. Once again, under the standard for evaluating this motion to dismiss, the parties never agreed to the forum-selection clause.

If the contract was formed in Massachusetts, purchase order 55 constitutes an offer rather than a purported acceptance. In this scenario, Belcher-Robinson could either accept or reject that purchase order. Once again, under the standard for evaluating this motion to dismiss, the Court must find that Belcher-Robinson rejected the offer made by purchase order 55. In the alternative, Belcher-Robinson might have purported to accept the offer while proposing alterations, one of which would be the exclusion of the forum-selection clause. If the exclusion of the forum-selection clause were a material change, Belcher-Robinson's objections constitute a rejection and counter-offer. CISG, Art 19. If the exclusion of the forum-selection clause does not materially alter the purchase order, Belcher-Robinson's purported acceptance constitutes an acceptance, and the terms of the contract are—in the absence of objections by Roctel to Belcher-Robinson's objections—the terms of the purchase order with the exclusion of the forum-selection clause. CISG, Art 19(2). There is no evidence that Roctel made any modifications or objections to those objections made by Belcher-Robinson. Therefore, whether Belcher-Robinson's objections constitute a rejection of the purchase order offer or a purported acceptance with modifications, the forum-selection clause drops out.

In sum, the evidence submitted still leaves open several possibilities for how Belcher-Robinson and Roctel formed a contract. Construing the evidence presented in Belcher-Robinson's favor, as the Court must under the standard for ruling on this motion to dismiss, the Court finds that the forum-selection clause is not included under any of those possibilities. Therefore, the motion to dismiss is due to be denied on the grounds of the forum-selection clause.

Questions

Q 19-5

(a) In the above case, did the court find that purchase order 55 constituted a counter-offer?
(b) What reasoning did it provide for its finding?

Q 19-6

Do you think a forum selection clause should fall within the scope of Article 19(3) CISG? Why or why not?

V. Battle of the Forms

C 19–5

Bundesgerichtshof (Germany),
9 January 2002,
CISG-online 651[78]

[Facts]

The plaintiff [buyer 1] and the assignor [buyer 2], both located in the Netherlands and trading in dairy products, purchased a total of 2,557.5 tons of powdered milk in the first half of

---

[78] Translation taken from CISG Pace (citations omitted).

1998, based on a number of contracts, from defendant [seller 1], which is headquartered in Germany, and its major shareholder [seller 1A]. Of this powdered milk, [buyer 1] and [buyer 2] sold 7.5 tons to the Dutch company I. and 2,550 tons to the Algerian company G.I., owned by P.L. S.p.A. (hereinafter G. S.p.A.), formerly known as O.R. S.p.A. The contents of the telephonic orders were recorded by [buyer 1] and [buyer 2] and/or by [seller 1] and [seller 1A] in written confirmations. The letters of confirmation of delivery of [seller 1] and [seller 1A] (whose production facility in L. [seller 1] acquired in the beginning of 1998 with all existing contractual relationships) each contained in the footer the following text:

'We sell exclusively pursuant to our general terms and conditions. Contrary statutory conditions or contrary general terms and conditions of the buyer are expressly not acknowledged and are therefore not part of the contract.'

The terms and conditions at issue contain the following warranty clause:

'VI. Warranty and Notification of Defects

The buyer must inspect the goods immediately upon delivery and note any complaints on the delivery note ... Defects that are not noticeable at the time of delivery can only be claimed before the printed expiration date ... The buyer must make available the goods at issue or enough samples of the goods at issue; if he does not do so, the buyer cannot make any warranty claims.'

Condition No. 8 in the so-called M.P.C. conditions referred to by [buyer 1] provides:

'Section 10. Sampling and Complaints

Notwithstanding any duty of the seller to pay back the purchase price, or a part thereof, the liability of the seller for damages suffered (and/or to be suffered) is at all times limited to the invoiced amount for the delivered goods.'

The powdered milk, which was packaged and delivered by [seller 1], was inspected through spot-checks by [buyer 1] and/or [buyer 2] with the assistance of 'I.S. Nederland B.V.' (hereinafter 'I.S.') without any special results, then it was newly palletised in the harbor of Antwerp and thereafter shipped to Algeria and, to the extent it was sold to I., to Aruba/Netherland Antilles.

After local subsidiaries of G S.p.A. processed the powdered milk delivered to Algeria, some of the produced milk had a rancid taste. Thereupon, G. S.p.A. complained to [buyer 1] and [buyer 2] about a total of 207.6 tons of powdered milk as well as part of the powdered milk that had already been processed into 10,000 liters of milk. On June 24 and August 19, 1998, representatives of G. S.p.A., of [buyer 1], of [buyer 2] and of [seller 1] had several meetings in A. to clarify the question of the compensation for G. S.p.A. The result of these negotiations, during which [buyer 1] and [buyer 2] each promised certain compensation to G. S.p.A., was recorded in four 'minutes of amicable settlement'; these documents were also signed by the representative of [seller 1]. By letter dated August 24, 1998, the legal department of [seller 1A], which was entrusted by [seller 1] with the resolution of the matter, informed [buyer 1] and [buyer 2] of the following, among other things:

'We acknowledge that a partial quantity of 177 tons of the total quantity of 3,495 tons of powdered milk, delivered pursuant to the letters of confirmation of delivery dated ... did not meet the contractual requirements.

'We do not deny that you have warranty claims because of the quality deviation, but the following two aspects must be considered:

[...]

2 All letters of confirmation of delivery mentioned above refer to our general terms and conditions, which must therefore govern our legal relationship. Thus, S. AG does not have to deal with any warranty or damages claims raised by company G. '... We expressly emphasise here that we are willing to rescind the contractual relationship with you and/or company A. because of the 177 tons of inadequate powdered milk. Further claims that company G. may raise against you or company A. are not substantively justified and will not be accepted by us.'

By letter dated September 1, 1998, [buyer 2] claimed damages from [seller 1] in the amount of $198,150.36; it assigned this claim to [buyer 1] on November 30, 1998. Company I. also complained to [buyer 1] regarding the delivery of 7.5 tons of powdered milk because of, among other things, a sour taste of the powdered milk, and claimed damages in the amount of Hfl [Dutch florin] 29,256, which [buyer 1] paid. [Buyer 1] alleged that the rancid taste, noticed by the ultimate buyers, was caused by an infestation of the powdered milk by lipase that already existed at the time of the transfer of the risk as a result of the faulty processing of the milk. This defect was only noticeable after the delivery and was immediately complained of by it. [Seller 1] acknowledged its warranty in the agreements recorded in Algeria as well as in its letter dated August 24, 1998. Under the rules of the CISG, [seller 1] is liable for the damages incurred by [buyer 1] and [buyer 2] that resulted from the payment of damages to the ultimate purchasers and the travel costs for the meeting in A., totaling DM [Deutsche Mark] 780,506.46; this was not excluded by [seller 1]'s general terms and conditions of delivery. [Seller 1] alleged that the lipase infestation of the powdered milk delivered to Algeria first occurred after the transfer of the risk, or at least it was not caused by it. The powder delivered to company I. could not be consumed because of an inSect infestation. In any case, the application of the CISG is excluded by its general terms and conditions. Thus, the German *Bürgerliches Gesetzbuch* governs, with the consequence that [buyer 1] has no claim for damages because the delivered powdered milk did not lack an assured quality. ...

[Judgment]

[...] 1. The Court of Appeals, however, correctly assumed that the compensation rules of the CISG for the claims of [buyer 1] are not excluded by its General Terms and Conditions ('M.P.C. conditions'), which provide considerable limitations of liability for the seller, inter alia, by restricting any compensation to the amount invoiced for the delivered goods.

a) The Court of Appeals correctly assumed that the partial contradiction of the referenced general terms and conditions of [buyer 1] and [seller 1] did not lead to the failure of the contract within the meaning of Art 19(1) and (3) CISG because of the lack of a consensus (dissent). His judicial appraisal, that the parties have indicated by the execution of the contract that they did not consider the lack of an agreement between the mutual conditions of contract as essential within the meaning of Art 19 CISG, cannot be legally challenged and is expressly accepted by the appeal.

b) The Court of Appeals further correctly stated that the warranty clauses in the M.P.C. conditions used by [buyer 1], which are beneficial to [seller 1], were replaced by the rejection clause of [seller 1]. The objections raised by the appeal in this regard are not persuasive. The question to what extent colliding general terms and conditions become an integral part of a contract where the CISG applies, is answered in different ways in the legal literature. According to the (probably) prevailing opinion, partially diverging general terms and conditions become an integral part of a contract (only) insofar as they do not contradict each other; the statutory provisions apply to the rest (so called 'knock out' rule). Whether there is such a contradiction that impedes the integration, cannot be determined only by an interpretation of the wording of individual clauses, but only upon the full appraisal of all relevant provisions. The appeal misunderstands this when it wants to compare only the limited rejection clause of [seller 1] to [buyer 1]'s warranty clauses, which are favorable to [seller 1]. As the Court of Appeals has correctly determined, the Dutch M.P.C. conditions contain substantial deviations from the CISG's warranty rules— which would essentially remain applicable based on the General Terms and Conditions of [seller 1]—and it cannot be assumed that [buyer 1] wanted to have the M.P.C. conditions, which are internally balanced, apply to it insofar as they are noticeably more detrimental than the statutory provisions without having the benefit of the clauses that are favorable to it. Vice versa, there is nothing to show that [seller 1] wanted those clauses of the M.P.C. conditions that are unfavorable to it apply to the contracts. The result is no different if one follows the contrary opinion ('last shot' doctrine). Certainly under the point of view of good faith and fair dealing (Art 7(1) CISG), [seller 1] should not have assumed that the question whether certain provisions of the opposing terms and conditions contradicted its own (even insofar as it served its Terms and Conditions last) could be answered in isolation for individual clauses with the consequence that the individual provisions that were beneficial to it would apply. [...]

Questions

Q 19-7

Explain what is understood by the 'battle of the forms'.

Q 19-8

What solutions are offered to the battle of the forms problem?

Q 19-9

What was the basis for the decision of the court in the above case (C 19-5)?

Q 19-10

What approach, according to this case (C 19-5), is to be taken when considering and comparing standard forms?

Q 19-11

(a) What is the approach to the problem of the battle of the forms under your domestic legal system?
(b) What similarities or differences are there between your domestic legal system and the CISG?

C 19-6

Amtsgericht Kehl (Germany),
6 October 1995,
CISG-online 162[79]

[Facts]

The [seller] plaintiff manufactures knitwear; the [buyer] defendant sells knitwear. Initially, the [buyer] ordered two sample sweaters from the [seller]; the [buyer] was charged DM [Deutsche Mark] 103. Based on these samples, the [buyer] then ordered 310 sweaters for a total price of DM 9765. The samples as well as the merchandise at issue were ordered through the [seller's] sales representative, Mr. M. The [seller] submits that the [buyer] later asserted that the goods did not conform to the contract. In the [buyer's] opinion, the material was not sufficiently resistant to washing. The [seller] objects to the [buyer's] notice of non-conformity as being unspecified and belated. The goods were not defective and were identical to the samples. Regarding the further details of the [seller's] pleadings, the Court refers to the [seller's] briefs of 8 September 1993, 24 February 1994, 18 May 1994, 8 September 1994 and 21 November 1994. The [seller] requests the Court to order the [buyer] to pay him DM 9,374.40 with 10% interest from 9 January 1993. The [buyer] requests the Court to dismiss the claim.

[Judgment]

The [seller's] claim is justified.

...

II.

1. The claim for interest is legitimate pursuant to Art 78 CISG. According to this provision, the party that fails to pay the price or any other sum in arrears shall pay the other party [at maturity] interest on these amounts. Pursuant to Arts 58, 59 CISG, the purchase price for the sweaters delivered on 8 December 1992 became due prior to the date from which the [seller] requests interest (9 January 1993).

2. Since Art 78 CISG does not provide for an interest rate, the matter is to be settled in conformity with the law applicable by virtue of the rules of German private international law.

a) German law would be applicable in the event that the [buyer's] General Conditions were effectively included in the contract. The [buyer] based her order on her General Terms of Purchasing for Finished Products. The [seller] submits to have accepted the order based on his own General Conditions, a point that the [buyer] contests.

aa) Assuming that [seller] had sent his General Conditions to the [buyer], this would have constituted a counter-offer in the sense of Art 19(1) CISG. However, it follows from the performance of the contract that both parties were in agreement about the essentialia negotii. Thus, it must be assumed that they waived the enforcement of their conflicting Standard Terms or that they derogated from the application of Article 19, taking advantage of their party autonomy under Art 6 CISG. In this case, the contract would have been entered into in accordance with the terms of the CISG.

---

[79] Translation taken from CISG Pace (citations omitted).

bb) If the [seller] did not send his General Conditions to the [buyer], it still cannot be assumed that the [buyer's] Terms for Purchasing became part of the contract. On the one hand, the [seller] denies having received the [buyer's] General Terms of Business; on the other hand, the [buyer] did not state that he had included an Italian translation of his Terms for Purchasing. Since the language of the contract in the present case was not German, the General Terms of Business written in German did not become part of the contract. ...

Questions

Q 19-12

What additional requirements does this case (C 19-6) set out for the incorporation of standard terms?

Q 19-13

What do you think would have been the case if, even if the language of the contract was not German, the seller had been able to understand German?

Q 19-14

Compare the case of the *Amtsgericht Kehl* (C 19-6) with the case of the *Oberster Gerichtshof* (C 14-9).

(a)   Which solution seems more correct to you?
(b)   Could the holding of the OGH (C 14-9) be applied to a battle of the forms situation?

Q 19-15

(a)   What role does the language of the negotiations play?
(b)   How is the battle of the forms resolved where the language of the negotiations and the language of the contract itself differ?

Article 20 CISG

(1) A period of time for acceptance fixed by the offeror in a telegram or a letter begins to run from the moment the telegram is handed in for dispatch or from the date shown on the letter or, if no such date is shown, from the date shown on the envelope. A period of time for acceptance fixed by the offeror by telephone, telex or other means of instantaneous communication, begins to run from the moment that the offer reaches the offeree.

(2) Official holidays or non-business days occurring during the period for acceptance are included in calculating the period. However, if a notice of acceptance cannot be delivered at the address of the offeror on the last day of the period because that day falls on an official holiday or a non-business day at the place of business of the offeror, the period is extended until the first business day which follows.

Article 20 CISG sets out the point in time at which the period for accepting an offer begins to run, and how this period is calculated. As with many other provisions of the CISG, the interpretation of the term 'reaches' attains significance in Article 20(1) CISG in the context of instantaneous communications. This issue is discussed in more detail under Article 24 CISG below. Article 20(2) CISG clarifies the basis for calculation of the acceptance period and provides for an extension of the acceptance period.

There are, at the time of writing, no reported cases applying this article.

CISG Advisory Council Opinion No 1: Electronic Communications under CISG:[80]

[...]

CISG Art 20(1) [...]

OPINION A period of time for acceptance fixed by the offeror in electronic real time communication begins to run from the moment the offer enters the offeree's server. A period of time for acceptance fixed by the offeror in e-mail communication begins to run from the time of dispatch of the e-mail communication. 'Means of instantaneous communications' includes electronic real time communication. The term 'reaches' is to be interpreted to correspond to the point in time when an electronic communication has entered the offeree's server.

---

[80] Taken from www.cisgac.com.

Art 10 UN Convention on the Use of Electronic Communications in International Contracts 2005:

Time and place of dispatch and receipt of electronic communications

1. The time of dispatch of an electronic communication is the time when it leaves an information system under the control of the originator or of the party who sent it on behalf of the originator or, if the electronic communication has not left an information system under the control of the originator or of the party who sent it on behalf of the originator, the time when the electronic communication is received.
2. The time of receipt of an electronic communication is the time when it becomes capable of being retrieved by the addressee at an electronic address designated by the addressee. The time of receipt of an electronic communication at another electronic address of the addressee is the time when it becomes capable of being retrieved by the addressee at that address and the addressee becomes aware that the electronic communication has been sent to that address. An electronic communication is presumed to be capable of being retrieved by the addressee when it reaches the addressee's electronic address. ...

ICC eTerms 2004:

A. Article 2—Dispatch and Receipt

2.1 An electronic message is deemed to be:

   (a) dispatched or sent when it enters an information system outside the control of the sender; and
   (b) received at the time when it enters an information system designated by the addressee.

2.2 When an electronic message is sent to an information system other than that designated by the addressee, the electronic message is deemed to be received at the time when the addressee becomes aware of the message.
2.3 For the purpose of this contract, an electronic message is deemed to be dispatched or sent at the place where the sender has its place of business and is deemed to be received at the place where the addressee has its place of business.

Questions

Q 20-1

How could Article 20(1) CISG be applied to email communications? Refer to CISG Advisory Council Opinion No 1, the UNCITRAL Model Law on Electronic Commerce and the Draft Resolution II, and the UN Convention on the Use of Electronic Communications in International Contracts.

Q 20-2

(a) Why are holidays included in the calculation? Consider the peculiarities of international trade accounted for in Article 20(2) CISG.
(b) What is the meaning and purpose of the exception in Article 20(2) CISG?

Article 21 CISG

(1) A late acceptance is nevertheless effective as an acceptance if without delay the offeror orally so informs the offeree or dispatches a notice to that effect.

(2) If a letter or other writing containing a late acceptance shows that it has been sent in such circumstances that if its transmission had been normal it would have reached the offeror in due time, the late acceptance is effective as an acceptance unless, without delay, the offeror orally informs the offeree that he considers his offer as having lapsed or dispatches a notice to that effect.

I. Overview

A. Content and Purpose of Article 21 CISG

Article 21 CISG operates as a proviso to Article 18(2), whereby an acceptance that does not reach the offeror on time is deemed ineffective. A clear distinction must be made between the two subsections of Article 21 CISG. Under Article 21(1) CISG, an acceptance that is dispatched late, or in such a way that it will definitely arrive late, is prima facie ineffective, but can still be accepted by the offeror when it expressly informs the offeree thereof. Under Article 21(2) CISG, an acceptance that would have otherwise arrived on time, but due to a delay in the mode of transmission arrives late, is deemed to be effective unless the offeror informs the offeree that this is not the case.

B. Domestic Laws

This approach can be compared with provisions in some domestic legal systems. In Germany, for example, § 149 BGB reflects the position under Article 21(2) CISG. Under English law, if the late acceptance was due to a delay in transmission, the mailbox rule would dictate that the contract was concluded at the time of dispatch, without the offeror having the option of making a declaration in the spirit of Article 21(2) CISG.

II. Article 21(1) CISG

CISG Advisory Council Opinion No 1: Electronic Communications under CISG:[81]

[...]

CISG Art 21(1) [...]

OPINION The term 'oral' includes electronically transmitted sound provided that the offeree expressly or impliedly has consented to receiving electronic communication of that type, in that format, and to that address. The term 'notice' includes electronic communications provided that the offeree expressly or impliedly has consented to receiving electronic messages of that type, in that format, and to that address.

Question

Q 21-1

Can information be given to the offeree in the form of an electronic message under Article 21(1) CISG?

III. Article 21(2) CISG

CISG Advisory Council Opinion No 1: Electronic Communications under CISG:[82]

[...]

CISG Art 21(2) [...]

OPINION The term 'writing' covers any type of electronic communication that is retrievable in perceivable form. A late acceptance in electronic form may thus be effective according to this article. The term 'oral' includes electronically transmitted sound and communications in real time provided that the offeree expressly or impliedly has consented to receiving electronic communication of that type, in that format, and to that address. The term 'notice' includes electronic communications provided that the offeree expressly or impliedly has consented to receiving electronic messages of that type, in that format, and to that address. The term 'dispatch' corresponds to the point in time when the notice has left the offeree's server. A prerequisite is that the offeree has consented expressly or impliedly to receiving electronic messages of that type, in that format, and to that address.

---

[81] Taken from www.cisgac.com.
[82] Taken from www.cisgac.com.

Questions

Q 21-2

Can you think of the reason for the mechanism of Article 21(2) CISG, taking into account the requirements of international trade?

Q 21-3

In electronic communications, what would be a typical situation in which acceptance could be delayed?

Q 21-4

What are the 'dispatch' requirements under electronic communications? See also the ICC eTerms in Article 20 CISG above.

Article 22 CISG

An acceptance may be withdrawn if the withdrawal reaches the offeror before or at the same time as the acceptance would have become effective.

This provision is the counterpart to Article 15(2) CISG, which contains a similar provision in respect of offers. There are no reported cases applying this article.

CISG Advisory Council Opinion No 1: Electronic Communications under CISG:[83]

[...]

CISG Art 22 [...]

OPINION The term 'reaches' corresponds to the point in time when an electronic communication has entered the offeror's server, provided that the offeror expressly or impliedly has consented to receiving electronic messages of that type, in that format, and to that address.

Question

Q 22-1

(a) Give a practical example of how an acceptance may be validly withdrawn.
(b) How can an acceptance be validly withdrawn in the context of electronic communications?

---

[83] Taken from www.cisgac.com.

Article 23 CISG

A contract is concluded at the moment when an acceptance of an offer becomes effective in accordance with the provisions of this Convention.

Overview

A. Content and Purpose of Article 23 CISG

Article 23 CISG requires interpretation by other provisions of the Convention. Read in conjunction with Article 18(2) CISG, a contract is concluded when acceptance of an offer reaches the offeror. As in Article 18(3) CISG, effective acceptance, and thereby the conclusion of the contract, can also take place by conduct. This provision was considered necessary precisely because the point in time of the conclusion of the contract is referred to numerous times throughout the CISG.

Question

Q 23-1

Where can you find references to the time of the conclusion of the contract in the CISG? See if you can find them all!

B. Domestic Laws

In most domestic legal systems, acceptance becoming effective and the conclusion of a contract coincide.

Question

Q 23-2

What is the situation in legal systems applying the mailbox rule?

In some legal systems, an exception to this principle applies to the conclusion of contracts where no express acceptance is required (that is acceptance by conduct).

Art 10 OR:[84]

1.   If a contract arises between absent parties, it shall come into effect at the time at which the declaration of acceptance is presented for dispatch to the other party.
2.   If an express acceptance is not required, the contract comes into effect upon receipt of the offer.

Questions

Q 23-3

What is the practical difference between Article 23 CISG and Article 10 OR?

Q 23-4

How would the point in time at which acceptance by conduct becomes effective be determined under the CISG?

Q 23-5

Using your references from the answer to Q 23-1, explain the significance of the time of the conclusion of the contract in the context of each provision.

---

[84] Author's translation.

Article 24 CISG

For the purposes of this Part of the Convention, an offer, declaration of acceptance or any other indication of intention 'reaches' the addressee when it is made orally to him or delivered by any other means to him personally, to his place of business or mailing address or, if he does not have a place of business or mailing address, to his habitual residence.

I. Overview

A. Content and Purpose of Article 24 CISG

Article 24 CISG defines, for the purposes of Part II of the CISG on the formation of contracts, when a communication 'reaches' the other party. Since Article 24 CISG is to be understood as the expression of a principle, it must also—in light of Article 7(2) CISG—apply to those declarations in Part III that are expressly required to reach the addressee, despite only referring to Part II of the CISG.

Questions

Q 24-1

List all the provisions relevant for a communication 'reaching' a party?

Q 24-2

(a) What is meant by an oral declaration?
(b) What is the situation when a declaration is received by an answering machine?
(c) Does an oral declaration need to be understood in order to be effective? Why or why not?

Q 24-3

What is the situation when the declaration arrives outside working hours?

B. Domestic Laws

Many domestic legal systems, such as the German legal system, do not have specific provisions concerning the 'receipt' of documents, but merely require receipt incidentally in order to determine other matters.

C. Drafting History

Article 24 CISG can be traced back to the definition of the expression 'to be communicated' in Article 12(1) ULF and was repeatedly amended in the Working Group. Particular consideration was given to oral declarations and the addressee's place of habitual residence.

II. Article 24 CISG in the Age of Electronic Communication

The rule of 'receipt' has necessitated at least some conceptual modifications in light of the ever-increasing proliferation of electronic means of communication, both under the CISG and under domestic legal systems.

CISG Advisory Council Opinion No 1: Electronic Communications under CISG:[85]

[...]

CISG Art 24 [...]

OPINION The term 'reaches' corresponds to the point in time when an electronic communication has entered the addressee's server, provided that the addressee expressly or impliedly has consented to receiving electronic communications of that type, in that format, and to that address. The term 'orally' includes electronically transmitted sound and other communications in real time provided that the addressee expressly or impliedly has consented to receive electronic communications of that type, in that format, and to that address.

Question

Q 24-4

(a)   What solution is proposed in CISG Advisory Council Opinion No 1?
(b)   What would argue against the application of this solution? Consider again the problems addressed in Q 15-3 above.

---

[85] Taken from www.cisgac.com.

Article 25 CISG

A breach of contract committed by one of the parties is fundamental if it results in such detriment to the other party as substantially to deprive him of what he is entitled to expect under the contract, unless the party in breach did not foresee and a reasonable person of the same kind in the same circumstances would not have foreseen such a result.

Overview

A. Content and Purpose of Article 25 CISG

Article 25 CISG is a key provision of the Convention and defines the concept of fundamental breach of contract, which is used in various provisions throughout the CISG (Arts 46, 49, 51, 64, 70, 72, 73). The existence of a fundamental breach of contract under the CISG entitles the non-breaching party, in certain circumstances, to declare avoidance of the contract, the ultima ratio remedy of the CISG. The operation of this provision cannot be discussed in isolation, but will be discussed in further detail in conjunction with the relevant articles below.

B. Domestic Laws

It is difficult to discern a trend amongst domestic legal systems as to when a party may avoid a contract due to a breach by the other party that destroys its own interest in the contract. However, the approaches can be basically divided into two concepts: the concept of 'fundamental breach', which is recognised in the Anglo-American systems, and the '*Nachfrist*' model, which is used in the Germanic systems. In any case, a common feature of most legal systems is that a breach must acquire a certain degree of seriousness before avoidance by the non-breaching party may be justified. This is in line with the general principle that avoidance is to be regarded as the ultima ratio remedy, with the general rule being that efforts should be taken to uphold the contract wherever possible.

Under modern, CISG-oriented laws, such as the Scandinavian Sales Law and the Dutch *Wetboek*, as well as the PICC 2010, fundamental breaches of contract, or similar concepts, are adopted as the central notion. The new German Civil Code is also based on this concept.

Art 7.3.1 PICC 2010:

[...]

(2) In determining whether a failure to perform an obligation amounts to a fundamental non-performance regard shall be had, in particular, to whether
  (a) the non-performance substantially deprives the aggrieved party of what it was entitled to expect under the contract unless the other party did not foresee and could not reasonably have foreseen such result;

[...]

C. Drafting History

The idea that a party could avoid a contract only where the disturbance is significant, whilst restricting it to damages where the breach is only minor, was first propagated by Rabel—whose work *Recht des Warenkaufs* laid the foundations for the unification of international sales law—and was found in the 1956 and 1962 drafts, and expressed in Article 10 ULIS as what the parties would have regarded as fundamental had they put their minds to it. Although this arguably advocates an objective standard of determination, even at this stage, dispute existed as to whether a subjective or an objective standard should be applied in determining the 'fundamental' nature of a breach. Ultimately it was decided that the seriousness of the breach should not be defined by reference to the (objective) extent of the damage, but rather to the (subjective) interests of the promisee as actually set out by the contract.

C 25-1

Bundesgericht (Switzerland),
15 September 2000,
CISG-online 770[86]

For a summary of the facts see C 7-5 above.

[...]

aa) [Fundamental breach of contract (Art 25 CISG)]

The concept of fundamental breach as defined in article 25 CISG must be interpreted in a restrictive way and, in case of doubt, it must be considered that conditions of such breach are not fulfilled (Neumayer/Ming, op. cit., n. 2 ad Art 25 CISG). The breach must concern

---

[86] Translation taken from CISG Pace database.

the essential content of the contract, the goods, or the payment of the price concerned, and it must lead to serious consequences to the economic goal pursued by the parties. The importance of the breach is not determinative; only the consequences of the breach to the damaged party are determinative. This means that a principal obligation must have been breached in such a way that the economic goal of the contract cannot be achieved; the damaged party being interested no longer in the performance of the contract. Absolute loss of all objective interests of the creditor is not required. Moreover, it does not matter whether or not the default is objectively reparable (Neumayer/Ming, op. cit., n. 3 ad Art 25 CISG).

According to that view, the breach of an ancillary obligation can only constitute a fundamental breach if it has some repercussions on the performance of the principal obligations in a such way that the interest of the creditor in the performance of the contract is lost, without the necessity that the latter suffers some monetary damage (Neumayer/Ming, op. cit., n. 4 and 7 ad Art 25 CISG). The motivation of the creditor must be identifiable by the debtor, so the debtor could have known or it would be possible to know that the creditor considered the performance of the breached contractual clause so essential that he would have refused the contract if he had known of such future breach (Neumayer/Ming, op. cit., n. 5 ad Art 25 CISG). To judge that point, at the place and at the time of the conclusion of the contract, the determining interest of each of the parties must be identifiable by the other (Neumayer/Ming, op. cit., n. 6 ad Art 25 CISG). Finally, the damage must be foreseeable by the breaching party or by any other reasonable person of the same kind in the same circumstances at the time the breach of contract is committed. The contract determines if there existed a risk of a substantial detriment to the reasons and interests of the affected party, which had encouraged that party to conclude the contract (Neumayer/Ming, op. cit.,n. 8 ad Art 25 CISG). [...]

C 25-2

Supreme Court of Poland,
11 May 2007,
CISG-online 1790[87]

[Facts]

On 19 January 2000, the Buyer M. W. D. GmbH & Co KG requested from the Seller a price estimate for 4,400 square meters of a specific type of leather which was to be delivered to a shoe manufacturer in Germany. In response, the Seller submitted an offer for the requested leather for the purpose of manufacturing military shoes for the German army (*Bundeswehr*). On 24 January 2000, the Buyer accepted the offer and the Seller sent the ordered goods to a third party manufacturer.

The Buyer did not inspect the goods after they were delivered to the manufacturer. After the shoes were manufactured, the German Federal Bureau for Technical Defense and Supply noticed that the goods did not conform to the specifications of the offer. On 12 May 2000, the Buyer notified the Seller that the goods were non-conforming, asked for a quality control certificate and fixed an additional time for the Seller to deliver conforming goods (15 May 2000). In the meantime, the *Bundeswehr* returned all the shoes (37,130 pairs). The Seller

---

refused to deliver substitute goods and on 17 December 2002, the Buyer sent the Seller a declaration of avoidance of the contract.

[REASONING]

In its analysis, the Court assumed that the CISG distinguishes between breach, including fundamental breach, and non-conformity of the goods. The Court stated that common law and civil law differ when it comes to the treatment of breach of contract. However, under the CISG there is no need to distinguish instances of non-performance from other breaches of contract. The Appellate Court ruling in this litigation acknowledged that the Convention provides for less serious legal consequences in the event the party performed but its performance nevertheless amounted to a breach of contract. The Supreme Court disagreed and stated that there should not be a distinction between failure to perform and other breaches of contract. Delivery of non-conforming goods is a breach of contract. This rule stems from Article 35 of the Convention which describes what characteristics goods should have in order to conform to the contract. Failure to fulfill those characteristics amounts to non-conformity. However, mere non-conformity does not entitle the buyer to require delivery of substitute goods under Article 46(2) of the Convention. This remedy is available only if the lack of conformity constitutes a fundamental breach of contract under Article 25.

Scholars agree that Article 25 is one of the most difficult provisions to interpret because it includes numerous undefined terms. At the same time, this article is one of the most important provisions because the matter of a fundamental breach, judged on the circumstances of the contract and expectations of the parties, determines which remedies are available, especially delivery of substitute goods and avoidance of contract without the requirement to give an additional time to perform. Having the freedom to choose remedies, the buyer, however, is bound to the contract and should not, acting in good faith and as a reasonable person, first request delivery of substitute goods and then, not waiting for delivery, declare the contract avoided.

There is no need to explain the whole process of the determination of a fundamental breach. It is enough to note that under Article 25, detriment (meaning a substantial deprivation of a party of what he is entitled to expect under the contract) cannot equal damages as they include all actual and potential negative consequences of a breach of contract. Therefore, a party claiming a fundamental breach of contract does not have to show that he suffered damages or did not receive benefits. Moreover, the notion of reasonable expectations of an obligee is not measured subjectively, but rather requires a full analysis of the text of the contract, any practices which the parties have established between themselves, usages, negotiations and all relevant circumstances of the case. Therefore, the concrete and ascertained legal relationship is crucial for this determination. The burden of proof is placed on the party seeking relief under the Convention.

[...]

Questions

Q 25-1

Why is Article 25 to be interpreted restrictively?

Q 25-2

(a) According to the Polish case (C 25-2), what should the court consider in determining whether a fundamental breach exists?
(b) Is the question of the existence of a substantial detriment relevant?

Q 25-3

(a) How does foreseeability come into play?
(b) Who bears the burden of proof?

Article 26 CISG

A declaration of avoidance of the contract is effective only if made by notice to the other party.

Overview

During the preliminary work on the CISG, the principle of *ipso facto* avoidance, present in many articles of ULIS, was widely criticised. After the completion of a new study on the topic, the Working Group finally agreed upon the principle that the injured party be required to give notice of avoidance to the party in breach. Such an explicit notice was deemed necessary to preserve certainty as to the parties' rights and obligations, thereby completely rejecting the principle of *ipso facto* avoidance for the CISG. As with Article 25 CISG, the operation of this provision will be discussed in further detail in conjunction with the relevant articles below.

Questions

Q 26-1

Why do you think there is a requirement to give notice under Article 26 CISG?

Q 26-2

Can a declaration of avoidance be revoked after the notice has reached the other party?

Article 27 CISG

Unless otherwise expressly provided in this Part of the Convention, if any notice, request or other communication is given or made by a party in accordance with this Part and by means appropriate in the circumstances, a delay or error in the transmission of the communication or its failure to arrive does not deprive that party of the right to rely on the communication.

I. Overview

A. Content and Purpose of Article 27 CISG

Article 27 CISG deals with post-contractual communications. It gives a party dispatching a notice or other communication in an appropriate manner the right to rely on its content. This provision of the CISG should be understood as only applicable to Part III of the CISG, as rules for acceptance and receipt under Part II are regulated (with one exception—Art 16(1) CISG) by Article 24 CISG, which applies to declarations and communications leading up to and associated with the conclusion of a contract (see Art 24 CISG above). Other communications are regulated under the general rule of Article 27 CISG, subject to express rules found in the individual provisions.

Question

Q 27-1

(a) What is the purpose of drawing a distinction between the effect of communications made pursuant to the offer/acceptance of a contract and other communications?
(b) What communications are covered by Article 27 CISG (give examples from the CISG)?

B. Domestic Laws

Article 27 CISG follows the traditional dispatch theory. In this respect it departs from the principle, present, for example, in the German legal system under § 130(1) BGB, that a communication (*Willenserklärung*), whether pre- or post-contractual, must reach the addressee.

C. International Principles

Art 1.10 PICC 2010:

(1) Where notice is required it may be given by any means appropriate to the circumstances.

(2) A notice is effective when it reaches the person to whom it was given.

(3) For the purpose of paragraph (2) a notice 'reaches' a person when given to that person orally or delivered at that person's place of business or mailing address.

(4) For the purpose of this article 'notice' includes a declaration, demand, request or any other communication of intention.

Question

Q 27-2

Which principle does Article 1.10 PICC 2010 follow?

II. Article 27 CISG and Instantaneous Communication

It is uncertain whether Article 27 CISG also applies to oral declarations made *inter praesentes* and to similar declarations made 'instantaneously'.

Questions

Q 27-3

(a) Look at the wording of Article 27 CISG. Are there any indications that would lead to the conclusion that oral communications do not fall within the ambit of Article 27 CISG?

(b) If so, what could these be?

Q 27-4

(a) What does the party relying on Article 27 CISG have to prove?

(b) How is proof to be provided?

Q 27-5

(a)   What are the 'means appropriate' in the circumstances?
(b)   What is appropriate from a language perspective?

Q 27-6

Does the issue of 'appropriate means' fall within the ambit of Article 27 CISG?

CISG Advisory Council Opinion No 1: Electronic Communications under CISG:[88]

[...]

OPINION A notice, request or other communication may be given or made electronically whenever the addressee expressly or impliedly has consented to receiving electronic messages of this type, in that format, and to that address. [...]

Art 5 UNCITRAL Model Law on Electronic Commerce:

Legal recognition of data messages

Information shall not be denied legal effect, validity or enforceability solely on the grounds that it is in the form of a data message.

Art 8 UN Convention on the Use of Electronic Communications in International Contracts 2005:

Legal recognition of electronic communications

1.   A communication or a contract shall not be denied validity or enforceability on the sole ground that it is in the form of an electronic communication. [...]

Art 10 UN Convention on the Use of Electronic Communications in International Contracts 2005:

Time and place of dispatch and receipt of electronic communications

1.   The time of dispatch of an electronic communication is the time when it leaves an information system under the control of the originator or of the party who sent it on behalf of the originator or, if the electronic communication has not left an information system under the control of the originator or of the party who sent it on behalf of the originator, the time when the electronic communication is received.
2.   The time of receipt of an electronic communication is the time when it becomes capable of being retrieved by the addressee at an electronic address designated by the addressee. The time of receipt of an electronic communication at another electronic address of the addressee is the time when it becomes capable of being retrieved by the addressee at that

---

[88] Taken from www.cisgac.com.

address and the addressee becomes aware that the electronic communication has been sent to that address. An electronic communication is presumed to be capable of being retrieved by the addressee when it reaches the addressee's electronic address. ...

Question

Q 27-7

What is the situation with respect to electronic means of communication and the e-commerce phenomenon?

Article 28 CISG

If, in accordance with the provisions of this Convention, one party is entitled to require performance of any obligation by the other party, a court is not bound to enter a judgement for specific performance unless the court would do so under its own law in respect of similar contracts of sale not governed by this Convention.

I. Overview

A. Content and Purpose of Article 28 CISG

A basic principle underlying the CISG is that the performance of each party's obligations under an international sale of goods contract is to be upheld. However, Article 28 CISG, in essence, places a limitation on the remedies available to a non-breaching party to a transaction. Despite the fact that one party may be entitled to require performance by the other party, a court will not be obliged to order such specific performance unless it would do so under its own domestic law. With respect to the specific issue of being able to claim for the purchase price, see Article 62 CISG below.

B. Domestic Laws

It was precisely the divergence in domestic laws on the issue of the right to require performance that prompted the introduction of Article 28 into the CISG.

(a) Continental European Legal Systems

Under many continental European legal systems, the right to require the performance of a contract is taken for granted under the principle of *pacta sunt servanda*. European legal systems recognise the right to specific performance of a contract as a matter of course, without a need to expressly refer to it in the law itself. Indeed, in the German legal system, an explicit exception to specific performance is only granted when the performance of the obligation becomes impossible.

§ 275(1) BGB:[89]

> A claim for specific performance is excluded if performance is impossible for the obligor or for any other person.

(b) Common Law Legal Systems

This view is not shared by all legal systems. The alternative view, advocated by Roman and Anglo-American law, focuses not on specific performance of the contract itself, but rather on monetary compensation representing the value of such performance. The general view is that only in cases where damages would be an inadequate remedy will specific performance be allowed; however, this is also a matter for the discretion of the courts granting this equitable remedy.

Sec 52 SGA:

> (1) In any action for breach of contract to deliver specific or ascertained goods the court may, if it thinks fit, on the plaintiff's application, by its judgement or decree direct that the contract shall be performed specifically, without giving the defendant the option of retaining the goods on payment of damages.
>
> [...]

§ 2-716 UCC:

> (1) Specific performance may be decreed where the goods are unique or in other proper circumstances.
> (2) The decree for specific performance may include such terms and conditions as to payment of the price, damages, or other reliefs as the court may deem just.
>
> [...]

Questions

Q 28-1

(a) What factor does the UCC focus on in order for a court to decide to award specific performance?
(b) What could be the reason for this?

Q 28-2

Discuss those cases in which specific performance is necessary, and those in which it would not make sense.

---

[89] Author's translation.

C. Drafting History

Article 28 CISG represents a compromise reached with the goal of bridging the differences between the continental European and the common law legal systems on the issue of the right to require performance of a contract. Due to the fundamentally different approaches to this topic, allowing reference to domestic law was considered the only compromise that enabled all diverging views to be given due regard. This clause does, however, act against the CISG's aim of harmonisation of international sales law, since Article 28 CISG permits the use of national limitations.

D. International Principles

As apparent, the reference to national law in Article 28 CISG presents considerable problems for the development of a 'uniform law' in this area, due not in the least to the fact that the law in this area, more so than other areas, differs quite considerably between different legal systems. In Articles 7.2.1 and 7.2.2 PICC 2010, an attempt was made to find a uniform solution to the problem of specific performance under the different legal systems.

Art 7.2.1 PICC 2010:

Where a party who is obliged to pay money does not do so, the other party may require payment.

Art 7.2.2 PICC 2010:

Where a party who owes an obligation other than one to pay money does not perform, the other party may require performance, unless
(a) performance is impossible in law or in fact;
(b) performance or, where relevant, enforcement is unreasonably burdensome or expensive;
(c) the party entitled to performance may reasonably obtain performance from another source;
(d) performance is of an exclusively personal character; or
(e) the party entitled to performance does not require performance within a reasonable time after it has, or ought to have, become aware of the non-performance.

Questions

Q 28-3

What is the difference between the duty to perform a monetary obligation and the duty to perform a non-monetary obligation?

Q 28-4

What is the difference between the duty to perform a monetary obligation and payment of damages?

Q 28-5

(a) For non-monetary obligations, what is the approach of Article 7.2.2 PICC 2010?
(b) Which legal system does the approach of Article 7.2.2 PICC 2010 reflect?

II. Situations of Applicability of Article 28 CISG

There is only limited case law on Article 28 CISG.

C 28-1

Magellan International Corporation v Salzgitter Handel GmbH,
US Dist Ct (ND IL), 7 December 1999,
CISG-online 439

For a summary of the facts see C 14-2 above.

[Judgment]

Count II: Specific Performance or Replevin Convention

Art 46(1) provides that a buyer may require the seller to perform its obligations unless the buyer has resorted to a remedy inconsistent with that requirement. As such, that provision would appear to make specific performance routinely available under the Convention. But Convention Art 28 conditions the availability of specific performance:

'If, in accordance with the provisions of this Convention, one party is entitled to require performance of any obligation by the other party, a court is not bound to enter judgment for specific performance unless the court would do so under its own law in respect of similar contracts of sale not governed by this Convention.'

Simply put, that looks to the availability of such relief under the UCC. And in pleading terms, any complaint adequate to provide notice under the UCC is equally sufficient under the Convention. Under UCC § 2-716(1) a court may decree specific performance 'where the goods are unique or in other proper circumstances.' That provision's Official Commentary instructs that inability to cover should be considered 'strong evidence' of 'other proper circumstances.' UCC § 2-716 was designed to liberalise the common law, which rarely allowed specific performance. Basically courts now determine whether goods are replaceable as a practical matter—for example, whether it would be difficult to obtain similar goods on the open market. Given the centrality of the replaceability issue in determining the availability of specific relief under the UCC, a pleader need allege only the difficulty of cover to state a claim under that Section. Magellan has done that. [...] It may perhaps be that when the facts are further fleshed out through discovery, Magellan's claims against Salzgitter will indeed succumb either for lack of proof or as the consequence of some legal deficiency. But in the current Rule 12(b)(6) context, Salzgitter's motion as to Counts I and II is denied, and it is ordered to file its Answer to the Complaint on or before December 20, 1999.

Questions

Q 28-6

In what specific situations does Article 28 CISG generally apply?

Q 28-7

(a) What factor gave rise to the applicability of Article 28 CISG in the above case (C 28-1)?
(b) Is this reasonable in international sales contracts?

Article 29 CISG

(1) A contract may be modified or terminated by the mere agreement of the parties.
(2) A contract in writing which contains a provision requiring any modification or termination by agreement to be in writing may not be otherwise modified or terminated by agreement. However, a party may be precluded by his conduct from asserting such a provision to the extent that the other party has relied on that conduct.

I. Overview

A. Content and Purpose of Article 29 CISG

Article 29(1) CISG concerns modifications and/or additions to contracts that have already been concluded. According to this provision, the mere consent of the parties suffices to incorporate such modifications or additions into the existing contract. The significance of this provision is, first, that no formal requirements need to be observed in modifying or terminating a contract and, secondly, that the common law doctrine of 'consideration', which also governs the issue of contractual modification, is not applicable under the CISG.

Notwithstanding this, Article 29(2) CISG still seeks to uphold the parties' agreement regarding form. To the extent that their contract provides that amendments may only be made in writing, this is to be complied with. However, if a party's conduct induces reliance by the other party on non-observance of formal requirements, the first party will be estopped from making a contrary assertion.

B. Domestic Laws

Under common law, the doctrine of consideration also applies to modifications of the contract. However, this principle has been statutorily amended in the US.

§ 2-209 UCC:

(1) An agreement modifying a contract within this Article needs no consideration to be binding.

(2)   A signed agreement which excludes modification or rescission except by a signed writing cannot be otherwise modified or rescinded, but except as between merchants such a requirement on a form supplied by the merchant must be separately signed by the other party.

(3)   The requirements of the statute of frauds Section of this Article (Section 2-201) must be satisfied if the contract as modified is within its provisions.

(4)   Although an attempt at modification or rescission does not satisfy the requirements of subSection (2) or (3) it can operate as a waiver.

(5)   A party who has made a waiver affecting an executory portion of the contract may retract the waiver by reasonable notification received by the other party that strict performance will be required of any term waived, unless the retraction would be unjust in view of a material change of position in reliance on the waiver.

Question

Q 29-1

Compare and contrast the wording of Article 29 CISG and Section 2-209 UCC. What similarities and differences can you find?

C. Drafting History

Despite the principle, obvious to many continental European lawyers, of the autonomy of the parties to amend or terminate a contract between them, the introduction of Article 29 CISG (which had no forerunner in ULF and ULIS) provoked debate during both the preparation of the CISG and at the Vienna Conference. The reason for the insertion of the provision into Part III, and not Part II of the CISG was to allow even those states who had opted out of the operation of Part II to make use of it.

   In the context of contractual amendments, the same rules apply as for the conclusion of a contract, see the discussion on Article 11 CISG above; namely, that unless the contract provides otherwise, any amendments/agreements to terminate need not be in writing.

II. Article 29(1) CISG

Whether agreement has been reached between the parties under Article 29(1) CISG to modify or terminate the contract is determined on the basis of the rules set out in Articles 14 to 24 CISG regarding offer and acceptance.

C 29-1

Oberlandesgericht Köln (Germany),
22 February 1994,
CISG-online 127

[Facts][90]

A seller and a German buyer reached an oral agreement for the sale of wood. The following day the seller sent a telefax confirming the agreement in writing. The goods were shipped four months later and reached Germany after another month; they were then delivered to a third party to which they had been resold in the meantime by the buyer. After examination of the goods the end purchaser notified the buyer of defects found in the goods. The buyer immediately informed the seller thereof. The seller's managing director replied announcing that he would go personally to Germany where he intended 'to market' the goods himself. The purchase price remained unpaid. The seller later on assigned its claim to a company (assignee) which commenced an action against the buyer to recover the price. The first instance court decided in favor of the assignee and the buyer appealed.

[Judgment][91]

[...]

1. According to the provisions of the CISG, the [seller's] claim for the purchase price arose here from the contract for the delivery of the wood to [buyer], but it was voided before the assignment to plaintiff because of the cancellation of the purchase contract. ... The parties, however, cancelled the contract by mutual agreement after [buyer's] notice of the defects. [Buyer] sufficiently set forth the claimed defects of the wood delivery and clearly expressed at the same time that she considered the defects to be material. On appeal, she further stated she had given notice of the defects to the [seller] on or before July 8, 1992, as proven by the [seller's] fax letter dated July 8, 1992, which is no longer contested by [seller's assignee]. The examination of the goods carried out by Company O in the beginning of July 1992 was still timely pursuant to CISG Art 38; the goods had to be sent on to [buyer's] customer from H—which was known by the [seller]—with the consequence that, according to CISG Art 38(3), the examination could be deferred until the wood delivery had arrived at Company O's facilities. The objection to the defects, which was raised on or before July 8, 1992, was made within a reasonable time after the discovery of the defects (CISG Art 39), particularly since July 4 and July 5, 1992 were a weekend. It is irrelevant whether [buyer's] cancellation of the agreement based on the alleged defects was timely, i.e., within a time equivalent to the reasonable time allotted for the notice of defects. Either way, following the notice of defects, the [seller] manifested her intention to cancel the purchase agreement, and [buyer] conclusively agreed hereto. This follows from the [seller's] written answer concerning the notice of defects, as well as from [buyer's] further conduct with respect to the agreement. The [seller] had already announced in her letter dated July 8, 1992 that she would come to Germany in order to market the wood herself. In a further faxletter dated July 27, 1992, the [seller] confirmed [buyer's] notice of defects—with reservations—after examination of the goods ('not as bad as you claim'), and informed her that she had found a Dutch company which would market

---

[90] Summary of facts taken from UNILEX.
[91] Translation taken from CISG Pace (citations omitted).

the wood for her. This was the latest indication from which [buyer] was able to infer that the [seller] did not want to be bound by the agreement any longer. Because the [seller's] intention to market the wood herself was expressed without a reservation or limitation, there was no reason, contrary to plaintiff's argument, to presume that the [seller] only wanted to assist in the marketing, while leaving the responsibility for the marketing with [buyer]. On the other hand, the [seller] could infer from [buyer's] conduct that [buyer] acquiesced in the cancellation of the agreement, since she neither objected to the letters dated July 8 and July 27, 1992, nor demanded replacement goods free of defects. CISG Art 29(1) expressly permits such a cancellation by agreement. The same rules apply to the formation of a contract to cancel an agreement as apply to the formation of the agreement itself. An offer to cancel can, therefore, pursuant to CISG Art 18(1), not be accepted by silence or inactivity of the other party; together with other circumstances, however, silence can indeed be important and may be interpreted as the acceptance of an offer of cancellation. Such circumstances exist here, because [buyer] not only remained silent but also refrained from further fulfillment of the agreement, specifically from insisting on the delivery of replacement goods or from asserting other warranty claims. Thus, the [seller] lost her claim to the purchase price. [...]

There are no specific requirements as to the form in which such agreement to modify/terminate the contract must be made. However, according to Art 29(2), if the written contract contains a clause that any changes to the contract must be made in writing, then the parties are bound by this agreement.

Question

Q 29-2

(a)   What was the contentious factor in the above case (C 29-1)?
(b)   What did the court conclude on this point?

C 29-2

Chateau des Charmes Wines Ltd v Sabaté USA Inc, Sabaté SA,
US CA (9th Cir), 5 May 2003,
CISG-online 767[92]

[...]

Factual Background and Procedural History

The material facts pertinent to this appeal are not disputed. Sabaté France manufactures and sells special wine corks that it claims will not cause wines to be spoiled by 'cork taint,' a distasteful flavor that some corks produce. It sells these corks through a wholly owned California subsidiary, Sabaté USA.

---

[92] Text taken from CISG Pace (footnotes omitted).

In February 2000, after some preliminary discussions about the characteristics of Sabaté's corks, Chateau des Charmes, a winery from Ontario, Canada, agreed by telephone with Sabaté USA to purchase a certain number of corks at a specific price. The parties agreed on payment and shipping terms. No other terms were discussed, nor did the parties have any history of prior dealings. Later that year, Chateau des Charmes placed a second telephone order for corks on the same terms. In total, Chateau des Charmes ordered 1.2 million corks.

Sabaté France shipped the corks to Canada in eleven shipments. For each shipment, Sabaté France also sent an invoice. Some of the invoices arrived before the shipments, some with the shipments, and some after the shipments. On the face of each invoice was a paragraph in French that specified that 'Any dispute arising under the present contract is under the sole jurisdiction of the Court of Commerce of the City of Perpignan.' On the back of each invoice a number of provisions were printed in French, including a clause that specified that 'any disputes arising out of this agreement shall be brought before the court with jurisdiction to try the matter in the judicial district where Seller's registered office is located.' Chateau des Charmes duly took delivery and paid for each shipment of corks. The corks were then used to bottle Chateau des Charmes' wines.

Chateau des Charmes claims that, in 2001, it noticed that the wine bottled with Sabaté's corks was tainted by cork flavors. Chateau des Charmes filed suit in federal district court in California against Sabaté France and Sabaté USA alleging claims for breach of contract, strict liability, breach of warranty, false advertising, and unfair competition. Sabaté France and Sabaté USA filed a motion to dismiss based on the forum selection clauses. The district court held that the forum selection clauses were valid and enforceable and dismissed the action. This appeal ensued.

Discussion

[...]

1. The question before us is whether the forum selection clauses in Sabaté France's invoices were part of any agreement between the parties. The disputes in this case arise out of an agreement for a sale of goods from a French party and a United States party to a Canadian party. Such international sales contracts are ordinarily governed by a multilateral treaty, the United Nations Convention on Contracts for the International Sale of Goods ('C.I.S.G.'), which applies to 'contracts of sale of goods between parties whose places of business are in different States ... when the States are Contracting States.' C.I.S.G., Art 1(1)(a), 15 U.S.C.App., 52 Fed.Reg. 6262 (March 2, 1987). The United States, Canada, and France are all contracting states to the C.I.S.G. 15 U.S.C.App. (Parties to the Convention). And none has acceded to the Convention subject to reservations that would affect its applicability in this case. Moreover, because the President submitted the Convention to the Senate, which ratified it, see Public Notice 1004, U.S. Ratification of 1980 United Nations Convention on Contracts for the International Sale of Goods: Official English Text, reprinted in 15 U.S.C.App.; Letter of Transmittal from President Reagan to the Senate of the United States (Sept. 21, 1983), reprinted in 15 U.S.C.App., there is no doubt that the Convention is valid and binding federal law. Accordingly, the Convention governs the substantive question of contract formation as to the forum selection clauses.

[...]

II. 2. Under the C.I.S.G., it is plain that the forum selection clauses were not part of any agreement between the parties. The Convention sets out a clear regime for analyzing international contracts for the sale of goods: 'A contract of sale need not be concluded in or evidenced by writing and is not subject to any other requirement as to form.' C.I.S.G., Art 11. A proposal is an offer if it is sufficiently definite to 'indicate[ ] the goods and expressly or implicitly fix[ ] or make[ ] provision for determining the quantity and the price,' id., Art 14, and it demonstrates an intention by the offeror to be bound if the proposal is accepted. Id. In turn, an offer is accepted if the offeree makes a 'statement … or other conduct … indicating assent to an offer.' Id., Art 18. Further, 'A contract is concluded at the moment when an acceptance of an offer becomes effective.' Id., Art 23. Within such a framework, the oral agreements between Sabaté USA and Chateau des Charmes as to the kind of cork, the quantity, and the price were sufficient to create complete and binding contracts.

The terms of those agreements did not include any forum selection clause. Indeed, Sabaté France and Sabaté USA do not contend that a forum selection clause was part of their oral agreements, but merely that the clauses in the invoices became part of a binding agreement. The logic of this contention is defective. Under the Convention, a 'contract may be modified or terminated by the mere agreement of the parties.' Id., Art 29(1). However, the Convention clearly states that '[a]dditional or different terms relating, among other things, to … the settlement of disputes are considered to alter the terms of the offer materially.' Id., Art 19(3). There is no indication that Chateau des Charmes conducted itself in a manner that evidenced any affirmative assent to the forum selection clauses in the invoices. Rather, Chateau des Charmes merely performed its obligations under the oral contract.

Nothing in the Convention suggests that the failure to object to a party's unilateral attempt to alter materially the terms of an otherwise valid agreement is an 'agreement' within the terms of Article 29. Cf. C.I.S.G., Art 8(3) ('In determining the intent of a party or the understanding a reasonable person would have had, due consideration is to be given to all relevant circumstances of the case including the negotiations, any practices which the parties have established between themselves, usages and any subsequent conduct of the parties.'). Here, no circumstances exist to conclude that Chateau des Charmes' conduct evidenced an 'agreement.' We reject the contention that because Sabaté France sent multiple invoices it created an agreement as to the proper forum with Chateau des Charmes. The parties agreed in two telephone calls to a purchase of corks to be shipped in eleven batches. In such circumstances, a party's multiple attempts to alter an agreement unilaterally do not so effect. See *In re CFLC, Inc.*, 166 F.3d 1012, 1019 (9th Cir.1999).

Question

Q 29-3

(a) What does this case say about the interaction between Article 29(1) and Article 19 CISG?
(b) What is the implication for Article 19(2) in the context of modifications to a contract?
(c) Do you think this is the correct approach?

C 29-3

BTC-USA Corporation v Novacare et al,
US Dist Ct (Dist Minn), 16 June 2008,
CISG-online 1773[93]

[...]

II. BACKGROUND

BTC is a Minnesota corporation with its principal place of business in Minneapolis, Minnesota. Novacare and its subsidiary Mougeot-Copy are French entities with their principal places of business in France. Koehler is a German entity with its principal place of business in Germany. Greene resides in New York and is the Secretary, Executive Vice President, and Chief Executive Officer of Koehler America, a subsidiary of Koehler. Defosse resides in France and previously worked for Mougeot-Copy and currently works for Koehler.

BTC is a paper broker that sold carbonless paper during the time periods relevant to the current litigation. To sell carbonless paper, BTC needed a relationship with a paper mill that produces and supplies carbonless paper. In March 2003, a Mougeot-Copy representative approached BTC and proposed that BTC cancel its relationship with its current supplier and represent Mougeot-Copy's carbonless paper line instead. Defosse and Sebastien Courtois ('Courtois') conducted discussions with BTC regarding Mougeot-Copy's interest in forming an exclusive relationship with BTC. On three instances, Defosse traveled to Minnesota to meet with BTC and its customers, on two of those occasions Courtois joined Defosse. Throughout the negotiations Mougeot-Copy, through Defosse and Courtois, represented that it was interested in a long-term relationship with BTC and was committed to working with BTC in the United States. Finally, on or about March 2004, the parties orally agreed that Mougeot-Copy would be BTC's sole supplier and BTC would be Mougeot-Copy's sole distributor in the United States. Accordingly, BTC terminated its relationship with its previous supplier and began taking the necessary steps to sell Mougeot-Copy's paper. From July through September 28, 2004, BTC placed orders with Mougeot-Copy and received shipments of customer orders and inventory from Mougeot-Copy. During that time, Mougeot-Copy operated under an agreement with Koehler whereby Koehler would sell paper to Novacare, which would then market and distribute the paper under its proprietary trade mark 'Mougeot-Copy.' Koehler and Novacare agreed to terminate their relationship in May 2004 when Koehler decided to stop manufacturing carbonless paper for Novacare.

On September 28, 2004, Mougeot-Copy informed BTC that it was exiting the carbonless paper industry and would only supply BTC with carbonless paper until the end of 2004. Mougeot-Copy informed BTC that although it would no longer supply BTC with carbonless paper, BTC could purchase carbonless paper with Koehler. However, Koehler subsequently informed BTC that, contrary to Mougeot-Copy's representation, Koehler would not supply BTC with carbonless paper.

---

[93] Citations omitted.

BTC contends Mougeot-Copy deceived BTC to believe it intended to form a long-term partnership and used BTC to gain access to clients and business information, which it then used to its advantage when it began working with Koehler to sell carbonless paper in the United States. BTC contends that as a consequence, it suffered significant financial losses and serious, permanent damage to its reputation.

III. DISCUSSION

In its Motion to Dismiss, Novacare asserts the Court should dismiss the Amended Complaint for improper venue pursuant to Federal Rule of Civil Procedure 12(b)(3) or, in the alternative, for failing to state a claim upon which relief can be granted pursuant to Federal Rule of Civil Procedure 12(b)(6). Novacare contends that BTC agreed to a forum selection clause included in its purchase order agreements requiring that any disputes arising between BTC and Novacare be settled in France. Novacare also asserts that the Court should dismiss BTC's Amended Complaint because the allegations set forth fail to state a claim for which relief can be granted. Koehler, Greene, and Defosse submitted a motion to dismiss asserting that the Court should dismiss Defosse if it dismisses Novacare for improper venue and that the Court should dismiss Koehler and Greene because it lacks personal jurisdiction over them.

A. Forum Selection Clause—Novacare and Defosse

. [...]

When BTC needed paper supply from Mougeot-Copy it would place an order by fax or email indicating the quantity and quality of the paper sought and the time and place for delivery. After negotiating the details with BTC, Mougeot-Copy would send BTC a pro forma invoice, which detailed the specifics of the order. The pro forma invoice also included the general conditions of sales, which included the following provision:

JURISDICTION AND DISPUTES

Registered office of the Seller (Laval/Vologne, France) is to be considered as elected domicile.

All disputes arising between the Buyer and the Seller shall be exclusively settled by the competent court of Epinal (Tribunal de Commerce d'Epinal, Vosges).

Before filling BTC's order, Mougeot-Copy required that BTC confirm its agreement to the terms on the pro forma invoice by writing, email, or some other method. On four occasions, Ron Michlitsch ('Michlitsch'), BTC's vice president, provided the confirmation required by Mougeot-Copy by signing the pro forma invoice and initialing the general conditions of sales. In each instance, Michlitsch initialed the general conditions of sales adjacent to the forum selection clause.

Novacare contends that venue is improper because BTC agreed to the forum selection clause included with the pro forma invoices and thus agreed to resolve all disputes in France. BTC contends that because the forum selection clause was not included in the parties' March 2004 oral agreement and is not an implied term to the parties' contract, the forum selection clause is unenforceable. BTC acknowledges that Michlitsch initialed the general conditions of sales but argues that doing so does not mean that BTC expressly, freely, and consciously agreed to the forum selection clause. Novacare contends that even if the forum selection clause was not included in the March 2004 oral contract, BTC expressed assent to the clause (indicated by Michlitsch's initialing the general conditions of sales), and thus agreed to modify the contract. Novacare contends that because BTC expressly agreed to the forum selection clause, the clause is enforceable, and requires that the Court dismiss BTC's Amended Complaint for improper venue.

The key question to determining whether venue is proper is whether the parties agreed to the forum selection clause. Because this case involves a dispute regarding the international sale of goods it is governed by the United Nations Convention on Contracts for the International Sale of Goods ('CISG'). *Chateau Des Charmes Wines LTD v. Sabate USA, Inc.*, 328 F.3d 528, 530 (9th Cir. 2003) (stating that because the President submitted the CISG to the United States Senate, which ratified it, the CISG is valid and binding federal law). Pursuant to the CISG, parties may execute oral contracts and may modify contracts by 'the mere agreement of the parties.' CISG arts. 11, 29(1).

The Ninth Circuit addressed similar issues in Chateau Des Charmes Wines, 328 F.3d 528. In that case, the defendant included a forum selection clause in the invoices it sent to the plaintiff; however, unlike this case, there was no evidence that the plaintiff assented to the added term. Defendant argued that plaintiff's failure to object constituted an agreement to the forum selection clause; however, the Ninth Circuit disagreed. The court explained: 'Nothing in the [CISG] suggests that the failure to object to a party's unilateral attempt to alter materially the terms of an otherwise valid agreement is an "agreement" within the terms of Article 29. Here, no circumstances exist to conclude that Chateau des Charmes's conduct evidenced an "agreement."'

In the case at bar, when Michlitsch initialed the general conditions of sale BTC expressed its assent to the forum selection clause. Pursuant to Article 29, parties are free to agree to modify previously agreed upon contracts, even if the modification constitutes a material alteration. BTC assented to a material alteration of the oral contract.

BTC contends that the Court should not enforce the forum selection clause because doing so would result in hardship and surprise. Whether the clause would result in hardship and surprise is relevant to determining whether the clause constitutes a material alteration not expressly agreed upon by the parties under Uniform Commercial Code § 2-207. See *Marvin Lumber and Cedar Co. v. PPG Indus., Inc.*, 401 F.3d 901, 911 (8th Cir. 2005); *Revlon, Inc. v. United Overseas Ltd.*, No. 93 Civ. 0863, 1994 U.S. Dist. LEXIS 220, 1994 WL 9657 (S.D.N.Y. Jan. 12, 1994). Not only does this case not involve the application of § 2-207, or the analogous article of the CISG, there is no dispute that the forum selection clause materially altered the oral contract. Hardship and surprise may prevent enforcement in a case where a forum selection clause is unilaterally inserted into the contract without the express assent of the parties, it will not prevent enforcement in this case where BTC expressly agreed to the clause by initialing the general conditions of sales.

Next, BTC contends that Michlitsch did not assent to the forum selection clause when he initialed the general conditions of sales because he may not have read them and thus did not agree to them or he did not understand them to be an alteration because he did not negotiate the original contract. This argument ignores the general principle of contract law that, 'in the absence of fraud, misrepresentation or deceit, one who executes a contract cannot avoid it on the ground that he did not read it or supposed it to be different in its terms.' *N&D Fashions, Inc. v. DHJ Indus., Inc.*, 548 F.2d 722, 727 (8th Cir. 1976).

[...]

C 29-4

Solae, LLC v Hershey Canada, Inc,
US Dist Ct (Del), 9 May 2008,
CISG-online 1769[94]

[...]

Solae is a Delaware limited liability company with its principal place of business in St. Louis, Missouri. Hershey Canada is a Canadian corporation with its principal place of business in Mississauga, Ontario. For the past several years, Solae has supplied soy lecithin to Hershey Canada. In late 2005, Laurie Cradick ('Ms. Cradick'), Solae's account manager responsible for sales of soy lecithin products to, and the customer relationship with The Hershey Company ('Hershey'), and Kim McLucas ('Ms. McLucas'), of Hershey's commodities department, began negotiating the projected volume of soy lecithin products that Hershey and Hershey Canada would be ordering in 2006, and the sale price that would apply during that period. In December 2005, Ms. Cradick and Ms. McLucas reached agreement that 'for the period from January 1, 2006 to December 31, 2006 Hershey Canada would order up to 250,000 pounds of [soy lecithin] at a price of US $1.2565 per pound.' The parties dispute whether the terms of this agreement were reduced to writing. Ms. McLucas then notified James Kuehl ('Mr. Kuehl'), a materials analyst for Hershey Canada at its Smith Falls, Ontario manufacturing plant ('the Smith Falls plant'), of this agreement, which she referred to as contract '46044618,' by e-mail on January 20, 2006.

Under the 2006 agreement, as under agreements reached in previous years, Mr. Kuehl would fax a purchase order to Solae's customer service department, indicating, among other things, that the quantity ordered should be 'release[d] against contract 46044618.' After faxing Mr. Kuehl an order confirmation, Solae would ship the soy lecithin. Following shipment, Solae would send an invoice to the Smith Falls Plant. Solae's standard order confirmations and invoices refer to attached 'Conditions of Sale.' The parties do not dispute that these Conditions of Sale were not mentioned during negotiations between Ms. McLucas and Ms. Cradick.

This action arises largely out of Solae's September 27, 2006 shipment of 40,000 pounds of soy lecithin allegedly contaminated with Salmonella to Hershey Canada for use in chocolate products at its Smith Falls, Ontario manufacturing plant ('the Smith Falls plant'). The shipment was made pursuant to Mr. Kuehl's faxed purchase order on June 21, 2006, requesting delivery on September 29, 2006. Solae's order confirmation, sent June 23, 2006, did not include its Conditions of Sale, but did refer to them. The invoice sent to the Smith Falls Plant following shipment did contain the Conditions of Sale.

The contamination was discovered by Hershey Canada in October 2006 while conducting routine testing. Before the contamination was realized, Hershey Canada had incorporated this allegedly-contaminated soy lecithin into over two million units of Hershey Canada product shipped throughout Canada. This contamination resulted in a large-scale recall of Hershey Canada chocolate products, the temporary closure of the Smith Falls plant, and an extensive investigation by the Canadian Food Inspection Agency ('CFIA') and the Office of Food Safety and Recall ('OFSR'). Subsequently, Hershey Canada notified Solae of the con-

---

[94] Case abstract taken from UNILEX (citations omitted).

taminated soy lecithin, and informed Solae that it would hold Solae responsible for damages incurred as a result of the incident. Hershey Canada also refused to accept delivery or pay for any additional lots of soy lecithin, including a lot for which an order had been placed on October 17, 2006.

[...]

ANALYSIS

I. Forum Selection Clause

[1] The parties dispute the relevant contract governing this dispute. If the relevant contract contains a forum-selection clause, Hershey Canada's contentions regarding personal jurisdiction are largely irrelevant. When a party is bound by a forum selection clause, the party is considered to have expressly consented to personal jurisdiction. *Res. Ventures, Inc. v Res. Mgmt. Int'l, Inc.*, 42 F.Supp.2d 423, 431 (D.Del.1999). An express consent to jurisdiction, in and of itself, satisfies the requirements of Due Process. *Sternberg v O'Neil*, 550 A.2d 1105, 1116 (Del.1988). Such consent is deemed to be a waiver of any objection on Due Process grounds and an analysis of minimum contacts becomes unnecessary. See *Hornberger Mgmt. Co. v. Haws & Tingle General Contractors, Inc.*, 768 A.2d 983, 987 (Del.Super.Ct.2000) (stating '[a] party may expressly consent to jurisdiction by agreeing to a forum selection clause ... If a party consents to jurisdiction, a minimum contacts analysis is not required.'); *USH Ventures v Global Telesystems Group, Inc. C.A.* No. 97C-08-086, 1998 WL 281250, at *7, 1998 Del. Super. Lexis 167, at *22 (Del.Super.Ct. May 21, 1998) (same). Accordingly, the Court must determine whether Hershey Canada is bound by a forum selection clause.

According to Solae, the relevant contract is the invoice and 'Conditions of Sale,' mailed to Hershey Canada on or about September 27, 2006, concurrent with Solae's shipment of the allegedly-contaminated soy lecithin. Solae contends these Conditions of Sale set forth terms governing the transaction, and have been 'included in invoices from Solae to Hershey for soy lecithin and other soy-based products since approximately 2003.' The Conditions of Sale provide:

'This Agreement is to be construed and the respective rights of Buyer and Seller are to be determined according to the laws of the State of Delaware, USA, without regard to choice of law or conflict principles of Delaware or any other jurisdiction, and the courts of Delaware shall [have] exclusive jurisdiction over any disputes or issues arising under this Agreement.'

Solae contends that Hershey Canada accepted the September 2006 shipment of soy lecithin and rendered payment in full, without objecting to or rejecting the Conditions of Sale, and therefore the forum selection clause governs the transactions at issue.

Hershey Canada contends that a 'Quantity Contract' entered in January 2006 governed Solae's sale of soy lecithin to Hershey Canada for the year 2006, which contains no provision identifying Delaware as either a proper forum, or the source of governing law. Under the terms of the 2006 Quantity Contract, the parties agreed to the total volume of soy lecithin that Hershey Canada was obligated to purchase before December 31, 2006, the price at which Solae was obligated to sell such volume, and the freight terms of 'FOB Destination.' Hershey Canada contends that no modifications to the Quantity Contract were proposed after January 2006.

Hershey Canada points out that the Conditions of Sale that Solae contends govern the dispute arrived after the shipment of the allegedly-contaminated soy lecithin had been delivered, and were received by individuals with no authority to modify the existing 2006 Quantity Contract. Hershey Canada further contends that there was never an affirmative assent to modify the parties' existing contract, and that, under the United Nations Convention of Contracts for the International Sale of Goods, Solae's 'unilateral attempt to add terms through an invoice did not modify the parties' contract.'

In response, Solae contends that the Conditions of Sale were familiar to Hershey Canada through Solae and Hershey Canada's 'long history of dealing under Solae's terms.' Solae contends that the discussions between the parties regarding 2006 shipments to Hershey Canada did not give rise to a binding contract, and that the parties' course of dealing as to these shipments confirm that the annual volume discussions did not create binding agreements. Solae contends that it never received Hershey Canada's 2006 Quantity Contract, pointing to the incorrect address and fax number listed for Solae on the face of the contract, and that Solae's representative had not seen a document akin to the 2006 Quantity Contract prior to this litigation.

[2] The parties agree that the United Nations Convention of Contracts for the International Sale of Goods ('CISG') governs contract formation here. Under the terms of the CISG, 'a contract is concluded at the moment when an acceptance of an offer becomes effective in accordance with the provisions of this Convention.' CISG, Art 23. An offer must be 'sufficiently definite,' and 'demonstrate an intention by the offerer to be bound if the proposal is accepted.' Id., Art 14. An offer is accepted, and a contract is formed when the offeree makes a statement or other conduct, 'indicating assent to an offer.' Id., Art 18. The CISG does not contain a statute of frauds, stating that 'a contract of sale need not be concluded in or evidenced by writing and is not subject to any other requirement as to form.' Id., Art 11. Courts have held that a binding contract exists when the parties sufficiently agree to the goods, the quantity and the price. See, e.g., *Chateau des Charmes Wines Ltd. v Sabate U.S.A., Inc.*, 328 F.3d 528, 531 (9th Cir.2003).

Having reviewed the record in light of the applicable legal standard, the Court is not persuaded by Solae's contention that its Conditions of Sale control the disputed transaction. In her April 19, 2007 affidavit, Ms. Cradick states that, in or about mid-December 2005, the parties reached agreement as to 'the projected volume of soy lecithin … that would be ordered by manufacturing plants of … Hershey Canada during 2006, and the sale price that would apply during that period.' Ms. Cradick also states that Mr. Kuehl's June 21, 2006 purchase order was '[p]ursuant to' this agreement; this is further reflected in the actual purchase order, which indicates that the order should be 'release[d] against' the 250,000 pounds Hershey Canada was obligated to purchase under this agreement.

[3] The record is clear that Ms. Cradick and Ms. McLucas had reached agreement as to the amount of soy lecithin Solae was obligated to sell Hershey Canada during the calendar year 2006, and the price at which Solae was obligated to sell. Under this agreement, Hershey Canada was obligated to purchase a substantial quantity of soy lecithin from Solae at the price agreed upon. The Court concludes that this is sufficient to create a complete and binding contract under the CISG (the '2006 Contract').

[4] Because the 2006 Contract did not include a forum-selection clause, the Court must now determine if the forum-selection clause contained in the Conditions of Sale subsequently became part of the 2006 Contract under the CISG. As Hershey Canada points out, this issue was addressed by the Ninth Circuit in *Chateau des Charmes Wines Ltd.*, 328 F.3d 528:

Under the Convention, a 'contract may be modified or terminated by the mere agreement of the parties.' [CISG], Art 29(1). However, the Convention clearly states that '[a]dditional or different terms relating, among other things, to … the settlement of disputes are considered to alter the terms of the offer materially.' Id., Art 19(3). There is no indication that [the buyer] conducted itself in a manner that evidenced any affirmative assent to the forum selection clauses in the invoices. Rather, [the buyer] merely performed its obligations under the oral contracts. Nothing in the Convention suggests that the failure to object to a party's unilateral attempt to alter materially the terms of an otherwise valid agreement is an 'agreement' within the terms of Article 29.

Here, as in Chateau, Solae has set forth no substantive evidence indicating that Hershey Canada agreed to a modification of the terms of the 2006 Contract, beyond Hershey Canada's receipt of the Conditions of Sale. Solae has not set forth evidence refuting Mr. Kuehl's statement that he was not authorized to negotiate contractual terms or to commit Hershey Canada to Solae's Conditions of Sale, and the Court does not agree with Solae's contention that because multiple invoices and pre-shipment confirmations containing these Conditions of Sale were sent to Hershey Canada over 'years of sales and dozens of transactions,' these terms necessarily became part of the 2006 Contract. '[A] parties' multiple attempts to alter an agreement unilaterally do not so effect.' Chateau, 328 F.3d at 531. In sum, the Court concludes that Hershey Canada's continued performance of its duties under the 2006 Contract did not demonstrate its acceptance of the terms contained in the Condition of Sales, and the Court further concludes that Solae's Conditions of Sale did not modify the 2006 Contract to add a forum-selection clause.

Questions

Q 29-4

(a)   Was there a valid modification in the above cases (C 29-3 and C 29-4)?
(b)   If so, how did the modification come about?
(c)   How can the differences in findings of the two courts be explained?

Q 29-5

How did the court in *Solae, LLC v Hershey Canada, Inc* (C 29-3) distinguish the case from the *Chateau Des Charmes Wines* case (C 29-2)?

III. Article 29(2) CISG

The lack of requirements as to form set out in Article 11 CISG also generally applies to modifications and/or termination of the existing contract, see Article 29(1) CISG. However, according to Article 29(2) CISG, if the original contract contains any provision regarding the observance of formal requirements, it may not be otherwise modified or terminated. This provision shares many similarities with Article 2.1.18 PICC 2010.

Art 2.1.18 PICC 2010:

> A contract in writing which contains a clause requiring any modification or termination by agreement to be in a particular form may not be otherwise modified or terminated. However, a party may be precluded by its conduct from asserting such a clause to the extent that the other party has reasonably acted in reliance on that conduct.

For the interaction between these two articles (the equivalent of Art 2.1.18 PICC 2010 in PICC 1994), see the following case.

C 29-5

ICC International Court of Arbitration, Award No 9117/1998, CISG-online 777[95]

[Facts]

A Russian seller (Claimant) and a Canadian buyer (Respondent) entered into a contract for the sale of goods. The Claimant delivered part of the goods before the expiry of the US import licences, while the remaining part was delivered after the expiry. The Respondent refused to pay the full price alleging that the Claimant had failed to ship all the goods before the expiry of the import licences and had violated the Respondent's exclusive right to import the goods into the US. The Claimant commenced arbitration in accordance with the arbitration agreement contained in the contract, providing for arbitration under the ICC Rules of Arbitration and Reconciliation. The contract did not contain a choice of law clause. The Arbitral Tribunal stated that, pursuant to Art 13(3) and (5) of the ICC Rules for Reconciliation and Arbitration, and, in addition to the contractual provisions agreed upon by the parties, the relevant usages of trade and the CISG would apply. For the matters which had not been contractually agreed upon and which could not be determined by observing either trade usages or CISG, the law of the Russian Federation would apply. In dealing with the merits of the case, the Arbitral Tribunal corroborated the provisions of the CISG with the reference to the UNIDROIT Principles, stating that, although the UNIDROIT Principles of International Commercial Contracts shall [not] directly be applied, it is nevertheless informative to refer to them because they are said to reflect a world-wide consensus in most of the basic matters of contract law. Thus, the Arbitral Tribunal referred to Arts 2.17 (Merger clauses) and 2.18 (Written modification clauses) of the UNIDROIT Principles to confirm the rule laid down in Art 29 (2) CISG, according to which the Respondent could not rely on any kind of oral promises or assurances, or any kind of written references which were not at the same time reflected in an Amendment or Supplement to the Contract. Finally, reference was made to Art 4.3 (Relevant circumstances) of the UNIDROIT Principles to determine whether a course of dealing was established between the parties which could fairly be regarded as a common basis of understanding to interpret their statements and other conduct.

---

[95] English abstract taken from UNILEX.

[Judgment]

In the instant case, two provisions are of paramount importance: first, the so-called merger clause (sometimes called integration clause) and, second, the written modification clause. Both of them may be characterised as typical clauses, and there can be no doubt for any party engaged in international trade that the clauses mean, and must mean, what they say. [...] The parties are, however, free in extending an agreed form even in future amendments; see Article 2.18. Article 2.18 of the 1994 Unidroit Principles is the Article on the written modification clause to which reference will be made in the following paragraphs. The written modification clause in which the present Parties have also explicitly agreed on the framework of the Contract [...] has the same effects as the merger clause with regard to any future negotiations, promises and any other extrinsic evidence which otherwise might be adduced for supplementing, altering or contradicting the written contract. The significance of the written modification clause is explained in Article 29(2) CISG which reads as follows: A contract in writing which contains a provision requiring any modification or termination by agreement in be in writing may not be otherwise modified or terminated by agreement. However, a party may be precluded by his conduct from asserting such a provision to the extent that the other party has relied on that conduct.

[...] In the instant case, however, it is the Tribunal's opinion that there is no room whatsoever for applying the exception clause. The present Parties have agreed on the written requirement for any kind of modifications, and there is no evidence of a conduct which could be of a nature as to do away with that specific requirement. Again, it is useful to realise that a written modification clause is another typical element in international contracts. The comparison [with] the 1994 Unidroit Principles again seems appropriate. Article 2.18 states the following: (Written modification clause). A contract in writing which contains a clause requiring any modification or termination by agreement to be in writing may not be otherwise modified or terminated. However, a party may be precluded by its conduct from asserting such a clause to the extent that the other party has acted in reliance on that conduct. As can be seen, Article 2.18 of the 1994 Unidroit Principles is quite close to Article 29(2) CISG.

[...] The Majority Arbitrators further considered whether under the general duty to act in good faith Claimant would have been under an obligation to accelerate the shipment [...] so to allow a customs clearing prior to the expiry of the US import license. For instance, parties to a contract might be or become bound by a particular course of dealing which they have established as between themselves, by virtue of their previous commercial practices and conduct, and which can fairly be regarded as a common basis of understanding for interpreting their expression and other conduct. This notion, for instance, is also reflected in Article 4.3 of the 1994 Unidroit Principles (which are not directly applicable in the instant case, but nevertheless express a communis opinion and consensus). The question thus arises whether such a particular course of dealing (which might have been considered or applied by this Tribunal) had been established between the Parties. The answer to this question is, however, negative, for three reasons. First, it is from the outset hardly conceivable that a conclusive (and in the end legally binding) commercial practice can be established overriding the terms of a straightforward sales contract; typically, such practices emerge in the framework of long-term contracts such as those in the construction industry. Second, the explicit integration clause and the written modification clause, as contained in the Contract, operate as a bar against the assumption that a certain behaviour or practice could reach the level of becoming legally binding between the Parties. Third, the contractual relationship, as it had been examined by this Tribunal, did not reveal any particular commercial practices between the Parties, and there is no evidence before the Tribunal that the Parties had established a particular conduct which could have become legally binding on them.

Questions

Q 29-6

What are the similarities and differences between a merger clause and a written modification clause?

Q 29-7

(a)   What was the relevant fact in the above case (C 29-5)?
(b)   What part of Article 29 CISG did the court rely on to reach its conclusion?

Q 29-8

(a)   What impact does a course of dealing between the parties have on a written modification clause?
(b)   Can a written modification clause be overthrown by a usage of trade?

C 29-6

Oberlandesgericht Innsbruck (Austria), 18 December 2007, CISG-online 1735[96]

For a summary of the facts see C 3-3 above.

[…]

POSITION OF THE PARTIES BEFORE THE COURT OF FIRST INSTANCE

Position of the [Seller]

The Plaintiff [Seller] requested that the Defendant [Buyer] be held liable to pay the differences accrued due to the unilateral reductions amounting to EUR 191,866.10 as well as to pay a further EUR 1,243.33 in respect to invoice number 80962 of 1 June 2006, which had been unduly reduced by the [Buyer].

The [Seller] alleged in respect to the amount of EUR 191,866.10 that, according to the agreement of 29 March 2005, a price of EUR 682.50 per ton would apply. This agreement had been binding and the invoices had been based thereon. The issuing of a closing invoice had not been agreed on. In the aftermath of 29 March 2005, no new agreement in respect to the price had been reached, wherefore the reductions of the [Buyer] had not been justified. In particular, an oral negotiation between the parties on 29 November 2005 had not resulted in a new agreement. It was true that the [Buyer] had falsely claimed in a note that a new

---

[96] Translation taken from CISG Pace (footnotes omitted).

agreement had been reached; however, the [Seller] had sent a timely objection in writing. The parties had not agreed on the Austrian standard B 2110. In the alternative, the note of the [Buyer] constituted neither an effective modification of the contract nor an effective waiver on behalf of the [Seller] in respect to its claims arising out of the contract.

Position of the [Buyer]

The [Buyer] requested the court to dismiss the claim.

The [Buyer] alleged that the price reduction had been effected in accordance with the international decline of steel prices. It had successfully convinced the [Seller] on 29 November 2005 that it would be entitled to the respective reduction. In the course of these negotiations, the parties had agreed that, on the one hand, the [Buyer] had to pay EUR 40,000.00 net in respect to the reductions effected between May and 15 November 2005, but, on the other hand, a price of EUR 497.50 per ton (laying not included) should apply in respect to all deliveries subsequent to 16 November 2005. In addition, the [Buyer] had guaranteed an option contract to the [Seller] in respect to the delivery of four tons of construction steel for four years. It had been intended that the CEO of the [Seller] drafted this option contract in writing and that he further discussed it with the [Buyer]. The agreed payment of EUR 40,000.00 net had been due upon receipt of this draft. The [Buyer] had sent a note in respect to this agreement on 1 December 2005, which had not been objected to by the [Seller] until 17 January 2006. The objection had not been effected in due time according to item 5.5 of the Austrian standard B 2110, which had been included in the contract. According to the agreement of 29 November 2005, the payment of EUR 40,000.00 would not be due as the [Seller] had failed to draft the priority right and would hence be in default. In addition, according to the agreed Austrian standard B 2110, the [Seller] had been obliged to issue a final invoice including all necessary proof. Due to the fact that such proof had not been brought, the [Buyer] would be entitled to the reductions calculated on the basis of its own records. Furthermore, the [Buyer] would be entitled to counterclaims which surpassed the amount claimed. The [Buyer] therefore declared a set-off in eventu.

[…]

REASONING OF THE APPELLATE COURT

[…]

2. In respect to the legal assessment

[…]

According to Article 29(2) CISG, a contract in writing which contains a provision requiring any modification or termination by agreement to be in writing may not be otherwise modified or terminated by agreement. An oral modification or termination does not have any legal effect if a written contract or a contract which falls under Article 3(1) CISG stipulates, that it may only be altered by written agreement.

However, Article 29(2) does not define the term written agreement on a modification or termination of the contract. The Article does not provide for a specific type of written form. Article 29(2) CISG is supplemented by Article 13 CISG in this respect as it states that writing includes telegram and telex for the purpose of the Convention. Therefore, a unilateral confirmation of a modification or termination by agreement (e.g., via telegram or telex) meets the requirements of Article 29(2) CISG.

It is in any case decisive what the parties themselves determined as written form and how this agreement has to be interpreted by applying Article 8 CISG (Schlechtriem/Schwenzer,

Kommentar zum Einheitlichen UN-Kaufrecht, Article 13, margin number 2; Schlechtriem, Internationales UN-Kaufrecht, margin number 67).

In the present case, the clause in respect to written form provides for the requirement that modifications or amendments to the contract need to be confirmed in writing by both parties. According to this clause, a unilateral written confirmation of a modification or termination by agreement in the sense of Article 13 CISG would not suffice to meet the requirement of a written form.

Nevertheless, not only the order of the [Buyer] but also the Austrian standard B 2110 forms part of the contract. The latter provides in item 5.5 that the requirement in respect to written form is met if an oral agreement is confirmed in writing by one contractual partner within a reasonable period of time if the other contractual partner does not object thereto within a reasonable period of time. It is true that the order prevails over the Austrian standard B 2110 as regards contradictions. However, item 5.5 of the Austrian standard B2110 does not contradict the clause in respect to written form of the order but only amends it. Hence, the clause has to be interpreted as follows:

In general, a modification or an amendment of the contract needs to be confirmed in writing by both parties; nevertheless, it suffices if one contractual partner confirms an oral agreement in writing if the other contractual partner does not object to this. Thus, these two provisions can be applied simultaneously and do not contradict each other. It is true that Item 5.5 of the Austrian standard B 2110 weakens the requirement as to form as contained in item 12 of the order, however, it does not deviate from the requirement of a bilateral agreement as a sole unilateral written confirmation of an agreement—as provided for by Article 13 CISG—does not suffice. The requirement as to form is only met if the other contractual partner does not object to the written confirmation within a reasonable period of time.

Therefore, according to this interpretation, the requirement in respect to written form according to Article 29(2) CISG is met in the present case if an oral modification of the contract is confirmed in writing by one contractual partner and not contested by the other party.

The [Buyer] has compiled the note of 1 December 2005 in respect to the agreement of 29 November 2005. This note reached the [Seller] on 6 December 2005. The [Seller], however, failed to object until 17 January 2006. This objection has not been effected within due time, as a period of six weeks cannot be considered as reasonable in respect to the fast-moving building industry, where a fast decision is necessary and usual.

As a consequence to the late objection against the written note of the [Buyer] of 1 December 2005, the requirements as regards the written form in the sense of the contractual agreement of the parties and according to Article 29(2) CISG have been met according to item 5.5 of the Austrian standard B 2110.

Question

Q 29-9

(a)   On what basis did the court in the *Innsbruck* case come to the conclusion that the contract had been validly modified?

(b)   Why were the seller's objections invalid?

Article 30 CISG

The seller must deliver the goods, hand over any documents relating to them and transfer the property in the goods, as required by the contract and this Convention.

I. Overview

Article 30 CISG outlines the main obligations of the seller. It emphasises that it is the contract that is decisive for determining the scope of these obligations.

II. The Seller's Obligations in Detail

A. 'Delivery' of the Goods

Delivery comprises solely the obligation of giving the buyer the means of taking possession of the goods. The actual completion of performance, whereby the buyer takes over possession of the goods and the property in them, is not part of the notion of 'delivery'.

What the delivery obligation actually comprises is often clarified by the use of the ICC Rules for the Use of Domestic and International Trade Terms (INCOTERMS®).

Cl A4 EXW INCOTERMS® (2010):

Delivery. The seller must deliver the goods by placing them at the disposal of the buyer at the agreed point, if any, at the named place of delivery, not loaded on any collecting vehicle. If no specific point has been agreed within the named place of delivery, and if there are several points available, the seller may select the point that best suits its purpose. The seller must deliver the goods on the agreed dated or within the agreed period.

Cl A4 FOB INCOTERMS® (2010):

Delivery. The seller must deliver the goods either by placing them on board the vessel nominated by the buyer at the loading point, if any, indicated by the buyer at the named port of shipment or by procuring the goods so delivered. In either case, the seller must deliver the goods on the agreed date or within the agreed period and in the manner customary at the port.

If no specific loading point has been indicated by the buyer, the seller may select the point within the named port of shipment that best suits its purpose.

Cl A4 DAT INCOTERMS® (2010):

Delivery. The seller must unload the goods from the arriving means of transport and must then deliver them by placing them at the disposal of the buyer at the named terminal referred to in A3 a [for contract of carriage] at the port or place of destination on the agreed date or within the agreed period.

Question

Q 30-1

Compare and contrast the three delivery obligations under INCOTERMS® above. What is the significance of 'delivery' in each context for the obligations of the seller?

B. 'Handing over' Documents

Article 30 CISG not only obliges the seller to deliver, but also to hand over all documents relating to the goods. Again, to the extent that INCOTERMS® are incorporated into the contract between the parties, they provide more detail as to the content of this obligation.

Cl A3 CIF INCOTERMS® (2010):

Contracts of carriage and insurance. [...] b) Contract of insurance. The seller must obtain, at its own expense, cargo insurance complying at least with the minimum cover provided by Clauses (C) of the Institute Cargo Clauses (LMA/IUA) or any similar clauses. The insurance shall be contracted with underwriters or an insurance company of good repute and entitle the buyer, or any other person having an insurable interest in the goods, to claim directly from the insurer.

When required by the buyer, the seller shall, subject to the buyer providing any necessary information requested by the seller, provide at the buyer's expense any additional cover, if procurable, such as cover as provided by Clauses (A) or (B) of the Institute Cargo Clauses (LMA/IUA) or any similar clauses and/or cover complying with the Institute War Clauses and/or Institute Strikes Clauses (LMA/IUA) or any similar clauses.

The insurance shall cover, at a minimum, the price provided in the contract plus 10% (i.e., 110%) and shall be in the currency of the contract.

The insurance shall cover the goods from the point of delivery set out in A4 and A5 to at least the named port of destination.

The seller must provide the buyer with the insurance policy or other evidence of insurance cover.

Moreover, the seller must provide the buyer, at the buyer's request, risk, and expense (if any), with information that the buyer needs to procure any additional insurance.

Cl A8 CIF INCOTERMS® (2010):

Deliver document. The seller must, at its own expense, provide the buyer without delay with the usual transport document for the agreed port of destination.

This transport document must cover the contract goods, be dated within the period agreed for shipment, enable the buyer to claim the foods from the carrier at the port of destination and, unless otherwise agreed, enable the buyer to sell the goods in transit by the transfer of the document to a subsequent buyer or by notification to the carrier.

When such a transport document is issued in negotiable form and in several originals, a full set of originals must be presented to the buyer.

Cl A8 DDP INCOTERMS® (2010):

Delivery document. The seller must provide the buyer, at the seller's expense, with a document enabling the buyer to take delivery of the goods as envisaged in A4/B4.

Cl A10 DDP INCOTERMS® (2010):

Assistance with information and related costs. The seller must, where applicable, in a timely manner, provide to or render assistance in obtaining for the buyer, at the buyer's request, risk and expense, any documents and information, including Security-related information, that the buyer needs for the transport of the goods to the final destination, where applicable, from the named place of destination.

The seller must reimburse the buyer for all costs and charges incurred by the buyer in providing or rendering assistance in obtaining documents and information as envisaged in B10.

Question

Q 30-2

(a)   Outline the main differences in the documents required under CIF and those under DDP.
(b)   Are there any other documents that might be relevant? List any documents which may be relevant in an international sales contract.

C. 'Transfer of Property' in the Goods

The seller is also obliged to transfer the property in the goods. The transfer of property is not governed by the CISG (see Art 4(b)) and is thus subject to the law applicable under the rules of private international law of the forum. Domestic law, therefore, determines whether the property passes when the contract is concluded, which documents may be necessary for the transfer of property, and other related matters, especially the question of retention of title or other security interests of the seller (see in detail Art 4(b) CISG above).

However, whether a retention of title clause has been validly agreed upon in the sales contract and whether alleging a retention of title will constitute a breach of contract are matters that may be settled by reference to the CISG. For the common law approach, see Section 18, Rules 1 and 5(1) SGA and Section 2-401(2) UCC.

Sec 18, Rule 1 SGA:

> Where there is an unconditional contract for the sale of specific goods in a deliverable state the property in the goods passes to the buyer when the contract is made, and it is immaterial whether the time of payment or the time of delivery, or both, be postponed.

Sec 18, Rule 5(1) SGA:

> Where there is a contract for the sale of unascertained or future goods by description, and goods of that description and in a deliverable state are unconditionally appropriated to the contract, either by the seller with the assent of the buyer or by the buyer with the assent of the seller, the property in the goods then passes to the buyer; and the assent may be express or implied, and may be given either before or after the appropriation is made.

§ 2-401(2) UCC:

> Unless otherwise explicitly agreed title passes to the buyer at the time and place at which the seller completes his performance with reference to the physical delivery of the goods, despite any reservation of a Security interest and even though a document of title is to be delivered at a different time or place; and in particular and despite any reservation of a Security interest by the bill of lading
>
> (a) if the contract requires or authorises the seller to send the goods to the buyer but does not require him to deliver them at destination, title passes to the buyer at the time and place of shipment; but
> (b) if the contract requires delivery at destination, title passes on tender there.
>
> The continental European approach is demonstrated by § 929 BGB and Art 1583 CC.

§ 929 BGB:[97]

> Agreement and transfer. For the transfer of property in moveable goods, it is necessary that the owner hand over the goods to the purchaser and that both parties are in agreement that

---

[97] Author's translation.

property in the goods should be transferred. If the purchaser already has the goods in its possession, then agreement as to the transfer of property in the goods is sufficient.

Art 1583 CC:[98]

[The sale] is complete between the parties, and ownership is acquired as of right by the buyer with respect to the seller, as soon as the thing and the price have been agreed upon, although the thing has not yet been delivered or the price paid.

Question

Q 30-3

(a)   When does title pass to the buyer according to these domestic legal rules?
(b)   Which systems recognise a property transfer through the mere conclusion of a contract, and which require the actual handing over of the goods?
(c)   What system of property transfer does the US legal system apply?

---

[98] Translation taken from www.legifrance.gouv.fr.

Article 31 CISG

If the seller is not bound to deliver the goods at any other particular place, his obligation to deliver consists:

(a) if the contract of sale involves carriage of the goods—in handing the goods over to the first carrier for transmission to the buyer;

(b) if, in cases not within the preceding subparagraph, the contract relates to specific goods, or unidentified goods to be drawn from a specific stock or to be manufactured or produced, and at the time of the conclusion of the contract the parties knew that the goods were at, or were to be manufactured or produced at, a particular place—in placing the goods at the buyer's disposal at that place;

(c) in other cases—in placing the goods at the buyer's disposal at the place where the seller had his place of business at the time of the conclusion of the contract.

I. Overview

A. Content and Purpose of Article 31 CISG

Article 31 CISG specifies, in the absence of express or implied agreement by the parties on this point, both the content of the seller's delivery obligation and the place of performance of this obligation.

B. Domestic Laws

Domestic laws adopt diverging approaches to the content and the place of performance of the seller's delivery obligation.

(a) Carriage of the Goods

Under US law, Section 2-504 UCC sets out the seller's obligations.

§ 2-504 UCC:

> Where the seller is required or authorised to send the goods to the buyer and the contract does not require him to deliver them at a particular destination, then unless otherwise agreed he must
>
> (a)   put the goods in the possession of such a carrier and make such a contract for their transportation as may be reasonable having regard to the nature of the goods and other circumstances of the case; and
> (b)   obtain and promptly deliver or tender in due form any document necessary to enable the buyer to obtain possession of the goods or otherwise required by the agreement or by usage of trade; and
> (c)   promptly notify the buyer of the shipment. Failure to notify the buyer under paragraph (c) or to make a proper contract under paragraph (a) is a ground for rejection only if material delay or loss ensues.

The position is similar under Section 32 SGA and Article 141 PRC CL.

Sec 32(1) SGA:

> Where, in pursuance of a contract of sale, the seller is authorised or required to send the goods to the buyer, delivery of the goods to a carrier (whether named by the buyer or not) for the purpose of transmission to the buyer is prima facie deemed to be delivery of the goods to the buyer.

Art 141 PRC CL:[99]

> The seller shall deliver the subject matter at the prescribed place.
>
> Where the place of delivery was not prescribed or clearly prescribed, and cannot be determined in accordance with Article 61 hereof, the following provisions apply:
>
> (i)   If the subject matter needs carriage, the seller shall deliver the subject matter to the first carrier for transmission to the buyer. ...

(b) Delivery by Placing Goods at Buyer's Disposal

As a general rule, 'placing the goods at the buyer's disposal' also involves an obligation to notify the buyer. US law supports this position.

§ 2-503 UCC:

> (1)   Tender of delivery requires that the seller put and hold conforming goods at the buyer's disposition and give the buyer any notification reasonably necessary to enable him to take delivery. ...

The German law on this point is not as detailed because it merely focuses on a 'place for performance' (*Leistungsort*) of the contract.

---

[99] Translation taken from www.novexcn.com/contract_law_99.html.

§ 269(1) BGB:[100]

> If the place for performance is neither certain nor can be determined from the circumstances, particularly from the nature of the contractual relationship, then performance is to take place at the seller's place of residence at the time of the conclusion of the contract.

II. Article 31(a) CISG

Under Article 31(a) CISG, for contracts of sale involving the carriage of goods, subject to any other agreement, the seller delivers the goods for the purposes of the CISG when it hands them over to the first carrier for transmission to the buyer.

Questions

Q 31-1

(a)   When is delivery effected in cases of multiple carriers?
(b)   When is delivery effected in cases of transport by the seller's own employees?
(c)   When is delivery effected in handing goods over to a freight forwarder?

Q 31-2

Could delivery be effected in the case of non-conforming goods? Compare and contrast the CISG and the UCC in this respect.

C 31-1

Handelsgericht Zürich (Switzerland),
10 February 1999,
CISG-online 488[101]

[Facts]

1. [Seller's claim] During the years 1995 and 1996, the [seller]—and in part company A. S.p.A., who the [seller] merged with on 23 December 1995—received various commissions by the [buyer], who is acting as a publishing house for art books. The orders concerned the printing, binding and delivery of art books and catalogues. With his claim, [seller] demands payment of outstanding invoices regarding various commissions. The dates of the invoices

---

[100] Author's translation.
[101] Translation taken from CISG Pace (citations omitted).

submitted lie in the period between 24 October 1995 and 25 June 1996. The [buyer] does not deny that the contracts were formed and deliveries were made. However, [buyer] claims that she is able to set-off various claims for damages as well as reductions in price. The background of the dispute is the [buyer]'s allegation that the [seller] repeatedly failed to deliver art books, respectively art catalogues, in time for exhibition openings or presentations. [Buyer] claims that, as a result, she lost the trust of extremely important private art patrons and consequently suffered large damages. [...]

[Judgment]

[...]

3. Claims set off by the [buyer]

3.1 Christian Vogt 'In Camera' [...] d) aa) The buyer may claim damages under Art 45(1) (b) in connection with Arts 74–77 CISG, if the seller fails to perform his delivery obligation. In principle, the liability for damages is a liability for the guaranteed performance of the seller's obligations, which is independent of the seller's fault. In the meaning of this provision, 'obligations of the seller' are all obligations which the seller is subject to because of the specific legal transaction. They may result from an explicit provision or interpretation of the contract, from the supplementary provisions of the Convention as well as the relevant trade usages or the usages established between the parties. bb) Regarding the handing over of the goods, none of the parties plead that the [seller] was to perform the carriage of the goods. It is however disputed which party was to bear the risk for the forwarding agent. The [seller] is of the opinion that a dispatch ex-works was agreed upon. [Seller] submits that he organised the forwarder solely as a favor and without a corresponding obligation. The [buyer] in turn argues that the commission of the forwarding agency and the responsibility for its actions was the [seller]'s obligation. cc) Art 31 CISG, which deals with the content of the seller's delivery obligation, distinguishes between contracts that involve the carriage of goods and such contracts where carriage is not necessary. Art 31 CISG does not include a situation where the seller himself has to deliver the goods to one of the buyer's places of business. Such a form of delivery of the goods owed is not provided for in Art 31. In doubtful cases, such an obligation cannot be assumed: If the contract requires carriage of the goods at all, it is an obligation to dispatch the goods; in other cases the goods are to be placed at the buyer's disposal at the seller's place of business. The seller's delivery obligation therefore consists in initiating the transport of the goods: He must hand over the goods to the first carrier for transmission to the buyer. By handing over the goods to the carrier for transmission to the buyer, the seller fulfills his delivery obligation. For this reason, the buyer may no longer hold the seller liable for non-performance under Art 45(1)(b) CISG, if the goods are destroyed or misdirected during transport or if the handing over to the buyer is delayed. The carrier's mistakes are therefore not within the liability sphere of the seller. The question of whether the contract was fulfilled in time is therefore also determined by the timely dispatch and not by the time of arrival of the goods. dd) It is evident from the files and the corresponding statements of the parties that 28 September 1995 was agreed as 'ready for shipping'. The [buyer] does not plead that the seller did not keep to this date, instead [buyer] even acknowledges that the seller made the goods ready for dispatch in time. [Buyer] further does not contend that the [seller] accepted a contractual obligation to effect delivery of the goods at the place specified by the [buyer]; she solely holds the view that the [seller] assumed the organization and the responsibility for the forwarding agent. It is therefore undisputed that the [seller] on 28 September 1995 handed over the goods to the carrier commissioned by him. By this action, [seller] fulfilled his obligations under the law and therefore performed within time.

Question

Q 31-3

According to the above case (C 31-1), what situations are excluded from the scope of Article 31 CISG?

III. Article 31(b) and (c) CISG

Under Article 31(b) CISG, where specific goods or goods from a specific stock are contracted for and the parties knew at the time of the conclusion of the contract where these goods were held or produced, the seller fulfils its delivery obligation by placing the goods at the buyer's disposal at that place.

Questions

Q 31-4

Article 31(b) CISG covers four different scenarios. Describe these.

Q 31-5

Are goods in transit covered by Article 31(b) CISG?

Q 31-6

What does 'placing the goods at the buyer's disposal' actually mean?

If the contract does not require the goods to be transported, no specific place of delivery has been agreed, and the specific requirements of Article 31(b) CISG are not fulfilled, then the place of delivery is determined under Article 31(c) CISG. Here, the place of delivery and performance of the delivery obligation is the seller's place of business.

IV. INCOTERMS® and Article 31 CISG

Article 31 CISG only applies if the seller is 'not bound to deliver the goods at any other particular place'. If the place of delivery is determined by a delivery obligation under INCOTERMS®, and INCOTERMS® apply to the contract, an analysis of the interaction between INCOTERMS® and Article 31 CISG is required.

In a number of cases, the INCOTERMS® delivery terms lead to the same place of delivery and the same delivery obligations that would apply by default under Article 31 CISG. Since, in such a case, the parties have failed to agree upon 'another particular place', Article 31 CISG continues to apply and the relevant INCOTERMS® assume a merely supplementary function.

Cl A4 EXW INCOTERMS® (2010):

Delivery. The seller must deliver the goods by placing them at the disposal of the buyer at the agreed point, if any, at the named place of delivery, not loaded on any collecting vehicle. If no specific point has been agreed within the named place of delivery, and if there are several points available, the seller may select the point that best suits its purpose. The seller must deliver the goods on the agreed dated or within the agreed period.

Cl A4 CPT, CIP INCOTERMS® (2010):

Delivery. The seller must deliver the goods by handing them over to the carrier contracted in accordance with A3 on the agreed date or within the agreed period.

Question

Q 31-7

Compare the above provisions of INCOTERMS® to the provisions of Article 31 CISG. What are the similarities and differences?

V. Place of Performance as Place of Jurisdiction

In practice, establishing the place of performance under Article 31 CISG is not only of significance for the performance of the seller's obligations, but can also establish jurisdiction in some circumstances. If the civil procedural law applicable to disputes arising out of the contract provides for jurisdiction at the place of performance, and if the substantive law of the contract, which determines the place of performance, is the CISG, then the place of performance will be determined by reference to the place of the seller's delivery obligation under Article 31 CISG. In EU Member States, the 1968 Convention on jurisdiction and the enforcement of judgments in civil and commercial matters (the Brussels Convention) was recently replaced by the Council Regulation (EC) No 44/2001 on jurisdiction and the recognition and enforcement of judgments in civil and commercial disputes (the Brussels Regulation).

Art 5(1) Brussels Convention (1968):

A person domiciled in a Contracting State may, in another Contracting State, be sued:

1.   in matters relating to a contract, in the courts for the place of performance of the obligation in question; in matters relating to individual contracts of employment, this place is that where the employee habitually carries out his work, or if the employee does not habitually

carry out his work in any one country, the employer may also be sued in the courts for the place where the business which engaged the employee was or is now situated.

[...]

Art 5(1) Brussels Regulation (2001):

A person domiciled in a Member State may, in another Member State, be sued:

1. (a) in matters relating to a contract, in the courts for the place of performance of the obligation in question;
   (b) for the purpose of this provision and unless otherwise agreed, the place of performance of the obligation in question shall be:
       — in the case of the sale of goods, the place in a Member State where, under the contract, the goods were delivered or should have been delivered,
       — in the case of the provision of services, the place in a Member State where, under the contract, the services were provided or should have been provided,
   (c) if subparagraph (b) does not apply then subparagraph (a) applies.

C 31-2

Oberster Gerichtshof (Austria),
14 December 2004,
CISG-online 1018[102]

[Facts]

[Seller] seeks payment due to delivery of goods to the total amount of EUR 65,413.36. [Seller] asserts that due to an agreement upon the place of performance pursuant to Art 5(1)(b) Brussels Regulation, the Trial Court had jurisdiction. [Buyer] had ordered goods—among others laser devices—according to the usual practice between the parties. [Seller] had accepted the [buyer]'s offer by written confirmation. Usually the confirmation notice had contained the terms 'EXW W [a location in Austria]' and 'LIEU DE PAIEMENT ET TRIBUNAL: W'. Even if one assumes no agreement on the place of performance, pursuant to Art 5(1)(b) Brussels Regulation in connection with 31 CISG, W was the place where the [Seller] handed the goods to the carrier, likewise the place of delivery. Apart from that, the order confirmation contained the express reference to the Incoterm CPT ('Carriage paid to'). Thus, the place of delivery was the place where the goods were handed to the carrier. [Buyer] objects the jurisdiction of the Trial Court because W neither was the stipulated nor the actual place of performance. The goods were handed to the [Buyer] in Italy; the actual place of delivery was located there. [Buyer] alleges that [Buyer]'s place of business has to serve as place of performance. [Seller] effected the transmission to this destination by contracting with a carrier.

---

[102] Translation taken from CISG Pace (citations omitted).

[Judgment]

The Austrian Trial Court held that it is competent to hear the case. It ascertained that an established business relationship existed between [Seller] and [Buyer]. In total, eleven invoices or confirmation letters, respectively, were exchanged between the parties during the period between 24 January and 10 June 2002. All of them contained the term 'LIEU DE PAIEMENT ET TRIBUNAL COMPETENT: W'. In addition to this, these documents contained several references to terms of delivery (Incoterms®), so that W__ was agreed upon as place of performance. Apart from that, [the Austrian location] W __ also was the forum of the place of performance pursuant to Art 5(1)(b) Brussels Regulation.

The Appellate Court reversed the decision of the Trial Court and dismissed the claim. It held that the appeal against its decision is admissible. The rules of the Brussels Regulation, which prevail the domestic law, were to apply exclusively. Accordingly, the claim must be lodged at the place of residence, unless Arts 5 to 24 Brussels Regulation provide otherwise. For sales contracts, Art 5(1) Brussels Regulation stipulates that the place of performance must be determined autonomously by means of actual criteria. All contractual claims can be lodged at this place. The default rule of Art 5(1) Brussels Regulation does not govern if the parties agreed upon the place of performance. The adoption of the Brussels Regulation was accompanied by the idea to prevent determination of the place of performance according to the lex causa. First and foremost, one always has to establish whether the parties have agreed upon the place of performance. If they did not do so, the place of performance, unless the goods were already delivered, is where the goods had to be delivered according to the contract. In case of successful delivery and [Buyer]'s acceptance of the goods, the actual place of handing over the good is decisive. The agreement upon the place of delivery, which then also serves as place of performance can be made by incorporating Incoterms®. These are established terms for use in contracts, to which reference can be made by stating the full title of the term, supplemented by the chosen place, or by reference to the three letter abbreviation offered for every term. However, it is not beyond doubt whether Incoterms® can be treated as common law or established trade usage. The validity of an agreement is governed by the proper substantial law. Since Austria and Italy were Contracting States to the CISG, this Convention was to govern the agreement upon the place of business. Pursuant to Art 14 CISG, a contract is concluded by offer and acceptance. The incorporation of terms into the contract requires the user's intent to make them part of the offer, which must be known to the other party, and the other party's acceptance. A reply that deviates from the content of the offer is a rejection and constitutes a counter-offer, Art 19 CISG. To conclude a contract, the counter-offer itself needs to be accepted. Only mutually agreed terms shall be effective. The [Seller] did not rely on an agreement upon the forum pursuant to Art 23 Brussels Regulation. The [Seller] assumed the agreement upon the place of performance due to the established practice of [Buyer] ordering goods and [Seller] accepting by means of order confirmations. These confirmations usually contained Incoterms® referring to [the Austrian location] Wels as the place of performance. Opposed to the eleven invoices on which the payment that is sought is based, there are only three order confirmations. That is why the assertion of the [Seller] that it replied to the [Buyer]'s offers by order confirmation was only true concerning these three cases. Especially the most mature part-claim (and invoice) was not accompanied by an order confirmation. A contract cannot be concluded by invoices only; three order confirmations as such cannot establish a practice between the parties, since in multiple cases the order was not replied by a confirmation. Consequently, one cannot assume that the [Buyer] implicitly consented to a modification of the contract. For that reason, the [Seller] cannot rely on the incorporation of terms which were indicated on the three order confirmations. The [Seller] failed to prove an effective agreement upon the place of performance. Accordingly, the default rule of Art 5(1)(b) applies. The destination of the supplies was Italy. The [Seller] placed the transmission order under the Incoterm 'CPT'. Due to the lack of agreement upon the place of performance, this would mean that pursuant to Art 31(a) CISG, the place of performance is located at the [Seller]'s place of business. However, for reasons of the place of performance pursuant to Art 5(1)(b) Brussels Regulation, the lex causa is not decisive. The place of performance needs to be determined autonomously by means of actual criteria. In any event, [the Austrian location] W was not the actual place of delivery. That is why the [Austrian] Trial Court had no jurisdiction to hear the case. The [Seller]'s appeal is admissible but unfounded. As to [Seller]'s assertion that by way of incorporating the mentioned Incoterms®, the parties have agreed upon W as the place of performance, the Appellate Court correctly held that the invoices and three order confirmations displaying the terms, do not amount to an agreement upon the place of performance. ... Where, like here, the place of performance was not agreed upon separately, then pursuant to Art 5(1)(b) Brussels Regulation, the place of performance for obligations under a sale of movable goods is the place where, according to the contract, the goods were delivered or where they had to be delivered. Opposed to Art 5 Brussels Convention, which assigns the determination of the place of performance to the proper national law, for sales contracts this place now needs to be determined by use of actual criteria. For procedural reasons, place of performance is the place where the characteristic obligation was performed or needed to be performed. The place where the performance regarding the goods in fact was executed, represents the decisive criteria for ascertaining the international jurisdiction [...]. The place of delivery is to be understood in the actual sense of the wording. It is the place where the buyer takes delivery and confirms the conformity of the goods. Usually, this is the place of delivery agreed upon by the parties. ... Since the goods were transmitted to the place of business of the [Buyer] in Italy, it is certain that the parties have agreed upon this place to be the place of destination. There is no indication to the effect that the parties to the contract have chosen the place where the [Seller] handed over to goods to the carrier to serve as the place of performance. For that reason, the place where the goods were actually destined is the decisive place of performance. ... The national rules governing the place of performance for mail-order purchases are irrelevant, since they were contrary to the provisions of the Brussels Regulation and would introduce the criteria of the lex causa. The governing idea is that the place of performance is determined by facts and is not subject to legal criteria. ... Commentators—particularly due to the ill-drafted wording of Art 5(1)(b) Brussels Regulation—expresses opposing views. ... The court however cannot follow these views, since these interpretations were contrary to the intention of the drafter to determine the place of performance for reasons of jurisdiction autonomously and without recourse to national substantive law. [...]

Questions

Q 31-8

Compare and contrast Article 5(1) Brussels Convention with Article 5(1) Brussels Regulation.

Q 31-9

How is the relationship between jurisdictional seat and place of performance resolved under Article 5(1) Brussels Convention and Article 31 CISG?

Q 31-10

What actions are governed by Article 5(1) Brussels Regulation in the case of the sale of goods?

Q 31-11

How does Article 5(1) Brussels Regulation define the place of performance for contracts involving the sale of goods?

Q 31-12

(a)   What do the above cases have to say regarding the interaction between Article 5(1) Brussels Convention, Article 5(1) Brussels Regulation and the CISG?
(b)   Is this convincing?

Article 32 CISG

(1) If the seller, in accordance with the contract or this Convention, hands the goods over to a carrier and if the goods are not clearly identified to the contract by markings on the goods, by shipping documents or otherwise, the seller must give the buyer notice of the consignment specifying the goods.

(2) If the seller is bound to arrange for carriage of the goods, he must make such contracts as are necessary for carriage to the place fixed by means of transportation appropriate in the circumstances and according to the usual terms for such transportation.

(3) If the seller is not bound to effect insurance in respect of the carriage of the goods, he must, at the buyer's request, provide him with all available information necessary to enable him to effect such insurance.

I. Overview

Article 32 CISG elaborates on the additional obligations of the seller in situations where carriage of the goods is involved. Under Article 32(1) CISG, the seller has an obligation to notify the buyer of the consignment specifying the goods in the absence of other clear identification. Under Article 32(2) CISG, if the parties have agreed that the seller is to be responsible for arranging carriage of the goods, then it is under an obligation to conclude the appropriate contracts. Under Article 32(3) CISG, to the extent that the seller is not responsible for insuring the goods, it is obliged to provide the buyer with all the information needed to enable it to insure the goods. Again, whether the provisions of Article 32 CISG can actually be applied, depends upon the agreement between the parties and the remainder of the Convention.

II. Article 32(1) CISG

Article 32(1) CISG only applies to cases in which the seller delivers the goods by handing them over to a carrier for transmission to the buyer. Whether the seller 'delivers' by this act will be determined by reference to the contract between the parties, or to the Convention.

Cl A7 FOB INCOTERMS® (2010):

Notice to the buyer. The seller must, at the buyer's risk and expense, give the buyer sufficient notice either that the goods have been delivered in accordance with A4 or that the vessel has failed to take the goods within the time agreed.

Cl A4 FOB INCOTERMS® (2010):

Delivery. The seller must deliver the goods either by placing them on board the vessel nominated by the buyer at the loading point, if any, indicated by the buyer at the named port of shipment or by procuring the goods so delivered. In either case, the seller must deliver the goods on the agreed date or within the agreed period and in the manner customary at the port.

If no specific loading point has been indicated by the buyer, the seller may select the point within the named port of shipment that best suits its purpose.

Questions

Q 32-1

What circumstances require a notice of dispatch?

Q 32-2

Compare Article 32(1) CISG with the notice and delivery provisions of the FOB clause of INCOTERMS® (2010).

Q 32-3

What consequences does the giving of notice have for the passing of the risk in the goods? See also the discussion on Article 67(2) CISG below.

III. Article 32(2) CISG

Article 32(2) CISG clarifies that, to the extent that the seller has to arrange for the carriage of the goods, the conclusion of a contract of carriage comprises part of this obligation.

C 32-1

Bezirksgericht Saane (Switzerland),
20 February 1997,
CISG-online 426

[Facts][103]

An Austrian company, plaintiff, entered into a contract for the purchase and transport of spirits to Russia with the Swiss branch of a company that had its headquarters in Liechtenstein. The contract was never performed because a dispute arose among the parties regarding the mode of transport and the final date of performance. The Austrian buyer sued the Swiss seller for repayment of an advance payment, while the defendant claimed damages for breach of contract. [...] The factual issue in dispute was whether the parties had agreed that the goods were to be transported by truck, as the buyer claimed, or whether the choice of the mode of transport had been left to the seller. The court held that, as the CISG does not contain rules on the burden of proof, it is necessary to rely on the rules of private international law of the forum, which, in this case, led to the application of Swiss domestic law (article 7(2) CISG). Since the buyer was unable to meet the burden of proof evidencing an agreement to transport the goods by truck, the court found that the choice of transportation mode had been left to the seller (article 32(2) CISG).

[Judgment][104]

After the [buyer] had contacted the [seller], the [seller] submitted a written offer within a pro-forma invoice dated 17 December 1993. The [buyer] countersigned this written offer and sent it back to the [seller] on 17 December 1993. Therefore, the parties entered into an agreement. Thereby, the parties agreed upon:

— The form, kind and quantity of the product (300,000 one-litre bottles of 'Alkohol Royal Feinsprit 96%');
— The price as consideration (acquisition and transportation price in total: US$ 339,000); and
— The destination for delivery of the goods sold (Moscow). The parties further agreed to the following prerequisites for the goods to be delivered ex factory by 15 January 1994 at the latest:
— A payment on the [seller]'s account to be effected in the amount of 7% of the overall purchase price due, i.e., US$ 23,730 on 17 December 1993; and
— A letter of credit (irrevocable, confirmed, transferable and divisible) to be opened with a western European universal bank, whereby this letter of credit should be payable at the delivery of the goods ex factory and presentation of the relevant CMR documents. In the light of those further agreements, the parties also agreed on (i) the amount that the [buyer] should pay in advance, (ii) the time period for the delivery of the goods, (iii) the place for and date of payment as well as (iv) the mode of payment. However, the parties did not agree in writing on the mode of transportation and the period for the delivery of the goods.

---

[103] Summary of facts taken from UNILEX.
[104] Translation taken from CISG Pace (citations omitted).

4.1 [Legal classification of the sales contract] The agreement, which the parties entered into on 17 December 1993, is to be classified as an international sales contract (delivery of and transfer of title on the goods against payment of the purchase price).

The Court found that the CISG was applicable.

[...]

The District Court can base its decision on the issue whether or not the parties agreed to a specific mode of transportation merely on the presented documents and files besides the opposing statements of the parties:

aa) [Impact of the CIF clause to the question whether or not there is an agreement to a specific mode of transportation]

In the pro-forma invoice, the parties agreed that the purchase price for the sold goods should be US$ 339,000. The parties further agreed therein that this purchase price is calculated on the basis as being 'CIF Moscow'. The [seller] argues that this provision means that the purchase price payable under the sales contract comprises 'all costs for the goods sold, for their insurance and for the freight to the main station of Moscow'. According to Incoterms® 1990, this CIF clause refers to an offshore or inland transportation on vessels and shall mean: 'Cost, Insurance and Freight ... (named port of destination).' In the light of such a CIF clause, the risk of loss of the goods should pass to the [buyer] at the place of delivery. The purchase price should include all costs for the delivery of the goods to the specified place of destination and the [seller] is to have the goods insured. Since Moscow is not a seaport, the CIF clause could not mean that the goods should be transported on a vessel. Consequently, the provision in the pro-forma invoice ('the price is calculated on the basis as being CIF Moscow') shall mean that, on the one hand, the purchase price of US$ 339,000 includes all transportation costs; and, on the other hand, this provision addresses the place for delivery, the pass over of the risk of extinction, the costs for and the insurance of the goods. However, this CIF clause does not give any hints to the agreed mode of transportation.

bb) [Impact of a new submitted offer of the seller to the aforementioned question]

In the [seller]'s fax dated 21 December 1993, he stated the quantity of the goods, sold under the sales contract, as '14,000 bottles/container, 2 Container/truck.' Therein, the [seller] explicitly defined the mode of transportation. But the purchase price of DM 615,000, as stated therein, was not in compliance with the already agreed purchase price for the goods, as set forth in the pro-forma invoice of 17 December 1993. According to an assumed average exchange rate between DM and US$ at 1.7097 in December 1993, this altered purchase price corresponded to a total amount of US$ 359,712.20, i.e., US$ 1.199 per bottle of Alkohol Royal Feinsprit. The [buyer] has never accepted this new and altered offer of the [seller].

cc) [Impact of [D]'s letter of 27 December 1993 to the aforementioned question]

[D] was the company that charged [mandated] the [buyer] to acquire and arrange the transportation of the goods. In the light of the letter [D] addressed and sent to the [buyer] dated 27 December 1993, one has to conclude that [D] did not make a decision in respect of the mode of transportation to be used under the sales contract. In fact, [D] expressly excluded therein a combined transportation by train and truck. However, [D] did not stipulate a specific mode of transportation. Therefore, this issue was still unsettled. [D] did not clarify which mode of transportation should be used instead of a combined transportation for the delivery of the goods under the sales contract. One concludes the aforementioned fact of lack of clarification by [D] according to No. 2 of the aforementioned letter. Therein, [D] stipulated that the goods should be transported exclusively by truck, only if [D] determined that such a mode of transportation should be used. Furthermore, [D] asked for the costs of transportation by train calculated on a basis as being CIF Chop, CIF Moscow, or CIF Irkutsk. The fact that [D] as the [buyer]'s mandator mentioned the expression 'CIF Moscow' with regard to a transportation of goods by train, can be interpreted in two different ways: This fact may indicate either that the abbreviation 'CIF' did not have any impact to a possible agreement between the [seller] and the [buyer] to a specific mode of transportation, or that the parties also considered transportation by train through the expression 'CIF Moscow', as used in the pro-forma invoice of 17 December 1993. In her letter of 31 December 1993, the [buyer] asked the [seller] to submit a new offer for the transportation of the goods by truck calculated on the basis as being 'CIF Moscow.' Therein, the [seller] should separately indicate the price for the transportation. The [seller] responded and informed the [buyer] that the net sum, to be paid for one litre of the goods ex factory, was US$ 0.99. Transportation of the goods to Moscow might amount to DM 12,000 or DM 13,000 per truck. However, it is extremely burdensome to organise trucks, hence the [seller] is only in the position to deliver the goods sold by train (container) (act. 3/15). The [seller] submitted a new and revised offer to the [buyer] in his letter of 7 January 1994. Thereupon, the [seller] might only sell the Alkohol Royal Feinsprit on the term ex factory for a purchase price of US$ 0.99 (in total: US$ 297,000) and the [buyer] should be obliged to pay the transportation costs, i.e., US$ 0.24 per litre, directly to the relevant carrier. The [seller] gave reasons for this new offer insofar as the increased transportation costs might not be covered by the agreed purchase price of US$ 1.13 (in total: US$ 339,000). Hence, in the light of a transportation by truck, the purchase price amounts to US$ 0.99 plus additional transportation costs of US$ 0.24 (total sum: US$ 1.23 per litre).

The [buyer] rejected this offer too, because it was not in compliance with the agreed provisions of 17 December 1993. The [buyer] in her letter of 9 January 1994 requested that the [seller] enter into a sales contract directly with 'G. T D i A' in respect of the 300,000 litres of Alkohol Royal Feinsprit. Thereupon, the goods should be delivered by exclusively truck and the purchase price should amount to US$ 1.21 (in total: US$ 363,000). The [seller] did not even react to this request. All activities of the parties, as carried out after 21 December 1993, indicate that both parties petitioned for a supplement to the sales contract of 17 December insofar as they both wanted to agree on a specific mode of transportation by truck. The parties could not agree by virtue of dissenting opinions in respect of the purchase price. Under the assumption of a fixed sales price of US$ 297,000 for the Alkohol Royal Feinsprit, one can ascertain that the transportation costs—as indicated in the [seller]'s offer letters dated 21 December 1993 and 7 January 1994 and in the [buyer]'s offer letter of 9 January 1994—were approximately US$ 20,000 or US$ 30,000 more expensive than the transportation costs as indicated in the pro-forma invoice. Such a great difference might be an indication that the purchase price of US$ 339,000, as set out in the pro-forma invoice, could not have included transportation by truck. The statements of the parties are in opposition to each other in respect of the agreed mode of transportation. In the light of the files of the Court, there are even more indications for than against [the conclusion] that the parties did not agree to transportation by truck within the pro-forma invoice of 17 December 1993. The District Court, however, has not reached the necessary certainty regarding this issue which is in dispute between the parties. As a result, the general rules for the allocation of the onus of proof do apply. The CISG does not contain any rules regarding the onus of proof. Therefore, one has to reconsider the private international law of the relevant jurisdiction of the lawsuit pursuant to Art 7(2) (Second part) CISG. According to Art 118 IPRG in connection with Art 3 S. 2 Hague Convention, Swiss substantive and procedural law is applicable. According to Art 8 ZGB, the party that asserts the existence of a fact and claims to derive any rights from this fact bears the onus of proof, unless as otherwise provided by law.

ee) [Conclusion of the Court regarding the choice of the mode of transportation] The [buyer] has not given evidence for the fact, on which her claim is inter alia founded, that the parties in their agreement of 17 December 1993 agreed to an exclusive transportation of the goods by truck. Hence, the [buyer] has to bear the consequences of this lack of giving evidence

(BGE 107 II 275). As a result, the dispositive law of the CISG is applicable in this case, in particular, Art 32(2) CISG. Under Art 32 CISG, a seller who is obliged to provide for the transportation and delivery of the goods, must enter into any agreements which might be necessary to meet his obligation, i.e., the transportation of the goods to the determined destination. Thereby, a seller has to choose such a means of transportation as appears appropriate in the specific circumstances and necessary to the general terms for such transportation. In this case, the [seller] had to provide for the transportation and delivery of the goods. The District Court gathers the aforementioned fact from the statements of the parties in the hearing of the Court of 19 June 1996 as well as from the correspondence of the parties after 17 December 1993. Hence, the choice of the mode of transportation was in the [seller]'s own discretion, who, in opposition to the [buyer], already had experience with regard to transactions with Alkohol Royal Feinsprit in Russia. Therefore, one cannot blame the [seller] with an anticipated breach of contract because of his choice of the mode of transportation, i.e., transportation of the goods by train.

[...]

Cl A3 CFR, CIF INCOTERMS® (2010):

Contracts of carriage and insurance.

a) Contract of carriage. The seller must contract or procure a contract for the carriage of the goods from the agreed point of delivery, if any, at the place of delivery to the named port of destination or, if agreed, any point at that port. The contract of carriage must be made on usual terms at the seller's expense and provide for carriage by the usual route in a vessel of the type normally used for the transport of the type of goods sold.

[...]

Cl A3 CPT, CIP INCOTERMS® (2010):

Contracts of carriage and insurance.

a) Contract of carriage. The seller must contract or procure a contract for the carriage of the goods from the agreed point of delivery, if any, at the place of delivery to the named place of destination or, if agreed, any point at that place. The contract of carriage must be made on usual terms at the seller's expense and provide for carriage by the usual route and in a customary manner. If a specific point is not agreed or is not determined by practice, the seller may select the point of delivery and the point at the named place of destination that best suit its purpose.

[...]

Question

Q 32-4

How did the court interpret 'appropriate means of transportation' in the above case (C 32-1)?

Article 33 CISG

The seller must deliver the goods:

(a) if a date is fixed by or determinable from the contract, on that date;
(b) if a period of time is fixed by or determinable from the contract, at any time within that period unless circumstances indicate that the buyer is to choose a date; or
(c) in any other case, within a reasonable time after the conclusion of the contract.

I. Overview

Article 33 CISG specifies the time within which the seller is to fulfil its obligation to deliver the goods. Here again, it is primarily up to the parties to fix a date or a time for performance in their individual contract. Only in cases where no delivery date has been contractually agreed will the CISG 'step in' with the standard of 'reasonable time' for performance after the conclusion of the contract.

Question

Q 33-1

(a) What do you believe is the purpose of a provision like Article 33 in the CISG?
(b) For which of the buyer's rights is it significant?

II. Article 33(a) CISG

Under Article 33(a) CISG, the seller is obliged to deliver goods on the date fixed or determined by the contract. Thereby, reference is not only to be had to contracts in which the date is expressly stipulated, but also to implicit determinations on a construction of the contractual terms. This subsection also covers the situation where the buyer is to 'call up' the goods.

Question

Q 33-2

What kind of circumstances could give rise to a determination of the date by reference to the contractual terms?

III. Article 33(b) CISG

Article 33(b) CISG requires the seller to make delivery within a contractually-agreed fixed period of time. In such a case, the right to choose an actual date of delivery within the agreed fixed period generally rests with the seller.

Questions

Q 33-3

Under which circumstances might the right to choose the date for delivery lie with the buyer?

Q 33-4

Look at the following examples and state whether, in your opinion, each one falls within the ambit of Article 33(a) or Article 33(b) CISG:

(a) 'Wednesday after Easter';
(b) 'Within 10 days after Easter';
(c) 'At the latest 10 days after sight of sample'.

IV. Article 33(c) CISG

Article 33(c) CISG applies where, based upon the contract between the parties, neither (a) nor (b) can be used. In this case, reference is made to a reasonable time after the conclusion of the contract, within which the seller is to effect delivery. What is reasonable will depend on the circumstances of the individual case.

The following cases provide guidance as to the interpretation of this obligation in the case of seasonal goods.

C 33-1

Audiencia Provincial de Barcelona (Spain), 20 June 1997, CISG-online 338

[Facts][105]

The dispute concerns a possible lack of conformity of textile dyes supplied late by the foreign seller to the Spanish buyer. The buyer's judicial claim for damages was not admitted by the Court.

[Judgment][106]

[...]

II. Having reviewed all the submissions and the judgment of the Court below, the [buyer's] appeal must be rejected. This Court agrees with the factual and legal reasoning of the Court of First Instance.

The evidence shows that both parties maintained commercial relationships, that [seller] supplied goods, and that [buyer] did not pay for them. [Buyer] alleges that he did not need to pay for them since [seller] had previously breached the contract. This breach had allegedly two aspects: first, there was a late dispatch of the goods, and second, the goods that arrived were defective and not fit for the purpose for which they had been ordered. Regarding the first reason, according to the abundant documentary evidence provided by the parties, the usual practice was that [buyer] would place the order. [Seller] would then confirm it and would indicate the date of dispatch. This was not the case with the orders numbers 256, 257 and 258, because the proximity of Christmas meant that the supplier could not undertake to dispatch the goods on a specific date, and did not do so. The last dispatch was received by [buyer] in January 1993, and was accepted without any objection. In the trade of printing seasonal fabrics, time is an important consideration. However, there is no doubt that, since there was no specific date fixed for the arrival of the goods, one must turn to Article 33(c) of the Vienna Convention on the International Sale of Goods (11 April 1980). According to that Article, in the absence of an express agreement, the [seller] should deliver the merchandise in 'a reasonable time' after the formation of the contract, as it was done in this case. It is common ground that the goods were accepted by the [buyer].

Question

Q 33-5

(a) Which aspects did the court consider relevant in assessing the 'reasonable time' in the above case (C 33-1)?
(b) How is this reconcilable with the general notion of 'reasonableness' under the CISG?

---

[105] Summary of facts taken from UNILEX.
[106] Translation taken from CISG Pace (citations omitted).

C 33-2

Oberlandesgericht Naumburg (Germany),
27 April 1999,
CISG-online 512

[Facts][107]

A German buyer and a Danish seller concluded a contract for the sale of a car. Pursuant to the offer of the buyer, the seller was to deliver the car within March 1997. The seller sent the buyer a confirmation of order in which April 1997 was the time of delivery and reserved the right to change the period of delivery. The buyer signed this confirmation and sent it back to the seller without objecting to the discrepancy. In the middle of March, the buyer informed the seller that it would declare the contract avoided, if the car would not be delivered by the end of March. In April 1997, the buyer declared the contract avoided, as the car had not been delivered yet. In the middle of May 1997, the seller informed the buyer that the car was ready to be collected. After fixing several periods for payment and collection, the seller entered into a replacement sale at a lower price. The seller sued the buyer claiming payment of the difference and alleged that no time for delivery had been fixed in the contract and that it had never received a declaration of avoidance.

[Judgment][108]

[...] On the other hand, the alteration does not bring forward a fixed date for delivery and because the stipulated delivery period was qualified as 'reserved', the date is not determinable from the contract (Art 33 (a) CISG). Thus the delivery was to be effected within a reasonable time after the conclusion of the contract (Art 33(c) CISG). The contract was concluded with the receipt of [seller's] acceptance on 29 January 1997. While the [buyer's] request for delivery no later than 15 March 1997 did not become part of the contract, it has to be considered in determining the reasonable time for performance under Art 33(c) CISG. Because it was clearly important to the [buyer] that the delivery take place within this time frame (29 January 1997–15 March 1997), the [seller] would have had to deliver by that date in order to have delivered within a reasonable time. It is irrelevant whether delivery delays of two to four weeks are common in the international sale of vehicles. When determining a reasonable time for delivery, it is of the essence to consider the statements of the parties and the concrete contractual circumstances. A delivery by 15 May or 3 June would no longer have been reasonable. ... The appeal thus was denied.

Question

Q 33-6

(a)   Do you agree with the provision that the court in C 33-2 relied on?
(b)   Why or why not?
(c)   Do you agree with the interpretation of the 'delivery date'?

---

[107] Summary of facts taken from UNILEX.
[108] Translation taken from CISG Pace (citations omitted).

C 33-3

*Alpha Prime Development Corporation v Holland
Loader Company, LLC,*
US Dist Ct (Col), 6 July 2010,
CISG-online 2111[109]

OPINION

ORDER ON MOTION FOR PARTIAL SUMMARY JUDGMENT

I. Introduction

THIS MATTER is before the Court on Plaintiff's Motion for Partial Summary Judgment and Supporting Memorandum filed October 2, 2009. This motion seeks summary judgment on the first claim for relief for delivery of nonconforming goods against [Seller].

Plaintiff [Buyer] asserts that summary judgment on the first claim is proper based on Seller's admitted failure to deliver a refurbished piece of coal mining equipment—termed a 'Holland 610 Loader' ['Loader']—that [Buyer] purchased from [Seller] and [Seller]'s admitted refusal to refund [Buyer]'s money. [Buyer] seeks judgment in the amount of $552,344.50 plus pre-judgment interest, which includes the purchase price of the equipment ($475,000) and costs associated with delivery.

[...]

[Buyer] claims, however, that even if the parties agreed that the Loader was to be refurbished in Mexico, summary judgment is still appropriate. It relies on the provision that when a contract governed by the CISG does not fix a particular date or period of time for delivery of goods, '[t]he seller must deliver the goods ... within a reasonable time after the conclusion of the contract.' CISG Art 33. [Buyer] asserts that in no way can it be a reasonable time for delivery of the goods since the Loader was purchased in July 2008 and was still not delivered in May 2009 when [Buyer] asserts that it exercised its right to avoid the contract (and in fact, the Loader has still not been delivered).

Turning to my analysis, '[w]hat is a reasonable time depends on what constitutes acceptable commercial conduct in the circumstances of the case.' Official Commentary to 1978 Draft of CISG Art 33, P 8, reprinted at 2 Guide to the Int'l Sale of Goods Convention 20-240 (West 2009). Again, I find that there are genuine issues of material fact that preclude entry of judgment as to this issue, i.e., whether under the circumstances of this case [Seller] acted within a reasonable time frame as to delivery of the Loader. There is evidence in the record that the refurbishing would take some time (120 to 180 days) and that [Buyer] had indicated to [Seller] that it had no immediate need for the Loader due to a purported lack of commercially viable surface mineable coal in its Mexican concessions. Under these circumstances, a reasonable jury could find that [Seller]'s delay in refurbishing the Loader was reasonable. There is also the fact that in May 2009 [Buyer] indicated that it rejected the goods; if this is the case [Seller] arguably no longer had a duty to deliver the Loader to [Buyer]. Accordingly, I also deny summary judgment on this issue. See, e.g., *Gonzales v Duran*, 590 F.3d 855, 861 (10th Cir. 2009) (a jury question exists 'when a disputed issues of material fact concerning the objective reasonableness of the defendant's actions exists') (quotation omitted); *Trout*

---

[109] Case taken from UNILEX.

v Nationwide Mut. Ins. Co., 316 Fed. Appx. 797, 2009 WL 721551, at *5 (10th Cir. 2009) (reasonableness of defendant's conduct 'is a quintessential jury question which we would expect to survive summary judgment'); *Yumukoglu v Provident Life & Acc. Ins. Co.*, 36 Fed. Appx. 378, 2002 WL 1150814, at *3 (10th Cir. 2002) (reasonableness is generally a question for the jury). [...]

Question

Q 33-7

What factors did the court consider in the above case (C 33-3) to determine whether or not a 'reasonable time' was complied with under Article 33(c) CISG?

Article 34 CISG

If the seller is bound to hand over documents relating to the goods, he must hand them over at the time and place and in the form required by the contract. If the seller has handed over documents before that time, he may, up to that time, cure any lack of conformity in the documents, if the exercise of this right does not cause the buyer unreasonable inconvenience or unreasonable expense. However, the buyer retains any right to claim damages as provided for in this Convention.

I. Overview

A. Content and Purpose of Article 34 CISG

Article 34 CISG specifies the seller's duty to deliver documents, provided such an obligation exists under the contract. According to the first sentence, the delivery of such documents is to take place in conformity with the contract. If the seller has delivered non-conforming documents before the date contractually agreed, it may cure the lack of conformity before this date, provided that this is possible without causing the buyer unreasonable inconvenience or expense.

B. Domestic Laws

Most domestic legal systems do not contain an explicit provision regulating the seller's obligation to hand over documents, nor any explanation as to the consequences of breach. However, the principle of party autonomy certainly allows the parties to agree upon the delivery of documents in their individual circumstances.

§ 2-503(5) UCC:

> Where the contract requires the seller to deliver documents
>
> (a) he must tender all such documents in correct form [...]
> (b) tender through customary banking channels is sufficient and dishonor of a draft accompanying the documents constitutes non-acceptance or rejection.

C. Drafting History

The first sentence of Article 34 CISG is essentially the same as Article 50 ULIS. The requirement that the contract be decisive for the form of handing over has been added; however, the predominant view in both ULIS and CISG is that this sentence is only there for clarification purposes. In contrast to Article 50 ULIS, the reference to trade usages has been omitted.

Questions

Q 34-1

Which documents does Article 34 CISG relate to?

Q 34-2

(a)   Do you think that trade usages could still be relevant in the context of Article 34 CISG?
(b)   Why or why not?

II. Time, Place and Form of Handing over Documents

Article 34 CISG places an obligation on the seller to hand over the 'documents relating to the goods' at the time and place and in the form set out in the parties' contract.

C 34-1

International Court of Commercial Arbitration Chamber of Commerce and Industry of the Russian Federation, Award No 27/2001, 24 January 2002, CISG-online 887[110]

[Facts]

[Buyer], a Russian firm, brought the claim against [Seller], a Hungarian firm based on the contract for the international sale of goods made by the parties on 12 October 1999. The claim was brought because the [Buyer], who made a 100% advance payment for the goods to be delivered CIP place of destination in Russia as required by the contract, did not receive the

---

[110] Translation taken from CISG Pace (citations omitted).

goods. The goods were delayed during the transportation and kept at a customs warehouse at a transit point in Russia. The [Buyer] demanded a refund of the payment for the goods as well as penalties for the delay in delivery. In the [Buyer]'s opinion, his claims are reasonable since the [Seller] failed to make a delivery to the place of destination stated in the contract. The [Seller] contested the [Buyer]'s claim. The [Seller] argued that he duly fulfilled all the obligations under the contract.

[Judgment]

[...]

3.3 The dispute between the parties concerns division of obligations between the seller and buyer under their contract for the international sale of goods. In the [Buyer]'s opinion, the [Seller] failed to fulfill his obligations and did not deliver the goods to the place of destination agreed upon and [this circumstance] gives the [Buyer] the right to demand a refund of the price of goods paid by the [Buyer] in advance. Non-delivery of the goods resulted from failure to carry out customs formalities required to import the goods into the [Buyer]'s country. [...]

Article 34 CISG sets forth the [...] obligation of the seller to hand over to the buyer the documents relating to the goods. Pursuant to Article 34, if the seller is bound to hand over documents relating to the goods, he must hand them over at the time and place and in the form required by the contract. As follows from the materials of the case and from the arguments made by the parties' representatives at the proceeding, the [Seller] fulfilled this obligation when he handed over an airway bill and other documents to the [Buyer]'s representative. [The representative] was authorised by the [Buyer] to assist in carrying out customs formalities required to import the goods and in delivering the goods to the place of destination agreed upon. The [Buyer] has submitted no evidence denying the fact that the [Seller] handed over to the [Buyer]'s representative the documents relating to the goods. For the above stated reasons, the Tribunal comes to the conclusion that the Respondent [Seller] has fulfilled his obligations under the contract, CISG and INCOTERMS®-90. [...]

Question

Q 34-3

Which documents were required to be delivered under the contract discussed in the above case (C 34-1)?

III. Seller's Right to Cure

The second sentence of Article 34 CISG clarifies that a seller who has handed over non-conforming documents 'early' has the right to cure the lack of conformity until the time for handing over agreed upon in the contract.

Questions

Q 34-4

(a)   Which trade sectors would generally displace the dispositive rule of the second sentence of Article 34 CISG?
(b)   Why?
(c)   Must this be done contractually, or is there another way?

Q 34-5

Is the inclusion of Article 34 in the CISG necessary at all? Why or why not?

Q 34-6

Do you think the CISG is suited to deal with documentary sales? Why or why not?

For details as to the content of the seller's right to cure after the date for delivery has passed, please refer to the discussion on Article 48 CISG below.

Article 35 CISG

(1) The seller must deliver goods which are of the quantity, quality and description required by the contract and which are contained or packaged in the manner required by the contract.

(2) Except where the parties have agreed otherwise, the goods do not conform with the contract unless they:

    (a) are fit for the purposes for which goods of the same description would ordinarily be used;

    (b) are fit for any particular purpose expressly or impliedly made known to the seller at the time of the conclusion of the contract, except where the circumstances show that the buyer did not rely, or that it was unreasonable for him to rely, on the seller's skill and judgement;

    (c) possess the qualities of goods which the seller has held out to the buyer as a sample or model;

    (d) are contained or packaged in the manner usual for such goods or, where there is no such manner, in a manner adequate to preserve and protect the goods.

(3) The seller is not liable under subparagraphs (a) to (d) of the preceding paragraph for any lack of conformity of the goods if at the time of the conclusion of the contract the buyer knew or could not have been unaware of such lack of conformity.

I. Overview

A. Content and Purpose of Article 35 CISG

Article 35 CISG sets out when goods delivered by the seller are deemed to conform to the contract in terms of type, quantity, quality and packaging. It is based on a uniform concept of 'lack of conformity' that includes not only discrepancies in quality, but also in quantity, delivery of an *aliud* (totally different good) and packaging defects. However, as is the case in many domestic systems, and in the ULIS, the CISG upholds the distinction between goods possessing defects in quality, and defects in title, which is discussed in greater detail under Article 41 CISG below.

B. Domestic Laws

The CISG presents some material differences to the approaches to the issue of lack of conformity under domestic legal systems. Domestic laws draw different distinctions regarding lack of conformity that are not expressly recognised in Article 35 CISG. In those sales laws that are still largely based upon Roman legal principles, a distinction is attached to the difference between the ordinary characteristics of the goods (*Sacheigenschaft*) and a specific warranty as to the existence of certain characteristics (*Zusicherung*). Furthermore, the distinction, still used in many legal systems, between *peius* (non-conforming good) and *aliud*, is also of no significance under the CISG.

Art 197(1) OR:[111]

> The seller is liable to the buyer for any breach of warranty of quality and for any defects that would materially or legally negate or substantially reduce the value of the object or its fitness for the designated purpose.

Art 1641 CC:

> A seller is bound to a warranty on account of the latent defects of the thing sold which render it unfit for the use for which it was intended, or which so impair that use that the buyer would not have acquired it, or would only have given a lesser price for it, had he known of them.

Art 1643 CC:

> He is liable for latent defects, even though he did not know of them, unless he has stipulated that he would not be bound to any warranty in that case.

In common law systems, the approaches differ yet again. US law distinguishes between express and implied warranties.

§ 2-313 UCC:

> (1) Express warranties by the seller are created as follows:
>   (a) Any affirmation of fact or promise made by the seller which relates to the goods and becomes part of the basis of the bargain creates an express warranty that the goods shall conform to the affirmation or promise.
>   (b) Any description of the goods which is made part of the basis of the bargain creates an express warranty that the goods shall conform to the description.
>   (c) Any sample or model which is made part of the basis of the bargain creates an express warranty that the whole of the goods shall conform to the sample or model.
> (2) It is not necessary to the creation of an express warranty that the seller use formal words such as 'warrant' or 'guarantee' or that he have a specific intention to make a warranty, but an affirmation merely of the value of the goods or a statement purporting to be merely the seller's opinion or commendation of the goods does not create a warranty.

---

[111] Translation taken from www.admin.ch/ch/e/rs/2/220.en.pdf.

§ 2-314 UCC:

(1) Unless excluded or modified (Section 2-316), a warranty that the goods shall be merchantable is implied in a contract for their sale if the seller is a merchant with respect to goods of that kind. Under this Section the serving for value of food or drink to be consumed either on the premises or elsewhere is a sale.

(2) Goods to be merchantable must be at least such as
  (a) pass without objection in the trade under the contract description; and
  (b) in the case of fungible goods, are of fair average quality within the description; and
  (c) are fit for the ordinary purposes for which such goods are used; and
  (d) run, within the variations permitted by the agreement, of even kind, quality and quantity within each unit and among all units involved; and
  (e) are adequately contained, packaged, and labeled as the agreement may require; and
  (f) conform to the promise or affirmations of fact made on the container or label if any.

(3) Unless excluded or modified (Section 2-316) other implied warranties may arise from course of dealing or usage of trade.

§ 2-315 UCC:

Where the seller at the time of contracting has reason to know any particular purpose for which the goods are required and that the buyer is relying on the seller's skill or judgment to select or furnish suitable goods, there is unless excluded or modified under the next Section an implied warranty that the goods shall be fit for such purpose.

Under English law, a distinction is drawn between warranties and conditions, which give rise to different consequences in the event of breach.

Sec 14 SGA:

(1) Except as provided by this Section and Section 15 below and subject to any other enactment, there is no implied term about the quality or fitness for any particular purpose of goods supplied under a contract of sale.

(2) Where the seller sells goods in the course of a business, there is an implied term that the goods supplied under the contract are of satisfactory quality.

(2A) For the purposes of this Act, goods are of satisfactory quality if they meet the standard that a reasonable person would regard as satisfactory, taking account of any description of the goods, the price (if relevant) and all the other relevant circumstances.

(2B) For the purposes of this Act, the quality of goods includes their state and condition and the following (among others) are in appropriate cases aspects of the quality of goods—
  (a) fitness for all the purposes for which goods of the kind in question are commonly supplied,
  (b) appearance and finish,
  (c) freedom from minor defects,
  (d) safety, and
  (e) durability.

(2C) The term implied by subsection (2) above does not extend to any matter making the quality of goods unsatisfactory—
  (a) which is specifically drawn to the buyer's attention before the contract is made,
  (b) where the buyer examines the goods before the contract is made, which that examination ought to reveal, or

(c) in the case of a contract for sale by sample, which would have been apparent on a reasonable examination of the sample.

(2D)–(2F) [...]

(3) Where the seller sells goods in the course of a business and the buyer, expressly or by implication, makes known—
(a) to the seller, or
(b) where the purchase price or part of it is payable by instalments and the goods were previously sold by a credit-broker to the seller, to that credit-broker,

any particular purpose for which the goods are being bought, there is an implied term that the goods supplied under the contract are reasonably fit for that purpose, whether or not that is a purpose for which such goods are commonly supplied, except where the circumstances show that the buyer does not rely, or that it is unreasonable for him to rely, on the skill or judgement of the seller or credit-broker.

(4) An implied term or warranty about quality or fitness for a particular purpose may be annexed to a contract of sale by usage.

(5) The preceding provisions of this Section apply to a sale by a person who in the course of a business is acting as agent for another as they apply to a sale by a principal in the course of a business, except where that other is not selling in the course of a business and either the buyer knows that fact or reasonable steps are taken to bring it to the notice of the buyer before the contract is made.

(6)–(8) [...]

Sec 15 SGA:

(1) A contract of sale is a contract for sale by sample where there is an express or implied term to that effect in the contract.

(2) In the case of a contract for sale by sample there is an implied term—
(a) that the bulk will correspond with the sample in quality;
(b) *repealed*;
(c) that the goods will be free from any defect, making their quality unsatisfactory, which would not be apparent on reasonable examination of the sample.

(3), (4) [...]

Sec 15A SGA:

(1) Where in the case of a contract of sale—
(a) the buyer would, apart from this subsection, have the right to reject goods by reason of a breach on the part of the seller of a term implied by Section 13, 14 or 15 above, but
(b) the breach is so slight that it would be unreasonable for him to reject them,

then, if the buyer does not deal as consumer, the breach is not to be treated as a breach of condition but may be treated as a breach of warranty.

(2) This Section applies unless a contrary intention appears in, or is to be implied from, the contract.

(3) It is for the seller to show that a breach fell within subsection (1)(b) above.

(4) [...]

Question

Q 35-1

(a)   Compare Article 35 CISG to the national solutions set out above. Which do you think were influential in the drafting of Article 35 CISG?
(b)   What differences and/or problems can you perceive between the national solutions and the CISG?

Germany revised its law of obligations and sales law provisions in 2002.

§ 434 BGB:[112]

(1)   The thing is free from material defects if, upon the passing of the risk, the thing has the agreed quality. To the extent that the quality has not been agreed, the thing is free of material defects
   1.   if it is suitable for the use intended under the contract,
   2.   if it is suitable for the customary use and its quality is usual in things of the same kind and the buyer may expect this quality in view of the type of the thing.

   Quality under sentence 2 no. 2 above includes characteristics which the buyer can expect from the public statements on specific characteristics of the thing that are made by the seller, the producer (Section 4(1) and (2) of the Product Liability Act [*Produkthaftungsgesetz*]) or his assistant, including without limitation in advertising or in identification, unless the seller was not aware of the statement and also had no duty to be aware of it, or at the time when the contract was entered into it had been corrected in a manner of equal value, or it did not influence the decision to purchase the thing.
(2)   It is also a material defect if the agreed assembly by the seller or persons whom he used to perform his obligation has been carried out improperly. In addition, there is a material defect in a thing intended for assembly if the assembly instructions are defective, unless the thing has been assembled without any error.
(3)   Supply by the seller of a different thing or of a lesser amount of the thing is equivalent to a material defect.

Question

Q 35-2

(a)   What is the origin of § 434 BGB?
(b)   Compare § 434 BGB and Article 35 CISG. Describe the similarities and differences.

The PRC unified its contract law in 1999.

---

[112] Translation taken from www.gesetze-im-internet.de/englisch_bgb/.

Art 153 PRC CL:[113]

The seller shall deliver the subject matter in compliance with the prescribed quality requirements. Where the seller gave quality specifications for the subject matter, the subject matter delivered shall comply with the quality requirements set forth therein.

Art 154 PRC CL:

Where the quality requirements for the subject matter were not prescribed or clearly prescribed, and cannot be determined in accordance with Article 61 hereof, Item (i) of Article 62 hereof applies.

Art 61 PRC CL:

If a term such as quality, price or remuneration, or place of performance etc. was not pre-scribed or clearly prescribed, after the contract has taken effect, the parties may supplement it through agreement; if the parties fail to reach a supplementary agreement, such term shall be determined in accordance with the relevant provisions of the contract or in accordance with the relevant usage.

Art 62 PRC CL:

Where a relevant term of the contract was not clearly prescribed, and cannot be determined in accordance with Article 61 hereof, one of the following provisions applies:

(i) If quality requirement was not clearly prescribed, performance shall be in accordance with the state standard or industry standard; absent any state or industry standard, performance shall be in accordance with the customary standard or any particular standard consistent with the purpose of the contract;

(ii)–(vi) [...]

Art 156 PRC CL:

The seller shall deliver the subject matter packed in the prescribed manner. Where a packing method was not prescribed or clearly prescribed, and cannot be determined in accordance with Article 61 hereof, the subject matter shall be packed in a customary manner, or, if there is no customary manner, in a manner adequate to protect the subject matter.

Art 168 PRC CL:

In a sale by sample, the parties shall place the sample under seal, and may specify the quality of the sample. The subject matter delivered by the seller shall comply with the sample as well as the quality specifications.

---

[113] Translation taken from www.wipo.int/wipolex/en/text.jsp?file_id=182632.

Question

Q 35-3

Compare the provisions of the PRC CL relating to the conformity of the goods with other domestic provisions and Article 35 CISG. Explain the similarities and differences.

C. Drafting History

In substance, Article 35 CISG is largely based on Article 33 ULIS, although the approach to the question of conformity can be distinguished. Whereas the starting point in Article 35 CISG is the basic rule that the goods must conform to the contract, Article 33 ULIS was, instead, used as a 'catch-all' provision. A further difference can be found in the consequences of the delivery of non-conforming goods under the two provisions. Whilst Article 33 ULIS regarded this as a failure to fulfill the delivery obligation, non-conforming goods have no effect on the delivery obligation under Article 35 CISG, but rather give rise to remedies under Article 45 *et seq.* CISG.

II. Article 35 (1) CISG

A. General

Article 35(1) CISG requires a seller to deliver goods that meet the specifications of the contract regarding description, quality, quantity and packaging. An often disputed issue is what the contract actually 'required'.

C 35-1

Bundesgericht (Switzerland),
22 December 2000,
CISG-online 628[114]

[Facts]

A. The [buyer], whose place of business is in Haldenwang [Germany], trades in textile machinery. The [seller], with seat in Goldach [Canton St. Gallen, Switzerland] tried to sell his used textile machines in the year 1998. After the parties had made contact in December of

---

[114] Translation taken from CISG Pace (citations omitted).

1998, the [seller] sent to the [buyer], in the beginning of January 1999, a list of the machinery offered for sale including a 'price offer'. On 12 January 1999, the [buyer's] manager viewed various machines together with two prospective customers from Iran. On the following day, [buyer's] manager declared that he was interested in certain machines, but did not agree with the offered prices.

With letter of 24 February 1999, the [buyer] again contacted the [seller] and—by referring to the machinery list—expressed an interest in a rotary printing machine '*Stork*' RDIV Airflow A 640.000 including equipment. This letter, as well as a confirmation of order by the [seller] dated 1 March 1999, reveals that the machine was supposed to be sold to the interested persons from Iran. After the [seller] had confirmed his willingness to sell the machine in writing on 26 February 1999, the [buyer] faxed to the seller, on 9 March 1999, a 'purchase confirmation' with a detailed description of the furnishings of the machine and the equipment. It was furthermore noted that the machine contained a 'rapport equipment 641 mm—1018 mm' and that the machine was 'complete and operating as viewed.'

[The sales contract]

On 9 March 1999 the [seller] and the [buyer] signed a sales contract which read in part:

'The parties agree the sale of
— 1 piece rotary printing machine, brand *Stork*, Type RD-IV Airflow A 640.000, Rapportausrüstung 641 mm—1018 mm, [...], with the following equipment:
— [...]
from the [seller's] property to the [buyer] at a price of DM [Deutsche Mark] 233,000.00—

'The following conditions apply:

1. The price is ex works excluding dismantling, loading, transport, insurance etc. These obligations are to be performed by the buyer or a company commissioned by buyer. The costs accrued are born by the buyer in their entirety.
2. The collection has to occur—after a prior agreement on the date—by 30 June 1999 at the latest.
3. The purchase price is payable:
   — 30% down payment = DM 69,900.00—immediately
   — 70% final payment = DM 163,100.00—before dismantling
   — If the machine is not collected by the date named under clause 2., the seller is entitled to terminate the contract without meeting any further requirements. In this case, the down payment goes to the seller as a stipulated penalty.
4. [...]
5. The goods for sale are taken over by the buyer in the present conditions, any guarantee or rights to remedy are waived.'

After the [buyer] made the down payment in the amount of DM 69,900.00 on 11 March 1999, the [buyer's] manager viewed the machine again fourteen days later and realised that it was only equipped for a rapport length of 641 mm. With letter of 12 April 1999, the [buyer] complained to the [seller] that the stencil holders for a rapport length of 1018 mm were missing. [Buyer] referred to the contract, in which a 'rapport equipment 641 mm—1018 mm' had been assured. Because used stencil holders were not available and new holders would cost DM 99,000.00, the [buyer] gave the [seller] the following options:

'Alternative 1:

You accept that the sales contract does not correspond to the agreement and you withdraw from the contract and reimburse the down payment in the amount of DM 69,900.00.

'Alternative 2:

You accept a reduction in price in the amount of DM 60,000.00, with which you contribute to the purchase price of new stencil holders. This means that you bear roughly 60% of the additional costs, while the [buyer] bears approx. 40%.'

With letter of 13 April 1999, the [seller] turned down these proposals and held to the contract. [Seller] noted that the [buyer] had declared on 9 March 1999 that [buyer] would buy the machine 'complete and operating as viewed.' The remark regarding the rapport equipment in the sales contract referred solely to the technical bounds, but did not allow any conclusions to be drawn as to the measurements of the existing stencil holders.

On 26 April 1999, the [buyer] wrote to the [seller] that [buyer] would not take the machine and, under OR Art 107, refused the belated performance unless the [seller] assured [buyer] by 10 May 1999 that 'a machine is sold conforming to the contract, which contains an operating rapport equipment between 641 mm and 1018 mm.' When the [seller] insisted on his position, the [buyer], in accordance with OR Art 107(2), on 4 June 1999 declared that she refused the belated performance. On 1 July 1999, the [seller] declared in writing that [seller] terminated the contract of 9 March 1999 in reliance on contract clause 3 and that [seller] would keep the down payment as the stipulated penalty.

[...]

[Judgment]

[...]

However, as the Court of First Instance correctly held, the prerequisites and the remedies for breach of contract result not from OR Art 197, but from CISG Art 35. According to CISG Art 35, the seller must deliver goods which are of the quantity, quality and description required by the contract and which are contained or packaged in the manner required by the contract. Which characteristics of the goods were agreed upon and are part of the contract needs to be established—if necessary—by interpretation of the parties' statements under CISG Art 8. In contrast to OR Art 197, CISG Art 35 does not contain a specific rule for war-ranted characteristics. Instead, the seller generally vouches for all qualities which the buyer is entitled to expect from the goods under the contract. The Court of First Instance adopted this—objective—interpretation in deciding that the [buyer] was not entitled to expect that she would be able to print rapport length of 1018 mm on the acquired machine without installing additional holders. The Court of First Instance held that the [seller] was entitled to assume that the [buyer] realised that the remark regarding the rapport equipment was meant to refer to the bounds of possible rapport length, which could be printed if the necessary equipment existed. The [buyer] does not submit, nor is it apparent, how the Court of First Instance vio-lated the provisions of the CISG, in particular CISG Art 8(2), according to which statements made by a party are to be interpreted according to the understanding that a reasonable person of the same kind as the other party would have had in the same circumstances. The [buyer] is an expert and knew that she was not offered a new machine, but one which was built fourteen years ago and consequently did not conform to the latest technical expectations. It was there-fore up to [buyer] to inform herself about the operation and equipment of the machinery, an act that the [buyer] apparently embarked on only after the contract had been concluded. In view of these facts, it is without doubt compatible with CISG Art 8(2) if the Court of First Instance finds that the [seller] was entitled to expect that the [buyer] concluded the contract in full knowledge of the technical possibilities of the machinery and its equipment. For these reasons, the Supreme Court concurs with the Court of First Instance that the sold machine was offered to the [buyer] in conformity with the specifications of the contract. The [buyer's] claim for remedy for breach of contract is, therefore, unfounded.

[...]

C 35-2

Oberlandesgericht München (Germany), 13 November 2002, CISG-online 786[115]

[Facts]

[Buyer] claims damages from Respondent [Seller] out of a sales contract concerning the shipment of organic barley used for brewing. Claimant [Buyer] could not use the barley because of doubts regarding its origin. It was laid down in the facts of the appealed judgment of the *Landgericht* [District Court, Court of First Instance]. Under the supplement and delivery contract dated 14/31 July 2000, [Buyer] purchased 150 tons of organic barley from [Seller]. Shipment was to take place in August/September 2000. As to quality, the parties agreed that:

'The goods will meet the requirements under Council Regulation EEC No. 2092/91 on organic production of agricultural products, state of origin Germany.'

[Buyer] received, as ordered by [Seller], 150 tons of barley divided into six partial shipments of 28 and 29 September, 3 and 9 October, 30 November and 20 December 2000. [Seller] on its part had purchased the barley from Estate R, which in turn had purchased a substantial part from a company located in Gotha. With the last partial shipment of 20 December 2000, [Buyer] received a certificate affirming that these last delivered goods met the standards of Council Regulation EEC No 2092/91. For the first five partial shipments, [Buyer] received no such certificates. [Buyer] only claims damages concerning the first five partial shipments.

In a letter dated 6 February 2001, [Buyer] was ordered by the inspection body of the Belgian Ministry of Agriculture to neither process nor resell these five shipments of barley. This was done because of doubts whether the barley was of organic origin or rather because the requisite proof of this by certificate was missing. [Buyer] notified [Seller] of these facts on 15 February 2001 as a notice of defect. Whether the shipments in question were actually of organic origin was not ascertained in this proceeding. In the relevant wholesale business, quality as organic barley is proven only by certificates accompanying the goods, issued by companies admitted for certification. Conventionally grown barley has substantial less market value than organic barley; this is likewise applicable to the malt products produced out of this barley. [Buyer] calculated out of difference between the value of the goods delivered and that of the goods contracted for, additionally costs for repurchase of barley to fulfil other contractual commitments and further expense damages at a total amount of 48,480 DM [Deutsche Mark].

[...]

[Judgment]

The barley that was delivered did not comply with the quality required under the contract. [...]

1. The barley that [Seller] delivered did not conform to the contract as required by Article 35(1) CISG. Goods were to be supplied that complied with Council Regulation EEC

---

[115] Translation taken from CISG Pace (citations omitted).

No 2092/91 on organic production of agricultural products. Following the parties' statements, it is certain that [Buyer] received a CMR-bill of lading on delivery. But this note does not fulfil the requirements of Annex III No. 8.

The delivery notes submitted by [Seller] only concern the delivery from Estate R to the [Seller]. There were no delivery notes submitted from [Seller] to [Buyer]. [Buyer] mentions unsigned delivery notes in its last written submission but does not submit such despite the instruction of the Court concerning the importance the Court places on the covering documents.

The shipment of organic barley without covering documents as defined by Annex III No. 8 violated the minimum inspection requirements for the inspection scheme according to Article 9. Therefore, the barley lost the privilege of being declared as 'organic'. The Belgian inspection bodies were obliged to have the notes of organic origin removed from the goods (Article 9 IX Council Regulation EEC No 2092/91). As a consequence, the barley did not comply with the quality required under the contract.

This very formal construction is justified also in content. Organic barley cannot be distinguished from other barley, at least not by usual methods and with proportional expenditure. The system of the Regulation is not based on the assumption of inspecting the goods but proceeds from a system of certification of companies at production, trade and processing. The fact that goods originate from a certified company and this company confirms that the goods were produced under the requirements of Article 6 Council Regulation EEC No. 2092/91 permits the declaration of 'organic' origin and thus a substantial higher price. In the case at hand, this amounted to 625 DM/t organic barley as opposed to 290 DM/t conventional barley. This applies to all stages of processing. [Buyer] alleges a selling price of 1,256 DM for one ton of organic malt and for conventional malt 605 DM.

In the final analysis, the relevant note about the established conformity in the inspection (Article 10 Council Regulation EEC No. 2092/91 in connection with Annex V) relied on by consumers depends on the observation of the inspection scheme in force. In other words, the consumer pays a substantially higher price for an organic product and not for a proven quality but for the observation of the inspection scheme at production, transport and processing. 'Certificates accompanying the goods' or 'party certificates' are not known to the Council Regulation. Even if these should be customary they can only be regarded as covering documents as defined by No. 8.2 of Annex III of the Council Regulation if they are presented with the goods. An issuing and presentation months after the shipment—as in the case at hand—does not meet the requirements. Retrospective establishment and control that Annex III wants to obtain is no longer possible. This is shown by the 'Certificates accompanying the goods' explicitly: This certificate accompanying the goods attests that the company from Gotha delivered organic barley whereas the company did not grow any barley in the year 2000. This was argued by the joint litigant to 2 in the oral hearing. The certificate contains no information whatsoever that the company from Gotha only acted as a trader with the necessary consequence of naming the producer.

[...]

Questions

Q 35-4

According to the case of the Swiss *Bundesgericht* (C 35-1) above, what other provision/s of the CISG can be applied to determine what the contract actually required under Article 35(1) CISG?

Q 35-5

(a)   What exactly was relied on to establish the lack of conformity under Article 35(1) CISG in the case of the *Oberlandesgericht München* (C 35-2) above?

(b)   Under which 'head' (quantity, quality or description) of Article 35(1) CISG did the lack of conformity fall?

B. *Peius* and *Aliud*

According to the CISG, every type of deviation—even a deviation in kind—constitutes a lack of conformity with the contract. Consequently, the distinction between *peius* and *aliud*, which is still so important in the Swiss and Austrian legal systems—and formerly under German law—is of no importance under the CISG.

C 35-3

Bundesgerichtshof (Germany),
3 April 1996,
CISG-online 135

[Facts][116]

The Dutch plaintiff was the assignee of a Dutch company, which had sold four different quantities of cobalt sulphate to the [buyer], a German company. It was agreed that the goods should be of British origin and that the plaintiff should supply certificates of origin and of quality. After the receipt of the documents, the [buyer] declared the contracts to be avoided since the cobalt sulphate was made in South Africa and the certificate of origin was wrong. The [buyer] also claimed that the quality of the goods was inferior to what was agreed upon. The plaintiff demanded payment.

[Judgment][117]

[Buyer's] position is incorrect. Contrary to German domestic law, the CISG does not differentiate between delivery of different goods and delivery of goods that do not conform to the contract. Under the CISG, an *aliud* delivery does therefore, at least generally, not constitute a non-delivery, but constitutes a delivery of non-conforming goods. The CISG is different from German domestic law, whose provisions and special principles are, as a matter of principle, inapplicable for the interpretation of the CISG (Art 7 CISG). The Court does not need to resolve whether, in the event of a blatant divergence from the contractual condition, a non-delivery in the meaning of Art 49(1)(b) CISG can arise. Such a violation of contract did not occur in the present case. The [buyer] bought cobalt sulfate 21%; this

[116]   Summary of facts taken from UNILEX.
[117]   Translation taken from CISG Pace (citations omitted).

has been delivered by the [seller]. According to the [buyer's] submissions in the final appeal proceedings, the Court must assume that the [buyer] did not order the delivered fodder quality, but technical quality; i.e., goods without the flow auxiliaries. This divergence is certainly not severe enough to regard the delivery not only as non-conforming, but as not having been made at all.

NB: This case was decided under the old German Civil Code.

Question

Q 35-6

What would be the consequences of considering delivery of an *aliud* as non-delivery rather than as non-conforming delivery?

III. Article 35(2) CISG

Article 35(2) CISG provides standards relating to the goods' quality, function and packaging that are deemed to apply when the parties have not otherwise agreed.

A. Article 35(2)(a) CISG

Article 35(2)(a) CISG requires the seller to deliver goods 'fit for the purposes for which goods of the same description would ordinarily be used'.

(a) 'Average Quality', 'Merchantable Quality', 'Merchantability'

Whether the purposes for which the goods would ordinarily be used encompass various quality standards recognised in domestic law is disputed in the literature. Many domestic legal systems (for example, the German, Austrian, French and Swiss Civil Codes) contain an express provision that generic goods are to be of average type and quality. Common law systems, however, require that the goods be 'merchantable', which includes being fit for the 'ordinary purposes' (US: § 2-314 UCC) or of 'satisfactory quality', including fit for 'all the purposes for which goods of the kind in question are commonly supplied' (UK: Sec 14 SGA). Under the CISG, the scope of Article 35(2)(a) CISG has been subject to considerable debate.

C 35-4

Netherlands Arbitration Institute, Case No 2319, 15 October 2002, CISG-online 740/780[118]

[Facts]

[...]

[36] The following sets forth the facts as they are understood by the Arbitral Tribunal.

[37] [Sellers] are all active in the exploration of offshore gas fields in the Netherlands continental shelf. They have been granted production licenses for certain blocks. In order to spread risks, exploration and production generally take place in the form of joint venture contracts with one company being the operator responsible for operational and financial issues. Products are being allocated between the joint venture partners in accordance with their proportionate ownership interest. However, sales are the sole responsibility of each of the companies.

[38] [Buyer] is a major international player in the field of exploration, production and refining of crude oil and distribution of oil products and gas.

[39] Condensate is an associated liquid product derived from the exploration of gas fields after separation from the gas stream by the producer. Condensate from the fields operated by [sellers] and subject of the dispute is referred to as 'Rijn Blend'.

[40] In 1993 and 1994, [sellers] (or their predecessors) concluded twelve sales contracts with [buyer] in relation to the abovementioned Rijn Blend. There are—according to the Request for Arbitration—13 [sellers] while there are 12 sales contracts. This is related to the fact that 1) affiliated companies (i.e., the ... companies, the ... companies and the ... companies) only concluded one contract, and 2) that some contracts have been assigned from the original seller (the contracts with ... respectively with ... BV ['Besloten Vennootschap' (Dutch limited liability company)]) to one of the [sellers] (C. BV respectively Y. BV). Reference is in this respect made to Exhibit 2 of the Statement of Claim.

[41] As far as the Arbitral Tribunal understands, the condensate came from various offshore gas fields [...] operated by [sellers] in the Netherlands continental shelf. The condensate streams were brought together at the P15-D platform in the North Sea where they were commingled with one another and with crude oil produced from an offshore oil field. From the platform, the blend was transported through a single pipeline to Tank 101 of the ... Company (a joint venture of ... NV ['Naamloze Vennootschap' (Dutch limited liability company)] (65%) and ... BV (35%), hereafter referred to as 'Q') terminal in Europoort where it was delivered 'ex storage tank' to [buyer] as a condensate/crude oil mix, hereafter named the 'Rijn Blend'. The delivery and lifting of the Rijn Blend at Europoort took place jointly for all sellers in accordance with a pre-established nomination procedure. The Rijn Blend is subsequently refined on behalf of [buyer] at the Q. refinery and derivate products are sold by [buyer] to users.

---

[118] Citations omitted.

[42] [Buyer] alleges that at the Q. refinery the Rijn Blend is blended with other crude oils to optimise the refining process. Subsequently, the refining process results in the production of LPG, light naphtha, heavy naphtha, kerosene, light gas oil, heavy gas oil and residue. All light naphtha produced at Q. is sold to CH. ... GmbH, a joint venture between KK. ... AG and Deutsche ... AG, a subsidiary of CH. ... GmbH also has other suppliers for its light naphtha requirements.

[43] [Sellers] were not the only sellers of Rijn Blend to [buyer]. One other seller was K. ... BV who was also the operator of the P15-D platform. After the merger of [buyer]'s parent company and K., K. ... BV was renamed '... BV' and has taken a neutral position regarding the disputes between [sellers] and [buyer].

[44] The sale contracts of [sellers] with [buyer] were identical or almost identical. There was no detailed product description and only a few specifications for the product. All contracts provided for application of Dutch law and for NAI arbitration.

[45] Apparently, from 1993 or 1994 on and for a long time, there had been no problems regarding the sale contracts between [sellers] and [buyer].

[46] [Buyer] alleges that CH. ... GmbH was encountering processing problems at its plant as of Spring 1997 resulting in rapid de-activation of catalysts and corrosion (causing operational and environmental concerns) and that as of May 1997, Q. had been contacted since the light naphtha produced at Q. might have caused the problems. As of November 1997, a possible link was made with mercury levels in the Rijn Blend used at Q. [Buyer] further alleges that the link was established as of May 1998 and that solutions (both long and short term) were envisaged in cooperation with K. ... BV.

[47] The disputes between [sellers] and [buyer] relate to deliveries as of June 1998. On June 11, 1998, [sellers] were informed by K. ... BV that [buyer] had indicated that it would not take the next lifting of the Rijn Blend because of levels of mercury in the Rijn Blend, which made it unacceptable for further processing or sales.

[48] Because of alleged lack of storage facilities, the Rijn Blend—on June 13, 1998—was loaded onto a vessel chartered for that purpose. Also, it is alleged that storing on a chartered vessel was a cheaper option than shutting down production at the gas fields. Because of the alleged absence of short-term local market opportunities, the Rijn Blend was transported to the United States where it was sold to LL. Petroleum Corp. at a price substantially lower than the price under the contract. In this respect, [sellers] allege that they suffered losses of US $1,100,000.

[49] On June 16, 1998, [buyer] informed [sellers] that it would suspend taking delivery of the Rijn Blend until a solution for the mercury problem had been found.

[50] Since a solution was not found regarding the mercury problem, [buyer] terminated the contracts or led the contracts to expire in accordance with the contract termination provisions or the contract provisions regarding renewal. In the intermediate period, [sellers] sold the condensate not taken by [buyer] to third parties (such as one further sale to LL. Petroleum Corp., two to M. International AG and all others to H.... BV) at an alleged loss as compared to the contract price. On top of the US $1,100,000 on the June 1998 cover sale, the Arbitral Tribunal gathers from the information provided by [sellers] that other cover sales caused losses alleged to be in excess of US $5 million resulting in an alleged overall loss of US $6,333,178.58.

[...]

[Judgment]

[…]

5.1 Issue 1: Conformity of the Rijn Blend

[62] Article 35(1) CISG provides that the seller should deliver goods, which are of the quantity, quality and description required by the contract. All twelve contracts do not contain quality specifications but only define Rijn Blend as a 'Mix of … condensates and/ or crude oil …', '… condensates and crude oil' or 'condensates' and refer to the blocks from where the Rijn Blend originate. The contracts also refer to the gravity of the Rijn Blend for price calculation purposes but parties agree that this element is of no relevance for the present purposes. Consequently, article 35(1) CISG is not applicable to the conformity issue.

[63] Article 35(2) CISG provides in relevant parts that the goods do not conform with the contract unless they: (a) are fit for the purposes for which goods of the same description would ordinarily be used; or (b) are fit for any particular purpose expressly or impliedly made known to the seller at the time of the conclusion of the contract, except where the circumstances show that the buyer did not rely, or that it was unreasonable for him to rely, on the seller's skill and judgement.

[…]

[67] As to Article 35(2)(b) CISG, the Arbitral Tribunal notes that the particular purpose of the goods must have been made known to the seller at the time of the conclusion of the contract. The question then arises whether [buyer], at that time (i.e., 1993 and 1994) expressly or impliedly indicated to the respective [sellers] the use it intended to make of the Rijn Blend. The Arbitral Tribunal is of the opinion that it did not. […] Consequently, the Arbitral Tribunal rules that, absent contract quality specifications, Article 35(2)(b) CISG is not the proper basis to assess non-conformity issues in international sales of commodities such as Rijn Blend.

[68] The Arbitral Tribunal, thus, finds that the dispute between the parties is to be analysed under Article 35(2)(a) CISG which requires that the goods are fit for the purposes for which goods of the same description would ordinarily be used. In this respect, three interpretations exist. According to a first line of thought, Article 35(2)(a) requires that the seller delivers goods which are of a *merchantable quality*. This interpretation goes back to the drafting history of CISG. During the negotiations of CISG, the question arose how the provision of the draft on conformity of goods, absent contract specification or particular purpose, should be interpreted. At that time, it became clear that the English common law countries favoured merchantable quality whereas the civil law continental European rule was to the effect that average quality is required. In order to clarify the draft, the Canadian delegation proposed to endorse the civil law rule by also including an average quality rule. However, during the negotiations, the Canadian amendment was withdrawn. This background has been mentioned in the German *New Zealand Mussels* case but was considered not to be relevant there because the mussels were both merchantable and of average quality. No case law could be found which inferred from the *travaux préparatoires* that the continental rule was not to be adopted and that merchantable quality is sufficient.

[69] The Second view is that the *average quality* rule is to be adopted in relation to CISG cases.

[70] Scholarly writings have mentioned the problem but later publications, even among civil law scholars, are divided between merchantable and average quality with a majority of Germanic writers endorsing the average quality rule based upon similar rules in the

German, Austrian and Swiss civil codes. Some other authors have taken positions similar to the majority view but with some qualifications based on the concrete circumstances of the case such as a buyer ordering goods from a specialised manufacturer (entitled to above-average quality) or a buyer who under specific circumstances could not expect average quality (entitled to below-average but still satisfactory quality). Finally, some French authors have specifically stated that the average quality rule of the French Civil Code is not applicable to CISG cases.

[71] Finally, a third theory rejects both opinions mentioned above and states that neither merchantability nor average quality fit within the CISG system. This theory rather suggests a reasonable quality. One case has endorsed this theory in holding that the buyer's reasonable expectations are to be taken into account.

[72] Contrary to Article 35(2)(b) CISG, Article 35(2)(a) does not require that quality requirements are determined at the time of the conclusion of the contract. Thus, factual elements occurring after the conclusion of the contract may be taken into account to determine quality standards.

[...]

[80] The Arbitral Tribunal therefore proceeds on the basis that the Rijn Blend contained increased levels of mercury and, thus, must answer the question whether Rijn Blend with increased levels of mercury still meets the standard of Article 35(2)(a) CISG requiring products to fit ordinary purposes of goods of the same description. The Arbitral Tribunal is thus facing the question mentioned above whether merchantable, average or reasonable quality is required.

[81] As a starting point of the analysis, it should be noted that condensate is a commodity with multiple purposes. It can be used in the refining process but it may also be used by chemical and other companies. Thus, condensate may be characterised as a multi-purpose commodity.

[...]

[87] The Arbitral Tribunal now proceeds with the application to Rijn Blend of the three quality standards under Article 35(2)(a) CISG.

[88] As to the standard of merchantability, it should be noted that the primarily Germanic theory of average quality is based on the assumption that in the English common law merchantability implies that goods are conforming if there is a substitute market. It would be the expression of the *caveat emptor*-rule under which buyers assume the risk of quality problems if they fail to specify quality requirements in their contracts or inspect goods before concluding the contract. This rule was, however, changed in 1910 in the *Bristol Tramways Carriage Co. Ltd v Fiat Motors Ltd.* case (1910 2 KB 831) where the test was developed whether a reasonable buyer would have accepted the goods if he had fully examined the goods. As to commodities, the English common law developed the rule that goods conform if a reasonable buyer would have concluded the contract if he had known the quality of the goods without bargaining for a price reduction.

[89] Thus, a merchantability test under CISG based on English common law, if any, would raise the question whether a reasonable buyer would have concluded contracts for Rijn Blend at similar prices if such a buyer had been aware of the mercury concentrations. In this respect, the substitute cover sales made to LL. Petroleum Corp., M. International AG and H. ...BV are relevant. [Sellers] have argued that these cover sales have been contracted on an arm's length basis. From [Sellers]' Exhibit 5a to the Statement of Claim, it appears that the cover sale to LL. Petroleum was made at a 31% discount (US $9 as compared to the price

of US $13.04 under the contracts). Although the first sale might have been a distress sale, the subsequent 15 sales were made at discount within a range of 14% (October 1998) to 44% (February 1999). It is conjectural to what extent these discounts may be attributed to the mercury levels of the Rijn Blend but, in the opinion of the Tribunal, [sellers] sufficiently have established that these cover sales were made at discounts and on an arm's length basis without that evidence being rebutted by [buyer]. For that reason, the Arbitral Tribunal is ready to accept that [sellers] have met their burden of proof that these ranges indicate that there was no market for Rijn Blend with increased mercury levels at prices comparable to the sales contracts when the increased levels were disclosed to prospective alternate buyers.

[90] From this evidence, the Arbitral Tribunal accepts that the goods were not merchantable as this concept is generally used in common law countries having a law based on English common law. Apparently, other buyers in the market for Rijn Blend were—at times comparable to the June 1998 contemplated lifting—unwilling to pay the price [sellers] had agreed with [buyer].

[91] Consequently, if a merchantability test (as understood in the common law) were to be used for interpreting article 35(2)(a) CISG, it would lead to the conclusion that the delivery of Rijn Blend with increased mercury levels did not conform to the sales contracts.

[92] As to average quality, the evidence presented to the Arbitral Tribunal by both parties indicates and—sometimes—emphasises that quality of condensates such as Rijn Blend may differ from one region to another due to geological or other reasons. The Arbitral Tribunal will thus limit its analysis to the relevant geographical market. As suggested by the evidence presented and the expectations of the parties, the geographical market may be limited to the North Sea market.

[93] As has been indicated before, only the product market for so-called 'full range' condensates will be taken into account. In determining average quality, the relevant product is to be looked upon. The presence of mercury in other products such as gas, may be relevant for purposes such as determining the awareness in the industry of mercury content but not for determining the quality of a different product such as condensate.

[...]

[97] In order to prove that the Rijn Blend in June 1998 did not conform with the contracts, [buyer] would have to prove: 1) the mercury levels in or around June 1998, 2) the above average levels of those levels, and/or an unacceptable increase of those levels over the lifetime of the contract.

[98] The mere fact that the Arbitral Tribunal is prepared to accept (see supra Nos. 74-80) that the problems at CH. ... were caused by increased levels of mercury attributable to Rijn Blend sold by [sellers], does not imply that these levels by logical necessity or on the basis of other considerations are to be held above average or unacceptably high and consequently turning Rijn Blend into a condensate of below average quality. The mere fact that K. ... BV investigated the matter and also looked for solutions, does not imply that it accepted that the goods did not conform. K. ...'s attitude may well have been inspired by commercial reasons to keep an important long-term customer.

[99] [Buyer], thus, under the average quality standard, has the burden of proof to establish that the goods in June 1998 were likely to be below average quality.

[100] In the opinion of the Arbitral Tribunal, [buyer] has failed to meet that burden of proof. From the evidence, it is unclear whether there is a common understanding in the refining industry what average quality for blended condensates (such as Rijn Blend) should have been

and what levels of mercury are tolerable. Also, it has not been proven what margins from an average standard, if any, are permissible.

[101] The Arbitral Tribunal's conclusion above is not altered by the fact that [sellers] have attempted to prove that in the industry, at the time the Contracts were concluded in 1993/1994, there was a general awareness of mercury levels in condensates and their consequences in refining processes. Even if that had been proven, it would not change the Tribunal's conclusion because still no average quality standards and the acceptable levels of mercury therein have been established.

[102] Not having met its burden of proof, [buyer], under an average quality standard, were to be held liable for not accepting delivery of the Rijn Blend in June 1998, provided the Arbitral Tribunal would accept such an average quality standard under Article 35(2)(a) CISG.

[103] The Arbitral Tribunal is thus faced with a choice between merchantable quality and average quality since both tests lead to different conclusions. However, the Tribunal is of the opinion that neither test is to be applied in CISG cases.

[104] First, the interpretation of Article 35(2)(a) CISG is to be guided by Article 7(1) CISG which suggests that the international character of the Convention and the need to promote uniformity in its application and the observance of good faith in international trade are to be taken into account in the interpretation process.

[105] The need to ensure uniformity would indicate that, since there are no clear-cut cases or uniform scholarly opinions, neither standard at first sight should prevail.

[106] Thus, Article 7(2) CISG may be invoked. Article 7(2) provides that matters governed by CISG but not expressly settled in it, are to be solved in conformity with the general principles on which CISG is based or, in the absence of such principles, in conformity with the law applicable by virtue of the rules of private international law.

[107] This provision imposes first an intro-interpretation with respect to interpretation issues or gaps (i.e., solutions are first to be sought within the CISG system itself). Absent general principles on which CISG is based, recourse may be had to domestic law indicated by virtue of principles of private international law.

[108] This provision would seem to exclude the average quality rule. Although it is embodied in the law of both Germanic and Romanistic legal systems, Heuzé—as referred to above— has rightly indicated that national notions regarding quality of goods are not controlling in CISG cases. For that reason, the average quality standard cannot be accepted. It is a theory, which imports a domestic notion, which is not sufficiently universal into the CISG system in violation of Article 7(2) CISG. Furthermore, recent codifications in civil law countries such as in The Netherlands have abolished the average quality rule of Article 1428 old Civil Code in favour of a reliance standard.

[109] The same argument against domestic conformity notions, of course, must be used in relation to the merchantability standard of the English common law. Thus, English common law based jurisdictions such as Canada, Australia, New Zealand or Singapore cannot use their merchantability criteria *ne varietur* in CISG cases.

[110] In solving this interpretation issue, attention is also to be paid to Articles 31 and 32 of the Vienna Convention on the Law of Treaties dated May 23, 1969.

[111] Article 32 of the 1969 Vienna Treaty permits to resort to the *travaux préparatoires* of treaties to explain ambiguous or unclear treaty provisions. Article 35(2)(a) CISG may thus

be interpreted on the basis of the preparatory work during the negotiations leading to CISG. In this respect, the Canadian proposal is to be recalled which was worded as follows:

'For the purposes of paragraph (2)(a), the goods are reasonably fit for the purposes for which the goods of the same description would ordinarily be used if,

(a) they are of such quality and in such condition as it is reasonable to expect having regard to any description applied to them, the price and all other relevant circumstances;

and without limiting the generality of clause (a),

(b) if the goods, (i) are such as pass without objection in the trade under the contract description, (ii) in the case of fungible goods, are of fair average quality within the description, ...'

[112] There being no consensus on the Canadian proposal, it was withdrawn. The records of the 15th meeting of the Diplomatic Conference under No. 45 indicate in this respect that the proposal was withdrawn after consultation with several other delegations from common law countries.

[113] Two arguments may be advanced in relation to the *travaux préparatoires*. On the one hand, one may argue that the fact that the proposal was not adopted indicates that CISG chose for the standard of merchantability.

[114] The counterargument would be that the non-adoption and withdrawal of the proposal establishes non-consensus regarding the issue and that the drafters of CISG intentionally created an ambiguity or gap without taking a position on it.

[115] The latter proposition seems to be more likely. First, the Canadian proposal cannot be interpreted as defending the traditional English law requirement of merchantability but rather attempted to clarify it. In this respect, the text of the Canadian proposed amendment borrowed heavily from the text of §2-314 of the U.S. Uniform Commercial Code which is not a strict merchantability criterion but more an open-textured provision, referring also to average quality (see infra). One may infer from the text of the Canadian proposal that the strict merchantability criterion was not even proposed and its withdrawal, consequently, cannot endorse the theory of strict merchantability.

[116] On the other hand, the Canadian proposal and its withdrawal can also not be invoked for the proposition that CISG adopted a criterion of average quality. At least, it did not exclude it. Thus, the drafting history of CISG does not permit to draw a clear conclusion regarding the intentions of the drafters and, consequently, it does not help to explain the ambiguity of Article 35(2)(a) CISG.

[117] On the basis of the arguments above, the Tribunal holds that neither the merchantability test nor the average quality test are to be used in CISG cases and that the reasonable quality standard referred to above (see No. 71) is to be preferred.

[118] The choice in favour of a test of reasonable quality is supported by the authors and the case cited above in No. 71 as well as by those scholarly writings that have rejected the average quality test. It is compatible with the *travaux préparatoires* since the Canadian amendment does not exclude an interpretation in favour of reasonable quality since it provided that under article 35(2)(a) CISG goods are fit for their ordinary use if it is reasonable to expect a certain quality having regard to price and all other relevant circumstances. Also, any such interpretation complies with article 7(1) CISG imposing to take into account the international character of CISG and its reluctance to rely immediately on notions based on domestic law. Furthermore, the interpretation preferred by the Arbitral Tribunal is consistent with Article

7(2) CISG, which primarily refers to the general principles of CISG as possible gap fillers. In this respect, it may be noted that CISG often uses open-textured provisions referring to reasonableness (e.g., Articles 8, 18, 25, 33, 34, 37, 38, 39, 43, 44, 46, 48, 49, 65, 72, 75, 77, 79, 86, 87 and 88). Finally, even if one were to rely on domestic law by virtue of article 7(2) CISG, Dutch law would be applicable and would also impose a standard of reasonable quality.

[119] The question then arises whether the Rijn Blend delivered in 1998 did meet the reasonable quality requirement. The Arbitral Tribunal is of the opinion that it did not for at least two reasons: price and the long-term nature of the sales contracts.

[120] As to price, it has been sufficiently proven that the price as determined by the price formula agreed upon by the parties in all likelihood—even taking into account transportation costs—could not [have] been obtained for cover transactions when the mercury levels were disclosed to alternate prospective buyers. This is an objective element to be taken into account when determining the quality of the Rijn Blend. Apparently, Rijn Blend with increased mercury levels has a significant lower value than Rijn Blend without increased mercury levels and a discount is to be paid for the buyer's costs in removing the mercury or a buyer's alternate use. Consequently, the Arbitral Tribunal finds that [sellers] could well insist upon the performance of the sales contracts if—in relation to the contract price—they had been willing to bear the costs of removing the mercury from the Rijn Blend. Alternatively, the parties could have agreed upon a price reduction to reflect the decreased value of the Rijn Blend. Both options apparently have been discussed during negotiations between the parties but no solution could be found. Therefore, it is the opinion of the Arbitral Tribunal that [buyer], based on the price to be paid under the contracts, could insist upon removal of the mercury or price reduction and alternatively could refuse delivery of the Rijn Blend.

[121] The long-term nature of the sales relationships between the parties corroborates the findings of the Arbitral Tribunal set forth in the preceding paragraph. Apparently, there have been no quality problems related to the levels of mercury in the Rijn Blend in the initial years of the Contracts as of 1993/1994. At the least, [buyer] has sufficiently proven or made it sufficiently probable that CH. ... was its downstream customer over the lifetime of the contracts or the least as of 1995. Over that sufficiently long period, a pattern had developed under which—in the opinion of the Arbitral Tribunal—[buyer] could expect that the Rijn Blend met the quality requirements it was or had become used to over the years. In this respect, the Arbitral Tribunal finds that the [buyer] has sufficiently proven or at least sufficiently has established the probability that the Rijn Blend delivered to it had sudden increased mercury levels. The Arbitral Tribunal has not read in the evidence submitted by [sellers] that there were increased mercury levels well before 1998. Consequently, the Tribunal holds that [buyer] was entitled under the contracts to a constant quality level of the Rijn Blend corresponding to the quality levels that had been obtained during the abovementioned initial period of the Contracts and on which [buyer] and its customers could reasonably rely. This conclusion is not altered by the fact, as emphasised by [sellers] during the June 2001 hearing, that [buyer] never measured the mercury content upon or before conclusion of the Contracts. This fact, in the opinion of the Arbitral Tribunal, is of no importance. On the basis of the arguments above, it is clear that the results of these measurements at that time would not have indicated the abovementioned increase of mercury levels.

[122] Since [buyer] was claiming relief (i.e., suspension of performance) only as of the June 1998 deliveries when as of April 1998 it had in its mind become established that there were increased levels of mercury in the Rijn Blend (and no other causes for the increase were present), it

could invoke such relief as of that date. In this respect, it has not been established that [buyer] had waived its rights by taking delivery as of 1996 or as of April 1998. The Tribunal, on the contrary, is of the opinion that [buyer] acted in a constructive manner in trying to solve the problem (albeit only with K. ... BV) rather than to claim relief for past damages.

[123] On the basis of the contract price and the nature of the relationship between the parties, the Tribunal finds that the risks associated with changing compositions of the Rijn Blend thus laid with [sellers] who should have monitored that composition or should have agreed to removal of the mercury or to price reduction. Since it has been established that the increased levels of mercury were to be sought before the point of delivery, the risks of any such increased levels are to be allocated to the [sellers] who had control only over its possible causes and were thus in the better position to detect the increased levels and their causes and to remedy any such quality problem. Although [buyer] could also have taken precautionary measures to detect changes in the composition of the Rijn Blend, that would not have solved the liability issue (including [buyer]'s right to suspend performance) and the question where the loss had to fall. Under the circumstances, the Tribunal finds that the sellers rather than the buyer had the obligation to remove the mercury in order to be able to deliver the Rijn Blend at a quality level the buyer reasonably could expect in view of the price it was bound to pay and the quality levels it had been used to.

[124] Consequently, the Arbitral Tribunal holds that [sellers] did not comply with their obligations to deliver Rijn Blend conforming to the contract under Article 35(2)(a) CISG as of and including the June 1998 lifting.

[...]

Questions

Q 35-7

What common law approach shares similarities with the approach taken under Article 35(2)(a) CISG?

Q 35-8

List the differences between merchantable, average and reasonable quality.

Q 35-9

How did the tribunal in the Netherlands Arbitration case (C 35-4) try to reconcile the different approaches concerning fitness for ordinary purpose?

(b) Public Law Requirements

Several decisions have discussed whether the quality standard prevailing in the buyer's or the seller's jurisdiction is to apply when determining lack of conformity under Article 35(2)(a) CISG. This is especially relevant to the issue of compliance with particular public law provisions.

C 35-5

Bundesgerichtshof (Germany),
8 March 1995,
CISG-online 144[119]

[Facts]

Defendant [buyer], who runs a fish import business in D. [Germany], bought 1,750 kilograms (kg) New Zealand mussels for U.S. $3.70 per kg from Plaintiff [seller], who resides in Switzerland. [Seller] delivered the goods, as agreed, in January 1992 to a storage facility belonging to [buyer] and located at Company F. in G.G., and invoiced [buyer] on January 15, 1992 in the amount of U.S. $6,475 payable within 14 days.

At the end of January 1992, Company F. informed [buyer] that the federal veterinary agency of G.G. had taken samples of the goods for examination purposes. After the veterinary agency confirmed at the end of January/beginning of February 1992, upon [buyer's] request, that an increased cadmium content was discovered in the mussels and that further examinations by the responsible veterinary examination agency of Southern Hesse were necessary, [buyer] informed [seller] of these facts by facsimile dated February 7, 1992. According to the report by the veterinary examination agency of Southern Hesse, which was received by [buyer] on February 26, 1992 and forwarded to [seller] by [buyer], cadmium contents of between 0.5 and 1.0 milligram per kg (mg/kg) were ascertained in four of the examined bags of mussels; these contents did not yet exceed twice the amount of the 1990 standard of the federal public health agency, but further examinations by the importer were found necessary. An examination commissioned by [seller] and conducted by the federal agency for veterinary matters in Liebefeld-Bern determined a cadmium content of 0.875 mg/kg.

By facsimile dated March 3, 1992, [buyer] announced to [seller] that she was going to send the mussels back at [seller's] expense since the veterinary agency had declared them 'not harmless' due to their high cadmium content; simultaneously, she complained that the goods were 'no longer in their original packaging as required' and that, furthermore, the packaging was unsuitable for frozen food. Thereafter, [seller] informed [buyer] by telephone that she would not accept the goods. Consequently, [buyer] did not return the goods. According to a report of the chemical examination laboratory of Dr. B. dated March 31, 1992, which had been commissioned by [buyer] for further examination, three samples revealed 1 mg of cadmium per kg; a doubling of the federal public health agency standards could not be 'tolerated,' and at least 20 additional samples of the entire delivery had to be examined.

[Buyer] requested that [seller] cover, among other things, the future expenses of the examination; [seller] did not reply.

In the complaint, [seller] demands payment of the purchase price of U.S. $6,475 plus interest. She claimed that the mussels were suitable for consumption because their cadmium content did not exceed the permitted limit; furthermore, [buyer] had not given timely notice of the defects. [Buyer], on the other hand, declared the contract avoided due to a fundamental breach of contract because the mussels were defective and had been complained of by the responsible authorities. Thus, the mussels were not permitted to be delivered out of the

---

[119] Translation taken from CISG Pace (citations omitted).

storage facility. And by now, the 'expiration date of 12/92,' affixed to the merchandise by [seller], had come and gone anyway.

The Trial Court (here the '*Landgericht*') obtained an expert opinion from the federal public health agency. With respect to the question whether the mussels were suitable for consumption having the reported cadmium content, the federal public health agency elaborates that the ZEBS (central registration and evaluation office of the federal public health agency for environmental chemicals) standards are guidelines indicating an unwanted concentration of harmful substances in food for purposes of preventative consumer health protection. Occasionally exceeding the individual standard which are not toxicologically explainable, usually does not lead to harmful effects on one's health, even if the measured concentration reaches twice the amount of the standard. If twice the amount of the standard is exceeded, the responsible state control authorities usually declare that, analogous to the procedure legally required for enforcement of the meat hygiene regulations (*Fleischhygiene Verordnung*), the relevant food can no longer be considered suitable for consumption according to the foodstuffs and consumer goods law ('*Lebensmittel- und Bedarfsgegenständegesetz*' or 'LMBG') § 17 (1) (Nr.1).

The Trial Court ruled against [buyer] in accordance with [seller's] petition. On appeal, buyer claimed, as a precaution and with offer of proof, that the cadmium content of the mussels was even higher than 1 mg/kg. The Court of Appeals (*Oberlandesgericht*) dismissed [buyer's] appeal. In the appeal to this Court, [buyer] continues to move for a dismissal, whereas [seller] pleads for a dismissal of the appeal.

[Judgment]

The appeal is unsuccessful.

I. The Court of Appeals has explained:

The U.N. Convention on Contracts for the International Sale of Goods dated April 11, 1980 (CISG) applies to the legal relationship between the parties. According to CISG Art 53, [seller] is entitled to the purchase price. [Buyer] can only declare the contract avoided pursuant to CISG Art 49(1)(a) in case of a fundamental breach of contract by seller. It is true that a delivery of goods that do not conform with the contract can be a fundamental breach of contract within the meaning of CISG Art 25; in case of a lack of express agreement, CISG Art 35(2) governs the question whether the goods conform with the contract. The question whether only goods of average quality are suitable for ordinary use (CISG Art 35(2)(a)) or whether it is sufficient that the goods are 'marketable' may be left open. The delivered mussels are not of inferior quality even if their cadmium content exceeds the examination results known so far. The reason for this is that the standard for cadmium content in fish, in contrast to the standard for meat, does not have a legally binding character but only an administratively guiding character. Even if the standard is exceeded by more than 100%, one cannot assume that the food is no longer suitable for consumption, because mussels, contrary to basic food, are usually not consumed in large quantities within a short period of time and, therefore, even 'peaks of contamination' are not harmful to one's health. That is why it is no longer relevant whether the public law provisions of those countries, to which an export was possible at the time of conclusion of the contract, have no influence on the conformity of the goods with the contract according to CISG Art 35(2)(a).

The fact that the standard was exceeded is similarly not relevant to the elements of CISG Art 35(2)(b) (fitness for a particular purpose). There is no evidence that the parties implicitly agreed to comply with the ZEBS-standards. Even if [seller] knew that [buyer] wanted to market the goods in Germany, one cannot make such an assumption, especially since the standards do not have legal character.

The demand to declare the contract avoided is also not legally founded based on [buyer's] allegation that the goods were not packaged properly. [Buyer's] pleadings in this respect are not substantiated and can, therefore, not be accepted. In any event, the statement to declare the contract avoided is statute-barred by CISG Art 49(2). This is so because on March 3, 1992, Defendant (buyer) gave notice for the first time that the packaging of the goods delivered in the beginning of January did not conform with the contract; therefore, she did not give notice within a reasonably short time.

II. These elaborations hold up against a legal re-examination with respect to the result.

1. The application of the CISG provisions to the contract between the parties is expressly no longer questioned and is also correct (CISG Art 1(1) (a)). The prerequisite to [buyer's] right to declare the contract avoided pursuant to CISG Art 49(1)(a) due to the cadmium contamination of the delivered mussels is, therefore, a fundamental breach of contract by [seller] within the meaning of CISG Art 25. This is the case when the purchaser essentially does not receive what he could have expected under the contract, and can be caused by a delivery of goods that do not conform with the contract. Not even non-conformity with the contract within the meaning of CISG Art 35 can, however, be determined.

a) In this respect, an agreement between the parties is primarily relevant (CISG Art 35(1)). The Court of Appeals did not even find an implied agreement as to the consideration of the ZEBS-standards. [Buyer] did not argue against this finding, and it is not legally objectionable. The mere fact that the mussels should be delivered to the storage facility in G.G. does not necessarily constitute an agreement regarding the resalability of the goods, especially in Germany, and it definitely does not constitute an agreement regarding the compliance with certain public law provisions on which the resalability may depend.

b) Where the parties have not agreed on anything, the goods do not conform with the contract if they are unsuitable for the ordinary use or for a specific purpose expressly or impliedly made known to the seller (CISG Art 35(2)(a) and (b)). The cadmium contamination of the mussels, that has been reported or, above that, alleged by [buyer], does not allow us to assume that the goods, under this rule, do not conform with the contract.

aa) In the examination of whether the goods were suitable for ordinary use, the Court of Appeals rightly left open the question—controversial in the legal literature—whether this requires generic goods of average quality or whether merely 'marketable' goods are sufficient. Even if on appeal, goods of average quality were found to be required, [buyer] has still not argued that the delivered mussels contain a higher cadmium contamination than New Zealand mussels of average quality. It is true that, according to the report from the examination laboratory of Dr. B., submitted by [buyer] to the trial court, and the contents of which is thereby alleged, 'there are also other imported New Zealand mussels on the market … that do not show a comparable cadmium contamination.' It does not follow, however, that average New Zealand mussels on the market contain a smaller amount of cadmium than the mussels delivered to [buyer].

The appeal wrongly requests that [seller] submit a statement that New Zealand mussels usually have such a high cadmium contamination. After taking delivery without giving notice of the lack of conformity, the buyer must allege and prove that the goods do not conform with the contract and the seller does not have to allege and prove that they do conform with the contract. Contrary to [buyer's] contention at trial, she accepted the mussels by physically taking delivery (CISG Art 60(b)) at the place of destination in G.G., and she did not give notice of the lack of conformity of the goods at that time.

bb) Admittedly, from the point of view of salability and, therefore, resalability of the mussels and contrary to the Court of Appeals' opinion, even if twice the amount of the

ZEBS-standard is exceeded, as [buyer] alleged, this would not change anything regarding the suitability of the mussels for consumption pursuant to LMBG §17(1)(1), and, considering the report from the federal public health agency and the documented administrative practice of the state health agencies, there would be reservations, if the public law provisions of the Federal Republic of Germany were relevant. This, however, is not the case. According to the absolutely prevailing opinion in the legal literature, which this Court follows, the compliance with specialized public law provisions of the buyer's country or the country of use cannot be expected.

Some uncertainties, noticeable in the discussions in the legal literature and probably partly caused by the not very precise distinction between subsections (a) and (b) of CISG Art 35(2), do not require clarification in the evaluation of whether this question must be integrated into the examination of the ordinary use of the goods or the examination of the fitness for a particular purpose. There is, therefore, no need to finally decide whether, within the scope of CISG Art 35(2)(a), as most argue, the standards of the seller's country always have to be taken into account, so that it is not important for the purposes of subsection (a) whether the use of the goods conflicts with public law provisions of the import country. In any event, certain standards in the buyer's country can only be taken into account if they exist in the seller's country as well or if, and this should possibly be examined within the scope of CISG Art 35(2)(b), the buyer has pointed them out to the seller and, thereby, relied on and was allowed to rely on the seller's expertise or, maybe, if the relevant provisions in the anticipated export country are known or should be known to the seller due to the particular circumstances of the case. None of these possibilities can be assumed in this case:

aaa) [Buyer], who bears the burden of proof, did not allege that there are any Swiss public law provisions concerning the contamination of mussels with toxic metals. The appeal similarly does not mention anything in this respect.

bbb) The agreement regarding the place of delivery and place of destination is in itself, even if it could be viewed as an indication by [buyer] of the anticipated marketing in Germany, neither under subsection (a) nor under subsection (b) of CISG 35(2) sufficient to judge whether the mussels conform with the contract pursuant to certain cadmium standards used in Germany. Decisive is that a foreign seller can simply not be required to know the not easily determinable public law provisions and/or administrative practices of the country to which he exports, and that the purchaser, therefore, cannot rationally rely upon such knowledge of the seller, but rather, the buyer can be expected to have such expert knowledge of the conditions in his own country or in the place of destination, as determined by him, and, therefore, he can be expected to inform the seller accordingly. This applies even more in a case like this, where, as the reply to the appeal rightly points out, there are no statutes regulating the permissible cadmium contamination and where, instead, the public health agencies apply the provisions, that are only valid as to the meat trade, 'analogously' and, seemingly, not uniformly in all the German *Länder* (federal states) to the exceeding of standards in the fish and mussels trade and where the legal bases for measures of the administrative authorities do not seem completely certain.

ccc) This Court need not decide whether the situation changes if the seller knows the public law provisions in the country of destination or if the purchaser can assume that the seller knows these provisions because, for instance, he has a branch in that country, because he has already had a business connection with the buyer for some time, because he often exports into the buyer's country or because he has promoted his products in that country. [Buyer] did not allege any such facts.

ddd) Finally, the appeal argues unsuccessfully that the mussels could not be sold due to the 'official seizure' and were, therefore, not 'tradable.' There is no need to go into great detail with respect to the question whether [buyer] has even alleged a seizure of the goods and whether she could have reasonably and with a chance of success attacked such a measure. In any event, a seizure would have been based on German public law provisions which, as set forth above, cannot be applied in order to determine whether the goods conformed with the contract (*supra*, specifically II(1)(b)(bb)(bbb)).

2. The Court of Appeals also correctly denied the [buyer's] right to declare the contract avoided because of the improper packaging of the goods.

[...]

Questions

Q 35-10

(a) Which party's public law provisions was the court relying on in C 35-5 to determine whether there was a breach of contract?
(b) Why do you think this was the case?
(c) What are the exceptions?

Q 35-11

The court did not take a position as to whether Article 35(2)(a) or Article 35(2)(b) CISG applies to public law provisions. Discuss this question.

C 35-6

RJ & AM Smallmon v Transport Sales Ltd,
High Court of New Zealand, 30 July 2010,
CISG-online 2113[120]

[Facts]

[1] [The buyers] carry on a road transport and earthmoving business in Queensland, Australia. They purchased four trucks to use in their business from a New Zealand company, [the seller].

[...]

[7] Before a vehicle can be driven on the road in Queensland it must be registered, and in order to be registered it must meet a number of requirements. These include a requirement [that] vehicles manufactured after a certain date [...] must be fitted with a compliance plate.

[...]

---

[120] Translation taken from CISG Pace (citations omitted).

[9] As for the compliance plate, this is a metal tag attached to the vehicle at the time of manufacture. Essentially, it is a certificate that the vehicle was manufactured to Australian Design Rules [ADR].

[...]

[11] In April 2006, [the buyer] saw a prominent advertisement in the Australian edition of a trade magazine, advertising trucks for sale. The advertisement had been placed by [the seller] [...]. It showed a photograph of a truck and gave [the seller's] contact details, stating:

Late model 8x4 cab & chassis available. Some on Spring some on Airbag. Most have Alloys and Med km. Prices available ex New Zealand or Landed at Brisbane, Melbourne or Sydney. These trucks are good buying!!!!!!!

Dealer inquiry welcome.

Phone Grant and discuss your requirements.

[12] At the time, the [buyers] were looking to upgrade their existing fleet. [...]

[13] [The buyer] duly contacted [the seller] in New Zealand.

[...]

[19] [The buyer] duly met with [the seller] at a truck yard in Auckland. [...]

[20] [The buyers] [...] inspected the trucks [...]. During the course of their inspection, the [buyers] noted black plates screwed on the inside door of the trucks, which they [mistakenly] assumed were the compliance plates because they were in the same place where in their experience compliance plates are normally located. [In fact the compliance plates were missing.]

[...]

[23] [...] [The seller] told [the buyers] he could put them in touch with Australian contractors who had brought in the other trucks he had sold to Australians. One was a customs broker, a Mr Tucker, and the other was Mr Walsh who [was an ADR compliance engineer].

[...]

[25] At the conclusion of the meeting, the [buyers] verbally agreed to purchase four trucks for the sum of $72,000 per truck, with a deposit of 10 per cent payable immediately and the balance to be paid before the trucks left New Zealand. [The seller] was to arrange and pay for the cleaning of the trucks and the shipping.

[...]

[32] The day after the meeting with [the seller] at the truck yard, the [buyers] paid the 10 per cent deposit.

[33] [The buyers] received an invoice for the balance of $259,220 on 31 August 2006, and paid it on 18 September 2006.

[...]

[36] The trucks left New Zealand on 29 September 2006.

[37] They arrived in Brisbane on 2 October 2006.

[...]

[43] On 20 October 2006, [the buyer] went to register the first of the trucks at Queensland Transport. However, much to her dismay, she was informed that she was not able to register the truck because it did not have compliance plates attached [...].

[58] The [buyers] say that had they known the trucks were not capable of being fully registered, they would never have purchased them. [...] They consider the trucks worthless and are seeking recovery of the full purchase price.

[...]

[Judgment]

[...]

[80] Article 35(2)(a) requires that the goods be fit for the purposes for which they are ordinarily used.

[81] Trucks are ordinarily used for carting goods on the road. These trucks were mechanically capable of being driven on the road. However, the [buyers] contend that because the trucks were not registrable at the point of sale, and never could be fully registered, they could not be driven and were therefore not fit for the ordinary purpose.

[82] The issue of whether conformity with Article 35(2)(a) [CISG] can be determined by reference to regulatory requirements prevailing in the buyer's jurisdiction has been considered in a number of overseas decisions and articles: for example, the 'New Zealand mussels case' (*Bundesgerichtshof* (German Supreme Court), 8 March 1995, VIII ZR 159/94), the 'Italian Cheese Case' (Court of Appeal, Grenoble, 13 September 1995, 93/4126) and *Medical Marketing v Internazionale Medico Scientifica* (Federal District Court, Louisiana, 17 May 1999, 99-0380). See also commentary on Article 35(2)(a) in P Schlechtriem & I Schwenzer Commentary on the UN Convention on the International Sale of Goods (2nd ed, OUP, 2005) at 418 and P Schlechtriem & P Butler UN Law on International Sales (Springer, 2009) at [139].

[83] The following principles can be distilled from these authorities: [...] As a general rule, the seller is not responsible for compliance with the regulatory provisions or standards of the importing country even if he or she knows the destination of the goods unless:

a. The same regulations exist in the seller's country.
b. The buyer drew the seller's attention to the regulatory provisions and relied on the seller's expertise.
c. The seller knew or should have known of the requirements because of special circumstances.

Special circumstances may include:

i.   The fact the seller has maintained a branch in the importing country.
ii. The existence of a long-standing connection between the parties.
iii. The fact the seller has often exported into the buyer's country.
iv. The fact the seller has promoted its products in the buyer's country.

[...]

[93] It follows that if the [buyers] are to succeed in establishing a breach of Article 35(2)(a) [CISG], it must be on the grounds that [the seller] ought to have known because of special circumstances.

[94] What is alleged to amount to special circumstances are the facts that [the seller] advertised in Australia and that [the seller] had exported trucks previously into Australia. The evidence established that prior to the transaction [in dispute], [the seller] had exported seven Volvo trucks into Australia.

[95] As the authorities make clear, these are circumstances capable of amounting to special circumstances.

[96] However, in my view, they are outweighed by two other considerations. The first is the terms of the advertisement which stated 'landed' at Brisbane. The second is that [the seller] expressly recommended Australian contractors who would be able to assist the [the buyers] with importation and ADR compliance. He was thereby delineating the parties' respective responsibilities, as well as delineating his own field of expertise and knowledge, and in my view in those circumstances it would be wrong to say that [the seller] ought to have known.

[97] The same consideration also applies to Article 35(2)(b) [CISG]:

[...]

[98] The [buyers] made known they wanted to use the trucks in Australia and therefore 'use in Australia' could be said to be a particular purpose.

[99] However, in my view, the circumstances show it was unreasonable for the [buyers] to rely on [the seller's] skill and judgment. The [buyers] were experienced transport operators. They were in a much better position to know the registration requirements of their own country than [the seller]. The fact the trucks did not have compliance plates was not hidden from them, but was there to be seen. As experienced transport operators, they could be expected to be able to identify a compliance plate. [...]

[100] In those circumstances, any reliance placed on [the seller's] expertise or knowledge [...] about the regulatory requirements in Australia would not in my view be reasonable.

[...]

[117] For the reasons already traversed, [...] the [...] claims made by the [buyers] are dismissed.

[...]

Question

Q 35-12

(a) What were the special circumstances which prima facie justified an exception of the general rule that the seller is not obliged to deliver goods in compliance with regulatory provisions or standards of the importing country that the court applied at hand?
(b) What were the considerations the court found to outweigh these special circumstances?
(c) How could these considerations be abstracted from the current case and be described in a more general way?

C 35-7

Bundesgerichtshof (Germany),
2 March 2005,
CISG-online 999[121]

[Facts]

[Seller's assignee] seeks payment of the purchase price for various meat deliveries based on the assigned rights of the Belgian wholesale meat distributor [Seller].

In April 1999, [Buyer] ordered a larger amount of pork from [Seller]. The goods were to be delivered directly from the [Buyer] to the [Buyer]'s customer, H. in K ..., and from there, further distributed to a trading company in Bosnia-Herzegovina/Republic of Srpska. The delivery was made in partial amounts on 15 April, 27 April and 7 May 1999. [Seller] issued invoices to [Buyer] for the above deliveries for Deutsche Mark [DM] 49,106.20, DM 29,959.80 and DM 49,146.75 respectively, referencing the delivery dates, and the invoices were payable at the latest on 25 June 1999, and were accompanied by so-called certificates of fitness for consumption. The goods arrived in Bosnia-Herzegovina at the latest on 4 June 1999. [Buyer] paid DM 35,000 towards the total amount due of DM 128,212.75. [Seller] assigned its claim to the remaining amount of DM 93,212.75 (Euro 47,658.92) to [Seller's assignee].

Starting in June 1999, the suspicion arose in Belgium and Germany that the meat produced in Belgium was contaminated with dioxin. As a result, in Germany, an ordinance for the protection of consumers from Belgian pork was issued (effective 11 June 1999) in which the meat was declared to be unmarketable, insofar as no certificate was presented declaring the meat to be free of contaminants. In this regard, the European Union issued an ordinance about the necessity of certificates of fitness for consumption, confirming dioxin-free goods. Finally, on 28 July 1999, identical ministry ordinances were issued in Belgium about the confiscation of fresh meat and meat products from beef and pork that, among other things, also contained provisions regarding meat that had already been exported abroad at that point in time.

[Seller's assignee] demands payment of the remaining amount. [Buyer] claims that the purchased pork was placed in a customs storage facility, and a confirmation that the meat was free of dioxin was demanded for customs clearance in Bosnia-Herzegovina at the end of June 1999. On 1 July 1999, a notification was received from Bosnia-Herzegovina that prohibited the sale of the delivered goods. After receipt of the notification of the prohibition of sale, [Buyer] requested numerous times that [Seller] produce a health clearance certificate. Since [Seller] did not provide such a certificate, the goods were finally destroyed.

The Court of First Instance gathered evidence by questioning a number of witnesses and obtaining an official notification from the German Federal Ministry of Health and then dismissed the complaint. The appeal by [Seller's assignee] against this decision was rejected by the Court of Appeals. [Seller's assignee] is now prosecuting its application for relief to the full extent after the Panel found the appeal to be procedurally permissible.

---

[121] Translation taken from CISG Pace (citations omitted).

[Judgment]

[...]

It is true that a seller is generally not liable for the goods meeting the public law regulations valid in the country of consumption. In this case, however, the product itself caused the issuance of protective regulations under public law, and not only in the ultimate buyer's country (Bosnia-Herzegovina), but also throughout the entire European Union, including the country of origin, Belgium. The fact that the ordinance at issue was enacted in Belgium only very late—at the end of July 1999—is irrelevant; in any case, the prescribed comprehensive confiscation is a strong indication that dioxin contamination already existed when the disputed deliveries were made. Through the evidence gathered in the lower court proceeding, it was finally proven that [Buyer] attempted unsuccessfully to obtain from [Seller] a certificate guaranteeing the absence of dioxin in the goods.

[...]

2. As to the substance, the Court of Appeals, without expressly clarifying this, but obviously in agreement with the Court of First Instance, assumed that [Buyer] was justified in reducing the purchase price because the delivered goods did not conform with the contract (Arts 35, 36, 50 CISG).

[...]

3. b) In its conclusion, the Court of Appeals correctly assumed that the pork delivered by [Seller] did not conform with the contract; this applies, however, only to the deliveries made on 15 and 27 April 1999. This does not apply to the last delivery made on 7 May 1999, according to the submission by [Seller's assignee], which, in this respect, has not been controverted (compare below at 4).

According to Art 35(1) CISG, goods (only) conform with a contract if they are of the quantity, quality and description required by the contract. If the parties have not agreed otherwise, the goods only conform with the contract if they are fit for the purposes for which goods of the same description would ordinarily be used (Art 35(2)(a) CISG). In international wholesale and intermediate trade, an important part of being fit for the purposes of ordinary use is resaleability (tradeability). In the case of foodstuffs intended for human consumption, resaleability includes that the goods are unobjectionable as to health, i.e., at least not hazardous to health. Insofar as the compliance with public regulations is relevant here, the circumstances in the Seller's country are generally controlling because the Seller cannot be generally expected to know the relevant provisions in the Buyer's country or—in a case where the wholesaler sells directly to the client/consumer at the retailer's request—in the country of the ultimate consumer. The situation is only different, however, if the provisions in the Seller's and the Buyer's country are essentially the same, or if the Seller is familiar with the regulations in the Buyer's country based on certain circumstances. The provisions of the country Bosnia-Herzegovina, which were, according to the [Buyer]'s disputed allegation, the reason behind the confiscation and destruction of the entire goods, are therefore not applicable.

[...]

d) Accordingly, it was also clear for the Belgian territory, at the latest by the end of July 1999, that the meat delivered to [Buyer] by [Seller] in April 1999 was not resaleable and thus did not conform with the contract within the meaning of Art 35(1) and 35(2)(a) CISG. The characteristics that led to the confiscation and the loss of tradeability were already attached to the meat at the time the risk passed because, objectively, already at this point in time, it was clear that it originated from the dioxin contaminated inventory. The fact that the suspicion became known only weeks later and led to far-reaching official precautionary measures in Germany, the European Union and finally also in Belgium, does not change the existence of the character of the goods as potentially harmful to health at the time the risk passed. Whether and to what extent the meat delivered to [Buyer] was actually contaminated with dioxin is irrelevant because the suspicion alone, which excluded the marketability, which became apparent later and which was not invalidated by the Seller, has a bearing on the resaleability and tradeability.

We also do not need to decide whether the suspicion that certain goods may be harmful to health always represents a breach of contract with regard to foodstuffs. At least if the suspicion—as in this case—has led to public measures that preclude the goods' tradeability, the goods must be viewed as not conforming with the contract for the area of wholesale and intermediate trade.

4. The situation is different with respect to the 7 May 1999 delivery. To that extent, [Seller's assignee] had already submitted in the court of first instance, without objection, that the meat had already been processed on 12 January 1998, to which the appeal correctly points, with reference to the corresponding note in the invoice of 7 May 1999. Because the delivery included a certificate, customary at the time and deemed sufficient, stating the goods were fit for human consumption, the goods were resaleable and unaffected by the precautionary measures ordered in Germany and Belgium in June and July 1999 for meat originating from animals slaughtered after 15 January 1999. If, however, as [Buyer] claims, this delivery was also confiscated and destroyed in Bosnia-Herzegovina, this was certainly not the result of a breach of contract on the side of the Seller.

5. Based on the above, [Buyer] correctly reduced the purchase price to zero for the deliveries made on 15 and 27 April 1999. On the other hand, it owes—as the Panel itself can decide because further determinations are not expected—to [Seller's assignee] the full purchase price for the delivery made on 7 May 1999 in the amount of DM 49,146.75.

[…]

Question

Q 35-13

The court discusses the question of controlling public law requirements. Is this case (C 35-7) comparable to the New Zealand mussels case (C 35-5)?

C 35-8

Medical Marketing International, Inc v Internazionale Medico Scientifica, Srl, US Dist Ct (ED LA), 17 May 1999, CISG-online 387[122]

[Facts]

[Buyer] is a Louisiana marketing corporation with its principal place of business in Baton Rouge, Louisiana. [Seller] is an Italian corporation that manufactures radiology materials with its principal place of business in Bologna, Italy. On January 25, 1993, [buyer] and [seller] entered into a Business Licensing Agreement in which [seller] granted exclusive sales rights for Giotto Mammography H.F. Units to [buyer].

In 1996, the Food and Drug Administration (FDA) seized the equipment for non-compliance with administrative procedures, and a dispute arose over who bore the obligation of ensuring that the Giotto equipment complied with the United States Governmental Safety Regulations, specifically the Good Manufacturing Practices (GMP) for Medical Device Regulations.

[...]

[Buyer] does not dispute that CISG applies to the case at hand. Under CISG, the finder of fact has a duty to regard the 'international character' of the Convention and to promote uniformity in its application. CISG Article 7. The Convention also provides that in an international contract for goods, goods conform to the contract if they are fit for the purpose for which goods of the same description would ordinarily be used or are fit for any particular purpose expressly or impliedly made known to the seller and relied upon by the buyer. CISG Article 35(2).

[Judgment]

[...]

[Seller] argued that CISG did not require that it furnish [buyer] with equipment that complied with the United States GMP regulations. To support this proposition, [seller] cited a German Supreme Court case, which held that under CISG Article 35, a seller is generally not obligated to supply goods that conform to public laws and regulations enforced at the buyer's place of business. In that case, the court held that this general rule carries with it exceptions in three limited circumstances: (1) if the public laws and regulations of the buyer's state are identical to those enforced in the seller's state; (2) if the buyer informed the seller about those regulations; or (3) if due to 'special circumstances,' such as the existence of a seller's branch office in the buyer's state, the seller knew or should have known about the regulations at issue.

---

[122] Citations omitted.

The arbitration panel decided that under the third exception, the general rule did not apply to this case. The arbitrators held that [seller] was, or should have been, aware of the GMP regulations prior to entering into the 1993 agreement, and explained their reasoning at length. [...]

Question

Q 35-14

On what basis was it argued in the *Medical Marketing* case (C 35-8) that the goods had to conform to public laws at the buyer's place of business?

B.   Article 35(2)(b) CISG—'Fitness for a Particular Purpose'

Article 35(2)(b) CISG requires that the goods be fit for 'any particular purpose expressly or impliedly made known to the seller at the time of the conclusion of the contract'. The common law systems contain comparable provisions (see above).

The relevant Section of the UCC (§ 2-315) introduces a concept that is worthy of discussion in respect of its counterpart in Article 35(2)(b) CISG. The UCC makes reference to the seller having 'reason to know'. The comparative standard of knowledge is expressed in the CISG as 'expressly or impliedly made known to the seller', which closely equates with the wording of Section 14(3)(a) SGA 1979 ('expressly or by implication, makes known'). Under these three approaches, therefore, it would seem that no problems are posed when the seller has express knowledge of the particular purpose/s. Problems arise only with respect to implicit knowledge.

Questions

Q 35-15

(a)   In a comparison of all three provisions (Art 35(2)(b) CISG, § 2-315 UCC and Sec 14(3) SGA), which condition/s for a finding of fitness for particular purpose is/are common to all of them?
(b)   How do they differ?

Q 35-16

In this respect, where the seller did not know of the particular purposes for the goods, but should in fact reasonably have known, can it still be held liable under the CISG?

C 35-9

Landgericht München (Germany),
27 February 2002,
CISG-online 654[123]

[Short summary of the seller's claim and buyer's counterclaim]

The parties involved in these proceedings are in dispute about the execution and performance of an international sales contract. The [seller] asks for payment of the purchase price; [buyer 2] requests restitution of the sales contract, after she had declared the avoidance of the contract in question: she asks for return of her pre-payment under the sales contract against return of the goods delivered and received.

[Identification of the parties]

The [seller], a limited liability company under Italian law, carries on business as reputable and respectable interior decorator. [Buyer 1] is an international car rental agency; [buyer 2] is one of her subsidiaries.

[Facts]

During late summer in 1998, the [seller] was developing a metallic, sphere cantilever for a video screen in accordance with Ms. ____'s request (Ms. ____ is [buyer 1]'s representative with general authority [*Prokurist*] and [buyer 2]'s managing director). The cantilever [hereinafter referred to as 'Globe'], when assembled into a smaller or respectively larger frame, was supposed to rotate around its own centre like a ventilator. The [seller] produced a prototype of such a Globe, presented it at [buyer 1 and 2]'s office in Munich on 30 October 1998 and left it behind. [Buyer 1] and [buyer 2] were therefore in the position to try and test this prototype of the Globes. Concurrently, the [seller] made [buyer 2] an offer to produce, deliver and sell these Globes. The offer encompassed the prospective purchase price to be staggered so that it should reflect the actual amount of Globes being delivered. On 15 December 1998, [buyer 1] ordered at first 20 large Globes at Italian Lira [*Lire*] 4,500,000.—as well as 15 small Globes at *Lire* 3,800,000. [Buyer 2] extended that offer to 60 Globes of each size on 18 March 1999. The [seller] delivered the overall amount of 119 Globes, namely:

(i)   19 large Globes on 27 March 1999;
(ii)   39 small Globes on 21 April 1999;
(iii)   40 large Globes on 7 October 1999; and
(iv)   21 small Globes on 23 November 1999.

[...]

[Buyer 1 and buyer 2's allegations of non-compliance of the goods]

[Buyer 1] complained about technical problems after the first deliveries of the Globes on 18 May 1999, 2 June 1999, 16 September 1999, 30 June 1999, 13 July 1999 and 23 July 1999 by fax. She asserted that the Globes did not entirely sway from one side to the other side, or in fact did not move at all after the lapse of just a few days. In [buyer 1]'s letter of 18 May 1999, she additionally alleged that the Globes were flawed due to construction failures. [...]

---

[123] Translation taken from CISG Pace (citations omitted).

[Seller's counter-arguments as to the lack of compliance of the goods]

The [seller] brought before the Court that the delivered Globes were not defective. The examination of one rejected Globe in ____ led to the result that it operated absolutely fine without any reported malfunction. Consequently, [buyer 1 and buyer 2] had stated a lack of conformity of the good truly without substance. [...]

[Buyer 1 and buyer 2's pleading and response to the seller's claim]

They ask the Court to dismiss the [seller]'s claim.

[Buyer 1] and [buyer 2] contend the Globes were defectively constructed, that the Globes were particularly inappropriate for a continuous use and operation within a presumed minimum operational life of two years. They additionally proclaim the flawed process of developing the Globes, and that they notified the [seller] of the lack of conformity and the defects several times in their letters and via telephone. One of [buyer 1 and buyer 2]'s employees declared the avoidance of the sales contract via telephone in August 1999. This notification took place well before the delivery of the last two batches of the Globes. They assert that the delivered Globes bear only a face value of a maximum of *DM* 150,000.

[...]

[Judgment]

The [seller]'s claim is admissible but only partially founded—in an amount of *EUR* 75,273.74. [Buyer 2]'s counterclaim is admissible in fact but entirely unfounded.

[...]

The [seller]'s claim for payment shall be considered thoroughly in turn:

—[Lack of conformity of the Globes]

The delivered Globes did not comply with the provisos in the sales contract because the motor used was not appropriate and suitable for a long-term use and operation of the Globes. The [seller] had positive knowledge that [buyer 1] ordered the Globes with her intention to have them displayed as respectable exhibits in the showrooms of her branches situated in several different countries (Art 35(2)(b) CISG). For this reason, it was made crystal clear and recognizable to the [seller], that [buyer 1] might not use these expensive and sophisticated exhibits just for a relatively short advertising campaign—a few months—but sought to acquire them as a permanent part of furniture for her offices. It was implied to the sales contract that the parties agreed to a long-term—several years—operational life of the Globes, although the parties had not particularly agreed to a specific provision dealing with their intended lifetime. In the light of the high transportation costs to each of [buyer 1]'s branches—the large Globes weighed almost 290 Kg including their wrapping—the Court assumes an impliedly agreed operational lifetime of the Globes of three years on average.

—[Description of the defect of the Globes with regard to their motor]

The Court concludes from the examination and test carried out by the expert Prof. Dr. ____ that the [seller] assembled a cheap collector motor. This motor was not proper and suitable for a long-term use and operation. Further, it was impossible even to render any services with regard to the motor. [Buyer 1] intended to use the Globes oscillating. This intended use leads to a significant strain of the Globes during the shift of their rotation direction. Henceforth, the [seller] should have used electronically commutated direct or alternating current motors combined with squirrel-cage (*hamster wheel*) rotors [*Kurzschlussläufer*]. In addition, the motors should have been provided with wheels and tracks (*Kugellagerung*). The motors, assembled with the Globes and sent to the expert within their original wrapping did, however, operate without any failure and malfunction throughout 2,730 hours.

The Court assumes nonetheless a defect and lack of compliance of the Globes. During his hearing at the Court, the expert gave comprehensive evidence that all of the motors of the Globes had a maximum operational lifetime of 5,000 hours. This equals to a daily overall operating time of less than one year, since [buyer 1], as a car rental agent, keeps her salesroom open to the public for seven days per week. Even if one considers the fact, that (i) the maximum operational lifetime of the motors is merely based on the expert's guess; and (ii) thus this actual figure may vary from time to time, the motors assembled cannot suffice to the intended operational requirements and their lifetime under any circumstances. The unit encompassing the motor, gear and worm wheel is an extremely simple construction. The Court was able to learn of this fact during its formal inspection of the motors on 31 January 2002. One could also informally describe this sort of conduct as quasi-delictual. The motors seem in actual contrast to the remainder of the product, which is of a complex nature and bears a high value.

[…]

The exemption from liability contained in Art 35(2)(b) CISG also plays an important role. Under Art 35(2)(b) CISG, the seller will not be liable for a lack of conformity if the circumstances show that the buyer did not rely, or that it was unreasonable for it to rely on the seller's skill and judgment.

C 35-10

Handelsgericht Aargau (Switzerland), 5 November 2002, CISG-online 715[124]

[Facts]

[…]

2. In June 1999, P. contacted the [seller] as the agent for the [buyer], asking if the [seller] would be in the position to manufacture inflatable triumphal arches, to be used as advertising media during car racing events. On 9 June 1999, the [seller] presented a cost estimate. He offered the manufacturing and labeling of one triumphal arch, the appropriate supercharger as well as the so-called 'service expenditure' for the positioning, maintenance and taking down of one triumphal arch.

On 6 April 2000, the [buyer] confirmed the order for the manufacturing of three triumphal arches for the total price of *Sf* [Swiss francs] 127,157.50. This order confirmation included only the manufacturing and the labeling of the three arches as well as the appropriate supercharger. In addition, the [buyer] demanded that a test be carried out on the site of the Hockenheimring, at which '*inter alia*, the best possible security of the advertising medium is

---

[124] Translation taken from CISG Pace (citations omitted).

developed and shown'. This test was realized on 2 May 2000. On Friday, 26 May 2000, the [seller] delivered the three triumphal arches to the Hockenheimring site, where the [seller] set up the arches and briefed the employees of one of the companies called in by the [buyer] to position the arches and handle the supercharger. One triumphal arch was set up above the access road of the pit stop area; the other arches were set up on the green space next to the racing circuit. On Saturday, 27 May 2000, one of the arches next to the circuit collapsed. As a result, the race management center insisted that all arches be removed. In a fax of that same day, the [buyer] complained of the defects that had occurred. The [buyer] also responded by letter dated 29 May 2000, whereupon on 14 June 2000, by authorized proxy, the [seller] declared the contract suspended.

[...]

[Judgment]

[...]

3. The [buyer] asserts the defectiveness of the work delivery. The [seller] denies this; [seller] alleges perfect performance of the contract.

a) According to Art 35(1) CISG, the seller must deliver goods of the quantity, quality and description required by the contract. Unless the parties have agreed otherwise, the goods provided for a certain purpose are only considered in conformity to the contract if they are suitable for the certain purpose of which the seller has been made aware at the conclusion of the contract explicitly or otherwise, except where the circumstances show that the buyer did not rely, or that it was unreasonable for the buyer to rely, on the seller's skill and judgment (Art 35(2)(b) CISG).

b) In the case under consideration, it is clear that the purpose of the use of the goods to be manufactured or produced was known to the [seller]; namely, use as advertising media next to and across the racing track. As safety is of vital importance in this enterprise, a test was carried out at the site of the Hockenheimring on 2 May 2002. As a result, it became evident that additional safety measures needed to be taken; it was generally agreed to install a safety wire in order to avoid a breakdown of the arch that was to be set up across the racing track in case of a failure of the supercharger, as well as to raise the so-called site stamps in order to prevent sagging. The question of 'statics', respectively, 'static calculation', remained open, in fact—as far as the cost absorption as well as the realization by a German specialist on-site or a Swiss specialist was concerned. Moreover, it is not contested that the [seller] requested an offer for the optimal fixation of the arches to the ground at the S. consortium in Herisau of 5 April 2000, which the [seller] submitted to the [buyer] after the test of 2 May 2000. The additional costs according to that offer totaled *Sf* 23,798.80 per arch. The [buyer] rejected this additional charge of more than the half of what was agreed to as the price for a single arch.

Yet, all these circumstances do not have any impact on the purpose of use of the arches. In spite of the question that remains open in connection with a static calculation, the subject matter of the contract remains the supply of three triumph arches, which were supposed to be used as advertising medium next to and across the racing track. The rejection by the [buyer] of additional costs for an optimal fix does not entail either that after the conclusion of the contract the [buyer] did not trust or must not have trusted the [seller]'s experience as a specialist for such advertising media. In fact, the [buyer] might still have acted on the assumption that the [seller] would carry the analytic expertise necessary for the manufacturing and supply of arches suitable for the agreed purpose and that the [seller] would deliver arches suitable for the target use. Otherwise, the [seller] would have had to point out his missing expertise and to explicitly express his reservation concerning the applicability of the arches for the agreed purpose. It is neither asserted nor proved that the [seller] did so.

c) The D2-arch, delivered by the [seller] and set up on 26 May 2002 on a lawn next to the Hockenheimring collapsed on the morning of 27 May 2002 at the connection of the inflatable arch and the so-called 'stamp'. This occurred after the race (training and preliminary heat) had started. The arch lost air and drifted with the wind towards the racing track. The Arcor-arch, which was mounted above the access road of the pit started to vibrate because of the racing cars going through with a reduced speed of 60 km/h. As a result, the concrete elements used for the fixation of the Arcor-arch began to falter. For this reason, the race organizers demanded that all three arches be removed. Thus both a quality or manufacturing flaw as well as an insufficient stability of the arch set up above the pit access occurred. The suitability of all three arches for the agreed target use—next to and above the racing track— was not given at that point of time. Consequently, it was a case of non-compliance with the contract (defects), for which the [seller] was liable according to Art 35(2)(b) in connection with Art 36(1) CISG.

C 35-11

Schmitz-Werke GmbH & Co, Plaintiff-Appellee, v Rockland Industries, Inc; Rockland International FSC, Inc, Defendants-Appellants, US Ct App (4th Cir), 21 June 2002, CISG-online 625[125]

[Facts]

[Seller] is a Maryland corporation that manufactures drapery lining fabric. In the early to mid 1990s, [seller] manufactured a type of drapery fabric called Trevira Blackout FR (Trevira). 'Blackout' refers to the fabric's ability to block light completely. The fabric was manufactured to meet European flame resistance standards, and was intended for sale in European markets. [Seller] no longer manufactures this fabric, and claims that this is because the product did not meet its volume requirements, while [buyer] maintains that [seller] discontinued Trevira because of numerous problems with the material.

[...]

[Buyer] initially placed an order for about 200 meters. On receipt of the [seller's] fabric for testing, the sample was shipped to PMD. [Buyer] notified [seller] that there were several problems with the fabric but that in general they were satisfied with the material. After this test, [buyer] placed an initial order of 15,000 meters of Trevira, which was shipped via ocean freight in mid-August 1994. [Buyer] noted some additional problems with this initial shipment, but decided to go ahead and print the material. After the printing, additional problems with the fabric became apparent, and a [seller] representative was offered a chance to inspect the fabric. There was conflicting testimony at trial about the results of a meeting between [buyer] and [seller's] representative that followed in October of 1994, but the district

---

[125] Citations and footnotes omitted.

court credited [buyer's] version of events. According to [buyer], despite some problems with the Trevira fabric, [seller] urged [buyer] to continue printing the fabric, and claimed that the lower quality portions of the Trevira fabric could successfully be transfer printed with patterns (as opposed to being printed with solid colors). In November 1994, after this meeting, [buyer] placed another order of Trevira fabric, this time for 60,000 meters.

PMD, meanwhile, was continuing to print the original shipment of the fabric. In December 1994, PMD told [buyer] about some of the problems it observed with the fabric. In February 1995, [buyer] had WKS, another German company, inspect part of the new order that [seller] had sent as part of the November 1994 order. On March 20, 1995, WKS issued its report, which indicated that it had found some problems with the Trevira fabric. By April of 1995, the post-printing percentage of fabric that was classified as 'seconds' (lower-grade material) was between 15% and 20%.

On June 21, 1995, [buyer] contacted [seller] and indicated that they wanted to return approximately 8,000 meters of fabric, and eventually [buyer] shipped that amount back to [seller]. There were extended discussions between [seller] and [buyer] about how to settle this dispute, but eventually these discussions broke down and this suit followed.

[Judgment]

Causation

[Seller] argues that [buyer] must demonstrate both the existence and the nature of the defect in the fabric before it can recover for breach of warranty—and that to show the nature of that defect, expert testimony is required. Article 35 of the CISG governs the duty of the seller to deliver goods that conform with the contract. Article 35(2) lists various reasons goods may not conform with the contract, including goods which were expressly or impliedly warranted to be fit for a particular purpose. In response, [buyer] argues that all it need show is that the goods were unfit for the particular purpose warranted—transfer printing—and that it need not show precisely why or how the goods were unfit if it can show that the transfer printing process the goods underwent was performed competently and normally. [Seller] is correct that [buyer] did not provide any evidence at trial that would establish the exact nature of the defect in the Trevira fabric. The text of the CISG is silent on this matter. See CISG, 15 U.S.C. App., Art 35(2).

Under Maryland law, [seller] is correct that a plaintiff in a products liability case must show that the product in question is defective, even if the cause of action is for breach of an express or implied warranty. However, [seller's] resort to Maryland law does not aid its argument— there is no support in Maryland law for [seller's] claim that the plaintiff in such a case must always provide expert testimony describing the exact nature of the defect. The district court in this case did not rule that expert testimony was not required to show the nature of the problem with the Trevira fabric. Instead, the district court held that since [buyer] had submitted sufficient evidence of the competence of PMD's transfer printing process, it was proper to infer that the fabric was not suited for that process, even without direct evidence of the precise nature of the fabric's unsuitability. [Buyer] argues that since it did submit expert testimony regarding the transfer printing process, even if such testimony is required, [buyer] has satisfied its burden, and the district court's ruling in their favor is supported by the evidence. We agree with [buyer].

Under either the CISG or Maryland law, [buyer] may prevail on a claim that the fabric was unfit for the purpose for which it was expressly warranted (transfer printing) by showing that when the fabric was properly used for the purpose [seller] warranted, the results were shoddy—even if [buyer] has introduced no evidence as to just why or how the fabric was unfit. [Buyer] has shown that the fabric was defective—the fabric's defect was that it was unfit for transfer printing. [Seller] attempts to counter this argument by claiming that this improperly shifts the burden of proof. [Seller's] concerns are misplaced—[buyer] still must prove that the transfer printing process was ordinary and competently performed, and still must prove that the fabric was defective—it just permits [buyer] to do so without proving the exact nature of the defect.

There was significant evidence regarding PMD's transfer printing process presented at trial (including expert testimony), and the court's finding that the PMD printing process was ordinary and competent is not clearly erroneous. The district court found that [seller] warranted its fabric to be fit for transfer printing, that the fabric was transfer printed in a normal and competent way, and that the resulting printed fabric was unsatisfactory. This is enough to support the district court's factual finding in favor of [buyer] on the warranty claim—the fabric was not fit for the purpose for which it was warranted. The district court's findings as to defect in this respect are not clearly erroneous; nor did the district court err in law in regard thereto.

Reliance

[Seller] also argues that even if the court properly found that the Trevira fabric was not particularly well suited for transfer printing as warranted, [buyer] cannot recover on such a warranty because it did not in fact rely on [seller's] advice as required under CISG Article 35(2)(b). [Seller] is correct that Article 35(2)(b) of the CISG requires that the buyer reasonably rely on the representations of the seller before liability attaches for breach of a warranty for fitness for a particular purpose. See CISG Art 35(2)(b). The district court explicitly found that [buyer] relied on the statements of [seller's] representative that the Trevira fabric was particularly well suited for transfer printing. The court also found that [buyer] continued to print the fabric with the express consent of [seller] after it discovered and reported problems with the fabric. The district court's finding that [buyer] relied on [seller's] statements proclaiming the Trevira fabric's suitability for transfer printing is supported by the evidence and was not clearly erroneous.

[...]

Questions

Q 35-17

What was the result of the seller's implicit knowledge in the *Landgericht München* case (C 35-9)?

Q 35-18

(a)   What were the circumstances in the *Aargau* case (C 35-10) that might lead to the conclusion that the buyer did not rely on the seller's knowledge?
(b)   Do you agree with the court's reasoning?

Q 35-19

What facts must the buyer prove if it wants to rely on Article 35(2)(b) CISG?

C. Article 35(2)(c) CISG: Sale by Sample or Model

Article 35(2)(c) CISG provides that, in order to conform to the contract, goods must 'possess the qualities of goods which the seller has held out to the buyer as a sample or model'.

Question

Q 35-20

Are you aware of similar provisions under national laws?

C 35-12

Landgericht München (Germany),
27 February 2002,
CISG-online 654[126]

For a summary of the facts see C 35-9 above.

[Judgment]

[Extreme noise emission of the Globes is, however, deemed accepted by the buyers]

However, neither [buyer 1] nor [buyer 2] can contend a further defect of the Globes with regard to their extreme noise emission, although the hearing judge had the impression these emissions were very burdensome, irritating and disturbing. [Buyer 1] and [buyer 2] were in a position to test and examine a prototype of the Globes, before they actually ordered them. Notwithstanding the (assumed) knowledge of the extreme noise emission, [buyer 1] and [buyer 2] ordered the Globes. Thus, they are deemed to have accepted such an extreme noise emission as being in compliance with the provisions of their sales contract. Hence, they must have become aware of this emission, at any rate when they conducted even a relative short testing operation of the Globes (see intended statutory purpose of Art 35(2)(c) CISG).

[...]

Question

Q 35-21

What was the effect of applying Article 35(2)(c) CISG in the *Landgericht München* case (C 35-12)?

---

[126] Translation taken from CISG Pace (citations omitted).

D. Article 35(2)(d) CISG: Packaging

Article 35(2)(d) CISG includes appropriate packaging in determining the goods' conformity with the contract.

Question

Q 35-22

(a)   Which domestic sales laws also recognise a provision similar to Article 35(2)(d) CISG?
(b)   How are defects in packaging dealt with under your domestic law?

C 35-13

Cour d'appel de Grenoble (France),
13 September 1995,
CISG-online 157[127]

[Facts]

The [buyer], domiciled in Brignoud (Isère), imports Italian food products under the name Tomatopasta, for resale in France. To this end, he has business dealings with the Invernizzi Company the [seller], established in Moretta, Italy.

[...]

[Judgment]

[...]

CONSIDERING, on the lack of conformity of the delivered goods, that on 20 July 1992, the [buyer] sent a facsimile to the [seller] to notify them that the delivered Provolone cheeses were mouldy and weighed 30 kg instead of the 20 kg ordered; That, by facsimile the same day, the [seller] offered to take back the contested goods on one of its next trips to Italy, and took up the obligation to allow the [buyer] a claim. That, by facsimile of 13 July 1992, the [seller] had agreed a claim of 693 000 lira, corresponding to six cartons of Ricotta cheese which had been returned; That the total amount of these claims, in French francs, 14,312.76 FF, which according to the [buyer] the [seller] had agreed to, is not contested by SFF company;

---

[127] Translation taken from CISG Pace (citations omitted).

THAT the SFF company indicates, on one hand, that they 'correspond to the goods cited in earlier invoices, as is commonly done'; but that the SFF had produced no earlier invoice establishing such a fact; that it indicates on the other hand, that 'these claims cannot be invoked against SFF in its capacity as factor'; but that, moreover, such claims some liquid and due, by agreement between the parties, before the notification of the assignment, give rise to compensation under Article 9 paragraph 2 of the Ottawa Convention;

THAT, concerning the [buyer's] alleged claim of 8,400 FF on the grated parmesan cheese, which had not been labeled in accordance with French Law on the composition and expiry date of food products, it is clear from an exchange of correspondence of 25 November 1992 between the [buyer] and the [seller], that the latter claims an agreement that the grated parmesan be packaged in 'unmarked sachets'; But that, given the complaint of the [buyer], this agreement is not established; That it is thus appropriate to ascertain what the intent of the contracting parties was from the indications which they have been able to provide.

THAT it is indisputable, by virtue of the relations pursued by the parties for at least several months, that the [seller] knew that the parmesan sachets ordered by the [buyer] would be marketed in France; That this knowledge imposed the duty on him, according to the provision of Article 8(1) of the Vienna Convention, to interpret the order as pertaining to goods, which have to comply with the marketing regulations of the French market;

THAT in omitting to place labels on the sachets as to the composition and expiry date, the [seller] had delivered non-conforming goods in the meaning of Article 35 of the Vienna Convention which particularly regulates packaging.

[...]

Question

Q 35-23

(a) What requirements did the packaging in the case above (C 35-13) have to live up to?
(b) Compare this case with the cases on public law requirements discussed above (C 35-5 to C 35-8).

IV. Article 35(3) CISG

Article 35(3) CISG exempts the seller from liability for a lack of conformity in the goods where the buyer 'knew or could not have been unaware' of the non-conformity at the time of conclusion of the contract.

C 35-14

Tribunal Cantonal de Vaud (Switzerland),
28 October 1997,
CISG-online 328[128]

[Facts]

An Italian seller and a Swiss buyer concluded orally a contract for the sale of a second hand Caterpillar bulldozer. The parties agreed that, before delivery, the seller would substitute three defective parts of the bulldozer, which the buyer had tested at the seller's premises before the contract was concluded. The parties also agreed that an advance partial payment would be made upon the seller's issuing an invoice, and that the remainder of the price would be paid in two installments at certain dates after delivery. The buyer paid the advance partial payment two weeks after the issue of the invoice by the seller. The bulldozer was delivered with the new parts, but the buyer refused to pay the remainder of the price and brought an action against the seller claiming damages for [...] lack of conformity.

[Judgment]

As to the buyer's claim of damages for non-conformity, the Court held that the CISG has abandoned the notion of guarantee in some domestic laws, in favor of a new, common notion of non-conformity (Art 35 CISG). The Court further noted that Art 35(3) CISG provides that the seller is not liable for any lack of conformity if at the time of concluding the contract the buyer knew or could not have been unaware of the lack of conformity. In the case at hand the seller had expressly informed the buyer about the current state of the second hand bulldozer, which the buyer had even tested before making its purchase order. Except for the replacement of three specific parts, the parties had not agreed on repair of further defects before delivery. On this ground the Court concluded that the goods delivered conformed to contract specifications (Art 35(1) CISG).

The Court further held that, in any event, the buyer had lost its right to rely on a lack of conformity of the goods under Arts 38 and 39 CISG, since it had not given notice of the defects.

The seller was entitled to payment of the full purchase price, plus interest (Art 78 CISG) accruing from the due date of payment fixed by the contract.

[...]

Question

Q 35-24

Based on the analysis of the court's approach above (C 35-14), how can the buyer's state of knowledge be determined under Article 35(3) CISG?

---

[128] English abstract taken from UNILEX.

V. Burden of Proof and Evidence of Lack of Conformity

The CISG does not prescribe specific rules regarding the allocation of the burden of proof with regard to lack of conformity in goods.

The following case considers the allocation of the burden of proving lack of conformity.

C 35-15

Bundesgericht (Switzerland),
13 November 2003,
CISG-online 840[129]

[Facts]

Company *A-GmbH*, domiciled in Germany, sold a used laundry machine of the brand Seco SS 240 to Company *B & Co.* domiciled in Switzerland. This was adapted to use KWL as a substance and thus additionally required a distillation plant and a nitrogen generator. The purchase price was fixed at Deutsche Mark [DM] 55,600. The machine was delivered to the Buyer on 29 July 1996. By letter dated 26 August 1996, the Buyer gave notice that the distillation of the machine was defective and that the stainless steel (*Nieroster*) container leaked and urgently needed to be replaced.

On 29 August 1996, a representative of the Seller examined the machine in order to compile a 'findings report'. By letter dated 5 September 1996, under the heading 'UNUSABLE MACHINE DELIVERY', the Buyer communicated the following to the Seller:

'As you are aware from the letter dated 28 [sic—correct: 26] August 1996 and from various telephone conversations, the machine delivered is not usable. Your visit on 29 August 1996 with our Ms. D., together with information provided over the telephone between you and Mr. D., has shown that the machine distillation system does not work. You have confirmed that several things were forgotten when making delivery and that you are under an obligation to complete this. We are happy to list the defects for you again.
(a) The distillation control unit (floating head) is defective and the consequences of this are: the distillation does not automatically turn off and pulls air into the system, [which] in turn leads to further consequential damages.
(b) The stainless steel (*Nieroster*) container for the light ends is leaking (The consequences: flooding the ground with KWL).
(c) The condensed water is not being separated.
(d) The booster pump for the cleaner was not connected and adjusted.
(e) The impregnating pump was not delivered [...].

[...]

'To this day, we have still not received the pump.

---

[129] Translation taken from CISG Pace (citations omitted).

[...]

'Our advice from legal services has shown that we can immediately avoid the contract if these guarantee obligations are not performed within 10 days.

'We will exercise this right if there is no other way to solve the problem. We will offset the entire invoice, since the delivered machine components do not work.

[...]

'We give you 10 days in which to remedy all grievances; otherwise we shall be forced to institute legal proceedings.'

On 6 September 1996, the Seller assigned its claim for the purchase price to C, situated in Germany. On 9 September 1996, the Seller was declared insolvent.

In its letter dated 18 September 1996, the Buyer basically communicated to the Seller that it would assert a claim for damages in the amount of DM 59,600 based on the failure to repair the machine, which was to be settled within 30 days. In addition, the Buyer indicated that it would have the machines disposed of if no repairs were carried out by 30 September 1996.

With its letter dated 27 September 1996, [Seller's assignee] C requested the Buyer to pay the purchase price that had been assigned to him by 4 October 1996.

With its letter dated 19 October 1996, the Buyer sent a reminder to the Seller regarding the claim for damages and set a final 10-day payment deadline. In addition, the Buyer basically stated that, as the Seller had shown no interest in resuming possession of the machine, it would dispose of it as indicated.

On 16 April 1998, [Seller's assignee] C brought a claim against D at the Lucerne-Land Local District Court (*Amtsgericht*) for payment of the purchase price. The claim was dismissed with costs on 21 January 1999 due to D's lack of capacity to be made a Defendant (*Passivlegitimation*).

B. On 2 August 1999, [Seller's assignee] brought a claim against the Buyer at the Lucerne-City Local District Court (*Amtsgericht*) for payment of the purchase price of DM 55,600 plus interest at a rate of 4% since 30 July 1996. In addition, the [Seller's assignee] claimed damages in the amount of Swiss Francs [CHF] 12,902 plus interest at a rate of 5% since 21 January 1999.

[...]

[Judgment]

[Non-conformity was not proven]

According to the principle that a party has to prove the elements of a provision acting in its favor, a seller who demands the purchase price must prove that delivery was made in conformity with the contract and a buyer who bases a defense (e.g., for rescission of the contract or for a reduction of the price) on the lack of conformity of the goods must prove the lack of conformity. Thereby, according to the principle mentioned, both parties bear the burden of proving conformity with the contract, to the extent that they derive rights from the presence or lack of such conformity. Consequently, as there is no exception in the present case, the allocation of the burden of proof regarding the lack of conformity of the goods is to be ascertained by reference to proximity to the evidence. Following this principle, the transfer of the goods to the buyer's sphere of control is decisive. This is in accordance with the jurisprudence of the German Federal Supreme Court (*BGH*), whereby a buyer who has accepted the goods without objection has then to prove their lack of conformity. Acceptance under Art 60(d) [sic—correct: Art 60(b)] CISG means the physical assumption of the goods. In contrast thereto, the view has been supported that an acceptance of the goods without notification of lack of conformity can only be assumed after the period for examining the goods and notifying the lack of conformity has expired without having being made use of. If defects were to have been notified within this period, then the seller would be obliged to prove that these defects were not in existence at the time of the passing of the risk. However, this view does not take account of the situation that, after being accepted by the buyer, the goods are solely within his sphere of control and he is therefore in a better position to prove the existence of a lack of conformity than the seller is to prove the absence of such. Particularly during the reasonable period of time in which the buyer is to notify defects under Art 39 CISG, the seller then has no possibility to secure evidence. According thereto, it is justified that the buyer, who has accepted the goods and has obtained control over them, be required to prove the lack of conformity of the delivered goods, to the extent that he asserts rights on this basis.

5.4 It follows from the above that the [Buyer] who has accepted and taken possession of the delivered machine, must also be required to prove its lack of conformity, to the extent that he based his right to avoid the contract or reduce the purchase price on this. Therefore, in the end result, the Court of Appeal (*Obergericht*) has allocated the burden of proof in conformity with federal law. However, it is insignificant that the machine was disassembled by the [Buyer], as this act only made its own submission of evidence more difficult, and not that of the [Seller's assignee]. It is also irrelevant whether the Seller delivered diagrams, as the [Buyer] did not give timely notice of the absence of these plans and cannot, therefore, derive any rights from this from an evidentiary law perspective.

[...]

Questions

Q 35-25

(a)   In the absence of rules under the CISG, how should we decide on matters concerning the burden of proof?
(b)   Are there general principles from which we could derive an approach to burden of proof issues (see discussion on Article 7 CISG above)?
(c)   Based on these general principles, how do you think burden of proof issues should be resolved under Article 35 CISG?

Q 35-26

Compare the Swiss *Bundesgericht* case (C 35-15) with the case of the German *Bundesgerichtshof*, 8 March 1995, CISG-online 144 (detailed excerpt C 35-5). There, the court stated:

After taking delivery without giving notice of the lack of conformity, the buyer must allege and prove that the goods do not conform with the contract and the seller does not have to allege and prove that they do conform with the contract. Contrary to [buyer's] contention at trial, she accepted the mussels by physically taking delivery (CISG Art 60(b)) at the place of destination in G.G., and she did not give notice of the lack of conformity of the goods at that time.

How does this case approach the issue as to which party is to bear the burden of proof?

How the buyer can prove lack of conformity will also be significant in many cases, as goods may have been destroyed, dismantled and so on. Expert opinion may be accepted in order to establish a lack of conformity.

C 35-16

Chicago Prime Packers, Inc v Northam Food Trading Co, et al, US Dist Ct (ND IL), 21 May 2004, CISG-online 851

For a summary of the facts see C 7-1 above.

[Judgment][130]

[...]

1. Northam has failed to prove that the ribs were non-conforming at the time of transfer

To carry its burden, Northam relies primarily on the report and testimony of Dr. Maltby. As set forth above, Dr. Maltby concluded that the product he inspected arrived at Beacon in a rotten condition. However, Chicago Prime points out several problems with Northam's reliance on Dr. Maltby's conclusion. Most significantly, neither Dr. Maltby nor anyone else could confirm that the meat Dr. Maltby inspected was in fact the product that was sold to Northam by Chicago Prime, and evidence was produced at trial to suggest that they were not the same ribs. Even though the rib boxes were labeled with Brookfield establishment numbers, the evidence showed that Beacon had purchased and received other loads of ribs originating from Brookfield prior to April 25, 2001. Furthermore, some of the ribs examined by Dr. Maltby (from one of the Intact Pallets) were stacked both horizontally and vertically. Brookfield packages its loin back ribs only horizontally. Dr. Maltby had no personal knowledge of how or where the meat was stored from April 25, 2001 to May 23, 2001, and the first time any government inspector viewed the meat was on May 4, 2001. According to Dr. Maltby, loin back ribs, if kept at room temperature, could spoil in five to seven days. Surprisingly, Northam did not present any witness affiliated with Beacon to address those issues.

Chicago Prime produced evidence, through the testimony of Steve Moughler, Brian Boomsma, and USDA Inspector Scott Elliott, that the ribs delivered by Brookfield were processed and stored in acceptable conditions and temperatures from the time they were processed until they were transferred to Northam on April 24, 2001. Mr. Moughler, Brookfield's Director

---

[130] Citations omitted.

of Quality Assurance, testified that the ribs were appropriately processed and maintained in acceptable temperatures while at Brookfield; and no other meat products that were processed and stored at the same time and under the same conditions as the ribs were found to be spoiled or objectionable. Furthermore, Inspector Elliott, who was assigned to the Brookfield facility from October 2000 through July 2001, testified that, during the relevant time period, he did not notice any 'bad meat.' Finally, Mr. Boomsma, President of Dutch Farms, which owns B & B, testified that, based on a review of the temperature records of B & B, 'we did what we were supposed to do' from the time the ribs were received by B & B and picked up by Brown Brother's.

Northam attempts to discredit the testimony of Mr. Moughler and Mr. Boomsma by pointing out deficiencies in the record keeping of Brookfield and B & B during the relevant time period. But, even if the records are incomplete, there is nothing in the evidence demonstrating that Brookfield, B & B or Fulton did anything improper with respect to the ribs or that the ribs were spoiled prior to being transferred to Northam. Northam argues that Chicago Prime has 'utterly failed to establish that the ribs were damaged while at Beacon.' That argument ignores the fact that Northam carries the burden of proving that the ribs were non-conforming at the time of receipt.

Notwithstanding Dr. Maltby's testimony, Northam has failed to carry its burden of demonstrating that the ribs that are the subject of this lawsuit were spoiled at the time Brown Brother's took possession of them on April 24, 2001. In addition, even if the ribs were spoiled at the time of transfer, Northam has failed to prove that it examined the ribs, or caused them to be examined, within as short a period as is practicable under the circumstances, or that it rejected or revoked its acceptance of the ribs within a reasonable time after it discovered or should have discovered the alleged non-conformity.

[…]

Question

Q 35-27

How could the buyer have proven the non-conformity in this case (C 35-16)?

VI. Concurring Remedies

Under most domestic legal systems the buyer may alternatively rely on other remedies, especially remedies arising from tort law such as negligence or misrepresentation. Whether the buyer may rely on these concurring remedies in case of non-conformity of the goods in a CISG contract is still an open question.

C 35-17

Electrocraft Arkansas, Inc v Super Electric Motors, Ltd et al, US Dist Ct (AR), 23 December 2009, CISG-online 2045

[Facts]

Plaintiff buyer purchases electric motors from defendant seller, which he supplies to manufacturers of refrigerators. In 2008, the buyer began to receive notices from its customers asserting that the motors purchased from the seller were failing at an unacceptable rate. The failures turned out to result from manufacturing defects and were confirmed to be incurable. Consequently, the buyer took back the defective motors rendering himself incapable of fulfilling its contractual obligations. The buyer claims that the seller although confirming the motors' defectiveness denied to cure the situation, to refund for paid invoices, or to void the unpaid invoices but instead demanded payment for the motors that were delivered. It alleges that the seller has caused it damage by way of the loss of the existing customers as it was forced to pay significant amounts to resolve customer claims and to remedy customer complaints, as well as damage to its business reputation. It therefore files, amongst others, a breach of warranty and a negligence/strict liability claim against the seller.

[Judgment][131]

[...]

Whether [the buyer's] negligence/strict liability claim [...] falls within the scope of the CISG and is preempted presents a more difficult question given the relationship of tort and contract and respective remedies. [...] Commentators differ on the preemptive effect of the CISG on tort remedies. For example, one pair of commentators argue that '[i]f one seeks to achieve the greatest level of uniformity, it cannot be left to the individual states to apply their domestic laws, whether contractual or based on tort' and that the need to promote uniformity as it is laid down in CISG Article 7(1) thus requires that 'the CISG displaces any domestic rules if the facts that invoke such rules are the same that invoke the Convention.' 'In other words, wherever concurring domestic remedies are only concerned with the nonconformity of the goods—such as negligence in delivering non-conforming goods [...]—such remedies must be pre-empted by the CISG'. *Id.*

Another commentator argues that contractual and delictual remedies have coexisted in many jurisdictions for centuries, and a given State's ratification of the sales Convention does not imply its intention to merge contract with tort [...].

Despite differing viewpoints concerning the preemptive effect of the CISG on tort remedies, there is agreement that concurring state contractual claims are preempted by the CISG. Thus, a tort that is in essence a contract claim and does not involve interests existing independently of contractual obligations [...] will fall within the scope of the CISG regardless of the label given in the claim and therefore not require a determination concerning the preemptive effect of the CISG on tort remedies. The question for this Court, then, is whether [the buyer's]

---

[131] Citations omitted.

negligence/strict liability claim is, as argued by [the seller] 'actually … a breach-of-contract claim in masquerade.'

[…] '[W]hether an action is based on contract or tort depends on the right sued upon, not the form of the pleading or relief demanded.'. 'If based on breach of promise it is contractual; if based on breach of a non-contractual duty it is tortious.' The purpose of the law of contract is to see that promises are performed, whereas the law of torts provides redress for various injuries. Owing to that distinction, the measure of damages in contract cases differs from that in tort cases. In tort cases, the purposes of the law is to compensate the plaintiff for the injury inflicted even though it may have been unexpected, but in contract cases the special damages must have been in contemplation of the parties when the agreement was made.

The Court has considered the matter and determines that [the buyer's] negligence/strict liability claim is based on contract. [The buyer] 'concedes that its breach of contract and warranty claims are rooted in the CISG,' and 'it further concedes that its negligence [and, necessarily, strict liability […] claim— is based on the same factual allegations: that [the seller] had a duty to provide conforming goods to [the buyer], it failed to do so and such failure caused [the buyer] to sustain damages.' But these are not allegations of wrongdoing that are extra-contractual or otherwise amount to a breach of duty distinct from or in addition to the breach of contract claim at issue in this action. Rather, the obligation of the seller to deliver goods conforming to the contract and the interests of the buyer to use, consume, or to resell the goods purchased, and therefore to receive them conforming to the contract, as alleged by [the buyer], are economic interests that are basically contractual and regulated by the CISG and its rules and remedies for international sales. In addition, [the buyer] seeks identical damages for its negligence/strict liability claim as it seeks for its breach of contract and warranty claims. It is clear, then, that [the buyer's] negligence/strict liability claim is based on breach of contract, not breach of a non-contractual duty, and [the buyer's] negligence/strict liability claim […] is thus preempted by and subsumed within the CISG.

[…]

Question

Q 35-28

(a) Why is it essential that the CISG pre-empts concurring domestic remedies?
(b) What are the purposes of the law of contract and the law of torts?
(c) How do you determine whether a claim is of tortious or contractual nature?

Article 36 CISG

(1) The seller is liable in accordance with the contract and this Convention for any lack of conformity which exists at the time when the risk passes to the buyer, even though the lack of conformity becomes apparent only after that time.
(2) The seller is also liable for any lack of conformity which occurs after the time indicated in the preceding paragraph and which is due to a breach of any of his obligations, including a breach of any guarantee that for a period of time the goods will remain fit for their ordinary purpose or for some particular purpose or will retain specified qualities or characteristics.

I. Overview

A. Content and Purpose of Article 36 CISG

Article 36 CISG deals with the time at which a lack of conformity must have existed in order for the seller to be held responsible for it. Paragraph (1) reiterates the general rule that a seller is liable for any lack of conformity existing at the time that the risk in the goods passes to the buyer. For more detail of the passing of risk issue, refer to the discussion under Chapter IV of the CISG below. Paragraph (2) restates the rule present in most domestic legal systems that the seller is also liable for any lack of conformity subsequently appearing due to a breach of the seller's obligations, including of a guarantee given to the buyer.

Most case law on this area only discusses Article 36 CISG in the periphery and therefore, reference should be made to case law on Articles 35, 38 and 39 CISG. Again, under this provision, scholarly opinion is divided as to whether the allocation of the burden of proof should be settled by reference to the domestic law applicable under the rules of private international law, or whether the general principle of the party who asserts a fact bears the burden of proving its existence applies.

B. Domestic Laws

With respect to Article 36(1) CISG, most domestic legal systems are in congruence with the approach under the CISG.

§ 434(1) BGB:[132]

> The thing is free from material defects if, upon the passing of the risk, the thing has the agreed quality. [...]

Article 36(2) CISG makes the seller liable for a lack of conformity occurring after the passing of risk, provided that the lack of conformity is in breach of one of the seller's obligations, including a guarantee. This paragraph is also a formulation of the principle often referred in domestic legal systems as the 'durability rule', whereby the goods are warranted as remaining fit for the contractually-agreed purpose for a certain period of time after the risk has passed. However, the approach can be differentiated according to different countries.

II. Operation of Article 36 CISG

C 36-1

Bundesgerichtshof (Germany), 2 March 2005, CISG-online 999[133]

For a summary of the facts see C 35-7 above.

[Judgment]

[...]

c) At the decisive point in time of the passing of the risk—here: at the time of the delivery of the goods at the Seller's Belgian domicile to the first forwarding agent (Art 67, first sentence CISG) in April 1999—there was neither the suspicion of a harmful dioxin contamination of the pork, nor—more importantly—had the relevant ordinances yet been enacted in Belgium, Germany and the EU. This circumstance, however, does not contradict the goods' lack of conformity with the contract as assumed by the lower courts; that is so because the non-conformity is already given, as expressly clarified in Art 36(1), last clause CISG, at the point in time the risk passes if it already exists at this point in time but only later becomes apparent, i.e., if it is a hidden defect.

Exactly this was the case here, insofar as it relates to the deliveries made on 15 and 27 April 1999; according to the invoices, the meat in question was processed and frozen on 3 March 1999. The suspicion of dioxin contamination harmful to health existed for all pigs slaughtered between 15 January and 23 July 1999. The meat was, to the extent it was still in Belgium, confiscated for precautionary reasons; it was only to be sold if, by 31 August 1999, at the latest, by tracing the origin of the goods or through lab analysis, the suspicion of dioxin con-

---

[132] Translation taken from www.gesetze-im-internet.de/englisch_bgb/.
[133] Translation taken from CISG Pace (citations omitted).

tamination was dispelled vis-à-vis the responsible control authorities. To the extent the suspicion proved to be true, meat already exported was supposed to either be destroyed abroad or shipped back to Belgium, where it would also be confiscated and destroyed. It is undisputed that the Seller failed to produce proof of the absence of dioxin as required by it.

[...]

Questions

Q 36-1

Discuss the cases in which Article 36(1) or (2) CISG could come into play.

Q 36-2

Describe and analyse the distinction between Article 36(1) and 36(2) CISG.

Q 36-3

(a)   Describe some of the usual guarantees that manufacturers give.
(b)   How does the warranty of durability under Article 35(2) CISG relate to a guarantee in the sense of Article 36(2) CISG?

Article 37 CISG

If the seller has delivered goods before the date for delivery, he may, up to that date, deliver any missing part or make up any deficiency in the quantity of the goods delivered, or deliver goods in replacement of any non-conforming goods delivered or remedy any lack of conformity in the goods delivered, provided that the exercise of this right does not cause the buyer unreasonable inconvenience or unreasonable expense. However, the buyer retains any right to claim damages as provided for in this Convention.

Article 37 CISG allows the seller to cure any lack of conformity or deficiency in the goods up until the date for delivery, provided the seller has delivered before this date. The seller's right to cure applies to all breaches of contract, that is, in contrast to Article 48 CISG, this right exists regardless of whether or not the breach of contract amounts to a fundamental breach. However, what this provision does not do is give the seller a right to cure after the date of delivery; in this respect, see Article 49(1)(a) CISG for more detail.

Questions

Q 37-1

What are the consequences of the seller's right to cure under Article 37 CISG?

Q 37-2

What are the consequences of the buyer refusing to allow the seller to remedy the defects?

Articles 38 and 39 CISG

Article 38 CISG

(1) The buyer must examine the goods, or cause them to be examined, within as short a period as is practicable in the circumstances.
(2) If the contract involves carriage of the goods, examination may be deferred until after the goods have arrived at their destination.
(3) If the goods are redirected in transit or redispatched by the buyer without a reasonable opportunity for examination by him and at the time of the conclusion of the contract the seller knew or ought to have known of the possibility of such redirection or redispatch, examination may be deferred until after the goods have arrived at the new destination.

Article 39 CISG

(1) The buyer loses the right to rely on a lack of conformity of the goods if he does not give notice to the seller specifying the nature of the lack of conformity within a reasonable time after he has discovered it or ought to have discovered it.
(2) In any event, the buyer loses the right to rely on a lack of conformity of the goods if he does not give the seller notice thereof at the latest within a period of two years from the date on which the goods were actually handed over to the buyer, unless this time-limit is inconsistent with a contractual period of guarantee.

I. Overview

A. Content and Purpose of Articles 38 and 39 CISG

Article 38 CISG sets out the buyer's obligation to examine goods delivered under a contract of sale by the seller. However, the goods delivered cannot merely sit in the buyer's storeroom until it gets around to looking at them; the obligations under Article 38 CISG are, indeed, quite onerous: the buyer must examine the goods 'within as short a period as is practicable in the circumstances'.

Article 39 CISG establishes the obligation to give notice and addresses the issue of the periods for giving notice in order for the buyer to be able to rely on a lack of conformity. Article 39 CISG also makes reference to time: the buyer must give notice of any lack of conformity 'within a reasonable time'. The period for giving notice under Article 39 CISG begins to run when the buyer discovers or ought to have discovered the defect.

As the question of whether Article 38 CISG has been satisfied usually arises incidentally in the context of Article 39 CISG, these two provisions are often dealt with together, both in case law and in scholarly opinion.

B. Domestic Laws

An express, independent duty to *examine* is very rarely found in domestic legal systems. However, difficulties in interpretation arise due to differing domestic concepts of notice requirements. In many countries, there is no duty to give notice at all; in those countries that do recognise such a duty, the position is aptly summarised in the following CISG Advisory Council Opinion.

CISG Advisory Council Opinion No 2: Examination of the Goods and Notice of Non-Conformity: Articles 38 and 39:[134]

COMMENTS

1. Introduction

The provisions regarding the notice that should be given by the buyer to the seller of goods in case of their alleged lack of conformity to the contract were among the most disputed matters in the preparation of the CISG. The proper interpretation of those provisions is in turn one of the most controversial matters in its implementation since it involves both fact and law, as shown in the appendix to this opinion.

2. Domestic Legal Systems

2.1. The differences of opinion in the drafting of the notice requirement and in its interpretation arise largely out of differences in the domestic law of sales. Those laws take three different approaches to the matter:

1. The buyer must give a notice specifying the nature of the alleged lack of conformity within a short period of time after delivery of the goods. The allowable period of time may be specified, e.g., eight days, or a word such as 'immediately' may be used.
2. The buyer must give a notice of the alleged non-conformity before 'acceptance' of the goods in order to reject them, an action that normally brings with it the avoidance of the contract. However, the buyer is under no obligation to examine the goods and no notice of lack of conformity within any particular period of time need be given in order to claim damages.
3. The buyer must give a notice of the alleged lack of conformity. The notice may not need to be as specific as in the legal systems of the first group and it must be given within a period that may be described as 'a reasonable time'.

---

[134] Taken from www.cisgac.com.

2.2. Legal systems in the first group emphasise the security of the transaction for the seller. Claims of lack of conformity that are raised any significant period of time after the delivery of the goods are suspect, do not allow the seller to verify the lack of conformity as of the time of delivery and reduce the possibility that the consequences of lack of conformity can be minimised by repair or the supply of substitute goods.

2.3. Legal systems in the second group emphasise the right of the buyer to receive compensation for the seller's failure to deliver conforming goods. Depriving the buyer of all remedies because notice is not given within some specified period of time is considered to be too harsh a result. The buyer automatically has a reduced possibility of recovery if no claim for lack of conformity is filed for a significant period of time since the buyer, who has the burden of proof, would have more difficulty to substantiate that the goods were not conforming at the time of delivery. Since the buyer has the obligation to mitigate damages, any increase in damages that occur after the buyer is aware of the lack of conformity are not compensated. This group of legal systems contains a number of industrialised countries, as well as many developing countries.

2.4. Legal systems in the third group attempt to strike a balance between security of the transaction for the seller and assuring that the buyer can recover compensation for the seller's failure to deliver conforming goods. The requirement of giving notice is sometimes explained as designed to defeat commercial bad faith on the part of the buyer.

[...]

(a) Civil Law Legal Systems

Some Germanic legal systems recognise an explicit duty on the buyer to examine the goods. In Germany, this duty is, however, limited to sales between merchants. Under German law, a 'prompt' (*unverzüglich*) examination is required.

§ 377 HGB:[135]

(1) If a sale is a business transaction for both parties, then the buyer must promptly examine the goods after receipt from the seller, to the extent that this represents the ordinary business practice, and if a lack of conformity is discovered, promptly notify the seller thereof.

(2) If the buyer omits to notify, the goods are deemed to be accepted unless a lack of conformity existed which was not recognizable by an examination.

(3) If such lack of conformity subsequently becomes apparent, then the notification must take place promptly after the discovery thereof; otherwise the goods will also be deemed accepted in respect of this lack of conformity.

(4) For the assertion of rights by the buyer, the timely dispatch of the notification suffices.

(5) If the seller fraudulently concealed the lack of conformity, it cannot rely on these provisions.

In contrast, under Swiss law, an examination 'in accordance with the usual course of business'[136] is sufficient.

The PRC modelled its provisions on examination and notice on the CISG.

---

[135] Author's translation.
[136] Art 201 OR.

Art 157 PRC CL:[137]

Upon receipt of the subject matter, the buyer shall inspect it within the prescribed inspection period. Where no inspection period was prescribed, the buyer shall timely inspect the subject matter.

Art 158 PRC CL:

Where an inspection period was prescribed, the buyer shall notify the seller of any non-compliance in quantity or quality of the subject matter within such inspection period. Where the buyer delayed in notifying the seller, the quantity or quality of the subject matter is deemed to comply with the contract.

Where no inspection period was prescribed, the buyer shall notify the seller within a reasonable period, commencing on the date when the buyer discovered or should have discovered the quantity or quality non-compliance. If the buyer fails to notify within a reasonable period or fails to notify within 2 years, commencing on the date when it received the subject matter, the quantity or quality of the subject matter is deemed to comply with the contract, except that if there is a warranty period in respect of the subject matter, the warranty period applies and supersedes such two year period.

Where the seller knew or should have known the non-compliance of the subject matter, the buyer is not subject to the time limits for notification prescribed in the previous two paragraphs.

In other civil law legal systems, even if a duty to examine the goods exists, the duty is included incidentally in the provision concerning the duty to notify of any lack of conformity. The Dutch *Burgerlijk Wetboek* (Civil Code) and the new Austrian *Unternehmensgesetzbuch* (Corporate Code) follow this trend.

§ 377 UGB:[138]

(1) If the sale is a business transaction for both parties, then the buyer must give notification to the seller of defects that it detected or should have detected, in the usual course of business after delivery upon examination within a reasonable period of time.

(2) If the buyer fails to give notice, it no longer has the right to bring claims of guarantee (§§ 922 ff ABGB), of damages owing to the defects (§ 933a Abs 1 ABGB), as well as those arising from a mistake due to the defect (§§ 871 f ABGB).

(3) If such a defect subsequently becomes apparent, this defect must also be notified within a reasonable period of time; otherwise, the buyer no longer has the right to bring the claims described in subs. 2 in respect of this defect either.

(4) In order to retain its rights, it is sufficient if the buyer dispatches the notification on time; this also applies if the notification does not reach the seller.

(5) The seller cannot rely on this provision if the buyer proves that the seller deliberately or in a grossly negligent manner caused or concealed the defect, or if the defect concerned is a defect in livestock (*Viehmangel*), for which a rebuttable presumption (*Vermutungsfrist*) (§ 925 ABGB) exists.

---

[137] Translation taken from www.wipo.int/wipolex/en/text.jsp?file_id=182632.
[138] Author's translation.

Art 7:23(1) BW:[139]

> The buyer may no longer invoke the fact that what has been delivered does not conform to the contract, unless he has notified the seller thereof within a reasonable period after he has or reasonably should have discovered this. However, where the thing proves to lack a quality which according to the seller it possessed, or where the deviation pertains to facts which the seller knew or ought to know but has not communicated, the notification must take place within a reasonable period after the discovery.

(b) Anglo-American Legal Systems

Under Anglo-American law, reference is not made to an actual duty on the buyer to examine, but rather to a notification of defects to be made within a 'reasonable time', which necessarily presupposes the undertaking of an examination. Under English law, the seller is under an obligation to give the buyer time to examine the goods. However, the buyer is only required to give notice of any lack of conformity if it wishes to avoid the contract.

Sec 35 SGA:

(1)   The buyer is deemed to have accepted the goods subject to subsection (2) below—
    (a)   when he intimates to the seller that he has accepted them, or
    (b)   when the goods have been delivered to him and he does any act in relation to them which is inconsistent with the ownership of the seller.
(2)   Where goods are delivered to the buyer, and he has not previously examined them, he is not deemed to have accepted them under subsection (1) above until he has had a reasonable opportunity of examining them for the purpose—
    (a)   of ascertaining whether they are in conformity with the contract, and
    (b)   in the case of a contract for sale by sample, of comparing the bulk with the sample.
[...]
(4)   The buyer is also deemed to have accepted the goods when after the lapse of a reasonable time he retains the goods without intimating to the seller that he has rejected them.
(5)   The questions that are material in determining for the purposes of subsection (4) above whether a reasonable time has elapsed include whether the buyer has had a reasonable opportunity of examining the goods for the purpose mentioned in subsection (2) above.
[...]

Under US law, the obligation is to give timely notice of a breach of contract.

---

[139] Translation taken from *New Netherlands Civil Code*, PPC Haanappel and Ejan Mackaay (trans) (1990).

§ 2-607(3) UCC:

> Where a tender has been accepted:
> (a) the buyer must within a reasonable time after he discovers or should have discovered any breach notify the seller of breach or be barred from any remedy;
>
> [...]

Questions

Q 38/39-1

Compare the domestic solutions and their practical consequences.

Q 38/39-2

Based on a comparison of the domestic law approaches described above, can you specify which countries are referred to in each of the three approaches described in the CISG Advisory Council Opinion No 2?

C. Drafting History

Owing to the greatly divergent solutions under domestic law, the drafting of Articles 38 and 39 CISG proved very controversial. In contrast to Article 38 ULIS, which provided for the goods to be examined 'promptly', the CISG merely requires examination to take place 'within as short a period as is practicable in the circumstances'. The requirement of 'reasonable time' otherwise prevalent in the CISG was omitted from the examination requirement under Article 38 CISG due to perceived problems with perishable goods. The CISG also says nothing about the requirement of how the goods are to be examined; the requirement under ULIS that the method of examination be governed by the law of the place where the examination was to take place, was omitted.

   With regard to the duty to give notice of defects, the leading participants in the preparation of ULIS were from the Germanic systems outlined above that recognise a strict notice requirement in their domestic laws. Due to the greater diversity in the legal systems represented during the preparation of the CISG at UNCITRAL, and above all, the presence of a number of developing countries, this strict notice requirement was modified to the 'milder' form currently found in Article 39 CISG. Consequently, a compromise was reached in this respect.

   The requirement of 'prompt' notice under Article 39 ULIS was amended to 'within a reasonable time', to be determined by reference to the circumstances of the individual case. Under Article 44 CISG, the notice requirements of Article 39(1) CISG will not prevent the buyer from claiming a reduction in the price or damages except for lost profit if he has a reasonable excuse for his failure to give such notice (see discussion on Art 44 below).

II. Examination of the Goods

A. Period for Examination

The buyer's obligation to examine the goods forms the basis of his obligation to notify the seller of defects under Article 39 CISG. The time by which the buyer must have completed the examination under Article 38 CISG corresponds to the time under Article 39 CISG, by which it ought to have discovered any lack of conformity and triggers the 'reasonable time' period for giving notice of defects. Courts and tribunals have applied differing approaches concerning the nature and detail of the examination required under Article 38 CISG. In particular, the extent to which the buyer is required to undertake certain procedures in order to determine any lack of conformity has been discussed by the courts.

C 38/39-1

Oberlandesgericht Karlsruhe (Germany),
25 June 1997,
CISG-online 263[140]

[Facts]

The plaintiff [buyer] asserts a claim for damages against the defendant [seller], due to a delivery of adhesive foil covers which did not conform to the terms of the agreement. [Seller is a German firm, buyer an Austrian firm.] In March of 1995, the [buyer] ordered 7,500 square meters of foil from the [seller], for a price of 0.57 DM per square meter. The foil was supposed to be self-adhesive, and suitable for being peeled from polished premium steel sheets so that no adhesive residue would remain. The foil, which was delivered on March 28, 1995, did not meet these specifications because the acrylic adhesive which was applied was not suitable for that particular purpose.

The [buyer] inspected the foil for correct quantity and readily apparent defects, but did not conduct an experimental removal of the foil from the metal sheets. On April 20 1995, the [B. Metal and Baths Construction Corporation] [B. GmbH Company], which has a contract with the [buyer], informed the [buyer] that after removal of the foil 'the entire adhesive residue remained on the polished surface, like an adhesive film.' On April 21, 1995, the [buyer] informed the [seller] of the lack of conformity. B. GmbH Company cleaned the steel sheet surfaces at a cost of 492,240 Austrian Schillings [sA], for which they were reimbursed by the [buyer].

The parties attempted to reach an agreement. In the various conversations and written correspondence that ensued, the [seller] never mentioned that she found fault with the fact that the [buyer] had first informed her of the lack of conformity on April 21, 1995.

---

[140] Translation taken from CISG Pace (citations omitted).

The [buyer] demands compensation of 492,240 *sA* from the [seller]. She maintains that this amount was absolutely necessary for the cleaning of the metal sheets. Furthermore, the [buyer] contends that the complaint about the defective quality was made within the period prescribed by the CISG, given that the General Business Terms and Conditions established by the [seller], which indisputably provide for a deadline of complaint of eight days, did not become part of the contract. The defect only became apparent after further processing of the adhesive film.

[…]

[Judgment]

The [seller's] appeal from the decision of the Heidelberg trial court, October 2, 1996, is justified. Even though the protective foil, which was delivered by the [seller] on March 28,1995, was defective, the [buyer] is not entitled to damages due to the lack of conformity. She did not notify the [seller] of the lack of conformity within as short a period as was practicable and has thus lost her right to claim damages (Article 38 and Article 39 of the CISG).

[…]

II. The defective protective foil did not conform to the contract as required by Article 35 and Article 36 of the CISG. According to Article 38 of the CISG, the buyer 'must examine the goods, or cause them to be examined, within as short a period as is practicable in the circumstances.'

This duty to examine, which also includes a sample test, was not performed in a timely manner by the [buyer]. She lost the right to rely on a lack of conformity of the goods according to Article 39(1) of the CISG, since she did not notify the seller 'within a reasonable time after [s]he ha[d] discovered it or ought to have discovered it.' The inspection 'within as short a period as is practicable in the circumstances' should make it clear between the parties of the sales contract, whether or not the delivered goods will be accepted as conforming.

[…]

In fact, the [buyer] did not 'examine the goods within a short time.' Although she received the protective foil on March 28, 1995, her first written notice of the defect is dated April 21, 1995. On that same date, the [buyer] telephoned the [seller] and relayed that her customer, the B. GmbH Company, had discovered adhesive residue on the metal surfaces during the processing of the mounted foil. The B. GmbH Company had informed the [buyer] of this problem on April 20, 1995. This claim for lack of conformity, therefore, was made twenty-four days after the delivery of the goods.

a) Even though the time periods indicated in Article 38 and Article 39 of the CISG 'are formulated less stringently' than in Paragraph 377 HGB, and are in particular cases more flexible to administer, the buyer is obliged to examine the goods for non-conformity within a short period of time. The 'median value' for this time frame for examination according to Article 38(1) of the CISG can, even regarding durable goods, be based on a three-to-four-day time period. This figure can be corrected upward or downward as the particular case requires.

b) The extent and intensity of the examination are determined by the type of goods, packaging and the capabilities of the typical buyer. Even though the parties have had a long-standing business relationship, random tests are always required. A so-called test processing is necessary if the lack of conformity which is to be detected is only apparent after the processing.

The [buyer] did not examine the adhesive foil. Above all, she did not perform a test process or an adhesive experiment, even though she was undoubtedly in a position to do so. She could have performed the adhesion process which would have led to the discovery of any defect in the product. The supporting expert opinion which the [buyer] procured from the *österreichischen Kunststoffinstitutes* on August 21, 1995, confirms that such an adhesion test was possible: examinations performed between August 11 and August 17, 1995, resulted in 'large amounts of organic residue' on the sheet metal surfaces, and these stain formations are objectionable. It is a fact then, that the test examination, which was incumbent upon the [buyer], would have resulted in the discovery of the stains after a maximum of seven days. If the [buyer] had begun with the test process after three or four days, she would have been able to notify the [seller] of the lack of conformity within ten or eleven days at the latest. H., a technician at B. GmbH Company, who was called as a witness during the trial, confirmed this: 'We pull[ed] off the foil from one metal sheet after each charge. It revealed, in fact, that the adhesive stuck.' Thus, it is proven that a hidden defect did not exist.

2. The [buyer's] notice of the lack of conformity was too late. According to Article 39(1) of the CISG, the time limit for giving notice begins at that point in time at which the lack of conformity could have been discovered. This is at the latest ten or eleven days after the delivery; therefore on April 7th or 8th, 1995.

[...] Therefore, the complaint of April 21, 1995, is several days too late. The [buyer's] omission of the test process resulted in a failure to meet the time period for notification.

[...]

4. According to Article 44 of the CISG, and notwithstanding Article 39(1), the buyer can sue for damages if [s]he has a 'reasonable excuse' for the omission of the required notice. The [buyer] was unable to furnish such an excuse. Article 44 of the CISG relieves the buyer only from the omission or neglect of the notice requirements stated in Article 39(1) of the CISG. The buyer is not excused, however, if [s]he did not duly execute the examination required by Article 38 of the CISG: If the belated notice is caused by the fact that the buyer did not inspect the goods in the mandatory manner, [s]he cannot rely on Article 44. This is the case here. The required examination of the quantity and defects in the goods did not encompass all of the steps for inspection required by Article 38 of the CISG, which also includes a test process.

[...]

Questions

Q 38/39-3

How would you describe the approach of the *Oberlandesgericht Karlsruhe* (C 38/39-1)?

Q 38/39-4

Against what background must this decision be understood?

B. Manner of Examination

C 38/39-2

Landgericht Paderborn (Germany),
25 June 1996,
CISG-online 262[141]

[Facts]

The [seller's] claim is for payment of the purchase price. The [seller] delivered PVC plastic to the [buyer] in 1993 and in the beginning of 1994, which the [buyer] used to manufacture rods destined for *Rolladen* [roll-down shutters]. [Translator's note: *Rolladen* are a type of heavy shutters one rolls down in front of a window to block out rays of light.]

[Seller] delivered PVC granules in colors of gray, beige and white. [Seller's] invoices remain outstanding in part in the amount of 22,437.66 DM [Deutsche Mark].

The [seller] submits that the [buyer] repeatedly promised to pay the outstanding sums. In particular, [buyer's] employee A acknowledged [seller's] right to payment during a telephone conversation on 9 March 1994 and promised to send a check. Seller maintains that the [buyer] is obliged to pay him the requested amount on the basis of this acknowledgement.

The [seller] requests the Court to order the [buyer] to pay him DM 22,437.66, with 5% interest from 9 March 1994 onwards.

The [buyer] requests the Court to dismiss the claim.

The [buyer] alleges that it is not true that she had made a promise to pay the outstanding sums. [...]

[Buyer] is furthermore of the opinion that the [seller] is not entitled to payment of the purchase price, because he failed to conclusively carry out his delivery obligations.

Alternatively, the [buyer] declares a set-off against [seller's] claim with her claim for damages. [Buyer] alleges that the deliveries relating to [seller's] invoices of 5 October 1993 and 9 November 1993 concerning PVC granules in amounts of 5,295 kg and 6,496 kg in color 'blanc' [white] did not correspond to the sample agreed upon. The parties had agreed that the goods would have the same qualities as the granules of [buyer's] former supplier, Firm L. The goods delivered by [seller] did not correspond to this requirement. The [buyer] produced *Rolladen* shutter rods out of this material, which she delivered to Firm F. Firm F manufactured *Rolladen* shutters out of these rods and installed them at several building projects. The shutters manufactured from the white rods did not completely block the light. Instead, the light shimmered through in a red tone, especially when the sun was shining. The reason was that the PVC granules delivered by the [seller] had too low a titanium dioxide content.

Firm F was obliged to remove the *Rolladen* shutters at the building sites and has charged the accrued expenses to the [buyer]. Additionally, Firm F has returned non-processed rods to the [buyer] and requested reimbursement of the purchase price. [Buyer] submits that the seller is

---

[141] Translation taken from CISG Pace (citations omitted).

liable for these costs accrued by Firm F's rightful complaint and for [buyer's] additional costs resulting from acquiring new conforming goods.

[...]

The [buyer] declares a set-off against the [seller's] claim in this amount.

In the alternative, [buyer] declares that she reduces the price of the non-conforming granules 'blanc' [white] to zero under Art 50 CISG.

[...]

In any event, the [buyer] did not satisfy her obligation [under Arts 38 and 39 CISG] to examine the goods and to provide to [seller] timely notification of the non-conformity.

Additionally, the [seller] disputes the amount of damages claimed by the [buyer].

[...]

[Judgment]

[Seller's] claim for payment by [buyer] is unfounded.

[...]

However, the [buyer], according to Article (45)(1)(a) and Article 74 CISG, has a claim for damages at least in the amount of her statement of claim on the basis of [seller's] non-conforming performance of the contract. According to the Court's taking of evidence, the titanium dioxide content of the granules was below 6%, the amount which [seller] himself considers necessary. The expert had taken two samples and determined the amount of titanium dioxide, coming up with figures of 5.51% and 5.38%. The photos taken by the expert indicate that the shutters manufactured out of the granules let light through. The reason for this according to the expert was, on the one hand, that the granules delivered by the [seller] had too low a titanium dioxide content and, on the other hand, that the profile of the *Rolladen* shutters was too thin in comparison to similar products manufactured by other producers. The effective strength of the rods is in part only 1.3 mm when it should customarily be at least 1.6 mm. However, even if the rods had possessed a strength of 1.6 mm, the damage could not have been avoided, because the light shone through also in those places where the strength was 1.6 mm or more.

The Court must conclude that despite the less than customary strength of the rods, [buyer's] customers would not have issued complaints if the titanium dioxide content had been sufficient. This follows from the fact that in the course of using the granules delivered by Firm L (her former supplier), the [buyer] had not experienced this problem, as [buyer's] manager testified in the oral hearing.

Whether the insufficient strength of the rods contributed to the damage is furthermore irrelevant under the law. Contrary to German sales law, under the CISG the [seller] guarantees the conformity of the goods (Arts 35, 45(1), 74) in a way that the seller is liable for damages that the buyer suffers as a result of non-conformity of the goods. The [buyer's] damages mainly consist of compensation for her customers, caused by the [seller's] delivery of granules with an insufficient percentage of titanium dioxide. Therefore, the [seller] has to pay damages irrespective of the fact that the rods would have been less likely to have light shine through had the [buyer] manufactured them at a strength of 1.6 mm and above.

The [buyer] has not lost her right to remedies under the CISG for failure to examine the goods and notify the seller of lack of conformity of the goods in a timely manner as provided by Articles 38 and 39 of the CISG. The expert convincingly explained that the [buyer] was unable to establish without quantitative chemical analysis that the goods did not contain the correct amount of titanium dioxide. In the circumstances, such an analysis could not have been required from the [buyer] as a criteria for fulfilling her duty to examine the goods within the short period [seller] alleges.

[...]

C 38/39-3

Oberster Gerichtshof (Austria),
27 August 1999,
CISG-online 485[142]

[Facts]

In September and October of 1995, plaintiff [seller] delivered, pursuant to the order of defendant [buyer], approx. 28,000 pairs of trekking shoes made in Bulgaria directly to a Scandinavian company, which operates more than 240 retail stores. Because the initial delivery date (end of September 1995) could not be adhered to, the parties agreed on its postponement for approximately one month. The [seller] charged the various partial deliveries with partial invoice to the [buyer], whereby 13 of these invoices from the period between September 28 and October 31, 1995 were paid by the [buyer]. On December 13, 1995, the [seller] granted a credit entry for a further partial invoice dated October 31, 1995, for 3,012 pairs of trekking shoes for juveniles and took the entire partial delivery that had been charged by this invoice back after the [buyer] had given notice to the [seller] dated October 10, 1995, that it would not accept any more shoe deliveries after October 20, 1995. Two partial invoices (dated September 8 and September 18, 1995) concerning trekking shoes for adults remained unpaid.

[Judgment]

[...]

This Panel also concurs with the court of appeals' elaborations concerning the manner of the examination that must be performed by the buyer. Primarily relevant for the type of examination are the agreements between the parties. In the absence of any such agreements, the required manner of examination can be gleaned from trade usage and practices. Insofar as the court of appeals deemed—in this sense—a clarification of the question to be necessary as to whether the merely visual examination is a customary examination in the case of large quantity shoe purchases, because the expert's opinion did not give a clear answer in this respect, this Panel cannot oppose this—well founded—opinion. But should this question have to be answered in the negative, then this Panel must follow the court of appeals' opinion that a reasonable examination, which must be thorough and professional, must definitely take place. Although costly and expensive examinations are unreasonable, the buyer must, in the

---

[142] Translation taken from CISG Pace (citations omitted).

case of a large quantity shoe purchase as here, call in experts in the broadest sense (experts skilled in the shoe trade) in order to comply with its obligation to examine. By demanding such an examination procedure, the demands for an examination the buyer must perform are not carried too far. The court of appeals correctly elaborated in this connection that the defendant as the buyer must prove that the defects noticed later could not have been discovered by the required professional spot-check-like examination. The burden of proof that the notice of lack of conformity was given timely and properly rests always with the buyer.

Contrary to [buyer's] opinion, it is necessary to ascertain the arrival dates of the partial deliveries that contained defective shoes at the place of destination in Scandinavia, because in the case of partial deliveries, the buyer must examine each delivery separately.

[...]

Questions

Q 38/39-5

How does the *Landgericht Paderborn* case (C 38/39-2) determine the limits of examination?

Q 38/39-6

According to the case of the *Oberster Gerichtshof* (C 38/39-3), upon which circumstances will the scope of examination required depend?

Q 38/39-7

List all the circumstances that may be relevant in determining the buyer's duty to examine.

C 38/39-4

International Court of Commercial Arbitration Chamber of Commerce and Industry of the Russian Federation, Award No 54/1999, 24 January 2000, CISG-online 1042[143]

[Facts]

The action has been brought by a firm, registered in the USA (the buyer), against a Russian company (the seller) on the basis of the contract, which was concluded in January 1998 and which provided for the delivery of two instalments of the goods under the FCA condition

---

[143] Translation taken from CISG Pace (citations omitted).

(according to Incoterms® 1990); the railway station of dispatch—at the seller's place. The requirements with respect to the quality of the goods were fixed in the contract in the clause 'Quality of the Goods' by means of a reference to concrete Technical Conditions (TC) which are in force in Russia. The goods were to be shipped to an overseas country by means of their dispatch to an exterior Russian port indicated in the contract. The seller bore an obligation to examine, before the shipment, whether the quality of the goods was in accordance with the requirements of the TC and to provide the buyer with verifying documents of title. Under the contract, the goods were considered to be of conforming quality if they were in accordance with the documents of title. Alongside with that, the buyer was given a right to inspect the goods by a recognised neutral control organisation, of the SGS type [*Société Générale de Surveillance*], or an analogous organisation at the port of shipment or on loading of the goods.

According to the buyer, since the inspection of the first instalment of the goods turned out to be impossible at the port of shipment due to technical reasons, this inspection was performed in the country of destination of the goods. Selective examination of the instalment of the goods revealed substantial deviations from the requirements of the contract. As a result, this instalment was accepted by the ultimate consumers with a considerable reduction of its price. With respect to the first instalment, the buyer, in his statement of claim, demanded compensation of the sum of the reduction of the price which was equal to the amount unpaid by the ultimate consumers. With regard to the second instalment, the buyer demanded from the seller the reimbursement of loss in the form of loss of profit caused by the fact that the delivery of the goods of non-conforming quality in the first instalment had led to the loss of reputation of the production of the given manufacturer in the market. This had caused substantial delay in its realisation and sale under considerably lower prices.

In addition to the statement of claim, the buyer demanded the reimbursement of the loss caused by transportation of the first instalment of the goods on the territory of Russia and its storage and unloading at the exterior Russian port.

The seller objected to the buyer's claims and asked for a dismissal of the claim. In the seller's opinion, the buyer having violated the rules of the inspection of the quality of the goods did not prove the fact of the goods being of non-conforming quality. Moreover, the buyer did not bring forward the claim within the time limit fixed by the contract. The seller also contested the documents produced by the buyer as proof of the non-conformity of the first instalment of the goods and the admissibility of bringing forward the claim, taking into account the terms of the contract on franchise. The seller also relied on the buyer's having proved neither the fact that the delay in sale of the second instalment of the goods had been caused by non-conforming quality of the first instalment, nor the fact that market prices had changed for the period of sale of the second instalment. The buyer submitted explanations with respect to all points of objections of the seller. In the proceedings of the ICCA, the representatives of the seller contended that the buyer's explanations were not substantiated.

[Judgment]

[…]

3.1. The manner (methods) of examination of the goods by the buyer

The buyer justly points out that the clause of the contract 'Conditions of Handing Over-Acceptance of the Goods' contains no instructions on the manner of examining the quality of the goods by the buyer. At the same time, the clause of the contract 'Quality of the Goods' provides that the quality must be in accordance with the State Standards (GOST) and/or the TC, indicated in specifications, and must be verified by the documents of title issued by the seller. The specifications to the contract contain concrete references to the TC, which stipulate the manner (methods) of examination of the quality of the goods. The Vienna Convention 1980 does not contain any direct instructions on manner (methods) of examination of the quality of the goods by the buyer, whereas the Civil Code of the Russian Federation (paragraph 4 Article 474) provides that the manner as well as other conditions of examination of the quality of the goods, performed by both buyer and seller, must be the same. This provision of the Civil Code of the RF is in accordance with a long practice of the Arbitration Court at the Chamber of Commerce & Industry of the RF (Chamber of Commerce & Industry of the USSR), which is based upon the rule that the terms of the contract, according to which the quality of the goods must meet a certain standard, mean that examination of the quality, both in the country of the seller and in the country of the buyer, must be performed in pursuance with the instructions of this standard. At that, in the concrete decisions of the Arbitration Court, it has been particularly pointed out that operation of other instructions in the buyer's country does not matter, because the parties have directly agreed upon subjecting their relations concerning the issues of quality to the provisions of a particular standard which establishes a method of examining the quality.

Accordingly, the fact that the parties could have agreed upon different terms with regard to the way of acceptance than those stipulated by the TC, cannot serve as a basis for recognising the buyer as being entitled, in the absence of the term on the manner of acceptance in the contract, to base himself on some other practice different from the requirements of the TC to which a direct reference has been made in the contract at determining the requirements for the quality of the goods.

As follows from the documents produced by the buyer, the buyer himself, contrary to his assertions, proceeded from the condition that the inspection of the quality of the goods, if the buyer wanted to perform it, had to be implemented by SGS methods established in the country of origin of the goods. In particular, such a term was directly provided for in a draft of the contract that the buyer presented to the ICCA [International Council for Commercial Arbitration] and sent to a firm of a third country. At that, the ICCA notes that the complainant buyer had included such a term in the draft of the contract before the first instalment of the goods arrived at the destination port, the document on discovery of the defects was drawn up and the notification thereof was sent to the seller.

The same term is contained in two contracts, concluded by the buyer in April and June 1998 with contracting parties both from the same country to which the first instalment was delivered, and from another country. These contracts were presented to the ICCA by the buyer himself.

[...]

Question

Q 38/39-8

How was the method of examining the goods determined in the Russian Federation case (C 38/39-4)?

C. Postponement of Examination

Article 38(2) CISG allows examination of goods sold under a contract involving carriage of the goods to be postponed until the goods arrive at their destination. Under Article 38(3) CISG, where goods are redirected in transit or redispatched by the buyer without him having a reasonable opportunity to examine the goods, examination of these goods will also be postponed until the goods reach their final destination.

Question

Q 38/39-9

(a)   What prerequisites can you identify in Article 38(2) and (3) CISG?
(b)   What potential problems could arise in this context?

C 38/39-5

Oberlandesgericht Stuttgart (Germany),
12 March 2001,
CISG-online 841[144]

[Facts]

The [seller], whose place of business is in W. [Austria], demands from the [buyer], whose place of business is in H. [Germany], payment of delivered goods. [Seller] asserts a claim for payment of the purchase price for apple juice concentrate delivered in January of 1997 in the overall amount of 174,053.10 Deutsche Mark [*DM*] and a claim for the remainder of the purchase price for strawberries delivered in April of 1997 in the amount of 33,261.19 *DM*.

In January of 1997, the [buyer] ordered from the [seller] 100,000 kg Polish apple juice concentrate at a price of 1.69 *DM* per kilogram. The [seller] confirmed the order in writing on 16 January 1997. The [seller] purchased the juice concentrate from a company H., whose place of business is in L. [Poland] and who in turn had the juice produced by a business in K. [Poland]. It was here where the goods were loaded upon four tank wagons. In accordance with the parties' agreement, the first tanker supply was delivered to the [buyer]'s customer, the S. Ltd. in P., on 24 January 1997; the further tankers arrived on 27 January 1997.

Upon the goods' arrival, [buyer]'s customer had samples taken, which were initially subjected to a rough or control analysis by the company F.-L. Ltd. At least at that point in time, company F.-L. Ltd. was almost exclusively acting for [buyer]'s customer. During this initial control analysis, which lasted approximately two to two and a half hours, only a few parameters were checked and no conspicuousness was detected. Afterwards, the goods were filled into stationary tanks and mixed with the products from other suppliers. Furthermore,

---

[144] Translation taken from CISG Pace (citations omitted).

[buyer]'s customer started diluting the concentrate to drinking strength and filled the product into individual tetra packs.

It was then discovered through the fine analysis finished by company F.-L. Ltd. on 28 January 1997, that glucose syrup had been added to the apple juice concentrate delivered by the [buyer]. The result of this analysis was confirmed by an inspection carried out by the company GfL Ltd. on behalf of [buyer]'s customer on 6 February 1997. Reserve samples kept by [buyer]'s customer were used for this inspection. After the [buyer]'s customer complained to the [buyer] of the added sugar with fax of 28 January 1997, [buyer] herself gave notice complaining of the lack of conformity to the [seller] with letter of 29 January 1997. As the results of the analysis undertaken by the company GfL Ltd. arrived, the [buyer] again notified the [seller] of the non-conformity with letter of 6 February 1997. The letter ends with the closing remark: 'We will now approach the unwinding of this complaint cautiously and step-by-step and will keep you updated in accordance with our own level of information.'

With letter of 26 February 1997 the [buyer] requested the [seller] to make a substitute delivery of the agreed amount of apple juice concentrate and fixed an additional period of time for the performance; [buyer] announced that she would declare the contract avoided in case the [seller] failed to effect the substitute delivery within the stipulated period of time. At the same time, the [buyer] informed the [seller] that her customer had already produced 501,000 tetra packs at 0.75 liters each from the goods delivered by the [seller] and mixed them with other supplier's products. For the time being, the sale of these packages was frozen and the goods stored, which was why [buyer]'s customer had announced a considerable damages claim against the [buyer]. However, the [buyer] had been able to reach an agreement with her customer that all—including future—reciprocal claims resulting from the non-conforming deliveries were considered settled and the deliveries were to be regarded as not having occurred. This agreement did not extend to the transport, customs and analysis costs born by the [buyer], which—in the [buyer]'s opinion—had to be reimbursed by the [seller].

Since a substitute delivery had not been effected up until that point in time, the [buyer] declared the contract avoided by letter of 26 March 1997.

The [seller] requests full payment of her deliveries, both with respect to the apple juice concentrate and the strawberries. The District Court (*Landgericht*) partially granted the claim in the amount of 108.806,65 *DM* and dismissed the remainder of the claim.

The [buyer]'s appeal is without success.

[Judgment]

The appeal is not successful.

[...]

3. However, the [buyer] in any case lost the right to declare the contract avoided under Art 82(1) CISG.

a) In accordance with Art 82(1) CISG, the buyer loses the right to declare the contract avoided if it is impossible for him to make restitution of the goods substantially in the condition in which he received them. In the present case, the delivered goods were mixed with the products of different suppliers by the [buyer]'s customer and contractual partner, company S., so that a restitution of the goods in its original condition is no longer possible following the [buyer]'s own submissions.

b) Art 82(1) CISG does not apply if the goods or part of the goods have been sold in the normal course of business or have been consumed or transformed by the buyer in the course of normal use before he discovered or ought to have discovered the lack of conformity (Art

82(2)(c) CISG)). Once it has been established that the preconditions of Art 82(1) CISG are met, the burden of proof for the exceptions provided by Art 82(2) CISG is upon the party who, for the reasons stated in that paragraph, nevertheless holds on to its wish to declare the contract avoided. In the present case, the onus of proof is on the [buyer], who was unable to establish such proof.

aa) The [buyer] may not rely upon the argument that she sold the goods in the normal course of business before she discovered or ought to have discovered the lack of conformity. This is because the case concerns a so-called '*Streckengeschäft*'; that is, the [seller] was also aware of the fact that the goods were not to be delivered to the [buyer], but directly to the [buyer]'s customer, company S. in P. The sale to company C. can therefore not be considered a sale in the normal course of business in the meaning of Art 82(2)(c) CISG. If one took the opposing view—as the [buyer] does—the duty to examine the goods would not exist in case of a '*Streckengeschäft*'. Such a result is certainly not intended by Art 82(2)(c) CISG.

bb) The [buyer] is furthermore unable to prove that she consumed or transformed the goods in the course of normal use before she discovered or ought to have discovered the lack of conformity. As has already been explained, the case concerns a so-called '*Streckengeschäft*', with the result that the [buyer]'s customer, company S., was under the duty to examine the goods. This is particularly true as the examination of the goods was deferred under Art 38(2) CISG until the arrival of the goods at the place of business of [buyer]'s customer. The conduct, respectively misconduct, of [buyer]'s customer therefore needs to be attributed to the [buyer].

cc) In the case at hand, [buyer]'s customer mixed the concentrate delivered by the [seller] with the goods delivered by other suppliers even though she ought to have discovered the lack of conformity of the goods beforehand. It is the Court's opinion that [buyer]'s customer ought to have had the concentrate delivered by the [seller] examined with regard to a possible sugar content. [Buyer]'s customer also ought to have waited for the corresponding analysis results before mixing the product with the apple juice concentrate delivered by other suppliers.

It is true that [buyer]'s customer waited for the result of the so-called control analysis undertaken by company F.-L. Ltd. before [seller]'s goods were mixed with the goods delivered by other suppliers. In this first control analysis—which takes roughly two to two and a half hours following the [buyer]'s submissions—the goods were solely examined with respect to a few parameters. At the time, this constituted the standard procedure of [buyer]'s customer, respectively of the company F.-L. Ltd. It is undisputed that the goods were initially not examined for sugar additives. It was only established in the so-called fine analysis that glucose syrup had been added to the apple juice concentrate. The first results of this fine analysis—also with respect to the loading of the first tank wagon that had already arrived on 24 January 1997—were available on the evening of 27 January 1997. At this point in time, the goods had already been mixed with the goods delivered by other suppliers.

Admittedly, there are no statutory provisions that prescribe an examination of apple juice concentrate before it is processed. However, in the Court's opinion [buyer]'s customer was held under Art 38 CISG, §377 HGB to undertake at least an examination of the goods delivered by the [seller] confined to the most important parameters. In doing so, [buyer]'s customer was held to examine the sugar level of the goods, and to wait for the corresponding results before mixing the goods with other products and processing them. This follows from the fact that all parties involved—including the [buyer] in her capacity as the trader—have to ensure the correctness of the goods under the laws for food production and distribution. Since drinks produced from sugared concentrate may not be called 'apple juice', but may solely be traded as 'fruit juice drink' or 'fruit juice nectar', it had to be and could reasonably have been expected that [buyer]'s customer would examine the concentrate delivered by the [seller] for added sugar before she would begin with the processing or even with mixing the goods.

Due to the explanations of the expert witness Prof. Dr. M., who was commissioned by the Court, the Court is convinced that sugar additives in apple juice concentrate were not as unusual and exceptional in the relevant period of time, that is in January 1997, that such an adulteration could not or could hardly have been expected. [...]

By not waiting for the results of the analysis regarding the sugar level and by mixing the goods delivered by the [seller] with the product of other suppliers, the [buyer]'s customer therefore acted at her own risk. This was particularly true in view of the fact that the goods could not be returned to the [seller] for this reason. As the conduct of [buyer]'s customer is to be attributed to the [buyer], [buyer] also needs to bear this risk with the consequence that [buyer] is unable to prove that she consumed or transformed the goods in the course of normal use before she ought to have discovered the lack of conformity. If [buyer]'s customer had waited for the results of the examination regarding the sugar level of the goods, the lack of conformity would have been discovered before the consumption, respectively the transformation of the goods. As [buyer] was consequently unable to prove that an exception in the meaning of Art 82(2)(c) CISG applies, [buyer] lost the right to declare the contract avoided following Art 82(1) CISG.

[...]

C 38/39-6

ICC International Court of Arbitration, Award No 9187/1999, CISG-online 705[145]

[Facts]

The contract concerned the sale by Defendant to Claimant of a quantity of coke supplied by a third company also a signatory to the contract. The contract provided for a reduction in the purchase price in the event of discrepancy between the actual moisture, ash, sulphur volatile and micum 40 and 10 levels and those stated in the contract. Weight and quality were to be analyzed at the loading port and recorded in a certificate of analysis binding on Claimant and Defendant. This was done by A. An inspection by B of the quality of the coke upon arrival revealed an important discrepancy as against the weight and quality analyses carried out at loading. A further inspection was carried out jointly by A and B and confirmed the findings made upon the goods' arrival. Claimant refused to accept the coke. In response, Defendant argued that it was merely the seller and not the supplier of the cargo and therefore was not responsible for quantity or quality. An independent examination of the cargo was carried out, confirming the results of the earlier joint inspection.

[Judgment]

[...]

According to Art 38/1 CISG, it is the buyer's duty to examine the goods after taking receipt of them, within as short a period of time as is practicable under the circumstances. If the contract includes the carriage of the goods, the examination may be postponed until after the moment when the goods arrived at their destination (Art 38/2 CISG). According to

---

[145] Taken from CISG-online (citations omitted).

Art 6 CISG the parties may derogate from the provisions of the CISG fully or partially, in particular from Art 38 CISG.

It follows from Art 5 of the Contract, that delivery had to be effectuated 'Free on Board' (FOB, Incoterms® 1990), meaning that Defendant, as seller, fulfilled its obligation to deliver when coke in the quantity and quality as set forth in the Contract passed over the ship's rail at the ... port. From that point of delivery on, Claimant bore all costs, including the costs associated with risks of loss of or damage to the goods.

In line with the agreed moment in which the risk passed, the examination of the goods had to take place by [A] at the port of loading: As far as the time of the inspection is concerned, Art 9 of the Contract has to be reasonably interpreted as the stipulation of a pre-shipment inspection in the sense of Art 38/1 CISG. However, in regard to the party responsible for inspection, the Arbitral Tribunal finds that—in derogation from Art 38 CISG according to which the buyer has to inspect the goods—the conformity of the coke, its quantity and quality, was to be assessed by a neutral inspection body as third party (appointed by both Claimant and Defendant) when the coke was loaded onto the vessel. Such common examination through seller and buyer is possible and common in certain businesses.

With the Arbitral Tribunal's above interpretation, Claimant's argument of Art 9 of the Contract being a (invalid) disclaimer does not have to be discussed any further.'

With respect to the quality discrepancy

1. Actual Quality of Coke at Loading Port

[...] The Arbitral Tribunal concludes that the actual quality of the coke loaded onto the vessel did not conform with the terms of the Contract and that, thus, Defendant did not deliver the goods in conformity with the specifications of the Contract. [A]'s Certificate of Analysis issued based on samples during the loading was obviously incorrect.

2. Binding Character of [A]'s Certificate of Analysis

As mentioned above ..., the parties were—according to Art 9 of the Contract bound in principle by the quantity and quality determination of [A] which inspected the coke as a commonly appointed neutral inspection body. However, Claimant asserts that based on the gross inaccuracy of [A]'s certification which according to the Claimant was manipulated by Defendant, it is not bound by this quality determination.

Whether this argument is of any help must be assessed in the light of the applicable legal stipulations. The Contract is silent to the applicability of its Art 9 in case of incorrect certification through the appointed inspection body and, as a consequence it has to be referred to the CISG in order to answer this question.

In principle, the buyer has to bear the consequences of an incorrect examination in the sense of Art 38 CISG performed by third parties; it is bound by the examination and has approved the (non-contractual) delivery. However, this finding does not apply if the parties have jointly appointed the neutral inspection body or if the seller alone has insisted on the third party; the quality determination, if wrong, renders it non-binding to the parties. This was also concluded by the Arbitration Panel of Hamburg pursuant to which the stipulation of final quantity and quality determination through a certificate of analysis is binding upon the parties in its nature as an Arbitral certificate (*Schiedsgutachten*) unless it proves to be incorrect. The Arbitral Tribunal is of the opinion that [A]'s certificate does not determine the actual quality of the coke. Because the inspection of the coke through a third party was mutually agreed by the parties in Art 9 of the Contract, and not suggested by Claimant alone ..., Claimant is not bound by [A]'s quality determination. Consequently, it does not have to bear the consequences of the wrong certificate in the sense that it automatically has lost any and all of its legal remedies for non-contractual delivery of the coke after the risk passed from Defendant to Claimant.

On the other hand, it cannot be concluded from the above that Claimant can base its claims on the quality determinations carried out in ... as if Art 9 of the Contract had not existed The impact of the incorrect examination through [A] on Claimant's duty to give valid notice of the non-conformity of the coke still has to be assessed.

Question

Q 38/39-10

(a)   Compare the above two cases (C 38/39-5 and C 38/39-6). Who undertook the examination in the first case?
(b)   And in the second?
(c)   Was the examination binding on the buyer in both cases?

III. Reasonable Period of Time under Article 39 CISG

As with the difficulties in interpreting the examination requirements of Article 38 CISG, Article 39 CISG has also suffered from the tendency of national courts to interpret the notification requirements in accordance with the understanding under their domestic legal system.

C 38/39-7

Bundesgerichtshof (Germany),
8 March 1995,
CISG-online 144

For a summary of the facts see C 35-5 above.

[Judgment][146]

[...]

2. The Court of Appeals also correctly denied the [buyer's] right to declare the contract avoided because of the improper packaging of the goods. The question whether [buyer's] allegations were sufficient for a conclusive statement of a fundamental breach of contract

---

[146] Translation taken from CISG Pace (citations omitted).

(CISG Art 25) or of any lack of conformity with the contract at all (CISG Art 35(2)(e) [sic]) may remain unanswered. In any event, Defendant (buyer) lost her rights that might have resulted from these allegations due to untimeliness. This does not, however, result from the 'untimeliness' of the declaration to avoid the contract pursuant to CISG Art 49(2)(b)(i), but from the untimeliness of the notice of the lack of conformity required by CISG Art 39(1), which must be considered first.

In that respect, it does not make any difference whether the mussels were delivered 'in the beginning' of January 1992, as the Court of Appeals assumed, or not until January 16, 1992, as the appeal alleges pointing to the 'Betreff' ('Re.') Section of [buyer's] facsimile dated February 7, 1992. The first notice of the lack of conformity of the packaging in the facsimile dated March 3, 1992 was untimely even if the latter date of delivery was decisive. [Buyer] had to examine the goods or had to have them examined within as short a period after they arrive at the place of destination as practicable under the circumstances (CISG Art 38(2) in connection with subsection (1)). At least during the working week from January 20 to 24, 1992, [buyer] could have easily done this, whether by herself at the storage facility not far from her place of business or by a person employed by company F. and designated by [buyer]. The allegedly improper packaging could have easily been ascertained in an external examination. The time limit for the notice of the lack of conformity, which starts at that moment (CISG Art 39(1)), as well as the time limit to declare the contract avoided pursuant to CISG Art 49(2) should not be calculated too long in the interest of clarifying the legal relationship of the parties as quickly as possible. Even if this Court were to apply a very generous 'rough average' of about one month, taking into account different national legal traditions, the time limit for the notice of the lack of conformity with the contract had expired before March 3, 1992.

The appeal's reference to an examination of the mussels already carried out by the public health agency as well as [buyer's] earlier notice of the increased cadmium content do not affect the assumption that the notice of lack of conformity was untimely. If the goods do not conform with the contract in various aspects, it is necessary to state all defects individually and describe them. The buyer cannot claim those defects, of which he gave untimely notice.

[…]

Questions

Q 38/39-11

(a) What reason did the court in the above case (C 38/39-7) give for a short calculation of the period of time for giving notice?
(b) On a consideration of the requirements of international trade, can you think of any reasons as to why the court took this approach?

Q 38/39-12

What insight did the court in the above case (C 38/39-7) provide as to the development of a general 'rule of thumb' for the calculation of a reasonable period of time under Article 39 CISG?

C 38/39-8

Bundesgerichtshof (Germany),
3 November 1999,
CISG-online 475[147]

[Facts]

Plaintiff [buyer's assignee] is a paper converting company and produces, inter alia, H.-moist tissues. It purchases the required semi-finished moist tissue-crepe from T. paper factory in B./Switzerland [buyer] in an ongoing business relationship; for the manufacture of the semi-finished product, the [buyer] uses cellulose material that is refined in a PM 3 paper machine in several production stages. This machine contains three grinding gears which are connected in series, so-called double-disk refiners, which are equipped either with model EWR 5/76/60 grinding devices of the manufacturer E. or with model E 6533 R/L grinding devices of the defendants [sellers].

On March 31, 1993, the [buyer] ordered one E 6533 R/L grinding device set from the [sellers] at the price of DM [Deutsche Mark] 3,065; at the time, the [sellers] did not know that this grinding device was intended for the production of moist tissues. The grinding device, which was delivered on April 7, 1993, was assembled on April 13, 1993 into the PM 3 paper machine as double disk refiner No. 1, which is connected in series prior to double disk refiners Nos. 2 and 3, and was put into operation on April 17, 1993. On April 25, 1993, the [buyer] first discovered a total loss of double disk refiner No. 2, which had been equipped with a grinding device supplied by company E.; as a result, the defective grinding device was replaced on April 26, 1993. On April 26, 1993, the grinding device which had been delivered by the [sellers] suffered a total loss; as a result, it was replaced by a grinding device supplied by company E.

From April 19 until April 22, 1993, the [buyer] produced with the aforementioned PM 3 paper machine a total of 243.51 tons of semi-finished moist tissues, of which the [buyer] delivered 120.953 tons in April and May 1993 to the [buyer's assignee]. On May 17, 1993, the [buyer's assignee] gave notice by telephone to the [buyer] that the already processed H. semi-finished moist tissues showed patches of rust and that the not yet processed semi-finished moist tissue-crepe also showed a tendency to brownish specking. On May 27, 1993, the [buyer] commissioned company P. in M. to identify the patches of rust and, for this purpose, had the grinding device inspected together with other things that had been delivered by the [sellers]. After receipt of the test report prepared by company P. dated June 9, 1993, which the [buyer] received on June 11, 1993, the [buyer] contacted the [sellers] by letter dated June 14, 1993 and, as a precaution, stated that it held them liable for the damages incurred because the [buyer] suspected that the grinding device delivered by the [sellers] on April 7, 1993 was defective. After the [buyer] assigned to the [buyer's assignee] all of its claims arising from the purchase agreement concluded with the [sellers] on March 31, 1993, the [buyer's assignee] claims a partial amount of DM 100,000 as damages arising from the lack of conformity of the grinding device with the contract. The [sellers] opposed this claim on the grounds that, inter alia, neither the [buyer] nor the [buyer's assignee] had met their obligations to examine and to give timely notice; the [buyer's] notice to the [sellers] of the defect was untimely. Further, the [sellers argued,] no particular specification of the grinding device delivered on April 7, 1993 had been agreed upon; in addition, the [buyer] had overloaded the delivered grinding device during its use.

---

[147] Translation taken from CISG Pace (citations omitted).

The Regional Court dismissed the complaint, and the [buyer's assignee's] appeal against that decision was unsuccessful. On appeal, the [buyer's assignee] pursues its claims further.

[Judgment]

II. These elaborations do not withstand scrutiny.

1. The Court of Appeals correctly and undisputedly applies the United Nations Convention on Contracts for the International Sale of Goods of April 11, 1980 (CISG), which became effective for the Federal Republic of Germany on January 1, 1991 and for Switzerland on March 1, 1993, to the purchase agreement entered into by the [buyer] and the [sellers] dated March 31, 1993.

2. In the absence of a contrary ascertainment of facts by the court of appeals, it must be assumed, for purposes of the proceedings on appeal, that the grinding device's defect claimed by the [buyer's assignee] is a latent defect that could not have been discovered by an appropriate examination (Art 38(1) CISG) either upon delivery on April 7, 1993 or upon the installation on April 13, 1993 or during its use. If, thereafter, the lack of conformity with the contract of the delivered grinding device showed up for the first time at the time of the total loss on April 26, 1993, the beginning of the examination and notice period under Arts 38(1), 39(1) CISG cannot yet be assumed at April 26, 1993.

a) In this context, it can be left undecided whether, under UN Sales Law, latent defects must, as the appeal argues, be brought to the [sellers'] attention only after actual discovery in each specific case, so that the reasonable period of time referred to in Art 39(1) CISG only begins at the time of the (later) actual discovery of the defect, or whether, as the court of appeals assumes, the time at which the latent defect could be discovered is relevant to the beginning of the reasonable period of time.

b) Even if the [buyer] were not allowed to let the total loss of April 26, 1993 rest, but rather had to take measures to detect the cause of the damage, the court of appeals should not have assumed, as the appeal correctly argues, on the basis of the facts ascertained so far, that a possible operating error of the [buyer's] own employees 'could have been clarified without difficulty,' so that the defectiveness of the delivered grinding device must have suggested itself to the [buyer] already on the day of the loss.

aa) A possible reason for the total loss on April 26, 1993 was, as the [buyer's assignee] submitted uncontestedly, and as the court of appeals also discussed, either an operating error or a lack of conformity with the contract of the delivered grinding device. The independent evidentiary process later initiated by the [buyer's assignee] was supposed to clarify which of the two reasons for the loss was the case; even in the instant lawsuit, the [sellers] still claimed improper handling because the grinding discs moved at a very short distance (quasi-zero-zero-distance) in opposite direction. If hence an operating error could also have occurred unnoticed, it is not evident how such an error could have been excluded immediately after the damage occurred, without special effort, by merely questioning the [buyer's] employees.

bb) Even if the [buyer] could have excluded a possible operating error quickly by internal investigation and without commissioning an expert opinion, it had to be allotted, in any case, a certain period of approximately one week for the decision as to what to do next and for the initiation of necessary measures—e.g., the selection and commissioning of an expert—followed by the two weeks assumed by the Court of Appeals for the expert's investigation, followed by the—regular—one-month notice period pursuant to Art 39(1) CISG. But in that case, the [buyer's] notice letter to the [sellers] dated June 14, 1993—seven weeks after the total loss—was not untimely.

[...]

C 38/39-9

Bundesgericht (Switzerland),
13 November 2003,
CISG-online 840[148]

For a summary of the facts see C 35-15 above.

[Judgment]

3.

3.1 Under the UN Sales Law, the buyer must examine the goods, or cause them to be examined, within a short a period as is practicable in the circumstances (Art 38(1) CISG). It loses the right to rely on a lack of conformity of the goods if it does not give notice to the seller specifying [in the German version: precisely] the nature of the lack of conformity within a reasonable time after it has discovered it or ought to have discovered it (Art 39(2) [sic—correct: Art 39(1)] CISG). Whether these time periods have been complied with is for the court to decide in its own discretion. The Federal Supreme Court (*Bundesgericht*) is generally free to examine discretionary decisions in appellate proceedings. However, it thereby exercises restraint and only intervenes if the previous instance has deviated from the principles recognized in academic opinion and jurisprudence without reason, if it has taken account of facts that should not have played any role in the decision in the case at hand, or if it, conversely, has failed to consider circumstances that it would have been obliged to consider. The Federal Supreme Court (*Bundesgericht*) will also intervene in discretionary decisions if they prove to be obviously inequitable or manifestly unjust (BGE 127 III 351 Reason 4a p 354, with further references).

3.2 Upon a consideration of academic opinion and jurisprudence, the Court of Appeal (*Obergericht*) assumed in the present case that a period of examination of one week and a period of notification of one month could be accepted, in which case the notification dated 26 August 1996 took place in good time. In addition, on 5 September 1996, the [Buyer] gave a new, more detailed notification of defects, which was, in any case, one month after it would have had to have been assumed that it had discovered the defects notified. Upon a consideration of the circumstance that a representative of the Seller examined the machine again on 29 August 1996, the second and more detailed notification of the defects dated 5 September 1996 would also in no way appear to have been made too late. In respect of this finding, the Court of Appeal (*Obergericht*) does not appear to have exceeded its discretion. This has also not been asserted by the [Seller's assignee].

4.

4.1 The Court of Appeal (*Obergericht*) accepted that, with the notification of defects dated 5 September 1996, the [Buyer] had notified that the distillation regulator was defective, that the stainless steel (*Nieroster*) container leaked, that the condensed water was not being separated off, that the booster pump for the cleaner was not connected and adjusted and that the impregnating pump was not delivered. In addition, the Court of Appeal (*Obergericht*) indicated that although the experts stated that the functionality of the machine was not guaranteed, as it did not meet the requirements of a standard prototype, the [Buyer] nevertheless failed to notify the [Seller's assignee] of this defect. Similarly, the [Buyer] also failed to notify the [Seller's assignee]

---

[148] Translation taken from CISG Pace (citations omitted).

that the measuring cells on the nitrogen generator were defective and that the nitrogen genera-tor itself was dirty and had been poorly maintained. Therefore, contrary to the view of the Local District Court (*Amtsgericht*), the [Buyer] could not derive any rights from this defect.

4.2 The [Buyer] alleges that the Court of Appeal (*Obergericht*) incorrectly only examined the defects that were individually mentioned in its letter dated 5 September 1996. The court failed to consider that, in this letter, the [Buyer] had generally notified of an 'unusable machine delivery' and that the individual defects were only to be understood as referring to the problem areas, to which, in the opinion of the [Buyer], the lack of functionability could be attributed. Thereby, the [Buyer] gave sufficient notice that the machine was unusable.

[...]

C 38/39-10

Oberster Gerichtshof (Austria),
27 August 1999,
CISG-online 485[149]

For a summary of the facts see C 38/39-3 above.

[Judgment]

[Buyer's] appeal is not justified.

The lower courts stated correctly that the provisions of the CISG apply to the purchase agreement, since neither the [seller's] General Conditions of Sale were included in the pur-chase agreement nor a trade usage existed which—in accordance with the CISG's optional character—prevails over the provisions of this treaty.

This Panel concurs with the court of appeals' elaborations concerning the duration of [buyer's] period to examine and to give notice pursuant to Arts 38 and 39 CISG. The court of appeals correctly named the relevant criteria in accordance with the judicial guidelines developed by the Austrian Supreme Court in JBl 1999, 318: Hence, the short period for the examination depends on the size of the buyer's company, the type of the goods to be examined, their complexity or perishability or their character as seasonal goods, the type of the amount in question, the efforts necessary for an examination, etc. Here, the objective and subjective circumstances of the concrete case must be considered, in particular the buyer's personal and business situation, characteristic features of the goods, the amount of the delivery of goods or the type of the chosen legal remedy. Although the periods for the required examina-tion and notice must be viewed less rigidly than pursuant to § 377 HGB ('immediately'), the reasonable periods pursuant to Arts 38 and 39 CISG are not long periods. The reasonable period pursuant to Art 39 CISG has to be adapted according to the circumstances. Insofar as no specific—above mentioned—circumstances speak for a shorter or longer period, one in fact must assume a total period of approximately 14 days for the examination and the notice. That is, it must not be overlooked that, even in spite of the CISG's 'buyer-friendly tenden-cies', Art 38 as well as Art 39 shall serve the purpose of achieving clarity concerning whether performance was properly made; claims and disputes based on later defects, which could be

---

[149] Translation taken from CISG Pace (citations omitted).

explained by the buyer's improper handling or the buyer's failures, should be excluded as far as possible. Besides, the [buyer] itself assumes that the shoes it had ordered are 'seasonal goods' (*see* response to the appeal p. 6 and appeal p. 3); particularly in such a case, a longer period than the 14-day period granted by the court of appeals would not comport with the purposes of Arts 38 and 39 CISG, as attention shall be paid to the buyer's interest in the use of 'seasonal goods' in the current season. In the appellate proceedings, the parties doubt neither that the examination period pursuant to Art 38 CISG commenced upon the arrival of the goods in Scandinavia (Art 38(3)), nor the [buyer's] obligation as a middleman to examine the goods itself or have them examined by its customer.

[...]

On the other hand, this Panel cannot agree with the [seller's] argument that the telefax dated November 8, 1995, should not be viewed as a notice of lack of conformity. In this respect, the elaborations of the court of appeals are also logical and legally flawless. The notice of lack of conformity is specified insofar as it described the lack of conformity quite exactly. However, it must be noted that the notice of lack of conformity preserves only the right to claim the sufficiently specified defects and that a 'notification of other defects afterwards' is not possible.

In all, this Panel shares the court of appeals' legal opinion that the defendant as the buyer lost its right to rely on a lack of conformity of the goods insofar as it did not give notice of lack of conformity of the purchased shoes properly and timely. In that case, it has lost all legal remedies it would have had under Art 45 CISG.

[...]

Questions

Q 38/39-13

Does the Swiss court (C 38/39-9) share the view of the earlier German (*BGH*) case (C 38/39-7)?

Q 38/39-14

Does the Austrian court (C 38/39-10) share the view of the German and Swiss courts?

Q 38/39-15

Does the court in the Austrian case (C 38/39-10) distinguish between the period for examination and that for giving notice?

Q 38/39-16

(a)   How does the *BGH* in the 1999 case (C 38/39-8) calculate the period for examination of the goods; and the period for giving notice?
(b)   When did the period for giving notice commence in the 1999 case (C 38/39-8)? Compare this approach to the position of the earlier *BGH* case (C 38/39-7).

For the position under Roman legal systems, refer to the following cases.

C 38/39-11

Cour de Cassation (France), 26 May 1999, CISG-online 487[150]

[…]

On the sole grounds of appeal:

—WHEREAS [buyer] had ordered, on 5 August 1992, 196 rolled metal sheets from [seller]; delivery took place between 28 October 1992 and, for the greater part, 4 December 1992; [buyer] revoked the contract by letter of 1 December 1992 principally for the reason that the goods did not conform to the order, neither in quantity, nor in quality; by its behavior on 15 December 1992 it had established an avoidance of the sale;

—WHEREAS [seller] challenges the judgment of the Court of Appeals of Aix-en-Provence, 21 November 1996, for having set aside the plea invoked by [seller] on the basis of Articles 38 and 39 CISG, according to [seller's] grounds, that the Court of Appeals, which found the time between inspection tests performed by [buyer] on 9 and 11 November 1992 and the imprecise reporting of the 'non-conformity in the agreed quality, dimensions and quantities' made by the [buyer] on 1 December 1992, did not draw the proper legal conclusions from its own assertions, in violation of the aforementioned provisions;

—WHEREAS we find that the Court of Appeals only used its sovereign discretion in maintaining, after having recalled the chronology of the facts, that the buyer *had* inspected the goods in a prompt and normal period of time, bearing in mind the handling that the [goods] required and that [buyer] *had* alerted [seller] of the non-conformities within a reasonable time in the meaning of Article 39(1) CISG;

—NOW THEREFORE the grounds for appeal cannot be accepted.

FOR THESE REASONS:

—REJECTS the appeal;

[…]

Judgment of lower court included for legal reasoning regarding Art 39(1) CISG.

Cour d'appel d'Aix-en-Provence 21 novembre 1996

[…]

[Facts]

[Buyer] had on 5 August 1992 ordered, through DAMSTAHL FRANCE's intermediary, 196 laminated metal sheets CUAL 9 N13 Fe2 of which—98 of dimension 12/240/101 and—98 of dimension 25/245/1036.

---

[150] Translation taken from CISG Pace (citations omitted).

The order was accepted by [seller] on 6 August 1992 under reservation of cover insurance that had been realized by the credit insurer of that company and LYONNAISE DE BANQUE's Security as far as concerns [buyer].

Delivery was made between 26 October 1992 and 4 December 1992.

As to the reasons that the delivery times had not been respected, and that the delivered goods were not conforming, neither in quantity, nor in quality with respect to what [buyer] ordered, [buyer] had renounced the contract by letter of 1 December 1992, then fixed on 15 December 1992 in avoidance [*résolution*: avoidance, or cancellation *ex tunc*] of the sale and subsequent invalidity of the bank security.

[...]

[Buyer] further seeks to have the court hold that the obligation of the 'brief time' [*dans un délai raisonnable*: 'within a reasonable time'] required by Art 39 CISG, applicable in the instant case, was respected;

[...]

And [seller maintains that [buyer] did not conduct that test and bring to [seller's] attention the defects of the goods in the 'brief time' [*dans un délai raisonnable:* 'within a reasonable time'] required by the CISG;

[...]

[Judgment]

[...]

Under application of Art 39 CISG:

— That law applicable in the area of international sale of goods envisions in its Art 38 that the buyer must inspect the delivered goods within as short a period as is practicable in the circumstances [*dans un délai aussi bref que possible au égard aux circonstances*];
— And in its Art 39 which a buyer forfeits the right to rely on a defect of conformity if it does not notify the seller specifying the nature of that defect within a reasonable period beginning at the moment either when it was noticed, or should have been noticed.

From the exhibits adduced at trial—fax, correspondence, delivery order—it follows:

— That a first part of the order had been delivered 28 October 1992 with some reservations of 'quality control, conformity and quantity' contained on the C.M.R.;
— That some tests of the plates had been conducted on 9 and 11 November 1992 by [buyer];
— That some faxes seeking information had been exchanged between [buyer] and DAMSTAHL on 16 and 19 November 1992;
— That the annulment of the contract for 'non-conformity in quality dimensions and established quantities', had been made known to the seller by letter of 1 December 1992;
— That finally, the notice of avoidance of the sale for non-conformity had been sent on 15 December.

This chronology of facts shows that the buyer had inspected the goods which it had received within a quick and normal period of time, bearing in mind the heavy handling of the plates called for, and some incompressible periods of time which the inspection required, and had warned its seller of the non-conformities that it deemed unacceptable, within a period sufficiently reasonable so that no forfeiture clause could be opposed to it.

The grounds drawn from Art 39 CISG are thus to be set aside.

[...]

C 38/39-12

Cour d'appel Grenoble (France),
13 September 1995,
CISG-online 157

For a summary of the facts see C 35-13 above.

[Judgment][151]

[...]

2. CONSIDERING

[...]

THAT in omitting to place labels on the sachets as to the composition and expiry date, the [seller] had delivered non-conforming goods in the meaning of Article 35 of the Vienna Convention which particularly regulates packaging; That the buyer issued the written complaint the month following delivery; That this had thus been done within a reasonable time period in the sense of Article 39 of the Vienna Convention;

THAT moreover, the prefixed time period of two years mentioned in the Second paragraph of this article does not envisage a legal action.

For the American approach, see the following case.

C 38/39-13

Shuttle Packaging Systems, LLC v Jacob Tsonakis, Ina SA and INA Plastics Corp,
US Dist Ct (WD MI), 17 December 2001,
CISG-online 773[152]

[Facts]

Plaintiff's Verified Complaint alleges that on November 1, 2000, it agreed to a purchase agreement with Defendants. Plaintiff alleges that under the purchase agreement Defendants were required to supply thermoforming line equipment for the manufacture of plastic gardening pots together with the technology and assistance to use the equipment. The equipment included a 'double line' having an annual output capacity of 1,800,000 lbs.

---

[151] Translation taken from CISG Pace.
[152] Citations omitted.

and a 'trade gallon line' having an annual output capacity of 3,270,000 lbs. The aggregate purchase price for the equipment was $1,200,000 for the double line and $1,800,000 for the trade gallon line. The Contract also included other terms relating to payment schedules, non-competition, warranties, notices, expenses, interest, and an integration clause. The non-competition term did not include the specific terms for non-competition, but required the further execution of a non-competition agreement. Although it was not alleged in the Complaint, the Court notes for clarification sake that, based on other exhibits filed by the parties and their briefing, the trade gallon line was intended to manufacture 2.5 liter pots and the double line was intended to manufacture 11 centimeter pots on one line and 4 inch pots on the other line.

[…]

[Judgment]

[…]

Defendants' final argument relating to likelihood of success is that the Plaintiff committed the first material breach of the contract and, as such, Defendants are no longer bound by the terms of the non-competition agreement. Defendants also make a related argument that because Plaintiff delayed in complaining about the performance of the equipment, it is not entitled to suspend payment of money owed under the purchase agreement.

This related argument concerns Articles 38 and 39 of the Convention, which require the buyer to 'examine the goods ... within as short a period as is practicable in the circumstances' and which further state the buyer 'loses the right to rely on a lack of conformity of the goods if he does not give notice to the seller specifying the nature of the lack of conformity within a reasonable time.' Article 39 also provides a two-year time period as the outer limit of time for a buyer to notify the seller of a lack of conformity (unless the goods are subject to a longer contractual period of guarantee).

This related argument fails. The wording of the Convention reveals an intent that buyers examine goods promptly and give notice of defects to sellers promptly. However, it is also clear from the statute that on occasion it will not be practicable to require notification in a matter of a few weeks. For this reason, the outer limit of two years is set for the purpose of barring late notices. In this case, there was ample reason for a delayed notification. The machinery was complicated, unique, delivered in installments and subject to training and on-going repairs. The Plaintiff's employees lacked the expertise to inspect the goods and needed to rely on Defendants' engineers even to use the equipment. It is also wrong to say, in light of this record, that notification did not occur until July 6, 2001. Long before the July 6 correspondence, there was a steady stream of correspondence between the parties relating to the functioning of the equipment which may have constituted sufficient notice of the complaints. The international cases cited by Defendants are not apposite to this discussion because they concern the inspection of simple goods and not complicated machinery like that involved in this case.

[…]

Questions

Q 38/39-17

(a) Based on the above cases decided under the French legal system (C 38/39-11 and C 38/39-12), how would you characterise the approach to Article 39 CISG under the Roman law tradition?
(b) Compare this approach to the approach of the German and Austrian courts (C 38/39-7, C 38/39-8 and C 38/39-10).

Q 38/39-18

(a) What are the relevant criteria according to the court in *Shuttle Packaging* (C 38/39-13) when determining the period of notice?
(b) How can the general approach of the US District Court be characterised and compared to the approaches of the other courts outlined above?

IV. Specificity of Notice

Article 39(1) CISG states that the notice must 'specify the nature of the lack of conformity'. A large number of decisions have sought to interpret and apply this language. Again, most of the case law concerning specificity stems from the German-speaking countries.

C 38/39-14

Landgericht Hannover (Germany),
1 December 1993,
CISG-online 244[153]

[Facts]

An Italian seller and a German buyer concluded a contract for the sale of shoes. The parties agreed that in case of apparent defects, notice of non conformity should be given in writing within ten days of delivery, while in case of hidden defects, immediately after discovery. The buyer refused to pay alleging that six weeks after the delivery it had given written notice that the shoes were not of the quality required by the contract. The seller, after making two

---

[153] English abstract taken from UNILEX.

requests for payment, commenced an action against the buyer claiming payment of price with interest and expenses for the requests.

[Judgment]

In the Court's opinion, the buyer had lost its right to rely on a lack of conformity.

The Court found that a notice of non conformity is valid only if made within the time limit fixed in the contract. Since the defects were apparent, the buyer could have easily found them out by properly examining the goods after delivery (Art 38 CISG). The buyer should have given notice of non conformity within the fixed time limit, instead of doing so following customer complaints six weeks later. The Court further held that it was not sufficient to give notice of the mere fact of non conformity. The buyer should have described the precise nature of the defects, as required by Art 39(1) CISG. Therefore the buyer was obliged to pay the price according to Art 53 CISG and interest at the Italian statutory interest rate. Finally, the Court held that expenses incurred in consequence of the requests for payment could not be claimed. As the time of payment was determinable from the contract, no formal request was necessary (Art 59 CISG).

C 38/39-15

Bundesgerichtshof (Germany), 4 December 1996, CISG-online 260[154]

[Facts]

Plaintiff [seller's assignee] demands payment of the purchase price from defendant [buyer] for a computerized printing system including software arising out of an assigned right.

On November 11, 1992, the [buyer], located in Vienna, ordered a printing system called 'dynamic page printer' from Company A [hereinafter seller], located in P. near N. for the total price of DM [Deutsche Mark] 65,100. The unit consisted of a thermal transfer printer, a color monitor, a computer and a software package. [Seller] confirmed the order by letter dated November 22, 1992. With respect to the warranty, the order confirmation contained the following arrangement, which indisputably became part of the contract:

'The warranty covers software and hardware as a unit. The warranty period is 6 months and starts with the non-defective functioning of the system. The start of the warranty period is calculated from the installation and operational handover.

In the event that a subsequent malfunction or a defect appears later, the buyer shall give prompt written notice of this fact to [seller] .... If cure of the defect fails twice, the buyer may then, according to his choice, reduce the purchase price or declare the contract avoided.'

On January 30, 1993, the printing system was installed at the [buyer's] offices, and on February 8, 1993, it was handed over for the purpose of commencing operation. By letter

---

[154] Translation taken from CISG Pace (citations omitted).

dated February 9, 1993, the [buyer] already informed [seller] of eight—4 'open points,' among others under Point 4 'Documentation of the Printer,' and requested resolution by February 25, 1993 at the latest. [Seller] commented on this by letter dated February 11, 1993; it announced that the delivery of the documentation would take place during the 7th calendar week 1993.

By further letter dated March 2, 1993, the [buyer] complained that despite the additional period of time set until February 25, 1993, [seller] had not remedied the defects listed under Points 1, 2, 3, 5 and 8 of the letter dated February 9, 1993; at the same time, [the buyer] declared the contract avoided 'because of non-compliance with the additional time period granted.' [The buyer] did not mention the Documentation of the Printer any more.

Until now, the [buyer] has neither in total nor in part paid the purchase price, which was due in installments of 20% upon receipt of the confirmation of the order, of 60% upon announcement of delivery, and of 20% after the installation and operational handover. The Regional Court [*Landgericht*] granted the claim for payment of DM 65,100 in all respects. On appeal by the [buyer], the Higher Regional Court [*Oberlandesgericht*] revised the decision of the Regional Court and dismissed the complaint. On appeal, the [seller's assignee] requests that the judgment of the Trial Court be reinstated.

[Judgment]

[…]

[The Court stated that] the [buyer] had given timely notice of the defect of incomplete documentation. Under an objective and reasonable view, the chosen term 'Documentation of the Printer' referred to the entire system, i.e., to the hardware as well as to the software; it was timely and sufficiently detailed. Since [seller] did not deliver complete documentation despite the [buyer's] notice of the defect, the [buyer] repudiated the contract rightfully on account of a fundamental breach of contract. [The Court held that,] besides—if it still mattered—the second attempt to cure the defect failed as well, since the [seller's assignee] also remained inactive after the [buyer's] second demand of August 24, 1994. This letter by the [buyer] was also still timely; specifically, the claim for delivery of complete documentation was not time-barred. Finally, the failure to mention the insufficient documentation in the [buyer's] letter of repudiation dated March 2, 1993 did not constitute a waiver of the right to assert the defect. After all this, the [buyer] (once again) declared the contract avoided by letter dated October 12, 1994, which amounts to an avoidance under CISG Art 64(1)(a). Therefore, pursuant to CISG Art 81(1), it was freed from the obligation to pay the purchase price.

II. These statements do not withstand legal scrutiny.

[…]

2. On the merits, the appeal is successful. The Court of Appeals based its opinion, that the [buyer] rightfully declared the contract avoided, only on the failure to deliver complete documentation of which the [buyer] gave notice. The appealed decision cannot be based upon this reasoning.

[…]

b). If the [buyer] has warranty claims against the seller—and of what kind—primarily depends upon the warranty terms and conditions of [seller], which became part of the contract. They have priority over the CISG provisions (CISG Art 6).

The contractual provisions merely regulate the extent, the beginning and the duration of the warranty, the obligation of the buyer to give immediate notice of the defects occurring after the handover, as well as the buyer's right to reduce the purchase price or to declare the contract avoided after attempts to cure failed twice. Apart from that, the warranty provisions of the CISG remain applicable.

aa). The latter initially apply to the timeliness of the notice of those defects that already exist at the goods' handover. To that extent, CISG Art 38(1) provides that the buyer must examine the goods within as short a period of time as the circumstances will allow. He must give notice to the seller of any defect within a reasonable period after this point in time (CISG Art 39(1)).

The [buyer] already complained about the 'Documentation of the Printer' as an 'open point' by letter dated February 9, 1993, i.e., one day after the February 8, 1993 handover of the system and instructions by an employee of the seller. Therefore, the timeliness of the notice is beyond question.

bb). We cannot agree, however, with the court of appeals insofar as it deemed the [buyer's] notice to be detailed enough with respect to the lack of complete documentation for the printer unit.

Pursuant to CISG Art 39(1) (last clause), the buyer must, in his notice, describe with particularity the kind of lack of conformity with the contract. That way, the seller shall be enabled to get an idea of the kind of breach of contract and to take the necessary steps, e.g., to initiate a substitute or subsequent delivery. On the other hand, the demands of specificity must not be carried too far. The determination as to whether a notice of defects complies with this standard is primarily made by the trial judge.

The Court of Appeals held that the term 'Documentation of the Printer' under Point 4 of the [buyer's] notice of defects dated February 9, 1993 referred to the whole unit including the software. This interpretation does not hold up against the arguments on appeal [here].

Since the printer unit delivered by the [seller] consisted of a thermal transfer printer, a color monitor, a computer and a software package, the term 'printer'—as the court of appeals did not correctly see—was, without further specification, at least ambiguous because it could relate to the unit as well as to the individual element. Therefore, in order to meet the requirements of CISG Art 39(1), the [buyer] would have been obligated to describe the defect in such a detailed manner that any misunderstandings were impossible and to enable the seller to determine unmistakably what was meant. Special knowledge on the part of the [buyer] was not necessary for this task because anyone who handles these kinds of systems is able to distinguish the printing system from the printer itself as an individual component. Therefore, the ambiguity of the term 'printer' goes against the [buyer].

Up to now, the Court of Appeals has not reached any findings from which one could discern that the parties nevertheless understood the [buyer's] notice of defects unambiguously in the sense of the missing documentation for the entire printer unit. The [seller's assignee's] submission in the lower courts indicates the opposite, i.e., that the notice of defect really only covered the documentation for the printer. The [seller's assignee] already claimed at trial that [seller] had sent the demanded documentation for the printer by letter dated February 22, 1993 in order to settle the notice of defects concerning Point 4 of the letter dated February 9, 1993. It additionally referred to this allegation in its reply to the notice of appeal in an admissible manner. If the seller, in reaction to the [buyer's] notice of defects, sent documentation for the 'printer' as an individual component—which must be presumed for the appeal to this court—and if the [buyer] did not mention Point 4 anymore in its letter of rescission dated March 2, 1903 but objected to five of the formerly eight defects as 'not cured,' one must infer that what the [buyer] received from [seller] corresponded to what it had asked for in its letter dated February 9, 1993.

In any event, we cannot assume, based on the facts known so far, that the notice of defects dated February 9, 1993 referred to the documentation for the entire printer system with the clarity CISG Art 39(1) requires in the interests of the seller.

c).

aa). In the opinion of the Court of Appeals, however, the [buyer] had the right to revive the notice of defective documentation by letter dated August 24, 1994—after the issuance of the first judgment dated July 26, 1994—and to grant the [seller] another period for subsequent improvement.

In this respect, the legal starting point of the Court of Appeals is already incorrect: It assumes that the beginning of the time period is the time of the delivery of the complete documentation and relies on the decision of the Federal Court of Justice dated November 4, 1992—VIII ZR 165/91. In doing so, it overlooks that HGB § 377, upon which the decision was based, refers to the time of 'delivery,' which requires the complete delivery of the goods into the buyer's sphere of influence (decision of the Federal Court of Justice, *supra*, at II.2.b). In contrast, CISG Art 39(1) speaks of a 'reasonable time after (the buyer) has discovered or ought to have discovered (the lack of conformity of the goods).' Recourse to the mentioned jurisprudence is, therefore, for this reason alone not possible.

It is obvious, that the limitations period of CISG Art 39(1) had run by August 1994; upon a reasonable examination, the [buyer] could have, within a short period of time, recognized the complained-of alleged breach of contract regarding 'the documentation, i.e., the operating or service instructions,' which was noticed in the letter dated August 24, 1994. The question whether this period of time had expired on the day of the [buyer's] letter of repudiation dated March 2, 1993, can be left open. It can further be left open whether the [buyer] has forfeited its right to give notice of defects by basing its repudiation exclusively on other defects, without reserving its right to raise warranty claims concerning any defects with respect to the documentation. The Court of Appeals' assumption that the [buyer] validly declared the contract avoided in its letter dated October 12, 1994 after the notice of defects dated August 24, 1994 and the failure to cure, is therefore incorrect.

[...]

C 38/39-16

Bundesgerichtshof (Germany),
3 November 1999,
CISG-online 475[155]

For a summary of the facts see C 38/39-8 above.

[Judgment]

[...]

3. The notice letter dated June 14, 1993 also met the substantive requirements of Art 39(1) CISG, an issue the Court of Appeals was able to leave open based on its legal point of view. By means of this provision, pursuant to which the buyer must specify 'the nature of

---

[155] Translation taken from CISG Pace (citations omitted).

the lack of conformity,' the seller shall be enabled to get an idea of the lack of conformity in order to take the necessary steps. In that context, the buyer, in any case, must specify the complained-of deviation of quality; concerning machinery and technical equipment, only an explanation of the symptoms can be demanded, not an explanation of the underlying causes. Here, the [buyer] gave notice to the [sellers] by letter dated June 14, 1993 that a customer had found steel splinters in the semi-finished goods that had been produced using the grinding device in dispute and that, as a result, when processing the semi-finished goods into moist tissues, patches of rust occurred thereon. At the same time, the [buyer] expressed the suspicion that the grinding device delivered on April 7, 1993 was defective, so that the [buyer], as a precaution, stated that it held the [sellers] liable for all damages incurred and to be incurred in the future. Thus, the complained-of lack of conformity of the shipment was sufficiently specified in accordance with the [buyer's] state of knowledge at that time, so that the [sellers] were able to learn from the letter dated June 14, 1993 the delivery item as well as the complained-of lack of conformity with the contract.

[...]

C 38/39-17

Bundesgericht (Switzerland),
13 November 2003,
CISG-online 840[156]

For a summary of the facts see C 35-15 above.

[Judgment]

[...]

4.3 The UN Sales Law was drafted in Arabic, English, French, Spanish, Russian and Chinese. It was also translated into German, among other languages. In the case of ambiguity in the wording, reference is to be had to the original versions, whereby the English version, and, secondarily, the French version are given a higher significance as English and French were the official languages of the Conference and the negotiations were predominantly conducted in English. According to the German translation of Art 39(1) CISG, the buyer must precisely specify the nature of the lack of conformity in the notice to the seller. The English and French texts of the Convention talk about 'specifying the nature of the lack of conformity' and '*en précisant la nature de ce défaut*', respectively. Thereby, the notice must specify the nature, type or character of the lack of conformity. What must be considered is that the verbs 'specify' and '*préciser*' can not only be translated as '*genau bezeichnen*' (precisely describe), but also with '*bezeichnen*' (describe) or with '*angeben*' (indicate). Consequently, the original versions do not require the description to be as precise as could be expected from the German translation. According to those texts, a notification of defects that (precisely) indicates the nature or the character of the lack of conformity is sufficient. The wording of Art 39(1) CISG does not require a more precise circumscription. This is also not necessary, as in this day and age of electronic communication, the seller can be expected to ask questions

---

[156] Translation taken from CISG Pace (citations omitted).

in any case if he desires more precise instructions from the buyer. In order to circumscribe the nature or type of the lack of conformity, it is sufficient if the buyer communicates that a machine or parts thereof are not functioning and indicates the appropriate symptoms. It is not necessary that he also elaborate the causes of the functional faults. To the extent that the seller is not aware of the intention of the buyer's declaration, its notification of defects and other behavior is to be interpreted in the way a reasonable person in the same position as that of the seller under the same circumstances would have understood it (Art 8(2) CISG).

4.4 The [Buyer] indicated in its letter dated 5 September 1996 that the delivered machine was not usable. This statement is to be appreciated in its context. Additionally, the [Buyer] then stated the individual functional faults or missing parts, respectively, and demanded the removal of the problems. It is evident from the request to make repair and the faults listed individually that the [Buyer] was not notifying the [Seller's assignee] of the general lack of functionability based on its construction, but rather regarded the machine as defective but generally functional. Therefore, the Court of Appeal (*Obergericht*) correctly accepted that the lack of functionality of the machine owing to the failure to meet a pro- totype standard, which was determined by the experts, was not notified by the [Buyer]. The fact that the [Buyer] indicated the defects again, shows that the list of defects was to be understood as exhaustive. As the nitrogen generator was not included in this list, the [Seller's assignee] could have assumed that there was no objection in this regard. Thereby, the Court of Appeal (*Obergericht*) correctly found that to this extent, a notification of defects was lacking, and that the Buyer, therefore, could not derive any rights from the defectiveness of the nitrogen generator and the insufficient technical standard of the machine.

[...]

Questions

Q 38/39-19

Can you see any relationship between the cases cited above concerning the period for giving notice (C 38/39-7–13) and those concerning the specificity of notice (C 38/39-14–17)?

Q 38/39-20

According to the *BGH* case of 3 November 1999 (C 38/39-16), what are the minimum requirements exist for the content of a notice?

Q 38/39-21

How would you describe the approach of the *BGH* (C 38/9-15 and C 38/39-16)?

Q 38/39-22

(a)   Summarise the arguments presented in the *Bundesgericht* case (C 38/39-17) interpreting the specificity of notice requirement.
(b)   In light of the reasoning in Section 4.3 of the *Bundesgericht* case (C 38/39-17), would you have expected the outcome of this case?

V. Form of Notice

Article 39 CISG does not specify the form of the notice of lack of conformity that is required; of course, the parties are free to agree on a particular form if they wish. What is significant here is the ability to prove that notice was, in fact, given.

C 38/39-18

Landgericht Frankfurt am Main (Germany),
13 July 1994,
CISG-online 118[157]

[Facts]

An Italian seller and a German buyer concluded a contract for the sale of shoes. After taking delivery, the buyer complained over the telephone lack of conformity of the goods and refused to pay the price. The seller commenced legal action to recover the contract price.

[Judgment]

The court held that, in principle, notice of non conformity may also be given via telephone. However, in the case at hand, the court stated that the buyer could not rely on lack of conformity. In fact, the buyer had not proved evidence either to have given notice within a reasonable time, or to have specified the nature of the lack of conformity, as required in Art 39(1) CISG. Therefore, the buyer was obliged to pay the price according to Art 53 CISG.

CISG Advisory Council Opinion No 1: Electronic Communications under CISG:[158]

[...]

CISG Art 39(1)

[...]

OPINION

---

[157]   English abstract taken from UNILEX.
[158]   Taken from www.cisgac.com.

The term 'notice' includes electronic communications provided that the seller expressly or impliedly has consented to receiving electronic messages of that type, in that format, and to that address.

[...]

Question

Q 38/39-23

(a) What does the *Frankfurt am Main* case (C 38/39-18) have to say about the form that notice of lack of conformity can, and should, be given in?
(b) Who bears the burden of proof?
(c) How can notice be proven?

VI. Article 39(2) CISG Time Limit

Article 39(2) CISG creates a cut-off date for the giving of notice of lack of conformity at two years from the date the goods were handed over to the buyer, subject to any contractual period of guarantee. The cut-off period hereunder is, however, not to be confused with the limitation periods for bringing warranty claims, which determine the period within which the buyer must bring an action before the courts in order to be able to enforce its existing claims. These questions are not dealt with in the CISG, but rather by the UN Convention on the Limitation Period in the International Sale of Goods, to the extent that the parties are situated in Contracting States to this Convention. Otherwise, the domestic law applicable under the rules of private international law is to be used.

The interaction between the two-year cut-off period for giving notice of lack of conformity and domestic rules concerning limitation periods for the bringing of actions has also caused some controversy in the courts. There is no problem where the domestic limitation period exceeds the two-year limit under Article 39(2) CISG. However, it can be problematic in cases in which the domestic limitation period is *shorter* than the two-year cut-off period for giving notice of lack of conformity, such as under Swiss law, in which the domestic limitation period is one year.[159]

---

[159] *Cf* Art 210 OR.

C 38/39-19

Bundesgericht (Switzerland),
18 May 2009,
CISG-online 1900

[Facts][160]

A Swiss seller and a Spanish buyer concluded a contract for the sale of a packaging machine in December 2000. Under the contract, the seller was to install the machine and prepare its operation at buyer's factory. Subsequently, a dispute arose between the parties regarding the exact performance of the machine. The buyer asserted that an output of 180 vials per minute had been promised by the seller, but the seller contended that this was neither possible nor had it been agreed upon. Thereafter, the seller attempted on several occasions to increase the performance of the machine which remained, however, well below the buyer's expectations. Finally, on 23 March 2003, the buyer declared the contract terminated and claimed restitution of the purchase price plus damages. The seller counterclaimed for the outstanding purchase price along with damages.

Both the Court of first instance and the Court of appeal ruled in favor of the buyer on the basis of CISG's provisions. The seller then appealed to the Swiss Federal Supreme Court.

[...]

Furthermore, [Seller] asserts that the provisions of Art 210(1) OR has been violated. [Seller] claims that any claims on the part of [Buyer] were already subject to limitation and that the Appellate Court failed to apply the one-year limitation period of Art 210 OR to the present case.

[...]

[Judgment][161]

[...]

10. [No violation of provisions governing the limitation period]

10.1 The CISG does not govern the limitation of claims arising out of contracts for the international sale of goods. Therefore, the assessment of whether an asserted claim arising out of a contract governed by the CISG is in fact subject to a time-bar must be decided in accordance with the domestic substantive law applicable by virtue of the conflict of laws rules of the forum State. If the conflict of laws rules of the forum State lead to the application of the substantive law of a Contracting State to the United Nations Convention on the Limitation Period in the International Sale of Goods of 14 June 1974, the issue of limitation is to be determined in accordance with this Convention.

10.2 [Seller] has its habitual residence in Switzerland. Thus, the Appellate Court has correctly decided that the issue of limitation of the right to declare the contract avoided is governed by Swiss law. Since Switzerland has not become a Contracting State to the United Nations Convention on the Limitation Period in the International Sale of Goods of 14 June 1974, its

---

[160] Summary of the facts taken from UNILEX.
[161] Translation partly taken from CISG Pace (citations omitted).

four-year limitation period concerning all claims arising out of contracts for the international sale of goods cannot apply in the present case. It means that the question of limitation of claims arising out of the contract concluded between [Buyer] and [Seller] is governed by the Swiss Code on the Law of Obligations of 30 March 1911.

10.3 [Seller] has submitted before the Court that the limitation period was governed by Art 210 OR.

Pursuant to Art 210 OR, a buyer's claims arising out of a lack of conformity of the goods become time-barred one year after the goods have been delivered to it by the seller. In certain cases, an application of this one-year limitation period (Art 210 OR) to contracts governed by the CISG will be problematic: It might happen that claims arising out of a lack of conformity of the goods would already be time-barred whereas the period for notification under Art 39(2) CISG has not even expired. As stated beforehand, the buyer loses the right to rely on a lack of conformity of the goods in accordance with Art 39(2) CISG if he does not give the seller notice thereof at the latest within a period of two years from the date on which the goods were actually handed over to the buyer. Therefore, legal scholars tend to argue that Art 210 OR should be inapplicable to sales contracts governed by the CISG. The Court holds that this is an appropriate solution. The one-year limitation period provided for in Art 210 OR cannot be applied at least to those cases where it would subject a claim to limitation even before the two-year notification period of Art 39(2) CISG has expired. Otherwise, there would be a violation of provisions of public international law.

There are various possible solutions to adapt the rule contained in Art 210 OR. For instance, some scholars propose that the general limitation period of ten years under Art 127 OR should apply instead of Art 210 OR. Others suggest that the period under Art 210 OR should either be extended to two-years or that the one-year period of Art 210 OR should not already commence at the time of delivery but only by the time when the lack of conformity has been notified.

In the present case, it may remain undecided which of these solutions should be applied. In particular, it is immaterial whether the relevant limitation period is two or ten years. The Appellate Court has correctly reasoned that the laws of Switzerland also govern a possible suspension of the running of the limitation period. Art 135 OR provides that the running of a limitation period will be suspended either if the debtor acknowledges the existence of the claim or if the creditor files an action with respect to the claim. The debtor may acknowledge the existence of a claim against itself by virtue of any conduct which may be reasonable understood by the creditor as a confirmation of its liability in law. By virtue of its final attempt to cure the lack of conformity of the machine on 31 October 2002, [Seller] has suspended the running of the limitation period. [Buyer] has also filed an action with respect to the questionable claim on 9 February 2004. Consequently, the asserted claim would not be subject to a time-bar even if a two-year limitation period were applied.

10.4 Therefore, [Buyer]'s claims and other rights following the existence of a fundamental breach of contract are not time-barred. [Seller] has not raised any objection against the magnitude of the demanded sums. The Appellate Court has made a correct decision also with respect to the issue of limitation.

[...]

As a consequence, the Swiss Federal Supreme Court dismissed the [Seller]'s appeal as unfounded.

Question

Q 38/39-24

(a)   Why would the application of a domestic one-year limitation period violate public international law?
(b)   Which solutions exist to reconcile a short domestic limitation period with Article 39(2) CISG?

VII. Application of Articles 38 and 39 CISG by Analogy?

From their wording as well as their systematic position Articles 38/39 CISG only apply to the initial delivery of non-conforming goods. There may, however, be situations where an application by analogy is called for.

C 38/39-20

Hof van Beroep Ghent (Belgium),
14 November 2008,
CISG-online 1908

[Facts]

In June 2004 the buyer, a German trader, purchased from the seller, a company under Belgian law, two freezing chambers to be installed at the Hamma bakery. Following a complaint of the buyer asserting the goods' non-conformity, the seller effected repairs of the goods on 27 January 2005 and confirmed the same to the buyer on 2 February 2005. On 31 May 2005 the Hamma bakery informed the buyer about its discontent regarding the result of the repairs. The buyer alleges that the repairs were conducted in an uncompleted manner and foremost that he raised non-conformity of the goods in time, *i.e.* both prior to the repairs conducted by the seller on 27 January and after these repairs by means of his letters of 7 July 2005 and 7 November 2005. The court in the first instance held that the buyer was to pay to the seller the sum agreed upon for the 'project Hamma bakery'. Against this the buyer argues in the appeal.

[Judgment][162]

[...]

[The court held that], [i]t is reasonable to also apply Art 39 of the CISG in case of defective repairs. After a defective repair by the seller, the buyer can again rely on all of his rights as

---

[162] Translation taken from CISG pace (citations omitted).

creditor. For this purpose, the buyer must inform the seller within a reasonable time of the fact that the repairs have been performed in a defective or unsatisfactory way. Art 39 must therefore be applied by analogy.

[...]

When [Buyer], as a merchant, does not [...] protest in time and in a sufficiently specific manner [...] against the [...] notice [...] from the repairing [Seller], in which it was stated that the reported non-conformities to the freezing chambers have been repaired, this must be considered as an acceptance by [Buyer] that all of the reported non-conformities had been repaired.

[...]

The Hamma bakery apparently informed [Buyer] on 31 May 2005 of its discontent with the result. At that moment, *i.e.*, 31 May 2005, there can therefore be no doubt that [Buyer] was aware of the non-conformity of the repairs. [...] Insofar as it can be accepted that [Seller] did in fact get knowledge of the contents [of the alleged note dating 7 November [2005]] it was not made within the reasonable time frame required by the CISG. To no avail, [Buyer] is [...] referring to [...] a letter that he alleges to have written to [Seller] on 7 July 2005. [...] In the disputed writing [...], insofar it is real and has actually been sent, it is only stated that [an] invoice ... was being sent back, as this invoice related to necessary repairs. Insofar as this would relate to the current dispute [...], it is in any case not a notice of non-conformity of repairs made including the necessary specifications. At the very least for reasons of apparent inertia, [Buyer] did in the given circumstances lose his right to rely on the fact that the repairs of the goods delivered by [Seller] do not conform to the agreement (Art 39 CISG).

[...]

The judgment of the first judge must therefore be confirmed in this sense.

[...]

Question

Q 38/39-25

Which reasons speak for applying Article 39 by way of analogy?

VIII. CISG Advisory Council

CISG Advisory Council Opinion No 2: Examination of the Goods and Notice of Non Conformity: Articles 38 and 39—Black Letter Rules:[163]

Article 38

1. Although a buyer must examine the goods, or cause them to be examined, within as short a period as is practicable in the circumstances, there is no independent sanction for failure to do so. However, if the buyer fails to do so and there is a lack of conformity of the goods that an examination would have revealed, the notice period in article 39 commences from the time the buyer 'ought to have discovered it'.

2. Whether and when it is practicable, and not just possible, to examine the goods depends on all the circumstances of the case. It is often commercially practicable to examine the goods immediately upon receipt. This would normally be the case with perishables. In other cases, such as complicated machinery, it may not be commercially practicable to examine the goods except for externally visible damage or other non-conformity until, for example, they can be used in the way intended. If the goods are to be re-sold, the examination will often be conducted by the sub-purchaser. Another example is dealt with in article 38(3).

3. The period for examining for latent defects commences when signs of the lack of conformity become evident.

Article 39

1. The period for giving notice under article 39 commences when the buyer discovered or 'ought to have discovered' the lack of conformity. The buyer 'ought to have discovered' the lack of conformity upon the expiration of the period for examination of the goods under article 38 or upon delivery where the lack of conformity was evident without examination.

2. Unless the lack of conformity was evident without examination of the goods, the total amount of time available to give notice after delivery of the goods consists of two separate periods, the period for examination of the goods under article 38 and the period for giving notice under article 39. The Convention requires these two periods to be distinguished and kept separate, even when the facts of the case would permit them to be combined into a single period for giving notice.

3. The reasonable time for giving notice after the buyer discovered or ought to have discovered the lack of conformity varies depending on the circumstances. In some cases notice should be given the same day. In other cases a longer period might be appropriate. No fixed period, whether 14 days, one month or otherwise, should be considered as reasonable in the abstract without taking into account the circumstances of the case. Among the circumstances to be taken into account are such matters as the nature of the goods, the nature of the defect, the situation of the parties and relevant trade usages.

---

[163] Taken from www.cisgac.com.

4. The notice should include the information available to the buyer. In some cases that
    may mean that the buyer must identify in detail the lack of conformity. In other cases
    the buyer may only be able to indicate the lack of conformity. Where that is the case, a
    notice that describes the symptoms is enough to specify the nature of the lack of con-
    formity.

Question

Q 38/39-26

Compare CISG Advisory Council Opinion No 2 to the above case law.

Article 40 CISG

The seller is not entitled to rely on the provisions of articles 38 and 39 if the lack of conformity relates to facts of which he knew or could not have been unaware and which he did not disclose to the buyer.

I. Overview

Article 40 CISG operates to relieve the buyer from the consequences of failing to observe Articles 38 and 39 CISG in cases where the seller knew or could not have been unaware of the lack of conformity and did not disclose this to the buyer. This provision has been expressed as a reflection of the principle of 'fair trading' found in many domestic legal systems and underlying many other provisions of the CISG.

II. Operation of Article 40 CISG

C 40-1

Stockholm Chamber of Commerce Award (Sweden),
5 June 1998,
CISG-online 379[164]

[Facts]

According to a contract dated February 21, 1990 (the 'Contract'), Beijing Light Automobile Co., Ltd. ('BLAC') agreed to purchase from Connell Limited Partnership ('Connell'), through a division of Connell with the trading name 'Danly Machine' ('Danly'), a 4,000 ton rail press (the 'Press') designed to make frame rails to be used by BLAC in the manufacture of light trucks at its factory outside Beijing.

---

[164] Taken from CISG Pace (citations omitted).

[...]

The Press was constructed and first assembled at [seller's] Chicago plant. In late spring and early summer 1991 the plant was visited by [buyer's] representatives during the final stages of construction and assembly. In June 1991 final set-up and verification tests were made in order to ensure that the Press' functions then were in accordance with the Contract specifications. After completion and approval of the tests, the Press was disassembled so that it could be transported to China and in July 1991 delivery began and was concluded by shipment from the port of New Orleans on August 16, 1991. The Press arrived in the port of Tianjing in China on October 14, 1991, and reached [buyer's] plant outside Beijing in March 1992.

Assembly of the Press started in spring 1992. Assembly work was performed by [buyer] with the help of another Chinese company, China Mechanical Industry Installation Company ('CMIIC'). When the representatives of [seller] arrived at the plant for the installation supervision provided for in the Contract, at the end of June 1992, the assembly was substantially completed and the [seller] personnel was mainly involved in the subsequent tests and checks leading up to the final approval on July 23, 1992 by both parties.

[Buyer] began to operate the Press on January 10, 1993. For almost three years, [buyer] used the Press continuously without incident. On November 10, 1995, the Press failed (for reasons further discussed below), resulting in damage to the Press. [Buyer] requested that [seller] send technicians to assist in the repair of the Press but the parties failed to agree on the terms for such assistance, and [buyer] had the Press repaired with the help of technicians available in China. The Press returned to operation on August 15, 1996.

Shortly after the break-down of the Press, [buyer] asserted that the failure was caused by a deficiency for which [seller] was liable. [Seller] rejected any such liability and some correspondence took place in spring and summer 1996 in an effort to try to settle the matter amicably, however without success. On February, 1997, [buyer] addressed a Request for Arbitration to the Arbitration Institute of the Stockholm Chamber of Commerce, claiming damages from [seller].

[Judgment]

[...]

6.3 Applicability of Article 40

It is undisputed that [buyer's] notice of the alleged non-conformity was made well beyond the two year limitation period under Article 39(2) of CISG (and, of course, the 18-month guarantee period under the Contract). Therefore, [seller] will be liable for any non-conformity only if it relates to facts that [seller] could not have been unaware of and that were not disclosed to [buyer]. The Tribunal will address in turn the issues of non-conformity, [seller's] awareness and disclosure to [buyer].

[...]

b) [Seller's] awareness

Article 40 of CISG is, as stated above, to be considered a safety valve for the buyer. Its application results in a dramatic weakening of the position of the seller, who loses his absolute defences based on often relatively short-term time limits for the buyer's examination and notice of non-conformity, and instead is faced with the risk of claims only precluded by the general prescription rules under applicable domestic laws or possible international conventions (such as the 1974 Convention on the Limitation Period in the International Sale of Goods).

It follows that Article 40 of CISG should only be applied in special circumstances. A seller is normally (through his employees) aware of the actual state of goods delivered from his plant, but the fact that he also may be aware that some part of the goods may fail to meet the standard set by CISG cannot automatically lead to Article 40 being applicable. In such case the time limits for claims under many contracts governed by CISG would become illusory.

The doctrine on the issue of the seller's awareness according to Article 40 also reflects the difficulty in reaching a common denominator for the qualification of the necessary 'awareness'. There is, not unexpectedly, general consensus that fraud and similar cases of bad faith will make Article 40 applicable. But some authors are of the opinion that also what can be described as gross negligence or even ordinary negligence suffices, while others indicate that slightly more than gross negligence (approaching deliberate negligence) is required. As a clear case of the requisite awareness has been mentioned a situation where the non-conformity has already resulted in accidents in similar or identical goods sold by the seller and been made known to him or to the relevant branch of the industry. But also in the absence of such relatively clear cases awareness may be considered to be at hand if the facts relating to the non-conformity are easily apparent or detected. Some authors indicate that the seller is not under an obligation to investigate possible instances of non-conformity but others say that he must not ignore clues and some go so far as to suggest that the seller, at least in certain cases, has an obligation to examine the goods to ascertain their conformity.

In this case, [seller] had not for several years before the Contract built a 4,000 ton press and there is no evidence that a P-52 lockplate has been used in or intended for presses of similar sizes before or after the Contract. The intended, 'foolproof' design involved the A-5750 key retainer and a keyway with corresponding width. [Seller] has stated that the problem resulting in the change to the P-52 appeared at the stage where the lock-nut was to be secured in its position on the shaft tightly against the hub of the gear. The ninth slot and the two unthreaded holes on the lock-nut bear the mark of improvised efforts to solve the problem. [Seller] has stated that it would have been possible to remove the shaft and machine a new key way for the A-5750 key retainer but this would entail a cost of some USD 2,000–3,000 and a delay of 2-3 days. Instead [seller] tried to solve the problem with the P-52 lockplate. No record has been found of the exchange of the locking devices.

However, this does not conclusively prove that [seller] foresaw the ultimate failure of the P-52 lockplate if improperly installed. In fact, one possible explanation for the absence of any information or, as contended by [seller], of any subsequent inspection of the installation of the lockplate is that [seller] itself did not fully appreciate the risk. But the alternative positioning marked by the two unthreaded holes on the lock-nut indicates that [seller] realized the necessity or at least desirability of a correct positioning of the lockplate, and it stands to reason that this was caused by the concern that impact forces otherwise could have a detrimental effect on the durability in the long run of the lockplate.

Whatever the reason for the absence of records or information or follow-up on the P-52 lockplate, the Tribunal is of the opinion that it is not defensible to replace, apparently in an impromptu fashion, in a new and 'custom made' press of a size that [seller] for many years had not built, a planned design intended for an important security function with a new device without ascertaining its performance or installation. These are the circumstances that in the Tribunal's opinion distinguishes this case from the situation where a seller is generally 'aware' that the goods manufactured in his ordinary course of business are not of the best quality or leave something to be desired. But that is not in itself enough to meet the test under Article 40. The requisite state of awareness that is the threshold criterion for the application of Article 40 must in the Tribunal's opinion amount to at least a conscious disregard of facts that meet the eyes and are of evident relevance to the non-conformity.

The absence of any document or witness showing [seller's] internal deliberations when replacing the A-5750 with the P-52 lockplate does not prevent the application of Article 40. The article as phrased is intended to alleviate the burden of proof on the buyer in respect of the seller's awareness, a burden that otherwise often would be impossible. If the evidence and the undisputed facts show that it is more likely than not that the seller is conscious of the facts that relate to the non-conformity, it must be up to the seller to show that he did not reach the requisite state of awareness. It is in the nature of things when applying Article 40 that considerable time may have passed since manufacture or delivery of the goods and that the evidentiary situation may be difficult. But once the buyer has sufficiently established the basis for his claim under Article 40, it is the seller that must assume the risk of not being able to counterbalance this with evidence on his own design and manufacturing process that, after all, he is in a better position to secure than the buyer.

In this matter, the Tribunal can draw no other conclusion from the available facts than that [seller], when substituting the P-52 for the A-5750 arrangement, was aware that the positioning of the P-52 lockplate was critical (as indeed also is stated by [seller] in its briefs). Yet there is no evidence or even claim from [seller] that [seller] either intended or made any effort to ascertain that the P-52 was in fact properly installed. It must therefore be assumed that [seller] did not have any such intention. It is not for the Tribunal to speculate on the reason for this. What is relevant is that [seller] cannot have been unaware of the fact that proper installation was critical, the fact that the possibility of improper installation by [buyer] could not be ruled out, the fact that there was a clear risk that this could lead to serious failure of the Press within a period of time that certainly differed from what [buyer] was entitled to expect under the Contract, and that [seller] did not do anything to eliminate this risk. The Tribunal therefore concludes that [seller] must be assumed to have consciously disregarded apparent facts which were of evident relevance to the non-conformity and which, in fact, caused the failure of the Press.

c) Disclosure

In order to avoid liability for non-conformities of which the seller cannot be unaware, he must disclose them to the buyer. It is not sufficient that the buyer should be able, from documents available to him, to deduce that some alteration has been made in the design of a machine or such like. The fact that 'A 5750' was indicated in the service manual and that the actual locking device in the same place was stamped 'P-52' does not amount to a disclosure by [seller] to [buyer] of the non-conformity in this case. As already stated in the foregoing, the non-conformity of the P-52 relates to the installation, and it is thus the failure by [seller] to instruct on or supervise installation that has resulted in the non-conformity being permitted to cause the failure of the Press. In other words, even if [seller] had informed [buyer] of the exchange as such (and without any further information on proper installation or the risks involved in the arrangement, etc.) this would not be enough; to disclose in the sense of Article 40 is to inform the buyer of the risks resulting from the nonconformity.

Question

Q 40-1

(a)   According to this decision (C 40-1) what are the requirements for Article 40 CISG?
(b)   Under which circumstances would there be a disclosure?

Article 41 CISG

The seller must deliver goods which are free from any right or claim of a third party, unless the buyer agreed to take the goods subject to that right or claim. However, if such right or claim is based on industrial property or other intellectual property, the seller's obligation is governed by article 42.

I. Overview

A. Content and Purpose of Article 41 CISG

Although the CISG does not cover the question of transfer of title to goods, Article 41 CISG governs the seller's duty to deliver goods that the buyer can enjoy in undisturbed possession and ownership. This provision is only concerned with rights to the goods themselves; intellectual and industrial property rights are governed by Article 42 CISG (see discussion below).

B. Domestic Laws

Under German law, reference is made to rights of third parties.

§ 433(1) BGB:[165]

The sales contract places the seller of goods under an obligation to hand over the goods to the buyer and to transfer the title in the goods. The seller must sell the goods free from physical defects and third-party rights.

---

[165] Author's translation.

§ 435 BGB:[166]

> The goods are free from third-party rights if third parties cannot assert any rights against the buyer in relation to the goods, or only those assumed under the sales contract. [...]

Under US law, 'good title' is warranted by the seller.

§ 2-312(1) UCC:

> Subject to subsection (2) there is in a contract for sale a warranty by the seller that
>
> (a) the title conveyed shall be good, and its transfer rightful; and
> (b) the goods shall be delivered free from any security interest or other lien or encumbrance of which the buyer at the time of contracting has no knowledge.

Under English law, a term is implied into the contract that goods are free from rightful possessory or proprietary claims of a third party, apart from those known or disclosed between the parties.

Sec 12(2) SGA:

> In a contract of sale, other than one to which subsection (3) below applies, there is also an implied term that
>
> (a) the goods are free, and will remain free until the time when the property is to pass, from any charge or encumbrance not disclosed or known to the buyer before the contract is made, and
> (b) the buyer will enjoy quiet possession of the goods except so far as it may be disturbed by the owner or other person entitled to the benefit of any charge or encumbrance so disclosed or known.

II. Operation of Article 41 CISG

C 41-1

Oberster Gerichtshof (Austria),
6 February 1996,
CISG-online 224

For a summary of the facts see C 9-3 above.

---

[166] Author's translation.

[Judgment][167]

[...]

Furthermore, the non-issuance of the letter of credit was not the cause for non-fulfillment of the contract. In accordance with the holdings of the lower courts, this Court finds that the [sellers] are responsible for the non-fulfillment of the contract, because they did not obtain clearance of their supplier for export of the liquid gas into Belgium. According to Art 30 CISG, the seller is obligated to deliver the goods in accordance with the terms of the contract. The argument of the [sellers] in their appeal to the effect that the prohibition of export into Belgium and the resulting consequences are part of the sphere of the [buyer], because the latter did not make the possibility of export into Belgium a condition of the contract, is without merit. Upon conclusion of a contract of sale, the buyer can generally assume in the absence of special circumstances (embargo, legal restrictions, general restrictions known to the industry) that the further use the goods is unlimited and is not subject to further restrictions. It is not the duty of the buyer to obtain an assurance that further delivery restrictions do not exist. To the contrary, it is the obligation of the seller to mention such restrictions of delivery, which limit the normally unrestricted use of the goods. If the seller omits to mention such restrictions, the buyer can justifiably assume that such restrictions do not exist. According to Art 41 CISG, the seller has to deliver goods, which are not subject to the rights of third parties, unless the buyer has previously agreed to accept such goods in fulfillment of the contract. If the supplier of the seller has restricted the export of the goods, then the goods are burdened with such a restriction. This consequently means that the delivery of goods, which are subject to such a restriction, constitutes non-fulfillment of the contract in the absence of the buyer's consent.

[...]

Questions

Q 41-1

Compile a list of possible rights or claims by third parties that may fall under Article 41 CISG.

Q 41-2

(a)   How did the court in the above case (C 41-1) expand the application of Article 41 CISG?
(b)   What other Article of the CISG could be considered instead?

The first sentence of Article 41 CISG places an obligation on the seller to deliver goods not only free from any right, but also free from any claim of a third party. Whether such claim is derived from a third party's right is irrelevant for the purposes of this article. Consequently, not only normal, founded claims, but even unfounded claims can give rise to liability under Article 41 CISG.

---

[167] Translation taken from CISG Pace (citations omitted).

Questions

Q 41-3

(a) How would the situation in which a mere claim is made be resolved under your domestic law where it turns out that the third party does not have a right over the goods?
(b) How would this situation be resolved under the CISG?

Q 41-4

Some authors want to exclude 'frivolous' claims from the ambit of Article 41 CISG. Discuss this question.

Article 42 CISG

(1) The seller must deliver goods which are free from any right or claim of a third party based on industrial property or other intellectual property, of which at the time of the conclusion of the contract the seller knew or could not have been unaware, provided that the right or claim is based on industrial property or other intellectual property:

    (a) under the law of the State where the goods will be resold or otherwise used, if it was contemplated by the parties at the time of the conclusion of the contract that the goods would be resold or otherwise used in that State; or

    (b) in any other case, under the law of the State where the buyer has his place of business.

(2) The obligation of the seller under the preceding paragraph does not extend to cases where:

    (a) at the time of the conclusion of the contract the buyer knew or could not have been unaware of the right or claim; or

    (b) the right or claim results from the seller's compliance with technical drawings, designs, formulae or other such specifications furnished by the buyer.

I. Overview

A. Content and Purpose of Article 42 CISG

Article 42 CISG states the general duty of the seller to deliver goods to the buyer that are free from third party industrial and intellectual property rights and claims. This duty will only be held to exist in cases where the seller knew or could not have been unaware of the existence of such a right or claim in the contemplated state of resale or use of the goods. Similarly, the seller will not be liable where the buyer knew or could not have been unaware of the right or claim.

B. Domestic Laws

Most domestic legal systems do not explicitly provide for a warranty that the goods are free from intellectual or industrial property rights. Rather, any warranty in this regard forms part of the general liability for defects in title.

An explicit reference to industrial rights is, however, made in US law.

§ 2-312(3) UCC:

> Unless otherwise agreed a seller who is a merchant regularly dealing in goods of the kind warrants that the goods shall be delivered free of the rightful claim of any third person by way of infringement or the like but a buyer who furnishes specifications to the seller must hold the seller harmless against any such claim which arises out of compliance with the specifications.

Questions

Q 42-1

Can you think of any reasons to differentiate between defects in title and encumbrances by intellectual property rights?

Q 42-2

What differences between the CISG and the US approach are apparent from the provision above (§ 2-312(3) UCC)?

II. Mere Claims

As is the case under Article 41 CISG, it is also sufficient here that a third party makes a *claim* against the buyer; whether or not a *right* actually exists is irrelevant.

III. Territorial Limitations

A significant restriction on the seller's liability results from the fact that it can only be liable for rights and claims in certain states. Under Article 42(1)(a) CISG, this is the state of resale or use, provided that this was contemplated at the time of conclusion of the contract. Failing such contemplation, the buyer's state will also become relevant according to Article 42(1)(b) CISG.

C 42-1

Oberster Gerichtshof (Austria),
12 September 2006,
CISG-online 1364

[Facts][168]

An Austrian buyer bought CD-Media from a German seller. The German seller's supplier was its Taiwanese parent company, authorized to produce and distribute the CD-Media under a license agreement stipulated with a licensor. A dispute arose between the parties since the buyer failed to pay for some invoices. The buyer asserted that it had refused payment since the goods acquired from the seller in the year 2000 had not been properly licensed. Indeed, in March 2000, the license agreement had been terminated due to a dispute concerning the license fees. The seller replied that all CD-media delivered to the buyer were properly licensed and that the buyer's claims were excluded under Art 42(2)(a) CISG because, when the goods had been ordered, the buyer knew of the dispute over the payment of the license fees. In addition, the buyer had not complied with its duty to give notice to the seller of the nature of the right or claim of the third party within a reasonable time as required by Art 43 CISG.

[Judgment][169]

The Court of First Instance [...] dismissed [Seller]'s request for [the payment of the outstanding invoices]

[...]

The Appellate Court held that [Seller]'s appeal was justified and amended the judgment of the Court of First Instance in a way that [Seller] was awarded the sum of EUR 283,606.71, now being the matter in dispute. [...] The reasoning on the merits is based on the finding that under the special provision of Art 42 CISG [...] the seller was liable if an attempt is made to restrict the buyer in the use of the goods. As, in general, unjustified third-party claims may already trigger the seller's liability, the same legal consequence had to be effected *a fortiori* in cases where an industrial property right actually existed. As a result, a deficiency in title occurred whenever an industrial property right existed, or if the buyer is being sued by the proprietor or if both aspects are met at the same time. The burden to prove a deficiency in title was on the buyer. The liability of the seller for deficiencies following the property right was territorially limited under Art 42(1)(a) and (b) CISG. Therefore, the seller had to guarantee that no third-party rights existed only with reference to certain countries, but not on a worldwide level. First, it was liable for deficiencies in title caused by industrial property rights according to the law of the country in which the goods should be used or marketed. This would apply if the parties at least recognizably considered this country as a potential place for resale at the time of conclusion of contract, which is to be substantiated by the buyer. Subsidiarily, the seller was liable for conflicting property rights in the buyer's country.

In the case at hand, [Buyer] successfully proved that the said blank CD media delivered by [Seller] were burdened with a patent right of [Licensor]. It was established that [Licensor] possessed a European Processing Patent. It consisted of a batch of national patents. It was not

---

[168] Summary of facts taken from UNILEX.
[169] Translation taken from CISG Pace (citations omitted).

determined whether the European Processing Patent for blank CD media held by [Licensor] also applied in Austria. Likewise, [Buyer], which had the burden of proof, failed to deliver procedural submissions on that point. In any case, it was definitely determined that [Licensor]'s European patent had entered into effect in Germany. It can be assumed that the parties took into consideration a resale of the blank CD media within Germany, although [Seller] had delivered the goods ordered by [Buyer] to Austria. Both [Buyer] and [Seller] supplied retailers in Germany. Following this common market, [Seller] could have been aware of the fact that [Buyer] would resell the blank CDs *inter alia* in Germany. Such awareness is further supported by the fact that [Seller] even delivered part of the goods to Germany which can already be concluded from [Seller]'s submissions in regard to invoice no. 1. By virtue of this invoice, [Seller] requested payment of the German VAT, which in turn would have never occurred if delivery had been effected to Austria. Since [Seller] had been aware or could have been aware that [Buyer] resold the purchased goods *inter alia* in Germany, it can be assumed that the parties took that country into consideration at the time of the conclusion of the contract. Therefore, the prerequisites were met in order to assume that the blank CD media were deficient in title.

[...]

[Reasoning of the Federal Supreme Court]

The [Buyer]'s appeal is admissible; it is also justified in respect to a repeal of the judgment of the Appellate Court.

[...]

It is therefore of critical relevance whether [Seller] had breached its contractual duty. Generally, under the CISG the burden to prove the factual prerequisites of a provision is on the party that intends to employ it to its own advantage. Consequently, the burden to prove the breach of contract is on [Buyer]. [...]

[Buyer] argued that it had to assume that at least those goods which were delivered by [Seller] during the year 2000 had not been licensed. [Liquidator of Seller's assets] responded that [Licensor] would not even hold patent and license rights on all storage media and it apparently had not registered its rights in all countries.

This submission by [Buyer] requires some further discussion and ascertainment. In general as mentioned above, the burden to prove the extent of an alleged industrial property right of [Licensor] establishing the lack of conformity is on [Buyer] being the party relying on the breach. The industrial property rights under Art 42 CISG refer to patents of any kind. These can likewise be processing patents, as patent protection also embodies the direct products manufactured by a patented process. In that respect, the Appellate Court made a proper legal assessment when it territorially limited the seller's liability for deficiencies in title following a third-party right in terms of Art 42(1)(a) and (b) CISG. The seller merely has to guarantee a corresponding conformity in certain countries, but not on a worldwide level. It is primarily liable for any conflict with property rights under the law of the State in which (not: 'into which'!) it is being resold or in which it is supposed to be used, provided that the parties took this State into consideration at the time of the conclusion of the sales contract. The burden of proof in this respect is on the buyer.

In this respect, a discussion of the undifferentiated submission of [Buyer] is necessary. The assumption by the Appellate Court that the parties allegedly had—recognizably for the [Seller]—considered Germany as the State in which the blank CD media were to be used is inadmissible without a corresponding discussion with the parties. Therefore, this cannot be employed as an indicating factor pointing to a lack of conformity.

[...]

Furthermore, the Appellate Court's assessment was correct when it held that a seller would breach the contract at any rate if an industrial property right of a third person actually existed; under the additional requirements of Art 42 CISG the seller is also liable if any industrial property right is being unrightfully claimed. It is part of the seller's sphere of risk to deal with the third party in such cases.

[...]

Following the necessary discussion of the parties' submissions: [a] Regarding the existence of a deficiency because of the alleged industrial property right of [Licensor], and [b] Regarding the country that the parties considered for the use of the blank CD media there is further need for a hearing in the first instance. Hence the judgments made in the second instance have to be repealed. [...]

Question

Q 42-3

(a)   In which way is the seller's liability under Article 42 CISG restricted?
(b)   What is the reasoning behind the restrictions imposed by Article 42 CISG?

IV. Knowledge of the Seller

The seller's liability under Article 42 CISG is further limited by the fact that it is only liable for claims of which it knew or could not have been unaware at the time of the conclusion of the contract.

Question

Q 42-4

What is the reasoning behind this restriction imposed by Article 42 CISG?

Article 43 CISG

(1) The buyer loses the right to rely on the provisions of article 41 or article 42 if he does not give notice to the seller specifying the nature of the right or claim of the third party within a reasonable time after he has become aware or ought to have become aware of the right or claim.

(2) The seller is not entitled to rely on the provisions of the preceding paragraph if he knew of the right or claim of the third party and the nature of it.

Article 43(1) CISG is analogous to Article 39(1) CISG and is applicable to the case of third party rights and claims. Reference should therefore be had to the much more extensive case law cited under Article 39 CISG above.

Article 43(2) CISG, in turn, parallels Article 40 CISG.

Question

Q 43-1

Why do you think there is no parallel provision to Article 38 CISG with respect to third party rights and claims?

C 43-1

Bundesgerichtshof (Germany),
11 January 2006,
CISG-online 1200

[Facts][170]

A Dutch car dealer bought from a German seller [a] used car. Approximately two months later the car was seized by the police due to the suspicion that it could have been a vehicle previously stolen in Paris. Later on the buyer, formally requested by the insurance company—which had indemnified the owner—to return the car, refused alleging acquisition in good faith. A dispute brought before a Dutch court on this issue was still pending at the time of the present decision.

---

[170] Summary of facts taken from UNILEX.

Meanwhile, two months after the seizure the buyer asked the seller in writing for restitution of the price already paid and later filed a suit in a German court to obtain termination of the contract and damages.

[Judgment][171]

[...]

8. [The Court of Appeals]' explanations withstand legal scrutiny, so that the appeal by [Buyer] must be dismissed.

9. [...] [Buyer] cannot declare the contract avoided based on a fundamental breach of contract pursuant to Art 45(1)(a), Art 49(1)(a) CISG, and it is also not entitled to damages pursuant to Art 45(1)(b), Art 74 CISG, because it did not give notice of a legal defect within the meaning of Art 41 CISG in a timely manner pursuant to Art 43(1) CISG.

10. Pursuant to Art 41 (first sentence) CISG, a seller must deliver goods free from any right or claim of a third party. If, however, the buyer fails to meet its obligation imposed in Art 43(1) CISG to give notice of the right or claim of the third party, it cannot invoke its rights under Art 41 CISG.

11. The conclusion of the Court of Appeals that [Buyer] did not give timely notice to [Seller] of the legal defect—primarily the existing interest of a third party in the car—must be followed. The reasonable time of Art 43(1) CISG begins to run when the buyer becomes aware or ought to become aware of the legal defect. [Buyer] asserts that it learned of the alleged theft of the car in Paris, which is disputed by [Seller], upon its seizure on August 23, 1999. However, [Buyer]'s notification in a letter by its attorney of October 26, 1999, approximately two months after the seizure, is then, as the trial court correctly states, no longer within the reasonable time period.

12. The circumstances of each individual case are decisive in measuring the time period, so that a schematic fixing of the time for the notice of defect is impossible. The buyer must be granted a certain time period within which he can get a general picture of the legal situation; the type of legal defect must also be considered. Based on these standards, the Court of Appeals determined legally correctly that a time period of more than two months after the seizure was not within a reasonable period of time.

13. The appeal claims in vain that, in cases of cross-border traffic of goods, a protracted legal evaluation with the involvement of attorneys with specialized knowledge is necessary. As the trial court accurately stated, even for a legal layperson such as [Buyer], the suspicion of theft, made obvious by the police seizure, was easily recognized as an especially significant occurrence without the need to secure legal advice.

[...]

17. After all of this, the Court of Appeals correctly left undecided whether [Buyer] had become the rightful owner of the car, as claimed in the litigation with the legal successor to C.

18. The Court of Appeals further correctly assumed that [Buyer] could have a claim because the French insurance company C., by letter dated May 16, 2000, demanded that [Buyer] turn over the car to it, but the Court also correctly denied existence of a timely notice in this context.

[...]

---

[171] Translation taken from CISG Pace (citations omitted).

20. [Buyer] cannot, however, derive any rights from the demand for the car by C. because it did not notify [Seller] of this in a timely manner. A claim for the turnover of the car was raised against [Buyer], according to the findings of fact, by letter dated May 16, 2000. [...] This letter was received by [Buyer] on May 17, 2000. It has not been determined, and is also not referenced by the appeal in [Buyer]'s submissions in the trial court, that [Buyer] contacted [Seller] based on C.'s turnover demand on May 16, 2000, aside from the (later withdrawn) complaint of December 2000. Whether the December 2000 complaint, served on [Seller] on December 14, 2000, satisfied the content requirements of Art 43(1) CISG and must therefore be viewed as the notice of legal defect can remain undecided; that is so because [Buyer], in any event, did not meet the deadline of Art 43(1) CISG triggered by the turnover demand of May 2000, as correctly stated by the Court of Appeals. Nearly seven months had elapsed from the turnover demand to the complaint.

21. The deadline by which notice had to be given regarding C.'s claim to the vehicle is not to be viewed as complied with by [Buyer] having already informed [Seller] of the police seizure by letter dated October 26, 1999. In that letter, [Buyer] based its claim solely on the police suspicion of theft. In that letter, [Buyer] was not able to notify [Seller] of C.'s third-party claim, which was raised later. It is not enough that [Seller] was generally advised of the alleged theft. The notice of a third party claim is supposed to allow the seller to make contact with the third party and to defend the claim against the buyer. The notice must therefore set forth the name of the third party and inform the seller of the steps taken by the third party. These requirements are not met by the earlier letter of October 26, 1999. The letter never mentioned the claim of a third party that would have created a legal defect within the meaning of Art 41 CISG; this is clearly based on the fact that such a claim had not been raised against [Buyer] at that time. Additionally, the identity of the claimant was missing. In this context, the statement that the car was 'provided to the entitled party'—which, by the way, was based on an error by [Buyer]'s attorney and did not reflect the facts—was not enough. It is obvious that [Buyer] does not have an excuse for the untimely notice regarding C.'s turnover demand within the meaning of Art 44 CISG.

Questions

Q 43-2

Describe the purpose of Article 43(1) CISG. How does it contribute to the seller's interests?

Q 43-3

Compare and contrast Article 39(1) and Article 43(1) CISG. What similarities and differences can you find?

Article 44 CISG

Notwiths tanding the provisions of paragraph (1) of article 39 and paragraph (1) of article 43, the buyer may reduce the price in accordance with article 50 or claim damages, except for loss of profit, if he has a reasonable excuse for his failure to give the required notice.

I. Overview

A. Content and Purpose of Article 44 CISG

Article 44 CISG operates to 'relieve' the somewhat onerous consequences for the buyer arising from a failure to comply with the provisions of Articles 39(1) and 43(1) CISG by allowing a 'reasonable excuse' for the failure to give notice under those provisions. However, the buyer is not excused entirely; upon proving such reasonable excuse, its remedies are limited to damages, except for loss of profit, or a reduction of the purchase price.

B. Domestic Laws

Article 44 CISG has no predecessor in national sales laws. Under English law and many of the related common law systems, an obligation to examine the goods and notify lack of conformity is not expressly recognised, and such omission certainly does not lead to loss of legal rights.

C. Drafting History

The provision does not have a predecessor in ULIS either, and was introduced into the CISG solely as a compromise for what some countries viewed as the 'harsh consequences' of the notification provisions in Article 39 CISG. The concern was expressed that Article 39 CISG could turn into a 'booby trap' for buyers, particularly from developing countries, in which the buyer would acquire machines and other technical equipment, and owing to lack of knowledge, would not discover the lack of conformity or would not be able to describe it with the requisite precision.

II. Operation of Article 44 CISG

The interpretation of 'reasonable excuse' has caused problems in the case law under this provision, mainly due to the diverging national law views on this concept.

C 44-1

Oberlandesgericht München (Germany),
8 February 1995,
CISG-online 142[172]

[Facts]

A German seller and an Austrian buyer entered into a contract for the purchase of Polypropylen-Plastic granulate to be manufactured in accordance with the chemical compositions specified under the contract. According to the contract, the seller had the duty to examine the goods and to deliver them to a Danish company with which the buyer entertained a permanent supply agreement. The seller delivered the goods without examining them before. About one month after delivery, the Danish company notified the buyer that the goods did not conform with the specifications set forth under the contract and asked for damages. The buyer gave the seller notice of the non conformity of the goods and of the claim for damages of the Danish customer only about two months later.

[Judgment]

[...]

Finally, the Court addressed the issue of whether the buyer had a reasonable excuse for its failure to give a timely notice (Art 44 CISG). In answering this question, it considered the fast-paced nature of the buyer's business which required quick decisions and prompt actions. For this reason the Court determined that the buyer did not have a reasonable excuse. It noted that in taking into account the relevant circumstances and equitable considerations, it would be easier to allow such an excuse to a single trader, an artisan, or to a free professional.

---

[172] English abstract taken from UNILEX.

C 44-2

International Court of Commercial Arbitration Chamber of Commerce and Industry of the Russian Federation, Award No 54/1999, 24 January 2000, CISG-online 1042

For a summary of the facts see C 38/9-4 above.

[Judgment][173]

[...]

—*Thirdly*, the materials of the case confirm that, according to the requirements of the TC the inspection of the goods at the port of shipment (as well as on loading on board the vessel) was, evidently, technically and economically unreasonable. In the opinion of the ICCA, which took into consideration one of the general principles of the Vienna Convention 1980 on application of the rule of reasonableness at the evaluation of the conduct of the parties [...], the postponement of the inspection of the quality of the goods till their arrival at the port of destination or at the consumers' enterprises in the country of destination must be recognised as reasonable. Taking into consideration the fact that there were no concrete time limits for the inspection of the goods in the contract, the ICCA deemed it possible to apply the principles used in Article 38 of the Vienna Convention 1980, in order to approach this issue.

—*Fourthly*, the contract does not stipulate the consequences of the seller's [recte: buyer's] breach of the time limit for bringing forward the claims (*pretenzii*). Considering this issue with regard for the above said and taking into account the provisions of the Vienna Convention 1980 (Article 44), the ICCA concluded that the buyer had a reasonable justification of why he had not notified the seller within the period fixed by the contract for bringing forward the claims (*pretenzii*). At the same time, the ICCA did not deem it possible to agree with the buyer in that Article 40 of the Vienna Convention 1980, which bars the seller's right to rely on Articles 38 and 39 of the Convention, when non-conformity of the goods is connected with the facts of which he knew or could not have been unaware and of which he did not inform the buyer, applied in the present case. As follows from the materials of the case and the results of their consideration by the ICCA, the fact of the presence of the defects in itself, the nature of the defects, the volume of the defective production and its evaluation, applied by the parties, cannot lead to the conclusion, suggested by the buyer, that the seller 'deliberately did not indicate the presence of the defects in the documents of title.'

3.7. The amount of the sum to be paid by seller to buyer with respect to first instalment of the goods

—*Fourthly*, having failed to examine the goods and to notify on the discovered non-conformity of the goods within the time limit fixed by the contract for bringing forward a claim (*pretenziya*) and having produced justification thereof recognised by the ICCA as substantiated, the buyer, in virtue of Article 44 of the Vienna Convention 1980, had the right to reduce the price

---

[173] Translation taken from CISG Pace (citations omitted).

in accordance with Article 50 of the Convention or to claim damages, except for loss of profit. Having demanded the reduction of the price, the buyer thereby waived his claim, formulated in his Supplement to the statement of claim, for compensation of expenses in accordance with Article 45, in excess of payment of the amount of reduction of the price. The buyer's reference in the Supplement to the statement of claim to Articles 75 and 76 of the Convention cannot be recognised as substantiated because these articles, as they clearly indicate, are applicable only in cases where the contract has been avoided.

C 44-3

ICC International Court of Arbitration, Award No 9187/1999, CISG-online 705

For a summary of the facts see C 38/39-6 above.

[Judgment][174]

[...]

3. Notice of Non-Conformity

Pursuant to Art 39 CISG the buyer loses its legal remedies for non-contractual delivery if it fails to give valid notice of such non-conformity to the seller within a reasonable period after the moment when such non-conformity was or should have been detected. This provision has two relevant exceptions, though: Firstly, if the lack of conformity relates to facts of which the seller knew or ought to have known and which it did not disclose to the buyer, the seller is not entitled to rely on Art 39 CISG (Art 40 CISG). Secondly, under Art 44 CISG the buyer does not lose its right to claim damages (except for loss of profit), if it has a reasonable excuse for its failure to give the required notice pursuant to Art 39 CISG.

Claimant contends that it acted in compliance with Art 39 CISG by giving notice to [Y] that the quality of the coke jointly examined by [A] and [B] was inconsistent with [A]'s quality determination at the port of loading and, therefore, by refusing the cargo of coke. However ... the Contract required in its Art 9 that the examination took place in China and, consequently, any non-conformity should have been notified upon examination in China. Therefore, the Arbitral Tribunal finds that Claimant's notice was given too late.

As a consequence it has to be examined whether any of the above mentioned exceptions to Art 39 CISG are applicable; i.e. if Defendant knew or ought to have known the non conformity of the coke when it was handed over to Claimant, after inspection and loading and failed to disclose this fact to Claimant (Art 40 CISG) or whether Claimant had a reasonable excuse for not duly notifying Defendant (Art 44 CISG).

In order to decide whether there was a reasonable excuse for not notifying the seller in due time (Art 44 CISG) the Arbitral Tribunal has to consider the extent of the violation of the seller's [recte: buyer's] duty, the importance of the loss of seller's [recte: buyer's] legal remedies and the buyer's [recte seller's] interest in prompt and exact information. Schwenzer answers

---

[174] Citations omitted.

the existence of a reasonable excuse to the positive in cases where a national inspection body, based on which the buyer approves the goods and takes delivery, incorrectly examines them. The burden of proof in regard to the existence of circumstances for a reasonable excuse lies with the buyer.

Claimant has sufficiently shown that it had in good faith relied on the accuracy of [A]'s certification; otherwise, it would hardly have effected payment of the purchase price. Despite of [sic] Art 9 of the Contract, according to which [A]'s quality determination would be binding and final for both parties, such legal consequence is barred since [A]'s analysis was incorrect ... Taking into account that both parties had agreed on a neutral inspection body—thereby relieving Claimant from bearing the consequences of an incorrect examination alone—the Arbitral Tribunal concludes that Claimant's lack of due notice is to be reasonably excused in the sense of Art 44 CISG.

[...]

Questions

Q 44-1

(a)   What were the relevant considerations of the court in applying Article 44 CISG in the German case (C 44-1)?
(b)   What criteria would you consider in this case?

Q 44-2

What does the Russian Arbitration case (C 44-2) say generally about the interpretation of Article 44 CISG?

Q 44-3

(a)   What was the factor relied upon in the ICC case (C 44-3) to establish excuse under Article 44 CISG?
(b)   Who bore the burden of proof and for which reasons?

Q 44-4

What is the relationship between Articles 40 and 44 CISG?

Article 45 CISG

(1) If the seller fails to perform any of his obligations under the contract or this Convention, the buyer may:
    (a) exercise the rights provided in articles 46 to 52;
    (b) claim damages as provided in articles 74 to 77.
(2) The buyer is not deprived of any right he may have to claim damages by exercising his right to other remedies.
(3) No period of grace may be granted to the seller by a court or arbitral tribunal when the buyer resorts to a remedy for breach of contract.

I. Overview

This provision serves to give an overview of the remedies available to the buyer in the event of the seller's breach of contract due to non-performance of its contractual obligations. By referring to other provisions, it provides the buyer with a starting point when seeking to exercise any remedy against the seller. Article 45(1)(a) CISG provides reference to the buyer's remedies regarding performance, avoidance of the contract, or a price reduction, whilst Article 45(1)(b) CISG concentrates solely on damages. Article 45(2) CISG clarifies that Article 45(1)(a) and (b) can operate concurrently, a question that was disputed in the national Germanic legal systems. Article 45(3) CISG alludes to and clarifies the position under legal systems based on French law.[175]

II. Article 45(1) CISG

The remedies referred to in Article 45(1) CISG are available to the buyer if the seller fails to fulfill any of its obligations under the contract or the CISG.

---

[175] *Cf* Art 1184(3) *CC.*

C 45-1

ICC International Court of Arbitration,
Award No 9978/1999,
CISG-online 708[176]

[Facts]

A dispute arose as a result of non-delivery of the goods for the subject matter of the contract of sale between Claimant (purchaser) and Respondent (seller). The contract contained a special clause providing that, in the event of non-delivery, seller would be liable to a penalty of 2% of the contract value in full and final settlement. The goods were to be paid for by letter of credit (L/C) upon presentation of certain documents, including a forwarder's certificate of receipt specifying that the goods had been taken over for the free disposal of the beneficiary (i.e. Respondent). The documents were presented and payment made, but the goods were never delivered to Claimant. Negotiations were undertaken for the sum paid to be refunded. An initial amount was repaid and an agreement made for the transfer to Claimant of sums purported to be owed to Respondent by a third party. Claimant subsequently initiated arbitration proceedings asking for the refund of amounts paid under the L/C (plus interests), bank interest paid in connection with the L/C, detention charges, deadfreight and a 2% penalty for non-delivery. Claimant based its claim for damages on Art 45(1)(b) CISG in conjunction with Art 74, invoking Articles 78 and 84(1) in support of its request for interest. Alternatively, it claimed repayment under Articles 49 and 81(2), maintaining that it had avoided the contract in accordance with Articles 26 and 49(1)(a) CISG and arguing that this too entitled it to damages. It considered its claim for damages was not barred by the special condition for non-delivery contained in the contract, since the damages were claimed not for non-delivery, but for breach by Respondent of an obligation arising at law under the Convention. Respondent rejected these claims, maintaining that it did not own the goods when they were sold to Claimant and invoking force majeure to disclaim liability for detention charges and deadfreight. It further claimed exemption from any liability in excess of the 2% contractual penalty.

[Judgment]

With respect to Claimant's claim for damages under Articles 45(1)(b) and 74 CISG

'Claimant has no claim for damages against Respondent. Damage claims for non performance arising out of the contract in dispute are governed by the "UN-Convention on Contracts for the International Sale of Goods" (CISG). The CISG applies to the contract as part of the applicable German law according to its Art 1(1)(b). Pursuant to Art 6 CISG the parties to an international sales contract may derogate from the provisions on damages in Art 45(1)(b) CISG through inclusion of a penalty/liquidated damages (pld) clause. This is what the parties have done in the case before the Tribunal with the inclusion of the special conditions for non-delivery.

This pld-clause is valid under the applicable German law and precludes any further damage claims for non-performance which the Claimant may have against Respondent.

---

[176] Citations omitted.

The validity of this clause is not governed by the CISG but by German law as the law governing the contract ... Art 4(a) CISG provides that the Convention is not concerned with the validity of individual provisions contained in the contract. This also applies to pld-clauses.'

[...]

Claimant maintains that in addition to this claim for restitution of the amount paid to Respondent under the L/C, it is entitled to damages for the interest payments to [bank] and the refinancing costs incurred due to the South-East Asian financial crisis under Art 45(2), 74 CISG. This view is based on the wording of Art 45 (1) CISG. This Article provides that the buyer may, among other remedies, claim damages if the seller '...fails to perform any of his obligations under the contract or this Convention ...'. In Claimant's view, this reference to the seller's obligations at law, i.e. under the UN-Sales Convention, includes the seller's duty to restitute amounts received from the buyer in case of avoidance of the contract by the buyer under Art 81(2) CISG. A violation of this duty under the Convention would, in Claimant's view, trigger a claim for damages. This claim for damages would be due, not for non-delivery, but for Respondent's violation of a duty under the Convention. The damage claim would, therefore, be outside the special condition contained in the contract, the scope of which is limited to damages for non-delivery.

The Tribunal does not follow this view. It is based on a misconception of the relationship between the seller's primary obligations under the contract, the buyer's right to claim damages under Art 45 (2), 74 CISG and the buyer's right to avoid the contract pursuant to Art 49 CISG.

The reference made in Art 45 (1) CISG to the seller's obligations 'under the contract or this Convention' takes up the wording of Art 30 CISG *in fine*. Art 30 CISG outlines the seller's primary and principal obligations to deliver the goods, hand over the documents and transfer the property in the goods sold. The wording of Art 30 CISG makes it clear that the scope and substance of these primary obligations are determined chiefly by the terms of the contract (see Art 6 CISG). The sole purpose of the reference to the seller's obligations under 'this Convention' is to make it clear that the Convention's provisions governing the seller's obligations in Art 30 et seq. CISG apply only in so far as the contract contains no other specific provision. ... It follows from this interconnection between Art 30 and Art 45 CISG that the buyer has a right for damages under Art 45 (1) CISG if the seller fails to perform any of these primary obligations determined by the provisions of the contract or, absent such agreement of the parties, by Art 30 et seq. CISG. In the case before the Tribunal it is the non-delivery of the goods by Respondent.

The identical wording of Art 30 and 45 CISG also makes it clear that the buyer's right to damages is triggered only in case of the seller's failure to perform these primary obligations. The wording '... or this Convention ...' in Art 45 (1) CISG refers to the primary obligations of the seller laid down in Art 30–44 CISG [sic] or some ancillary obligations provided for in the Convention (e.g. Art 85, 88(2)) or in the contract. The duty to restitute amounts paid to the seller under Art 81(2) CISG does not constitute such a primary obligation arising out of the contract or the Convention. This duty is triggered by a fundamental breach of the seller and therefore does not fall within the catalogue of primary obligations listed in Art 30 et seq. CISG or agreed upon by the parties. Rather, the duty to restitute is a secondary obligation arising upon the seller's breach of contract. Such secondary obligations are not meant by the reference in Art 45 (1) CISG to the seller's obligations 'under ... the Convention'. This view is confirmed by the relationship between damage claims and restitution within the Convention's system of remedies. The drafters of the Convention were well aware that the buyer might have a justified claim for damages in addition to restitution. They have made it clear in Art 45 (2) CISG that the buyer's right to claim damages which is triggered by the seller's failure to perform one of his primary obligations under Art 30 et seq. CISG is not foreclosed by the buyer exercising other remedies. This general rule is put in more specific terms for the buyer's right to avoid the contract in Art 81(1) CISG. This provision provides that avoidance of the contract by the buyer releases both parties from their obligations under the contract, 'subject to any damages which may be due'. This wording does not refer to a new claim for damages arising due to the seller's failure to refund the purchase price received from the buyer. Rather, this wording provides for the continuation of any claims for damages which may exist due to the seller's violation of his primary obligation under the contract or under Art 30 et seq. CISG. This continuing claim for damages covers the part of the loss which exceeds the interest claim under Art 84 (1) CISG. New claims for damages may arise after avoidance only with respect to the violation of those contractual duties which already existed prior to the avoidance of the contract and which are left untouched by the avoidance according to Art 81(1) CISG.

Thus, under the system of remedies established in the UN Sales Convention, it is the same event (i.e. Respondent's non-delivery as a fundamental breach) which triggers Claimant's right for damages and its right to avoid the contract. Art 81(1) CISG makes it clear that the one (right to avoid) does not interfere with the other (right to damages). As has been explained in detail above …, Claimant's claim for damages under Art 45 (1) (b), 74 CISG, triggered by Respondent's fundamental breach of contract, is precluded by the special condition for non-delivery contained in the contract.

[…]

Question

Q 45-1

What did the court decide in the above case (C 45-1)?

III. Article 45(2) CISG

Under Article 45(2) CISG, the right to claim damages can also be combined with any other remedy.

Question

Q 45-2

(a)   What general principle of the CISG does Article 45(2) CISG embrace?
(b)   Is this general principle also a feature of your own domestic law?

IV. Article 45(3) CISG

In view of the French law (Art 1184(3) *CC*), Article 45(3) CISG disallows a court from granting the seller a period of grace where the buyer makes a claim for breach of contract.

Article 46 CISG

(1) The buyer may require performance by the seller of his obligations unless the buyer has resorted to a remedy which is inconsistent with this requirement.

(2) If the goods do not conform with the contract, the buyer may require delivery of substitute goods only if the lack of conformity constitutes a fundamental breach of contract and a request for substitute goods is made either in conjunction with notice given under article 39 or within a reasonable time thereafter.

(3) If the goods do not conform with the contract, the buyer may require the seller to remedy the lack of conformity by repair, unless this is unreasonable having regard to all the circumstances. A request for repair must be made either in conjunction with notice given under article 39 or within a reasonable time thereafter.

I. Overview

A. Content and Purpose of Article 46 CISG

Article 46 CISG grants the buyer the right to require the seller to actually perform its obligations (Art 46(1)); to make a substitute delivery (Art 46(2)); or to repair a lack of conformity (Art 46(3)).

B. Domestic Laws

Domestic laws were of great significance in the drafting of Article 46(1) CISG and the right to require performance of the contract. The regulation of this right represents a mixture of various legal traditions. Whereas the right, in itself, is derived from continental European legal systems, the construction of the right as a remedy is based on common law.

With respect to the right to require delivery of substitute goods or repair, Article 46(2) and (3) CISG formed the basis for the modification of the German sales law in 2002.

§ 439(1) BGB:[177]

> As supplementary performance, the buyer may, at its option, demand the removal of the defect or the supply of goods free from defects.

Question

Q 46-1

What is the crucial difference between § 439(1) BGB and Article 46(2) CISG?

II. Performance of the Contract—Article 46(1) CISG

Article 46(1) CISG only grants the buyer the right to require performance of the contract if it has not resorted to a remedy 'inconsistent with this requirement'.

Questions

Q 46-2

What remedies could be inconsistent with the right to require performance?

Q 46-3

Consider the requirements of Article 28 CISG in light of Article 46(1) CISG. How does this represent a further limitation of Article 46(1) CISG?

III. Claim to Substitute Delivery—Article 46(2) CISG

Article 46(2) CISG, like Article 46(3), outlines one particular aspect of the right to require performance under Article 46(1). It primarily applies in circumstances where generic goods are delivered that lack conformity with the contract.

---

[177] Author's translation.

Questions

Q 46-4

Can you outline the preconditions for requiring substitute delivery under Article 46(2) CISG?

Q 46-5

Why does Article 46(2) CISG restrict the buyer's right to substitute delivery?

Q 46-6

How is a 'reasonable time' determined for the purposes of Article 46(2) CISG?

IV. Repair—Article 46(3) CISG

The obligation to repair under Article 46(3) CISG comprises the buyer's right to demand repair by the seller of goods that do not conform to the contract under Article 35 CISG.

C 46-1

Oberlandesgericht Hamm (Germany),
9 June 1995,
CISG-online 146[178]

[Facts]

[Seller], a manufacturer of windows and doors located in South Tyrol/Italy, asserts a balance of purchase price claim against [buyer] (located in Germany). [Buyer] ordered 19 window elements altogether from [seller] for the building project of his customer F. The window elements were delivered by [seller] between July 9 and July 19, 1991, and, after that, were installed by [buyer]. On July 5, 1991, [seller] billed [buyer] in the amount of DM [Deutsche Mark] 15,363.80 for the window elements. After the installation of the window elements by [buyer], it was discovered that a part of the ISO window-panes had defects. Because of [buyer's] complaint, [seller] delivered new window-panes which were installed by [buyer] himself.

[...]

---

[178] Translation taken from CISG Pace (citations omitted).

[Buyer] set off his claim for the costs of the installation of the replacement window-panes against [seller]'s claim.

[Judgment]

[…]

The admissible appeal of [buyer] is, in its essential part, legally justified.

[…]

II. [Seller's] purchase price claim under CISG Art 53 (the basis and amount of which is not in dispute between the parties) was voided by way of set-off by [buyer] with a counterclaim of at least an equal amount.

[…]

2. The counterclaim, which, pursuant to *Bürgerliches Gesetzbuch* § 387, is necessary for a set-off, is legally justified. [Buyer] is, contrary to the trial court's (the *Landgericht*) view, entitled to demand the costs and expenses for the exchange of the ISO windows.

a) An explicit basis for a claim for reimbursement of the costs is, however, not contained in the CISG.

b) But CISG Art 46(2) provides that if the goods do not conform to the contract, the buyer may require delivery of substitute goods if the lack of conformity constitutes a fundamental breach of contract and a request for substitute goods is made either in conjunction with notice given under CISG Art 39 or within a reasonable time thereafter. Pursuant to CISG Art 46(3), the buyer may require the seller to remedy the lack of conformity by repair if the goods do not conform to the contract. In the case at bar, it is not disputed that the ISO window-panes delivered by [seller] do not conform to the contract; [seller] has agreed to deliver goods that conform to the contract, and there is no need to decide whether this is considered a delivery of substituted goods or a repair.

One can conclude from CISG 48(1) that the seller bears the costs for the delivery of substitute goods or for the repair. Moreover, according to subparagraphs 1(b) and 2 of CISG Art 45, the seller must reimburse the buyer for all other damages caused by nonconformity of the first delivery in so far as they cannot be remedied by a delivery of substituted goods or a repair. Those damages include the costs for the exchange of the ISO window-panes by [buyer]. This applies at least where, as in this dispute, the buyer's own performance does not injure the [seller's] interests. [Seller] did not allege such a scenario. […]

c) As a result, [buyer's] set-off has voided the claim in full (*Bürgerliches Gesetzbuch* § 389).

[…]

d) Further, [buyer's] counterclaim, which he set off against [seller's] claim, is not barred by the statute of limitations

[…]

Questions

Q 46-7

Under what circumstances might a request for repair be regarded as unreasonable?

Q 46-8

If the buyer is able to repair the non-conforming goods itself, is the seller thereby totally relieved of its obligations?

Article 47 CISG

(1) The buyer may fix an additional period of time of reasonable length for performance by the seller of his obligations.
(2) Unless the buyer has received notice from the seller that he will not perform within the period so fixed, the buyer may not, during that period, resort to any remedy for breach of contract. However, the buyer is not deprived thereby of any right he may have to claim damages for delay in performance.

I. Overview

A. Content and Purpose of Article 47 CISG

Article 47(1) CISG entitles the buyer to fix an additional period of time (commonly referred to as a *Nachfrist*) within which the seller must perform its obligations. The provision operates in conjunction with Article 46 CISG, but is particularly relevant for the right to terminate the contract under Article 49(1)(b) CISG. Article 47(2) CISG prohibits the buyer from exercising other remedies during the *Nachfrist* period, but allows it to retain its right to damages for the delay thereby caused.

B. Domestic Laws

The concept of a *Nachfrist* period has its origins in the Germanic legal systems. Under §§ 281(1), 323(1), 441(1) *BGB*, the general rule is that damages, rescission of the contract and reduction of the price can only be claimed for non-performance or performance in breach of the contractual obligations if the debtor has failed to perform within a reasonable *Nachfrist* set by the creditor.

Question

Q 47-1

Based on the outline above, what is the essential difference between the Germanic approach and the approach under Article 47(1) CISG?

II. Operation of Article 47 CISG

A. Necessity of a *Nachfrist*

C 47-1

Oberlandesgericht München (Germany),
1 July 2002,
CISG-online 656[179]

[Facts]

The parties argue about the [buyer]'s obligation to pay for shoes and collection models delivered by the [seller] as well as the [buyer]'s set-off with claims for damages.

[...]

[Judgment]

[...]

III. The Court of First Instance did not make any mistakes in its application of the CISG.

[...]

3. The [buyer] was not entitled to declare the contract avoided with respect to the shoes not yet delivered without fixing an additional period of time for performance by the [seller]. Until the declaration of avoidance with letter of 30 March 2001, the [buyer] did not fix an additional period of time for the performance of the [seller] of the outstanding deliveries. According to Art 49(1)(b) CISG, [buyer] would have been obliged to take such measures. While Art 47(1) CISG is a may-do provision, it follows from the reference in Art 49(2)(b) and also from Art 47(2) sent. 1 CISG that the fixing of an additional period of time is an indispensable requirement for the buyer's exercise of remedies for breach of contract by the [seller], unless the seller has declared that he will not deliver under any circumstance (there is no such statement on the part of the [seller] in the present case). It furthermore follows from a comparison between Art 49(1)(a) and Art 49(1)(b) CISG that a non-delivery or a late delivery does not in itself constitute a fundamental breach of contract in the meaning of Art 25 CISG. Otherwise, the provision in Art 49(1)(b) CISG would not have been necessary and would not have been legislated. The [buyer] furthermore does not make any submissions regarding a time bargain.

[...]

The [buyer's] failure to pay the invoices therefore led to the [seller]'s discontinuation of the delivery, a fact that was also expressed in the [seller]'s letters to the [buyer] of 19 March 2001 and 23 March 2001. Because of the [buyer]'s non-payment, the [seller] was therefore entitled to stop the delivery.

[...]

---

[179] Translation taken from CISG Pace (citations omitted).

Questions

Q 47-2

Explain the interaction between Article 47 CISG and the right to avoid under Article 49(1)(b) CISG.

Q 47-3

What are the consequences of the buyer failing to set an additional period under Article 47(1) CISG?

B. Additional Period of Reasonable Length

As under the other provisions of the CISG that make reference to 'reasonable' periods of time, what constitutes an additional period of reasonable length can only be determined by reference to the circumstances of the individual case.

C 47-2

Oberlandesgericht Celle (Germany),
24 May 1995,
CISG-online 152[180]

[Facts]

In 1992, a German dealer in used printing equipment concluded a contract with an Egyptian firm for the sale of five offset printing presses and four smaller pieces of equipment. The German seller agreed to deliver the items in two installments. The first installment was to include three of the presses and two smaller items, while the remaining equipment was to be sent in the second installment. The purchase price included freight and insurance. The buyer agreed to pay the total purchase price as follows: 350,000 DM [Deutsche Mark] before shipment of the first installment, 130,000 DM against documents, 90,000 DM before the second shipment, and the last 85,000 DM against documents.

Before the first installment the buyer paid the seller 464,000 DM, which covered the purchase price of the first three presses plus 70,000 DM. The buyer made this payment together with a request that the seller include in the first installment one of the small items that was to be sent in the second installment. The seller accepted the payment but responded that the additional item would mean finding another container and the seller did not have enough time to do so. As a consequence, the first installment included only the three presses.

---

[180] Translation taken from CISG Pace (citations omitted).

The seller then delayed sending the second installment. After some consultations, the seller informed the buyer on 1 October 1992, that the seller was unable to acquire the two presses not yet delivered but could deliver three of the smaller items. The buyer rejected the offer and asked for its money back. With the notice of rejection on 4 December 1992, the buyer sent a notice giving the seller until 16 December to perform. The seller did not perform within this period and after subsequent negotiations failed, the buyer declared the contract avoided. The buyer brought a legal action to recover damages for the delay, for partial non-delivery, and for return of the 70,000 DM. The [Lower Court] rendered judgment for the buyer. The seller appealed.

[Judgment]

[...]

2.2. The [buyer] likewise effectively avoided the contract with respect to the other machines which [seller] had not delivered. This was done at the latest by a communication of the [buyer's] attorney on 26 January 1993, which rejected any further delivery and demanded the return of the excess price already paid. The [buyer] was entitled to do so.

2.2.1. Pursuant to Art 49(1)(b), the [buyer] may declare the contract avoided in the case of non-delivery if the [seller] does not deliver the goods within the additional period of time fixed by the [buyer] in accordance with Art 47(1) or the [seller] declares that he will not deliver the goods within the period so fixed. Where the [seller] has already delivered part of the goods, this rule also applies to that part of the goods which are missing (Art 51(1)). The [buyer] gave notice pursuant to Art 47(1) by the communication of his attorney on 4 December 1992. Such a notice is authorized if the [seller] has not satisfied his obligations under the contract (Art 45(1)(a)).

Where the contract fixes a period of time for delivery, the [seller] must deliver the goods within that period (Art 33(b)). The [seller] failed to satisfy this obligation. The [seller] was obligated to deliver the missing machinery by no later than August. The Lower Court's finding that the first installment was due by the end of May and the second by the end of August is convincing. The [buyer] was entitled to give a notice fixing an additional period of time for the seller to perform.

There remains the issue of whether the period fixed was too short. The [buyer] fixed a period from the time of the notice on 4 December to the time fixed in the notice of 16 December, a period which required shipment within eleven days.

With hindsight, this period was possibly too short to organize carriage by sea from [X] to [Y], given that the [seller] was dependent on the schedule of the ship and the existence of free space for freight. This does not make the notice ineffective where the notice has merely extended a period of time. In any case, when the [buyer] gave notice that the contract was avoided on 26 January 1993, a sufficiently long time (seven weeks) had elapsed. The [buyer] may declare the contract avoided even though the seller in the meantime has declared by its letter of 22 November 1992, that it was ready to deliver part of the goods. That letter offered to ship four of the machines originally ordered (for three of which there was an agreed partial avoidance) but it offered to substitute a different press for one of the presses originally agreed upon and the letter failed to mention (apparently by mistake, if one understands the [seller's] argument) the last of the machines ordered.

[...]

Questions

Q 47-4

What criteria should be used to determine whether the period of additional time was of a reasonable length?

Q 47-5

What are the consequences for the buyer of failing to set a 'reasonable' additional period of time?

C. Effect of Setting an Additional Period of Time

The setting of an additional period of time under Article 47(2) CISG prevents the buyer from exercising any other remedy until the period expires without the seller performing. However, under certain circumstances, the buyer may be excused from waiting until the expiry of the additional period of time.

Question

Q 47-6

Describe the circumstances in which a buyer could avoid sitting out the additional period before having recourse to remedies.

Article 48 CISG

(1) Subject to article 49, the seller may, even after the date for delivery, remedy at his own expense any failure to perform his obligations, if he can do so without unreasonable delay and without causing the buyer unreasonable inconvenience or uncertainty of reimbursement by the seller of expenses advanced by the buyer. However, the buyer retains any right to claim damages as provided for in this Convention.

(2) If the seller requests the buyer to make known whether he will accept performance and the buyer does not comply with the request within a reasonable time, the seller may perform within the time indicated in his request. The buyer may not, during that period of time, resort to any remedy which is inconsistent with performance by the seller.

(3) A notice by the seller that he will perform within a specified period of time is assumed to include a request, under the preceding paragraph, that the buyer make known his decision.

(4) A request or notice by the seller under paragraph (2) or (3) of this article is not effective unless received by the buyer.

I. Overview

A. Content and Purpose of Article 48 CISG

Article 48(1) CISG gives the seller the right to cure even after the due date for delivery, provided that it can do so without causing unreasonable delay or other inconvenience. This right does not affect any claim the buyer may have for damages. Under Article 48(2) CISG, the buyer is barred from exercising any remedy inconsistent with the seller's performance if the seller has asked that the buyer accept performance and the buyer has remained silent. Article 48(3) and (4) CISG concern the question of interpretation of a notice to perform, and the receipt rule, which we have already discussed in the respective context of many other provisions of the CISG.

B. Domestic Laws

On the one hand, the seller's right to remedy the defect, even after the date of delivery, is often regulated by the general terms and conditions of delivery, that is by the parties' autonomy. On the other hand, many national laws also recognise an actual right to cure.

§ 2-508(2) UCC:

> Where the buyer rejects a non-conforming tender which the seller had reasonable grounds to believe would be acceptable with or without money allowance the seller may if he seasonably notifies the buyer have a further reasonable time to substitute a conforming tender.

As stated above in the context of Article 47 CISG, under German sales law, a reasonable period in order to allow 'late' performance of obligations must generally be tolerated before having recourse to other remedies.

C. International Principles

Uniform laws also recognise the need to take these factors into consideration.

Art 7.1.4 PICC 2010:

(1) The non-performing party may, at its own expense, cure any non-performance, provided that
  (a) without undue delay, it gives notice indicating the proposed manner and timing of the cure;
  (b) cure is appropriate in the circumstances;
  (c) the aggrieved party has no legitimate interest in refusing cure; and
  (d) cure is effected promptly.
(2) The right to cure is not precluded by notice of termination.
(3) Upon effective notice of cure, rights of the aggrieved party that are inconsistent with the non-performing party's performance are suspended until the time for cure has expired.
(4) The aggrieved party may withhold performance pending cure.
(5) Notwithstanding cure, the aggrieved party retains the right to claim damages for delay as well as for any harm caused or not prevented by the cure.

Question

Q 48-1

Name some similarities and differences between Article 48 CISG and Article 7.1.4 PICC 2010.

II. Article 48(1) CISG

A. 'Subject to Article 49'

According to the wording of Article 48(1) CISG, the seller's right to cure is made 'subject to Article 49'. Whether the buyer's right to avoid the contract prevails over the seller's right to cure is subject to debate in scholarly opinion and case law.

C 48-1

Handelsgericht Aargau (Switzerland),
5 November 2002,
CISG-online 715[181]

For a summary of the facts see C 35-10 above.

[Judgment]

[...]

4. a) In case of a seller's non-compliance with a contract or CISG obligation, in principal the following five legal remedies (defects rights) are at the buyer's disposal:

— Right to performance (Art 46(1) CISG);
— Right to cure (Art 48 CISG);
— Right to avoid the contract because of a fundamental breach of contract (Art 49(1)(a) CISG);
— Right of price reduction (Art 50 sentence 1 CISG);
— Right to damages (Art 45(1)(b) in connection with Arts 74-77 CISG).

In the present case, the [buyer] declared the contract's avoidance, due to the existence of a fundamental breach of contract, analogously already in his notification of defects dated 27 May 2000 and unmistakably, in the letter of his legal representative dated 14 June 2000. As, according to Art 48(1) CISG, the seller 'subject to Art 49' may remedy any failure even after the date for delivery, the question arises concerning the relationship between the seller's right to cure (according to Art 48(1) CISG) and the buyer's right to avoid the contract (according to Art 49(1)(a) CISG). About this the following may be stated.

b) aa) The term fundamental breach of contract according to Art 49(1)(a) CISG is defined in Art 25 CISG. According to this Article, the condition for a fundamental breach of contract is an especially weighty impairment of the buyer's interest in the performance. Yet, besides the objective weight or importance of a defect, it is decisive of the substantiality of a breach of contract, whether the defect can be removed by subsequent repair or substitute delivery. The UN Sales Law proceeds from the fundamental precedence of preservation of the contract, even in case of an objective fundamental defect. When in doubt, the contract is to be maintained even in case of fundamental defects, and an immediate contract avoidance should stay exceptional. Because, as long as and so far as (even) a fundamental defect can still be removed by remedy or replacement, the fulfillment of the contract by the seller is still possible and the buyer's essential interest in the performance is not yet definitively at risk. According to doctrine as well as jurisdiction of the UN Sales Law, an objective fundamental defect does not mean a fundamental breach of contract when the defect is removable and the seller agrees to remedy this defect without creating unreasonable delay or burden on the buyer. That the buyer is obliged to accept a remedy (subsequent cure of the defect) offered by the seller results from Art 48(2) CISG. According to this provision, when the seller notifies the buyer of his readiness for performance, the buyer may not within a reasonable period of

---

[181] Translation taken from CISG Pace (citations omitted).

time 'resort to any remedy which is inconsistence with performance by the seller'. For this reason, the buyer does not have the right to avoid the contract even in case of an objective fundamental defect as long as and as far as the seller comes up with a remedy (subsequent cure of the defect) and such is still possible.

c) In the present case, both the quality problem or manufacturing defect (tearing out of the connection of the D2-arch with the 'stamp') which occurred on 27 May 2000, and the lacking stability of the Arcor-Arch could have been remedied. And it is certain that the [seller] reacted immediately to the notice of defects dated 27 May 2000 and made different proposals ('as I see it') in his writing dated 29 May 2000, through which the 'goal jointly', i.e., the subsequent performance, could be reached. The [buyer] reacted to the [seller]'s readiness to remedy on 14 June 2000 by declaring the contract avoided. [Buyer] was not entitled to do so according to the explained priority of the entitlement to subsequent cure or remedy over the entitlement of contract avoidance that forms the basis of the UN Sales Law, even in the case of an objective fundamental defect.

d) aa) According to UN Sales Law doctrine, a buyer's right of immediate contract avoidance is conceded by way of exception, without having to wait for the seller's readiness to remedy or the remedy itself. Yet, these exceptional facts of the case require that a remedy not be possible, if it is refused by the seller, or is not reasonable for the buyer. An entitlement to immediate contract avoidance is conceded by Schlechtriem/Huber if:

— The date of delivery has a fundamental importance (usual practice in the trade or similar cases);
— The remedy of the defect by the seller is not reasonable from an objective point of view; for example because of the uncertainty about the refund of the expenses in the sense of Art 48(1) CISG;
— It is not reasonable for the buyer to agree with the remedy of the defect; for example, because it is obvious that the seller is not capable of this;
— The seller refuses to remedy the defect seriously and finally.

bb) The parties did not agree upon a date of delivery in the sense of a fixed trade usage that would exclude a subsequent performance. The arches were supposed to be used as advertising media in several races during the entire season. If a remedy would have been carried out after the first use on 27 May 2003 within a useful period of time, the arches could have been used during further races. Therefore, the inadequate performance of the agreed delivery of the arches for the car racing in Hockenheim on the 27/28 May 2000 did by no means exclude the subsequent performance during the following races during the 2000 season. It was not a case of complete impossibility, but only a partial impossibility. As far as the still possible part of the owed performance is concerned, the [seller] can rely on his entitlement to remedy. As [seller] has—as stated (see 4c, *supra*)—at least analogously declared his readiness to remedy, the [buyer] has to bear the onus of assertion and proof concerning the existence of an exceptional fact of the case. But a corresponding state of affairs, which in the case of a fixed usage could justify the priority of [buyer]'s right to avoid the contract over [seller]'s entitlement to remedy the defect, was not substantiated or proven in the proceedings.

5. a) For this reason, the [buyer] was not able to declare the contract avoided in a legally binding way in his writing of 14 June 2000. In this case, the legal consequences depend on the reaction of the seller. Only if the seller consents to the avoidance of the contract will the contract get avoided. If, however, the seller disagrees with the avoidance of the contract or does not declare the contract avoided himself, the contract consequently will continue.

In this proceeding, the [seller] asks the [buyer] for performance: payment of the purchase price. Thus, [seller] holds on to the continued existence of the contract, and consequently the primary duty of the [buyer]: to pay the [seller] for the goods. Based on the contract concluded by the parties and according to Art 53 CISG, the [buyer] is bound to pay the purchase price and to receive the goods. The fact, that—with the exception of the right to avoid the contract—the [buyer] is entitled to certain rights in the event of defects, does not alter the situation.

b) The [seller] submitted claims for damages, but he did not substantiate them nor did he reserve the assertion of these claims 'in further proceedings'. Claims against the [buyer] for damages, as defined by Art 45(2)(b) in connection with Art 74–77 CISG, consequently are not to be judged in the present lawsuit.

[...]

Questions

Q 48-2

Do you agree with the position of the *Handelsgericht Aargau* (C 48-1) that Article 48 CISG provides a legal remedy for the buyer granting it a right to cure?

Q 48-3

(a)   How did the court (C 48-1) judge the relationship between Articles 48(1) and 49(1)(a) CISG?
(b)   What other interpretations can you think of?

B. Reasonableness

The seller is only granted a right to cure when this can be done without unreasonable delay and inconvenience.

Questions

Q 48-4

Why do you think this is the case?

Q 48-5

What criteria should be used to determine 'unreasonable delay and inconvenience'?

III. Article 48(2), (3) CISG

A seller who has failed to perform a contractual obligation on time cannot force the buyer to accept late performance; however, under Article 48(2) and (3) CISG, the buyer may, by its conduct, be held to late performance by the seller.

C 48-2

Amtsgericht Nordhorn (Germany),
14 June 1994,
CISG-online 259[182]

[Facts]

The [seller] runs a shoe factory situated in Italy. On 21 March 1993, the [seller] formed a sales contract regarding the delivery of 280 pairs of various shoes with the [buyer], who is a shoe retailer in Bad Bentheim [Germany]. The sales contract, which is written in the Italian language, contains a remark in handwriting '*prima ferie non dopo*' ['before the holidays, no later'] under the heading '*Consegna approssimativa senza impegno*' [approximate delivery, non-binding]. In the shoe trade in Italy, such wording means that the delivery is supposed to be effected before August.

On 5 August 1993, the [seller] delivered a first installment and invoiced the [buyer] on the same day with an amount of Italian Lira [*It£*] 14,953,000. On 30 November 1993, the [buyer] paid *It£* 14,504,410 subtracting 3% discount for immediate payment. The [seller] claims payment of the remaining *It£* 448,590.

[Seller] delivered the remaining goods on 24 May 1993 [*Translator's note*: the Court probably means 24 September 1993] and invoiced the [buyer] with an amount of *It£* 3,940,000 on the same day. The goods did not arrive at the [buyer]'s place of business until the beginning of October. By that time, the [buyer] had declared the contract avoided with a fax sent to the [seller] on 28 September 1993.

[Seller's position]

The [seller] furthermore claims payment of the remaining purchase price for deliveries invoiced in the previous season in the amount of *It£* 392,195. The [buyer] has withheld this amount because of three complaints regarding the conformity of the goods. With respect to the [buyer]'s defenses, the [seller] relies on the [buyer]'s failure to give a timely notice of lack of conformity and on the statute of limitations.

The [seller] contends that the [buyer] was not entitled to declare the contract avoided. The preconditions for avoidance set out by the [seller]'s standard terms, which had validly been incorporated into the contract, had not been met.

---

[182] Translation taken from CISG Pace (citations omitted).

The [seller] requests that the [buyer] is ordered to pay him *It£* 4,780,795 plus 10% interest on the following sums: on *It£* 3,940,000 from 25 November 1993, on *It£* 14,953,000 from 6 October 1993 until 30 November 1993, and on *It£* 448,590 from 1 December 1993.

[Buyer's position]

The [buyer] requests that the [seller]'s claim be dismissed.

The [buyer] is of the opinion that the parties agreed on a fixed delivery date and that [buyer] was therefore entitled to an immediate avoidance of contract. Regarding the non-conformities, [buyer] submits that the [seller] never before referred to such time limits, but always accepted and credited goods returned. The [seller]'s current refusal therefore constituted a breach of good faith.

With respect to the further details of the case the Court refers to the content of the parties' briefs and attachments.

[Judgment]

The [seller]'s claim is predominantly justified.

[...]

[Seller's standard terms]

The Court may leave open the question of whether the prerequisites of Art 49 CISG were met. Under clause 4 of the [seller]'s standard terms and conditions, the customer is entitled to avoid the contract in case of a late delivery only if she previously announces her intention to declare the contract avoided and if the goods are not dispatched by the seller within fifteen working days after receipt of the customer's warning.

[...]

The Court can find no indication that the clause used by the [seller] is invalid. [Seller] has a legitimate interest in the announcement of an intended declaration of avoidance and the granting of an additional period of time. This interest results from the fact that, in cases where a buyer is entitled to declare the contract avoided under Art 49 CISG, the buyer may do so even if the delivery has already been effected, pursuant to Art 49(2)(a) CISG. The seller to that extent bears the risk that his deliveries will be refused in case of late performance. The provision in clause 4 of the [seller]'s standard terms is suited to minimize that risk. At the same time, it does not have an unreasonable adverse effect on the customer, because the wording of the clause does not exclude the possibility of an announcement that precedes the expiry of the delivery period. Consequently, there are no reservations regarding the validity of that provision.

The Court does not need to decide whether the clause would also find application to a time bargain. The remark 'before the holidays, no later' does not constitute a fixed delivery date. Such a fixed date could only be assumed if the transaction was supposed to 'stand and fall' with a delivery by that date. This was not the intention of the parties. Firstly, the wording is ambiguous. Secondly, the [buyer]'s conduct after the expiry of that date shows that a fixed delivery date was not intended. The [buyer], on the one hand, still accepted a delivery made on 5 August 1993 and, on the other hand, failed to refuse an additional period of time for performance by the [seller] of his obligations until 10 September 1993, as required by Art 48(2) and (3) CISG.

The [buyer] did not comply with her obligation under clause 4 of the [seller]'s standard terms to warn the [seller] of her intention to declare the contract avoided. The [buyer]'s obligation to do so did not lapse because the [seller] notified the [buyer] with letter of 5 August 1993 that he would perform the delivery until 10 September 1993, and because the [seller] was consequently entitled to remedy his failure to perform his obligation under Art 48(2) and (3) CISG. After that date had expired, it was still unclear to the [seller] whether the [buyer] would declare the contract avoided under Art 49 CISG. Thus, it cannot be assumed that the requirement under clause 4 of the [seller]'s standard terms was satisfied. Moreover, the [buyer] had the opportunity to warn the [seller] of her intention to declare the contract avoided within that period of time. The [buyer]'s failure to fulfil this obligation cannot be to the [seller]'s detriment.

[...]

Question

Q 48-6

(a)   According to the court (C 48-2), what should the buyer have done in order to be able to avoid the contract?

(b)   Would the outcome be different under Article 48 CISG?

Article 49 CISG

(1) The buyer may declare the contract avoided:
    (a) if the failure by the seller to perform any of his obligations under the contract or this Convention amounts to a fundamental breach of contract; or
    (b) in case of non-delivery, if the seller does not deliver the goods within the additional period of time fixed by the buyer in accordance with paragraph (1) of article 47 or declares that he will not deliver within the period so fixed.
(2) However, in cases where the seller has delivered the goods, the buyer loses the right to declare the contract avoided unless he does so:
    (a) in respect of late delivery, within a reasonable time after he has become aware that delivery has been made;
    (b) in respect of any breach other than late delivery, within a reasonable time:
        (i) after he knew or ought to have known of the breach;
        (ii) after the expiration of any additional period of time fixed by the buyer in accordance with paragraph (1) of article 47, or after the seller has declared that he will not perform his obligations within such an additional period; or
        (iii) after the expiration of any additional period of time indicated by the seller in accordance with paragraph (2) of article 48, or after the buyer has declared that he will not accept performance.

I. Overview

A. Content and Purpose of Article 49 CISG

Article 49(1) CISG sets out the conditions under which a buyer may declare a contract avoided for breach of contract. Avoidance may be made, first, where a fundamental breach of the seller's obligations is established under Article 49(1)(a) CISG; and secondly, if there is no initial fundamental breach, in the case of non-delivery of the goods within an additional period of time under Article 49(1)(b) CISG. Article 49(2) CISG sets out the various circumstances under which the buyer loses the right to declare the contract avoided.

B. Domestic Laws

(a) Continental Legal Systems

There have been significant differences of opinion among domestic legal systems concerning the circumstances under which the buyer may avoid the contract in case of any non-conforming tender. In continental legal systems, which were originally based upon Roman sales law principles, in the case of defects in the quality of the goods, the buyer always had the right either to demand reduction of the purchase price (*actio quanti minoris*) or to avoid the contract (*actio redhibitoria*).[183]

Art 205 OR:[184]

(1) In a case where the goods do not conform to the contract, the buyer has a choice between rescinding the contract by bringing an action for rescission of the contract or demanding compensation for the reduced value of the goods by bringing an action for reduction of the purchase price.

(2) Even if an action for rescission is asserted, the judge is free to merely grant compensation for the reduced value if the circumstances do not justify a rescission of the sale.

(3) [...]

Art 1644 CC:[185]

In the cases of Articles 1641 and 1643, the buyer has the choice either of returning the [goods] and having the price repaid to him or of keeping the [goods] and having a part of the price repaid to him, as appraised by experts.

(b) The Approach under English Law

In contrast to the 'continental' approach, the common law legal systems are based upon different principles. In England, the initial state of the law was that the remedies available for lack of conformity depended on whether the non-conformity could be classified as breach of a 'condition' or breach of a 'warranty'. The interpretation of these terms requires an examination of both the statute and case law on this area. Under the SGA, breach of a condition gives rise to a right to reject the goods and treat the contract as repudiated. In contrast, breach of a warranty can only give rise to a right to claim damages.

---

[183] *Cf* Germany: former § 462 *BGB* (in force until 31 December 2001); France: Art 1644 *CC*; Switzerland: Art 205 *OR*. But see Austria: Art 932 *ABGB*, only giving a right to avoid the contract in cases where repair is not feasible and a proper use is not possible.

[184] Author's translation.

[185] Translation taken from www.legifrance.gouv.fr.

Sec 11(3) SGA:

> Whether a stipulation in a contract of sale is a condition, the breach of which may give rise to a right to treat the contract as repudiated, or a warranty, the breach of which may give rise to a claim for damages but not to a right to reject the goods and treat the contract as repudiated, depends in each case on the construction of the contract; and a stipulation may be a condition, though called a warranty in the contract.

The case law on this area applies yet another interpretation. In *Cehave N.V. v Bremer Handelsgesellschaft mbH,*[186] attention was paid to the vast majority of stipulations that do not fall so neatly into the two categories of warranty and condition, the so-called 'innominate terms'. The remedy available for breach of an innominate term depends on the seriousness of the effect of the breach. To the extent that the lack of conformity results from breach of an innominate term, only where the breach substantially deprives the buyer of the whole benefit of the entire contract will avoidance be available.

The legislature has recently gone one step further with Sec 15A SGA, inserted in 1994 by the Sale and Supply of Goods Act, which states that, with respect to implied conditions, if the buyer does not deal as a consumer, the breach may not be treated as a breach of condition if the breach was so slight that it would be unreasonable for the buyer to reject the goods.

An interesting limitation of these principles is found in the context of acceptance.

Sec 11(4) SGA:

> [...] [w]here a contract of sale is not severable and the buyer has accepted the goods or part of them, the breach of a condition to be fulfilled by the seller can only be treated as a breach of warranty, and not as a ground for rejecting the goods and treating the contract as repudiated, unless there is an express or implied term of the contract to that effect.

As can be seen from Section 11(4) SGA, once the buyer has accepted the goods, even a breach of condition will only give rise to a claim in damages. Thus, the interpretation of the term 'acceptance' is the crucial issue here.

(c) The Approach under US Law

US sales law, although based on similar principles as the SGA, does not distinguish between conditions and warranties. Under Section 2-601 UCC, the so-called 'perfect tender rule' applies, giving the buyer the right to reject the goods if they do not conform to the contract in any respect. In recent times, however, US courts have limited the perfect tender rule by applying the good faith principle, especially in cases of a rightful and effective cure by the seller in accordance with Section 2-508 UCC. However, if the buyer has accepted the goods, avoidance of the contract is only possible if the non-conformity amounted to a fundamental breach or 'substantial

---

[186] *Cehave NV v Bremer Handelsgesellschaft mbH* [1976] 1 QB 44.

impairment' (§ 2-608(1) UCC). Thus, as with the English approach, acceptance is a key notion unknown in the continental legal systems.

§ 2-601 UCC:

> Subject to the provisions of this Article on breach in installment contracts (Section 2-612) and unless otherwise agreed under the sections on contractual limitations of remedy (Sections 2-718 and 2-719), if the goods or the tender of delivery fail in any respect to conform to the contract, the buyer may (a) reject the whole; or (b) accept the whole; or (c) accept any commercial unit or units and reject the rest.

§ 2-608(1) UCC:

> The buyer may revoke his acceptance of a lot or commercial unit whose non-conformity substantially impairs its value to him if he has accepted it:
> (a) on the reasonable assumption that its non-conformity would be cured and it has not been reasonably cured; or
> (b) without discovery of such non-conformity if his acceptance was reasonably induced either by the difficulty of discovery before acceptance or by the seller's assurances.

(d) Modern Solutions and International Principles

The previously sharp contrast between civil and common law has changed with the enactment of modern statutes, such as the German Statute on Modernisation of the Law of Obligations, the Scandinavian Sales Laws,[187] and the Netherlands *Wetboek*,[188] which apply the notion of fundamental breach or similar key concepts within the framework for avoidance or cancellation of the contract. The same is true for ongoing projects for the unification of the law.

§ 323 BGB:

> (1) If, in the case of a reciprocal contract, the obligor does not render an act of performance which is due, or does not render it in conformity with the contract, then the obligee may revoke the contract, if he has specified, without result, an additional period for performance or cure.
> (2) The specification of a period of time can be dispensed with if
>   1. the obligor seriously and definitively refuses performance,
>   2. the obligor does not render performance by a date specified in the contract or within a specific period and the obligee, in the contract, has made the continuation of his interest in performance subject to performance being rendered in good time, or
>   3. there are special circumstances which, when the interests of both parties are weighed, justify immediate revocation.
> (3)–(6) […]

---

[187] § 39 Norwegian Sale of Goods Act 1988; s 39 Finnish Sale of Goods Act 1987.
[188] Art 6:265 *BW*.

Art 7.3.1 PICC 2010:

(1)   A party may terminate the contract where the failure of the other party to perform an obligation under the contract amounts to a fundamental non-performance.

(2)   In determining whether a failure to perform an obligation amounts to a fundamental non-performance regard shall be had, in particular, to whether
    (a)   the non-performance substantially deprives the aggrieved party of what it was entitled to expect under the contract unless the other party did not foresee and could not reasonably have foreseen such result;
    (b)   strict compliance with the obligation which has not been performed is of essence under the contract;
    (c)   the non-performance is intentional or reckless;
    (d)   the non-performance gives the aggrieved party reason to believe that it cannot rely on the other party's future performance;
    (e)   the non-performing party will suffer disproportionate loss as a result of the preparation or performance if the contract is terminated.

(3)   In the case of delay the aggrieved party may also terminate the contract if the other party fails to perform before the time allowed it under Article 7.1.5 has expired.

Art 7.3.2 PICC 2010:

(1)   The right of a party to terminate the contract is exercised by notice to the other party.

(2)   If performance has been offered late or otherwise does not conform to the contract the aggrieved party will lose its right to terminate the contract unless it gives notice to the other party within a reasonable time after it has or ought to have become aware of the offer or of the non-conforming performance.

Question

Q 49-1

Compare the modern approaches regarding the circumstances under which avoidance of contract may take place. What are the similarities and differences?

C. Drafting History

Concerning the avoidance of the contract, the CISG clearly deviates from the ULIS, as only in cases of non-delivery does the fixing of an additional period of time 'elevate' an otherwise potentially non-fundamental breach to a fundamental one, thus giving the buyer the right to avoid the contract. This right to avoid the contract because of expiry of an additional period can only be asserted in cases of non-delivery, and not, as under the ULIS, in any other situations of breach, such as the delivery of non-conforming goods.

II. Avoidance for Fundamental Breach—Article 49(1)(a) CISG

A. Operation of Article 49(1)(a) CISG

The notion of the right to avoid for fundamental breach under Article 49(1)(a) CISG must be understood in conjunction with Article 25 CISG. Under Article 25 CISG, a breach is fundamental if it deprives the party (under Art 49, the buyer) of what it was entitled to expect under the contract. Case law has provided helpful interpretation as to what will constitute a fundamental breach entitling the buyer to avoid. In general, violation of a duty that the seller was obliged to fulfil under the contract is the first element in establishing a fundamental breach.

In light of the requirements of international trade, upon which basis the CISG was drafted, the avoidance of the contract is to be regarded as the *ultima ratio* remedy, or remedy of last resort. Not only Article 49(1)(a) CISG, but also many other provisions confirm that the CISG will allow contract avoidance only under narrow conditions and as a last resort (see Arts 25, 34, 37, 47, 48, 49, 63, 64 CISG).

B. Non-conforming Goods

The tender or the delivery of non-conforming goods under Article 35 CISG can result in a fundamental breach of contract under Article 49(1)(a) CISG. However, in light of the *ultima ratio* nature of the avoidance remedy, not every lack of conformity will be regarded as a fundamental breach. Here, a distinction needs to be drawn between a 'non-fundamental' lack of conformity, which merely gives rise to a claim for damages or a reduction of the purchase price, and a fundamental lack of conformity, which entitles the non-breaching party to declare the contract avoided. If the lack of conformity frustrates the buyer's expectations under the contract, it will depend on the specific circumstances as to whether the breach will be regarded as fundamental. The interaction between the provisions of Article 35 CISG and Article 49(1)(a) CISG has long been the source of debate in the courts.

C 49-1

Bundesgerichtshof (Germany),
3 April 1996,
CISG-online 135[189]

For a summary of the facts see C 35-3 above.

---

[189] Translation taken from CISG Pace (citations omitted).

[Judgment]

[...]

II. These findings withstand the test of legal review in all major points.

[...]

2. [...]

a) The Court of Appeals also correctly held—and was insofar unchallenged by the final appeal—that only Art 49 CISG can constitute the legal basis for the [buyer's] avoidance of contract. An application of Art 72 CISG is not possible, because the [seller] complied with his contractual obligation to store the goods in a warehouse in Antwerp and to notify the [buyer] that she could pick up the goods, while at the same time sending the documents. With this, the [seller] performed his delivery obligation, even though this performance was defective. Thus, there is no room to assume only an imminent future breach of contract, which is required for the preventive avoidance of contract under Art 72.

b) Nevertheless, the [buyer] in her appeal expresses the opinion that the seller can only request payment of the purchase price if he fulfills his obligation to deliver goods that conform to the contract (Art 30 CISG). Buyer alleges that as long as the seller does not submit and, if necessary, prove such delivery of conforming goods, the breach constitutes a case of non-delivery, entitling the buyer to avoid the contract under Art 49(1)(b) CISG. Therefore, [buyer] asserts that it is irrelevant whether the [seller's] breach of contract was fundamental in the sense of Art 25, 49(1)(a) CISG.

[...]

c) aa) As a legal basis for the [buyer's] avoidance of the contract, only the provision of Art 49(1)(a) CISG remains. This provision states that the buyer may declare the contract avoided if the failure by the seller to perform any of his obligations under the contract amount to a fundamental breach. A breach is fundamental according to the definition of Art 25 CISG, if it results in such a detriment to the other party, as to substantially deprive him of what he is entitled to expect under the contract, unless the party in breach did not foresee and a reasonable person of the same kind in the same circumstances would not have foreseen such a result. Basically, contractual obligations of every kind are to be considered for the determination of a substantial contractual interest, irrespective of whether they constitute a main or ancillary obligation or concern quality, quantity, time of delivery or other manners of performance. The agreement of the parties is of first and foremost relevance (Art 35(1) CISG). Except where the parties have agreed otherwise, the goods do not conform with the contract unless they are fit for the purposes for which goods of the description would ordinarily be used; unless they possess the qualities of goods which the seller has held out to the buyer as a model or sample; and unless the goods are packed in the usual and necessary manner (Art 35(2) CISG). If the non-conformity results from a divergence from the contractual quality or another deficiency of the goods, it needs to be ascertained whether a different method of processing or sale of the goods was possible and reasonable in the normal course of business, even if it had to be combined with a price reduction.

bb) For the final appeal proceedings, it has to be assumed that the goods delivered by [seller] did not conform with the contractual agreement pertaining to their origin and condition. However, as the Court of Appeals correctly stated, the [buyer]—who is insofar burdened with the obligation to submit and prove the facts—did not substantially submit that she was substantially deprived of what she was entitled to expect under the contract as a result of the [seller's] breaches.

cc) The [buyer] did not make use of the—useful—opportunity to expressly state in the contracts which obligations she considered essential. An implicit agreement to this extent cannot be concluded from the circumstances of the contracts.

dd) In the absence of express contractual stipulations, the Court needs to determine whether the seller's breach of contract substantially deprives the buyer of what she was entitled to expect under the contract. In doing so, regard is to be had to the CISG's tendency to limit avoidance of contract in favor of other possible remedies, in particular a reduction of the purchase price or a claim for damages (Art 50, 54(1)(b) CISG). As the Court of Appeals correctly stressed, avoidance of contract is only supposed to be the [buyer's] last resort to react to a breach of contract by the other party which is so grave that the [buyer's] interest in the performance of the contract essentially ceases to exist. Only if the buyer has substanti-ated and, if necessary, proven these prerequisites, does the question arise whether the seller foresaw or could have reasonably foreseen this result. This has to be assumed according to Art 25, last part of the sentence, CISG.

The [buyer's] appeal holds that it is solely decisive for the differentiation between a funda-mental and a non-fundamental breach whether the defect can be remedied by the seller. The Court does not follow this position. The present case does not warrant a decision on whether the possibility of a subsequent remedy of the goods excludes the assumption of a funda-mental breach, either completely or for a period of time. Even if, as in the dispute at hand, a subsequent remedy of the non-conformity is impossible, it does not necessarily follow that the [buyer's] performance interest essentially ceases to exist (quite independent of the kind and extent of the non-conformity). 'Fundamental' in the meaning of Arts 49 and 25 CISG requires a considerable breach of contract—both when interpreting the wording, and when looking at the purpose of the CISG's provisions regarding the buyer's legal remedies. Such gravity can be derived from the contract itself, from the relevant circumstances (Art 8 CISG), or from the reasons listed in Art 35(2) CISG. If a considerable breach does not follow from these criteria, then even a defect of the goods which cannot be remedied does not entitle the buyer to avoid the contract under Art 49(1)(a) CISG.

It is mainly up to the trial judge to determine whether a breach of contract is deemed funda-mental according to the above standard. The circumstances of the case are always decisive. In particular, it has to be considered whether it can be expected for the buyer to put the goods to another reasonable use. The Court of Appeals has followed these principles. Thus, its finding that in the present case there is no fundamental breach cannot be rejected as an error of law.

aaa) Concerning the origin of the goods: The [buyer's] submission that she exports and sells 'primarily' to India and South East Asia and that she would have had 'unforeseeable' difficulties there due to the South Africa embargo, is not sufficient to demonstrate that the possibility to export the goods to one of these countries constituted an essential part of the contract for her. The [buyer] neither named potential customers in one of these countries nor specified her previous export business, nor did the [buyer] submit that a disposal in Germany or an export to another country was not possible or only possible with unreason-able difficulties.

bbb) Concerning the condition of the goods, the above said also applies. A remedy of the goods (removal of the auxiliary flow) is not possible. Not even the [buyer] submits that a certain quality was expressly agreed upon (Art 35(1) CISG). But the [buyer] pleaded and offered corresponding proof that, failing the specification of a certain condition, technical quality was agreed upon (Art 35(2)(a) CISG). However, under the present circumstances it cannot be concluded that the—allegedly non-conforming—delivery of cobalt sulfate with auxiliary flow (fodder quality) constitutes a fundamental breach in the meaning of Art 49(1)

(a) CISG. A major indication to the contrary is the fact that the [broker's] final remark on the contract of 10 January 1992 (concerning the delivery of 2,000 kg cobalt sulfate 21%) regarding the description of goods contains the addendum 'feed grade'. The [buyer] did not object to this specification.

[...]

e) It is questionable, whether—as the [buyer] asserts—the fraudulent foisting of non-conforming goods (here: South African origin) always constitutes a fundamental breach of contract under Arts 25, 49 CISG. The question does not have to be decided in the present case, as the [buyer] did not show any fraudulent behavior by the seller. Such behavior would require that the seller consciously took advantage of the [buyer's] alleged ignorance of the South African origin of the goods. The [buyer] pleaded and rendered proof that neither she, nor the broker knew that the cobalt sulfate delivered by the [seller's] supplier, firm M, is produced exclusively in South Africa, and that this was also not general knowledge. Furthermore, the [buyer] holds that the [seller's] assertion that firm M only delivers cobalt sulfate stemming from South Africa is incorrect. The [buyer's] submission has to be interpreted—following its general context—in the way that the supplier also deals with English goods. This assumed, there was still no fraudulent behavior on the part of the seller. The [buyer] neither submitted nor provided any proof that the [seller] had ordered South African goods from firm M or even knew that the delivery was going to be made from there. On the other hand, if one follows the [seller's] argument that firm M exclusively distributes cobalt sulfate produced in South Africa and affixes an English certificate of origin, then the assumption of fraudulent behavior fails for lack of the subjective requirements. If this was the case, there would be a misconception about the origin of the goods on the part of the [buyer], but not a conscious exploitation of this misconception on the part of the [seller]. The [seller] submitted—undisputed by the [buyer]—that the [buyer] was aware of these practices. In doing so, the [seller] plausibly explained the incorrectness of the origin of the goods, which consisted either already in the contractual agreement about goods stemming from England, or at the latest in the delivery of a false Certificate of Origin. It would have been the task of the [buyer] to contradict this explanation.

f) Thus the [buyer] did not substantially submit a tortious act by the [seller]. Contrary to the [buyer's] opinion, the Court of Appeals consequently did not have to examine whether the [buyer] was entitled to refuse payment of the purchase price under the aspect of damages from tort under German or Dutch domestic law.

[...]

Question

Q 49-2

What circumstances of the above case (C 49-1) did the court consider and how did it treat them when dealing with fundamental breach?

(a) Express Stipulations

It is up to the parties to stipulate what they consider to be the essence of the contract. If the seller then fails to deliver in accordance with the express stipulations given, it cannot argue that it did not foresee any detriment that occurs to the buyer.

C 49-2

Oberlandesgericht Stuttgart (Germany), 12 March 2001, CISG-online 841[190]

For a summary of the facts see C 38/39-5 above.

[Judgment]

The appeal is not successful.

I. [...]

II. The Court furthermore agrees with the district court that the [seller] was unable to prove that the delivered apple juice concentrate conformed to the contract at the time of the passing of risk. [...]

III. In the opinion of the Court, the [buyer] was nevertheless not entitled to declare the contract avoided by virtue of Art 49 CISG.

1. Regarding goods that do not conform to the specifications of the contract, the CISG does not distinguish between the delivery of defective goods and the delivery of different kinds of goods. The delivery of an *aliud* does in any case not constitute a non-delivery in the meaning of Art 49(1)(b) CISG. Therefore, the avoidance of contract can in the present case only be based upon Art 49(1)(a) CISG. In the Court's opinion, the [buyer] is not entitled to declare the contract avoided because there is no fundamental breach of contract in the meaning of Art 49(1)(a) CISG. Following the definition in Art 25 CISG, a breach of contract is fundamental if it results in such detriment to the other party as substantially to deprive him of what he is entitled to expect under the contract, unless the party in breach did not foresee and a reasonable person of the same kind could not have foreseen such a result. The goods delivered by the [seller] had been mixed with glucose syrup and could therefore no longer be referred to as apple juice concentrate; drinks produced from it could not be traded as apple juice. Consequently, the goods did not conform to the contract. If the breach of contract—as in the present case—consists of a lack of conformity of the goods, it is decisive whether the buyer was without unreasonable expenditure able to process the goods differently or sell them in the normal course of business, if only with a price discount, and if the buyer could reasonably be expected to take such measures. It is true that the [buyer] submitted before the Court of First Instance that her customer, company S., had been unable to use the delivered concentrate, so that the goods had to be destroyed. However, before the first hearing in the appellate proceedings, the [buyer]'s attorney in his brief of 6 April 2000 pleaded that the goods were in the end used—in a permissible way—for the production of apple fruit drinks after all [translator's note: these drinks, in contrast to 'apple juice' may contain sugar additives]. It is the Court's opinion that the fact that [buyer]'s customer did in the end process and trade the goods speaks against assuming a fundamental breach of contract in the meaning of Art 49(1)(a) CISG in the present case.

2. Even if the delivery of the sugared goods was to be considered a fundamental breach of contract in the meaning of Art 49(1)(a) CISG—an opinion that could be based upon the

---

[190] Translation taken from CISG Pace (citations omitted).

fact that the [buyer] explicitly ordered apple juice concentrate, which was why the [seller] had to assume that the receipt of unsugared goods usable for the production of apple juice mattered to the [buyer]—the [buyer] would still not have been entitled to declare the contract avoided.

It needs to be said that the [buyer] did not lose the right to declare the contract avoided under Art 49(2)(b). [Buyer] declared the avoidance of contract with letter of 26 March 1997. This was after the additional period of time for the delivery of goods that conformed to the contractual specifications—which had been set on 19 March 1997 in accordance with Art 47 CISG until 26 March 1997—had expired without the [seller] performing a substitute delivery. If one assumes a fundamental breach of contract, the requirements for the setting of an additional period of time for the delivery of substitute goods in the meaning of Art 46(2) CISG are met: The [seller] was notified of the lack of conformity of the delivered concentrate with [buyer]'s letter of 29 January 1997 and the [buyer] required the [seller] to make a substitute delivery with letter of 26 February 1997.

[...]

Question

Q 49-3

What were the considerations concerning the fundamental breach in the above case (C 49-2)?

(b) Purpose for which Goods are Bought

C 49-3

Bundesgericht (Switzerland),
28 October 1998,
CISG-online 413[191]

[Facts]

Three German sellers and a Swiss buyer concluded a contract for the sale of meat to be further resold on the Egyptian market. After delivery the buyer complained about non-conformity of the goods caused by an excess of the fat and moisture content of the meat and declared the contract terminated. In the notice of non-conformity the buyer also offered to take delivery of the goods at a reduced price. As the buyer refused to pay the price the sellers filed suit against the buyer to recover the purchase prise plus interest. The buyer counter-claimed damages determined by defects of the goods and loss of profits.

---

[191] English abstract taken from UNILEX.

[Judgment]

The lower Court found that the buyer was only entitled to reduce the price of the defective goods. The Supreme Court affirmed the lower Court's decision and pointed out that in case of lack of conformity a fundamental breach entitling the buyer to terminate the contract under Arts 49 and 25 CISG can not be inferred when the processing or resale of the goods is still possible in the ordinary course of business without an excessive burden for the buyer. In the case at hand, the Court found that the defects of the meat only determined a loss of weight after its industrial processing and did not prevent its resale on the Egyptian market as was also proved by the buyer's offer to take delivery of the goods at a reduced price.

[…]

Questions

Q 49-4

Based on the above case (C 49-3), what will be decisive for a finding of fundamental breach in such cases?

Q 49-5

In the absence of express stipulations as to the characteristics of the goods, what other factors will be relevant in determining whether a fundamental breach has occurred in a specific case? Give examples of fact patterns in which these might be relevant.

C 49-4

Delchi Carrier SpA v Rotorex Corp,
US Ct App (2nd Cir), 6 December 1995,
CISG-online 140[192]

[Facts]

In January 1988, Rotorex agreed to sell 10,800 compressors to Delchi for use in Delchi's 'Ariele' line of portable room air conditioners. The air conditioners were scheduled to go on sale in the spring and summer of 1988. Prior to executing the contract, Rotorex sent Delchi a sample compressor and accompanying written performance specifications. The compressors were scheduled to be delivered in three shipments before May 15, 1988.

Rotorex sent the first shipment by sea on March 26. Delchi paid for this shipment, which arrived at its Italian factory on April 20, by letter of credit. Rotorex sent a second shipment of compressors on or about May 9. Delchi also remitted payment for this shipment by letter of credit. While the second shipment was en route, Delchi discovered that the first lot of compressors did not conform to the sample model and accompanying specifications. On May 13,

---

[192] Citations omitted.

after a Rotorex representative visited the Delchi factory in Italy, Delchi informed Rotorex that 93 percent of the compressors were rejected in quality control checks because they had lower cooling capacity and consumed more power than the sample model and specifications. After several unsuccessful attempts to cure the defects in the compressors, Delchi asked Rotorex to supply new compressors conforming to the original sample and specifications. Rotorex refused, claiming that the performance specifications were 'inadvertently communicated' to Delchi.

In a faxed letter dated May 23, 1988, Delchi cancelled the contract. Although it was able to expedite a previously planned order of suitable compressors from Sanyo, another supplier, Delchi was unable to obtain in a timely fashion substitute compressors from other sources and thus suffered a loss in its sales volume of Arieles during the 1988 selling season. Delchi filed the instant action under the United Nations Convention on Contracts for the International Sale of Goods ('CISG' or 'the Convention') for breach of contract and failure to deliver conforming goods. On January 10, 1991, Judge Cholakis granted Delchi's motion for partial summary judgment, holding Rotorex liable for breach of contract.

[...]

[Judgment]

[...]

Judge Cholakis held that 'there is no question that [Rotorex's] compressors did not conform to the terms of the contract between the parties' and noted that '[t]here are ample admissions [by Rotorex] to that effect.' We agree. The agreement between Delchi and Rotorex was based upon a sample compressor supplied by Rotorex and upon written specifications regarding cooling capacity and power consumption. After the problems were discovered, Rotorex's engineering representative, Ernest Gamache, admitted in a May 13, 1988 letter that the specification sheet was 'in error' and that the compressors would actually generate less cooling power and consume more energy than the specifications indicated. Gamache also testified in a deposition that at least some of the compressors were nonconforming. The president of Rotorex, John McFee, conceded in a May 17, 1988 letter to Delchi that the compressors supplied were less efficient than the sample and did not meet the specifications provided by Rotorex. Finally, in its answer to Delchi's complaint, Rotorex admitted 'that some of the compressors . . . did not conform to the nominal performance information.' There was thus no genuine issue of material fact regarding liability, and summary judgment was proper.

Under the CISG, if the breach is 'fundamental' the buyer may either require delivery of substitute goods, CISG Art 46, or declare the contract void, CISG Art 49, and seek damages. With regard to what kind of breach is fundamental, Article 25 provides:

A breach of contract committed by one of the parties is fundamental if it results in such detriment to the other party as substantially to deprive him of what he is entitled to expect under the contract, unless the party in breach did not foresee and a reasonable person of the same kind in the same circumstances would not have foreseen such a result.

In granting summary judgment, the district court held that '[t]here appears to be no question that [Delchi] did not substantially receive that which [it] was entitled to expect' and that 'any reasonable person could foresee that shipping non-conforming goods to a buyer would result in the buyer not receiving that which he expected and was entitled to receive.' Because the cooling power and energy consumption of an air conditioner compressor are important determinants of the product's value, the district court's conclusion that Rotorex was liable for a fundamental breach of contract under the Convention was proper.

[...]

Question

Q 49-6

What were the considerations concerning the fundamental breach in C 49-4?

(c) Possibility of Repair or Replacement

Question

Q 49-7

Discuss the findings that the *Handelsgericht Aargau* (C 48-1) makes with respect to the interaction between the seller's right to cure and the buyer's right to avoid the contract.

C. Non-conforming Documents

In some circumstances, the seller's duty to hand over documents can also be relevant for the determination of a fundamental breach.

C 49-5

Bundesgerichtshof (Germany),
3 April 1996,
CISG-online 135[193]

For a summary of the facts see C 35-3 above.

[Judgment]

[a)–c)] [...]

d) Furthermore, the [buyer] pleads that she was also entitled to avoid the contract because the seller had delivered false documents and had let elapse the fixed additional time to deliver four original Certificates of Analysis and four Certificates of Origin. The [buyer] pleads that the [seller] also failed to perform his contractual obligations in this regard, and that consequently the prerequisites of an avoidance of contract were present according to Art 49(1)(b) CISG.

aa) It is correct that the delivery of contractually stipulated documents can be an essential contractual obligation, which, if breached, may entitle the buyer to declare the contract

---

[193] Translation taken from CISG Pace (citations omitted).

avoided according to Art 49(1) CISG. However, it is not necessary to discuss in detail whether the present contracts constituted true documentary transaction with regard to the clause 'cash against documents', resp. 'CAD by cable transfer'. This is because the sales contracts of 10 January 1992 mentioned only the Certificate of Analysis as a document and the contracts of 14 January 1992 named solely the Certificate of Origin; neither mentioned the Certificate of Deposit, which the [buyer] needed in order to receive the goods at the place of deposit. The [buyer] did not plead in the trial phase that the seller withheld the Certificate of Deposit. But even if all four sales contracts were to be considered as typical documentary transactions there would be, contrary to [buyer's] assertion, no case of non-performance. The same principles apply to the documents which apply to the goods themselves: If the documents—though faulty—are handed over to the buyer, they are 'delivered' with the consequence that Art 49(1)(b) CISG does not apply. It is then relevant whether the buyer, through the defective documents, is substantially deprived of what she was entitled to expect under the contract. For this, one cannot solely consider the documents alone and whether the goods could be traded or not with the delivered documents. If the buyer can remedy the defect herself without difficulty by obtaining a correct document, she is able to sell the goods or the goods to be manufactured from them without difficulty, unless the goods themselves have grave defects. In such a case it cannot be said that the essential interest in the contract ceases to exist. It is also conceivable that the origin of the goods is irrelevant for the further disposal of the goods (sale or manufacturing). If that is the case, the faulty documents all the more so do not lead to a substantial deprivation of the contractual interest.

bb) This is how the matter lies in the dispute at hand. The [buyer] is correct when she points out that the Certificate of Origin from the Antwerp Chamber of Commerce, that was delivered by the [seller], was incorrect and that a use of this certificate in the course of the on-sale could not be expected from her. The term 'origin' is understood—both according to the normal usage as well as the relevant provisions of the EEC—to refer to the place of production or the place of the (essential) manufacturing. The [seller's] objection that one has to rely mainly on the correct import, and that the Certificate of Origin 'EEC' was therefore at the time of its issuance correct, is consequently not convincing. However, if the [buyer] herself was able to obtain a correct Certificate of Origin, as the [seller] submitted without the [buyer's] objection, then the [buyer's] substantial contractual interest was preserved as far as such a certificate was needed for the resale of the goods. The same principles apply to the Certificate of Origin as to the goods themselves. The [buyer] did not plead that she could not utilize the cobalt sulfate with a correct Certificate of Origin 'South Africa'.

cc) As far as the Certificates of Analysis to be presented by the [seller] are concerned, it has to be concluded that none of the four documents presented was in accordance with the contractual requirements. However, this fact also does not lead to the [buyer] being substantially deprived of what she was entitled to expect under the contract. At the [seller's] proposal, the parties agreed to have the delivered cobalt sulfate examined by an expert to be chosen by the [buyer]. The Court of Appeals held that the [buyer] received a correct Certificate of Analysis with the expert report and that therefore one cannot speak of a cessation of her contractual interest. This Court does not object to those findings. The fact that the [seller] did not hand over four Certificates of Analysis for the deliveries, which undisputedly stemmed from one production, provides even less justification for an avoidance of contract. At the [buyer's] order, the expert viewed all the goods in store, took samples and examined these samples. Therefore, his expert opinion included the deliveries pertaining to all four contracts for the sale of goods. Even if the [buyer] had intended to dispose of the four lots separately and would have needed a Certificate of Analysis for each of them, she could have produced additional certificates herself by making photocopies.

[...]

CISG Advisory Council Opinion No 5: The buyer's right to avoid the contract in case of non-conforming goods or documents—Black Letter Rules:[194]

1. In determining whether there is a fundamental breach in case of non-conformity of the goods giving the buyer the right to avoid the contract according to Art 49(1)(a) CISG, regard is to be given to the terms of the contract.
2. If the contract does not make clear what amounts to a fundamental breach, regard is to be given in particular to the purpose for which the goods are bought.
3. There is no fundamental breach where the non-conformity can be remedied either by the seller or the buyer without unreasonable inconvenience to the buyer or delay inconsistent with the weight accorded to the time of performance.
4. Additional costs or inconvenience resulting from avoidance do not influence per se whether there is a fundamental breach.
5. The issue of avoidance in case of non-conforming accompanying documents such as insurance policies, certificates etc., must be decided by resorting to the criteria set forth in 1. to 4.
6. In the case of documentary sales, there is no fundamental breach if the seller can remedy the non-conformity of the documents consistently with the weight accorded to the time of performance.
7. In the commodity trade, in general there is a fundamental breach if there is no timely delivery of conforming documents.
8. If the non-conformity does not amount to a fundamental breach, the buyer still has a right to withhold payment and to refuse to take delivery if reasonable under the circumstances.

Questions

Q 49-8

(a) What approach does the court take in the above case (C 49-5) with regard to the issue of non-conforming documents?
(b) According to this case, in which circumstances will non-conformity of documents result in a fundamental breach of contract?

Q 49-9

How do the black letter rules compare with the analysis of the foregoing case law?

---

[194] Taken from www.cisgac.com.

D. Late Delivery

In some circumstances, a late delivery, in itself, will constitute a fundamental breach of contract entitling a party to avoid. This is not to be confused with the requirements under Article 49(1)(b) CISG, according to which, after the lapse of the *Nachfrist* under Article 47 CISG, an otherwise non-fundamental non-delivery entitles the buyer to avoid the contract.

C 49-6

Corte di Appello di Milano (Italy),
20 March 1998,
CISG-online 348[195]

[Facts]

On 28 November 1990 an Italian buyer and a Hong Kong seller concluded a contract for the sale of knitted goods, with the following clause regarding delivery and payment: 'Delivery: 3rd December, 1990; Terms of payment: deposit: US $6,000.00; Balance: bank cheque'. Before the delivery date, the buyer issued a bank cheque in the amount of the deposit, but the goods were not delivered. After the date for delivery had expired, the buyer canceled the purchase order. The seller replied on 14 December 1990, stating that it would deliver the goods but only after payment of the entire purchase price.

In January 1991 the buyer brought an action before an Italian court claiming avoidance of the contract for breach by the seller and refund of the sum paid. The court of first instance rejected the buyer's claim, and the buyer appealed.

[Judgment]

[...]

The Court held that since the seller had failed to deliver the goods at the date fixed by the contract as required by Art 33 CISG, the buyer was entitled to declare the contract avoided on the ground of Arts 45(1) and 49(1) CISG, and that the cancellation of the purchase order sent by the buyer was equivalent to a notice of avoidance under Art 26 CISG.

The Court considered that, given the concise text of the delivery clause, the precise observance by the seller of the date for delivery was of fundamental importance to the buyer, who expected to receive the goods in time for the holiday season, as it had made apparent to the seller even after the conclusion of the contract. Therefore, the non-delivery at the date fixed by the contract amounted to a fundamental breach by the seller (Art 25 CISG).

The Court further held that the seller could not make payment of the full purchase price a condition for handing over the goods on the ground of Art 58(1) CISG. In fact, the seller had only specified such condition in its reply to the buyer's notice of avoidance. In any event, the seller cannot avail itself of the right set out in Art 58(1) CISG in such a manner that could

---

[195] English abstract taken from UNILEX.

cause a substantial detriment to the other party, because this would amount to a fundamental breach of contract (Art 25 CISG).

Questions

Q 49-10

When will late delivery constitute a fundamental breach?

Q 49-11

As a lawyer, how would you advise a buyer who comes to you and tells you that the seller has not delivered on time?

III. Avoidance after Additional Period of Time— Article 49(1)(b) CISG

Non-delivery, in itself, is not a fundamental breach of contract entitling the buyer to avoid. However, Article 49(1)(b) CISG provides a second ground under which a buyer can avoid the contract: in cases of non-delivery, the buyer may avoid the contract after allowing an additional period of time, in which the seller is requested to perform its obligations, to lapse without performance taking place. The buyer is thereby released from the burden of proving a fundamental breach of contract. The possibility of avoiding the contract by fixing an additional period of time is available to the buyer only if the seller fails to make delivery of all or part of the goods (see Art 51 CISG below), but not if the delivered goods are non-conforming within the meaning of Articles 35, 41, and 42 CISG (see discussion above; in these cases, generally only Art 49(1)(a) CISG applies).

C 49-7

Oberlandesgericht Celle (Germany),
24 May 1995,
CISG-online 152[196]

For a summary of the facts see C 47-2 above.

[Judgment]

---

[196] Translation taken from CISG Pace (citations omitted).

[...]

2.2. The [buyer] likewise effectively avoided the contract with respect to the other machines which [seller] had not delivered. This was done at the latest by a communication of the [buyer's] attorney on 26 January 1993, which rejected any further delivery and demanded the return of the excess price already paid. The [buyer] was entitled to do so.

2.2.1. Pursuant to Art 49(1)(b), the [buyer] may declare the contract avoided in the case of non-delivery if the [seller] does not deliver the goods within the additional period of time fixed by the [buyer] in accordance with Art 47(1) or the [seller] declares that he will not deliver the goods within the period so fixed. Where the [seller] has already delivered part of the goods, this rule also applies to that part of the goods which are missing (Art 51(1)). The [buyer] gave notice pursuant to Art 47(1) by the communication of his attorney on 4 December 1992. Such a notice is authorized if the [seller] has not satisfied his obligations under the contract (Art 45(1)(a)).

Where the contract fixes a period of time for delivery, the [seller] must deliver the goods within that period (Art 33(b)). The [seller] failed to satisfy this obligation. The [seller] was obligated to deliver the missing machinery by no later than August. The Lower Court's finding that the first installment was due by the end of May and the second by the end of August is convincing. The [buyer] was entitled to give a notice fixing an additional period of time for the seller to perform.

There remains the issue of whether the period fixed was too short. The [buyer] fixed a period from the time of the notice on 4 December to the time fixed in the notice of 16 December, a period which required shipment within eleven days.

With hindsight, this period was possibly too short to organize carriage by sea from [X] to [Y], given that the [seller] was dependent on the schedule of the ship and the existence of free space for freight. This does not make the notice ineffective where the notice has merely extended a period of time [...]. In any case, when the [buyer] gave notice that the contract was avoided on 26 January 1993, a sufficiently long time (seven weeks) had elapsed. The [buyer] may declare the contract avoided even though the seller in the meantime has declared by its letter of 22 November 1992, that it was ready to deliver part of the goods. That letter offered to ship four of the machines originally ordered (for three of which there was an agreed partial avoidance) but it offered to substitute a different press for one of the presses originally agreed upon and the letter failed to mention (apparently by mistake, if one understands the [seller's] argument) the last of the machines ordered.

If the [seller's] offer to deliver conformed with the contract, the [buyer] would not have the right to avoid the contract unless he could show that a partial delivery was a fundamental breach and therefore the missing press entitled him to avoid the entire contract (Art 51(2)). On the other hand, the [seller's] obligation of good faith (Art 7(1)) required him to await the [buyer's] answer to his offer before shipping.

However, the [seller's] offer was not in accordance with the contract. The [seller] wanted prepayment for the total price of the machines offered. This did not conform with the terms of the contract, which provided that part of the price was to be paid upon the tender of documents. The [buyer] was therefore entitled to declare the contract avoided by the communication of 26 January 1993. The [seller's] subsequent announcement on 3 February 1993, that he would be able to deliver the original press, came too late. In any event, this latter communication again demanded prepayment of the purchase price.

2.2.2. Only for the sake of completeness, it should be pointed out that [buyer's] right to demand repayment—if the right to this remedy had not already been created by [buyer's] rightful declaration of avoidance on 26 January 1993—would have been established, insofar as [seller] sold the contractual goods to other parties, based on that sale. In the [seller] having admitted having sold the goods to another party, lies the notice that [seller] is now incapable of fulfilling its contractual obligation at all. Such notice entitles the [buyer] to avoid the contract, even without setting an additional period of time (*Nachfrist*) […]. It is without consequence whether [seller] saw itself forced to sell elsewhere to minimize its damage. This would not change the fact that [buyer] is entitled to avoid the contract and demand repayment of the down payment, as [seller] is no longer able to deliver.

The contention of [seller] according to which it was still able to deliver, as [buyer] was not entitled to the specific machines mentioned in the contract, but only to delivery of comparable goods, cannot prevail. The contention is contrary to the clear wording of the contract, in which the machines are identified by serial number—as far as this is missing in regard to position no. 4, this still regards, according to [seller's] own statement, an individual machine, which could not be examined only because it was in England—and to the fact that [buyer] had individually examined the machines with the exception of position no. 4.

[…]

Question

Q 49-12

How did the court interpret the requirements of Article 49(1)(b) CISG in the above case (C 49-7)?

IV. Buyer's Observance of Time Limits—Article 49(2) CISG

According to Article 49(2) CISG, once the goods have been delivered, the buyer incurs certain obligations with respect to the observance of time periods if it wishes to exercise its right to declare the contract avoided. The buyer must declare the contract avoided within a reasonable time after the goods have been delivered, or, in the case of a late delivery, within a reasonable time after the buyer *becomes aware* that the goods have been delivered.

C 49-8

Bundesgericht (Switzerland),
18 May 2009,
CISG-online 1900[197]

For a summary of the facts see C 38/39-19 above.

[Judgment]

[...]

[Seller] further alleges that [Buyer] had not declared avoidance of the contract within a reasonable time on 23 March 2003. It is [Seller]'s position that, since the Appellate Court held that [Buyer] had not forfeited its right to declare avoidance, it committed a violation of Art 49(2)(b) CISG.

8.1 Under Art 49(2)(b)(i) CISG, the buyer loses the right to declare the contract avoided in respect to any breach other than late delivery, if he does not make that declaration within a reasonable time after he knew or ought to have known of the breach. The question of whether any given period of time may still qualify as 'reasonable' in terms of Art 49(2)(b) CISG must be determined in accordance with all circumstances of the individual case and the purpose of this provision. *Inter alia*, regard must be had to the nature of goods and lack of conformity as well as the conduct of the seller subsequent to the buyer's notice of non-conformity. Art 49(2)(b)(i) CISG provides that the relevant period of time commences as soon as the buyer has become aware or ought to have become aware of the breach of contract. This requires that the buyer has fully appreciated the existence, extent and scope of consequences of a breach of contract. Only if he has done so will he be capable of assessing whether there is actually a fundamental breach of contract which justifies avoidance of contract under Art 49(1)(a) CISG. In general, a period of one to two months will be necessary and reasonable for the buyer to sufficiently examine the situation, unless there is a special case which would objectively justify either an extended or a reduced period.

8.2 The Appellate Court confirmed the reasoning of the District Court. The latter has held that [Buyer] declared avoidance of the contract within a reasonable time. The District Court also held that [Buyer] properly notified the lack of conformity in accordance with Art 39(1) CISG. [Buyer] immediately notified [Seller] of the problems which had appeared after the packaging machine had been installed and after the first test-runs had been conducted. The first of these notifications was given on 5 October 2001. The following correspondence between the parties indicated that [Seller] persistently attempted to remedy the machine's lack of conformity. Until December 2002, [Buyer] sent more than twenty letters which contain detailed accounts of the still existing defects subsequent to the respective attempts to remedy. After [Seller] had undertaken these unsuccessful attempts for more than one year, it declared for the first time on 6 December 2002 that a performance of 180 vials per minute as demanded by [Buyer] could not be possibly achieved. At the same time, [Seller] made further proposals of how the actual

---

[197] Translation taken from CISG Pace (citations omitted).

performance might be increased. Thereupon, by letter dated 10 December 2002, [Buyer] referred to the extent of its losses which had been incurred until then by virtue of the lack of conformity of the machine. [Buyer] also demanded that [Seller] announce a definite date on which it would have accomplished the installation of a properly-operating machine. After a meeting at [Buyer]'s works, [Seller] made a proposal for an amicable settlement by letter dated 14 February 2003. However, [Seller] proposed a target performance which was once again well below the performance required by the contract. It turned out only by this point in time that [Buyer] would be substantially deprived of what it was entitled to expect under the contract. Therefore, the District Court concluded that the relevant period of time for a declaration of avoidance in terms of Art 49(2)(b) CISG commenced on 14 February 2003. Since [Buyer] declared avoidance of contract on 23 March 2003, it acted within a reasonable time. It had to be considered that the complexity of the case required considerable examinations in legal and commercial matters before a declaration of avoidance could have been expected. Consequently, [Buyer] had to be granted a period of almost one-and-a-half months.

8.3 [Seller] claims that the Appellate Court has wrongly and arbitrarily determined that [Buyer] had become aware of the fundamental breach of contract by 14 February 2003. [Seller] submits that it had pointed out already in its letter of 6 December 2002 that the packaging machine would never be capable of achieving an output of 180 vials per minute. As a consequence, its failure to perform the contract had become definitive. The District Court was not entitled to conclude that the fundamentality of the breach had become apparent only by 14 February 2003. This decision by the District Court was not consistent with its reasoning concerning the letter dated 6 December 2002. In that respect, the District Court came to an evidently incorrect and arbitrary determination of the facts.

[Seller]'s argument is unfounded. [Seller] has ignored that by virtue of the letter dated 6 December 2002, it merely turned out that the performance of 180 vials per minute as required by the contract could not be achieved. It was not readily apparent by this point in time which exact performance was possibly attainable by way of additional attempts to partially remedy the lack of conformity. Likewise, [Buyer] was not aware by that date about whether or not the breach of contract would turn out as a fundamental one. [Buyer] has become aware that the breach is indeed fundamental only subsequent to the meeting with [Seller]'s representatives and the latter's proposal for an amicable settlement. Therefore, neither the Appellate Court nor the District Court can be accused of an inconsistent—let alone an arbitrary—reasoning.

8.4 Given that [Buyer] had become aware of the fundamental breach of contract in terms of Art 49(2)(b)(i) CISG only by 14 February 2003, it has not forfeited its right to declare avoidance by making that declaration on 23 March 2003. [Buyer] has declared avoidance within a reasonable time as provided in Art 49(2)(b) CISG. Finally, even [Seller] has acknowledged that a period of between one and two months is generally reasonable.

[...]

As a consequence, [Seller]'s appeal is dismissed as unfounded.

Question

Q 49-13

(a) Article 49(2) CISG calls for the buyer to declare the contract avoided within a 'reasonable time'. Why do you think this requirement was written into the CISG?
(b) When does the period of time for declaring avoidance start running?
(c) Is there a general period of time which is considered as reasonable?

Article 50 CISG

If the goods do not conform with the contract and whether or not the price has already been paid, the buyer may reduce the price in the same proportion as the value that the goods actually delivered had at the time of the delivery bears to the value that conforming goods would have had at that time. However, if the seller remedies any failure to perform his obligations in accordance with article 37 or article 48 or if the buyer refuses to accept performance by the seller in accordance with those articles, the buyer may not reduce the price.

I. Overview

A. Content and Purpose of Article 50 CISG

Article 50 CISG enables the buyer to reduce the price where the seller has delivered goods that do not conform to the contract. Article 50 CISG is, however, subject to some limitations. It prevents the buyer from 'double-dipping' to the extent that, where the seller has cured the lack of conformity under Articles 37 or 48 CISG, or the buyer has refused cure thereunder, the price is not reduced.

B. Domestic Laws

The price reduction regulated in Article 50 CISG is a product of the legal systems of continental Europe. It has its origins in Roman law, which recognised the principle of *actio quanti minoris*. In contrast, the notion of price reduction, as a remedy, is unknown in common law legal systems. However, in such systems, this right is replaced by the right to claim damages.

§ 441 BGB:[198]

(1) Instead of avoiding the contract, the buyer can reduce the purchase price by way of a declaration made to the seller. […]

---

[198] Author's translation.

(2) [...]
(3) In the case of a price reduction, the purchase price is to be reduced in the proportion which the value of conforming goods at the time of the conclusion of the contract would have had to the actual value. [...]
(4) [...]

Art 205 OR:[199]

(1) In a case where the goods do not conform to the contract, the buyer has a choice between rescinding the contract by bringing an action for rescission of the contract or demanding compensation for the reduced value of the goods by bringing an action for reduction of the purchase price.
(2) [...]
(3) If the reduction in value claimed equals the purchase price, the buyer can only claim rescission.

§ 2-714(2) UCC:

The measure of damages for breach of warranty is the difference at the time and place of acceptance between the value of the goods accepted and the value they would have had if they had been as warranted, unless special circumstances show proximate damages of a different amount.

Question

Q 50-1

What are the practical differences between the solution under the CISG and that under common law?

C. International Principles

Unlike the CISG, the PICC 2010 do not contain the remedy of price reduction.

D. Drafting History

Article 50 CISG is based upon Article 46 ULIS, but differs in several respects from this earlier provision. The main difference lies in the additional reference to Article 37 CISG in Article 50, which was introduced by Germany as a logical extension of the inclusion of Article 48 CISG.

---

[199] Author's translation.

II. Requirements for a Reduction of the Price

Whether the goods in question lack conformity or not is to be determined by reference to Article 35 CISG, (see the discussion on this Article above). The price reduction can be invoked regardless of whether the lack of conformity amounts to a fundamental breach or a 'simple' breach of contract. The price reduction may even be claimed if the buyer did not give notice of the lack of conformity under Article 39(1) CISG, provided it had a reasonable excuse under Article 44 CISG. Finally, whether or not the seller can rely upon an exemption from liability under Article 79 CISG is irrelevant; the buyer may nevertheless reduce the price.

Question

Q 50-2

Do you think Article 50 CISG also applies in the case of encumbrances with third party intellectual or industrial property rights? Why or why not?

As provided for under Article 45(2) CISG, the buyer is able to combine the remedy under Article 50 CISG with other remedies in Articles 46 to 52 CISG. Thus, a claim for reduction of the price may be accompanied by a claim for damages, but only to the extent that the damages are not already reflected in the price reduction.

C 50-1

Oberster Gerichtshof (Austria),
23 May 2005,
CISG-online 1041[200]

[Facts]

[...]

The Defendant [Buyer], an Italian company with a branch in Austria, bought coffee machines for resale purposes from the Plaintiff [Seller], an Austrian company with a dependence in Italy, starting in early 1995. At first, the coffee machines were paid in cash; later on, dates for payment were granted. The resale to customers of the [Buyer] was at about cost-price. [Buyer]'s profit was to be made by also providing the customers with the coffee for the machines (which was also obtained from the [Seller]). This was known to the [Seller] from the beginning of the contractual relationship.

---

[200] Translation taken from CISG Pace (citations omitted).

About a month after the installation of the first coffee machines at the [Buyer]'s customers, the first complaints were made; mainly short circuits and water loss were named. These technical problems were known to the [Seller] from the very beginning and were constantly criticized by the [Buyer]. Attempts by the [Buyer], as well as by the [Seller], to repair the machines did not deliver enduring results; the repaired machines became defective again after a short time.

Set-up and construction of the coffee machines are very simple. However, the safety contact switch for the level of water in the water tank does not correspond to the state of engineering. Furthermore the mechanical devices (levers, coffee tablet holder) are implemented with high tolerances for adjusting, so that leakages may occur after the shortest intended use, which does not allow a continuous use for coffee preparation. The malfunctions are primarily caused by a conductive connection between the heating coil and the bottom flange of the heating container. Heat and lime deposits are sufficient to lead to a leak in the gasket. The escaping water causes conductive connections on the inner exposed parts of the electronic connections, and thus short circuits. From a technical point of view, the elimination of the construction flaws would be possible. For a short-time repair of these leakages, one hour of work per machine would be needed. A machine, repaired like this, could be used for some time, but not indefinitely.

[...]

By the end of 1996 and in early 1997, the [Buyer] decided to return to the [Seller] the broken machines as well as some unused and unpacked machines. However, after the delivery drive to Italy had already started, the [Buyer]'s employee was informed by the [Seller] by telephone that the machines would only be taken back if the invoices would be settled. After that, the machines were not returned.

There is no serious purchase interest in goods with such defects; because of that the machines are without value and unsalable.

[...]

[Judgment]

[...]

The assessment of the legal consequences concerning the delivery of the worthless goods has to be done in accordance with CISG Art 50, because—as it is likewise not contested in the revision proceedings—the [Buyer] failed to avoid the contract because of a fundamental breach within a reasonable time as imposed under CISG Art 49(2)(b). The [Buyer] bases its position in the appeal proceedings therefore only on CISG Art 50, whose first sentence reads:

'If the goods do not conform with the contract and whether or not the price has already been paid, the buyer may reduce the price in the same proportion as the value that the goods actually delivered had at the time of the delivery bears to the value that conforming goods would have had at that time.'

The CISG does not set a period of time for the buyer's desire to reduce price. In contrast to § 932 ABGB, it is not the date at which the contract was concluded that is crucial for reduction of price but date of delivery . At hand, the goods delivered by the [Seller] were at that date absolutely worthless and unsaleable.

The question is whether CISG Art 50 entitles the [Buyer] to reduce the price to zero when the goods are absolutely worthless.

— *On the one hand*, this question is answered in the affirmative by Müller-Chen, Magnus and Achilles and furthermore it is explained, that this kind of price reduction is beneficial for the buyer, when the avoidance of contract for whatever reasons is not possible, e.g., it did not adhere to the period of time given by CISG Art 49.

— *Contrary to that*, Schnyder/Straub maintain that this assessment is not acceptable at least for those cases in which the worthlessness of the goods could have been ascertained by the buyer through inspections that were to be conducted by it. They maintain that: A reduction of price by the whole price would equate the adjustment of the contract because of a price reduction with the avoidance of contract in its consequences for the buyer. But the avoidance of contract in the CISG is developed as *ultima ratio* of the legal remedies for the buyer and therefore was subjected to special formal requirements. Therefore, even with total worthlessness of the goods, the buyer would be held to the special periods of time given in CISG Arts 39, 49(2) for an avoidance of contract and to the obligation for restitution in accordance with CISG Art 82. These requirements especially with the goods being worthless could be easily met. It would not be expedient to bypass the valuations of the Convention concerning this matter by allowing the buyer to reduce the price especially in those cases, in which it did not satisfy the requisitions of the CISG.

— In case of an evident complete worthlessness of the goods, the enforceability of a price reduction is therefore excluded from the start. Because of the systematic precedence of the right to avoidance, the buyer in such cases could only have the legal remedy of avoidance at its disposal. CISG Art 83 would not oppose this, as the right to a price reduction never existed in the first place and therefore could not 'go on' existing after the loss of the right to avoidance.

— *Holding of this Court.* This Court, the recognizing Chamber of the Supreme Court, does not deem the latter opinion to be convincing.

The buyer's right to reduction of price in accordance with CISG Art 50 is not subordinate to the right to avoid the contract according to CISG Art 49. Even a—in this case only suggested—'systematic precedence of the right to avoidance', as Schnyder/Straub see it, could in no way lead to the result that a buyer of goods that are totally worthless because of a defect is worse off than a buyer of goods that are grossly defective but anyway have some minor worth. This is because CISG Art 50 gives the buyer the right to reduce the price even with an insignificant defect. The circumstance that CISG Art 50 does not provide for the return of the worthless goods to the seller is not relevant in this case, as the [Seller] never demanded the return of the worthless goods in return against the reimbursement of the contract price. Only if such a demand existed, i.e., if the return of the generally totally worthless goods would be a matter of importance (exceptionally) for the seller, could the demand for a return of the contract price on the legal grounds of price reduction to zero in accordance with CISG Art 50 be dependent on the return of the totally worthless goods to the seller.

The CISG creates substantive law and is to be interpreted autonomously in accordance with CISG Art 7. Therefore, discussions on the Austrian legal situation have to be omitted and it is to be primarily interpreted by its literal sense.

The legal remedy pursuant to CISG Art 50 is, according to its text, not restricted to certain cases. Summarizing, this Court, the recognizing Chamber of the Supreme Court, comes to the following conclusion:

CISG Art 50 allows a reduction of price to zero.

[…]

Questions

Q 50-3

How does the above case (C 50-1) explain the relationship between Article 49(1)(a) CISG and Article 50 CISG?

Q 50-4

If a fundamental breach is found to exist, what consequences does this have for any price reduction?

III. Calculation of Price Reduction

C 50-2

Handelsgericht Zürich (Switzerland),
10 February 1999,
CISG-online 488[201]

For a summary of the facts see C 31-1 above.

[Judgment]

[...]

Under Art 50 CISG, the reduction in price is determined by a proportional calculation. The reduced sales price is supposed to bear to the contractual purchase price the same proportion as the value that the goods actually delivered had at the time of the delivery bears to the value that conforming goods would have had at that time. This is the mandatory method of calculation and it is therefore inadmissible to instead simply use the estimated value of the delivered goods as the reduced purchase price, or to determine the reduced purchase price by subtracting the cost of repair from the contractually agreed price. The [buyer] claims damages in the amount of the binding costs without making a connection between the binding costs and the lower value of the goods. The [buyer] neither specifies the alleged lower quality of the goods, nor does she submit any indicators which would enable the Court to calculate the lower value according to the applicable proportional calculation method. The simplistic reference to the binding costs does not allow any conclusions as to the relation between the originally agreed reimbursement on the one hand and the gravity of the non-conformity on the other. The [buyer] therefore in no way managed to expound a lower value according to the respective provision of the Vienna Sales Law, which she herself referred to. Let alone did the [buyer] even come close to sufficiently substantiate the alleged lower value.

[...]

---

[201] Translation taken from CISG Pace (citations omitted).

Question

Q 50-5

(a) What does this case (C 50-2) state should be the method used to calculate the reduction of the price under Article 50 CISG?

(b) Is this solution workable in practice?

Article 51 CISG

(1) If the seller delivers only a part of the goods or if only a part of the goods delivered is in conformity with the contract, articles 46 to 50 apply in respect of the part which is missing or which does not conform.
(2) The buyer may declare the contract avoided in its entirety only if the failure to make delivery completely or in conformity with the contract amounts to a fundamental breach of the contract.

I. Overview

Article 51 CISG grants the buyer the same rights relating to a portion of the goods that the seller has failed to deliver in conformity with the contract as it has under Articles 46 to 50 CISG. Article 51(1) CISG sets out the general rule in this regard: apart from damages, all remedies of the buyer refer only to any part of the contract that lacks conformity or is not performed. In particular, where this is the case, the entire contract is not to be avoided; however, a 'partial avoidance' of the missing or non-conforming part is possible. The exception to this rule is contained in Article 51(2) CISG, namely that entire avoidance of the contract is only possible where the 'partial' breach is such as to amount to a fundamental breach of the entire contract.

II. Operation of Article 51 CISG

Article 51 CISG assumes that the seller has breached the contract, either by failing to deliver a part of the goods contracted for, or by delivering a part that lacked conformity with the contract. However, this presumes that the delivered goods can actually be 'physically and economically' separated into constituent parts.

C 51-1

Landgericht Heidelberg (Germany), 3 July 1992, CISG-online 38

[Facts][202]

In order to perform a contract with an Austrian enterprise, a German buyer ordered via fax from a US (Massachusetts) seller eleven computer components, indicating the price of five of the components. The seller delivered only five out of the ordered eleven components. The German buyer refused to pay the price of the five components, arguing that as a consequence of the partial delivery it had to obtain substitute goods to fulfil the contract with the Austrian enterprise. The US seller claimed payment of the price.

[Judgment][203]

The [Seller]'s claim is justified.

1. In the main issue, the [Seller] is entitled to payment of the purchase price by the [Buyer] in accordance with CISG Art 53. The Vienna UN Convention on the International Sale of Goods of 11 April 1980, which is to be applied to the situation on hand, is applicable law in the U.S.A. since 1 January 1988 and in Germany since 1 January 1991.

Regarding a decision in the present dispute, the question of whether the parties concluded a contract that only included the first five items of the fax letter of 10 July 1991 or if that contract was extended to all eleven items of the original enquiry later on may be left open. This being the case, even in the second alternative, as the [Buyer] was not entitled to avoid the entire contract in accordance with CISG Arts 45(1)(a), 49, there being in that case a so-called partial delivery by the [Seller].

Even if one alleges that the [Buyer] through M. E., who is named as a witness, set an additional period of time in accordance with CISG Art 49(1)(b) and after the expiration of that time informed the [Seller] within a reasonable period of time in accordance with CISG Art 49(2)(b)(ii) that it would avoid the contract, a right to avoid the contract is not present. In accordance with CISG Art 51(2), this would require that the partial delivery by the [Seller] at the same time constitute a fundamental breach of the entire contract. Evaluating all circumstances, this condition is not present in the case on hand.

The term fundamental breach is defined in CISG Art 25. Accordingly, the breach must have resulted in such detriment to the [Buyer] as substantially to deprive it of what it was entitled to expect under the contract. Specifically, the purpose for the purchase of the goods by the [Buyer] which also has to at least indirectly become clear out of the contract, must then be unobtainable because of the breach of contract by the [Seller]. To guarantee the achievement of the purpose of the contract in cases of a breach of contract by the seller, the buyer may be expected to make a substitute transaction. Ultimately, the buyer may claim possible additional costs due to a substitute transaction as damages caused by delay in accordance with CISG Art 74.

---

[202] Summary of facts taken from UNILEX.
[203] Translation taken from CISG Pace (citations omitted).

In the case at hand, the [Buyer], as it brought forth, wanted to use the ordered computer parts to fulfil an order placed by the company M. GmbH, Vienna. This contractual relationship was likewise concluded in July 1991; but the performance of the [Buyer] was not due until October 1991. It can meanwhile be seen from a letter by the [Buyer] of 11 August 1991 that in the beginning of August, the [Buyer] was already in possession of the missing computer parts because of a substitute purchase, that [Buyer]—as was submitted—was legally obligated to make; and therefore was in the position to fulfil the contractual obligations in regard to M. GmbH. The withdrawal by M. GmbH from its contract with the [Buyer]—and therefore the non-accomplishment of the purpose of the purchase targeted by the [Buyer]—only took place in January 1992 and therefore was obviously not a result of the breach of contract by the [Seller], as the [Buyer] had all the computer parts it needed to fulfil the order at hand.

Accordingly, there is no fundamental breach by the [Seller] in the sense of CISG Art 25. Therefore, an avoidance of the contract by the [Buyer] in accordance with CISG Art 51(2) was not possible.

Hence, in accordance with CISG Art 53, [Seller]'s suit for the purchase price is justified in the claimed and uncontested amount.

[...]

Questions

Q 51-1

According to the interpretation in this case (C 51-1), in which cases will avoidance for fundamental breach under Article 51(2) CISG be permissible?

Q 51-2

Consider the case of a defect in a component of a machine, which, although delivered separately, is necessary in order for the whole machine to function properly. Do you think such a case is subject to the provisions of Article 51 CISG, or rather to Article 49(1)(a) CISG?

Article 52 CISG

(1) If the seller delivers the goods before the date fixed, the buyer may take delivery or refuse to take delivery.
(2) If the seller delivers a quantity of goods greater than that provided for in the contract, the buyer may take delivery or refuse to take delivery of the excess quantity. If the buyer takes delivery of all or part of the excess quantity, he must pay for it at the contract rate.

I. Overview

Even in cases where the seller 'exceeds' its obligations under the contract, the issue of non-performance may still be relevant. Article 52 CISG refers to two such scenarios: either where the seller delivers too early, under subsection (1), or delivers too much, under subsection (2).

Question

Q 52-1

Under which provision of the CISG could the buyer have a duty to take possession of the goods notwithstanding its right to refuse to take delivery under Article 52(1) and (2) CISG?

II. Early Delivery—Article 52(1) CISG

The buyer has the right to refuse to take delivery under Article 52(1) CISG if the goods arrive before the contractually-agreed delivery date. If the buyer refuses to accept the goods delivered early, the seller is then obliged to redeliver at the agreed point in time. However, if the buyer accepts them, it is bound to pay the purchase price.

Question

Q 52-2

If the buyer accepts the seller's early delivery, is it thereby excluded from making any further claims due thereto? If not, what sort of claims could it assert?

III. Delivery of Excess Quantity

If the seller delivers more goods than contractually agreed, the buyer is entitled to reject the excess amount. This is consistent with the notion of non-conformity with the contractual agreement enunciated in Article 35(1) CISG. However, the contract itself may allow for certain deviations. Provided that any such deviation falls within the limits set out contractually, there is no overshipment.

C 52-1

La San Giuseppe v Forti Moulding Ltd,
Ontario Superior Court of Justice, 31 August 1999,
CISG-online 433

For a summary of the facts see C 1-1 above.

[...]

(5) At first, shipments were sent on a C.O.D. [Collect on Delivery] basis, followed by a requirement that payment be made within 30 days. Over the years, payments were not necessarily made within the 30 day period, but were made more or less currently until 1995. When an order was placed, it was understood by both parties that the amount shipped might vary above or below the ordered amount by up to 10%. There was no requirement that a specified quantity need be purchased at any time, except with respect to certain items made specially for Forti Moulding, where there were some minimum amounts that had to be ordered at one time.

[...]

[Judgment]

[...]

Overshipments

(42) Mr. Forti admitted that it was a term of the contract that he could be shipped 10% more or less of the product ordered. While he complained about overshipments in his testimony, he could point to a written complaint about a short shipment only once in 1994, for which he sought a credit of 54 metres. He claimed that there were overshipments in 1994, as well, pointing to a particular invoice, yet he did not make a written complaint. Given that he

made a complaint in writing about the quality of some of the goods in the same shipment in which he claimed an overshipment, I do not believe his claim with respect to overshipments in 1994.

(43) In any event, even if there had been overshipments, I find that the defendant accepted those goods and, in fact, paid for them. In accordance with Article 52(2) of the Convention and s. 29(2) of the *Sale of Goods Act*, there can be no complaint several years later.

(44) The only other overshipment alleged was in April, 1996, the last shipment. While there were complaints at trial about this, a careful reading of the invoice indicates that several of the items allegedly overshipped were within the 10% tolerance. As to the other items, given Mr. Forti's lack of forthrightness in his evidence generally and again, the lack of a complaint and a promise to pay, I do not accept that there was a problem of overshipment, and I find that the defendant accepted the quantity shipped. This claim is rejected as well.

[...]

Questions

Q 52-3

(a)   Upon what basis was the buyer unable to reject the goods in the above case (C 52-1)?
(b)   What other provision of the CISG could the court have relied upon regarding this issue?

Q 52-4

What happens if the buyer does not reject the goods?

Q 52-5

What happens if the buyer does reject the goods?

Article 53 CISG

The buyer must pay the price for the goods and take delivery of them as required by the contract and this Convention.

I. Overview

Article 53 CISG states the principal obligations of the buyer and serves as an introduction to the provisions set out in Chapter III of the Convention. It constitutes the counterpart provision of Article 30 CISG, which defines the seller's main obligations. Stating the essential obligations of the parties in Articles 53 and 30 CISG is helpful because the CISG does not define the term 'contract of sale' and the precise rights and obligations of the parties that arise from this relationship. As at various other occasions, the CISG stresses, in Article 53, that in defining the contractual obligations, primary regard shall be given to the contract agreed between the parties.

II. Parties' Agreement Prevails

Usually, the parties will have provided for the modalities of payment and taking delivery in their contract. They may do so by referring to internationally recognised trade terms, such as the INCOTERMS® or the UCP 600, or by specific contractual terms. In addition, the contract may impose obligations other than the payment of price and taking of delivery on the buyer, such as the issuance of securities or the supply of materials needed for manufacture or production of the goods (Art 3(1) CISG), or may require the buyer to provide specifications regarding the form, measurement or other features of the goods.

In case law, Article 53 CISG raises no particular difficulties. Numerous decisions refer to the provision in connection with judgements requiring the buyer to pay the price or fulfil another contractual obligation.

Questions

Q 53-1

Does Article 53 CISG allow any leeway to the parties to agree on specific rights and duties not mentioned in the provision?

Q 53-2

Does Article 53 CISG, by only mentioning the buyer's duty to pay the purchase price and take over the goods, treat a breach of these duties differently from other breaches of contract? See also Article 61 CISG.

C 53-1

CIETAC Arbitration Award, January 2007, CISG-online 1974[204]

[...]

I. FACTS OF THE CASE

The Claimant, as the supplier, and the Respondent, as the purchaser, signed the Contract on 26 February 2004, under which the Inner Mongolian ___ Company (the 'Inner Mongolian Company') was listed as the end-user of the subject equipment. According to the Contract, the [Seller] supplied the equipment to the [Buyer] who would then provide it to the end-user (i.e., the Inner Mongolian Company) for its use in the project to expand its Business & operation support system (the 'BOSS'). The Contract, among others, includes the following terms:

Clause 2.1: The total contract price would be US $2,689,021, of which the HPCSS service fee is US $591,514;

Clause 3.1: The [Buyer] is required to deliver an irrevocable sight L/C of 90% of the total contract price (i.e., US $2,420,119) issued by the Industrial and Commercial Bank of China, Inner Mongolian Branch in favor of the [Seller] within three weeks after the execution of the Contract;

Clause 3.2: The remaining 10% of the contract price (i.e., US $268,902) shall be paid against the presence of the original of the commercial invoice of the same amount and the initial inspection report issued by the end-user;

Clause 10.2: The seat of the arbitration is Beijing and the arbitral institution is CIETAC. The Contract shall be governed by the United Nations Convention on Contracts for International Sales of Goods (the 'CISG') made in 1980.

---

[204] Translation taken from CISG Pace.

The [Seller] alleged that the [Buyer] did not issue a L/C of US $2,420,119 in favor of the [Seller] as agreed in the Contract but only delivered a L/C of US $1,887,756.30 on 31 March 2004, and the [Buyer] failed to pay the remaining contract price (i.e., US $532,362.60) to the [Seller] by L/C or by other ways.

After its receipt of the L/C, the [Seller], still placing trust in the [Buyer], delivered the equipment for the [Buyer] on 30 April 2004 and performed the installation and test obligation according to the Contract even though it was negotiating with the [Buyer] on the amount of the L/C.

The project passed the initial inspection of the Inner Mongolian Company as the end-user and the original of the inspection report was issued to the [Seller] on 2 February 2005. It indicated the complete performance of the [Seller]'s obligations under the Contract. However, the [Buyer] only paid US $209,750.70 (i.e., the remaining 10% of the contract price other than the HPCSS service fees) to the [Seller].

Due to the [Buyer]'s breach of the Contract, the [Seller] requested the Inner Mongolian Company to pay the HPCSS service fees directly to it. The [Buyer] agreed to this and made the same request to the end-user. The Inner Mongolian Company paid RMB 479,912.24 (which equals US $59,151.40) to the [Seller]. To date, although the [Seller] has several times demanded that the [Buyer] make the remaining payment, the [Buyer] has still failed to pay to the [Seller] the remaining contract price which equals US $532,362.60.

As a matter of fact, the [Buyer] has asked the end-user to pay on 8 May 2005, 15 March 2005 and 21 July 2005, respectively, and the Inner Mongolian Company has agreed to pay and made the payment to the [Buyer]; however, the [Buyer] did not pay the outstanding contract price to the [Seller], which impaired the lawful interest of the [Seller].

[...]

The [Buyer] orally replied to the [Seller]'s allegations as follows:

Although the [Buyer] entered into the Contract as a purchaser, the [Buyer] was doing so as an agent of the end-user (i.e., the Inner Mongolian Company). The [Buyer] and the Inner Mongolian Company had entered into an Agency Agreement for Foreign Trade before the execution of the Contract. The Inner Mongolian Company had paid the [Buyer] the amount under the Contract; however, as there were other amounts unsettled between the [Buyer] and the Inner Mongolian Company, the [Buyer] refused to pay the price under the Contract to the [Seller].

The [Buyer] alleged that it has signed an Assignment Agreement with the Inner Mongolian Company and the Inner Mongolian Shengkaiyuan Decoration Company (the 'Decoration Company') on 23 February 2005 under which the Decoration Company agrees to assign the debt owing to it by the Chifeng Branch Company of the China Netcome Inner Mongolian Communication Company to the Inner Mongolian Company. Both the [Buyer] and the Decoration Company had notified the Inner Mongolian Company on 28 August 2006 of their agreement to its payment of the unsettled amount under the Contract to the [Seller] at any time.

Based on the above, the [Buyer] alleged that it was the Inner Mongolian Company but not the [Buyer] who should be responsible for paying the outstanding amount under the Contract, which was evidenced by the fact that the Inner Mongolian Company paid the 10% of the contract price directly to the [Seller].

In addition, the [Buyer] alleged that the outstanding amount claimed by the [Seller] was service fees the settlement of which was subject to a separate payment term and was not included in the total price of the Contract.

[...]

II. THE ARBITRATION TRIBUNAL'S OPINION

[...]

3. The [Seller]'s claims

(1) The outstanding amount of US $ 532,362.60 as claimed by the [Seller]

The Arbitration Tribunal notes that the [Buyer] has no objection to the allegation that the [Seller] had performed its obligations under the Contract and the [Seller] admits the fact that the [Buyer] has paid the contract price other than 90% of the HPCSS service fees under the Contract; and both parties confirmed at the court session that the amount of US $532,362.60 as claimed by the [Seller] was equal to 90% of the total amount of the service fees (i.e., US $591,514) under the Clause 2.1 of the Contract.

The Arbitration Tribunal also notes that the [Buyer] confirmed that the end-user, namely, the Inner Mongolian Company, had paid to it the contract price of US $532,362.60 already; however, the [Buyer] refused to pay the [Seller] for the excuse that the Inner Mongolian Company owed money to it under other transactions and the [Buyer] had signed an Assignment Agreement with the Inner Mongolian Company under which it assigned the debt owing to it by the China Netcome Inner Mongolian Communication Company to the Inner Mongolian Company in exchange for its agreement to pay the [Seller] the outstanding amount under the Contract. The [Seller] considered that the dispute between the [Buyer] and the Inner Mongolian Company under other transactions had no relation to this case and the amount owing to the [Buyer] by the Inner Mongolian Company was not the contract price in this case. The Assignment Agreement had no relation to this case and the [Seller] had no knowledge about this agreement. Therefore, the [Buyer]'s defenses for its non-payment were not substantiated.

After deliberation, the Arbitration Tribunal finds that the [Seller] has completely performed its obligations under the Contract and according to Article 53 of the CISG, the buyer must pay the price for the goods and take delivery of them as required by the contract and this Convention. Therefore, the [Buyer] shall pay the contract price according to terms of the Contract.

In addition, the Arbitration Tribunal notes that the [Buyer] alleged that according to the Agency Agreement for Foreign Trade in relation to the Phase III of the Project to Adjust the BOSS of China Mobile Company in Inner Mongolia, the Inner Mongolian Company should pay the [Seller] directly. The Arbitration Tribunal finds that this agency agreement has no relation with this case and it does not amend the provisions of the Contract on the rights and obligations of the [Seller] and the [Buyer]. The Inner Mongolian Company has transferred RMB 479,566.56 to ___ Technology (China) Company Ltd. on 23 August 2005, which as alleged by the [Buyer], indicated that the Inner Mongolian Company had become the person to pay under the Contract, the currency under the Contract had been changed to RMB from US dollars and the payee had been changed to ___ Technology (China) Company Ltd.

The [Seller] alleged that the ___ Technology (China) Company Ltd. was its subsidiary company and the [Seller]'s agreement to the Inner Mongolian Company's payment in RMB to its subsidiary in China was for obtaining the payment as soon as possible. This was the only payment made in this way and had been agreed by the [Buyer] in advance.

The Arbitration Tribunal finds that as the [Seller] submitted its written authorization to its subsidiary company and the all the parties agreed to do so, such change in payment method did not change the provisions of the Contract and the [Seller] and the [Buyer] shall continue to perform pursuant to provisions of the Contract and the [Buyer] shall pay the [Seller].

Based on the above, the Arbitration Tribunal does not support the [Buyer]'s refusal to pay the remaining part of the contract price of US $532,362.60 for the excuse that it had disputes with the Inner Mongolian Company under other transactions.

In addition, during the arbitration, the [Buyer] confirmed that it had the obligation to pay the contract price under the Contract to the [Seller] and it had received the payment of such price of US $532,362.60 from the end-user.

According to the above, the Arbitration Tribunal holds that the [Buyer] shall pay the unpaid amount of US $532,362.60 to the [Seller].

[...]

Question

Q 53-3

(a)   According to the above case (C 53-1), should account be taken of any other agreements when determining the buyer's obligations?
(b)   Why do you think this is the case?

III. Currency of Payment

A. Under the CISG

The CISG provides no explicit rule on the currency for payment. For its determination, the general rules apply: the parties may choose the currency in which the price is to be paid (Article 6). In the absence of such an agreement, whether the parties have established any practices between themselves in this respect, agreed on any usages (Article 9(1)) or are otherwise bound by international commercial usages (Article 9(2)) must be examined. If neither an agreement, nor any practices or usages to which the parties are bound exist, Article 7(2) CISG applies.

B. Comparison with Other Legal Provisions

Art 6.1.9(1) PICC 2010:

> If a monetary obligation is expressed in a currency other than that of the place for payment, it may be paid by the obligor in the currency of the place for payment unless:
>
> (a) that currency is not freely convertible; or
> (b) the parties have agreed that payment should be made only in the currency in which the monetary obligation is expressed. (2)–(4) ...

Art 6.1.10 PICC 2010:

> Where a monetary obligation is not expressed in a particular currency, payment must be made in the currency of the place where payment is to be made.

Question

Q 53-4

(a) Explain how the currency in which the price has to be paid is determined under the CISG.
(b) If the currency is to be determined according to Article 7(2) CISG, it is disputed whether the currency issue is to be resolved according to the general principles of the CISG or under the law applicable through the rules of private international law. Are there any provisions of the CISG which might establish a general principle as to the currency in which payment is to be made?
(c) How does the PICC 2010 answer the question of the currency in which payment is to be made?
(d) Why does it not seem advisable to derive a general principle from Articles 31(c), 57(1)(a) CISG with a view to determining the applicable currency rate? Consider their importance from a practical point of view.

Article 54 CISG

The buyer's obligation to pay the price includes taking such steps and complying with such formalities as may be required under the contract or any laws and regulations to enable payment to be made.

I. Overview

Article 54 CISG extends the buyer's duties by requiring it to comply with any formalities that may be necessary to enable payment to be made. It governs the actions preparatory to payment of the price specified in the contract or in any applicable laws and regulations. For example, the buyer must comply with any exchange, transfer and clearing provisions, or request any administrative authorisation required for a transfer of funds. The most common cases include the issuance of a guarantee or a letter of credit.

The goal of Article 54 CISG is twofold: first, and unless otherwise specified in the contract, it transfers fulfilment of payment formalities to the buyer, who must also bear the associated costs. Secondly, it clarifies that the steps that the buyer has to take are obligations, violation of which entitles the seller to resort to the remedies specified in Article 61 *et seq* CISG.

II. *'Obligation de moyen'* or *'obligation de résultat'*?

The question arises as to whether Article 54 CISG only obliges the buyer to carry out such steps as are necessary for the accomplishment of preparatory actions, but without making it responsible for any failure to make effective payment or to comply with any formalities necessary for payment to be made (*obligation de moyen*), or whether the buyer is held liable if the result, that is, effective payment or compliance with corresponding formalities, is not achieved (*obligation de résultat*). In other words, will the buyer be deemed in breach of its obligations if it does not, for example, deliver the letter of credit opened on behalf of the seller (*obligation de résultat*), or is it sufficient if the buyer has lined up payment, even if—for whatever reasonpayment cannot be made effectively (*obligation de moyen*)? See C 54-1 below in relation to this problem.

C 54-1

Downs Investments Pty Ltd v Perjawa Steel SDN BHD,
Supreme Court of Queensland (Australia), 17 November 2000,
CISG-online 587/859

[Facts][205]

An Australian seller and a Malaysian buyer concluded a contract for the sale of approximately 30,000 metric tonnes plus/minus 10% of scrap steel at the price of $164 per metric tonne C.N. F.F.O. Kemaman Malaysia. According to the written contract between the parties, shipment was to be made from any Australian port during July 1996 and payment was to be made by irrevocable letter of credit. As of July 1996, the buyer indicated that it would not issue the letter of credit. At this time, the seller had already agreed to charge a vessel. On 8 August, the seller asked the buyer to confirm by noon on 9 August as to whether it was prepared to honour the contract in question. As the buyer was not able to give its answer before the executive committee meeting, the seller terminated the contract on that same day.

[Judgment]

[...]

Article 54 of the Convention provides—'The buyer's obligation to pay the price includes taking such steps and complying with such formalities as may be required under the contract or any laws and regulations to enable payment to be made.' Failure to establish a letter of credit in the circumstances of this case was a failure by [buyer] to meet its 'obligation to pay the price' of the goods under the contract of sale. ... In my view the refusal by [buyer] to establish the letter of credit at a time when the 'Dooyang Winner' was standing by at Bells Bay in Tasmania to commence loading the scrap steel so that it might complete its loading programme either as advised on 18 July 1996 or as subsequently advised on 31 July 1996 was a clear breach by [buyer] of an essential term of the contract as varied. The excuse advanced on behalf of [buyer] for failing to meet its contractual obligation to supply the letter of credit, as it had promised to do on 22 July 1996, that a change of management structure in [buyer] required that an executive management committee approve the issue of letter of credit and that that committee refused to do so, in my view, is at law no excuse at all. Obviously [buyer], whatever changes were made in its management structure or internal arrangements for meeting its financial obligations whilst bound by the contract it had made with [seller] through its authorised officers, was obliged to perform its contractual obligation to procure the issue of a letter of credit as its former authorised officer had undertaken to do. ... I have already indicated that Datuk Abu told Mr Teo on the evening of 2 August 1996 that one of the committee members had objected to the contract because it had not been 'formalised' during the tenure of office of the current management committee. It is possible, if indeed not likely, that members of the committee in declining to meet the contractual obligations of [buyer] to provide the letter of credit to meet the cost of the scrap steel that was awaiting shipment to Kemaman from Australia were conscious of the fact that the contract price for that scrap steel was US $705,000.00 in excess of its then current market value. Was [seller] entitled to end the contract with [buyer] and recover damages on the ground of [buyer's] repudiation and/or non-compliance with an essential term of the contract?

---

[205] Summary of facts taken from UNILEX.

Whatever may be the explanation for the avowal of Mr Yunus that he had no knowledge of the contract between [buyer] and [seller] there is no doubt that on 24 July 1996 Mr Teo advised him of its existence. On 26 July 1996 Mr Teo handed to Mr Yunus copies of all documents, purchase orders, etc relating to that contract. He was then also advised that the shipment of the scrap steel the subject of the contract 'was so to speak actually on the way'. Thereafter in my view the evidence indicates a simple procrastination on the part of [buyer] to meet its contractual obligation. There is nothing in the evidence to suggest that the appropriate arrangements for the issue of the letter of credit could not have been made within a day or so. Indeed, Rohani Basir had undertaken to do that 'once you have confirmed the vessel of this contract'. In my view the most likely explanation for the refusal of [buyer] to issue the letter of credit without delay was the resolution of the executive committee on 2 August 1996 that the management be authorised 'to renegotiate and recommend appropriate action in relation to the supply of scrap' by [seller]. In my view [buyer] by the officers who succeeded Rohani Basir and Wan Ghani in its management clearly evinced an intention not to meet [buyer's] contractual obligation. It is clear when one reads the 'PAYMENT' clause and the letter from [seller] to [buyer] of 18 July 1996 that the provision of the letter of credit prior to the commencement of loading of the shipment to [buyer] of scrap metal was an essential term of contract. ... On 5 August 1996 the solicitors for [seller] in Malaysia sent a letter to [buyer] complaining of its failure to establish a letter of credit as requested—as it had undertaken to do on 22 July 1996. It advised that the vessel chartered by [seller] would commence to load the scrap steel under its contract with [buyer] on 8 August 1996. It requested that the letter of credit be established by close of business on 7 August 1996. It advised that should [buyer] fail to establish a letter of credit by that date then [seller] would treat [buyer] as having repudiated the agreement and would then take steps to dispose of the scrap steel, cancel the vessel charter if possible and then seek to recover damages from [buyer]. At the same time [seller] commenced to make inquiries about other possible purchasers of the scrap steel that was it was holding to fulfil its contract with [buyer]. On 7 August 1996 [buyer's] legal representatives replied to the letter of 5 August 1996 advising that [buyer's] new management was 'still studying this matter'. On 8 August 1996 [seller's] legal representatives asked [buyer's] legal representatives 'to revert by 12 noon of Friday, the 9th August 1996 as to whether your clients are prepared to honour the contract in question'. [Buyer's] lawyers immediately responded 'unfortunately we are unable to obtain any positive instructions from the defendant Steel SDN BHD [buyer] within this short time. We understand that the Board is meeting some time later this month. In the circumstances we will regret that we are unable to provide any repose to your query either way'. Upon receipt of this correspondence [seller's] legal representatives replied purporting to accept [buyer's] repudiation of its contractual obligations and terminated the contract. In my judgment [seller] was entitled to avoid the contract and to recover the loss it suffered as a consequence of [buyer's] repudiation and/or non-compliance with an essential term of its contract with [seller].

[...]

Questions

Q 54-1

Explain the purpose and scope of Article 54 CISG.

Q 54-2

If the contract provides, for example, for the opening of a letter of credit and the buyer does not comply with its duty, what are the seller's remedies?

Q 54-3

(a)   Is the buyer's duty to take the steps necessary to enable the seller to be paid an *obligation de résultat* or an *obligation de moyen*?
(b)   What was the position of the Supreme Court of Queensland (C 54-1)?

Article 55 CISG

Where a contract has been validly concluded but does not expressly or implicitly fix or make provision for determining the price, the parties are considered, in the absence of any indication to the contrary, to have impliedly made reference to the price generally charged at the time of the conclusion of the contract for such goods sold under comparable circumstances in the trade concerned.

I. Overview

Article 55 CISG embodies the subsidiary rule that, where a determined or determinable purchase price of the goods is lacking, the purchase price is deemed to be the market price at the time of the conclusion of the contract. Right from the very beginning of the unification process in sales law, the issue of an undetermined purchase price was highly disputed. There are disparities in the various legal systems: while some require at least a determinable market price, others are less strict. A very flexible solution embodied in Article 57 ULIS, according to which the buyer, in the absence of an agreement on the price, had to pay the price that the seller usually charged at the time of the conclusion of the contract, was modified at the Drafting Conference to the CISG. Contrary to ULIS, Article 14 CISG requires an express or, at least, implicit provision of the purchase price.

II. Interaction between Articles 14 and 55 CISG

The interplay between Articles 14 and 55 CISG has been extensively discussed in literature. The difficulties allegedly arising from the discrepancy between Articles 14 and 55 CISG seem to have been quite exaggerated. In case law, at least, the contradictory co-existence of both provisions does not cause any particular problems. Instead, it is consistently pointed out that one must refer, first and foremost, to the intention of the parties (Art 14(1)). Where an agreement on the purchase price is lacking but the buyer accepts the goods without objecting to any price indicated by the seller, the buyer will be deemed to have consented to that price. Article 55 CISG does not, therefore, enable the court or tribunal to establish a price where it has already been determined, or made determinable, by the contracting parties, nor does it authorise the judicial panel to establish a price according to Article 55 if the circumstances do not show that the parties had any intention to be contractually bound.

III. Comparison with Other Legal Provisions

Art 57 ULIS:

> Where a contract has been concluded but does not state a price or make provision for the determination of the price, the buyer shall be bound to pay the price generally charged by the seller at the time of the conclusion of the contract.

Art 5.1.7(1) PICC 2010:

> Where a contract does not fix or make provision for determining the price, the parties are considered, in the absence of any indication to the contrary, to have made reference to the price generally charged at the time of the conclusion of the contract for such performance in comparable circumstances in the trade concerned or, if no such price is available, to a reasonable price.

§ 2-305(1) UCC:

> The parties if they so intend can conclude a contract for sale even though the price is not settled. In such a case the price is a reasonable price at the time for delivery if
>
> (a) nothing is said as to price; or
> (b) the price is left to be agreed by the parties and they fail to agree; or
> (c) the price is to be fixed in terms of some agreed market or other standard as set or recorded by a third person or agency and it is not so set or recorded.

Art 1591 CC:[206]

> The price of a sale must be determined and stated by the parties.

Art 1474 Codice Civile:[207]

> (1) If the contract refers to goods which the seller regularly sells, and if the parties have neither determined the price nor the method of its determination, and if it [the price] is not fixed by official decree (Art 1339) or corporative standards, it is presumed that the parties intended to refer to the price usually charged by the seller.

---

[206] Translation taken from www.legifrance.gouv.fr.
[207] Author's translation.

(2)   If goods with a stock exchange or market price are involved [...], the price is the price of the lists or market reports of the place where delivery is to take place, or of those [lists or market reports] of the nearest place with a stock exchange or market.

C 55-1

Supreme Court of the Czech Republic,
25 June 2008,
CISG-online 1848[208]

RESOLUTION

[...]

The [Seller]'s extraordinary appeal is dismissed.

[...]

REASONS FOR THE DECISION

[...]

[Ruling of the Supreme Court]

[...]

Although the [Seller] has not raised an issue of fundamental legal importance that would supersede the case law, [Seller]'s objections are directed to the fact that the lower courts determined the conclusion of the purchase agreement to be in contrariety with substantive law (the CISG).

According to Article 18(2) of the CISG:

'An acceptance of an offer becomes effective at the moment the indication of assent reaches the offeror. An acceptance is not effective if the indication of assent does not reach the offeror within the time he has fixed or, if no time is fixed, within a reasonable time, due account being taken of the circumstances of the transaction, including the rapidity of the means of communication employed by the offeror. An oral offer must be accepted immediately unless the circumstances indicate otherwise.'

According to Section (3) of this Article:

'However, if, by virtue of the offer or as a result of practices which the parties have established between themselves or of usage, the offeree may indicate assent by performing an act, such as one relating to the dispatch of the goods or payment of the price, without notice to the offeror, the acceptance is effective at the moment the act is performed, provided that the act is performed within the period of time laid down in the preceding paragraph.'

---

[208] Translation taken from CISG Pace.

In Article 55 of CISG it is stated that:

'Where a contract has been validly concluded but does not expressly or implicitly fix or make provision for determining the price, the parties are considered, in the absence of any indication to the contrary, to have impliedly made reference to the price generally charged at the time of the conclusion of the contract for such goods sold under comparable circumstances in the trade concerned.'

From the cited provision of the CISG, it follows that Article 55 concerning the purchase price is applicable only on the condition that the agreement has been validly concluded. Therefore, it is first necessary to assess from the legal point of view whether there was a purchase agreement, i.e., whether such an agreement has been concluded and whether it is valid. In this regard, it was necessary to apply in the given case not only Article 18, Section (2) but also Section (3) of this Article concerning acceptance of an offer by performing an act (sending of goods, payment of purchase price, etc.). In such a case, it is necessary to examine practices established between the parties, namely their usages, ensuing from business so far undertaken between them including subsequent conduct of the parties after submitting the order (namely after the conclusion of agreement). In this sense, it was also necessary to take into consideration [Seller]'s document dated 9 May 1993, by which the acceptance of an order no. 93/1/0754 dated 4 May 1993 (in file under no. 1.75) was made, and the further document dated 14 May 1993 requesting 'the change of paint WG 24-9100 wrapping' (in file under no. 1.122) and [Seller]'s subsequent letter (in file under no. 1.123).

If, on the basis of evidence considered, the Appellate Court has come to the conclusion that the agreement has not been concluded, such a legal consideration cannot be challenged as flawed because the reasoning does not contradict substantive law, i.e., Article 18 of the CISG. The [Seller] has objected to the ruling of the Appellate Court (as well as the ruling of the Court of First Instance) alleging that they have failed to properly consider relevant evidence and contends that the proceedings suffered from flaws that could have caused an incorrect legal consideration of the matter in the sense of Article 241a, Section 2, letter a) of the ACP. That is, however, without any legal meaning with regard to solving the issue of admissibility of the extraordinary appeal pursuant to Article 237, Section 1, letter c) of the ACP.

[...]

C 55-2

Tribunal cantonal Valais (Switzerland), 27 April 2007, CISG-online 1721[209]

[...]

I. Ruling on the facts

1. a) [Seller]'s business consists of manufacturing, repairing, acquiring and selling kitchen equipment.

---

[209] Translation taken from CISG Pace database (footnotes omitted).

[Buyer] manages Public Utility E in ___. F presides over the board of directors of the company as sole signatory. Mrs. F also manages the company Hotel G, which operates a hotel of the same name. Mrs. F's husband, H, is the manager of this hotel. At the time in which the facts of this case are placed, Mr. H was also the commercial manager of Public Utility E. He was authorized to give orders to the personnel of both companies. Between 2001 and 2003, I worked as executive chef in Hotel G. He was, among other things, responsible for the facilities, the materials and the purchases for the kitchen of Public Utility E.

At a time not documented in the records of this case, but in any case prior to March 2002, [Seller] maintained contractual relations with Hotel G, and even with [Buyer]. On the occasion of works having been carried out at the Hotel G, Executive Chef I had, in particular, invited [Seller] to make offers regarding kitchen equipment. Hotel G accepted these offers by returning them to the offeror, signed and stamped by the company. The price of the material delivered by [Seller] amounted to about 60,000 to 80,000 Sf.

b) On Friday, 8 March 2002, the oven in the kitchen of Public Utility E had a breakdown. In the afternoon, Executive Chef I asked [Seller] to repair the defective equipment or to replace it. This was one day before the weekend, in the middle of the high season; urgent action was required. Under circumstances not documented in the records of the case, Executive Chef I rejected the repair of the oven. K, representative of [Seller], contacted its oven supplier, Company L in ___. Talking to the sales manager M, K indicated the reasons why it was necessary to deliver a replacement oven to Switzerland the next day (M, file 4, p. 166: '... I remember that the oven of the end customer did not work anymore and that it had to be replaced urgently.'). Company L only had one oven available, displayed in its exhibition hall. K proposed this oven—of the brand and type Lainox ME 110 P, to Executive Chef I. As the person responsible for the kitchen facilities at Public Utility E, after consulting with Mr. H, the manager of Hotel G—who authorized him to proceed—Executive Chef I accepted K's proposal.

On Saturday, 9 March 2002, at 7 h 50, [Seller]'s representative K took possession of the oven in dispute from Manufacturer L. The manufacturer handed out the transport document. It specified that the article had been sold (document 5, p. 17: '*causale del trasporto: Vendita*' ['reason for transportation: Sold'). Afterwards, K headed to Public Utility E. There, K discovered that, due to its volume, the equipment could not fit through the kitchen door. The parties agreed to postpone the installation. In the meanwhile, Executive Chef I placed the oven in the localities of Hotel G. The day before Easter—31 March 2002—the employees of that company broke the embrasure of the kitchen door at Public Utility E and could thus install the oven. During transport they damaged the handle bar of the oven. A few days later, [Seller]'s representative K repaired the oven and put it into operation.

For about 15 to 30 days the oven worked well. Then, the users were confronted with a breakdown caused by the relay. [Buyer] asked [Seller] to repair the defect; the technician proceeded with the repair. Thereafter, Executive Chef I 'finished the season' without being aware of any further breakdowns.

[...]

e) It has to be determined, on the basis of the circumstances of the case, whether the parties agreed to a complimentary concession, from [Seller] to [Buyer], of the right to use the oven or rather to a transfer of the property in the oven against payment. The following indicators (aa to ee) are sufficient to convince the court that [Seller] intended to obtain payment for the oven Lainox ME 110P, against title to the oven, and that this intention was well understood by [Buyer]. The common and real intention of the parties can therefore be inferred from the facts of the case.

[...]

ee) The behavior of the parties, after 8 March 2002, also helps the court to reveal their intentions.

[Seller] paid the transport costs and custom duties. [Buyer] never offered to reimburse [Seller] for these costs. [Buyer] neither alleged nor, *a fortiori*, established the existence of any agreement to that effect. If the parties had agreed on a rental, [Buyer] would have had to bear these costs (cf., with regards to national law, Higi, Commentaire zurichois, at Art 305 CO, para. 92). In the following, [Buyer] did not restitute the oven at the place where it was at the moment of the contract conclusion, although for rental contracts, if the parties did not specify anything, the obligation of restitution is a *dette portable* (Higi, at Art 305 CO, para. 48 et seq.).

II. Ruling on the law

[...]

4. [Seller] requests payment of 10,151.20 Sf. [Buyer], by way of pleading in the alternative, relies on the provisions on non-conforming goods.

a) Art 53 CISG provides that the buyer must pay the price for the goods and take delivery of them as required by the contract and the CISG. The CISG comprises the rule of concurrent performance (*'trait pour trait'*) (*Venturi* Commentaire romand, para. 63 at Art 184 CO, cf. also *Neumayer/Ming*, para. 2 at Art 58 CISG). Subject to a contrary provision, payment therefore has to be made at the time when the goods are made available to the buyer (Art 58(1) CISG). If the buyer passes an order of generic goods which he never acquired before and without any reference to a price, for example in case of urgency, this order constitutes an invitation to bid and the seller makes an offer to contract by delivering the goods: the buyer then accepts this offer by accepting the delivered goods, by using them or by reselling them. If the seller does not indicate the price of the delivered goods, the price is deemed to be the price currently practiced for such goods: the buyer thus bears the risk to pay more than foreseen if he accepts the delivered goods (*Neumayer/Ming*, para. 9 at Art 14 CISG). Furthermore, a sales contract can be validly concluded without any reference to the price (express or implicit) by the parties; the price is then objectively determined by reference to a medium price: this is the price generally charged at the time of the conclusion of the contract for such goods sold under comparable circumstances in the country of the seller. This provision protects the buyer from paying too much; and it does not permit the buyer to benefit from a very advantageous price (*Neumayer/Ming*, para. 2 at Art 55 CISG; cf. *Brunner*, para. 3 at Art 55 CISG; Venturi, para. 64 at Art 184 CO).

The CISG does not contain any provision concerning the currency or the statutory means of payment. In the absence of contractual conditions specifying the currency of the payment, it is determined by the national law, designated by the rules of conflict of laws (RVJ 2006 p. 188 consid. 6a; RVJ 1999, p. 227 consid. 3c; *Neumayer/Ming*, op. cit., para. 4 at Art 54 CISG).

[...]

Questions

Q 55-1

(a)   Under what circumstances does Article 55 CISG apply?
(b)   According to the Czech Supreme Court case (C 55-1), what is the pre-requisite for Article 55?
(c)   What does the Swiss case (C 55-2) say about the risk allocation under Article 55 CISG?

Q 55-2

(a)   Divide the corresponding provisions from the other legal systems into two groups: a liberal group which allows for a contract where the contract price has not been determined, and a group representing a narrower interpretation.
(b)   Where, on a scale of very strict to flexible provisions, would you place Article 55 CISG?

Q 55-3

(a)   Sometimes, courts or tribunals try to determine a missing price with a view to 'saving' the contract or rendering it effective. Under what circumstances will there definitely be no contract under the CISG, notwithstanding Article 55?
(b)   In which of the provisions from other legal systems referred to above is this legal position made particularly clear?

Q 55-4

(a)   How is the missing contract price to be determined under Article 55 CISG?
(b)   To what do the other legal provisions refer?
(c)   On the determination of the sales price, see, in particular, Article 57 ULIS. What changes have been made in Article 55 CISG? Is there another domestic sales law provision providing for a similar solution to Article 57 ULIS? Is there still a difference between Article 57 ULIS and that other domestic rule?
(d)   Do you regard Article 55 CISG as giving clear instructions on how to establish the missing purchase price? See Article 5.1.7 PICC 2010.

Article 56 CISG

If the price is fixed according to the weight of the goods, in case of doubt it is to be determined by the net weight.

I. Overview

This article constitutes a rule of interpretation for determining the contract price. 'Net weight' means the total weight less the weight of packaging. The provision seldom causes difficulties. The rule is subsidiary; the parties' intent (Art 6); practices which the parties have established between themselves; usages to which they have agreed (Art 9(1)); and commercial usages (Art 9(2)) prevail.

II. Comparison with Other Legal Provisions

§ 380 HGB:[210]

(1) If the purchase price is to be calculated according to the weight of the goods, the weight of packaging (weight of tare) is to be subtracted, subject to the terms of the contract or the trade usage at the place where the seller must perform.

(2) Whether and, if so, in which amount the weight of tare is to be subtracted according to a certain measure or percentage rather than according to exact calculation as well as whether and, if so, how much is to be calculated for the buyer's benefit or can be claimed as compensation for defective or useless pieces ... is subject to the contract or the trade usage at the place where the seller must perform.

---

[210] Author's translation.

Art 212 OR:[211]

(1)   [...]
(2)   If the purchase price is to be calculated according to the weight of the goods, the weight of packing (weight of tare) is to be subtracted.
(3)   A reservation is made for particular commercial usages with regard to certain trade products providing for a deduction of a fixed sum or a sum calculated as a percentage of the total weight or providing for charging the total weight in the calculation of the price.

Questions

Q 56-1

What is the purpose of Article 56 CISG?

Q 56-2

To what extent is the rule stated in Article 56 CISG subsidiary?

Q 56-3

Compare Article 56 CISG to the other legal provisions set out above.

(a)   Does Article 56 CISG reflect a rule generally acknowledged in commercial trade?
(b)   What is the reason underlying Article 56 CISG?

---

[211] Author's translation.

Article 57 CISG

(1) If the buyer is not bound to pay the price at any other particular place, he must pay it to the seller:
   (a) at the seller's place of business; or
   (b) if the payment is to be made against the handing over of the goods or of documents, at the place where the handing over takes place.
(2) The seller must bear any increase in the expenses incidental to payment which is caused by a change in his place of business subsequent to the conclusion of the contract.

I. Overview

In international trade, it is vital that the place of payment is well-defined. Therefore, Article 57 CISG lays down a threefold rule. In the first instance, the place of payment must comply with the parties' agreement (Art 6) or with any practices or usages to which they are bound (Art 9). If no such agreement, practices or usages exist and the contract has to be performed concurrently, payment is to be made at the place where the handing over of the goods takes place (Art 57(1)(b)). Only if one of the parties has to perform in advance does the rule of Art 57(1)(a), according to which payment is to be made at the seller's place of business, apply.

Article 57(2) CISG anticipates the possibility that the seller might change its place of business following the conclusion of the contract, and it imposes on the seller any increase in the expenses incidental to payment that are caused by such a change.

II. Article 57(1)(a) CISG

The subsidiary rule in Article 57(1)(a) CISG applies where the contract is not performed concurrently. It governs, for example, the situation where the seller dispatches the goods together with the bill, or where it waives its right of retention referred to in Article 58(2) CISG.

Article 57(1)(a) makes it clear that payment should be made at the creditor's domicile. The buyer bears the risk of loss or delay of payment.

III. Article 57(1)(b) CISG

Article 57(1)(b) CISG states that payment is to be made at the place where the goods are handed over. Since Article 58(1) lays down the principle that payment is to be made at the time delivery of the goods is made, if the parties agree on the place of delivery, they have, at the same time, made an agreement on where payment is to be made (see Art 58 CISG below). The same applies where the contract involves carriage of the goods and the seller dispatches them on terms whereby the goods, or documents controlling their disposition, will not be handed over except against payment (Art 58(2) CISG).

The documents that fall within the scope of Article 57(1)(b) CISG are disputed. Certainly, a bill of lading and a warehouse receipt are such documents; they are genuine documents of title to goods, and their delivery replaces the delivery of the goods. There are, however, further documents in international trade that, without being documents of title to goods, are utilised to effect delivery of the goods, for example, delivery orders, delivery warrants, bills of delivery (for example Art 4 *et seq.* Montreal Convention)[212], or a consignment note according to Article 4 *et seq.* CMR;[213] Article 12 *et seq.* CIM;[214] or Article 5 *et seq.* Warsaw Convention.[215]

Therefore, Article 57(1)(b) applies to all documents that are delivered in fulfilment of the seller's obligation (Arts 30, 34 CISG). These include all documents which enable the buyer exclusive access to the goods to the exclusion of the seller.

IV. Article 57(1) CISG as a General Principle
Valid for Other Monetary Claims

The CISG contains no explicit rule on where sums other than the purchase price are to be paid. There is a dispute in case law as to whether Article 57(1) CISG establishes, beyond payment of the price at the seller's place of performance, a general principle for other monetary obligations emerging from the contract of sale, such as compensation for breach of contract, or refund of the sales price following avoidance of the contract. See, in this respect, the following case abstract.

---

[212] Convention for the Unification of Certain Rules for International Carriage by Air (Montreal Convention).

[213] Convention on the Contract for the International Carriage of Goods by Road (CMR).

[214] Uniform Rules concerning the Contract for International Carriage of Goods by Rail (CIM).

[215] Convention for the Unification of Certain Rules Relating to International Carriage by Air (Warsaw Convention).

C 57-1

Cour d'Appel de Grenoble (France),
23 October 1996,
CISG-online 305

[Facts][216]

A French buyer and a German seller concluded a contract for the sale of industrial equipment. After delivery of the goods, the buyer commenced an action against the seller claiming restitution of a part of the purchase price paid in excess. The seller objected on the ground that the French Court had no jurisdiction to hear the case.

[Judgment][217]

[...] Considering [...] that [seller] wrote in its conclusions that the [buyer]'s claim is a payment claim after all in dispute; that the eventual obligation for payment is performed at the place of the debtor; ... [t]hat the Vienna Convention on Contracts for the International Sale of Goods of 11 April 1980, by its article 1(1)(b), governs the contract, ... [t]hat, contrary to French and German law, the Vienna Convention determines the place of payment of the price at seller's premises (article 57(1)); That the usual interpretation of this rule is that it expresses the general principle that payment is fulfilled at the place of business of the creditor ..., extended to other international commercial contracts in article 6.1.6 of the Unidroit Principles of International Commercial Contracts: 'If the place of performance is neither fixed by, nor determinable from, the contract, a party is to perform ... a monetary obligation, at the obligee's place of business ...' That [buyer's] action aims to hold the restitution of an overpayment; that it is constant between the parties that it is a demand for payment; that the place of fulfillment of the obligation in dispute is the province of the Court of First Instance of Valence where [buyer] is established; that it results from application of article 5(1) of the Brussels Convention that the Court of this place is competent to resolve the motion of [buyer] against [seller].

[...]

V. Means of Payment

The CISG contains no rule on the means of payment. The parties are free to agree on the means of payment (Art 6) or may be bound by practices or usages (Art 9). The drafters' general understanding was of payment in cash, although the transfer of money and other cashless means of payment have almost entirely displaced this understanding. Where the buyer does not pay in cash, payment is deemed to have been made at the time the sum is recorded on the seller's account.

---

[216] Summary of facts taken from UNILEX.
[217] Translation taken from CISG Pace (citations omitted).

VI. Article 57(1) CISG and Determination of Jurisdictional Competence

According to various domestic rules, the place of performance establishes a jurisdictional seat. For example, the European Council Regulation 44/2001 of 22 December 2001 on jurisdiction and the recognition and enforcement of judgments in civil and commercial matters (Brussels Regulation), which entered into force on 1 March 2002 and which replaced the 1968 Brussels Convention, provides an alternative jurisdictional competence at the place of performance of obligations (Art 5(1)). The Brussels Regulation applies whenever the defendant has its place of business in a Member State, regardless of the defendant's nationality. See the discussion under Article 31, section V above.

There are a large number of cases in which Article 57(1) CISG has been held to establish a jurisdictional seat. However, the jurisdictional effect of Article 57(1)(a) CISG has been criticised; the determination of the place of payment should only be relevant for determining who carries the risk of loss or delay of payment. Another critical aspect has been pointed out, namely the instability arising from the fact that the seller's change of place of business may establish a new judicial forum. At the Drafting Conference of the CISG, it was clear that there should be no confusion between substantial and procedural rules: Germany had opted for a clarification that the place of payment does not establish a jurisdictional seat. The proposal was dismissed, arguing that matters of jurisdiction were not within the scope of the CISG. Fortunately, with the entry into force of the Brussels II Convention, the discussion on whether the place of performance and payment should provide a jurisdictional seat has lost much of its significance with regard to sales contracts.

C 57-2

Oberster Gerichtshof (Austria),
3 April 2008,
CISG-online 1680[218]

[...]

[Facts]

The [Seller] claimed for the payment of the purchase price of 32 violins.

The [Seller] alleged that it had delivered 32 violins to Germany to the [Buyer]. The [Buyer] had accepted the instruments in order to resell them on its own behalf and for its own account. The agreed purchase price had been due in partial payments dependent on the progress of the resale. The [Buyer] had failed to pay. The [Seller] claimed that the Court would have jurisdiction according to Article 57 CISG in conjunction with Article 5 Brussels Regulation.

---

[218] Translation taken from the CISG Pace database.

The [Buyer] alleged inter alia that the Court would not have jurisdiction over the case.

[...]

Reasoning

[...]

The [Seller] alleges that an Austrian exporter would be allowed to claim for the payment of the purchase price in an Austrian court lacking any contrary agreements according to Article 57(1) CISG. The Convention on Contracts for the International Sale of Goods would represent a uniform substantive law which prevailed in respect to solely procedural provisions.

This allegation has to be commented as follows:

The Supreme Court stated in its judgment 1 Ob 94/04m—which also dealt with facts that had to be assessed according to the CISG—that the very place, where the characteristic performance of a contract has to be effected or should have been effected, is to be considered as being the place of performance from a procedural point of view.

The place where the performance has actually been effected was the decisive criteria for the international (choice of) jurisprudence. It was of particular importance, that the place of performance could be assessed pragmatically according to actual criteria, namely autonomously, and thus not according to legal criteria.

The contrary opinion of some scholars—in particular as far as reference is made to the unclear wording of article 5 No 1b Brussels Regulation—cannot be affirmed, as such an interpretation would constitute a blatant contrast to the intention of the legislator, namely to regulate the place of performance that is decisive in respect to jurisdiction autonomously, i.e. without any reference to substantive national law (compare 4 Ob 147/03a; 7 Ob 112/07g).

There is no reason to deviate from this preceding jurisdiction. The Supreme Court will not comment on recent critical remarks of scholars in respect to distance selling contracts (such as Ferrari, in: ecolex 2007, p. 303), in particular, as the present case does not involve a distance selling contract.

If goods are delivered to the domicile of the buyer according to the contract, a forum actoris arises. This applies as well if the case is regulated by the CISG (Geimer/Schütze, Europäisches Zivilverfahrensrecht 2, Article 5 EuGVVO margin number 87). Article 57(1) CISG cannot be applied in the case of a claim for payment of the purchase price, as the place of delivery is decisive in respect to all obligations under the contract as long as Article 5 No 1b Brussels Regulation is applied (Kropholler, Europäisches Zivilverfahrensrecht 8, Article 5 EuGVVO margin number 49).

As a conclusion to this, the extraordinary appeal of the [Seller] is not justified.

[...]

Question

Q 57-1

What does the above case (C 57-2) say about the interaction between Article 57 CISG and Article 5(1)(b) Brussels Regulation?

VII. Article 57(2) CISG

Article 57(2) CISG imposes any increase in the expenses incidental to payment which is caused by the seller's change of its place of business on the seller. The rule implies that, if the seller changes its place of business after the conclusion of the contract, the buyer must pay the price at the seller's new place. Any increase in expenses caused by this rests on the seller. However, Article 57(2) CISG has no effect on the rule that the buyer bears the risk of loss or delay of payment. For example, the buyer may have to execute payment of the purchase price earlier in order to be on time at the seller's new place of business; but it may then be compensated for any loss of interest (Art 57(2) CISG).

If the seller has assigned the right to receive payment of the purchase price to a third party, the question arises as to whether the place of payment changes from the seller's to the assignee's place of business. See C 57-2, A 57-1.

C 57-3

Oberlandesgericht Celle (Germany),
11 November 1998,
CISG-online 507[219]

[Facts]

A Portuguese seller and a Dutch buyer, defendant, concluded a contract for the sale of concentrated apple juice. The Portuguese seller then assigned his claim by contract to another company (the plaintiff), which started legal action as the defendant failed to pay the purchase price. The defendant intended to set off a claim in action. The latter claims derived from contracts of sale where the Portuguese had been the buyer and two German companies had been the sellers. The German sellers had assigned their claims by contract to the defendant.

[Judgment]

The Court of first instance decided that the defendant had to pay the full purchase price. With respect to the attempted set-off the Court declined jurisdiction.

In confirming the first instance decision, the Court of Appeal stated that the defendant had to pay the full purchase price and could not declare set-off due to the lack of jurisdiction. In order to determine whether it had jurisdiction over the declared set-off, the Court applied Art 5(1) of the EC Convention on Jurisdiction and Enforcement of Judgements in Civil and Commercial Matters (Brussels, 1968). According to this article a person domiciled in a Contracting State (in the case at hand: the plaintiff) may be sued in the court of the place of performance of the obligation in question. In the case at hand the set-off claims originated from the contracts between two German companies (in those contracts: the sellers) and the Portuguese company (in those contracts: the buyer). The Court applied Art 57 CISG to

---

[219] English abstract taken from UNILEX.

determine the place of payment. Originally, the Court had jurisdiction, as the seller's place of business was Germany. But after the German creditors had assigned the claims to the Dutch defendant, the German Court lost jurisdiction. Thus the international jurisdiction was vested in the Dutch Court.

A 57-1

Martin Gebauer, 'Uniform Law, General Principles and Autonomous Interpretation' *Uniform Law Review* 4 (2000) 683, 698 *et seq.*[220]

[...] Was the Celle court right in holding that the place of payment is changed under CISG when the claim for the price is assigned? Such assignment itself is a matter not governed by the Convention and hence is governed by domestic law, to be determined by the private international law rules of the forum. However, the Convention does govern the determination of the place of payment, and as a consequence, the impact of a valid assignment on the place of payment could also fall within its scope. There are three opinions regarding this issue. The first argues that it is governed by domestic law, since assignment and its consequences are matters not governed by the Convention. The second opinion affirms, as did OLG Celle, that in cases of assignment under CISG, the place of payment changes from seller's place of business to that of the assignee. And according to the third opinion, the determination of the place of payment cannot be influenced by an assignment and remains at seller's place of business. The second and third opinions do have one thing in common. They both regard the question implicitly as a matter settled, or at least governed, by CISG. For the first opinion, by contrast, the question is not a matter of interpretation or gap-filling, but of scope of application. Following the first opinion can lead to somewhat strange results. If it is left to domestic law to decide whether the place of payment is situated at the old or new creditor's place of business, it will be impossible to reach a decision if the domestic law situates the place of payment in general at the debtor's place of business. If the original place of payment is governed by the uniform law, it would appear that a coherent solution for the question of a change can only be found within the uniform law. CISG expressly settles a similar situation in Article 57(2)[,] [...] implying that in this case there is a change in the place of payment. It could be argued that Article 57(2) is a specific rule and conclusive in the sense that in all other cases not mentioned by it the place of payment will not change, thus favoring an autonomous interpretation ex contrario. There would however also be good grounds for stating that the issue at stake, i.e. a change in the place of payment caused by an assignment, is not expressly settled by the Convention and as such constitutes a gap in the sense of Article 7(2) CISG—in which case the unsolved question is supposed to be settled if possible by means of an analogical application of specific provisions or by resorting to the general principles on which the Convention is based. As far as application by analogy is concerned, the same Article 57(2) CISG springs to mind, arguing that it makes no difference for the determination of the place of payment whether it is the seller's place of business that is changed, or the person of the creditor. The contrary argument, however, would focus on the differences between the two situations, stating that the incidence of a third person as a creditor not chosen by the debtor is important enough to justify a different solution. In support of this it could also be affirmed that the place of payment is part of the obligation, and that the substance of the obligation cannot be changed by assigning the claim for the price. Supporters of this argument would probably call it a general principle on which the Convention is based. ...

---

[220] Footnotes omitted.

VIII. Comparison with Other Legal Provisions

Art 6.1.6 PICC 2010:

(1) If the place of performance is neither fixed by, nor determinable from, the contract, a party is to perform:
(a) a monetary obligation, at the obligee's place of business;
(b) [...]

§ 2-310 UCC:

Unless otherwise agreed

(a) payment is due at the time and place at which the buyer is to receive the goods even though the place of shipment is the place of delivery; and
(b) [...]
(c) if delivery is authorized and made by way of documents of title otherwise than by subsection (b) then payment is due at the time and place at which the buyer is to receive the documents regardless of where the goods are to be received; and
(d) [...]

§ 270 BGB:[221]

(1) In case of doubt, money must be delivered to the creditor at its domicile at the debtor's risk and expense.
(2) If the obligation accrued at the creditor's business and the creditor's place of business differs from its domicile, the place of business replaces the domicile.
(3) If the creditor's domicile or place of business changes after accruement of the obligation, thereby leading to an increase in costs or risk of delivery, the creditor bears, in the first case, the additional costs, in the second case the risk.
(4) The provisions on place of performance remain unaffected.

Art 1247 CC:[222]

(1) Payment must be made in the place designated by the agreement. Where a place is not designated, payment, if it is for a thing certain and determined, must be made at the place where the thing forming the object of the obligation was at the time of that obligation.
(2) [...]
(3) Apart from those cases, payment must be made at the domicile of the debtor.

---

[221] Author's translation.
[222] Translation taken from www.legifrance.gouv.fr.

Art 1182(3) Codice Civile:[223]

An obligation to pay must be fulfilled at the creditor's domicile at the time the obligation becomes due. If this domicile differs from the one the creditor had at the time of accruement of the obligation and if this impedes fulfilment, the debtor may, subject to prior notice to the creditor, make payment at its own domicile.

Art 74 OR:[224]

(1) The place of performance is determined by the parties' agreement as made expressly or derived from the circumstances.

(2) Absent an agreement to the contrary, the following principles apply:
1. Monetary obligations are to be paid at the place where the creditor has its domicile at the time of performance; 2. [...]

(3) If the creditor changes its domicile at which it can claim performance after accruement of the obligation and if this imposes considerable burden on the debtor, the debtor may perform at the original domicile.

§ 905(2) ABGB:[225]

In case of doubt, the debtor must perform monetary obligations at the creditor's domicile (place of business) at its own risk and expense. If it [the domicile] has changed after accruement of the obligation, the creditor bears the increase in risk and expense resulting therefrom.

Art 160 PRC CL:[226]

The buyer shall pay at the prescribed place. Where the place of payment was not prescribed or clearly prescribed, and cannot be determined in accordance with Article 61 hereof, the buyer shall make payment at the seller's place of business, provided that if the parties agreed that payment shall be conditional upon delivery of the subject matter or the document for taking delivery thereof, payment shall be made at the place where the subject matter, or the document for taking delivery thereof, is delivered.

Questions

Q 57-2

How does the CISG determine the place where payment of the purchase price is to be made?

---

[223] Author's translation.
[224] Author's translation.
[225] Author's translation.
[226] Translation taken from www.novexcn.com/contract_law_99.html.

Q 57-3

(a) To what extent is Article 57 CISG a subsidiary rule? See the corresponding provisions from the other legal systems.

(b) According to the INCOTERM® 'EXW' (Ex Works (insert named place)), the seller delivers when it places the goods at the disposal of the buyer at the seller's premises or another named place (ie works, factory, warehouse, etc). What does that mean in relation to where the buyer has to pay the purchase price?

Q 57-4

(a) How can we distinguish Article 57(1)(a) from Article 57(1)(b) CISG?

(b) Why is Article 57(1)(b) CISG of higher practical importance than Article 57(1)(a)?

Q 57-5

What kind of documents are referred to in Article 57(1)(b) CISG? (See C 58-1).

Q 57-6

(a) Does the CISG address the issue of where monetary obligations other than the purchase price are to be paid?

(b) What possible solutions are there to this question?

(c) Compare Article 57(1) CISG with the corresponding provisions of the PICC 2010, OR, and ABGB. To what extent are they broader than Article 57(1) CISG?

Q 57-7

Compare Article 57(1) CISG with the other legal provisions.

(a) Is it commonly acknowledged that the purchase price is paid at the seller's place of business?

(b) In particular, are there differences between Article 57(1) CISG, on the one hand, and the UCC and the French CC, on the other
  — with regard to the structure of the corresponding provisions?
  — in substance?

Q 57-8

If the seller's place of business changes after the conclusion of the contract, where is payment to be made:

(a) according to Article 57(2) CISG?

(b) according to the corresponding provisions of the BGB, ABGB, Codice Civile, and OR?

(c)   In which cases is the place of payment the creditor's new domicile?
(d)   In all other cases, where is the debtor to make payment? Are there any differences between the various provisions?

Q 57-9

What happens if there is not only a change in the seller's place of business, but a change in the person of the creditor itself?

(a)   What did the court in C 57-2 decide?
(b)   What other possibilities are there, according to A 57-1?

Article 58 CISG

(1) If the buyer is not bound to pay the price at any other specific time, he must pay it when the seller places either the goods or documents controlling their disposition at the buyer's disposal in accordance with the contract and this Convention. The seller may make such payment a condition for handing over the goods or documents.
(2) If the contract involves carriage of the goods, the seller may dispatch the goods on terms whereby the goods, or documents controlling their disposition, will not be handed over to the buyer except against payment of the price.
(3) The buyer is not bound to pay the price until he has had an opportunity to examine the goods, unless the procedures for delivery or payment agreed upon by the parties are inconsistent with his having such an opportunity.

I. Overview

Article 58 CISG defines the moment at which the price becomes due if the parties have made no stipulations to that effect. It determines the time of payment and establishes the principle that time of payment and time of delivery are interdependent. At the same time, it determines the point in time at which interest under Article 78 CISG starts to accrue.

II. Article 58(1) CISG

Article 58(1) CISG establishes the principle of simultaneous handing-over of the goods, or the documents controlling their disposition, and payment of the price. It embodies a principle recognised in many domestic sales laws. The seller is not obliged to hand over the goods if the buyer does not simultaneously pay the price; the buyer, conversely, does not have to pay if the goods, or the documents controlling their disposition, have not been placed at the buyer's disposal.

As Article 58(1) CISG makes clear, party agreement on the time of payment, or practices or usages by which the parties are bound, prevail. For example, where the parties include trade terms, such as INCOTERMS®, in their contract, these terms take priority.

INCOTERMS® (2010):

Rules for Sea and Inland Waterway Transport

CFR. Cost and Freight (insert named port of destination). 'Cost and Freight' means that the seller delivers the goods on board the vessel or procures the goods already so delivered. CIF. Costs Insurance and Freight (insert named port of destination). 'Cost, Insurance and Freight' means that the seller delivers the goods on board the vessel or procures the goods already so delivered. FAS. (Free Alongside Ship (insert named port of shipment). 'Free Alongside Ship' means that the seller delivers when the goods are placed alongside the vessel (e.g., on a quay or a barge) nominated by the buyer at the named port of shipment. FOB. Free On Board (insert named port of shipment). 'Free on Board' means that the seller delivers the goods on board the vessel nominated by the buyer at the named port of shipment or procures the goods already so delivered.

Rules for any Mode or Modes of Transport

CPT. Carriage Paid To (insert named place of destination). 'Carriage Paid To' means that the seller delivers the goods to the carrier nominated by the seller at an agreed place (if any such place is agreed between the parties) and that the seller must contract for and pay the costs of carriage necessary to bring the goods to the named place of destination. CIP. Carriage and Insurance Paid To (insert named place of destination). 'Carriage and Insurance Paid To' means that the seller delivers the goods to the carrier nominated by the seller at an agreed place (if any such place is agreed between the parties) and that the seller must contract for and pay the costs of carriage necessary to bring the goods to the named place of destination.

The term 'documents' is used in the same way as in Article 57 CISG (see Art 57 above). The place where the goods are handed over is the one agreed upon by the parties or, absent such an agreement, the place defined in accordance with Article 31 CISG.

C 58-1

Bundesgerichtshof (Germany), 3 April 1996, CISG-online 135[227]

For a summary of the facts see C 35-3 above.

[Judgment]

[...]

3. Also without merit is the appeal's objection that [buyer] was at least entitled to exercise a right of retention according to Art 58(1) CISG. According to this provision, the buyer is only bound to pay the purchase price when the seller places the goods or the documents controlling their disposition at the buyer's disposal. Documents in this sense are mainly the so-called true transfer documents, besides this, also similar documents granting the buyer a right of

---

[227] Translation taken from CISG Pace (citations omitted).

disposition to the goods and excluding the seller from same. ... Among these are in particular the Warehouse Receipt, but not the Certificate of Origin or of Quality: their tender is normally neither necessary nor sufficient to found the maturity of the purchase price. ... The [buyer] never pleaded in the course of the trial phase that the [seller] was not able and willing to turn over the Warehouse Receipt against concurrent payment of the purchase price. The [buyer's] assertion that the goods were no longer available was apparently made without any actual basis; the [buyer], and also the hired expert, could have ascertained the existence of the goods by inspecting them at any time. Whether the [buyer] would have been entitled to retain the payment of the purchase price because of the initially incomplete documents or the false EEC Certificate of Origin, even though the payment clause 'cash against documents,' respectively CAD was agreed, does not have to be decided. At any rate, such a right of retention would have ceased to exist prior to the end of the trial phase. The [buyer] received the correct Certificate of Analysis with the expert's report. The [buyer] herself would have been able to obtain the correct Certificate of Origin at the latest after the issue of the origin of the goods was resolved.

III. Article 58(2) CISG

A. Operation

Article 58(2) CISG deals with the situation where the contract involves carriage of the goods by an independent carrier. It establishes the seller's right to retain the goods as long as the buyer has not made payment, and thereby protects the seller from having to deliver without receiving payment.

B. Article 58(2) CISG—a General Principle of Retention?

There is a discussion about whether a general principle within the meaning of Article 7(2) CISG may be derived from Article 58(2) CISG, whereby one party may suspend its performance as long as the other party does not comply with its duties under the contract. See the following abstract.

CISG Advisory Council Opinion No 5: The buyer's right to avoid the contract in case of non-conforming goods or documents:[228]

OPINION

[...]

---

[228] Taken from www.cisgac.com.

8. If the non-conformity does not amount to a fundamental breach, the buyer still has a right to withhold payment and to refuse to take delivery if reasonable under the circumstances. Comments ...

4.19 The CISG recognises a right to withhold performance in several provisions. Art 58 CISG embodies the principle of 'payment against delivery' as concurrent conditions. According to Art 71 CISG, a party may also suspend its own performance if performance by the other party is insecure. Further rights to withhold performance are contained in Arts 81(2) Second sentence CISG, 85 second sentence and 86(1) second sentence CISG. The prevailing literature derives a general principle of a right to withhold performance according to Art 58(2) CISG from such provisions. ...

IV. Article 58(3) CISG

Generally, the buyer is not bound to pay the price until it has had an opportunity to examine the goods (Art 58(3) CISG). The examination in Article 58(3) CISG differs from Article 38 CISG, in that it is intended only to be a quick and cursory check.

The parties are allowed to derogate from this rule by including clauses such as 'payment against handing over of documents' or 'payment against handing over of the delivery slip'. Difficulties arise where the goods have to be forwarded to a third party and the parties have agreed on 'payment against handing over of the goods at their arrival'. If the buyer asserts its rights under Article 58(2) CISG, since the buyer cannot examine the goods other than upon arrival, the carrier must allow the buyer's prior examination before payment is made.

V. Comparison with Other Legal Provisions

Art 6.1.4(1) PICC 2010:

To the extent that the performances of the parties can be rendered simultaneously, the parties are bound to render them simultaneously unless the circumstances indicate otherwise.

See also Section 2-310 UCC (Art 57 CISG above).

Art 213 OR:[229]

(1) If no other point in time has been determined, the purchase price becomes due upon handing over the goods to the buyer.

---

[229] Author's translation.

(2) Notwithstanding the provision on late delivery owing to expiration of a certain due date, interest on the purchase price accrues without further notice if so entailed by usage or if the buyer can derive profits from the goods.

Art 66 PRC CL:[230]

Where the parties owe performance toward each other and there is no order of performance, the parties shall perform simultaneously. ...

Questions

Q 58-1

(a) Which principle does Article 58 CISG establish?
(b) Do you find a similar principle encapsulated in the provisions of the other legal systems set out above?

Q 58-2

The time at which goods, or the documents controlling their disposition, are placed at the buyer's disposal, thereby making the buyer's payment due, depends on the type of contract. Define when the buyer must pay in the following situations:

(a) The goods are delivered at the seller's place of business.
(b) The goods are delivered at the buyer's place of business.

---

[230] Translation taken from www.novexcn.com/contract_law_99.html.

Article 59 CISG

The buyer must pay the price on the date fixed by or determinable from the contract and this Convention without the need for any request or compliance with any formality on the part of the seller.

I. Overview

Article 59 CISG clarifies that the buyer has to pay the price without the need for any notice or compliance with any other formality on behalf of the seller. The seller may have recourse to all the remedies provided under the Convention if the buyer is in default of any of its obligations to pay the price. Furthermore, the interest provided for under Article 78 CISG begins to accrue as soon as the price becomes due. Article 59 CISG, although it is often quoted in case law, does not give rise to any noteworthy difficulties.

II. Determining when Payment becomes Due

The parties can agree on the date that payment becomes due (Art 6). Where the buyer is not bound to make payment on a certain date, Article 58 CISG states that performance of the contract is to be made at the time of payment. Therefore, the buyer will usually be informed of when it will have to pay, in that the seller will give notice of its intent to place the goods, or the documents controlling the disposition of the goods (Art 58(1), (2)), at the buyer's disposal and will request payment. If the parties are bound by an international trade usage, the time payment becomes due is determined by that usage. This is of particular importance with regard to the INCOTERMS® 2010, which have often been deemed to apply via Article 9(2) CISG (see Art 9 CISG above). Clause A1 of all INCOTERMS® requires that the seller send an invoice in order for the payment to become due.

INCOTERMS® (2010):

> A1 General obligations of the seller
>
> The seller must provide the goods and the commercial invoice in conformity with the contract of sale and any other evidence of conformity that may be required by the contract.
>
> Any document referred to in A1–A10 may be an equivalent electronic record or procedure if agreed between the parties or customary.
>
> B1 General obligations of the buyer
>
> The buyer must pay the price of the goods as provided in the contract of sale.
>
> Any document referred to in B1-B10 may be an equivalent electronic record or procedure if agreed between the parties or customary.

It is generally accepted that Article 59 CISG embodies a general principle within the meaning of Article 7(2) CISG, valid for any and all monetary claims which one party may have against the other, such as restitution of the price following dissolution of the contract, payment of compensation or repayment of sums expended for preservation of the goods.

Questions

Q 59-1

Which principle is embodied in Article 59 CISG?

Q 59-2

Why will the buyer, in practice, usually be notified by the seller that payment is due?

Article 60 CISG

The buyer's obligation to take delivery consists:

(a) in doing all the acts which could reasonably be expected of him in order to enable the seller to make delivery; and

(b) in taking over the goods.

I. Overview

Article 60 CISG imposes a twofold duty on the buyer to, first, undertake all acts to enable the seller to make delivery (Art 60(a)) and, secondly, to take delivery of the goods (Art 60(b)).

II. Article 60(a) CISG

A. Buyer's Involvement in the Delivery of the Goods

Usually, the parties will have stated the scope of the duties mentioned in Article 60(a) CISG in the contract. For example, some INCOTERMS® 2010 clauses provide for certain measures to be undertaken by the buyer in order to make delivery of the goods possible.

Cl B3 FOB and FAS INCOTERMS® (2010):

Contracts of carriage and insurance

a. Contract of carriage. The buyer must contract, at its own expense for the carriage of the goods from the named port of shipment, except where the contract of carriage is made by the seller as provided for in A3 a.

[...]

B. Article 60(a) CISG—A General Principle of Cooperation

It is generally accepted that Article 60 CISG reflects a principle of cooperation.

A 60-1

Denis Tallon, 'The Buyer's Obligations Under the Convention on Contracts for the International Sale of Goods' in Galston/Smit (ed), *International Sales: The United Nations Convention on Contracts for the International Sale of Goods* (1984) (New York: Matthew Bender), ch 7, pp 7-1 *et seq.*[231]

> [A]rticles 54 and 60(a) both deal with the preliminary acts required of the buyer for the exact performance of his obligation to pay the price and to take delivery. ... Article 54 compels the buyer to take all the necessary steps to enable payment to be made. Its predecessor gave examples such as the acceptance of a bill of exchange, the opening of a documentary credit or the giving of a banker's guarantee. Of greater importance still is the requirement of compliance with the sometimes burdensome formalities imposed by mandatory rules in many countries for payments to be made abroad. Performance of such acts in some cases depends only on the buyer's diligence; in others, it needs an administrative authorization, and here, the buyer cannot be held liable for a refusal of such authorization as long as he has taken all reasonable steps to obtain it. The notion is the same in 60(a) which imposes on the buyer the obligation to do 'all the acts which could reasonably be expected of him in order to enable the seller to make delivery.' Here the test of reasonableness is explicit. Such acts may include providing for carriage, for unloading, and for containers, according to the means of transportation prescribed, and also compliance with administrative formalities, such as obtaining an import license, when these are the responsibility of the buyer. For John Honnold, these preliminary obligations are applications of a general duty to cooperate which may be inferred from a series of other rules. Most of these obligations are obligations to give notice of some event or intent. Does this mean, in the words of Honnold, that '[t]hese many instances suggest that providing needed cooperation is one of the 'general principles on which [the Convention] is based',' under article 7(2)? The notion is found in the UCC in the title, although not in the text, of Section 2-311 ('cooperation respecting performance'). However, to speak of 'cooperation' is perhaps somewhat exaggerated. The term is used with a much stronger meaning in socialist countries, because in a planned economy both parties must collaborate throughout the period of the contract in order to realise the plan. In a free-market situation such as international trade, obligations are more one-sided; the basic rule is 'chacun pour soi.' It is normal that each party should try to get the utmost from the bargain, and to speak of cooperation is perhaps hypocritical. What is true is that both parties have an interest in the strict compliance with the contract and that they have to respect the rules of the game.

---

[231] Taken from CISG Pace (footnotes omitted).

III. Article 60(b) CISG

According to Article 60(b) CISG, the buyer must take over the goods. There are, however, limits to this obligation. If the goods do not conform to the contract, the buyer may reject them outright if the non-conformity amounts to a fundamental breach of the contract (Art 25), because a fundamental breach will enable it to avoid the contract (Art 49(1)(a)). If the seller delivers before the due date, or delivers a quantity of goods greater than that provided for in the contract, the buyer may reject the (excess quantity of) goods (Art 52). Where the non-conformity does not constitute a fundamental breach, the buyer will usually have to take over the goods and allow the seller to cure the breach (Art 48).

Where the buyer is supposed to take over documents instead of goods, it will, as a rule, not be forced to take them over if they are unclean because their 'uncleanness' will usually amount to a fundamental breach of contract. The INCOTERMS® state the buyer's right to reject unclean documents explicitly.

Cl A8 and B8 CPT INCOTERMS® (2010):

> A8 Delivery document. If customary or at the buyer's request, the seller must provide the buyer, at the seller's expense, with the usual transport document[s] for the transport contracted in accordance with A3.
>
> This transport document must cover the contract goods and be dated within the period agreed for shipment. If agreed or customary, the document must also enable the buyer to claim the goods from the carrier at the named place of destination and enable the buyer to sell the goods in transit by the transfer of the document to a subsequent buyer or by notification to the carrier. ...
>
> B8 Proof of delivery. The buyer must accept the transport document provided as envisaged in A8 if it is in conformity with the contract.

C 60-1

ICC International Court of Arbitration
Award No 13492/2006,
CISG-online 2141[232]

In 2004, a Swiss company (Claimant) agreed to sell iron ore to a Chinese company (Respondent) pursuant to a contract governed by the 2000 Incoterms® rules and the 1980 United Nations Convention on Contracts for the International Sale of Goods. Claimant sought reimbursement of demurrage costs incurred at the port of arrival due to Respondent's delay in taking delivery of the goods. Respondent argued that it was not given proper notification of the shipment

---

[232] Extract taken from ICC International Court of Arbitration Bulletin Vol 21/1 2010, pp 88–90.

and that under the applicable Incoterms® rule demurrage costs were to be borne by the seller, which was 'liable for the chartering of vessel'. The parties agreed that references to CNF in their contract were to be interpreted as an adulteration of C&F, which corresponded to DFR under Incoterms® 2000.

'Respondent's obligation to take delivery of the Goods and to pay demurrage charges

137. It is clear that Respondent was under an obligation to take delivery of the [Goods] upon arrival of the [ship] in the Port of. ..., including making all required arrangements for discharging the Goods. As submitted by Claimant, this conclusion follows from the CISG and the Incoterm CFR.

138. Article 53 CISG provides:

The buyer must pay the price for the goods and take delivery of them as required by the contract and this Convention.

139. Article 60 CISG provides:

The buyer's obligation to take delivery consists:

(a)   in doing all the acts which could reasonably be expected of him in order to enable the seller to make delivery; and

(b)   in taking over the goods.

140. Pursuant to Article 53 CISG, Respondent had the general obligation to take delivery of the Goods. Article 60(b) CISG provides that this obligation consists of taking over the Goods, that is, by physically accepting them.

141. The Incoterm CFR also sets out the seller's and buyer's obligations with respect to delivery of the Goods:

A4. Delivery. The seller must deliver the goods on board the vessel at the port of shipment on the date or within the agreed period.

B4. Taking delivery. The buyer must accept delivery of the goods when they have been delivered in accordance with A4 and receive them from the carrier at the named port of destination.

142. At the hearing, Respondent admitted that the buyer has 'the obligation to take delivery of the goods" (Tr. p. 15). Respondent added that it did '[take] delivery of the goods' (Tr. p.12) and discharged the cargo on 1 June 2004 (Tr. p. 20).

143. It is also clear that Respondent is liable for the costs of discharging the cargo. Indeed, 'FO' as appended to the term CNF in Article 2 of Appendix No. 1 of the Contract stands for "Free Out" which is a:

[q]ualification to a freight rate denoting that the cost of discharging the cargo from the ship's hold is not included in the freight but is payable by the charterer or shipper or bill of lading holder, as the case may be. When qualifying a term of sale, it denotes that the purchase price of the goods does not include this cost which is borne by the Buyer. Often, daily rates of discharging and demurrage are incorporated into such contracts. Abbreviated to FO (Peter Brodie, Dictionary of Shipping Terms, 4th ed., LLP, London, 2003, p.107).

144. The Incoterm CFR also addresses the issue of costs:

B6. Division of costs. The buyer must, subject to the provisions of A3 a), pay all costs relating to the goods from the time they have been delivered in accordance with A4, and ... unloading costs including lighterage and wharfage charges, unless such costs and charges were for the seller's account under the contract of carriage ...

145. Under the Incoterm CFR, delivery occurs when the goods pass the ship's rail in the port of shipment (Incoterms® 2000, p. 57). Demurrage costs are costs relating to the goods that are incurred after the goods have been delivered in accordance with the Incoterm CFR.

146. The Incoterms® 2000 also provide that under the term CFR:

[T]he buyer is bound to accept delivery of the goods and to receive them from the carrier and if the buyer fails to do so, he may become liable to pay damages to the seller who has made the contract of carriage with the carrier or, alternatively, the buyer might have to pay demurrage charges resting upon the goods in order to obtain the carrier's release of the goods to him (Incoterms® 2000, p. 9).

147. Accordingly, I find that under the Contract and the Incoterm CFR, with the qualification 'FO', Respondent had the obligation to take prompt delivery of the Goods by discharging the vessel. I further find that Respondent had the obligation to bear the costs of discharging the Goods and costs associated with delays, such as demurrage charges, attributable to Respondent.

148. This finding is reinforced by the B/L itself, Claimant's Exhibit 3, which stipulates that the Goods are to be:

... delivered in the like good order and condition at the aforesaid Port unto Consignees or their Assigns, they paying freight as indicated to the left plus other charges incurred in accordance with the provisions contained in this Bill of Lading.

And to the left of the above text the B/L provides:

DEMURRAGE USD 22,000

149. The consignee is the person to whom goods are to be delivered by the carrier at the destination. Although the B/L indicates 'TO ORDER' in the consignee box, Respondent was the intended recipient of the Goods at the destination, and Respondent referred to itself as the consignee at the Hearing (Tr. p. 19). Although I have already found that Respondent had a general duty to pay these charges under the Contract, Respondent also assumed responsibility for demurrage charges through presentation of the B/L in order to take possession of the Goods.

CISG Advisory Council Opinion No 5: The buyer's right to avoid the contract in case of non-conforming goods or documents:[233]

OPINION [...]

8. If the non-conformity does not amount to a fundamental breach, the buyer still has a right to withhold payment and to refuse to take delivery if reasonable under the circumstances.

---

[233] Taken from www.cisgac.com.

Questions

Q 60-1

(a)   What does the duty to take delivery, according to Article 60 CISG, consist of?
(b)   Which general principle can be derived from Article 60 CISG?

Q 60-2

(a)   Is there a limitation on what steps the buyer is obliged to take in order to enable delivery of the goods?
(b)   Is there a limit to the buyer's obligation to take over the goods?
(c)   In which provisions of the CISG do you find indications that the buyer's duty to take over the goods or documents is not infinite?

Q 60-3

What are the consequences of the buyer failing to comply with its duty as set out in Article 60 CISG?

Q 60-4

Who bears the risk if the buyer refuses to take over the goods or documents
—   and has the right to do so?
—   but is not entitled to do so?

Q 60-5

(a)   Why did the arbitral tribunal find in C 60-1 that the buyer had breached its obligations?
(b)   Did the tribunal base its decision on Article 60(b) CISG?

Article 61 CISG

(1) If the buyer fails to perform any of his obligations under the contract or this Convention, the seller may:
    (a) exercise the rights provided in articles 62 to 65;
    (b) claim damages as provided in articles 74 to 77.
(2) The seller is not deprived of any right he may have to claim damages by exercising his right to other remedies.
(3) No period of grace may be granted to the buyer by a court or arbitral tribunal when the seller resorts to a remedy for breach of contract

I. Overview

Article 61 CISG provides a cohesive catalogue of the principal remedies available to the seller if the buyer does not comply with any of its duties under the contract. It thereby mirrors Article 45 CISG, which lists all of the buyer's remedies for the seller's non-compliance. In addition to Article 61 CISG, the seller may be entitled to interest (Art 78) or to resell the goods (Art 88). Its rights in case of an anticipated breach of contract are set out in Articles 71, 72 and 73 CISG.

II. Article 61(1) CISG

Article 61(1)(a) CISG refers to the seller's right to require payment and specific performance of the buyer's other obligations, as well as to the seller's right to avoid the contract.

Article 61(1)(b) CISG establishes the seller's right to damages; for the calculation of damages, it refers to Articles 74 to 77 CISG.

III. Article 61(2) CISG

Article 61(2) CISG regulates the relationship between the various remedies available to the seller and allows for a claim for damages to be combined with other remedies. The possibility to combine various remedies is one of the CISG's salient features. The amount of damages will depend on which other remedy, if any, the seller chooses to invoke. According to the principle that the aggrieved party should not be overcompensated (see in detail Art 74 CISG below), the claim for damages will only comprise the loss that has not already been compensated for by the other remedy invoked.

IV. Article 61(3) CISG

A. Rationale of Article 61(3) CISG and Current Major Problems

According to Article 61(3) CISG, no court or arbitral tribunal may grant the buyer an extension of time for performance. Originally incorporated in the CISG as a clarification that, unlike some domestic legal systems, the CISG does not allow for any judicially-granted period of grace, the provision has gained significance in light of (mandatory) periods granted under some domestic laws.

C 61-1

Helen Kaminski v Marketing Australian Products, Pty Ltd Inc,
US Dist Ct (SD NY), 23 July 1997,
CISG-online 297

For a summary of the facts see C 1-2 above.

[Judgment]

[...]

MAP issued purchase orders for additional products and Helen Kaminski sent notice in October and November 1996 to MAP that the products were ready for shipment. Pursuant to the Distributor Agreement, MAP was to open a letter of credit seven days prior to shipment. When MAP failed to do so, on November 1, 1996, Helen Kaminski sent a Notice to Rectify within thirty days. On November 22, 1996, Helen Kaminski sent a notice of default requiring MAP to cure the defects under the Distributor Agreement. When MAP still did not cure, Helen Kaminski sent a notice of termination dated December 2, 1996 and commenced an action in Australia seeking a declaration that the Distributor Agreement was invalid and terminated. MAP filed for bankruptcy in the Southern District of New York on November 29, 1996. On January 28, 1997, MAP commenced an action against Helen Kaminski seeking a declaration that Helen Kaminski was subject to the automatic stay under Section 362,

Title 11, United States Code, and an order extending MAP's time to cure the defaults under the Distributor Agreement, pursuant to Section 108(b), Title 11, United States Code. Helen Kaminski then moved to dismiss this Complaint contending, among other arguments, that (1) the Convention on the International Sale of Goods ('CISG') superseded the Bankruptcy Code and therefore MAP could not have additional time to cure under Section 108(b), and (2) the automatic stay under Section 362 should not have an extra-territorial effect. On March 3, 1997, the Bankruptcy Court issued an Order ('March 3rd Order') which denied Helen Kaminski's motion to dismiss and determined that (1) Helen Kaminski was subject to the automatic stay and thus could not proceed with the action in Australia, and (2) extended MAP's time to cure the defaults pursuant to Section 108(b). Although the March 3rd Order does not state so explicitly, the parties agree that the bankruptcy court found that the CISG does not apply to the Distributor Agreement as it was not a contract for the sale of goods. Helen Kaminski now wishes to appeal this interlocutory order. ...

Discussion

Although Helen Kaminski presents four issues it wishes to appeal, this Court will reformulate these questions into the questions it believes are presented in Helen Kaminski's papers. Those questions are (1) whether the CISG applies to the Distributor Agreement, and if so, does the CISG supersede inconsistent provisions in the Bankruptcy Code, such that the bankruptcy court erred in giving MAP additional time to cure its default, and (2) if the CISG does not apply, whether the bankruptcy court erred in giving extra territorial effect to Section 362. ...

[Applicability of the CISG rejected.]

B. Extra-territorial Effect of Section 362

Helen Kaminski cites no authority for its contention that Section 362 of the Bankruptcy Code should not have extra-territorial effect, other than an argument that such a stay is superseded by the CISG. Since I have held that, in the circumstances of this case at least, the CISG does not apply, I need not reach this second issue. I note, however, that it is a general principle that all claims against a debtor should be handled in a single proceeding to insure equitable and orderly distribution of debtor's property.].

Conclusion

For the reasons given above, it is hereby

ORDERED that Helen Kaminski's motion for leave to appeal the March 3rd Order of the Bankruptcy Court is denied.

B. Comparison with Other Legal Provisions

Art 1184 CC:[234]

(1)   A condition subsequent is always implied in synallagmatic contracts, for the case where one of the two parties does not carry out his undertaking.
(2)   [...]
(3)   Avoidance must be applied for in court, and the defendant may be granted time according to circumstances.

---

[234] Translation taken from www.legifrance.gouv.fr.

Questions

Q 61-1

Explain the operation of Article 61 CISG.

Q 61-2

(a) What was the reason for including Article 61(3) CISG? See also Article 1184 CC.
(b) Which situations does Article 61(3) CISG currently deal with?

Q 61-3

(a) How did the US District Court in C 61-1 solve the conflict between Article 58(3) CISG and the US bankruptcy provisions?
(b) Keeping Article 7 CISG in mind, could you visualise an approach different from the one the court took in this case?

Article 62 CISG

The seller may require the buyer to pay the price, take delivery or perform his other obligations, unless the seller has resorted to a remedy which is inconsistent with this requirement.

I. Overview

Article 62 CISG contains a remedy generally recognised in civil law systems, namely the seller's right to require the purchase price and (other) specific performance of the contract. In contrast, as a general rule, common law countries allow for specific performance only in limited circumstances (see discussion in Art 28 CISG above).

II. Restrictions on Seller's Right to Payment and (Other) Specific Performance

Under the ULIS, if the buyer's non-payment of the purchase price amounted to a fundamental breach, the seller had to claim the purchase price immediately in order to avoid an automatic termination of the contract. Under the CISG, there is no *ipso facto* avoidance; avoidance of the contract will always require a notification (Arts 26, 49(2)(b), 64(2)(b) CISG). Still, the seller's right, as it is stated in Article 62 CISG, is limited in two ways: first, the seller is deprived of this right if it has resorted to a remedy which is inconsistent with insistence on specific performance, which will be the case where it has declared the contract avoided (Art 64 CISG) or fixed an additional period of time for performance (Art 63 CISG).

The second restriction accrues from Article 28 CISG, according to which a court is not bound to enter a judgment for specific performance unless the court would do so under its own law. The ratio of Article 28 CISG is the divergence in the various domestic laws mentioned above.

Under the law of several Contracting States, the remedy of 'specific performance' does not include the seller's claim for the purchase price (French, Anglo-American legal systems). English and US sales law, for example, essentially limit the seller's price action to cases where the risk has passed to the buyer (see Section III. below). However, an autonomous interpretation of the term 'specific performance' and the wording of Article 28 CISG strongly suggest that Article 28 CISG applies to the seller's claim for the purchase price in the same way that it applies to its other claims for specific performance.

Its application is certainly of practical importance: if the seller has the right to claim specific performance, it can force the buyer to perform the contract in its entirety.

III. Comparison with Other Legal Provisions

Art 7.2.1 PICC 2010:

Where a party who is obliged to pay money does not do so, the other party may require payment.

§ 2-709 UCC:

(1) When the buyer fails to pay the price as it becomes due the seller may recover, together with any incidental damages under the next section, the price
    (a) of goods accepted or of conforming goods lost or damaged within a commercially reasonable time after risk of their loss has passed to the buyer; and
    (b) of goods identified to the contract if the seller is unable after reasonable effort to resell them at a reasonable price or the circumstances reasonably indicate that such effort will be unavailing.

    [...]

Sec 49 SGA:

(1) Where, under a contract of sale, the property in the goods has passed to the buyer and he wrongfully neglects or refuses to pay for the goods according to the terms of the contract, the seller may maintain an action against him for the price of the goods.
(2) Where, under a contract of sale, the price is payable on a day certain irrespective of delivery and the buyer wrongfully neglects or refuses to pay such price, the seller may maintain an action for the price, although the property in goods has not passed and the goods have not been appropriated to the contract.

Questions

Q 62-1

(a) What kind of seller's rights does Article 62 CISG govern?
(b) Which generic term do we generally use for those rights?

Q 62-2

Why, from an international point of view, is Article 62 CISG not a self-evident provision?

Q 62-3

In what way are the seller's rights to specific performance restricted?

Q 62-4

Why could it be doubted whether Article 28 CISG applies to the seller's rights for specific performance?

Q 62-5

To which cases do the SGA and the UCC restrict the seller's price action?

Q 62-6

Which principle governs the seller's claim for the buyer to take over the goods and pay the purchase price under the PICC 2010?

Q 62-7

Can you find a provision under the CISG from which a general principle may be derived, possibly restricting the seller's claim to the purchase price?

Article 63 CISG

(1) The seller may fix an additional period of time of reasonable length for performance by the buyer of his obligations.
(2) Unless the seller has received notice from the buyer that he will not perform within the period so fixed, the seller may not, during that period, resort to any remedy for breach of contract. However, the seller is not deprived thereby of any right he may have to claim damages for delay in performance.

I. Overview

According to Article 63(1) CISG, the seller may fix an additional period of time of reasonable length to enable the buyer to perform its obligations. It mirrors Article 47 CISG, which states the buyer's corresponding right. The purpose of Article 63(1) CISG is to clarify that the seller (and not a court or arbitral tribunal, see discussion on Art 61(3) CISG above) is able to grant the buyer an additional period in which to perform its obligations under the contract where the buyer has not performed within the contractual period. Article 63(2) CISG makes it clear that, during this additional period, the seller cannot resort to any remedy that would make the buyer's performance impossible.

II. Article 63(1) CISG

Where the buyer does not fulfil its obligations, the seller has various options. It can insist on specific performance of the contract (Art 62); where the non-performance amounts to a fundamental breach of contract or it can avoid the contract (Art 64) and, for example, claim damages from a substitute transaction (Art 75). However, where uncertainties as to the fundamental nature of the breach of contract remain, the seller should proceed under Article 63 and grant the buyer an additional period of time for performance. After expiration of this period, it may avoid the contract if the buyer has failed to fulfil its obligation to pay the purchase price or take delivery of the goods within this time (Art 64(1)(b)). In all other cases, its right to avoid the contract will depend on whether the buyer's non-fulfilment of its duties in and of itself constitutes a fundamental breach of contract (Art 64(1)(a)).

The additional period of time fixed by the seller must be determined or at least determinable by calendar dates, and it must be of reasonable length. The reasonableness will depend on the circumstances of the case. Decisions on what constitutes a reasonable length of the additional period of time are rare. At any rate, it is acknowledged that, where the period is too short, a period of reasonable length is deemed to replace the period granted.

C 63-1

Corte di Appello di Milano (Italy),
11 December 1998,
CISG-online 430

[Facts][235]

An Italian seller and a French buyer concluded a contract for the sale of a printing press which the buyer intended to install in its new factory. The buyer made a partial payment but it failed to pay the balance and to take delivery of the press at the agreed date. Two months after the date for taking delivery and payment had passed, the seller, relying on a provision of the Italian Civil Code (diffida ad adempiere), sent a notice to the buyer demanding performance within the following 15 days and declaring that, in the event of non-performance by the buyer, the contract would be considered as avoided (terminated). The buyer failed to perform within the additional 15-day period and, after a few days, the seller sent a further notice of the same contents. As the buyer, again, failed to perform within the second additional period of time, the seller commenced legal action alleging avoidance (termination) of the contract for breach by the buyer and claiming damages.

[Judgment][236]

[...]

The [seller's] position is strengthened considerably by the intervened breach of the contract (in light of the new qualification given above) depending upon the notice of the [seller], pursuant to the provisions of Articles 61–64(1) and 26 of the Convention, and pursuant to Article 74 in relation to the breach committed by the [buyer]: consisting in the [buyer's] failure to pay the owed price and to pick up the goods, pursuant to Articles 53, 59 and 60. In particular, it appears that the [seller] granted the [buyer] an additional term to fulfill its obligations, and this term had a reasonable length within the meaning of Article 63 of the Convention. In addition, taking into account the term of delivery/payment (originally agreed for 5 September 1989) after a first notification dated 17 November 1989—instructing the [buyer] to pick up the goods within 15 days—an interlocutory behavior that *de facto* expanded the tolerance period already granted. On 6 December the [seller], in a letter to the [buyer], restated the content of the previous notice; also relevant is the final 15-day term, thus newly granted to the [buyer] by the [seller]. Therefore, the total extension granted after the deadline of the beginning of September, is two and a half months long, a term undoubtedly reasonable under the circumstances.

[...]

---

[235] Summary of facts taken from UNILEX.
[236] Translation taken from CISG Pace (citations omitted).

Seller is granted damages in the amount of £IT 88,000,000, plus interest accruing from 1 January 1990 until payment is completed.

III. Article 63(2) CISG

The fixing of an additional period of time is binding, in that it prevents the seller from resorting to other remedies during this period. The seller 'regains' such remedies if the period expires without the buyer performing or if the buyer indicates during the period that it will not perform. Article 63(2), sentence 2 CISG makes it clear that the fixing of an additional period is not classified as an extension for payment; therefore, the seller may still claim any damages arising from the buyer's non-compliance with the contract.

Questions

Q 63-1

In which cases will the seller proceed under Article 63 CISG?

Q 63-2

(a)   In what circumstances of non-compliance by the buyer may the seller fix an additional period of time?
(b)   In which cases does the expiration of an additional period, without action by the buyer, automatically amount to a fundamental breach of contract, thereby entitling the seller to avoid the contract?

Q 63-3

Consider situations where a period, in order to be reasonable, will be quite short, and others where it will be longer. On what will such reasonableness usually depend?

Q 63-4

Why is it not sufficient to request performance 'soon' or 'promptly', but rather to indicate a specific period or date? See also Article 47 CISG above.

Q 63-5

Is it possible to combine an additional period under Article 63(1) CISG with a declaration of avoidance in the event that the buyer fails to fulfil its contractual duties? See also C 63-1.

Article 64 CISG

(1) The seller may declare the contract avoided:
    (a) if the failure by the buyer to perform any of his obligations under the contract or this Convention amounts to a fundamental breach of contract; or
    (b) if the buyer does not, within the additional period of time fixed by the seller in accordance with paragraph (1) of article 63, perform his obligation to pay the price or take delivery of the goods, or if he declares that he will not do so within the period so fixed.
(2) However, in cases where the buyer has paid the price, the seller loses the right to declare the contract avoided unless he does so:
    (a) in respect of late performance by the buyer, before the seller has become aware that performance has been rendered; or
    (b) in respect of any breach other than late performance by the buyer, within a reasonable time:
        (i) after the seller knew or ought to have known of the breach;
        (ii) after the expiration of any additional period of time fixed by the seller in accordance with paragraph (1) of article 63, or after the buyer has declared that he will not perform his obligations within such an additional period.

I. Overview

Article 64 CISG pools together all cases in which the seller may declare the contract avoided when the buyer is in breach of one of its obligations. It reflects Article 49 CISG, which sets out the requirements for the buyer's right to avoid the contract. The seller is entitled to avoid the contract if the buyer has committed a fundamental breach of contract (Art 64(1)(a)). Where the buyer does not live up to its obligations to make payment or take over the goods, the seller may declare the contract avoided after expiration of an additional period of time within the meaning of Article 63 CISG (Art 64(1)(b)). If payment has been made but the buyer is late in the performance of one of its other obligations, the seller must avoid the contract before it learns of the buyer's ultimate performance (Art 64(2)(a)). In all other cases, its declaration of avoidance must be within a reasonable time after the seller knows or ought to have known of the buyer's breach (Art 64(2)(b)(i)), after the additional period has expired, or after the buyer has declared that it will not perform (Art 64(2)(b)(ii)).

The effects of the seller's avoidance are dealt with in Articles 81 to 84 CISG. All cases mentioned in Article 64 CISG require a declaration of avoidance within the meaning of Article 26 CISG.

II. Article 64(1)(a) CISG

According to Article 64(1) CISG, the seller may avoid the contract for two reasons: first, if the buyer has committed a fundamental breach of contract within the meaning of Article 25 CISG (a); and secondly, if the buyer does not pay the purchase price within an additional period of time fixed by the seller or does not take over the goods within that period (b). For the latter cases, see also Article 63 CISG above.

III. Article 64(1)(b) CISG

Article 64(1)(b) CISG governs the buyer's failure to pay the price or take over the goods. The seller has the right to avoid the contract if the buyer does not fulfil these obligations within an additional period of time fixed by the seller, or if the buyer declares that it will not do so within the period so fixed (Art 63(2)). The duty to pay the purchase price includes the duty to take the necessary steps for that purpose (Art 54), whereas the obligation to take over the goods involves all acts which could reasonably be expected of the buyer in order to enable the seller to make delivery (Art 60(a)). The following cases illustrate the operation of Article 64(1) CISG.

C 64-1

Shuttle Packaging Systems v Tsonakis et al,
US Dist Ct (WD MI), 17 December 2001,
CISG-online 773

[Facts][237]

Seller agreed to supply thermoforming lining equipment for the manufacture of plastic gardening pots to buyer. The buyer began to experience complications with the equipment and alleged that it failed to conform to seller's specifications and industry standards. After the buyer unilaterally suspended payment for the goods, the seller began to compete in the market for distribution of plastic gardening pots, which constituted an alleged violation of the non-competition agreement. In the motion before the Court, buyer sought to restrain the seller from selling pots in the North American market pending the outcome of the case.

---

[237] Summary of facts taken from UNILEX.

[Judgment]

[...]

Nevertheless, the Court does accept Defendants' contention that the Plaintiff's non-payment of progress payments on the machinery did constitute a 'fundamental breach of contract.' Article 25 of the Convention defines a 'fundamental breach of contract' as one 'which results in such detriment to the other party as substantially to deprive him of what he is entitled to expect under the contract...'. ... This is a significant definition in that Article 64 provides the seller a right to declare the contract avoided due to a 'fundamental breach of contract.' ... Article 64 is also specifically worded to give the implication that non-payment of the purchase price is the most significant form of a fundamental breach by a buyer, since, as to a serious non-payment, no additional notifications are required for avoidance of the contract. In this case, the buyer has had some legitimate complaints concerning the machinery throughout the delivery and training process. However, on the whole, the Court concludes that the evidence submitted best supports the proposition that these complaints did not constitute either a fundamental or even a substantial breach of the contract by the seller. This is particularly true since the context for this dispute—namely, the machinery has been successfully operated with Defendants' assistance and Plaintiff is a cash-strapped business raising performance questions only after formal inquiries have been made as to non-payment—tends to show that complaints about performance were opportunistic and not genuine in character. On the other hand, the Court determines that it is likely that non-payment of the large sums due for the performance payments was a fundamental breach of contract and that it excused Defendants' performance of non-competition obligations under the purchase agreement and non-competition agreement. As such, the Court concludes that Plaintiff is unlikely to succeed on the merits. ...

C 64-2

Oberster Gerichtshof (Austria), 28 April 2000, CISG-online 581[238]

[Facts]

An Austrian buyer and a German seller concluded a contract for the sale of jewellery. The seller was to deliver the jewellery after receiving payment from the buyer. The buyer sent the seller two cheques, but its bank dishonoured them for lack of funds. ... In his letter of 22 December 1997, [seller] informed [buyer] about these events and told her that as a result he would be unable to ship the goods. On 12 January 1998, [seller's] German attorney sent [buyer] the following letter:

'With reference to the contracts and invoices referred to above as well as to our client's letter of 17 November 1997, we point out that you have been delayed with your contractual obligations to pay the purchase price for the ordered jewelry since 10 November 1997. Furthermore you have sent our client two uncovered checks and thereby committed check fraud punishable by law. In order to avoid litigation and prevent any further damages, our client is willing to give you a final opportunity to fulfill your contractual obligations. In the name and with

---

[238] Translation taken from CISG Pace (citations omitted).

power of attorney of our client, we therefore fix a final additional period of time for payment of the above-mentioned invoices—until 2 February 1998. Should our client not receive the purchase price until that date, he will refuse to accept the performance of your obligation. Our client will then seek damages for non-performance or withdraw from the contract.'

[Buyer's] failure to take delivery of the selected jewelry caused a loss of profit on the part of [seller] in the amount of DM 21,314.75—the difference between the purchase price and his manufacturing costs. This damage arises regardless of a possible resale of the goods ordered to a subsequent buyer, as the later contract would have been formed independently of the [buyer's] order. ...

[Judgment]

[...]

The appeal against the decision of the Court of Appeal is not justified. ... Under Art 63(1) CISG, the seller may fix an additional period of time for performance by the buyer of his obligation. According to Art 64(1)(b) CISG, the seller may declare the contract avoided if the buyer does not, within the additional period of time fixed by the seller, perform his or her obligation to pay the price or take delivery of the goods. Avoidance of contract is effected by a unilateral declaration of the non-breaching party to the other party. The declaration of avoidance does not have to satisfy any form requirements and there are no time limits imposed—apart from Art 49(2) CISG, which is not relevant in the present case. The declaration must be unambiguous in that the [aggrieved party] does not wish to keep the contract on foot .... In the letter of 17 November 1997, [seller's] attorney declared that [seller] would refuse to accept payment of the purchase price should [buyer] not perform her obligation within the additional period of time fixed. As the Court of Appeal correctly pointed out, this is to be understood as a conditional declaration by [seller] to (then) avoid the contract. Insofar as the meaning of this declaration was blurred by the alternative ' ... or withdraw from the contract' this ambiguity was certainly resolved by the statement of claim, which unequivocally declared the contract avoided. As has already been pointed out, the declaration of avoidance is generally not bound to any specific form or time frame under the CISG, so that the statement of claim can replace the declaration of avoidance. [...]

C 64-3

Oberlandesgericht Brandenburg (Germany), 18 November 2008, CISG-online 1734[239]

[...]

FACTS AND CASE HISTORY

The parties are in dispute about reciprocal claims in the context of two contracts concluded between them on 1 December 2003 concerning the bottling of beer. The dispute further concerns [Seller]'s right to avoid these contracts.

---

[239] Translation taken from CISG Pace (citations omitted).

Both parties are breweries. [Seller] is a fully-owned subsidiary of T. Holding GmbH (hereafter: T.), which is domiciled in B. The two CEOs of [Seller], M. G. and K. U., are also the CEOs of company T.

[Buyer] is a company established under Belgian law and is registered with the commercial register in T___ (Belgium).

[...]

On 1 December 2003, [Seller] and [Buyer] concluded two written manufacturing and bottling service contracts. The date '1 December 2004' as indicated in one of the contracts is a mere typographical error. Both contracts concerned the manufacturing of beer and the provision of bottling services. One contract (hereafter: 'can contract') concerned the canning of beer. The other contract (hereafter: 'PET contract') concerned the bottling of beer into PET bottles.

[...]

The parties commenced execution of their can contract on 1 January 2004. [Seller] started to supply [Buyer] with PET bottles by June 2004.

[In August/September 2004, the parties entered into negotiations about the target quantities and purchasing plan for 2004. Disputes ensued about the target quantity that was to be purchased by the buyer.]

[...]

By fax dated 6 January 2005, [Seller] proposed to [Buyer] a seasonal formula for both bottling contracts and over the entire year 2005. [Buyer] responded by fax of 18 January 2005 and declared that it could not accept the proposed formulas, because the two contracts were considerably different from each other. In particular, different volumes had been stipulated for each of the contracts and this was not reflected in [Seller]'s proposal. The contract obliged the parties to confer with each other on the seasonal formula. Thus, [Buyer] proposed to schedule a meeting in due time.

[The parties continued to correspond about the quantity of beer to be purchased by the Buyer and about remedies for the existing discrepancies between actual and planned quantities purchased.]

[...]

By letter of 31 March 2005, [Seller] declared avoidance of both contracts with immediate effect. Reference is directed to the letter itself for the particulars. [Buyer] rejected this avoidance by letter dated 14 April 2005.

[...]

1. [Seller] asserts a right to declare avoidance of contract on the basis of three grounds: First, it relies on a breach by [Buyer] of its obligations to accept deliveries. Second, it relies on a breach of its obligation to pay. Third, [Seller] claims that [Buyer] breached its duty to cooperate in the process of determining a seasonal formula. With respect to the can contract, none of these assertions is founded.

a) [Seller] argues that throughout the year 2004 and the first three months of 2005, [Buyer] did not order and accept the required quantities of beer as designated in the contract. However, this does not justify avoidance under the relevant legal provisions of the CISG. In the course of proceedings before the Court of Second instance, [Buyer] no longer contests that the

CISG is applicable. Moreover, the District Court has correctly determined the application of the CISG. Reference is directed to that part of the contested judgment (pp. 7 and 8).

[...]

cc) Furthermore, [Seller] was not entitled to avoid the contract because of [Buyer]'s failure to comply with the target quantities for the year 2004 according to Art 64(1)(b) CISG. Under this provision, the seller may declare the contract avoided if the buyer does not perform his obligation to pay the price or take delivery of the goods within the additional period of time fixed by the seller. This provision does not apply inter alia because the term 'take delivery' means the physical handing over of goods which have already been produced. However, the breach of contract asserted by [Seller] refers to the act of ordering goods which is a precedent to production. The act of ordering is not connected to the act of delivering of the goods in terms of a physical handing over. Thus, it is not embraced by the term of taking delivery in Art 64(1)(b) CISG (cf. Honsell/Schnyder/Staub, Art 60 CISG para. 30).

dd) Finally, [Seller] has no right to declare avoidance under Art 64(1)(a) CISG. It provides that the seller may declare the contract avoided if the failure by the buyer to perform any of his obligations under the contract or this Convention amounts to a fundamental breach of contract in terms of Art 25 CISG. The CISG does not determine any relevant period of time within which this right must be exercised. It also does not require the seller to fix an additional period of time before avoidance may be declared. The provision applies to contracts for delivery of goods by installments as well. Thus, it applies in concurrence with Art 73 CISG.

[Buyer]'s failure to comply with the target quantities for the year 2004 does not fulfil the requirements of Art 64(1)(a) CISG. This breach of contract is not fundamental.

According to Art 25 CISG, a breach of contract committed by one of the parties is fundamental if it results in such detriment to the other party as substantially to deprive him of what he is entitled to expect under the contract, unless the party in breach did not foresee and a reasonable person of the same kind in the same circumstances would not have foreseen such a result. In general, any obligation under a contract may give rise to a relevant expectation, irrespective of their nature as primary obligations, ancillary obligations or mere modalities of performance (BGH, judgment of 3 April 1996, NJW 1996, 2364). In this respect, the general tendency of the CISG must be considered, which is to grant the right of avoidance only as an exceptional remedy, namely, when other remedies (price reduction or damages) are not desirable. Avoidance of contract shall be available only a last resort for either the buyer or the seller (BGH, judgment of 3 April 1996, cited above; Staudinger/Magnus, Art 64 CISG para. 4).

Primarily, it is for the court of first instance to decide whether a breach of contract is fundamental. It is determined by the circumstances of the individual case (BGH, judgment of 3 April 1996, cited above). In the present case, the breach by [Buyer] of its obligation to order and accept delivery of the stipulated annual target quantity does not amount to a fundamental breach.

As stated in the convincing expert opinion obtained by the District Court, it may be assumed that [Buyer] accepted deliveries of 225,030 hectoliters of beer in 0.33-liter cans and 83,948 hectoliters of beer in 0.5-liter cans from [Seller] throughout the year 2004. This means that [Buyer] was liable for a quantity shortage of 91,022 hectoliters in the light of a target quantity of 400,000 hectoliters. In fact, this amounts to a shortage of almost 23% for the year 2004. However, Art 64 CISG provides (insofar different from Art 73(2) CISG) that the whole contract must be taken into account instead of individual partial deliveries. Thus, the fundamentality of the breach must be determined in the light of the entire duration of the contract over three years. Only this broader consideration achieves a delineation of the scopes of Art 64 CISG, on the one hand, and Art 73 CISG, on the other hand. In total, [Buyer] was obliged to order 1,200,000 hectoliters of canned beer over a period of three years. The respective quantity shortage in 2004 only amounts to 7.5%. In the light of the considerable total volume of the contract, the Court does not find that this shortage (and the consequential damage incurred by [Seller]) may be seen as a substantial detriment.

[...]

IV. Article 64(2) CISG

Article 64(2) CISG makes the seller's right to declare the contract avoided conditional on its compliance with certain time limits. It thereby differentiates between cases of 'late delivery' and other cases. The provision is not very clear, and there is little case law to illuminate it. According to the majority of legal commentary, Article 64(2)(a) deals with the case where the buyer is in default with any obligation that would principally enable the seller to avoid the contract according to Article 64(1)(a) or (b) CISG, but then eventually performs this obligation. Late performance refers, in particular, to the situation where the buyer does not pay the purchase price or take over the goods within an additional period of time (Article 64(1)(b)), or to situations where the breach of a duty itself or the expiration of an unused *Nachfrist* set in order to fulfil such a duty amount to a fundamental breach (Art 64(1)(a)). In all of those cases of late but nonetheless effected performance, the seller may declare the contract avoided only if it did not know of the buyer's fulfilment of the outstanding duty. Where the buyer is late in performance of more than one duty and where the non-performance of each of these duties would enable the seller to avoid the contract, the seller is only then precluded from avoiding the contract if the buyer fulfils all of those duties and has notified the seller thereof.

Art 64(2)(b) CISG refers to cases other than late performance and in which payment has been made. This also excludes the buyer's failure to take over the goods and is thus restricted to cases of fundamental breach (Art 64(1)(a)). In these cases, the seller loses its right to avoid the contract if it does not declare so within a reasonable period of time starting from the moment when the seller knew or ought to have known of the breach (Art 64(2)(b)(i)) or, where an additional period of time was fixed (Art 63), following the expiration of that additional period (Art 64(2)(b)(ii)).

Questions

Q 64-1

In which cases is the seller entitled to avoid the contract?

Q 64-2

(a)   Does the buyer's mere non-payment of the purchase price allow the seller to avoid the contract? See also C 64-1.
(b)   Can a definite refusal to pay or take over the goods constitute a fundamental breach?
(c)   Does the buyer's failure to take over the goods entitle the seller to avoid the contract? See C 64-2.

Q 64-3

(a)   Could the buyer's violation of obligations other than the ones mentioned in Article 64(1)(b) CISG constitute a fundamental breach of contract?
(b)   If the seller has doubts as to whether such a breach amounts to a fundamental one, what can it do to clarify the situation?

Q 64-4

(a)   What should a seller, who does not receive payment or whose goods are not taken over in time, do with a view to obtaining the right to avoid the contract?
(b)   If the buyer does not comply with its duties other than to make payment and take over the goods, will an additional period of time (Art 63) automatically enable the seller to avoid the contract? Under which pre-conditions will the seller be entitled to terminate the contract? See also C 64-2.

Q 64-5

(a)   Which duties does the buyer's obligation to make payment include?
(b)   How broadly should the scope of the duties connected to the obligation to take over the goods be construed?

Q 64-6

(a)   Why was the seller unable to rely on Article 64 in C 64-3 above?
(b)   Do you think this is the correct approach?

Q 64-7

What factors did the court look at to determine whether or not there was substantial detriment?

Q 64-8

How can Article 64(2)(a) and Article 64(2)(b) CISG be distinguished?

Q 64-9

Decide whether the seller can avoid or has justifiably avoided the contract in the following situations:

(a)   Buyer has not paid timely, seller has fixed a reasonable additional period of time until yesterday and
    —   buyer has not made payment until today.
    —   buyer has made payment within the additional period granted and notified the seller thereof.
    —   buyer paid this morning at 11 am. The seller has declared the contract avoided before 11 am this morning.
    —   buyer made payment yesterday and notified seller thereof; the money is transferred today, but prior to transfer the seller has declared avoidance.
    —   same situation as before, but buyer does not notify the seller of its having made payment.
(b)   Buyer has neither paid timely nor has taken over the goods within an additional period of time. Shortly after,
    —   buyer pays, takes over the goods and notifies the seller thereof.
    —   buyer pays but does not take over the goods.
    —   buyer pays and takes over the goods, but is still in breach of another obligation which would allow it to avoid the contract.

Q 64-10

Since, generally, where the requirements of Article 64(1)(a) and (b) are met, the seller can freely choose whether it avoids the contract or claims specific performance of the contract, there might be a risk that it speculates to the detriment of the buyer by avoiding the contract at a date particularly favourable to it. For example, it could avoid the contract when the market price is particularly high and claim damages under Article 76(1) CISG. Is there a general principle under the CISG which obliges a party to keep the damage of the other party to a minimum?

Article 65 CISG

(1) If under the contract the buyer is to specify the form, measurement or other features of the goods and he fails to make such specification either on the date agreed upon or within a reasonable time after receipt of a request from the seller, the seller may, without prejudice to any other rights he may have, make the specification himself in accordance with the requirements of the buyer that may be known to him.

(2) If the seller makes the specification himself, he must inform the buyer of the details thereof and must fix a reasonable time within which the buyer may make a different specification. If, after receipt of such a communication, the buyer fails to do so within the time so fixed, the specification made by the seller is binding.

I. Overview

Article 65 CISG constitutes a special provision dealing with the shifting of the right to specify the goods from the buyer to the seller. The provision applies in cases where the contract leaves the specification to the buyer. Under the ULIS, the seller had the right to automatically avoid the contract if the buyer did not make a specification. The provision was criticised for being too harsh on the buyer, and was modified. Even Article 65 CISG met with considerable misgivings at the Drafting Conference of the CISG, but was, in the end, adopted.

Article 65 CISG presupposes that there is a valid contract, notwithstanding that the goods are not sufficiently specified. Its practical importance is that specifying the goods makes it easier for the seller to make a claim for performance of the contract or for damages, because the extent of such remedies is assessable only after the goods have been specified; for example, it is only then that a proper calculation of damages can be made.

II. Article 65(1) CISG

Article 65(1) CISG applies where the contract leaves it to the buyer to specify the goods and the buyer does not comply with this duty, either on the date agreed upon, or within a reasonable time after receipt of a request to do so. It gives the seller the right to then make the specification itself.

The wording 'after receipt of a request' makes it clear that the risk for delay or loss in transit of the request is borne by the seller (different from the rule in Art 27 CISG). The provision does not apply where the buyer is entitled to vary the specification of the goods at a later stage after the conclusion of the contract. Where the seller does not fix a specific period for complying with the request, the request is assumed to set a reasonable period in motion.

The seller's specification must be in accordance with the buyer's needs, to the extent that the seller is aware of those needs.

III. Article 65(2) CISG

According to Article 65(2) CISG, where the seller makes use of its right to specify the goods, it has to inform the buyer thereof and must fix an additional period of time in which the buyer has the possibility to contradict. Where the seller does not inform the buyer or grant an additional time limit for objections, its specifications are ineffective.

IV. Comparison with Other Legal Provisions

§ 2-311 UCC:

(1) An agreement for sale which is otherwise sufficiently definite (subsection (3) of section 2-204) to be a contract is not made invalid by the fact that it leaves particulars of performance to be specified by one of the parties. Any such specification must be made in good faith and within limits set by commercial reasonableness.

(2) Unless otherwise agreed, specifications relating to assortment of the goods are at the buyer's option and except as otherwise provided in subsections (1)(c) and (3) of section 2-319 specifications or arrangements relating to shipment are at the seller's option.

(3) Where such specification would materially affect the other party's performance but is not seasonably made or where one party's cooperation is necessary to the agreed performance of the other but is not seasonably forthcoming, the other party in addition to all other remedies

   (a) is excused for any resulting delay in his own performance; and

   (b) may also either proceed to perform in any reasonable manner or after the time for a material part of his own performance treat the failure to specify or to cooperate as a breach by failure to deliver or accept the goods.

Questions

Q 65-1

(a)   Why was Article 65 CISG disputed at the Drafting Conference?
(b)   Which party's interests come to the fore?

Q 65-2

Even if there is little chance that the buyer will be prepared to execute the contract, why is it helpful for the seller to make a specification of the goods?

Article 66 CISG

Loss of or damage to the goods after the risk has passed to the buyer does not discharge him from his obligation to pay the price, unless the loss or damage is due to an act or omission of the seller.

I. Overview of Chapter IV

Chapter IV (Arts 66 to 70) deals with the passing of the risk of damage to or loss of the goods from the seller to the buyer. 'Passing of risk' is the point in time in the performance of the contract from which the buyer has to pay the purchase price although the goods might be lost or damaged. Even if the risk, as will usually be the case, is covered by insurance, is it necessary to determine which of the two parties bears the risk if loss or damage actually occurs: the party who bears the risk must assert a claim against the insurer and may suffer depletion of current assets while waiting for settlement.

Articles 66 to 69 CISG regulate which party should bear the economic consequences in the event that the goods are accidentally lost, damaged or destroyed. The first article of the chapter (Art 66) governs the *consequences* after the risk of loss or damage passes to the buyer. The subsequent articles (Arts 67 to 69) set out rules governing the question of *when* the risk passes to the buyer. It must be noted that, with respect to the passing of risk, parties very often use international commercial terms, such as the INCOTERMS®, but may also use local terms or usages, which supersede the default rules of the CISG. Therefore, in the following, reference will repeatedly be made to such trade terms.

The last provision of the chapter (Art 70) deals with the allocation of the risk of loss or damage if the seller commits a fundamental breach of contract.

The rules of Chapter IV apply regardless of when title passes from seller to buyer (see Art 4(b) CISG); see also C 66-1 below. Furthermore, domestic rules, which allocate the risk to the owner of the goods, are irrelevant if the contract is governed by the CISG.

II. Article 66 CISG

As a general rule, the seller who has fulfilled its obligation to deliver the goods (Arts 31 to 34) will cease to bear the risk of loss or damage. Chapter IV and Articles 31 to

34 CISG often have almost identical wording. Article 66 CISG provides that, once the risk has passed to the buyer, the buyer must continue in the performance of its part of the contract unless the loss or damage was caused by the seller. A similar distinction is made in Article 36 CISG, according to which the seller remains liable for non-conformities existing at the time the risk of loss passes.

'Risk' has not been defined in the CISG. Article 66 CISG mentions loss of or damage to the goods. According to case law, 'risk' also includes diminution or shrinkage of the goods; theft or other disappearance of the goods (misplacing, transfer to a wrong address or person, mixing up with other goods); and also emergency discharge of the goods and similar casualties. As to the interpretation of the term 'risk', typically used insurance clauses (for example Institute Cargo Clauses, Institute War Clauses and Institute Strike Clauses)[240] may be important when determining whether a particular situation constitutes a 'casualty'.

From the wording of Article 66 CISG, it is at least uncertain whether it also refers to legal risks, as opposed to the physical risks just mentioned. Legal risks comprise intervention by state authorities, confiscation, or forbearance of possession, use, commercial exploitation and so on of the goods. The question has been dealt with in the case below (C 66-1).

C 66-1

Arbitration Court of the Chamber of Commerce and Industry of Budapest (Hungary), 10 December 1996, CISG-online 774[241]

[Facts]

Seller, a Yugoslav company, exported caviar to Buyer. Delivery took place on May 28, 1992, Hungarian customs clearance was affected on May 29, 1992. It was not contested by Buyer that delivery was according to the contract in every respect. The price agreed upon between Seller and Buyer was US $93,127—and it was never paid. ... Seller asked Buyer to pay the outstanding amount to four beneficiaries. Buyer agreed to it. On July 21, and on July 28, 1992 Buyer attempted to pay and gave orders to its bank to effect payment to the Cyprus beneficiaries, but failed. Buyer informed [the] beneficiaries the payments were not effected due to the UN sanctions against Yugoslavia. During the ... sanctions the parties made repeated endeavours to settle the outstanding debt of Buyer. The sanctions represented force majeure. In its letter of June 14, 1994 Buyer declared that 'the purchase of caviar stock has

---

[240] The most important insurance contracts in international trade include so-called Institute Clauses, which vary in scope. 'Institute Clauses' may refer to either the Institute of London Underwriters, which form the basis of the cargo insurance contract in many countries (sometimes also referred to as the 'London Clauses' or 'English Clauses'), or to the American Institute of Marine Underwriters, which are used in the USA and some other areas (also referred to as the 'American Institute Clauses' or 'American Clauses'). Though the American Clauses and the London Clauses may differ, they have a common stock on insurance clauses which are also the mostly used clauses in practice.

[241] Translation taken from CISG Pace (citations omitted).

happened, but declare that fulfillment of payment is limited by force majeure.' [...] After the UN sanction[s] were lifted, Claimant repeated its demands for payment on November 23, 1995, as well as on December 21, 1995.

[Judgment]

[...]

The Vienna Convention foresees in Art. 53 that the Buyer must pay the price for the goods and take delivery of them as required by the contract and this Convention. The contract of the parties definitely provided for the basis of the delivery as follows: 'The Buyer shall pick up the fish eggs at the Sellers address and bring the goods to his facilities in Hungary' (Point 2 of the Contract). The price was based FOB Kladovo (point 3 of the Contract). [...] The Buyer had to pay US $15,000 before the delivery and the remaining amount within two weeks after delivery of the goods [...] Art. 60 of the Vienna Convention confirms the Buyer's obligation to take delivery consists in taking over the goods. In the opinion of the Court of Arbitration taking over the goods means taking over the goods as foreseen in the Incoterms® Rules, which in our case was regulated by the Contract reading to pick up the goods at Sellers address, FOB Kladovo. [...]

Loss of or damage to the goods after the risk has passed to the Buyer does not discharge him from his obligation to pay the price, unless the loss or damage is due to an act or omission of the Seller (Art. 66 of the Vienna Convention). [...] The Court of Arbitration came to the conclusion that the risk and the ownership has passed to Buyer ... in accordance with the Contract at Kladovo. The Buyer could not exculpate itself proving the damage is due to an act or omission of Seller [...] In the opinion of the Court of Arbitration this means the damage caused by force majeure has to be borne by the party where the risk is at the moment the force majeure occurs. The Court of Arbitration finds it necessary [to] point out that the risk of the freight has to be borne by the Buyer unless the Contract of the parties or the applicable law otherwise provides (Art 67 of the Vienna Convention). Therefore, the Court of Arbitration stated that the claim of the Claimant is well founded and obliged [Buyer] to pay the Claimant the US $93,127 principal sum.

The *Kladovo* case links 'risk' to '*force majeure*' (see Art 79 CISG). Those two terms must not be confused: *force majeure* is an extraordinary event or circumstance beyond the control of the parties, an 'act of God'. In the case of *force majeure*, both parties are freed from liability. 'Risk' is a broader term which, although including *force majeure*, also covers less dramatic situations, for example a deterioration of the goods due to bad packaging by the carrier. The question that will then have to be decided is whether the buyer must pay the purchase price despite spoilage of the goods; as the *Kladovo* case shows, the answer will depend on whether risk has passed from seller to buyer.

III. Parties' Agreement on Passing of Risk

A. In General

The CISG's set of rules on the passing of risk is a supplementary, gap-filling principle that applies where the contract itself does not provide otherwise. The parties are free to make a contractual stipulation as to when the risk of loss of or damage to the goods passes from the seller to the buyer. They can make individual agreements, or they may include trade terms dealing with these aspects.

B. In Particular: INCOTERMS®

As far as the passing of risk in international trade is concerned, INCOTERMS® are of great importance. Their latest version—INCOTERMS® 2010—was published in January 2011. Other terms relating to the passage of risk may be used, such as the terms promoted by the Council of Mutual Economic Assistance (CMEA) in 1968 and 1976 or those promulgated by the United Nations Economic Commission for Europe. They are, however, less significant, as they are merely regional trade usages.

Under all of the INCOTERM® clauses, the rule is established that the risk passes from the seller to the buyer at the time delivery has been made in accordance with the chosen INCOTERM®. A5 and B5 of each INCOTERM® describe the time at which the risk passes, which, again, is linked to the moment at which delivery is made (a question dealt with in A4, B4 of each INCOTERM®). The said provisions read as follows:

INCOTERMS® (2010):

A5 Transfer of risks

The seller bears all risks of loss of or damage to the goods until they have been delivered in accordance with A4 with the exception of loss or damage in the circumstances described in B5.

B5 Transfer of risks

The buyer bears all risks of loss of or damage to the goods from the time they have been delivered as envisaged in A4.

If

(a)   the buyer fails to notify the nomination of a vessel in accordance with B7; or
(b)   the vessel nominated by the buyer fails to arrive on time to enable the seller to comply with A4, is unable to take the goods, or closes for cargo earlier than the time notified in accordance with B7;

then, the buyer bears all risks of loss of or damage to the goods:

(i)   from the agreed date, or in the absence of an agreed date,
(ii)   from the date notified by the seller under A7 within the agreed period, or, if no such date has been notified,
(iii) from the expiry date of any agreed period for delivery,

provided that the goods have been clearly identified as the contract goods.

A4 Delivery

The seller must deliver the goods either by placing them on board the vessel nominated by the buyer at the loading point, if any, indicated by the buyer at the named port of shipment or by procuring the goods so delivered. In either case, the seller must deliver the goods on the agreed date or within the agreed period and the manner customary at the port.

If no specific loading point has been indicated by the buyer, the seller may select the point within the named port of shipment the best suits its purpose.

B4 Taking delivery

The buyer must take delivery of the goods when they have been delivered as envisaged in A4.

C. Interpretation of Contract Terms with regard to Risk Allocation

Often, it is difficult to decide whether a particular contract term deals with the passing of risk or whether it merely refers to one party's duty to adequately insure the goods, or to the question of where delivery is to be made. The answer will depend on the interpretation of the contract term under Article 8 CISG. Where a 'codified' trade practice has been developed around a particular trade term, as is the case with INCOTERMS®, Article 8(3) CISG calls for full incorporation of those standard interpretations into the contract. That is, if the parties use a standard INCOTERM® such as EXW, FCA, CFR and so on, the questions settled by this INCOTERM®, including the passing of risk, will be interpreted according to established INCOTERMS® practice (see also C 66-1 above: 'In the opinion of the Court of Arbitration taking over the goods means taking over the goods as foreseen in the INCOTERMS® Rules, which in our case was regulated by the Contract reading to pick up the goods at Sellers address, FOB Kladovo.').

   If the contract provides for a term or clause other than an INCOTERM®, the question of whether such a term deals with the passing of risk or not is less clear. See, in this respect, C 66-2.

C 66-2

Oberlandesgericht Schleswig-Holstein (Germany), 29 October 2002, CISG-online 717[242]

[Facts]

The Plaintiff demanded of the Defendant the down payment for a stallion that, during the transport to the Defendant, died of colic whose cause could not be fully established. The District Court allowed the claim. [...] The Defendant now objects to this ruling [...]. [It claims that there had not] been any final and binding contract of sale between the Defendant and the Plaintiff, but rather an open purchase, as is usual in the sale of horses. [The Defendant further claims that] the conclusion of the contract was subject to the Defendant's approval of the stallion [and that] the risk could only pass to the buyer upon such approval. Due to the death of the horse, the approval [was] not given by the Defendant. The risk [had] therefore stayed with the Plaintiff. Thus, the Defendant [would] not [be] liable for damages.

---

[242] Translation taken from CISG Pace (citations omitted).

An agreement on the payment of the insurance [could not] alter the [...] distribution of the risk [as established by law]. [...] [As] it was unusual to insure a horse that needs to be transported against illness or death, [...] an explicit agreement would have been necessary, but there had not been such an agreement. A [possible] cargo insurance policy [...] would only have covered the risks of carriage, not a colic entailing death.

[Judgment]

The contract between the parties must be classified as a contract of sale containing additional agreements as to the maintenance of the stallion during the three months it was envisaged that it be in the care of the Defendant [Buyer].

The [CISG] is applicable to the parties' contract of sale. [...]

The Plaintiff [Seller] [claims] the payment of DM 30,000. [...]

The approval of the stallion by the Defendant [Buyer] cannot be a condition subsequent, as the contract between the parties is not a provisional contract of sale. The envisaged handing over of the stallion to the Defendant [Buyer] for three months was not motivated by the idea that Defendant [Buyer] should examine the stallion, but should improve the skills of the animal by appropriate training. The contract of sale between the parties was rather conditioned by the onward sale of the stallion. This is the result of an interpretation of the parties' contractual statements based on the understanding of a reasonable recipient of the statements (*cf.* [...] Arts. 8(1) through (3) of the CISG).

It emerges from the agreements that the legal validity of the contract was dependent on the onward sale of the stallion. At the time of the conclusion of the contract, the onward sale of the horse, on which hinged the remaining payment, was uncertain, and depended decisively on the success of the three months of training.

The decision as to whether [the resale of the horse] is a condition precedent or a condition subsequent must be made in accordance with the interests of the parties. The question of who is to bear the risk of the stallion dying before its onward sale without the fault of either party depends on this decision.

[Discussion of whether the resale of the horse is a condition precedent or a condition subsequent and conclusion that it was a condition precedent.]

[...]

As the condition, due to the death of the animal, undisputedly has not been fulfilled, the Plaintiff [Seller]'s claim for the payment of the price, lacking a binding contract of sale, has not legally arisen.

Nevertheless, the Seller's claim for the payment of [...] DM 30,000 is justified.

The Buyer's duty to pay, prior to the collection of the stallion, a down payment of DM 30,000 [...] was an independent obligation and was as such not conditioned on the onward sale of the stallion. This duty must be deemed to constitute an independent agreement between the parties concerning the passing of the risk during the time the contract was not yet finally binding. By way of this agreement, the parties evidently wanted to take into account the fact that the Seller was to [release] the horse into the care of the Buyer for an extended period of time, by which the latter obtained the opportunity to improve the horse in order to be able to achieve as high a price in the onward sale as possible. Given the constant danger of the horse being injured during training and of decreasing in value, the down payment was meant to constitute a just balancing of the interests of the parties, which avoided the Seller's risk of both losing the horse and not obtaining a claim for the payment of the purchase price. The risk was, thus, to be divided between the parties as of the moment of receiving or taking possession of the stallion. To this extent, the agreement as to the down payment was independent and [linked to] the onward sale of the stallion only to the extent the down payment was to be handed back in case the stallion was returned. The obligation of the Buyer, thus, was subject to the condition subsequent of the return of the stallion. As this condition, too, failed to materialize—due to the death of the animal—the duty of the Buyer to pay DM 30,000 is finally to be deemed to be unconditioned.

The risk passed when the horse was [...] taken over by the Buyer (*cf.* Arts. 66 and 69 of the CISG). The stallion was handed over at the time the Buyer had the carrier he assigned collect the horse at the stud farm. It was agreed that the stallion be collected by the Buyer. The fact that he made use of the services of a carrier, and therefore only obtained indirect possession, [complied] with the agreement of the parties and [did] therefore not prevent the passing of the risk. [...]

D. Usages in International Trade and Practices established between the Parties

Apart from the parties' individual agreement on the passing of risk, the passing of risk may also be governed by practices which the parties have established between themselves, or by trade usages on which the parties have agreed in the contract (Art 9(1)). According to Art 9(2) CISG, the parties are further bound by international trade usages which are widely observed, regardless of whether or not they agreed on them, if they knew or at least ought to have known of them.

There are a few cases in which the parties were considered bound by an INCOTERM® even absent express incorporation, simply by virtue of Article 9(2) CISG. However, the right view seems to be that even an INCOTERM® needs a clear reference in the contract and that, absent a contractual reference, an INCOTERM® could only be considered an international usage (Art 9(2)) if it were accepted by all actors in the particular trade sector to always apply.

Questions

Q 66-1

What are the consequences of the fact that the risk has passed to the buyer? See C 66-1 and C 66-2 in this respect.

Q 66-2

How do we find out whether a contract term concerns the passing of risk? See C 66-2.

Q 66-3

Who bears the burden of proving whether the risk passed from the seller to the buyer?

Q 66-4

How will the rules on passing of risk established in INCOTERM® clauses be interpreted in a CISG contract?

Q 66-5

Give an example of a loss of or damage to the goods which is neither due to an act or omission of the seller nor to natural forces and which remains out of the sphere of influence of the buyer. See C 66-1 in this respect.

Q 66-6

Articles 66 to 69 CISG govern the question of when the risk passes under an effectively concluded sales contract. Can the parties provide that the risk passes even before the contract has been concluded? See C 66-2.

Article 67 CISG

(1) If the contract of sale involves carriage of the goods and the seller is not bound to hand them over at a particular place, the risk passes to the buyer when the goods are handed over to the first carrier for transmission to the buyer in accordance with the contract of sale. If the seller is bound to hand the goods over to a carrier at a particular place, the risk does not pass to the buyer until the goods are handed over to the carrier at that place. The fact that the seller is authorised to retain documents controlling the disposition of the goods does not affect the passage of the risk.

(2) Nevertheless, the risk does not pass to the buyer until the goods are clearly identified to the contract, whether by markings on the goods, by shipping documents, by notice given to the buyer or otherwise.

I. Overview

Article 67 CISG governs the passing of risk if the contract involves the carriage of the goods. Article 67(1), sentence 1 CISG deals with the common situation where the goods must be forwarded and no particular place has been determined for them to be handed over to the carrier. Here, the risk passes with the handing over of the goods to the first carrier, regardless of who owns the goods. Article 67(1), sentence 2 CISG governs the exception where the seller is bound to hand over the goods to the carrier at a *particular place*. In such a case, the risk does not pass until handing over at that particular place has occurred. Article 67(1), sentence 3, states a common rule, namely that the retention of documents does not influence the passage of risk. Finally, according to Article 67(2) CISG, the risk remains with the seller until the goods can be clearly allocated to the contract. The consequences of the passing of risk are set out in Article 66 CISG.

II. Handing Over to the First Carrier (Article 67(1) CISG)

A. Article 67(1), Sentence 1 CISG

Article 67(1) CISG, like its counterpart provision in Article 31(a) CISG, does not define the situations in which a contract involves the carriage of goods. A contract will involve carriage if, either explicitly or implicitly, it provides for the transport of the goods after the conclusion of the contract. Virtually all INCOTERM® clauses constitute a typical explicit agreement that the goods will be forwarded (with the exception of the EXW clause). For goods which are sold afloat, Article 68 CISG provides special rules; those cases are not governed by Article 67 CISG.

Article 67(1), sentence 1, clarifies that the risk passes with the handing over to the first carrier. Thus, the CISG avoids divergences as to which party bears the risk during transport. The 'first carrier' is not an auxiliary person of the seller; Article 67(1), sentence 1, refers to an independent third person, whether this party is covering a domestic leg or international leg of the transport. Where the transport is carried out partly by the seller and partly by a third person, the risk passes with the handing over of the goods to the third person.

'Handing over' means the moment at which the carrier takes the goods into its custody. It will usually be sufficient to deposit the goods alongside the carrier's ship. However, where the parties have agreed on an INCOTERM®, 'delivery' is determined by Rule A4 of the particular INCOTERM® clause. For example, Rule A4 of the FOB, CFR, and CIF clause provides that the seller must hand the goods over on board, whereas under an FAS clause, delivery is made by placing the goods alongside ship. Other clauses leave it to the parties to determine the particular place of handing over the goods (EXW, FCA, CPT, CIP, DAP), or require delivery at the agreed terminal (DAT).

B. Interpretation of Contract Terms with Regard to Risk Allocation

Whether a contract term deals with the passing of risk, or whether it refers to one party's duty to adequately insure the goods or to the question of place of delivery, depends on the interpretation of the contract term according to Article 8 CISG.

C 67-1

Oberlandesgericht Karlsruhe (Germany), 20 November 1992, CISG-online 54[243]

[Facts]

A German buyer ordered over the telephone goods from a French seller. The conditions of delivery of the seller were 'franco domicile' ('frei Haus'), 'duty paid' ('verzollt'), 'non taxed' ('unversteuert'). The seller appointed a carrier for delivery of the goods. However the buyer failed to pay the price and denied that it had ever received the goods. The seller claimed payment of the price. As evidence of delivery of the goods the seller produced a delivery note on which the buyer had put a 'goods received' stamp ('Wareneingangsstempel') but without any signature of the buyer. [...]

---

[243] English abstract taken from UNILEX.

[Judgment]

The court held that the term 'franco domicile' covered not only the cost of delivery but also the passing of risk, so that the risk passed on to the buyer only upon delivery of the goods at its place of business. Therefore the parties had implicitly derogated from Arts 31(a) and 67(1) CISG concerning the passing of risk in contracts involving carriage of goods (Art. 6 CISG).

In reaching this conclusion, the court interpreted the term 'franco domicile' according to the understanding that a reasonable person would have had in the same circumstances (Art 8(2) CISG). In the court's opinion, a buyer entitled to the delivery of goods 'franco domicile' would not worry about transportation and insurance of the goods; [further,] the seller had insured the goods for transportation; finally the seller had often used its own transportation means in previous dealings with the same buyer.

The seller did not give evidence of delivery of the goods (the simple stamp without any signature of the buyer was held not to be sufficient evidence). The court therefore dismissed the seller's claim.

C. Particular Place (Article 67(1), Sentence 2 CISG)

Article 67(1), sentence 2 CISG refers to the situation where the seller must hand over the goods to the carrier at a particular place. The typical situation under Article 67(1), sentence 2 CISG involves the carriage of goods first on land and then by sea, whereby the seller is to deliver from port. The land transport is at the seller's risk. For those cases, the parties will often include an INCOTERM® in conjunction with a port (for example, 'FOB New York'). It must be noted that, where the parties agree on an INCOTERM®, they simultaneously derogate from Article 67(1), sentence 2 CISG to the extent that the place of handing over the goods (which coincides with the passing of risk) will be directly defined by that INCOTERM®. See also above, Article 66, III, C.

D. Documents Controlling the Disposition of the Goods (Article 67(1), Sentence 3 CISG)

Article 67(1), sentence 3 CISG states that the risk passes notwithstanding the fact that the seller might retain documents controlling the disposition of the goods. It is a widely acknowledged rule in international trade and is even accepted in countries whose domestic law connects the passing of risk with the passing of title.

III. Identification of the Goods (Article 67(2) CISG)

Article 67(2) CISG aims at protecting the buyer against the possibility of a seller presenting lost or damaged goods to it after the risk situation has occurred—with the result that the buyer is bound to pay the purchase price, although it is receiving damaged or diminished goods, or even no goods at all. The provision is of high practical importance in overseas trade, because, often, the seller does not identify the buyer as the receiver of the goods, but hands the goods to be shipped over to the carrier, and only subsequently identifies the recipients. The goods are not individualised until a notice has been dispatched that the goods have been loaded on ship. Without the existence of Article 67(2) CISG (and if the parties have not made an explicit stipulation), with dispatch of the notice, the risk would retroactively be imposed on the buyer from the moment the goods were handed over to the carrier. In order to avoid that result, Article 67(2) CISG requires that the goods be clearly identified to the contract by markings on the goods, shipping documents, by notice given to the buyer, or otherwise, before risk can pass to the buyer.

The rule of the Article 67(2) CISG leads to a division as to who bears the risk. This consequence is minimised, in that, normally, the notice of the goods loaded is effective at the moment of dispatching the goods: since Article 27 CISG provides that a notice becomes effective at the moment it is dispatched, the risk is usually on the buyer from the moment the goods are handed over to the carrier. Where a consolidated carriage of goods to several buyers has been agreed on, or where this conforms with an international trade usage, the risk passes with the allocation and identification of the consolidated cargo.

IV. Comparison with Other Legal Provisions

§ 2-509 UCC:

(1) Where the contract requires or authorizes the seller to ship the goods by carrier
  (a) if it does not require him to deliver them at a particular destination, the risk of loss passes to the buyer when the goods are duly delivered to the carrier even though the shipment is under reservation (Section 2-505); but
  (b) if it does require him to deliver them at a particular destination and the goods are there duly tendered while in the possession of the carrier, the risk of loss passes to the buyer when the goods are there duly so tendered as to enable the buyer to take delivery.

(2), (3) [...]

(4) The provisions of this section are subject to contrary agreement of the parties [...].

Art 185 OR:[244]

(1) The benefit and risk of the object pass to the buyer on conclusion of the contract, except where otherwise agreed or dictated by special circumstance.

(2) Where the object sold is defined only in generic terms, the seller must select the particular item to be delivered and, if it is to be shipped, must hand it over for dispatch.

(3) In a contract subject to a condition precedent, benefit and risk of the object do not pass to the buyer until the condition has been fulfilled.

---

[244] Translation taken from www.admin.ch/ch/e/rs/c220.html.

Art 1138 CC:[245]

(1) An obligation of delivering a thing is complete by the sole consent of the contracting parties.
(2) It makes the creditor the owner and places the thing at his risks from the time when it should have been delivered, although the handing over has not been made, unless the debtor has been given notice to deliver; in which case, the thing remains at the risk of the latter.

§ 447 BGB:

(1) If, at the buyer's request, the seller dispatches the thing sold to a place other than the place of performance, the risk passes to the buyer when the seller has handed the thing over to the forwarder, carrier or other person or body designated to dispatch the thing.
(2) If the buyer has given specific instructions as to the method of dispatching the thing and, without urgent reason, the seller fails to comply with this instruction, the seller is liable to the buyer for damage arising from that failure.

Questions

Q 67-1

Which situations are governed by Article 67 CISG?

Q 67-2

Who is meant by 'carrier'—is it a third party, or personnel under the seller's control?

Q 67-3

Article 67(1), sentence 1 CISG is said to state a generally accepted international rule. Why is it reasonable to impose the risk on the buyer as soon as the goods are handed over to carriers?

Q 67-4

How can the parties derogate from Article 67 CISG?

Q 67-5

What considerations guided the court in C 67-2 in holding that 'franco domicile' also governed the question of when the risk passed?

---

[245] Translation taken from www.legifrance.gouv.fr.

Q 67-6

With regard to Article 67(2) CISG, must the buyer have become the legal owner of the goods in order to say that the goods damaged or lost were 'the buyer's'?

Q 67-7

When does the risk pass in the following situations?

(a) Seller transports goods using its own equipment and personnel and delivers the goods at the agreed place of delivery.
(b) Seller initially transports goods and then hands them over to a third party who, after having carried them for a while, hands them over to another carrier.
(c) Seller is bound to hand the goods over to the first carrier at a particular place, but hands them over before the agreed place has been reached.
(d) Goods are handed over to the first carrier but have not yet been identified.

Q 67-8

In which of the above situations is the burden of the risk split during transport?

Q 67-9

Compare Article 67 CISG with domestic sales laws.

(a) Are there any similarities between Article 67(1) CISG and Section 2-509 UCC?
(b) What is the corresponding rule in the BGB?
(c) Why is the BGB clearer than the CISG with respect to the passing of risk in the case of handing the goods over to a freight forwarder?

Q 67-10

It has been stated that, under the CISG, although from a dogmatic view, the time of delivery and the time of passing of risk have been distinguished, in practice they will often coincide. This differs from French and Swiss law, which have settled the passing of risk in sales contracts differently.

(a) To what extent do Swiss and French law provide for a similar rule on the passing of risk?
(b) Which point in time is decisive as to whether the risk has passed to the buyer?
(c) Which rules are more suited for modern international trade, the French and Swiss ones or those found in Article 67 CISG and the other sales laws? Discuss.
(d) Under Swiss law, title to the goods will not pass until handing over the goods to the buyer. How does the CC settle the passing of title to goods? See Article 1138(1) CC.
(e) In light of your answer to (c) above, do you see a rationale in French law for how it handles the passing of risk?
(f) Which difficulty persists in Swiss law with regard to risk allocation between the buyer and the seller?

Article 68 CISG

The risk in respect of goods sold in transit passes to the buyer from the time of the conclusion of the contract. However, if the circumstances so indicate, the risk is assumed by the buyer from the time the goods were handed over to the carrier who issued the documents embodying the contract of carriage. Nevertheless, if at the time of the conclusion of the contract of sale the seller knew or ought to have known that the goods had been lost or damaged and did not disclose this to the buyer, the loss or damage is at the risk of the seller.

I. Overview

Article 68 CISG deals with the passing of risk when goods are sold afloat. The first sentence states the general rule that, in this case, the risk passes from the time of contract conclusion. However, 'if the circumstances so indicate', the risk is retroactively imposed on the buyer from the moment the goods are handed over to the carrier (sentence 2). In practice, sentence 2 of Article 68 is of greater significance than sentence 1. Finally, sentence 3 states that if the seller is held to have known of any deficiencies or losses of the goods without disclosing them at the time of the conclusion of the contract, 'the loss or damage is at the risk of the seller'.

Article 68 CISG is the result of a compromise achieved at the Drafting Conference. The ULIS provided for what has now become sentence 2 of Article 68, namely that, if goods are sold in transit, the risk should pass retroactively at the moment the goods are loaded on ship. Though a workable, clear rule, it had been criticised by import-oriented countries because the buyer bore the risk for a certain period prior to the conclusion of the contract. This is why the CISG opted for a passing of the risk at the moment of contract conclusion as a general rule and relegated the former ULIS rule to the level of exceptions. However, the broad wording of the exception leads to a retroactive imposition of the risk on the buyer in the majority of cases.

In practice, Article 68 is often superseded by an INCOTERM® or an individual contract clause. In fact, no prudent buyer would leave the question of risk allocation where goods are sold afloat to mere inference; this special type of transaction calls for an explicit provision on the passage of risk.

II. Passing of Risk at the Moment of the Conclusion of the Contract

The rule in Article 68, sentence 1 CISG leads to a division of who bears the risk. In matters of proof, this means that a seller claiming payment of the price must show that the goods were in good order at the moment of contract conclusion. If the buyer has already paid the price and then wishes to avoid the contract because of non-performance or non-conformity of the goods (Article 49(1)), it must prove that the loss of or damage to the goods occurred prior to the conclusion of the contract.

III. Retroactive Allocation of the Risk

The criterion used in sentence 2, 'if the circumstances so indicate', is rather vague. However, it is undisputed that sentence 2 applies if the buyer is entitled to an insurance claim directly from the insurer where the insurance contract covers all risks from the moment the goods are loaded on ship. This is the case with regard to contracts providing for a CIF or CIP INCOTERM®.

INCOTERMS® (2010):

> Clauses CIF (Costs Insurance and Freight) and CIP (Carriage and Insurance Paid to)
>
> **A3 Contracts of carriage and insurance**
>
> [...]
>
> Contract of insurance
>
> The seller must obtain, at his own expense, cargo insurance complying at least with the minimum cover provided by Clauses (C) of the Institute Cargo Clauses (LMA/IUA) or any similar clauses. The insurance shall be contracted with underwriters or an insurance company of good repute and entitle the buyer, or any other person having an insurable interest in the goods, to claim directly from the insurer.
>
> [...]

Article 68, sentence 2 CISG requires that the goods be handed over to 'the carrier who has issued the documents embodying the contract of carriage'. The documents referred to must be distinguished both from those mentioned in Article 58 CISG and from those referred to in Article 67 CISG. Article 58 CISG requires documents that represent the goods, and Article 67 refers to documents controlling the disposition of the goods. In contrast, Article 68 merely requires documents that prove the existence of the carriage contract. A similar provision can be found in certain INCOTERM® clauses.

INCOTERMS® (2010):

A8 Proof of delivery, transport document or equivalent electronic message (same wording as for CFR and CIF)

The seller must, at his own expense, provide the buyer without delay with the usual transport document for the agreed port of destination.

This transport document must cover the contract goods, be dated within the period agreed for shipment, enable the buyer to claim the goods from the carrier at the port of destination and, unless otherwise agreed, enable the buyer to sell the goods in transit by the transfer of the document to a subsequent buyer or by notification to the carrier.

[...]

For the purposes of Rule A8, the usual transport documents may be a receipt given by the carrier which proves the handing over of the goods to the latter, or a certificate of transport (for example, a bill of lading).

IV. Article 68, Sentence 3 CISG

Sentence 3 is an exception to sentences 1 and 2 of Article 68 CISG: if the seller knew or ought to have known that the goods had been lost or damaged at the time of conclusion of the contract, 'the loss or damage is at the risk of the seller'. With respect to damages, it is not clear what the consequences of that last phrase are: should the seller in such a case be liable only for the loss or damage occurred *during transit*, or should it also be liable for subsequent loss or damage? The question is yet to be clarified. Other than that, the fact that 'the loss or damage is at the risk of the seller' means that the buyer can exercise all remedies available in case of breach of contract (Art 45 CISG).

Questions

Q 68-1

As a general rule, when does the risk pass with regard to goods sold in transit?

Q 68-2

What are the diffculties with the general rule?

Q 68-3

What is the exception to the general rule?

Q 68-4

Why is the exception of greater practical relevance than the general rule?

Q 68-5

To which documents do Article 68, sentence 2, and Article 58, respectively, refer? Decide whether the following documents represent documents within the meaning of Article 58, or Article 68, sentence 2, or both:

(a) bill of lading;
(b) insurance policy insuring the goods in shipment;
(c) carriage contract document.

Article 69 CISG

(1) In cases not within articles 67 and 68, the risk passes to the buyer when he takes over the goods or, if he does not so in due time, from the time when the goods are placed at his disposal and he commits a breach of contract by failing to take delivery.

(2) However, if the buyer is bound to take over the goods at a place other than a place of business of the seller, the risk passes when delivery is due and the buyer is aware of the fact that the goods are placed at his disposal at that place.

(3) If the contract relates to goods not then identified, the goods are considered not to be placed at the disposal of the buyer until they are clearly identified to the contract.

I. Overview

Article 69 CISG governs the passing of risk in cases which do not fall under Articles 67 or 68 CISG. Sentence 1 addresses the situation where the place of delivery is the seller's place of business. Sentence 2 is the 'catch-all' provision covering all other cases. Article 69(3) CISG embodies the rule that the goods must be identified and thereby mirrors Article 67(3) CISG.

II. Article 69(1) CISG

Article 69(1) CISG deals with the passing of risk where the goods must be delivered at the seller's premises. The risk passes at the time the buyer takes over the goods or ought to take them over. The rationale behind this rule is that the risk should be borne by the party who has custody over the goods; that party will usually have insurance against loss of or damage to the goods. However, the risk does not pass where the goods have not been identified (Art 69(3)).

The rule of sentence 1 also applies where the goods are placed at the buyer's disposal and the buyer fails to take them over, thereby committing a breach of contract. The problem with this rule is the 'placement of the goods at the buyer's disposal' does not require that notice be given to the buyer of the fact that the goods are ready for collection. What is decisive is that the buyer is 'aware' of it. Therefore, the question is *when exactly* the buyer who is aware of the fact that the goods have been placed at its disposal but who fails to take them over, will be in breach of contract, as required by Article 69(1). Absent contractual stipulations, the standard will be that of a 'reasonable time', which will depend on the circumstances (the nature of the goods, distance, importance of time and so on).

Furthermore, sentence 1 also applies where the buyer is ready to take over the goods but refuses to pay the purchase price; it likewise applies where the buyer is excused from taking over the goods under Article 79 CISG: passing of risk and *force majeure* are distinct questions.

The situation to which Article 69(1) CISG refers is quite common where the seller is the manufacturer of the goods and the buyer is an export-trader. These parties may often include the Incoterm® 'EXW seller's premises' (its factory, mill, warehouse and so on) in their contract. Article 69(1) is then superseded by the interpretation rules of the Incoterms®. As regards the Incoterm® EXW, this means that the buyer will be responsible for loading the goods onto a truck or container at the seller's premises and for the subsequent costs and risks, although, in practice, it is not uncommon for the *seller* to load the goods on to a truck or container at its own premises without charging a loading fee.

It should be noted that, under the Incoterms®, the seller must notify the buyer that the goods have been delivered or made available. That is, in contrast to Article 69 CISG, the risk does not pass to the buyer, even if it is aware of the fact that the goods have been placed at its disposal, as long as it is not notified of this fact. The seller who fails to give such notice commits a breach of contract under the CISG!

III. Article 69(2) CISG

According to Article 69(2), the risk passes to the buyer when delivery is due and the buyer is aware of the fact that the goods are placed at its disposal at a place other than the seller's premises. Article 69(2) CISG governs all cases which do not fall under Articles 67, 68, or 69(1) CISG. The typical situation is where the goods are left with a third party, for example, at a warehouse.

C 69-1

Oberlandesgericht Hamm (Germany),
23 June 1998,
CISG-online 434[246]

[Facts]

Plaintiff, who has been assigned several debts by the seller, is asking for payment of the purchase price for a delivery of furniture.

---

[246] Translation taken from CISG Pace (citations omitted).

In the years 1992 to 1995 buyer, located in Steinheim, Germany, imported furniture manufactured in Hungary. [...]

The parties developed the practice to store the manufactured goods in a warehouse in Hungary until the buyer requested delivery. After the furniture had been stored in the warehouse, seller would issue storage invoices to the buyer. However, buyer would only pay the delivery invoices after the furniture had been delivered [to buyer's premises]. [The buyer] did not pay [any of] the storage invoices.

[...]

In her letter of 20 September 1994, buyer asked seller to stop sending her storage invoices. She told him that she would not pay such invoices [...] The furniture referred to in the invoices was not delivered to the buyer and she did not make any payment towards those invoices. The manufacturing company has gone bankrupt. The warehouse in Hungary was dissolved; there is no furniture left. [...]

[Judgment]

The appeal by [plaintiff] is unfounded. [...]

II. [...] 2. [Buyer] is not obliged under Art. 66 CISG to pay the purchase price despite the alleged loss of the goods. The burden of proof for the passing of risk is on the party that contends that the risk has passed [...]. Plaintiff did not submit and prove that the goods were destroyed after the risk had passed to the buyer.

(*Court holds that, from the provided evidence, the place of delivery of the furniture was in reality at the warehouse in Hungary.*)

[...]

The time of the passing of risk [must] be ascertained according to the rules of the CISG. The relevant provision in the case at hand is Art. 69(2) CISG, as the parties agreed that buyer would take possession of the goods at the warehouse in Hungary, that is, at a place other than the place of seller's business. The risk passes under Art. 69(2) CISG when the delivery is due and the buyer is aware of the fact that the goods are placed at her disposal at that place.

Even according to the plaintiff's submission, none of these requirements has been met. He has not proven that the deliveries were due. [...] Furthermore, plaintiff did not submit that seller had performed his obligation to deliver the furniture [...] According to the contracts, seller was to load the furniture on railway wagons or customer trucks and thereby place them at buyer's disposal. This never happened.

Furthermore, plaintiff has not explained at what point in time the furniture disappeared. Plaintiff admitted that plaintiff is unable to give any details in this regard. It is therefore— apart from the question whether a passing of risk has occurred in the first place—impossible to find out whether the loss of the furniture has occurred before or after the passing of risk.
[...]

IV. Article 69(3) CISG

Article 69(3) requires that the goods be identified; otherwise the risk remains with the seller. The goods are suffciently identified if they can be attributed to the buyer and the seller has informed the buyer thereof (see also above Art 67(3) CISG).

Questions

Q 69-1

Article 69(1) also applies where the buyer is exempt under Article 79 CISG—can you explain why?

Q 69-2

Analyse C 69-1:

(a) Where were the goods to be delivered?
(b) Did the question of whether delivery had been made become relevant for the question of whether the risk had passed to the buyer?
(c) Who bore the burden of proof as to whether the risk had passed?

Article 70 CISG

If the seller has committed a fundamental breach of contract, articles 67, 68 and 69 do not impair the remedies available to the buyer on account of the breach.

I. Overview

Article 70 CISG states the principle that the rules on the passing of risk do not impair the buyer's remedies for fundamental breach. Although not expressly stated, the rule of Article 70 CISG also applies where no delivery has taken place and the buyer wishes to exercise its remedies for non-performance (Art 49(1)(b) CISG).

II. Operation of Article 70 CISG

The effect of Article 70 CISG is that the risk passes retroactively to the seller where the buyer has resorted to the remedies of avoidance of the contract or has claimed substitute goods. Where the seller's delivery of non-conforming goods amounts to a fundamental breach of the contract, the buyer may, for example, claim substitute goods notwithstanding a loss of the delivered, non-conforming goods due to accident.

Article 70 CISG does not deal with loss of or damage to the goods which is *caused* by the seller's breach of contract, but solely with accidental losses or damages that occur *in spite of* a fundamental breach of contract.

A 70-1

Text of Secretariat Commentary on Article 82 of the 1978 Draft
   Draft counterpart of CISG Article 70[247]

---

[247] References omitted.

In essence, article 70 provides that where goods are damaged while in storage or transit and the buyer bears the risk of such damage, the buyer may, nevertheless, avoid the contract if, prior to such damage, there was a deficiency in the goods sufficiently serious to amount to a fundamental breach of contract. In this situation, 'the sense of the words used in article 70 is ... that the risks having passed back by the remedy of avoidance'. However, where the prior deficiency was not so serious as to amount to a fundamental breach of contract, the buyer cannot shift back responsibility for damage while in storage or transit by avoiding the contract.

So far, Article 70 CISG has never been applied in case law.

Article 71 CISG

(1) A party may suspend the performance of his obligation if, after the conclusion of the contract, it becomes apparent that the other party will not perform a substantial part of his obligations as a result of:
   (a) a serious deficiency in his ability to perform or in his creditworthiness; or
   (b) his conduct in preparing to perform or in performing the contract.
(2) If the seller has already dispatched the goods before the grounds described in the preceding paragraph become evident, he may prevent the handing over of the goods to the buyer even though the buyer holds a document which entitles him to obtain them. The present paragraph relates only to the rights in the goods as between the buyer and the seller.
(3) A party suspending performance, whether before or after dispatch of the goods, must immediately give notice of the suspension to the other party and must continue with performance if the other party provides adequate assurance of his performance.

I. Overview of Articles 71 to 73: Anticipatory Breach and Instalment Contracts

Articles 71 to 73 CISG deal with remedies available before performance by the other party is due. They are of great importance in practice. The provisions were discussed at length at the Drafting Conference. It was difficult to define the requirements of the provisions and to strike a balance between protecting the party conforming with the contract and protecting the interests of the debtor.

Article 71 must be read in context with Articles 72 and 73 CISG. The three provisions apply to both the seller and the buyer and deal with interferences in the run-up to the performance of the contract caused by endangerment of one party's rights (Art 71); anticipated breach of contract (Art 72); and interferences during the continuing performance of an instalment contract (Art 73).

II. Preliminary Remedy (Article 71 CISG)

Article 71 CISG deals with the situation in which performance of the contract is endangered. It does not deal with anticipated or actual breach of contract, which is covered in Articles 72, 45 *et seq.* and 61 *et seq.* CISG. Accordingly, the remedy provided in Article 71 is preliminary: the creditor is temporarily entitled to suspend performance, but it must resume performance as soon as the debtor is able and willing to perform.

The purpose of Article 71 CISG is to preserve the contract and, thus, performance of what is due. Article 71 emphasises the principle of concurrent performance. According to this principle, a party should not be obliged to perform if it is sufficiently clear that the promised counter-performance will not be rendered or will not conform to the contract.

Article 71 differentiates between the right to suspend performance (Art 71(1)) and the right to prevent the handing over of goods where they have already been dispatched (Art 71(2)). The effect of exercising one or both of these rights is that the creditor's performance does not become due as long as the creditor has grounds to rely on Article 71. The contract is in abeyance. The parties are expected to resume their obligations once the ground of suspension has been eliminated.

III. Right of Suspension (Article 71(1) CISG)

Article 71(1) CISG entitles the creditor to suspend performance of any of its obligations if, after the conclusion of the contract, it becomes apparent that the debtor will not perform a substantial part of its obligations. The danger of non-performance must be due either to 'a serious deficiency in [the debtor's] ability to perform or in its creditworthiness' (Art 71(1)(a)) or to the debtor's 'conduct in preparing to perform or in performing the contract' (Art 71(1)(b)).

The 'substantial part' referred to in Article 71(1) CISG is not congruent with the substantial deprivation referred to in Article 25 CISG. The threshold in Article 71 is lower: the contract must be considered as a whole; whether a 'substantial part' is at risk will depend on the importance which the contract itself attaches to a particular obligation, the parties' negotiations and on practices and/or trade usages, as well as on the parties' conduct subsequent to the emergence of the grounds which give rise to the expectation of non-performance.

The reasons for the debtor's unwillingness to perform may have already existed *before* the conclusion of the contract; however, the unwillingness itself must become apparent *after* the conclusion of the contract.

Article 71(1) CISG requires a prediction as to whether there is a strong possibility that the debtor will fail to fulfil a substantial part of its obligations, that is, its unwillingness must 'become apparent'. As will be seen, Articles 72 and 73 also provide for a prognosis with regard to a possible future breach of contract. The question of the different levels of probability under the three provisions will be discussed in connection with Article 73 CISG.

A. Serious Deficiency in the Ability to Perform or in Creditworthiness (Article 71(1)(a) CISG)

First, Article 71(1)(a) CISG refers to a 'serious deficiency in [the debtor's] ability to perform'. This means general obstacles in the performance of the contract, such as a strike, unpredictable loss of manufacturing facilities, outbreak of war and so on. Article 71(1)(a) also refers to a lack of creditworthiness, that is insolvency, bankruptcy of the debtor, or cessation of payment. This phrase is not necessarily tailored to the buyer; it may also be the seller who, at the outset of its performance, has to order raw materials or other goods and finds itself in unexpected financial straits.

As to whether mere delay in payment is enough to entitle the creditor to suspend its performance, see the following case abstract.

C 71-1

Oberster Gerichtshof (Austria), 12 February 1998, CISG-online 349[248]

[Facts]

[...]

The seller requested from the buyer the payment of DM 345,750 for the delivery of umbrellas during the period August 1992 until March 1993.

[...]

After several years of smooth cooperation, the [buyer] stopped paying for the deliveries. [...] [The seller] learned that the [buyer], having presented herself at the time of the conclusion of the sales contract as a flourishing and stable firm with sufficient financial means, had encountered considerable financial difficulties. This deteriorated financial condition was not known to [seller] at the time of the conclusion of the contract. By the end of 1992, there was a balance of payments due to [seller] in the amount of DM 128,169, which—apart from an amount of DM 254—resulted from invoices issued in the year 1992. Because [buyer] was in default of payment, [seller] himself had been unable to pay his suppliers, which led to a stop in deliveries. Already prior to the start of the deliveries for 1993, the [buyer] was informed that the balance due to [seller] had to be settled prior to a delivery. In February 1993, [buyer] requested [seller] to technically alter the already manufactured umbrellas. Due to the default in payment and because of this request for a modification of the contract, [seller] decided not to deliver. As the [buyer], in spite of many promises, did not pay the amount due from 1992, it was [seller's] understanding that the [buyer] was unable to effect payment. On 24 February 1993, [seller] was incorrectly informed by the [buyer] that there was an already executed bank payment order in favor of the [seller]. [Seller] therefore made further deliveries. The payment order, however, was not executed, because the [buyer] had revoked it. [...]

[Judgment]

[...]

Irrespective of the right to avoid individual installments of an installment contract, Art. 71 CISG offers a right of suspension [...]. According to this rule, a party has the right to suspend the performance of his obligations if, after the conclusion of the contract, it becomes apparent that the other party will not perform a substantial part of his obligations, as a result

---

[248] Translation taken from CISG Pace (citations omitted).

of (a) his serious deficiency in his ability to perform or his creditworthiness, or (b) his con-duct in preparing to perform or in performing the contract (Art. 71(1) CISG). Art. 71 CISG excludes all legal remedies of the applicable national law, which are envisaged for the situation that—subsequent to the conclusion of the contract—serious doubts arise whether the other party is able to perform her obligations. A recourse to broader retention rights of the national law is therefore excluded [...]. The right of suspension according to Art. 71 CISG exists inde-pendent of the right to avoid an installment contract pertaining to individual installments; the aggrieved party may choose between exercising one or the other legal remedy [...].

According to Art. 71 CISG, all 'serious' circumstances that put the orderly performance at risk may be considered as indicators that the performance is jeopardised, as well as economic difficulties including a lack of creditworthiness (Art. 71(1)(a) CISG). Furthermore, a risk may result from the debtor's conduct in performing or preparing to perform the contract (Art. 71(1)(b) CISG). A serious lack of creditworthiness, as alleged by the seller, is present if insolvency proceedings have been opened regarding the debtor's property or if the debtor has stopped his payments or deliveries [...]. Singular delayed payments or a sluggish mode of payment are normally not sufficient to show a serious loss of creditworthiness [...]. [T]he [buyer's] default in payment of the deliveries from the February and March 1993 [...] are not sufficient to legitimise a right of suspension according to Art. 71 CISG. Furthermore, the revocation of the payment order does also not show a serious lack of creditworthiness on the part of the [buyer] with high probability—such a degree is necessary in order to establish a right of suspension according to Art. 71 [...].

B. Conduct in Performing or in Preparing to Perform the Contract (Article 71(1)(b) CISG)

The rule may apply to both buyer and seller. A conduct on behalf of the buyer giv-ing rise to doubts as to whether it will perform may be its failure to pay for previous deliveries, to open a letter of credit at the contractually agreed date, or to provide the confirmation of a bank that it will open a letter of credit on occurrence of an event specified in the contract.

See also the following case abstract.

C 71-2

CIETAC Arbitration Award, 27 December 2002, CISG-online 2205[249]

[Facts]

On 15 September 1997, the [Buyer] and the [Seller] signed Contract No. 97TTNOR01, stipu-lating that the [Buyer] was to purchase from the [Seller] one BF700 item of Equipment for the Filling and Sealing of Oral Solutions for the total price of US $400,000 with a contract deposit in the amount of US $120,000. It was stipulated in the Contract that the main unit of the

---

[249] Translation taken from CISG Pace (citations omitted).

equipment was to be shipped no later than the end of October 1997, the widgets were allowed to be delivered to Hong Kong no later than the end of November 1997 and the installation and commissioning of the equipment were to be completed no later than Christmas of 1997.

Disputes arose during the performance of the Contract and the equipment was not delivered as scheduled.

The [Buyer] alleged that after the signing of the Contract, the [Seller] failed to deliver the goods as scheduled and that the package of the equipment was defective. The parties failed to reach agreement on the cooperation afterwards. On 27 May 1998, the [Seller] sent a facsimile to the [Buyer], informing that '*We are not going to deliver the first NBF700 Equipment this August as per the previous plan due to the concern that the expertise of our company for this type of equipment will be disclosed to another manufacturer.*'

In light of the above, on 20 July 1998, the [Buyer] formally notified the [Seller] requesting the delivery of the equipment on time in August 1998. The [Buyer] also stated that if the [Seller] failed to deliver the goods as scheduled for any reason, the [Buyer] would disclaim their agreement and shall retain the right to request the refund of the deposit under the Contract amounting to US $120,000 and the overdue fine by the [Seller].

The [Buyer] finally terminated [avoided] the contract because the [Seller] failed to deliver the equipment on time. The two parties negotiated over refund of the deposit and the return of moulds by the [Seller], but failed to reach an agreement.

[Facts according to seller:] The [Buyer] aimed for the innovation of a unique package difficult to imitate. Therefore, the [Seller] was asked to assist the [Buyer] with the accomplishment of the project plan, which included the development and design of the package. During the process of the project, a considerable number of alterations would have to be made even after the final determination of the selected package. The [Seller] had been taking charge of the research and development.

The [Seller] explained to the [Buyer] that a type of mould with high accuracy was requisite for pliability of the package. Therefore, the [Seller] urged the [Buyer] to use the moulds produced either by E... Co. in Austria or by a Japanese manufacturer. However, the [Buyer] selected the moulds from a Taiwanese manufacturer regardless of the [Seller]'s advice.

The testing of the package was conducted in Sweden by the [Seller]. The experiment of disinfection was conducted by an independent third party, G... The [Seller] advised the [Buyer] to adopt the disinfecting equipment provided by G... The [Seller] reported the testing result to the [Buyer]. According to the agreement between the [Seller] and the [Buyer], the product of the [Buyer], after the filling, was to undergo a high-temperature disinfecting process with the temperature exceeding 138°C. This was a strict requirement for the expertise of the package. G... and the [Seller] both mastered the necessary related expertise. Meanwhile, such expertise was provided to the [Buyer] as part of the agreement. Special experiments were conducted in the laboratory of G... to enable the [Buyer] to master the expertise of G.

The [Seller] and the [Buyer] were linked by Eastern Asia (Hong Kong) Co. (hereinafter referred to as Eastern Asia Co.). On 25 May 1998, Mr. B... F... of Eastern Asia Co. notified the [Seller] that the [Buyer] had purchased two filling machines from J... K... & Co. GmbH (hereinafter referred to as K...), a German corporation. In other words, the [Buyer] chose to purchase the product from the [Seller]'s competitor after two years' preparation by the [Seller] including research of the expertise, the comprehensive testing and the transfer of the expertise from the [Seller] to the [Buyer]. It was conspicuously intended by the [Buyer] to apply the package developed by the [Seller] to the filling machines provided by K..., so the [Seller] was concerned that K... and the [Buyer] would infringe upon the patent rights of the [Seller].

J... H... of the [Seller] expressed the concern in a facsimile sent to the [Buyer] on 28 May 1998 and J... H... wrote to the [Buyer] again on 4 June 1998. [...]

[Judgment]

[...]

4. Whether the [Seller] was entitled to refuse the delivery of equipment for fear of the disclosing of expertise

Another important reason for the failure to deliver the equipment was the possibility of disclosing expertise in addition to the aforesaid testing bottle issue. The [Seller] alleged that the [Buyer] purchased two filling machines from J... K... & GmbH Co., a competitor of the [Seller]. The [Buyer] did not deny this. [Buyer] stated that it was compelled to turn to other suppliers because of the long-term non-delivery by the [Seller]. The [Seller], however, asserted that since the [Buyer] intended to adopt the packages developed by the [Seller] to the filling machines provided by J... K... & GmbH Co., the [Seller] was concerned that they would infringe upon the patent rights of the [Seller], and expressed this concern to the [Buyer]. The Arbitration Tribunal holds that since both parties acknowledged that the purpose of purchasing the equipment by the [Buyer] was to distinguish the packages of the oral solution from the ones of the other domestic manufacturers and avoid the imitation of the products, both parties made considerable efforts for this purpose; but the adoption of the packages developed by the [Seller] in the filling machines of J... K... & GmbH Co. would expose the new expertise of the [Seller] to the attention of its competitors, which indeed posed a threat to the confidentiality of the [Seller]'s expertise. Therefore, the concern of the [Seller] was reasonable. In other words, the [Seller] was entitled to refuse the delivery of the equipment without protection of the confidentiality of its expertise.

[...]

A conduct of the seller that may give rise to fears that it will not perform a substantial part of its obligations was held to be, inter alia, the seller's late delivery of samples, or the delivery of defective samples, for approval by the buyer which would prevent the seller from manufacturing and delivering the goods on time; the seller's failure to obtain permission to export the goods, to nominate the port of loading as required by the contract, to comply with the time schedule for the contractually stipulated trial runs (thereby evoking reasons to believe that it was impossible for the seller to complete any adjustments that might be necessary on time); and the seller's failure to furnish certificates as to that the goods were free from rights or claims of third parties, or failure to procure the necessary licences or order the material needed in due time. Other indications are the use of unsuitable raw materials or inadequate means of transport.

IV. Right of Stoppage in Transit (Article 71(2) CISG)

Article 71(2) CISG deals with the seller's right to prevent the handing over of the goods to the buyer where they have been dispatched before the grounds described in Article 71(1) have become apparent (right of stoppage *in transitu*). If the right of stoppage is successfully exercised, the seller will regain access to the goods.

The effectiveness of this remedy is limited. Article 71(2) applies only between the seller and buyer, not to third parties such as the carrier, the buyer's creditors or state authorities. This gives rise to several situations in which the exercise of the right of stoppage will also depend on legal regimes other than the CISG, namely on transport law, insolvency law or property law. For instance, carriers will often secure their claims to payment of freight and of costs for stopping the goods by putting a lien on the goods; the seller's right to reacquire possession of the goods might then depend on its paying the costs for such stoppage. A further example where the right of stoppage might exist but not be successful is the case where the buyer becomes insolvent: it might be that the applicable (national) insolvency law does not recognise such a seller's right of stoppage and that the seller must join the schedule of creditors.

V. Notice Requirement: Providing Assurance (Article 71(3) CISG)

A. Giving Immediate Notice

Article 71(3) requires the creditor to immediately inform the debtor of its suspension of performance or prevention of the handing over of the goods. Notice may be given even before suspension. As to the form, and the risk of delay or error in the transmission of notice, Article 27 CISG applies. That is, the notice becomes effective from the moment of its dispatch.

If the creditor does not give such notice, the consequences are unclear. See, in this regard, the following abstracts.

C 71-3

Amtsgericht Frankfurt am Main (Germany),
31 January 1991,
CISG-online 34[250]

[Facts][251]

On September 25, 1988 a German buyer and an Italian seller concluded a contract for the sale of shoes at the price of DM 10107.19. The parties agreed that the goods should be delivered at the buyer's place of business, at the seller's expense. They also agreed that the carrier would not deliver the goods to the buyer until the buyer had paid 40% of the price. The balance was to be paid within 60 days of delivery of the goods. The seller handed over

---

[250] Translation taken from CISG Pace (citations omitted).
[251] Summary of facts taken from UNILEX.

the goods to the carrier together with an invoice for the amount of DM 10107.19. However, upon the seller's request, the carrier suspended delivery of the goods; [delivery] was resumed five months later, when the buyer had paid 40% of the agreed price. Following delivery of the goods, the buyer, instead of paying the remaining 60% of the price, only paid DM 1000. The seller commenced legal proceedings claiming payment of the balance of the purchase price.

[Judgment]

[...]

It is not necessary to decide whether or not it became apparent, after the [seller] had dispatched the goods, that there were in fact founded doubts about the creditworthiness of the [buyer] sufficient to entitle the [seller] to exercise his right to suspend the further delivery of the goods. Such a right of suspension is associated with a concurrent obligation of notification and information pursuant to Art. 71(3) CISG. If the [seller] wanted to exercise his right of suspension, the [seller] was obligated to inform the [buyer] about any existing or arisen doubts with regards to her creditworthiness or ability to perform her duties and liabilities under the sales contract. The [seller] has not demonstrated or given evidence that he gave any such notice and information to the [buyer]. Such a notification would have been an absolutely necessary prerequisite for exercising [seller]'s right of suspension for anticipatory breach.

In the light of the lack of such necessary notification and information, the [buyer] is entitled to claim for damages due to her loss of profit. [...]

C 71-4

Netherlands Arbitration Institute, Case No 2319, 15 October 2002, CISG-online 740/780[252]

For a summary of the facts see C 35-4 above.

[Judgment]

[...]

5.3 Issue 3: Could [buyer] refuse and/or suspend delivery for further deliveries? [...]

[137] Thus, the issue arises whether [buyer] gave immediate notice to [sellers] regarding the June 1998 delivery as required by Article 71(3) CISG when they did so on June 11, 1998 by fax to K. ... BV [...]. Since the problems with the increased mercury levels in the Rijn Blend were known well before that time, the Tribunal holds that the June 11, 1998 notification clearly was too late in order to enable [sellers] to take whatever action they deemed fit to protect their positions in relation to the June 1998 lifting to occur some days later.

[138] Consequently, the question arises whether the notification to K. ... BV and the subsequent discussions and negotiations with K. ... BV amounted to a notification to [sellers]. [...]

---

[252] Text taken from CISG Pace (citations omitted).

[145] The question of K. ... BV's capacity [...] boils down to the question whether [buyer] could rely upon the fact that when the operational problems regarding the increased levels of mercury could not be solved when the source of these levels became known, it was up to K. ... as the operator under the Terminalling, Off take and two of the three exploration Joint Operating Agreements to inform [sellers] at some point in time about the problems. If so, [sellers] would have reasonably led [buyer] to believe that they had been so informed and [buyer] could have relied on that.

[...]

(Buyer fails to prove that it informed seller according to Article 71(3) CISG.)

[148] On the basis of the above, the Arbitral Tribunal is of the opinion that [sellers] did not receive an immediate notification as required by Article 71(3) CISG. Consequently, [buyer] should have taken delivery of the June 1998 instalment and is liable for damages incurred upon [sellers] in that respect [...]

B. Providing Adequate Assurance

A party suspending performance must continue with its performance if the other party provides adequate assurance that it will perform. Such adequate assurance covers all sorts of security instruments, such as bank guarantees, suretyships, cessation of rights, the opening of an irrevocable letter of credit and so on. But 'adequate assurance' can, in fact, be furnished by any means, as long as it shows that the debtor will adhere to the contract. The time within which such assurance must be provided is not established in Article 71 CISG.

The case in which no assurance at all or, at least, no adequate assurance is furnished has not been settled either. Opinions are divided: while some hold that failure to provide adequate assurance automatically constitutes an anticipatory fundamental breach (Art 72 CISG), others suggest that this is not necessarily the case and that it will depend on the existence of further elements to decide whether the requirements of Article 72 CISG are fulfilled.

VI. Comparison with Other Legal Provisions

Art 7.3.4 PICC 2010:[253]

A party who reasonably believes that there will be a fundamental non-performance by the other party may demand adequate assurance of due performance and may meanwhile withhold its own performance. Where this assurance is not provided within a reasonable time the party demanding it may terminate the contract.

---

[253] *Cf* the virtually identical rule in Art 8:105 PECL.

Sec 44 SGA:

Subject to this Act, when the buyer of goods becomes insolvent the unpaid seller who has parted with the possession of the goods has the right of stopping them in transit, that is to say, he may resume possession of the goods as long as they are in course of transit, and may retain them until payment or tender of the price.

§ 2-609 UCC:

(1) A contract for sale imposes an obligation on each party that the other's expectation of receiving due performance will not be impaired. When reasonable grounds for insecurity arise with respect to the performance of either party the other may in writing demand adequate assurance of due performance and until he receives such assurance may if commercially reasonable suspend any performance for which he has not already received the agreed return.
(2) Between merchants the reasonableness of grounds for insecurity and the adequacy of any assurance offered shall be determined according to commercial standards.
(3) Acceptance of any improper delivery or payment does not prejudice the aggrieved party's right to demand adequate assurance of future performance.
(4) After receipt of a justified demand failure to provide within a reasonable time not exceeding thirty days such assurance of due performance as is adequate under the circumstances of the particular case is a repudiation of the contract.

§ 2-702(1) UCC:

Where the seller discovers the buyer to be insolvent he may refuse delivery except for cash including payment for all goods theretofore delivered under the contract, and stop delivery under this Article (Section 2-705).

§ 2-705(1) UCC:

A seller may stop delivery of goods in the possession of a carrier or other bailee when he discovers the buyer to be insolvent (Section 2-702) or if the buyer repudiates or fails to make a payment due before delivery or if for any other reason the seller has a right to withhold or reclaim the goods.

Art 82 OR:[254]

A party to a bilateral contract may not demand performance until he has discharged or offered to discharge his own obligation, unless the terms or nature of the contract allow him to do so at a later date.

---

[254] Translation taken from www.admin.ch/ch/e/rs/c220.html.

Questions

Q 71-1

What is the idea behind a right to withhold performance as stated in Article 71 CISG?

Q 71-2

See C 71-2 and Article 82 OR (Switzerland). Could the seller have withheld performance under Swiss law?

Q 71-3

(a) What are the differences between the two categories of suspension rights dealt with in paragraphs 1 and 2 of Article 71 CISG?
(b) Do the PICC 2010 provide for such a differentiation?
(c) Which of the two suspension rights mentioned in Article 71 CISG is dealt with in Section 2-705 UCC and Section 44 SGA?

Q 71-4

Is sluggish payment behaviour an indication of lack of creditworthiness within the meaning of Article 71(1)(a) CISG? See C 71-1.

Q 71-5

Article 71(3) CISG requires immediate notice of the conforming party's suspension of performance.

(a) What are possible consequences if the conforming party does not give the required notice? See C 71-3 on the one hand and C 71-4 on the other hand.
(b) Which of the two positions do you find more convincing?

Q 71-6

As regards the time span within which adequate assurance must be given, are there any differences between the Convention and the corresponding provisions in the PICC 2010 and Section 2-609(4) UCC? Which arrangement do you find more appropriate to the needs of international commercial parties?

Article 72 CISG

(1) If prior to the date for performance of the contract it is clear that one of the parties will commit a fundamental breach of contract, the other party may declare the contract avoided.
(2) If time allows, the party intending to declare the contract avoided must give reasonable notice to the other party in order to permit him to provide adequate assurance of his performance.
(3) The requirements of the preceding paragraph do not apply if the other party has declared that he will not perform his obligations.

I. Overview

Article 72 CISG allows the party that is confronted with an anticipatory fundamental breach of contract to declare the contract avoided. The provision was originally modelled on the Anglo-American rule of 'anticipatory breach of contract' (§ 2-610 UCC). Article 72 CISG is an expedient rule, since it allows a reaction to impending non-performance and enables the conforming party to free itself from a hapless contract at an early stage.

It must be noted that, once an anticipatory breach is impending, the avoidance of the contract is one possible choice. However, the conforming party may also choose to uphold the contract, await the date at which performance becomes due and, if the fundamental breach actually occurs, resort to other remedies, such as damages, a reduction of price and so on.

It is almost undisputed that the right to avoid the contract under Article 72 CISG must be exercised within a reasonable period after the imminent fundamental breach becomes clear, so as to prevent the opportunity for the creditor to speculate. The declaration of avoidance has to be made in conformity with Article 26 CISG.

II. Right to Avoid the Contract (Article 72(1) CISG)

Article 72(1) states the general rule that, for an avoidance of the contract, it must be clear that the other party will commit a fundamental breach of contract. Like Article 71(1)

CISG, it requires a prediction. As to the standard of prognosis required under Article 72(1), see *Schiedsgericht der Börse für landwirtschaftliche Produkte—Wien* at C 73-2.

Whether a breach is fundamental has to be assessed applying the standard of Article 25 CISG. In case law, the buyer was held to have committed an anticipatory breach where it had failed to pay for previous deliveries (C 74-5); where it refused to make payment while making false pretences that the goods were not conforming to the contract (C 64-1); or where, despite several requests on behalf of the seller, the buyer refused to open a letter of credit in the attempt to renegotiate the contract on a falling market (CISG-online 955). As for the seller, an anticipatory fundamental breach was seen in the fact that the seller's previous deliveries were defective to a point that the future delivery of conforming goods was not to be expected (C 71-4) or in the fact that the seller's provision of samples was so late that delivery of the goods could not possibly be made at the agreed date (C 72-1).

III. Notice Requirement (Article 72(2) CISG)

Article 72(2) CISG states the rule that, 'if time allows', the party intending to avoid the contract for anticipatory fundamental breach must give 'reasonable notice' to the other party. The idea behind the rule is that the party in anticipatory fundamental breach should have a chance to furnish adequate assurance of its performance to reassure the creditor that the contract will be honoured. Often, the creditor will expressly demand and specify the types of assurances and fix the period within which the debtor must furnish them.

There are several questions linked to this notice requirement: what does 'reasonable' notice mean? How is the term 'if time allows' to be understood? What happens if no 'reasonable' notice is given, or if no notice is given at all? What are the consequences of an inadequate or non-furnished assurance? There is some case law referring to those questions, but it is highly context-dependent, and its outcome is not always persuasive. However, with modern means of communication, situations in which time does *not* allow for giving notice will be rare. 'Reasonable' notice basically means 'communicated in an adequate way' and giving the debtor a real chance to provide adequate assurance. Where no notice is given, the consequences will depend on whether or not paragraph 3 of Article 72 applies (for a discussion of Art 72(3) see below). If paragraph 3 does not apply, it must be determined whether it would have been possible and reasonable to give notice. If it would, the creditor will be liable for breach of contract arising from its untimely avoidance. If not, the creditor can avoid the contract without further ado. This is also the consequence where no assurance has been provided.

Question

Q 72-1

Things are more complicated both where the notice given is unreasonably short and where the assurance provided by the debtor is insufficient. Should these two cases really be treated in the same way as those where no notice or no assurance at all were provided?

IV. Refusal to Perform (Article 72(3) CISG)

Article 72(3) CISG provides an exception to Article 72(2) CISG: the *declaration* of a party that it will not perform constitutes in itself an anticipated fundamental breach of contract. The declaration may be explicit or implicit, but it must make it definitely and unambiguously clear that the debtor will not fulfil its obligations. For an application of Article 72(3), see the following case abstract.

C 72-1

ICC International Court of Arbitration, Award No 8786/1997, CISG-online 749[255]

(*Facts were not provided in the case abstract.*)

[Judgment]

[...]

Claimant knew and had to anticipate that Defendant would not be able to give its green light for production by March 29 ... if Claimant delivered its samples only on March 10, respectively March 23 ... and if the samples were defective (at least) with respect to the first series of samples. As late as March 29 ... Claimant declared that delivery of the products within the time limit set in the Orders had become impossible. [...]

Claimant has made it clear in its fax dated March 29 ... that it would not be able to deliver the products at the date agreed upon and, therefore, that it would commit a fundamental breach of contract. According to Claimant's own statement of facts, it received, within two hours from its own fax, fax no [xx] of Defendant in which the latter declared to terminate the agreement. [...] The termination was based on delay ... Art. 72 para 1 CISG states: If prior to the date for performance of the contract it is clear that one of the parties will commit a fundamental breach of contract, the other party may declare the contract avoided.

Defendant terminated the agreement based on delay, i.e. based on late delivery of Orders. The termination of the agreement by Defendant therefore occurred on the basis of a fundamental breach of contract. Because Claimant itself declared that it would not meet the delivery deadline Defendant was under no obligation to ask for a bond from Claimant in accordance with Art. 72 para 2 CISG (Art. 72 para 3 CISG), as Claimant has alleged. Equally, Claimant's references to Art. 47 CISG ..., Art. 46 and 49 CISG ... are not

---

[255] English abstract taken from UNILEX.

applicable. The buyer is under no obligation to set an additional time limit to seller if seller has committed a fundamental breach of contract. Furthermore, Claimant's reference to Art. 26 CISG ... is without merit. Art. 26 CISG states: A declaration of avoidance of the contract is effective only if made by notice to the other party In the present case, termination of the agreement occurred by the telefax no ... which has been submitted as evidence by Claimant itself. Claimant has further admitted to have received this telefax.

[...]

V. Comparison with Other Legal Provisions

Art 7.3.3 PICC 2010:[256]

Where prior to the date for performance by one of the parties it is clear that there will be a fundamental non-performance by that party, the other party may terminate the contract.

§ 2-610 UCC:

When either party repudiates the contract with respect to a performance not yet due the loss of which will substantially impair the value of the contract to the other, the aggrieved party may

(a) for a commercially reasonable time await performance by the repudiating party; or
(b) resort to any remedy for breach (Section 2-703 or Section 2-711), even though he has notified the repudiating party that he would await the latter's performance and has urged retraction; and
(c) in either case suspend his own performance or proceed in accordance with the provisions of this Article on the seller's right to identify goods to the contract notwithstanding breach or to salvage unfinished goods (Section 2-704).

§ 2-703(1) UCC:

A breach of contract by the buyer includes the buyer's wrongful rejection or wrongful attempt to revoke acceptance of goods, wrongful failure to perform a contractual obligation, failure to make a payment when due, and repudiation.

§ 323(4) BGB:[257]

The obligee may terminate the contract before performance becomes due if it is obvious that the preconditions for termination will be satisfied.

---

[256] See also the almost identical wording of Art 9:304 PECL.
[257] Author's translation.

Questions

Q 72-2

Distinguish Article 72 CISG from Articles 71, 49 and 64 CISG.

Q 72-3

How must the requirement that an anticipatory fundamental breach be 'clear' be distinguished from the prerequisite in Article 71 CISG that it must 'become apparent' that one party will not perform a substantial part of its obligations?

Q 72-4

(a) What is the purpose of the 'notice' requirement in Article 72(2) CISG?
(b) In which cases will a notice within the meaning of Article 72(2) CISG not be required? See also C 72-1.

Q 72-5

(a) What are the consequences if no notice is given under Article 72(2) CISG?
(b) What happens if the debtor cannot furnish any adequate assurance?

Q 72-6

(a) How does the UCC settle the conflict between renewed willingness on behalf of the debtor to perform and the creditor's already having resorted to a remedy incompatible with the debtor's performance of the contract?
(b) Has this question been solved under the CISG? What could be a reasonable solution?

Article 73 CISG

(1) In the case of a contract for delivery of goods by instalments, if the failure of one party to perform any of his obligations in respect of any instalment constitutes a fundamental breach of contract with respect to that instalment, the other party may declare the contract avoided with respect to that instalment.
(2) If one party's failure to perform any of his obligations in respect of any instalment gives the other party good grounds to conclude that a fundamental breach of contract will occur with respect to future instalments, he may declare the contract avoided for the future, provided that he does so within a reasonable time.
(3) A buyer who declares the contract avoided in respect of any delivery may, at the same time, declare it avoided in respect of deliveries already made or of future deliveries if, by reason of their interdependence, those deliveries could not be used for the purpose contemplated by the parties at the time of the conclusion of the contract.

I. Overview

Article 73 CISG deals with the right to avoid the contract where the contract calls for the delivery of goods by instalments. Article 73 CISG provides three remedies in case of interferences associated with an instalment contract. According to Article 73(1) CISG, a fundamental breach in respect of a single instalment entitles the other party to avoid the contract in respect of that instalment. If such fundamental breach in respect of one instalment gives 'good grounds' to conclude that a fundamental breach will occur with respect to future instalments, the conforming party may avoid the contract for the future (Art 73(2) CISG). Article 73(3) CISG, finally, states that a buyer who avoids the contract in respect of one instalment may simultaneously avoid it in respect of prior or future instalments if, 'by reason of their interdependence', those instalments cannot be used for the purpose contemplated at the time of the conclusion of the contract.

The remedies provided in Article 73 CISG are additional remedies. This means that a party who is entitled to proceed according to Article 73 CISG might also prefer to resort to the general remedies (Arts 45, 61, 71, 72).

II. Definition of 'Instalment Contract'

An instalment contract provides for the delivery of goods in separate lots. The fact that more than one delivery is involved and the contract lasts for some time may lead to an increased interference. The difficulty lies in differentiating between instalment contracts and separate contracts based on an ongoing relationship. Case law has not been very precise in this respect. The following guidelines can be given: it is undisputed that an instalment contract calls for at least two separate deliveries at different points in time. This distinguishes it from an all-at-once contract. However, what are the elements that distinguish an instalment contract from a series of separate contracts? See C 73-1 in this respect.

C 73-1

Schiedsgericht der Börse für Landwirtschaftliche Produkte—Wien (Austria), 10 December 1997, CISG-online 351[258]

[Facts]

[...] Plaintiff [Seller] sold the Defendant [Buyer] a total of 6,300,000 kg Austrian summer-brew-barley harvest 1996, pure Maresi, loose per TADS-wagons for the price of Austrian schillings [sA] 225.—per 100 kg [...] to the dates January/February 1997 regarding the amount of 1,500,000 kg (Contract Attachment ./B) and March-June 1997 regarding the amount of 4,800,000 kg (Contract Attachment ./A), each according to the disposition of the buyer with weight set-off "according to the bill of lading final at departure" and parity "DAF Lichkov-Miedzylesie or Zebrzydowice". Regarding the quality of the goods, it was agreed: "healthy, customary in trade, at least 90% over 2.5 mm, 15% humidity at most, germination capacity at least 95%, stocking 29% at most, protein basis 11.5% 12% at most, quality final according to SGS-certificate." [...] The payment was supposed to be made by irrevocable and confirmed letters of credit for shipments of over 500 tons each.

[Judgment]

[...] VII. Issues of law present

1. The substance of the claim is a compensatory claim of the seller against the buyer, which is based in two respects on "breach of contract" by the buyer in the sense of para 50 et seq. of the "usages" of the market for farm products in Vienna: After delivery of two instalments of barley with a total weight of 500 tons, the buyer refused, as is undisputedly established, to accept further deliveries with the explanation that the goods delivered were defective and declared her "waiver" of further deliveries; after raising protest in the sense of para 50(1) and (2) of the "usages" and fixing an additional period of eight days for the performance of the

---

[258] Translation taken from CISG Pace (citations omitted).

contract (para 51 No. 1 of the "usages"). Following the buyer's "waiver" of further deliveries of goods, the seller finally declared the contract avoided.

1.1. Under these facts and circumstances, it is first to be examined, whether, according to the law to be applied to both contracts of sale, the buyer as purchaser of the barley had the right to avoid the contract with regard to the further installments which had not yet been delivered and which had not yet even been ready for delivery or acceptance, on grounds of the alleged qualitative defectiveness of the installments of 500 tons of the goods that had been already delivered, assuming the correctness of the buyer's allegation of defectiveness.

1.2. Neither the negotiated text of the contract, nor the 'usages' give an answer to this question, so that the CISG with its regulations in that regard has to be consulted. The regulations of the CISG are contained in Arts 72 and 73, which both provide for anticipated breach of contract as a reason for the avoidance of contract, while Art. 73, specifically for contracts for delivery of goods by installments, allows the avoidance of contract due to the apprehension of a future fundamental breach of contract in respect of future installments due to a fundamental breach of contract that has already occurred with installments already performed. According to the Arbitral Court's opinion, both contracts are to be considered a unitary transaction from an economic point of view, insofar as they provide for the delivery of the absolute same kind of goods in installments during the period January to June 1997 under the same legal terms—with slightly differing terms of payment—and they had been concluded the same day. Thus, these two contracts have to be regarded as a contractual unity, which actually comprise a total amount of barley as the object of sale, and they thus have to be subjected to the provision for contracts for delivery of goods by installment in the sense of Art. 73 CISG with regard to the installments, which had not yet been delivered. [...]

Apart from the criterion given in C 73-1, further elements which may indicate that the parties have concluded an instalment contract are the documentation of the delivery orders and the payment method: the fact that all of the goods are ordered on a single order form may suggest that the parties regard their contract as one single transaction rather than several separate ones. Likewise, the fact that the buyer agrees to pay for all deliveries in a lump sum is an indicator as to that the total of deliveries were intended to be treated as part of a single contractual agreement.

III. Fundamental Breach in respect of One Instalment (Article 73(1) CISG)

Article 73(1) CISG deals with interferences in respect of a single instalment. The residual contract remains in force and must be adjusted to the new situation.

'Fundamental breach' refers to the notion in Article 25 CISG. The fundamental breach must refer to one single lot. The assessment of whether this one particular instalment was 'fundamentally breached' is unproblematic where the contract as a whole consists of the delivery of the same kind of goods to be delivered in separate lots. However, the same assessment becomes difficult where the goods delivered in instalments are not similar in kind, for instance, where the contract provides for the sale and installation of complex equipment and the various parts are delivered in instalments. Whether a breach with regard to one single instalment is fundamental must then be assessed in light of the contract as a whole. The fundamentality would thus in general have to be denied where the instalment can be replaced or remedied.

IV. Good Grounds for Future Fundamental Breach (Article 73(2) CISG)

The avoidance of the contract as to future instalments is possible if the party seeking avoidance has 'good grounds' to conclude that the other party will commit a fundamental breach with respect to future instalments.

Article 73(2) CISG requires a prediction as to whether the fundamental breach in respect of the present instalment will encroach upon the future instalments.

The effect of an avoidance of the contract in respect of future instalments is a splitting of the entire contract. The original part remains unaffected. This includes the present instalment; the contract cannot be avoided in respect of the present instalment unless the requirements of Article 73(1) CISG are met. The contract will only be returned to status quo ante where there are exceptional circumstances such as an advance payment, the provision of devices, machinery, or licences with a view to serving the whole contract, etc.

The question most discussed in relation to Article 73(2) CISG is the required standard of prognosis: the contract can only be avoided for the future if there are 'good grounds' to conclude that a future fundamental breach will occur. Of particular relevance is the fact that Articles 71 and 72, which do also require a prognosis with regard to a future breach of contract, use different wording than Article 73(2) CISG ('becoming apparent' in Art 71, 'it is clear' in Art 72). Nowadays, it is undisputed that the difference in wording in the three provisions signals a different level of certainty regarding the future breach of contract. For an illustration of this differentiation, see once more *Schiedsgericht der Börse für Landwirtschaftliche Produkte—Wien.*

C 73–2

Schiedsgericht der Börse für Landwirtschaftliche Produkte—Wien (Austria),
10 December 1997,
CISG-online 351[259]

(*For a summary of the facts see C 73–1 above.*)

[Judgment]

Art. 73(2) CISG reads: "If one party's failure to perform any of his obligations in respect of any instalment gives the other party good grounds to conclude that a fundamental breach of

---

[259] Translation taken from CISG Pace (citations omitted).

contract will occur with respect to future instalments, he may declare the contract avoided for the future, provided that he does so within a reasonable time."

Should, as the buyer alleges, the already delivered barley really have a contract breaching defectiveness with regard to its quality, then this would have to be attributed to the seller as a fundamental breach of contract in the sense of the definition of Art. 25 CISG, because then the buyer is substantially deprived of what she was entitled to expect under the contract, i.e., barley of the agreed quality. Such a breach of duty, should it be regarded as proven, could in the Arbitral Court's opinion give the buyer "good grounds to conclude" that future install-ments might also be subject to equal or mostly similar defects in quality, especially with regard, that the breach of duty should have been present on two installments and still the seller did not weaken the buyer's apprehension, that the already proven defect on the install-ments already performed would also cling to future installments, by sufficient explanations and measures with respective probability.

According to the dominant opinion in the literature concerning the CISG, a less strict stan-dard is to be applied to the level of probability with which equal fundamental breaches of contract are to be expected on future installments after the breaches of duty so far, as is demanded in the case of Art. 72 CISG [...] which governs the anticipated breach of contracts which are not contracts for delivery of goods by installments. In that regard, a "common assumption" or "plausible reasons" are generally mentioned, sometimes also the opinion that the future breach of contract had to be "sure to expect" [...].

Honsell [...] is of the opinion, that the term "good grounds" in Art. 73(2) presupposes the least level of probability for the assumption of a future breach of contract, it suffices when for the reasons ascertained a defect in the performance of the future installments will occur with "predominant probability". The court of decision is of the same opinion; it thereby takes into consideration the buyer's regular impairment of confidence—due to the defective deliveries so far—in the seller's correct performance of contract, whose task it would be to weaken this apprehension of his contractual partner by sufficient explanations and measures, for example, through the proof that the goods to be delivered in the future would come from a different source (different producer, different trader, different silo-filling, etc.), so that equal defects are then not to be feared.

The burden of making sufficient allegations and the burden of proof for those facts, which can lead with sufficient probability to the assumption of future fundamental breaches of contract on the further installments ('good grounds') is, according to general rules, borne by the person who relies on those facts as a reason for the avoidance of contract; thus, in the present case the Defendant as buyer.

It would be the Plaintiff's obligation as seller then, to allege and prove those facts, which refute this assumption, i.e., the certified basis for prognosis. [...]

(Court affirmed the buyer's right to avoid the contract with regard to the future instal-ments according to Article 73(2) CISG.)

V. Avoidance of Past or Future Instalments due to their Interdependence (Article 73(3) CISG)

Simultaneously with an avoidance of the present instalment pursuant to Article 73(1) CISG, Article 73(3) CISG allows for an avoidance of instalments already made or of future instalments where, by reason of their interdependence, those instalments cannot be used for the purposes contemplated by the parties at the time of the conclusion of the contract. The avoidance of the entire contract according to Article 73(3) CISG presupposes the avoidance of a single instalment in application of Article 73(1). In contrast, a prognosis within the meaning of Article 73(2) is not required; the decisive element is the interdependence of the instalment avoided under Article 73(1) and the past or future instalments that are useless without the avoided instalment. 'Interdependence' must be assessed with a view to the purpose for which the buyer bought the goods. It will have to be denied where the goods in the defective instalment can be replaced or repaired within reasonable time: the defective instalment in itself may constitute a fundamental breach and allow for avoidance under Article 73(1); however, if it is reasonable for the buyer to buy replacement from another supplier, the instalments which are outstanding or have already been delivered cannot be regarded as having become useless, and thus, Article 73(3) cannot be relied on.

VI. Comparison with Other Legal Provisions

§ 2-612 UCC:

(1)   An 'installment contract' is one which requires or authorizes the delivery of goods in separate lots to be separately accepted, even though the contract contains a clause 'each delivery is a separate contract' or its equivalent.

(2)   The buyer may reject any installment which is non-conforming if the non-conformity substantially impairs the value of that installment and cannot be cured or if the non-conformity is a defect in the required documents; but if the non-conformity does not fall within subsection (3) and the seller gives adequate assurance of its cure the buyer must accept that installment.

(3)   Whenever non-conformity or default with respect to one or more installments substantially impairs the value of the whole contract there is a breach of the whole. But the aggrieved party reinstates the contract if he accepts a non-conforming installment without seasonably notifying of cancellation or if he brings an action with respect only to past installments or demands performance as to future installments.

Questions

Q 73-1

How do you distinguish 'instalment contracts' and simple contracts, several separate agreements, respectively? See also Section 2-612(1) UCC.

Q 73-2

Differentiate between the three situations mentioned in Article 73(1) to (3) CISG and explain their interaction.

Q 73-3

How do you distinguish Article 73 from Articles 71 and 72 CISG?

Q 73-4

(a) For which remedy does Article 73(1) CISG provide in case of fundamental breach in respect of a single instalment?
(b) Compare Article 73(1) CISG to Section 2-612(2) UCC with regard to requirements and available remedies.

Q 73-5

Article 73(2) CISG allows for an avoidance of the contract in respect of future instalments where there are 'good grounds' to conclude that a fundamental breach will occur with respect to future instalments. The question is whether this probability standard is higher or lower than the probability standard in Articles 71 and 72 CISG.

(a) See C 73-2: according to the tribunal, which of the three provisions provides for the lowest standard and which provides for the highest standard of prognosis?
(b) Note that the view adopted by the tribunal is a minority view. The majority in scholarly writing holds that the lowest probability standard applies in connection with Article 71 CISG and the highest under Article 72 CISG, with Article 73(2) somewhere in between. Explain why this order has been suggested and why, in particular, Article 71 CISG is considered to provide for the lowest level of prognosis.

Q 73-6

(a) Give an example of a situation that would give rise to avoidance pursuant to Article 73(3) CISG.
(b) Do you find similar solutions within the UCC?

Article 74 CISG

Damages for breach of contract by one party consist of a sum equal to the loss, including loss of profit, suffered by the other party as a consequence of the breach. Such damages may not exceed the loss which the party in breach foresaw or ought to have foreseen at the time of the conclusion of the contract, in the light of the facts and matters of which he then knew or ought to have known, as a possible consequence of the breach of contract.

I. Overview of Articles 74 to 77 and 79 CISG

The damages provisions enjoy a key position within the CISG's remedial matrix. The right to damages for the buyer, is laid down in Article 45(1)(b) CISG and for the seller, in Article 61(1)(b) CISG. These provisions clarify two matters: first, they make it clear that the remedy of damages may be coupled with other remedies. Secondly, they state the principle that the aggrieved party is entitled to damages if the contract is breached, regardless of whether there was fault on behalf of the breaching party (so-called no-fault rule). The function of Articles 74 to 77 CISG is to provide the formulae for the calculation of damages. The no-fault rule is limited by Articles 79 and 80 CISG, which allow the party in breach to be exempted from liability under very restricted conditions.

Article 74 CISG sets out the general rule applicable in all cases where the aggrieved party seeks to recover damages. Article 74 CISG is supplemented by Articles 75 and 76 CISG, which regulate the creditor's right to damages where the contract has been avoided and the aggrieved party has made a cover transaction (Art 75) or a market price for the goods (Art 76) exists. Article 77 CISG provides for a reduction of damages where it is shown that the aggrieved party has not complied with its duty to mitigate.

II. Article 74, sentence 1 CISG

A. Operation of Article 74, sentence 1 CISG

According to Article 74, sentence 1 CISG, the aggrieved party is entitled to a sum 'equal to the loss, including loss of profit, suffered by the other party as a consequence of the breach'. This provision embodies the principle of full compensation, whereby the creditor is to be placed in the same economic position as it would have been in if the contract had been properly fulfilled. The provision emphasises that a loss of profit is to be compensated as well, because certain domestic laws do not provide for such compensation.

B. Comparison with Other Legal Provisions

Art 7.4.1 PICC 2010:

> Any non-performance gives the aggrieved party a right to damages either exclusively or in conjunction with any other remedies except where the non-performance is excused under these Principles.

Questions

Q 74-1

Describe the damages concept of the CISG. In particular:

(a) what is the basic principle as to when a party will be entitled to damages?
(b) how is the no-fault rule attenuated?

Q 74-2

Compare the CISG to PICC 2010:

(a) with regard to the possibility of combining damages with other remedies.
(b) with regard to the exemption rule. Do the PICC 2010 embody the same features of the damages concept as the CISG?

III. Types of Losses

A. General Categorisations

Losses are typically divided into several categories. The CISG neither expressly distinguishes between various categories nor defines which groups of losses are covered. For a general overview of types of losses recoverable in case of breach, see the UCC, which provides a systematic list of losses.[260] The UCC starts with 'direct' loss in Section 2-714 UCC.

---

[260] This overview serves solely as a theoretical, systematic approach to the law of damages. It does not suggest that the UCC is an interpretative tool for Art 74 *et seq*.

§ 2-714 UCC:

(1) Where the buyer has accepted goods and given notification (subsection (3) of section 2-607) he may recover as damages for any non-conformity of tender the loss resulting in the ordinary course of events from the seller's breach as determined in any manner which is reasonable.

(2) The measure of damages for breach of warranty is the difference at the time and place of acceptance between the value of the goods accepted and the value they would have had if they had been as warranted, unless special circumstances show proximate damages of a different amount.

(3) In a proper case any incidental and consequential damages under the next section may also be recovered.

Section 2-714(2) UCC defines 'direct' loss as the compensation for the loss immediately caused by the breach. This comprises the costs for bringing about the situation that would have existed if the contract had been performed properly. Typical situations are the difference between the value of the goods delivered and the value conforming goods would have had, or the sum expended in curing the defect.

In addition, Section 2-714(3) UCC provides for 'incidental' and 'consequential' damages. These types of losses are quite clearly described in Section 2-715 (for the buyer) and Section 2-710 (for the seller).

§ 2-715 UCC:

(1) Incidental damages resulting from the seller's breach include expenses reasonably incurred in inspection, receipt, transportation and care and custody of goods rightfully rejected, any commercially reasonable charges, expenses or commissions in connection with effecting cover and any other reasonable expense incident to the delay or other breach.

(2) Consequential damages resulting from the seller's breach include

  (a) any loss resulting from general or particular requirements and needs of which the seller at the time of contracting had reason to know and which could not reasonably be prevented by cover or otherwise; and

  (b) injury to person or property proximately resulting from any breach of warranty.

§ 2-710 UCC:

Incidental damages to an aggrieved seller include any commercially reasonable charges, expenses or commissions incurred in stopping delivery, in the transportation, care and custody of goods after the buyer's breach, in connection with return or resale of the goods or otherwise resulting from the breach.

B. The Principle of 'Full Compensation' under the CISG

In principle, Article 74 CISG protects against all loss caused by the breach: 'damages for breach of contract by one party consist of a sum equal to the loss, including loss of profit, suffered by the other party as a consequence of the breach.' One often speaks of the 'full compensation' or 'full repair' principle of the Convention—a principle accepted by many domestic legal systems. The principle of 'full compensation' sets the benchmark for compensation: the aggrieved party should receive neither less (subject to Arts 79 and 80 CISG) nor more than the loss it suffered as a consequence of the breach.

The drafters of the CISG refrained from establishing specific guidelines for determining the loss that is recoverable because of the wide range of situations out of which losses can result. According to the traditional view, in order for the loss to be recoverable under the CISG, it must have a financial impact on the aggrieved party.

The purpose of this Section is to elaborate on the various kinds of losses compensable under Article 74 CISG. The following case neatly presents the range of losses claimable.

C 74-1

Delchi Carrier SpA v Rotorex Corp,
US Ct App (2nd Cir), 6 December 1995,
CISG-online 140

For a summary of the facts see C 49-4 above.

[...]

WINTER, Circuit Judge:

Rotorex Corporation, a New York corporation, appeals from a judgment of $1,785,772.44 in damages for lost profits and other consequential damages awarded to Delchi Carrier SpA following a bench trial before Judge Munson. The basis for the award was Rotorex's delivery of nonconforming compressors to Delchi, an Italian manufacturer of air conditioners. Delchi cross-appeals from the denial of certain incidental and consequential damages. We affirm the award of damages; we reverse in part on Delchi's cross-appeal and remand for further proceedings.

In a faxed letter dated May 23, 1988, Delchi cancelled the contract. Although it was able to expedite a previously planned order of suitable compressors from Sanyo, another supplier, Delchi was unable to obtain in a timely fashion substitute compressors from other sources and thus suffered a loss in its sales volume of Arieles during the 1988 selling season.

[Judgment]

BACKGROUND

[...]

After three years of discovery and a bench trial on the issue of damages, Judge Munson, to whom the case had been transferred, held Rotorex liable to Delchi for $1,248,331.87. This amount included consequential damages for: (i) lost profits resulting from a diminished sales level of Ariele units, (ii) expenses that Delchi incurred in attempting to remedy the nonconformity of the compressors, (iii) the cost of expediting shipment of previously ordered Sanyo compressors after Delchi rejected the Rotorex compressors, and (iv) costs of handling and storing the rejected compressors. The district court also awarded prejudgment interest under CISG art 78.

The court denied Delchi's claim for damages based on other expenses, including: (i) shipping, customs, and incidentals relating to the two shipments of Rotorex compressors; (ii) the cost of obsolete insulation and tubing that Delchi purchased only for use with Rotorex compressors; (iii) the cost of obsolete tooling purchased only for production of units with Rotorex compressors; and (iv) labor costs for four days when Delchi's production line was idle because it had no compressors to install in the air conditioning units. The court denied an award for these items on the ground that it would lead to a double recovery because 'those costs are accounted for in Delchi's recovery on its lost profits claim.' It also denied an award for the cost of modification of electrical panels for use with substitute Sanyo compressors on the ground that the cost was not attributable to the breach. Finally, the court denied recovery on Delchi's claim of 4000 additional lost sales in Italy.

[…]

Questions

Q 74-3

Explain the distinction between the various types of losses as under the UCC.

Q 74-4

Are there any losses that can only be allocated to one of those categories with difficulty?

Q 74-5

Why, in your opinion, does the CISG refrain from specifying particular types of losses?

Q 74-6

(a)   Read C 74-1. Is it possible to accumulate various types of losses, for example, consequential and incidental damages?
(b)   On which principle can the answer to (a) be based?
(c)   Based on these principles, do you agree with the reasoning of the first instance as reported in C 74-1?

C. Non-performance Loss

Non-performance loss is, first, the reduction of value of the goods due to their non-conformity. The aggrieved buyer is entitled to have the non-conformity cured at the expense of the seller. The promisee's delay in the performance of the contract also entitles the promisor to compensation for loss resulting from the delay.

D. Incidental Loss

(a) In General

According to the principle of full compensation set out in Article 74 CISG, incidental damages are also recoverable. Incidental damages include expenditure for making delivery, storing and preserving non-conforming goods, shipping and customs costs incurred when returning the goods, repairing any damage to goods that has since occurred, or installing substitute goods. The main question is whether the expenditures which the aggrieved party seeks to recover as loss have become futile due to the defective performance of the other party.

(b) Special Cases

(i) Expenditure for Debt Collection and Costs of Legal Proceedings

A prominent problem under the damages rules of the CISG is whether the expenditure for debt collection is recoverable. See in this respect the following case abstracts.

C 74-2

Schiedsgericht der Handelskammer—Hamburg (Germany), 21 June 1996, CISG-online 465[261]

[...] The Arbitral Tribunal had to decide on reimbursement by the buyer of the costs for legal assistance sustained by the seller. The Tribunal awarded the plaintiff reimbursement of the attorney's fees it incurred to pursue its claim out of court, proportionate to the degree it won. The Tribunal based the award on German domestic procedure law as well as on Art 74 CISG. Interpreting the arbitration agreement according to the understanding of a reasonable person (Art 8 CISG), the assistance of a specialized lawyer was to be expected, taking into account the circumstances of the case (involving complex legal questions dealt with by professional lawyers).

C 74-3

Amtsgericht Alsfeld (Germany), 12 May 1995, CISG-online 170[262]

[...] The Court did not award the seller recovery of the cost it incurred by hiring an Italian attorney for making a pre-trail demand for payment as, by doing so, the seller violated its duty to mitigate the loss (Art 77 CISG). The Court held that the cost of a pre-trail demand for payment would have been included in the attorney's fees of the

---

[261] English abstract taken from UNILEX.
[262] English abstract taken from UNILEX.

seller's German attorney and that it would have been reasonably possible for the seller's German attorney, who then filed the suit in the German Court, to demand payment from the buyer. [...]

A similar question is whether costs of legal procedure are recoverable under the CISG. See the following case.

C 74-4

Zapata Hermanos Sucesores SA v Hearthside Baking Co Inc, US Ct App (7th Cir), 19 November 2002, CISG-online 684[263]

[Facts]

Zapata, a Mexican corporation that supplied Lenell, a US wholesale baker of cookies, with cookie tins, sued Lenell for breach of contract and won. The district judge ordered Lenell to pay Zapata $550,000 in attorneys' fees. From that order, which the judge based both on a provision of the Convention on Contracts for the International Sale of Goods, Jan. 1, 1988, 15 USC App., and on the inherent authority of the courts to punish the conduct of litigation in bad faith, Lenell appeals.

[Judgment]

[...] Zapata brought suit under the Convention for money due under 110 invoices, amounting to some $900,000 (we round liberally), and also sought prejudgment interest plus attorneys' fees, which it contended are 'losses' within the meaning of the Convention and are therefore an automatic entitlement of a plaintiff who prevails in a suit under the Convention. At the close of the evidence in a one-week trial, the judge granted judgment as a matter of law for Zapata on 93 of the 110 invoices, totaling $850,000. Zapata's claim for money due under the remaining invoices was submitted to the jury, which found in favor of Lenell. Lenell had filed several counterclaims; the judge dismissed some of them and the jury ruled for Zapata on the others. The jury also awarded Zapata $350,000 in prejudgment interest with respect to the 93 invoices with respect to which Zapata had prevailed, and the judge then tacked on the attorneys' fees—the entire attorneys' fees that Zapata had incurred during the litigation.

[...] There is no suggestion in the background of the Convention or the cases under it that 'loss' was intended to include attorneys' fees, but no suggestion to the contrary either. Nevertheless it seems apparent that 'loss' does not include attorneys' fees incurred in the litigation of a suit for breach of contract, though certain pre-litigation legal expenditures, for example expenditures designed to mitigate the plaintiff's damages, would probably be covered as 'incidental' damages.

[...]

The Convention is about contracts, not about procedure. The principles for determining when a losing party must reimburse the winner for the latter's expense of litigation are usually not

---

[263] Citations omitted.

a part of a substantive body of law, such as contract law, but a part of procedural law. For example, the 'American rule,' that the winner must bear his own litigation expenses, and the 'English rule' (followed in most other countries as well), that he is entitled to reimbursement, are rules of general applicability. They are not field-specific. There are, however, numerous exceptions to the principle that provisions regarding attorneys' fees are part of general procedure law. For example, federal antidiscrimination, antitrust, copyright, pension, and securities laws all contain field-specific provisions modifying the American rule (as do many other field-specific statutes). An international convention on contract law *could* do the same. But not only is the question of attorneys' fees not 'expressly settled' in the Convention, it is not even mentioned. And there are no 'principles' that can be drawn out of the provisions of the Convention for determining whether 'loss' includes attorneys' fees; so by the terms of the Convention itself the matter must be left to domestic law (i.e., the law picked out by 'the rules of private international law,' which means the rules governing choice of law in international legal disputes).

US contract law is different from, say, French contract law, and the general US rule on attorneys' fee shifting (the 'American rule') is different from the French rule (loser pays). But no one would say that French contract law differs from US *because* the winner of a contract suit in France is entitled to be reimbursed by the loser, and in the US not. That's an important difference but not a contract-law difference. It is a difference resulting from differing procedural rules of general applicability.

The interpretation of 'loss' for which Zapata contends would produce anomalies, which is another reason to reject the interpretation. On Zapata's view the prevailing plaintiff in a suit under the Convention would [...] get his attorneys' fees reimbursed more or less automatically (the reason for the 'more or less' qualification will become evident in a moment). But what if the defendant won? Could he invoke the domestic law, if as is likely other than in the United States that law entitled either side that wins to reimbursement of his fees by the loser? Well, if so, could the plaintiff waive his right to attorneys' fees under the Convention in favor of domestic law, which might be more or less generous than Article 74, since Article 74 requires that any loss must, to be recoverable, be foreseeable, which beyond some level attorneys' fees, though reasonable ex post, might not be? And how likely is it that the United States would have signed the Convention had it thought that in doing so it was abandoning the hallowed American rule? To the vast majority of the signatories of the Convention, being nations in which loser pays is the rule anyway, the question whether 'loss' includes attorneys' fees would have held little interest; there is no reason to suppose they thought about the question at all.

For these reasons, we conclude that 'loss' in Article 74 does not include attorneys' fees [...]

(ii) Currency Devaluation

Whether loss resulting from the devaluation of currency may be recovered under the CISG is disputed. Read thereto the following case abstract.

C 74-5

Oberlandesgericht Düsseldorf (Germany),
14 January 1994,
CISG-online 119[264]

[Judgment]

[...]

III. [Other damages]

[...]

2. [Currency devaluation]

The [seller] also may not recover the currency devaluation of the Italian Lira against the German Mark in the amount of *It£* 1,382,250.

A currency devaluation can only be compensated if it leads to damages on the part of the creditor, for instance, if the creditor usually conducts his money transfers in a third currency and therefore always converts other currencies immediately after their receipt. In such a case, the currency devaluation has an unfavorable effect. Generally, however, an unfavorable development in the exchange rate does not lead to losses if the payment was to be effected in the creditor's currency. Usually, the creditor's currency is not converted into a different currency [...]. Nothing in the present case indicates that the [seller] suffered losses as a result of the exchange rate fluctuation. The [seller]'s contention that he needed German currency for visits to trade fairs and similar activities in Germany is irrelevant. The [seller] needed and bought those foreign currencies independently of the [buyer]'s breach of contract. In that respect, the [seller]'s damage consists solely in the fact that he had to take further bank credit. This damage does not have anything to do with the currency devaluation.

3. [Inflation rate]

It is irrelevant whether the [seller] made an alternative request for the domestic currency devaluation of the Italian Lira, that is, for inflation. The [seller] would in any case not be entitled to such compensation, because he claims to be using bank credit. Consequently, [seller] did not suffer any losses as a result of inflation, as the amount of the [seller]'s debts is not dependent on the inflation rate. [...]

Questions

Q 74-7

(a)   What is the decisive criterion for determining whether or not losses are to be compensated?

---

[264] Translation taken from CISG Pace (citations omitted).

(b)   Can the aggrieved party claim damages for expenditure that would have occurred in any case?
(c)   Can the aggrieved party claim damages for ongoing charges, such as renting localities, machinery and electricity bills?
(d)   What would be the situation if the buyer had launched a broad advertising campaign for various goods, including, but not limited to, the goods that the seller failed to deliver properly?

Q 74-8

On what do the courts focus when deciding whether or not debt collection costs should be recoverable? See C 74-2 and C 74-3.

Q 74-9

Is there any possibility of imposing attorneys' fees on the other party under Article 74 CISG? See C 74-4.

Q 74-10

Read the decision of the *Amtsgericht Alsfeld* in C 74-3, and answer the following questions.

(a)   Why was the aggrieved party denied its debt collection costs?
(b)   Would it have been able to recover them if the lawyer who represented it in court was the same lawyer who had tried to collect the outstanding sum? Which law would have governed that claim?

Q 74-11

What does C 74-4 state on the question of whether the aggrieved party will be compensated for the costs of legal proceedings? In particular:

(a)   which law governs the costs of legal proceedings?
(b)   for what crucial reason did the court refuse to allow damages for legal expenses?
(c)   why is it doubtful, according to C 74-4, that the USA would have signed the CISG if 'loss' was intended to include attorneys' fees?

Q 74-12

Do you see any practical difficulties resulting from extra-judicial legal costs being governed by the CISG?

Q 74-13

Are losses caused by currency fluctuations to be compensated? See C 74-5.

E. Consequential Damages

(a) Loss of Profit

Loss of profit, the most prominent 'indirect loss', is expressly recognised as recoverable under Article 74 CISG. Loss of profit is defined as the prevented augmentation of assets. Assessing loss of profit usually involves a prediction as to how the situation would have developed had the contract been fulfilled properly. On the interrelation between loss of profit and other damages, as well as on the calculation of lost profit, read the following case abstract.

C 74-6

Delchi Carrier SpA v Rotorex Corp,
US Ct App (2nd Cir), 6 December 1995,
CISG-online 140[265]

For a summary of the facts see C 49-4 above.

[Judgment]

[...]

On appeal, Rotorex argues that it did not breach the agreement, that Delchi is not entitled to lost profits because it maintained inventory levels in excess of the maximum number of possible lost sales, that the calculation of the number of lost sales was improper, and that the district court improperly excluded fixed costs and depreciation from the manufacturing cost in calculating lost profits. Delchi cross-appeals, claiming that it is entitled to the additional out-of-pocket expenses and the lost profits on additional sales denied by Judge Munson.

DISCUSSION

[...]

The Court of Appeals deems the district court's conclusion that Rotorex was liable for a fundamental breach of contract under the Convention proper.

We turn now to the district court's award of damages following the bench trial. [...]

The CISG provides: Damages for breach of contract by one party consist of a sum equal to the loss, including loss of profit, suffered by the other party as a consequence of the breach. Such damages may not exceed the loss which the party in breach foresaw or ought to have foreseen at the time of the conclusion of the contract, in the light of the facts and matters of which he then knew or ought to have known, as a possible consequence of the breach of contract. CISG Art 74. This provision is 'designed to place the aggrieved party in as good a position as if the other party had properly performed the contract.' [...]

---

[265] Citations omitted.

Rotorex argues that Delchi is not entitled to lost profits because it was able to maintain inventory levels of Ariele air conditioning units in excess of the maximum number of possible lost sales. In Rotorex's view, therefore, there was no actual shortfall of Ariele units available for sale because of Rotorex's delivery of nonconforming compressors. Rotorex's argument goes as follows. The end of the air conditioner selling season is August 1. If one totals the number of units available to Delchi from March to August 1, the sum is enough to fill all sales. We may assume that the evidence in the record supports the factual premise. Nevertheless, the argument is fallacious. Because of Rotorex's breach, Delchi had to shut down its manufacturing operation for a few days in May, and the date on which particular units were available for sale was substantially delayed. For example, units available in late July could not be used to meet orders in the spring. As a result, Delchi lost sales in the spring and early summer. We therefore conclude that the district court's findings regarding lost sales are not clearly erroneous. A detailed discussion of the precise number of lost sales is unnecessary because the district court's findings were, if anything, conservative.

Rotorex contends, in the alternative, that the district court improperly awarded lost profits for unfilled orders from Delchi affiliates in Europe and from sales agents within Italy. We disagree. The CISG requires that damages be limited by the familiar principle of foreseeability established in *Hadley v Baxendale*, 156 ER 145 (1854). CISG Art 74. However, it was objectively foreseeable that Delchi would take orders for Ariele sales based on the number of compressors it had ordered and expected to have ready for the season. The district court was entitled to rely upon the documents and testimony regarding these lost sales and was well within its authority in deciding which orders were proven with sufficient certainty.

Rotorex also challenges the district court's exclusion of fixed costs and depreciation from the manufacturing cost used to calculate lost profits. The trial judge calculated lost profits by subtracting the 478,783 lire 'manufacturing cost'—the total variable cost—of an Ariele unit from the 654,644 lire average sale price. The CISG does not explicitly state whether only variable expenses, or both fixed and variable expenses, should be subtracted from sales revenue in calculating lost profits. However, courts generally do not include fixed costs in the calculation of lost profits. [...] This is, of course, because the fixed costs would have been encountered whether or not the breach occurred. In the absence of a specific provision in the CISG for calculating lost profits, the district court was correct to use the standard formula employed by most American courts and to deduct only variable costs from sales revenue to arrive at a figure for lost profits.

In its cross-appeal, Delchi challenges the district court's denial of various consequential and incidental damages, including reimbursement for: (i) shipping, customs, and incidentals relating to the first and second shipments—rejected and returned—of Rotorex compressors; (ii) obsolete insulation materials and tubing purchased for use only with Rotorex compressors; (iii) obsolete tooling purchased exclusively for production of units with Rotorex compressors; and (iv) labor costs for the period of May 16–19, 1988, when the Delchi production line was idle due to a lack of compressors to install in Ariele air conditioning units. The district court denied damages for these items on the ground that they 'are accounted for in Delchi's recovery on its lost profits claim,' and, therefore, an award would constitute a double recovery for Delchi. We disagree.

The Convention provides that a contract plaintiff may collect damages to compensate for the full loss. This includes, but is not limited to, lost profits, subject only to the familiar limitation that the breaching party must have foreseen, or should have foreseen, the loss as a probable consequence. CISG Art 74; see *Hadley v Baxendale*, supra.

An award for lost profits will not compensate Delchi for the expenses in question. Delchi's lost profits are determined by calculating the hypothetical revenues to be derived from unmade sales less the hypothetical variable costs that would have been, but were not, incurred. This figure, however, does not compensate for costs actually incurred that led to no sales. Thus, to award damages for costs actually incurred in no way creates a double recovery and instead furthers the purpose of giving the injured party damages 'equal to the loss.' CISG Art 74.

The only remaining inquiries, therefore, are whether the expenses were reasonably foreseeable and legitimate incidental or consequential damages. [...]

The Court of Appeals held that these expenses are legitimate consequential damages that in no way duplicate lost profits damages.

[...]

CONCLUSION

We affirm the award of damages. We reverse in part the denial of incidental and consequential damages. We remand for further proceedings in accord with this opinion.

[...]

(b) Liability towards Third Parties; Loss of Reputation

Consequential damages may also arise in the form of loss of reputation or liability towards third parties. As examples of the latter, the seller might have to cancel its contract with its supplier, or the buyer who does not receive delivery from the seller might have to resell the goods or, where it receives non-conforming goods, may be held liable by its sub-purchaser for this non-conformity. A loss of reputation may consist of a loss of business reputation or commercial image. Read thereto the following abstract.

C 74-7

Landgericht Darmstadt (Germany),
9 May 2000,
CISG-online 560

[Facts][266]

A German seller and a Swiss buyer concluded several contracts for the sale of electronic products. Of the delivered goods 4000 video-sets had to be repaired by the buyer. When the seller claimed a reduced purchase price, the buyer claimed that the price reduction did not cover the costs of the entire reparation and asked for set-off with the additional costs. It put forward inter alia that due to the inferior quality of the products, its reputation in

---

[266] Summary of facts taken from UNILEX.

Switzerland had been damaged beyond repair. While the loss of reputation was difficult to calculate, it at least amounted to Sf 500,000.00 (DM 602,400.00).

[Judgment][267]

[...]

The Court does not follow [buyer's] argument regarding her allegedly damaged reputation. The [buyer] cannot claim a loss of turnover, on the one hand—which could be reimbursed in the form of lost profits—and then, on the other hand, try to get additional compensation for a loss in reputation. A damaged reputation is completely insignificant as long as it does not lead to a loss of turnover and consequently lost profits. A businessperson runs his business from a commercial point of view. As long as he has the necessary turnover, he can be completely indifferent towards his image. [Buyer] does not prove that her allegedly damaged reputation harmed her sales quotas. For this reason, she 'is unable to calculate the exact losses resulting from the damaged reputation.' It may very well be that if defective products are sold and marketed, the further development of the business does not correspond to the reasonable expectations. However, the Court expects at least a minimum of sufficiently substantiated submissions. The [seller] was right in pointing out that the [buyer] failed to fulfil that expectation. The generic claim that customers transferred their business to [buyer]'s competitors is not concrete enough to form the basis of a hearing of evidence. The fact that retailers wandered off to other suppliers could be documented easily enough from the [buyer]'s business papers. It does not require a 'survey evaluation'.

[...]

(c) Comparison with Other Legal Provisions

Art 7.4.2 PICC 2010:

(1) The aggrieved party is entitled to full compensation for harm sustained as a result of the non-performance. Such harm includes both any loss which it suffered and any gain of which it was deprived, taking into account any gain to the aggrieved party resulting from its avoidance of cost or harm.

(2) Such harm may be non-pecuniary and includes, for instance, physical suffering or emotional distress.

Art 7.4.3 PICC 2010:

(1) Compensation is due only for harm, including future harm, that is established with a reasonable degree of certainty.

(2) Compensation may be due for the loss of a chance in proportion to the probability of its occurrence.

(3) Where the amount of damages cannot be established with a sufficient degree of certainty, the assessment is at the discretion of the court.

---

[267] Translation taken from CISG Pace (citations omitted).

Questions

Q 74-14

(a) Define 'loss of profit'.
(b) Under what circumstances does the differentiation between loss of profit and other damages become relevant?
(c) Why is lost profit usually more uncertain than other damages?

Q 74-15

(a) Does Article 74 CISG state the standard of proof that the party claiming loss of profit must satisfy?
(b) Compare your answer to (a) with Article 7.4.3 PICC 2010. Are there, in practice, any differences to how the courts determine the level of proof under the CISG?

Q 74-16

(a) How did the Court of Appeals calculate *Delchi's* loss of profit in C 74-6, and on which rules did it base its calculation?
(b) The *Rotorex* case in C 74-6 deals, inter alia, with a so-called 'lost volume sale'. Can you explain what this means?

Q 74-17

Article 74 allows for liabilities towards third parties to be compensated. What are the requirements for this compensation, and how are such damages to be limited?

Q 74-18

(a) Is loss of reputation necessarily reflected in money?
(b) Does the CISG allow for (non-material) loss of goodwill? See C 74-7.
(c) Compare the solution under the CISG with the PICC 2010. Are there any differences?

Q 74-19

(a) Which level of proof did the court in C 74-7 apply for establishing loss of reputation?
(b) Why would it place an insurmountable burden on the aggrieved party if it were required to calculate the damages for loss of reputation exactly?

Q 74-20

In some legal systems, damages are awarded for the mere loss of a chance. For example, where a horse, as a result of delays in transport, arrives too late to run in a race, its owner may be able to recover a certain amount of the prize money if it can be established that the horse was the favourite to win.[268]

(a) Does the CISG cover the loss of a chance?
(b) Why does Article 7.4.3(2) PICC 2010 explicitly mention loss of a chance?
(c) If loss of a chance were not included in Article 74 CISG, how could this conflict with other principles underlying the CISG?

IV. Article 74, sentence 2 CISG

A. Operation of Article 74, sentence 2 CISG

The principle of full compensation is limited by the criterion that the loss was foreseeable at the time of the conclusion of the contract (Art 74, sentence 2). The drafters thereby adopted the Anglo-American contemplation rule established in the House of Lords decision of *Hadley v Baxendale*, 9 Ex 341, 156 ER 145 (1854) (see below). In accordance with the *Hadley* doctrine, the CISG's foreseeability standard is to be evaluated solely on the basis of information available to the party in breach at the time of the conclusion of the contract, in the light of the facts and matters which that party then knew or ought to have known.

C 74-8

Oberster Gerichtshof (Austria),
14 January 2002,
CISG-online 643

[Facts][269]

A German seller and an Austrian buyer concluded a contract for the sale of a cooling system to be specifically manufactured by the seller. According to the seller's standard terms, inter alia consequential damages were excluded. The seller failed to meet the date for delivery; when the cooling system was delivered, it showed some manifest defects (corrosion, poor finish) which the buyer immediately notified to the seller. Nevertheless, it installed the system in order to avoid the penalty provided by its contract with the intermediary. Subsequently additional technical defects appeared (lower capacity, noise level too high, and others) of which the buyer gave notice to the seller as soon as they were discovered. When the seller's attempts to repair proved to be unsuccessful, the buyer and the intermediary asked for the delivery of a substitute system, but the seller refused to do so. After another unsuccessful attempt to repair the system, the buyer and the constructor agreed to install temporarily the defective on the understanding that the buyer would later provide a substitute system. The

---

[268] See the example in the Official Comment to the PICC 2010, at Art 7.4.3, comment 1.
[269] Summary of facts taken from UNILEX.

seller was not involved in, nor informed about, this agreement. At the agreed date the system was remoulded by the buyer and newly installed. Since then, it has functioned properly. When the seller brought an action for payment of the invoices relating to other transactions between the two parties, the buyer refused to pay, and set-off against the obligation to pay those invoices the seller's obligation of reimbursement of the losses the buyer had suffered as a consequence of the delivery of the defective cooling system.

[Judgment][270]

[...] The opinion of the Appellate Court was that the [buyer] had a counterclaim under Arts 74 et seq. CISG since after rejection of an offer to correct the problem the [buyer] justifiably undertook to remedy the defect itself and then set off the [seller]'s claim out of court with its counterclaim. This opinion withstands all objections in these proceedings. Also, the [buyer]'s efforts to remedy the situation under the ascertained circumstances cannot be characterized as unreasonable.

The damages claim of the non-breaching party (here the [buyer]) under Art 74 CISG, which is independent of fault [...] and only to be paid in money damages [...] as a consequence of the other party's breach of contract (here the [seller]), functions as an equalizer. By way of money damages, the obligee should be put as closely as possible in the economic position in which he would have been, had the contractual obligations been properly performed [...]. The CISG is based on the principle of full compensation [...]: [...] Expenses incurred because of the contract can be recoverable if it is determined that they would not have been incurred were it not for reliance on performance of the contract and that they lost their purpose through the breach of contract. Moreover, from the viewpoint of a reasonable person in the same circumstances (Art 8(2) CISG), such expenses must have been appropriate and reasonable for the performance of the contract [...].

Under Art 74 CISG, however, (as the [seller] in this appeal rightly objects, asserting that the [buyer]'s damages claim many times exceeds the price of the table cooler at issue), the damages claim is limited to those losses which were foreseeable for the obligee at the time of the conclusion of the contract. With regard to the purpose of the contract, foreseeability must refer to losses that can be a possible consequence of a breach of contract. [...]. Foreseeability in Art 74 CISG refers therefore only to losses that at the time of the conclusion of the contract were an assessable consequence of a possible breach of obligation [...]. According to prevailing opinion, Art 74 CISG does not require precise and detailed foreseeability of losses, and certainly not a numbered sum on the extent of loss [...]. On the other hand, the invariably foreseeable possibility that a breach of contract will produce some type of loss is not sufficient. However, a (typical) loss due to non-performance is under prevailing opinion generally foreseeable [...]. It is necessary that the obligor could recognize that a breach of contract would produce a loss essentially of the type and extent that actually occurred [...]. Generally an objective standard is applied for foreseeability here. The obligor must reckon with the consequences that a reasonable person in his situation (Art 8(2) CISG) would have foreseen considering the particular circumstances of the case. Whether he actually did foresee this is as insignificant as whether there was fault [...]. Yet, subjective risk evaluation cannot be completely ignored: if the obligor knows that a breach of contract would produce unusual or unusually high losses, then these consequences are imputable to him [...].

Consequential damages are, insofar as they are pecuniary losses, also generally recoverable under the CISG if at the conclusion of the contract the loss could be viewed as a sufficiently probable consequence. For instance, a buyer of defective goods can foresee an obligation to

---

[270] Translation taken from CISG Pace (citations omitted).

pay damages to his own customers, as long as the obligation does not exceed the usual extent [...]. Since, however, in the present case, as already emphasized, the [seller]'s standard terms (which supercede the provisions of the CISG) exclude the recovery of consequential damages, the Appellate Court correctly rejected other such losses claimed by the [buyer] in the amount of DM 38,278.70. This is also no longer disputed in this appeal.

However, the Appellate Court failed to consider the limitation of damages through the foreseeability rule of Art 74 CISG. As just explained, the determination of the amount of the [buyer]'s set-off counterclaim also depends to a large degree on what possible losses a reasonable person would have foreseen at the time of the conclusion of this contract for work and materials. As also already explained, this foreseeability of loss within the meaning of Art 74 CISG is determined according to the particular circumstances at the time of the conclusion of the contract. However, the Trial Court, which erred in denying application of the UN Sales Law, failed to determine these. There was also no determination made regarding the [seller]'s subjective risk evaluation at the time of the conclusion of the contract. In particular, the [buyer]'s last claim brought was also not discussed, namely, that the [seller] knew at the conclusion of the contract where and under what conditions the table cooler was being installed and the [seller] therefore must have foreseen that in the event of defective performance a loss in the amount claimed could arise. The proceedings are in this regard yet incomplete, also regarding the extent of the rejection of DM 35,329.56 with the partial judgment.

[...]

From Art 74 CISG comes the necessity of determining to what degree a reasonable person within the meaning of Art 8(3) CISG in the circumstances known to the [seller] at the time of the conclusion of the contract could (or should) foresee such problems and expenses; and if need be, also whether or to what degree such damages (in this manner determinable, foreseeable, exceeding the loss, and resulting directly from the [seller]'s breach of contract) of the [buyer] were actually foreseeable for the [seller] at the time of conclusion of the contract. Since the time of the conclusion of the contract is the relevant moment, the circumstance emphasized by the Appellate Court, that the [seller] was informed of the threatening damages claims of the [buyer]'s customer, would only be of importance essential to the decision if this information was given prior to or during the conclusion of the contract.

In order to reliably answer the question of foreseeability within the meaning of Art 74 CISG according to these criteria, and thus determine the amount of the counterclaim from the out of court set-off, the Trial Court must clarify the questions of fact still left open in corresponding supplemental proceedings. The question of foreseeability of loss at the time of conclusion of the contract, which will then be judicable, will be of determining importance for the question of law identified by the Appellate Court as important within the meaning of § 502(1) ZPO regarding the reasonableness of the [buyer]'s claimed costs to remedy the defects. [...]

B. Comparison with Other Legal Provisions

England

Hadley v Baxendale, 9 Ex 341, 156 ER 145 (1854)

[...] ALDERSON, B.—[...] Now we think the proper rule in such a case as the present is this:— Where two parties have made a contract which one of them has broken, the damages which the other party ought to receive in respect of such breach of contract should be such as may fairly and reasonably be considered either arising naturally, i.e. according to the usual course of things, from such breach of contract itself, or such as may be supposed to have been in the contemplation of both parties, at the time they made the contract, as the probable result of the breach of it. Now, if the special circumstances under which the contract was actually made were communicated by the plaintiffs to the defendant, and thus known to both parties, the damages resulting from the breach of such a contract, which they would reasonably contemplate, would be the amount of injury which would ordinarily follow from a breach of contract under these special circumstances so known and communicated. But, on the other hand, if these special circumstances were wholly unknown to the party breaking the contract, he, at the most, could only be supposed to have had in his contemplation the amount of injury which would arise generally, and in the great multitude of cases not affected by any special circumstances, from such a breach of contract. [...]

Art 7.4.4 PICC 2010:

The non-performing party is liable only for harm which it foresaw or could reasonably have foreseen at the time of the conclusion of the contract as being likely to result from its non-performance.

Art 1150 CC:[271]

A debtor is liable only for damages which were foreseen or which could have been foreseen at the time of the contract, where it is not through his own intentional breach that the obligation is not fulfilled.

§ 351 Restatement 2d, Contracts:

(1) Damages are not recoverable for a loss that the party in breach did not have reason to foresee as a probable result of the breach when the contract was made.

Art 113 PRC CL:

Where a party failed to perform or rendered non-conforming performance, thereby causing loss to the other party, the amount of damages payable shall be equivalent to the other party's loss resulting from the breach, including any benefit that may be accrued from performance of the contract, provided that the amount shall not exceed the likely loss resulting from the breach which was foreseen or should have been foreseen by the breaching party at the time of conclusion of the contract.

[...]

§ 933a(1) ABGB:[272]

If there is fault on behalf of the party making delivery, the other party may also claim damages.

---

[271] Translation taken from www.legifrance.gouv.fr.
[272] Author's translation.

Art 208 OR:[273]

(1) [...]
(2) The seller must return the purchase price including interest and must bear the costs of legal proceedings, the expenses and seller's loss directly arising from the delivery of non-conforming goods.
(3) The seller must compensate for further loss if it cannot prove that there is no fault on its behalf.

Questions

Q 74-21

What is the underlying idea of the foreseeability test? See the English decision of *Hadley v Baxendale*.

Q 74-22

If one party—after the conclusion of the contract, but before committing the breach of contract—learns of circumstances which indicate a risk of extraordinary loss for the other party, is this relevant to the extent of the first party's liability? See C 74-8.

Q 74-23

(a) What kind of loss was at issue in C 74-8?
(b) How certain must the foreseeability of a loss be, according to C 74-8?

Q 74-24

Which party bears the burden of proving whether or not the loss was foreseeable?

Q 74-25

(a) Is there a way to derogate from Articles 74 to 77 CISG? See also C 74-8.
(b) What do we call such clauses, and what is their effect?
(c) What factors are relevant in determining the degree to which such a clause displaces the CISG provisions?
(d) Which law governs the question of whether or not such a contract clause is valid?
(e) If the limiting clause is found to be invalid, what law will displace it?

---

[273] Author's translation.

V. CISG Advisory Council

The above-explained principles have been laid down in the black letter rules of the CISG Advisory Council Opinion No 6.

CISG Advisory Council Opinion No 6: Calculation of Damages under CISG Article 74—Black Letter Rules:[274]

Article 74

1. Article 74 reflects the general principle of full compensation.

2. The aggrieved party has the burden to prove, with reasonable certainty, that it suffered a loss. The aggrieved party also has the burden to prove the extent of the loss, but need not do so with mathematical precision.

3. The aggrieved party is entitled to non-performance damages, which is typically measured by the market value of the benefit of which the aggrieved party has been deprived through the breach, or the costs of reasonable measures to bring about the situation that would have existed had the contract been properly performed.

   A. The aggrieved party is entitled to any net gains prevented as a result of the breach.

   B. Lost profits recoverable under Article 74 may include loss of profits that are expected to be incurred after the time damages are assessed by a tribunal.

   C. Lost profits include those arising from lost volume sales.

4. The aggrieved party is entitled to additional costs reasonably incurred as a result of the breach and of measures taken to mitigate the loss.

5. Under Article 74, the aggrieved party cannot recover expenses associated with litigation of the breach.

6. The aggrieved party is entitled to damages for pecuniary loss resulting from claims by third parties as a result of the breach of contract.

7. The aggrieved party is entitled to damages for loss of goodwill as a consequence of the breach.

8. If there has been a breach of contract and then the aggrieved party enters into a reasonable substitute transaction without first having avoided the contract, the aggrieved party may recover damages under Article 74, that is, the difference between the contract price and the substitute transaction.

9. Damages must not place the aggrieved party in a better position than it would have enjoyed if the contract had been properly performed.

   A. In calculating the amount of damages owed to the aggrieved party, the loss to the aggrieved party resulting from the breach is to be offset, in principle, by any gains to the aggrieved party resulting from the non-performance of the contract.

   B. Punitive damages may not be awarded under Article 74 of the Convention.

---

[274] Taken from www.cisgac.com.

Article 75 CISG

If the contract is avoided and if, in a reasonable manner and within a reasonable time after avoidance, the buyer has bought goods in replacement or the seller has resold the goods, the party claiming damages may recover the difference between the contract price and the price in the substitute transaction as well as any further damages recoverable under article 74.

I. Overview

Article 75 CISG comprises one of the two formulae for calculating damages in the case where the contract has been avoided. It calculates damages as the difference between the contract price and the price of a substitute transaction. The buyer can claim damages as the difference between the contract price and the higher price of the cover purchase. The seller is entitled to damages as the difference between the contract price and the lower price of the cover sale.

II. Operation of Article 75 CISG

A. Avoidance of the Contract

The wording of Article 75 CISG requires an effective avoidance of the contract prior to undertaking the substitute transaction. In practice, however, it might be reasonable for a party to enter into a cover transaction before avoiding the contract. In this respect see the following case abstracts.

C 75-1

ICC International Court of Arbitration,
Award No 8574/1996,
UNILEX[275]

[...]

With regard to the buyer's request for damages arising out of the higher price of the substitute transactions, the Arbitral Tribunal stated that it could not be based on Art 75 CISG, because the buyer had failed to make an effective declaration of avoidance (termination), which is a requisite under that provision. [...] Nevertheless, the Arbitral Tribunal awarded the buyer damages on the basis of Art 74 and Art 77 CISG, since the contract of sale was still in force in 1994 and the substitute transactions at a higher price than the one agreed upon in the contract could be considered as a measure undertaken to mitigate damages.

C 75-2

Oberlandesgericht Hamburg (Germany),
28 February 1997,
CISG-online 261

[Facts][276]

A German seller and an English buyer concluded a contract for the sale of Iron-molybdenum with a molybdenum content of at least 64%. The price agreed upon by the parties was 9.70 US$/Kg molybdenum. The standard terms of the seller contained a force majeure clause which exempted the seller for any responsibility following a failure and/or delay in delivery of the goods. A few days after the conclusion of the contract, the buyer refused a seller's proposal to increase the purchase price following a rise in market price. The seller further invited the buyer to accept a reduction of the molybdenum content together with a time delay. The buyer accepted the percentage reduction but fixed a shorter period of time for delivery. The seller informed the buyer that it needed an additional period of time and offered to pay the buyer a compensation. As the seller did not perform within the fixed period of time the buyer had to make a substitute purchase at a higher price in order to be able to perform a contract already concluded with a third party. The buyer commenced an action claiming damages and interest.

[Judgment][277]

[...]

The Court does not have to investigate whether the Buyer has avoided the contract before concluding a cover purchase, as Art 75 CISG would normally require. Doubts about a declaration

---

[275] www.unilex.info/case.cfm?pid=1&do=case&id=521&step=FullText
[276] Summary of facts taken from UNILEX.
[277] Translation taken from CISG Pace (citations omitted).

of avoidance before the conclusion of the cover purchase are caused by the fact that the fax of 17 January 1995 does not exactly prove when the Buyer informed the Seller of the cover purchase and thereby impliedly declared the contract avoided. The communications before—the faxes of 13 December 1994, 16 December 1994 and 29 December 1994—do not make clear that the Buyer intended to avoid the contract. A declaration of avoidance under the condition of performance which is generally admissible, […] was not made. Such a declaration cannot be seen in the fax messages mentioned above, nor in the fax message of 3 November 1994, because this would require that the Buyer actually wanted to lose its right to choose between contract fulfilment and damages by sending the messages. The communication submitted to the Court would contradict that conclusion because the Buyer insisted on its claim for 'performance of the contract'.

However, an explicit declaration of avoidance was not necessary because, before Buyer made the cover purchase, the Seller had seriously and finally refused to perform under the sales contract. Although the CISG does not make an exception from the requirement of a declaration of avoidance, the rule of the 'observance of good faith in international trade' (Art 7(1) CISG) leads to the result that a declaration of avoidance is not necessary, if it is certain that the other party will not perform its obligations in a case […].

The Seller uttered its serious refusal at the latest by the fax of 29 December 1994, which was the answer to the Buyer's fax of 16 December 1994, in which the Buyer continued to demand contract fulfilment and threatened to demand damages. It has not reacted to the Buyer's fax by a new offer to fulfil the contract but has merely offered the payment of a 'compensation'. While knowing that the Buyer obviously did not want to wait for the result of the negotiations between the Seller and its Chinese supplier, the Seller did not want to fulfil its obligations by acquiring the goods from a different source but only by paying damages or a compensation. In this situation, the Seller could not in good faith assume that it would still have the option to fulfil the contract, especially since it knew that the contract was a fixed-date transaction and since the Buyer had emphasized the importance of timely delivery several times.

Obviously, the Seller did not assume that it still had the option to fulfil the contract, as it has stated in a memorandum of 14 August 1995 that the Buyer could undisputedly no longer expect delivery in January 1995. Although the requirements to assume a refusal to deliver are high, at least the fax of 29 December 1994 has to be regarded as such a refusal. The Seller did not need the protection by a declaration of avoidance since it did not itself try to fulfil the contract.

[…]

C 75-3

Audiencia Provincial de Palencia (Spain), 26 September 2005, CISG-online 1673

[Facts][278]

A Spanish buyer entered into a contract with a US seller for the sale of a printing machine. Once delivered, the machine failed to function. The buyer sued the seller for breach of contract alleging lack of conformity of goods and claimed for damages, included the price of another printing machine bought from a third party. In response, the seller argued that

---

[278] Translation taken from UNILEX.

it did not breach the contract because it was the buyer's conduct (inappropriate conditions for placement, lack of adequate electricity and potable water) which led to the failure of the equipment, not the equipment itself.

The Court of First Instance ruled in favour of the buyer but awarded it only part of the damages claimed. Both of the parties appealed. The seller submitted the same issues argued before the lower court, while contesting the damages awarded to the buyer arguing that even assuming it had breached the contract, there was no direct link between the breach and the damages awarded to the buyer. The latter argued that the judgment in its favour should have included the cost of the replacement printing machine it had purchased.

[Judgment][279]

[...] this Court confirms the appealed sentence which supports the avoidance of the sales contract due to breach of the contract by the [Seller].

[...]

We also recognize that the second-hand printing machine purchased in Holland was acquired in July 1999 and the installation and that the proper functioning of the [Buyer]'s new machine bought from [Seller] was not at issue at that time. However, the beginning of the [Buyer]'s productive process, which commenced in March of each year, was suffering a great delay (more than three months). At that moment, the [Buyer]'s CEO took a risky decision to acquire a second-hand printer, which used a system sheet-to-sheet, for a high price (more than 50 million old *Pesetas*). This turned out to be a correct decision, due to the fact that the new printer could not be used and the [Buyer] needed to go to other printing companies, also the [Buyer] was at the limit of its production capacity to be able to produce all the printed paper needed to attend to its clients' demands. The decision of the [Buyer]'s CEO was not capricious. It was preventive and finally successful, and the evidence establishes that is not fair that the expense for the acquisition must be borne by [Buyer], when if the printer had functioned properly these expenses would not have been necessary. We rule that, by consequence, the said expense for damages should be included, with the price obtained for the sale of the second-hand printer to the Argentinean entity subtracted from this claim for added damages. The appeal lodged by the [Buyer] is thus sustained.

[...]

The Court sustains [Buyer]'s claim in its entirety and compels the [Seller] to pay the amount of €1,529,197.83, as a result of the breach of the contract.

[...]

Question

Q 75-1

(a)   Which situations does Article 75 CISG govern?
(b)   Was it necessary to establish Article 75 alongside Article 74 CISG?
(c)   If the aggrieved party does not proceed under Article 75 CISG, is it deprived of any other remedies available under the CISG?

---

[279] Translation taken from CISG Pace.

B. Reasonableness of the Cover Transaction

Article 75 CISG does not explicitly state that the price in the substitute transaction must be reasonable. Nonetheless, case law regularly requires that 'the buyer acts as a prudent and careful businessperson who sells goods of the same kind and quality, ignoring unimportant small differences in quality'.[280] As to what constitutes a reasonable time, see the following case abstract.

C 75-4

Oberlandesgericht Hamburg (Germany),
28 February 1997,
CISG-online 261

For a summary of the facts see C 75-2 above.

[Judgment][281]

(c) [The cover purchase]

The contract which was concluded by the Buyer on 11 January 1995 is an appropriate cover purchase in the sense of Art 75 CISG. Under this contract, which resembles the contract of 12 October 1994, (amended on 31 October 1994, Exhibits K 4 and K 6) with respect to the amount and the quality of the iron-molybdenum, the Buyer has acquired material from a third party, therefore the contracts suitability to cover the Buyer's fulfilment interest. Also the connection in time between the two contracts is so close that reasonable doubts concerning the contract's designation as a cover transaction are not present. With respect to the development of prices which is proven by the Seller's offer of 17 January 1995, no indication is given for the assumption that the cover purchase was not concluded in a manner in accordance to business usage. The cover purchase was also concluded within a reasonable period of time, approximately two weeks, after the refusal to deliver which replaces the declaration of avoidance in the instant case. This period of time has to be granted for orientation and consideration and for inviting offers, especially since—in contrast to §376 para. 3 HGB—the CISG does not require the Buyer to conduct the cover purchase 'immediately' [...].

III. Comparison with Other Legal Provisions

Art 7.4.5 PICC 2010:

Where the aggrieved party has terminated the contract and has made a replacement transaction within a reasonable time and in a reasonable manner it may recover the difference

---

[280] ICC Award No 8128/1995, UNILEX.
[281] Translation taken from CISG Pace (citations omitted).

between the contract price and the price of the replacement transaction as well as damages for any further harm.

§ 2-706(1) UCC:

Under the conditions stated in Section 2-703 on seller's remedies, the seller may resell the goods concerned or the undelivered balance thereof. Where the resale is made in good faith and in a commercially reasonable manner the seller may recover the difference between the resale price and the contract price together with any incidental damages allowed under the provisions of this Article (Section 2-710), but less expenses saved in consequence of the buyer's breach.

§ 2-712 UCC:

(1) After a breach within the preceding Section the buyer may 'cover' by making in good faith and without unreasonable delay any reasonable purchase of or contract to purchase goods in substitution for those due from the seller.
(2) The buyer may recover from the seller as damages the difference between the cost of cover and the contract price together with any incidental or consequential damages as hereinafter defined (Section 2-715), but less expenses saved in consequence of the seller's breach.
(3) Failure of the buyer to effect cover within this Section does not bar him from any other remedy.

Art 191(2) OR:[282]

The buyer in a commercial transaction is entitled to compensation of the difference between the sale price and the price he has paid in good faith to replace the object that was not delivered to him.

Art 215(1) OR:[283]

Where the buyer in a commercial transaction fails to discharge his payment obligation, the seller is entitled to compensation for the difference between the sale price and the price at which he has subsequently sold the object in good faith.

Questions

Q 75-2

(a) What factors are used to determine whether the cover transaction satisfies the 'reasonability test' in Article 75 CISG?
(b) On which other provision of the CISG can the requirement that the cover transaction be reasonable be based?

---

[282] Translation taken from www.admin.ch/ch/e/rs/2/220.en.pdf.
[283] Translation taken from www.admin.ch/ch/e/rs/2/220.en.pdf.

Q 75-3

What is the consequence if there is a significant difference between the contract price and the price in the substitute transaction?

Q 75-4

(a)   Is there a guideline as to what constitutes a reasonable time?
(b)   When will the reasonable time begin to run? See C 75-4.

Q 75-5

(a)   Compared to corresponding legal provisions from other legal systems, does Article 75 CISG constitute a generally acknowledged rule?
(b)   Do the domestic legal provisions also require a termination of the contract prior to the cover transaction?

IV. CISG Advisory Council

CISG Advisory Council Opinion No 8: Calculation of Damages under CISG Articles 75 and 76—Black Letter Rules:[284]

2.1   Under Article 75, an aggrieved party is entitled to recover as damages the difference between the contract price and the price of the substitute transaction.

2.2   The contract price is the price fixed in the contract or the price as determined under Article 55.

2.3   The price in any substitute transaction may be used to calculate damages under the formula set forth in Article 75 only if the aggrieved party made a substitute transaction in a reasonable manner and in a reasonable time.

2.4   In the event that the aggrieved party's substitute transaction was unreasonable, damages may be calculated according to Article 76 or Article 74.

3   An aggrieved party entitled to damages under Article 75 may also recover any further damages under Article 74.

---

[284] Taken from www.cisgac.com.

Article 76 CISG

(1) If the contract is avoided and there is a current price for the goods, the party claiming damages may, if he has not made a purchase or resale under article 75, recover the difference between the price fixed by the contract and the current price at the time of avoidance as well as any further damages recoverable under article 74. If, however, the party claiming damages has avoided the contract after taking over the goods, the current price at the time of such taking over shall be applied instead of the current price at the time of avoidance.

(2) For the purposes of the preceding paragraph, the current price is the price prevailing at the place where delivery of the goods should have been made, or, if there is no current price at that place, the price at such other place as serves as a reasonable substitute, making due allowance for differences in the cost of transporting the goods.

I. Overview

Article 76 CISG constitutes the second special rule to Article 74 CISG. It provides the formula for an abstract calculation of damages where the contract has been avoided. It dispenses with the requirement of an actual cover transaction and is based on the idea that the debtor should not benefit from the fact that the creditor abstains from undertaking a cover transaction.

II. Article 76(1), sentence 1 CISG

A. Avoidance of the Contract

As in Article 75 CISG, the wording of Article 76(1), sentence 1 CISG requires a proper avoidance of the contract prior to calculating damages.

C 76-1

Oberlandesgericht München (Germany),
15 September 2004,
CISG-online 1013

[Facts][285]

An Italian tannery (the plaintiff) sued a German manufacturer of upholstered furniture (the defendant) claiming the outstanding purchase price for a delivery of leather ordered in summer 2000. The action failed before the court of first instance because the defendant had successfully exercised a compensation defence. The set-off claim was based on the plaintiff's refusal to make further deliveries in accordance with a promise made in February 2000. The court of first instance regarded this refusal to perform as a fundamental breach of contract. Consequently, under article 76(1) CISG the defendant could recover the difference between the price fixed by the contract and the price paid for the covering purchase.

The question of law raised on appeal was whether articles 49(1)(a) and 76(1) CISG would require the buyer's express declaration of avoidance of the contract—which was missing in the case at hand—even if the seller definitely refuses to fulfil his obligations under the contract.

[Judgment][286]

[…]

2. […]

b) In addition, a claim for damages under Article 76 CISG does not fail due to the fact that the [Buyer] did not expressly declare the avoidance of the contract. As the [Seller] seriously and conclusively refused to perform its contractual obligations by disputing the existence of a binding contract, a declaration of avoidance of the contract by the [Buyer] was no longer necessary. The alternate view, which, for reasons of legal certainty and clarity, requires a declaration of avoidance of contract even in such cases, is not followed by the court.

If the obligor unambiguously and definitely declares that it will not perform its contractual obligation, it would be a mere formality to require a separate declaration of avoidance of the contract from the obligee. Legal certainty (determination of the point in time from which the obligee is entitled to make a substitute transaction or the point in time which is decisive for the determination of the current price according to Article 76 CISG, respectively) can still be maintained. On the one hand, an avoidance of the contract by the obligee is only unnecessary in cases in which the obligor clearly and conclusively refuses to perform. On the other hand, such a declaration from the obligor regardless whether in written or in oral form can usually be just as easily referenced to a particular date as an avoidance of the contract declared by the obligee.

The principle of the autonomous interpretation of the CISG does not conflict with such a view. Article 7(1) CISG expressly clarifies that, in the interpretation of this Convention, regard is to be had to the need 'to promote [...] the observance of good faith in international trade'. Although this does not open up the interpretation of the Convention to every single equitable consideration, it does, however, pave the way for the consideration of established and fixed principles of the national legal systems of the Contracting States, created as concrete ideals of

---

[285] Summary of facts taken from CLOUT 595.
[286] Translation taken from CISG Pace (citations omitted).

the principle of good faith. To this extent, it is recognized that, for example, the prohibition of *venire contra factum proprium* can apply to the interpretation of the provisions of the CISG. As a consequence thereof, a party who definitely refuses to perform the contract, or—as here—denies the very existence of contractual duties, cannot successfully rely on the argument that a declaration of avoidance of contract was not made by the opposing party.

In this context, the [Seller] cannot successfully rely on the argument that the [Buyer], in a letter dated 13 July 2000, refused a cancellation of the (outstanding) deliveries and insisted on complete delivery at the confirmed prices. This letter of the [Buyer] actually referred to the fax from the Italian agent, B., dated 22 June 2000, in which the latter had declared the cancellation of all ongoing transactions and a large part of the ongoing orders, by indicating quality problems with the [Seller]'s initial supplier and its requests for, from the perspective of the [Seller], 'unbearable price increases'. In contrast to this and in accord with the District Court, the court regards the letter of the [Seller] dated 13 July 2000 as a conclusive refusal of performance, in which the [Seller] comprehensively denies its contractual obligations. This letter was not received by the [Buyer] until 17 July 2000, as shown by the receipt stamp.

[...]

B. Current Market Price at the Time of Avoidance of the Contract

The current market price is the price generally charged on the market for goods of the same kind under comparable circumstances. The following case shows how difficult it may be to prove the existence of a current market price.

C 76-2

ICC International Court of Arbitration, Award No 8740/1996, CISG-online 1294

[Facts]

The parties entered into a contract for the sale of coal. A dispute arose: the buyer argued that since the delivered coal had a percentage of volatile matter of only 20.4% rather than the 32% which had been foreseen in the contract, it had the right to reject this delivery. The buyer claimed, *inter alia*, damages for breach of contract.

[Judgment][287]

[...] Claimants admit that only 13,758 mt were delivered under contract ... and that they defaulted on the balance of the contract quantity. [...]

The first issue on damages is whether Defendants are entitled to the difference between the contract price and estimated market value of the goods on the date of default as provided in Art 76 Vienna Convention. [...]

---

[287] Translation taken from UNILEX.

In view of Art 76 Vienna Convention the parties presented arguments for and against the existence of a market price for coal. Claimant argued that there is no such thing as uniform coal. The content in various elements (such as sulfur) differs from one type of coal to another. Even if one looks at volatiles which determine the caloric yield not all users have the same equipment and will necessarily prefer the coal with the highest percentage of volatiles. Moreover, coal is bulky and therefore the transportation costs for delivery at various places are an important element in the price. Consequently, Claimant argued, it has never been possible to establish a leading exchange as it for instance exists for gold, other metals and a number of commodities. Claimants argued that in sum, there is no market or current price for coal and that therefore Defendants can only recover damages if they can prove that they bought in replacement goods. Defendants argued against this that those involved in the sale and purchase of coal know about the prices practiced in the industry, and these prices are also published on a regular basis. This, they argued, makes it possible for an experienced trader to establish a price for a particular quality of coal to be delivered at certain times at a certain place. In the Arbitral Tribunal's view Defendant was not able to show that there is a market or current price within the meaning of Art 76 Vienna Convention, although there can be no doubt that in general the price of coal rose substantially between June and December 1994. It is undisputed that there is no commodity exchange and accordingly no commodity exchange price for coal. It is striking that Defendants were unable to state a market price for coal in general or for coal of a particular quality. Defendants were also unable to spot a contract of reference of contract quality. Defendants themselves point out that coal can have quite different specifications and that the requirements of the consumers may differ [...] Similarly, it is obvious that coal from different origins may have different heating values.

[...]

As a result, the Arbitral Tribunal comes to the conclusion that the pricing of a particular contract for the delivery of coal is primarily made in view of the particular contractual quality and the requirements of the respective purchaser. This leads to the conclusion that there is no relevant current market price. This view is confirmed by the following consideration:

The creditor is exempted from specifically evidencing the loss or damage suffered, if there is a market or current price. The idea is that a market or current price can be established by everyone, or at least by everyone in that particular trade. This in turn requires that the calculation of damages in the case of a market or current price (so-called abstract calculation of damages) must be possible with some certainty. Already in 1936 Ernst Rabel in his comparative study on the sale of goods (*Das Recht des Warenkaufs*, Berlin 1936, p 462) stated that the calculation of damages based on current prices instead of a calculation based on the actual cover purchase may in the interest of the debtor only be allowed if the current price can be established with some certainty.

[...].

Finally, the Arbitral Tribunal is of the opinion that generally, only a party that went out into the market to make a cover purchase has a credible case that it suffered damage. There is an exception to this, only where a commodity is in question which is regularly traded on the market, in other words, a commodity that has not just a market price but a regular market with many purchasers and sellers actively engaged in regular trading. Only when there is a market in this sense may one assume that whoever has goods may readily sell them and whoever needs goods may readily purchase them. The reason is that where there is a market of that nature it becomes easily believable that the aggrieved party's damages may be measured with reference to the market price, and it becomes unimportant to be able to pinpoint a particular cover purchase. The Arbitral Tribunal however does not find that there is a market for coal in this sense. Consequently, for legal purposes, the Arbitral Tribunal finds that the aggrieved buyer, Defendant, was required to show a cover purchase under the general rule and was not exempted from doing so under the exception of Art 76 Vienna Convention.

As a result the Arbitral Tribunal concludes that since there is no market or current price that could be applied Defendant cannot measure its damages on the basis of Art 76 Vienna Convention. Accordingly, Defendant must measure its damages on the basis of Art 75 Vienna Convention.

The only cover purchase that the Arbitral Tribunal can identify is in the contract dated 30 January, 1995, with a price of USD 41 per metric ton for 10,000 metric tons of ... coal. The Arbitral Tribunal does not find that the quality of that coal was inferior to ... coal. Accordingly, the damage measured by that cover purchase is, as calculated by Defendant, 10,000 metric tons x USD 41 per metric ton minus [contract pried per metric ton]. Defendant made no claim for further damages under Art 74 Vienna Convention.

[...]

III. Article 76(1), sentence 2 CISG

Article 76(1), sentence 2 CISG changes the relevant time for determining the market price in sentence 1 by stating that, where the aggrieved party has taken over the goods first and avoided the contract afterwards, the relevant point in time will be the time of taking over the goods.

IV. Article 76(2) CISG

The market price may differ from one state to another. According to Article 76(2), in the first instance, the 'place where delivery of the goods should have been made' is decisive. If there is no current price at that place, the relevant market price is the price at 'such other place as serves as a reasonable substitute'. Since the costs of transporting the goods are to be taken into account, the substitute place is usually the suitable place closest to the place of performance.

V. Comparison with Other Legal Provisions

Art 7.4.6 PICC 2010:

(1) Where the aggrieved party has terminated the contract and has not made a replacement transaction but there is a current price for the performance contracted for, it may recover the difference between the contract price and the price current at the time the contract is terminated as well as damages for any further harm.

(2) Current price is the price generally charged for goods delivered or services rendered in comparable circumstances at the place where the contract should have been performed

or, if there is no current price at that place, the current price at such other place that appears reasonable to take as a reference.

§ 2-708(1) UCC:

Subject to subsection (2) and to the provisions of this Article with respect to proof of market price (Section 2-723), the measure of damages for non-acceptance or repudiation by the buyer is the difference between the market price at the time and place for tender and the unpaid contract price together with any incidental damages provided in this Article (Section 2-710), but less expenses saved in consequence of the buyer's breach.

§ 2-713 UCC:

(1)   Subject to the provisions of this Article with respect to proof of market price (Section 2-723), the measure of damages for non-delivery or repudiation by the seller is the difference between the market price at the time when the buyer learned of the breach and the contract price together with any incidental and consequential damages provided in this Article (Section 2-715), but less expenses saved in consequence of the seller's breach.

(2)   Market price is to be determined as of the place for tender or, in cases of rejection after arrival or revocation of acceptance, as of the place of arrival.

§ 2-723 UCC:

(1)   If an action based on anticipatory repudiation comes to trial before the time for performance with respect to some or all of the goods, any damages based on market price (Section 2-708 or Section 2-713) shall be determined according to the price of such goods prevailing at the time when the aggrieved party learned of the repudiation.

(2)   If evidence of a price prevailing at the times or places described in this Article is not readily available the price prevailing within any reasonable time before or after the time described or at any other place which in commercial judgment or under usage of trade would serve as a reasonable substitute for the one described may be used, making any proper allowance for the cost of transporting the goods to or from such other place.

(3)   [...]

Art 191(3) OR:[288]

In the case of goods with a market or stock exchange price, the buyer need not buy the replacement object but is entitled to claim as damages the difference between the contractual sale price and the market price at the time of performance.

Art 215(2) OR:[289]

In the case of goods with a market or stock exchange price, the buyer is entitled to claim as damages the difference between the contractual sale price and the market price at the time of performance without needing to sell the object on.

---

[288] Translation taken from www.admin.ch/ch/e/rs/2/220.en.pdf.
[289] Translation taken from www.admin.ch/ch/e/rs/2/220.en.pdf.

Questions

Q 76-1

What is the idea underlying Article 76 CISG?

Q 76-2

(a)   When is it possible to claim damages under Article 76 CISG without declaring avoidance of the contract according to C 76-1?
(b)   If a calculation of damages under Article 76 CISG is not allowed, which calculation of damages will nonetheless be possible and on which provision will the claimant rely?
(c)   Does the methodological order of the damages provisions indicate whether the CISG favours the method of concrete calculation of damages over the abstract method, or vice versa?

Q 76-3

(a)   It has been said that there is a danger inherent in the method of determining the point in time relevant for determination of the market price (Art 76(1), sentence 1 CISG), in that the creditor speculatively delays avoidance of the contract. Explain this concern.
(b)   Which tool does the CISG provide to counter such abuse?
(c)   Might the creditor be obliged to avoid the contract before the time of performance?

Q 76-4

(a)   If the aggrieved party has undertaken a substitute transaction, is it still entitled to claim damages under Article 76 CISG? Consider, for example, the situation where the substitute transaction does not include all of the goods.
(b)   Which difficulties will the respondent who wants to hinder the claimant from claiming (higher) damages under Article 76 CISG (than it would be entitled to claim under Art 75) encounter if claimant is a 'permanent market trader', that is it buys and sells those kinds of goods continuously?

Q 76-5

(a)   Which criteria determine whether there is a current market price?
(b)   Who must prove the existence of a current market price?

Q 76-6

How will the damages be calculated if there is no market price for the goods in question, neither at the place of performance nor at the substitute place?

Q 76-7

Compare Article 76(2) CISG to the domestic law provisions.

(a) Do the other provisions also allow for additional damages other than those representing the difference between the contract and the market price?
(b) Do they require a termination of the contract prior to the abstract calculation of the difference between the contract and the market price?
(c) Which other provision contains a similar rule as to the determination of the market price?

IV. CISG Advisory Council

CISG Advisory Council Opinion No 8: Calculation of Damages under CISG Articles 75 and 76—Black Letter Rules:[290]

4.1 Under Article 76, an aggrieved party is entitled to recover as damages the difference between the price fixed by the contract and the current price.

4.2 In order for damages to be calculated pursuant to Article 76, the contract must fix, expressly or implicitly, a price for the goods.

4.3 The current price is the price generally charged for such goods sold under comparable circumstances in the trade concerned.

4.4 The time at which the current price is to be established is the time of avoidance, which is the moment when avoidance was declared; provided, however, that if the aggrieved party avoids the contract after taking over the goods, then the current price is to be determined at the time of such taking over.

4.5 (a) The location at which the current price is to be established is the place where the delivery of the goods should have been made.
 (b) If there exists no current price at the place of delivery, the current price is to be established at a reasonable substitute place.

5. If the contract does not fix a price or there is no current price within the meaning of Article 76, damages may be calculated under Article 74.

6. An aggrieved party entitled to damages under Article 76 may also recover any further damages under Article 74.

---

[290] Taken from www.cisgac.com.

Article 77 CISG

A party who relies on a breach of contract must take such measures as are reasonable in the circumstances to mitigate the loss, including loss of profit, resulting from the breach. If he fails to take such measures, the party in breach may claim a reduction in the damages in the amount by which the loss should have been mitigated.

I. Overview

Article 77 CISG embodies the principle that avoidable loss is not to be compensated. This means that, although the aggrieved party is not under an actionable 'duty' to mitigate its loss, if it fails to take reasonable steps to reduce such loss, it cannot recover damages in this regard.

II. Operation of Article 77 CISG

The following cases clearly illustrate which criteria are decisive for the question of whether the aggrieved party took reasonable measures to mitigate the loss.

C 77-1

Oberlandesgericht Braunschweig,
28 October 1999,
CISG-online 510

[Facts][291]

A Belgian buyer ordered frozen meat from a German seller. The seller's standard terms provided for advance payment by the buyer. When the seller requested advance payment, the buyer did not comply, alleging that the seller had unilaterally changed the place for delivery of the goods. The seller commenced a legal action to obtain damages.

---

[291] Summary of facts taken from UNILEX.

[Judgment][292]

[...]

a) When applying the CISG, the duty to pay damages is based on Article 74, in part also on Article 85. The Court does not follow the [buyer's] submission that the seller failed to take obvious steps to mitigate damages and that the reimbursement of his damages should consequently be reduced under Article 77 CISG. The [seller] was not obliged to undertake a substitute transaction. First, the [seller] did not have to agree to partial substitute sales of goods which he then would have possibly lacked, had the [buyer] desired to go through with the transaction after all. Second, Art 77 CISG does not principally oblige a party to enter a substitute transaction. It is only in exceptional circumstances that the seller is obliged to rescind his primary rights to performance for secondary rights in the form of damages [...]. Scholarly opinion correctly assumes that the seller is not obliged to enter a substitute transaction even if prices are falling, as this basically means putting himself in a position of inability to perform the contract. Exceptions apply if the promisee delays avoiding the contract without a plausible reason or speculatively, that is, if enough time has passed to expect a decision by him whether he intends to require performance or ask for remedies for breach of contract [...].

Such an exception is not given in the present case. In particular, the [seller] could not have been expected to decide during the last remaining days of the year 1995, whether to require the [buyer] to pay the purchase price and take over the goods or to declare the contract avoided and to confine himself to secondary remedies. As long as this decision had not been made—and he was not required to make it—the seller was not under a duty to sell the goods to third parties. In a similar manner, the [seller] was not under a duty to sell the goods under Art 88 CISG, because the meat in question could be preserved through freezing, because the cost of such preservation did not exceed 10% of the value of the meat, and because the decrease in prices in venison to be expected after the Christmas holidays does not constitute a deterioration in the meaning of Art 88 CISG [...].

[...]

C 77-2

Bundesgericht (Switzerland), 17 December 2009, CISG-online 2022

[Facts][293]

A Swiss manufacturer (seller) and a Ukrainian retailer (buyer) entered into a contract for the sale of watches. Despite having accepted the buyer's orders, the seller refused to deliver the goods on account of an exclusive distributorship agreement concluded with another Ukrainian company. The buyer then filed a suit against the seller, claiming damages amounting to the difference between the contractual price it should have paid to the seller and the retail value of the goods.

---

[292] Translation taken from CISG Pace (citations omitted).
[293] Summary of facts taken from UNILEX.

The first instance Court rejected the buyer's claim on the grounds that the buyer had failed to prove the retail price of the goods and had also failed to mitigate its loss by buying goods in replacement from the Ukrainian distributor. The buyer then appealed to the Federal Supreme Court.

[Judgment][294]

[...]

5. Under Art 77 CISG, the aggrieved party must take such measures as are reasonable in the circumstances to mitigate the loss, including loss of profit; if he fails to do so, the party in breach may claim a reduction in the damages in the amount by which the loss should have been mitigated.

When the goods are not delivered, this rule compels the buyer to purchase replacement goods if it is reasonably possible. The buyer is then entitled to damages [and interest] to be calculated under Art 75 CISG, i.e., the difference between the price agreed upon between the parties and the price of the replacement goods. If the buyer did not purchase replacement goods and if it would have been reasonable to do so, the damages [and interest] are reduced to the amount that would be due if he had purchased the replacement goods.

The Civil Court noted that [Buyer] had the opportunity to purchase watches of the same model as [Seller] refused to deliver in breach of its obligations, through the retailer that was awarded exclusivity in the Ukraine. The relevance of this fact is not substantially challenged before the Supreme Court because [Buyer] restricts its arguments to Swiss domestic law, yet the dispute is subject to the CISG. Consequently, [Buyer] is not entitled under Art 77 CISG to receive damages [and interest] calculated as the difference between the 'export' prices and the retail value, but rather calculated as the difference between the 'export' prices and the 'retail' prices that the retailer would have charged to deliver the same watches.

The dismissal of all claims is contrary to Art 74 and 77 CISG because [in that case] [Buyer] would not receive these reduced damages [and interest]. The Civil Court did not establish these 'retail' prices and the Supreme Court is, therefore, not in a position to rule on this matter. It does not appear at first sight that these prices were not invoked and that they cannot be invoked anymore according to cantonal procedural law.

[...]

C 77-3

Nova Tool & Mold Inc v London Industries Inc,
Ontario Court of Appeal, 26 January 2000,
CISG-online 582

[Judgment]

[...]

FINLAYSON J.A.:— Nova Tool & Mold Inc. appeals from the judgment of the Honourable Mr. Justice Zalev of the Ontario Court (General Division) dated December 16, 1998 which

---

[294] Translation taken from CISG Pace (citations omitted).

dismissed its action and granted judgment for the defendant London Industries Inc. on its counterclaim in the amount of $124,697.18 U.S., together with interest and costs.

The respondent is a parts supplier in the United States that supplies parts for Honda Motors. The respondent ordered a program of seven molds to be manufactured by the appellant with contractual payment terms in accordance with the industry norms as follows: a) one-third on the signing of the purchase order; b) one-third on the first try-out; and c) one-third on the final shipment.

As found by the trial judge, the appellant was slow in getting started on jobs numbered 619 and 620 and did not advise the respondent that these jobs would be delayed. Job 620 was not ready for its first try-out until December 4, 1996, more than a month behind schedule, at which time certain deficiencies were observed. The appellant was anxious to comply with the timetable called for in the contract but it became obvious to the respondent that it would be unable to do so. Problems persisted through two more try-outs in January 1997, despite the fact that Nova employees were working extra hours on the project. A further try-out originally scheduled for February 5, 1997 was postponed by Nova until February 10, 1997, but, as the respondent was under considerable pressure from its customer, Honda Motors, it began to seek an alternative subcontractor for job 620. Cambridge Tool and Die Corporation (an original bidder for the job) agreed to complete the work, but could only do so on a 'time and materials' basis because there was no time to provide a quote in advance of beginning work. The try-out on February 10 revealed that serious deficiencies and problems still existed in 620. London transferred the mold to Cambridge shortly after this try-out. London eventually paid Cambridge $335,220 US for completion of 620.

The issues between the appellant and the respondent crystallised when the final billing was issued by the appellant to the defendant for $367,834 U.S. with respect to the balance of six of the seven molds. Nova chose not to submit an invoice for the final one-third payment on 620, the other two-thirds having already been paid. The respondent asserted a counterclaim as set-off for 620, stating that it expended $335,220 U.S. to complete 620 at Cambridge, and also claiming damages for defects in job 619, ($15,600 U.S.), graining costs for three of the molds, and internal costs for late delivery of 620.

[…]

The appellant also argued that London had not acted reasonably in incurring the mitigation costs it paid to Cambridge in order to complete 620. In our view, this argument is without merit. The findings of the trial judge are very clear:

In any event, I find that it would have been extremely difficult to find a mold shop that would quote a fixed price on a transferred mold, particularly where it had no previous knowledge of it. In any event it would take about 4 or 5 weeks to get a quote. In view of Honda's schedule and the pressure London was in, getting a quote, or several quotes from mold shops which had time available, if any, was not an option. I find that Nova could not have corrected the problems and deficiencies in 619 and 620 on time even if it could work 24 hours per day. Those molds were required to be ready 18 weeks from first try-out. Nova did make efforts to its limits, but was not successful. It was not and would not ultimately be successful because its employees lacked the skill and talent necessary to do so. 620 had not improved significantly from the first try-out. It was scheduled for completion in May 1997. Honda needed a small number of parts at that time to begin with. It first made 5 to 30 cars to acquaint its workers with the new model, for advertising purposes and to do the tests necessary to comply with Government regulations before mass production could start London worked hand in hand with the Honda engineers to see what adjustments were necessary for mass production. Honda representatives attended each scheduled event and subsequent evaluations. Nova well knew that London was obliged to supply the parts necessary on time for each event according to Honda's schedule. If London did not have the parts ready to supply Honda, Honda could not pass Government regulations and be certified for mass production for the new model year.

Accordingly, what the respondent did was a necessary operation to mitigate its damages and the appellant's co-operation was in its own interests because the respondent faced a potential loss to Honda that was significant. Accordingly, we reject the appellant's arguments with respect to the respondent's action in contracting out the balance of Job 620 to Cambridge. [...]

III. Extent of Reduction of Damages

As Article 77 CISG expressly states, the party in breach may claim a reduction in the damages in the amount by which the loss could have been mitigated.

C 77-4

International Court of Commercial Arbitration Chamber of Commerce and Industry of the Russian Federation, Award No 54/1999, 24 January 2000, CISG-online 1042

For a summary of the facts see C 38/39-4 above.

[Judgment]

[...] [I]n accordance with Article 77 of the Vienna Convention 1980, if the party relying on the breach of the contract does not take measures reasonable in the circumstances to mitigate the loss, the party in breach is entitled to demand the reduction of damages in the amount by which they could have been reduced. In his reply to the claim and in the proceedings of the ICCA, the seller alleged that the buyer had not taken such measures. In this regard, the seller asked the Court to dismiss the buyer's claim. As follows from the materials of the case, the buyer did not provide the seller with documents confirming the validity of the claims in time and, accordingly, did not receive necessary information from the seller which could be used at negotiations with the consumers of the goods and conduce to solving the issue of decreasing the amount of reduction of the price. In particular, such a conclusion is also confirmed by the fact that [...] the issue of incorrectness of the applied method of the inspection of the quality of the goods was of decisive importance. The position set forth by the seller gives the ICCA grounds to conclude that Article 77 of the Vienna Convention 1980 is applicable to the present case.

With regard for all the above said considerations, the ICCA has come to a conclusion that it would be fair to fix the reduction of the price with respect to the quantity of the goods which had been, in fact, examined in the amount of 50% of the difference between the price of the goods under the contract in dispute and the price agreed to in the relations between the buyer and his customers. Thus, the seller must pay the buyer the above indicated discount under the claim related to the first instalment of the goods. [...]

IV. Comparison with Other Legal Provisions

Art 7.4.8 PICC 2010:

(1) The non-performing party is not liable for harm suffered by the aggrieved party to the extent that the harm could have been reduced by the latter party's taking reasonable steps.

(2) The aggrieved party is entitled to recover any expenses reasonably incurred in attempting to reduce the harm.

Questions

Q 77-1

(a) What concept underlies Article 77 CISG?
(b) What are the legal consequences if the aggrieved party fails to take 'such measures'?
(c) To what kind of remedies does Article 77 CISG apply?
(d) Are there similar provisions in domestic sales laws?

Q 77-2

(a) Specify the most important factors that a court must take into account in order to determine whether the aggrieved party acted in accordance with Article 77 CISG. See C 77-2.
(b) At what point in time are measures to mitigate damages to be taken? Consider seasonal goods, goods in a highly volatile market, non-perishable goods, the urgency in receiving the goods, etc.
(c) When will a cover transaction be necessary in order to comply with Article 77 CISG? See C 77-1.
(d) Is a party obliged to conclude a substitute transaction with the contract breacher?

Q 77-3

Decide whether the party complied with Article 77 CISG in the following cases:

(a) Seller does not resell the goods as long as the buyer, which is the party in breach, could still claim performance of the contract.
(b) Seller does not resell goods which had been made on the buyer's instructions.
(c) Seller collects debts through an agent or a lawyer where the legal situation is not particularly complicated.
(d) Buyer fails to resell defective, rapidly deteriorating goods.
(e) Buyer uses its own buffer stocks of coal where the seller is late in delivery.
(f) Buyer fails to look for replacement goods in markets other than the local region.

(g)   Buyer offers the goods delivered too late by the seller to its own buyer at a 10% discount.

(h)   Buyer fails to examine the shipments before mixing the shipments together.

Q 77-4

(a)   To what extent will the aggrieved party's damages be reduced if it fails to comply with Article 77 CISG? See C 77-4

(b)   Who bears the burden of proof for compliance with the duty to mitigate damages?

Q 77-5

Can the party who incurred expenses in order to comply with Article 77 CISG be compensated for these expenses? See also Article 88(3) CISG. On which provision(s) would the creditor base its calculation?

Article 78 CISG

If a party fails to pay the price or any other sum that is in arrears, the other party is entitled to interest on it, without prejudice to any claim for damages recoverable under article 74.

I. Overview

Article 78 CISG states the duty to pay interest on a sum which is due. It is supplemented by Article 84 CISG, which applies in cases where the contract has been avoided and obligates the seller to pay interest on the purchase price to be refunded.

II. History

At the Drafting Conference, the question of whether an obligation to pay interest should be established was strongly debated—to the extent that the whole meeting almost failed. Islamic countries, for reasons of religious law, were against a general duty to pay interest; other Contracting States objected to the application of the interest rate existing at the creditor's place of business. Whereas in the lead-up to the Drafting Conference, an agreement was reached on the inclusion of Article 84 CISG, the general duty to pay interest on sums in arrear stated in Article 78 CISG was not inserted until the last minute. With a view to those discrepancies, it is no surprise that Articles 78 and 84 CISG do not provide for a uniform interest rate—even the compromise reached was a considerable achievement.

III. Operation of Article 78 CISG

A. Scope of Application

Article 78 CISG applies to all monetary obligations, including payment of the purchase price, the sum by which the purchase price is reduced according to Article 50

CISG, and expenses paid in advance by one party but, pursuant to the contract, attributable to the other party.

B. Prerequisites

(a) Due Date

The only requirement established in Article 78 CISG is that the sum is due and that the debtor does not pay within the time provided, either by the contract or by the CISG.

(b) No Requirement for Formal Notice of Default

The duty to pay interest does not depend on prior notification of the debtor. With respect to the purchase price, express provisions are laid down in Article 59 CISG.

Questions

Q 78-1

Which duty does Article 78 CISG establish?

Q 78-2

What follows from the fact that the CISG itself has a provision on interest?

Q 78-3

On which sums is interest to be paid?

Q 78-4

Why has the applicable interest rate not been settled in Article 78 CISG?

Q 78-5

(a) When will the purchase price fall due? See Article 58 CISG.
(b) Has the question of the point in time at which other monetary obligations fall due been expressly settled in the CISG?
(c) Why will the debtor who is entitled to withhold its performance (Arts 71(1), 81(2), sentence 2 CISG) not be obliged to pay interest?

Q 78-6

Originally, a topic of dispute was whether a sum must have been made certain ('liquidated') in order to be interest-bearing. Can you explain why there used to be a controversy, due to this uncertainty, about whether or not interest could accrue? (It should be noted that, nowadays, the legal majority does not require a liquidated sum in order to incur interest.)

IV. Interest Rate

The interest rate has not been settled in Article 78 CISG. How the question is to be handled is a topic of debate. See, in this respect, the following cases.

C 78-1

Hof van Beroep Antwerpen (Belgium),
24 April 2006,
CISG-online 1258

[Facts][295]

A Belgian seller and a German buyer entered into a contract for the supply of construction materials. The contract was exclusively regulated by the seller's standard terms. According to those terms, the goods should have been delivered in 'November, December 1999 and January 2000'. The contract also provided for payment 'cash against documents (B/L)'. Since the buyer accepted and paid only for some of the shipments, the seller announced to the buyer that it would resell the goods within seven days but failed to do so. Nearly six months later, after granting the buyer a final period of time in which to perform, the seller invoked avoidance of part of the contract according to Art 64(1)(b) CISG, entered into a cover sale and claimed damages. On its part, the buyer invoked breach of contract by the seller in many respects.

The First Instance Court decided in favor of the seller, but denied it part of the damages it had claimed. Then the buyer appealed and the seller brought an incidental appeal to recover all the damages sought.

[…]

[Judgment][296]

[…]

According to the [Buyer], the [Seller] does not explain how the interest of US $31,305.29 is calculated. Moreover, according to the [Buyer], an excessive interest rate is used.

---

[295] Summary of facts taken from UNILEX.
[296] Translation taken from CISG Pace (citations omitted).

According to article 78 CISG, interest is due in case of late payment and interest commences to run without the need for an order. Since the interest rate is not determined by the CISG, it is determined by the *lex contractus, in casu* Belgian law.

The CISG does not forbid that the parties determine conventional interest. Moreover, article 6 CISG allows the parties to determine the damages themselves.

According to Belgian law, the conventional interest claimed by the [Seller] on the basis of article 5 of [Seller]'s general conditions—that are deliberately reduced to 9%—are certainly not exaggerated. Thus, the claimed interest rate of 9% is applied.

It is accepted that, if there is a resale in the sense of article [75] CISG, the interest runs from the payment of the resale. Accordingly, the [Seller] is only entitled to conventional interest at the rate of 9% from the date of payment of the resale till the date of full payment.

The debates are re-opened to allow the [Seller] to recalculate the claimed interest.

[...]

2. Compound interest

The [Seller] claims compound interests. After compound interest, the [Seller] claims payment of the main sum of US $256,652.95, increased with the interest at 9% since 20 February 2005 until the date of full payment. According to the [Buyer], the interest claimed by the [Seller] must be reduced and compound interests cannot be granted.

The CISG is silent on the question whether compound interests are possible. Article 78 CISG mentions 'interest on the price or any other sum', from which some authors conclude that no interest on interest is due. Other authors state that interests on interest can be framed in the practices between parties in the sense of article 9 CISG. However, it is required that the claimant prove that—because of the breach—he had to pay interest on interest himself to his financer for withdrawn credit. In any event, under the CISG, compound interest is not accorded automatically and the claimant, in this case the [Seller], has to prove that it is entitled to compound interest, e.g., because [Seller] had to pay extra interests itself since it lacked the payments that were due. In as much as the [Seller] has not proved this, the request for compound interest (which the [Seller] founds on Article 1154 of the Civil Code) is rejected.

[...]

C 78-2

Internationales Schiedsgericht der Bundeskammer der gewerblichen Wirtschaft—Wien (Austria),
SCH 4366, 15 June 1994,
CISG-online 121/691[297]

[...]

5.2.2. Article 78 of the CISG, while granting the right to interest, says nothing about the level of the interest rate payable. In international legal writings and case law to date it is disputed whether the question is outside the scope of the Convention—with the result that the interest

---

[297] Translation taken from UNILEX (citations omitted).

rate is to be determined according to the domestic law applicable on the basis of the relevant conflict-of-laws rules …—or whether there is a true gap in the Convention within the meaning of Article 7(2) so that the applicable interest rate should possibly be determined autonomously in conformity with the general principles underlying the Convention …. This second view is to be preferred, not least because the immediate recourse to a particular domestic law may lead to results which are incompatible with the principle embodied in Art 78 of the CISG, at least in the cases where the law in question expressly prohibits the payment of interest. One of the general legal principles underlying the CISG is the requirements of 'full compensation' of the loss caused (cf. Art 74 of the CISG). It follows that, in the event of failure to pay a monetary debt, the creditor, who as a business person must be expected to resort to bank credit as a result of the delay in payment, should therefore be entitled to interest at the rate commonly practiced in its country with respect to the currency of payment, i.e. the currency of the creditor's country or any other foreign currency agreed upon by the parties (cf. Art 7.4.9 of the Principles of International Commercial Contracts …). The information received from the leading Austrian banks is that the average 'prime borrowing rates' for US dollars and DM in Austria in the period in question were 4.5 % and 8 %, respectively. The interest due from the respondent should be calculated at those rates. …

C 78-3

Foreign Trade Court of Arbitration at Serbian Chamber of Commerce, 23 January 2008, CISG-online 1946

[Facts][298]

The dispute arose out of a contract for the sale of white crystal sugar. The Italian buyer commenced arbitration before a Serbian court of arbitration against the Serbian seller to recover the customs the buyer had to pay in Italy as a result of withdrawal by the Serbian authorities of the certificates of origin required by the contract and ensuring exemption from the payment of customs. The seller challenged the jurisdiction due to incorrect denomination of the court of arbitration, contested its liability for any damages suffered by the buyer as a result of the withdrawal, and disputed the amount of damages requested arguing that the buyer had already requested compensation for the same losses in another proceeding.

[Judgment][299]

…

7.3. Right to interest

The Arbitral Tribunal recognizes [Buyer]'s right to interest according to:

Article 9.508 of the Ole Lando Principles;

Article 7.4.9 of the UNIDROIT Principles;

---

[298] Translation taken from CLOUT 1022.
[299] Translation taken from CISG Pace (citations omitted).

Article 78 of the Vienna Convention 1980;

Article 2 paragraph 1(m) of the UML on International Credit Transfers; and

Article 277 paragraph 1 and Article 279 paragraph 2 of the LCT.

All of these provisions are very similar. All of them provide in a very similar manner that the obligor must pay the interest on the debt, payment of which is delayed.

Article 9.508 of the Ole Lando Principles determines that if payment of a sum of money is delayed, the aggrieved party is entitled to interest on that sum from the time when payment is due to the time of payment at the average commercial bank short-term lending rate to prime borrowers prevailing for the contractual currency of payment at the place where payment is due.

Article 7.4.9 of the UNIDROIT Principles provides that the rate of interest shall be the average bank short-term lending rate to prime borrowers prevailing for the currency of payment at the place for payment, or where no such rate exists at that place, then the same rate in the State of the currency of payment. In the absence of such a rate at either place the rate of interest shall be the appropriate rate fixed by the law of the State of the currency of payment.

The Vienna Convention of 1980 in Article 78 establishes the obligation of a party whose payment is in arrears, to pay interest on that amount, without further specification of the interest rate and of how it is to be determined.

Article 277 paragraph 1 and Article 279 paragraph 2 of the LCT, as well as the prior regulations and Principles, provide that the obligor who is in delay with payment is obliged to pay the default interest for the main debt from the date that it became due, and for the amount of interest that is not paid it can demand a default interest from the day that the claim for its payment was submitted to the court.

As none of the abovementioned Principles and regulations determine the interest rate, but rather make it definable, and because as of March 2001 there is no law in Serbia to fix such a rate for claims in a foreign currency, in the determination of the interest rate the Arbitral Tribunal has relied on the abovementioned principles as a safe indicator how to determine such a rate.

Article 9.508 of the Ole Lando Principle, as well as Article 7.4.9 of the UNIDROIT Principles clearly address the 'short term lending rate' which the Arbitral Tribunal has accepted as the method in which to determine the interest rate. Having in mind Article 2 paragraph 1(m) of the UML on International Credit Transfers, by which interest is defined as a time value of the funds or money involved, which, unless otherwise agreed, is calculated at the rate and on the basis customarily accepted by the banking community for the funds or money involved, therefore for the Euro. The Arbitral Tribunal is only left to determine the average interest rate.

In order to determine this, the Arbitral Tribunal, on its own initiative, acquired the Statistical Report of the European Central Bank for December 2007 according to which it determined how the amounts of the interest rate (EURIBOR) have changed from the submission of the claim until the end of November 2007—when the information was given to the Report. In the specified time period the interest rate of the Central European Bank was variable. The Arbitral Tribunal took as the most realistic interest rate for the time period from the submission of the claim until the end of November 2007, until the information existed, and determined the average interest rate of 4.62%—as stated in operative part of this Award under 1.

...

C 78-4

Landgericht Heidelberg (Germany),
2 November 2005,
CISG-online 1416[300]

[Facts]

[Seller] relies on claims for the purchase price from deliveries of natural stone to [Buyer].

[Seller] supplied [Buyer] with natural stone in the course of a lasting business relationship. In the time between February 2001 until July 2001 [Seller] issued to [Buyer] ten invoices over a total sum of Deutsche Mark [DM] 89,796. For these invoiced sums, a sum of EUR 26,766.85 has remained unsettled. By a letter dated 30 August 2001, [Buyer] accredited a partial sum of DM 42,409.93 (= EUR 21,683.85). For the relevant details, reference is made to the copies of this correspondence in the documents (exhibit K3). In this respect, [Buyer] proposed a settlement with the content described in exhibit K3, which meant that company ... would bear the unsettled invoice sums. The parties are in dispute about the conclusion and the validity of this settlement.

[Buyer] was reminded by letter dated 19 May 2003 (exhibit K5) to pay the partial sum of EUR 21,683.85. A time limit was set until 2 June 2003.

[...]

[Seller] requests that [Buyer] be ordered to pay [Seller] EUR 26,766.85 plus 5% interest above the prime lending rate since 3 June 2003 with respect to EUR 21,683.85 and with respect to EUR 5,083 since service of the action.

[...]

[Judgment]

[...]

1. Defendant [Buyer] is ordered to pay Plaintiff [Seller] EUR 26,766.85 plus interest of 5% above the base rate of interest with respect to EUR 21,683.85 since 3 June 2003 and to EUR 5,083 since 20 November 2003.

[...]

The claim for interest on the sum of EUR 21,683.85 since 3 June 2003 follows from Art 78 CISG. Pursuant to this provision, one party is entitled to interest if the other party fails to pay the price or any other sum that is in arrears. However, it is in dispute how the interest rate should be determined. The Court adheres [to] the position which favors a special link to the law that applies at the place of business of the debtor [...]. It seems convincing to the Court that the debtor operates with the money by profitably investing the sum to which the creditor is entitled in its own country instead of paying the sum to the creditor as required by the contract. Consequently, a special link must be drawn to that law which is applicable at the place of business of the debtor. Therefore, German

---

[300] Translation taken from CISG Pace (citations omitted).

law is applicable, meaning that the interest rate follows from § 288(1) BGB. With regard to the partial sum of EUR 5,083, the corresponding claim became mature with service of the judicial reminder on 20 November 2003 at the latest. As [Seller] requests interest only since service of the action, but an action has not been commenced here and, instead, the dispute was initiated by the service of a judicial reminder, [Seller]'s request must be interpreted in a way that interest was claimed at least since service of the judicial reminder. According to § 308 ZPO, interest may not be awarded for periods of time prior to the time mentioned in the request. These interest claims are awarded on the basis of Art 78 CISG, as well.

[...]

Art 7.4.9 PICC 2010:

(1)   If a party does not pay a sum of money when it falls due the aggrieved party is entitled to interest upon that sum from the time when payment is due to the time of payment whether or not the non-payment is excused.

(2)   The rate of interest shall be the average bank short-term lending rate to prime borrowers prevailing for the currency of payment at the place for payment, or where no such rate exists at that place, then the same rate in the state of the currency of payment. In the absence of such a rate at either place the rate of interest shall be the appropriate rate fixed by the law of the State of the currency of payment.

(3)   The aggrieved party is entitled to additional damages if the non-payment caused it a greater harm.

Questions

Q 78-7

Is compound interest possible under Article 78 CISG (See C 78-1)?

Q 78-8

(a)   Describe the different approaches in determining the applicable interest rate under the CISG.

(b)   What general principle of the CISG may be relied upon in determining the interest rate?

(c)   If this principle is applied, what effect does this have on the concrete interest rate?

(d)   Which interest rate is provided for in the PICC 2010 (Art 7.4.9(2))? Are there any problems in applying this rate?

(e)   What problems can you identify when relying on the subsidiary applicable domestic law?

(f)   Could there be a compromise between a truly uniform determination and reliance on the private international law/domestic law approach?

V. Relationship between Articles 78 and 74 CISG and Domestic Law

Article 78 CISG expressly provides for the possibility of the creditor claiming damages under Article 74 CISG, in addition to the right to claim interest under Article 78 CISG, if the creditor can prove that the debtor's non-payment caused it to incur a loss higher than the amount covered by the interest payment.

C 78-5

Amtsgericht Koblenz (Germany),
12 November 1996,
CISG-online 400[301]

[Judgment]

[Seller's] claim is justified. For his delivery according to [buyer's] order, the seller is entitled to receive the total purchase price [...]. The [seller's] claim for interest on the purchase price at a rate of 16.5% applicable to both invoices is legitimate on the basis of CISG Article 78 and Article 1284 of the Italian Civil Code. [...] According to Art 78 CISG, a party who fails to pay the price or any other sum in arrears is liable for interest to the other party. It is undisputed that at the time of the conclusion of the contract the parties had agreed on the terms of payment. The terms provided that payment within ten days entitled the buyer to a 3% discount, and that payment within 60 days meant a net payment. The period of payment for the purchase price consequently was 60 days from the billing date; therefore, for payment of the invoice of 4 April 1996, the date of payment was 5 June 1995; while payment of the invoice of 26 April 1995 was due on 27 June 1995. Contrary to German law, the only prerequisite for a claim for interest under Art 78 CISG is the maturity of the sum in arrears. Because Article 78 does not define the applicable rate of interest, Article 28 EGBGB leads to the application of Italian law. According to Article 128 of the Italian Civil Code, the statutory interest rate starting from 16 December 1990 is 10%. Nevertheless, the [seller] is entitled to the higher interest rate of 16.5% he requested. Article 78 does not exclude the possibility to demand reimbursement under Art 74 CISG for losses suffered through a bank credit at a higher rate than the statutory interest rate. In the parallel proceeding before the AG Bottrop [Germany], the [seller] submitted a bank certificate which proves that he is taking credit from his house bank in amounts exceeding the purchase price at an interest rate of at least 16.5%. The [seller] is therefore entitled to interest at the rate of 16.5% [...].

Domestic provisions may exist on interest that is to be paid during the legal process. It has been said that whether these provisions apply alongside Art 78 CISG should depend on whether they are qualified as purely procedural (e.g 'post-judgment interest' as it is known in US civil procedure, which obliges the debtor to pay some sort of penalty), or whether they are regarded as substantive provisions. In the latter case, Art 78 CISG supersedes domestic law.

---

[301] Translation taken from CISG Pace (citations omitted).

Questions

Q 78-9

Does the duty to pay interest on sums in arrears prejudice a claim for damages recoverable under Article 74 CISG? See C 78-5 and Article 7.4.9(3) PICC 2010.

Q 78-10

(a) To the extent that interest is recoverable, does the aggrieved party have a choice between Article 74 and Article 78 CISG?
(b) In which situations will the creditor prefer to proceed under Article 74 CISG? When will Article 78 CISG provide the only suitable basis?

Article 79 CISG

(1) A party is not liable for a failure to perform any of his obligations if he proves that the failure was due to an impediment beyond his control and that he could not reasonably be expected to have taken the impediment into account at the time of the conclusion of the contract or to have avoided or overcome it or its consequences.

(2) If the party's failure is due to the failure by a third person whom he has engaged to perform the whole or part of the contract, that party is exempt from liability only if:
    (a) he is exempt under the preceding paragraph; and
    (b) the person whom he has so engaged would be so exempt if the provisions of that paragraph were applied to him.

(3) The exemption provided by this article has effect for the period during which the impediment exists.

(4) The party who fails to perform must give notice to the other party of the impediment and its effect on his ability to perform. If the notice is not received by the other party within a reasonable time after the party who fails to perform knew or ought to have known of the impediment, he is liable for damages resulting from such non-receipt.

(5) Nothing in this article prevents either party from exercising any right other than to claim damages under this Convention.

I. Overview

Article 79 CISG deals with what has often been discussed in domestic sales law under the label of *force majeure*, impossibility, impracticability or excessive hardship. The provision specifies the circumstances in which a party is 'not liable' for the non-fulfilment of any of its obligations, as well as the remedial consequences if the exemption from liability applies. It establishes a limitation of the principle of 'strict liability' underlying the CISG, that is that the party who does not perform one of its duties is liable to pay damages regardless of whether there was fault on its behalf. Article 79 CISG is the result of a compromise between the proponents of 'strict liability' pursuant to the Anglo-American model (as settled in Art 74 CISG) and the proponents of fault-based liability, as it still exists, at least in theory, in several continental European legal systems (see also Art 74 CISG above).

II. Operation of Article 79 CISG

Article 79(1) CISG states the principle that a party is exempted only where its failure to perform rests on an impediment beyond its control. Article 79(2) CISG states the rule that, where the party in default has engaged a third party to perform the contract, it is only exempt if Article 79(1) applies to both the party in default and that third party. Article 79(3) CISG clarifies that the defaulting party is relieved not only where the impediment is permanent but also where it is merely temporary, but only for as long as the impediment continues to exist. Article 79(4) CISG requires that a notice of the impediment and the party's failure to perform be given within a reasonable time. Article 79(3) and (4) CISG have raised little discussion in case law. Article 79(5) CISG, finally, makes it clear that the effect of Article 79 CISG is limited, in that it affects only the question of damages, but not any other remedies available under the CISG.

III. Article 79(1) CISG

A. Impediment Beyond the Party's Control

Article 79(1) CISG states the general rule that, whenever one of the contractual duties cannot be performed and that failure is due to an impediment which was beyond the defaulting party's control, that party is exempt from liability if the impediment was neither foreseeable nor could have been avoided or overcome. The CISG does not differentiate among different contractual duties. The impediment must be an unmanageable risk or a totally exceptional event. If the impediment falls within the defaulting party's sphere of contemplation, the latter remains fully liable.

B. Unforeseeability

The impediment must not have been foreseeable. The contract terms, applicable practices and trade usages, as well as all relevant circumstances, must be considered in order to determine whether the defaulting party should have contemplated the existence or occurrence of the impediment.

C. Avoiding or Overcoming the Impediment

With respect to the possibility of avoiding or overcoming an impediment, case law applies a strict standard. It has been held reasonable that the party encountering the impediment incur even considerable additional costs or accept a bargaining loss in order to overcome it. Fluctuations in the market price or in the price of production, for example, are regularly raised as arguments, but are usually rejected because such factors are considered to be a normal risk of commercial activity. The *Secretariat Commentary* gives a contract which calls for the delivery of unique goods as an example of where the impediment could be neither avoided nor overcome. Prior to the time when the risk of loss would have passed, the goods are destroyed by a fire which is caused by events beyond the control of the seller.[302]

D. Practical Use

Article 79 CISG is raised quite frequently in case law, albeit with limited success. Often, courts or tribunals fail to clearly define in their decisions which of the requirements of Article 79 CISG is not fulfilled, whether the event is not regarded as an impediment, whether the impediment was not beyond the party's control, or whether the impediment was foreseeable or possible to overcome.

C 79-1

Bundesgericht (Switzerland),
12 June 2006,
CISG-online 1516

[Facts]

The buyer, a German Company ('Claimant'), and the seller, a Swiss Company ('Respondent'), had a business relationship for over 11 years. In January 2002 the Respondent obtained knowledge that a company in Italy offered 70 metric tons of Triethylen Tetramin (TETA). Respondent accordingly informed Claimant and after some negotiations Claimant sent to Respondent a sales confirmation for 60 metric tons. As Respondent's supplier failed to deliver, Respondent could not deliver the TETA to Claimant. Claimant subsequently held Respondent liable for the costs it incurred because its own customer concluded a cover purchase and claimed the difference in price to be paid as damages by the Claimant. Claimant thereupon claimed damages from Respondent.

[Judgment][303]

[...]

1.4 The previous instance had assumed that the sale was one for generic goods, which is contested by the Respondent. Since the goods were the remainder of the stock, it is, contrary to the view of the previous instance, irrelevant whether the Respondent was regularly delivered with goods of that kind. Rather, it is decisive that the Claimant could discern that the Respondent only wanted to sell the remainder of the stock of a certain supplier. Thus,

---

[302] Text of Secretariat Commentary on Art 65 of the 1978 Draft, para 9, Example 65A.
[303] Author's translation, citations omitted.

we are not dealing with a common sale of generic goods but with a sale of generic goods limited to a certain batch (*begrenzte Gattungsschuld*). Insofar as the entire stock was meant to be sold, the sale does in fact almost resemble a sale of specific goods, as this is claimed by the Respondent. However, this aspect is not of particular relevance and does not have to be definitely decided. The reason for the defect in performance was solely the behaviour of the supplier. Thus, the only relevant question is who bears the risk of the supplier's non-delivery. The liability for the supplier is part of the general procurement risk and thus lies with the seller. The seller is generally not excused if its supplier lets it down. If a debtor does not want to accept liability for such type of impediments that fall into its sphere of risk, it must exempt itself from liability by way of an adequate clause such as eg 'performance is subject to delivery by supplier'. Therefore, it remains to be ascertained whether the Claimant must have known from the overall circumstances that the Respondent did not want to accept the risk for delivery.

[...]

C 79-2

Macromex Srl v Globex International Inc,
American Arbitration Association, 23 October 2007,
CISG-online 1645[304]

[Facts]

Globex International ('Seller') is an American company engaged in the export of food products to multiple countries globally, including in Eastern Europe. Seller has contracts containing exclusivity agreements with companies in certain locales. In the ordinary course of business Seller developed a non-exclusive relationship with Macromex Srl. ('Buyer'), a Romanian company, and to ship, among other things, chicken leg quarters to Buyer. [...] After the conclusion of the Contracts between the parties, the price of chicken increased very substantially, and Seller's supplier failed to ship to it in a timely manner. Seller impacted this supply situation—unknowingly perhaps, at least initially—by allocating such product to two breakbulk shipments for itself, rather than to container sales for customers like Buyer. While Buyer did become more insistent regarding prompt delivery as the month of May progressed, Buyer did not formally claim breach; nor did Buyer set another delivery date prior to the issuance of a decree by the Romanian government, which established a chicken product importation ban with virtually no notice. To explain, an avian flu outbreak prompted the Romanian government to bar all chicken imports not certified as of June 7, 2006. The Romanian Bulletin addressing the restriction stated that: 'Transports loaded within 5 days of June 2, 2006 will be allowed to be imported into Romania.' An extension of one day was subsequently granted. Had Seller loaded the chicken within the two week window expressly provided for in the Contracts, or even within a week thereafter, the chicken would have been allowed into Romania. However, Seller was unable to certify all the remaining chicken in the order in time, so the final delivery was deficient. Buyer then proposed that Seller ship the balance of the chicken order to it at a location outside of Romania, suggesting certain ports. Another supplier to Buyer provided such alternative performance following implementation of

---

[304] Citations omitted.

the ban with respect to shipments on which it too was late. Seller ultimately refused the proposal, maintaining that the unfilled portions of the Contracts were voided by the Romanian government's action, which constituted a force majeure event. Seller thereafter sold the undelivered chicken to another buyer at a substantial profit. Buyer now seeks a damages remedy with respect to the undelivered product under the Contracts.

[Judgment]

[…]

B. Qualification for an 'Exemption' under the CISG

[…]

The Romanian government's decision to stop all chicken imports on virtually no notice to the industry was certainly beyond Seller's control, and it would not have been reasonably contemplated as a risk assigned to the Seller at the conclusion of the contract, as no prior ban experienced by either party was taken as precipitously. The third and fourth factors are closer questions, and are addressed in greater detail below (in reverse order) because of their ultimate importance to the determination of the merits.

i. Meeting the Fourth Factor of Causality

This requirement essentially requires a showing of causality between the impediment and the non-performance. The non-performance of the contract must be 'due to' the impediment. Causality exists here between Seller's inability to deliver the chicken and the Romanian government's ban on imports. The question is whether Seller's delay in performance beyond the shipment 'window' expressly provided for in the Contracts and/or by industry practice bars the Seller from claiming protection of the exemption by precluding Seller's ability to show causation.

Two cases have addressed whether a party can claim an exemption under Article 79 when it is in breach of the terms of the contract. In one case where the Buyer was supposed to have paid for a caviar delivery prior to the imposition of U.N. sanctions that made payment impossible, the court held that when 'Buyer was in default before the sanctions [the force majeure] became effective, he could have and should have paid at a date when payment was possible and his status of being a defaulting party cannot be changed by a later force majeure.' (Buyer was supposed to pay US $15,000 before delivery, while the balance was due 'within two weeks after delivery'.). A second court found that a party to a contract could not claim that a strike was an impediment because it occurred after the seller was already in arrears. However, these cases can be distinguished here since the seller is found not to be in fundamental breach prior to the occurrence of the impediment, and no CISG case was found directly addressing a fact pattern involving immaterial breach. Two scholarly approaches to access the ability of a seller to raise a force majeure exemption when the seller has already failed to perform some portion of the contractual obligations are also available and to be considered. Tallon argues that 'the exempting event must necessarily be the exclusive cause of the failure to perform. If goods not properly packaged are damaged following an unforeseeable and unavoidable accident, the seller remains nonetheless liable [...]The judge cannot reduce, even partly, the damages owed by the seller on account of that latter accident. The loss is attributable to the seller's failure to provide adequate accident-proof packaging.' Chengwei Liu adopts the position of *Enderlein & Maskow*, that 'on the contrary ... it cannot be required that the impediment is the exclusive cause of a breach of contract; '... the impediment should also be accepted when a cause overtakes another cause

... 'It is decisive ... whether the impediment lastly has caused the breach of contract. If this is so, it consumes other breaches of contract for which there are no grounds for exemption insofar as those no longer appear independently.' However, Chengwei Liu also stresses that '[t]he force majeure must have come about without the fault of either party. There will be no excuse if an unforeseeable event impedes performance of the contract when the event would not have affected the contract if the party had not been late in performing.' Chengwei Liu goes on to state that it is a general rule that 'a change in circumstances will not be taken into account if it occurred during a delay in performance of the person alleging application of the doctrine' due to the good faith requirements of the CISG, and that when 'the impediment occurs during the delay, its causality for the breach of contract is given only if it had an effect in the case of delivery within the period prescribed.'

[...]

ii. Meeting the Third Factor that Impediment Could Not Reasonably Be Overcome

The remaining key legal issue is whether the Seller should have complied with the Buyer's proposed alternative shipment to a location outside of Romania. Article 79 states that party will be exempted from liability if it 'could not reasonably be expected to ... have avoided or overcome it or its consequences.' There is very little case law under Article 79 defining what the Secretariat Commentary to the CISG terms a 'commercially reasonable substitute.'

[...]

The four corners of the CISG provide little guidance as to what constitutes a commercially reasonable substitute. The general principles of the CISG provide a preference for performance and the international character and promotion of good faith. These principles do little to advance the definition of commercially reasonable substitute in present circumstances. The Secretariat Commentary to the CISG provides some illuminating guidance, stating in pertinent part that:

'Even if the non-performing party can prove that he could not reasonably have been expected to take the impediment into account at the time of the conclusion of the contract, he must also prove that he could neither have avoided the impediment nor overcome it nor avoided or overcome the consequences of the impediment. This rule reflects the policy that a party who is under an obligation to act must do all in his power to carry out his obligation and may not await events, which might later justify his non-performance. This rule also indicates that a party may be required to perform by providing what is in all the circumstances of the transaction a commercially reasonable substitute for the performance, which was required under the contract.'

[...]

The facts of the instant case cut against the Seller in that another supplier to Buyer, Tyson, did deliver the chicken leg quarters to the Buyer in another locale. Even applying 'commercial practicability' as a test for excuse the shipment term was treated in fact as incidental aspect of performance despite the ban; an alternative unloading port was substituted as the destination consistent with U.C.C. § 2-614(1). While Seller raised the prospect that its agreements with other parties made substitute performance impossible without harm to Seller through breach of its other contracts, the Seller admitted that not all markets were covered by exclusive arrangements. Thus, under this approach Seller should have explored possible alternatives in this regard with Buyer, but failed to do so to Buyer's detriment and Seller's enrichment.

(c) Interpretation Aided by Sources Outside the Convention

If the CISG and its case law fail to provide the necessary information the next step is to look beyond that to private law. However, the CISG allows recourse to the rules of private international law only as a last resort. The analysis reaches that point.

[...]

The evidentiary record concerning what alternative steps were commercially reasonable in the limited time availability prior to the Romanian ban taking effect focused in substantial part on: (i) the Herculean effort to load as much product as possible from the supplier Seller had been using; (ii) the labeling requirements of the Romanian market as a factor limiting the ability to divert shipments at sea to Romanian customers; (iii) the logistical challenges attendant to identifying port docking space and refrigerated container availability if alternative manufacturers with product could even be found, particularly given the limited resources and time available to search for such alternatives instead of maximizing what could be loaded in timely fashion. The record in this regard reflects a commercially reasonable effort by Seller. However, the inquiry does not end here in searching for commercially reasonable alternatives. Buyer raised the prospect of accepting delivery of the product elsewhere to make subsequent shipment possible. Another American supplier facing the same Romanian ban as Seller shipped to another port. While that particular port may not have been a viable alternative for Seller, the evidence made clear there were ports where exclusivity arrangements would not have precluded such delivery. It was Seller's duty to do so here and it failed to do so, preferring to pocket the profit available in a market experiencing a dramatic rise in prices. In doing so Seller misappropriated a profit that should have been made available to Buyer through an alternative shipment destination. The law does not countenance such a result. Accordingly, Buyer is entitled to damages as a remedy. Article 74 of the CISG provides the applicable standard for the damages claim asserted by Buyer. Basically, under it Buyer is entitled to lost profits caused by Seller that were foreseeable at the time of entry into the Contracts The damages requested by Buyer meet the Article 74 standard and are adequately evidenced (See, e.g., Ex. 7). Seller's challenge to the damages sought, apart from a force majeure defense, is largely grounded upon the premise that market loss should not take into account a commercially reasonable phased release of product for sale. As such, Seller seeks to blur receipt of product with release of it into the market. However, there was no credible evidence on which to base that inference or to support such a finding. Seller's position is unpersuasive, and is divorced from commercial reality.

III. AWARD

A. Damages Accordingly, damages in the full amount requested of $608,323.00 are awarded.

[...]

IV. Comparison with Other Legal Provisions

Art 7.1.7 PICC 2010:

(1) Non-performance by a party is excused if that party proves that the non-performance was due to an impediment beyond its control and that it could not reasonably be expected to have taken the impediment into account at the time of the conclusion of the contract or to have avoided or overcome it or its consequences.

(2)   When the impediment is only temporary, the excuse shall have effect for such period as is reasonable having regard to the effect of the impediment on the performance of the contract.

(3)   The party who fails to perform must give notice to the other party of the impediment and its effect on its ability to perform. If the notice is not received by the other party within a reasonable time after the party who fails to perform knew or ought to have known of the impediment, it is liable for damages resulting from such non-receipt.

(4)   Nothing in this Article prevents a party from exercising a right to terminate the contract or to withhold performance or request interest on money due.

§ 2-614 UCC:

(1)   Where without fault of either party the agreed berthing, loading, or unloading facilities fail or an agreed type of carrier becomes unavailable or the agreed manner of delivery otherwise becomes commercially impracticable but a commercially reasonable substitute is available, such substitute performance must be tendered and accepted.

(2)   If the agreed means or manner of payment fails because of domestic or foreign governmental regulation, the seller may withhold or stop delivery unless the buyer provides a means or manner of payment which is commercially a substantial equivalent. If delivery has already been taken, payment by the means or in the manner provided by the regulation discharges the buyer's obligation unless the regulation is discriminatory, oppressive or predatory.

§ 2-615 UCC:

Except so far as a seller may have assumed a greater obligation and subject to the preceding Section on substituted performance:

(a) Delay in delivery or non-delivery in whole or in part by a seller who complies with paragraphs (b) and (c) is not a breach of his duty under a contract for sale if performance as agreed has been made impracticable by the occurrence of a contingency the non-occurrence of which was a basic assumption on which the contract was made or by compliance in good faith with any applicable foreign or domestic governmental regulation or order whether or not it later proves to be invalid.

(b) Where the causes mentioned in paragraph (a) affect only a part of the seller's capacity to perform, he must allocate production and deliveries among his customers but may at his option include regular customers not then under contract as well as his own requirements for further manufacture. He may so allocate in any manner which is fair and reasonable.

(c) The seller must notify the buyer seasonably that there will be delay or non-delivery and, when allocation is required under paragraph (b), of the estimated quota thus made available for the buyer.

§ 275(1) BGB:[305]

A claim for performance is excluded to the extent that performance is impossible for the obligor or for any other person.

§ 280(1) BGB:[306]

If the obligor breaches a duty arising from the obligation, the obligee may demand damages for the damage caused thereby. This does not apply if the obligor is not responsible for the breach of duty.

Art 119(1) OR:[307]

An obligation is deemed extinguished where its performance is made impossible by circumstances not attributable to the obligor.

Art 1148 CC:[308]

There is no occasion for any damages where a debtor was prevented from transferring or from doing that to which he was bound, or did what was forbidden to him, by reason of force majeure or of a fortuitous event.

Art 117 PRC CL:[309]

A party who was unable to perform a contract due to force majeure is exempted from liability in part or in whole in light of the impact of the event of force majeure, except otherwise provided by law. Where an event of force majeure occurred after the party's delay in performance, it is not exempted from liability.

For purposes of this Law, force majeure means any objective circumstance which is unforeseeable, unavoidable and insurmountable.

Art 118 PRC CL:

If a party is unable to perform a contract due to force majeure, it shall timely notify the other party so as to mitigate the loss that may be caused to the other party, and shall provide proof of force majeure within a reasonable time.

---

[305] Translation taken from www.gesetze-im-internet.de/englisch_bgb/.
[306] Translation taken from www.gesetze-im-internet.de/englisch_bgb/.
[307] Translation taken from www.admin.ch/ch/e/rs/2/220.en.pdf.
[308] Translation taken from www.legifrance.gouv.fr.
[309] Translation taken from www.wipo.int/wipolex/en/text.jsp?file_id=182632.

Questions

Q 79-1

(a) Which principle is laid down in Article 79 CISG?
(b) Describe the liability concept of the CISG, considering Articles 45, 61 and 79 CISG.
(c) Compare this liability concept to those found in domestic legal systems and the PICC 2010.

Q 79-2

To which contractual duties does Article 79 CISG apply?

Q 79-3

At which point in time must the impediment occur in order to fall under Article 79 CISG?

Q 79-4

Describe the circumstances under which an impediment in the sense of Article 79 CISG can be found.

Q 79-5

Could the seller be exempted under Article 79 CISG if its supplier fails (see C 79-1)?

Q 79-6

Could the debtor be exempted under Article 79 CISG if it was already in breach of contract when the impediment occurred?

Q 79-7

What obligations are imposed on the seller who is not able to deliver the goods as originally intended (see C 79-2)?

V. Hardship

Another category of impediment is a party's financial inability to perform. This impediment is usually called hardship. It is still disputed whether hardship may lead to an exemptiosn under Article 79 CISG and if so, what the relevant threshold should be. The consequences of hardship are also under discussion.

C 79-3

Oberlandesgericht Hamburg (Germany),
28 February 1997,
CISG-online 261[310]

For a summary of the facts see C 75-2 above.

[Judgment]

[...]

(d) [No force majeure or Art 79 exemption]

[...]

The Seller is also not exempted by the fact that acquiring the goods elsewhere would have led to considerable financial loss because it would have had to pay a higher price. The Seller generally bears the risk of considerable extra expenses in connection with acquiring the goods elsewhere, even the loss of transactions, as it has accepted the risk of acquiring the goods and the risk that they cannot be acquired at a certain price.

Despite of the triplication of market price that had to be paid for Chinese iron-molybdenum, an excess of the absolute limit of sacrifice is not given (*cf.* Schlechtriem-Stoll, Art 79 CISG para. 40). For parties doing business in a sector that has a very speculative aspect the limits of reasonability are very high. The contract was therefore not commercially unreasonable to an extent that it could be regarded as frustrated.

[...]

C 79-4

Cour de Cassation (Belgium),
19 June 2009,
CISG-online 1963

[Facts][311]

Buyer, a Dutch company, entered into several contracts with Seller, a French company, for the delivery of steel tubes. Subsequently, the price of steel unexpectedly rose by 70%. The contracts contained no price adjustment clause. The Court of First Instance, though admitting that the unforeseen price rise had caused a serious imbalance and continued performance of the contract at the contractual price would be harmful to the seller, excluded the seller's right to renegotiate the price, since the CISG, which governed the contract, was silent on the issue of hardship, and the Court did not determine the law applicable according to the relevant rules of private international law under which the seller might have been able to request renegotiation. The Court of Appeal referred to Article 7(2) of the CISG and

---

[310] Translation taken from CISG Pace (citations omitted).
[311] Summary of facts taken from UNILEX.

ruled that French law applied. Although French law does not provide for remedies in the case of hardship, in certain circumstances, such as in case of substantial imbalance of the contractual obligations, it imposed in accordance with the general principle of good faith the re-negotiation of the contract.

[...]

[Judgment][312]

[...]

1. Under Article 79(1) CISG [...] Changed circumstances that were not reasonably fore-seeable at the time of the conclusion of the contract and that are unequivocally of a nature to increase the burden of performance of the contract in a disproportionate manner, can, under circumstances, form an impediment in the sense of this provision of the Convention.

2. Article 7(1) states that:

'In the interpretation of this Convention, regard is to be had to its international character and to the need to promote uniformity in its application and the observance of good faith in international trade.'

Article 7(2) states that:

'Questions concerning matters governed by this Convention which are not expressly settled in it are to be settled in conformity with the general principles on which it is based or, in the absence of such principles, in conformity with the law applicable by virtue of the rules of private international law.'

Thus, to fill the gaps in a uniform manner adhesion should be sought with the general principles which govern the law of international trade.

Under these principles, as incorporated inter alia in the Unidroit Principles of International Commercial Contracts, the party who invokes changed circumstances that fundamentally disturb the contractual balance, as mentioned in paragraph 1, is also entitled to claim the renegotiation of the contract.

3. The judgment finds that:
— [Buyer] concluded with ... [Seller], a number of contracts of sale for the delivery of steel tubes;
— After the contracts had been concluded, the price of steel has unforeseeably increased by 70%;
— There was no clause in the contracts for price adaptation

The judges on appeal found that these unforeseen increases in the price gave rise to a serious imbalance which rendered the further performance of the contracts under unchanged conditions exceptionally detrimental for [Seller].

4. The Appellate Court judgment could, on the basis of these findings, without violation of the statutory provisions indicated in the plea, decide that [Buyer] must renegotiate the contractual conditions. The [Buyer]'s appeal from that judgment cannot be accepted. The Supreme Court rejects the [Buyer]'s plea in cassation.

[...]

---

[312] Translation taken from CISG Pace (citations omitted).

Art 6.2.2 PICC 2010:

> There is hardship where the occurrence of events fundamentally alters the equilibrium of the contract either because the cost of a party's performance has increased or because the value of the performance a party receives has diminished, and
> (a) the events occur or become known to the disadvantaged party after the conclusion of the contract;
> (b) the events could not reasonably have been taken into account by the disadvantaged party at the time of the conclusion of the contract;
> (c) the events are beyond the control of the disadvantaged party; and
> (d) the risk of the events was not assumed by the disadvantaged party.

Art 6.2.3 PICC 2010:

> (1) In case of hardship the disadvantaged party is entitled to request renegotiations. The request shall be made without undue delay and shall indicate the grounds on which it is based.
> (2) The request for renegotiation does not in itself entitle the disadvantaged party to withhold performance.
> (3) Upon failure to reach agreement within a reasonable time either party may resort to the court.
> (4) If the court finds hardship it may, if reasonable,
>   (a) terminate the contract at a date and on terms to be fixed, or
>   (b) adapt the contract with a view to restoring its equilibrium.

§ 313 BGB:[313]

> (1) If circumstances which became the basis of a contract have significantly changed since the contract was entered into and if the parties would not have entered into the contract or would have entered into it with different contents if they had foreseen this change, adaptation of the contract may be demanded to the extent that, taking account of all the circumstances of the specific case, in particular the contractual or statutory distribution of risk, one of the parties cannot reasonably be expected to uphold the contract without alteration.
> (2) [...]
> (3) If adaptation of the contract is not possible or one party cannot reasonably be expected to accept it, the disadvantaged party may revoke the contract. In the case of continuing obligations, the right to terminate takes the place of the right to revoke.

Questions

Q 79-8

Compare the prerequisites in Article 79(1) CISG, Articles 6.2.2 and 6.2.3 PICC 2010 and § 313 BGB.

---

[313] Translation taken from www.gesetze-im-internet.de/englisch_bgb/englisch_bgb.html#p1125.

Q 79-9

Compare C 79-3 and C 79-4.

(a)   What provisions do they apply to cases of hardship?
(b)   What is the relevant threshold beyond which hardship can be found?

Q 79-10

What are the consequences of hardship under Article 79(1) CISG, Article 6.2.3 PICC 2010 and § 313(3) BGB?

VI. Article 79(2) CISG

Article 79(2) CISG states the principle that, where the party in default has engaged a third party to perform the contract, it is only exempt if Article 79(1) applies to both the party in default and that third party. The provision applies to both the seller and the buyer, although, in practice, it is mostly the seller who relies on it. The requirements of Article 79(1) CISG must be met by both the seller and its supplier in order the seller to be exempt.

Whether this section can be extended to include a manufacturer or a sub-supplier has been discussed in a number of cases.

C 79-5

Bundesgerichtshof (Germany),
24 March 1999,
CISG-online 396

[Facts][314]

An Austrian owner of a vine nursery (the buyer) was in a longstanding business relationship with a German company (the seller) for the purchase of a special kind of wax, which it regularly used in order to prevent excessive drying out and limit danger of infection. As in the past, the buyer asked the seller to send an offer concerning 'ca. 5000 kg. black vinewax'. The wax was neither received nor inspected by the seller before delivery. It was delivered to the buyer in its original packaging directly from a third party, which the seller's supplier had entrusted with the production. The buyer partly used the delivered wax on its own vines fields and partly sold it on to other vine nurseries. After a large quantity of plants treated with the wax had suffered severe damage, the buyer complained thereof to the seller, then filed an action for damages. The seller objected, inter alia, that the vines had been damaged by a cause beyond its control.

---

[314] Summary of facts taken from UNILEX.

[...] 2. The appeal further asserts that defendant is, in any event, not liable for the damages caused by the use of the vine wax because it was only the intermediary and, therefore, the vine wax's non-conformity with the contract was beyond its control (CISG Art 79). This attack is also unsuccessful.

a) It may remain undecided whether CISG Art 79 encompasses all conceivable cases and forms of non-performance of contractual obligations creating a liability and is not limited to certain types of contractual violations and, therefore, includes the delivery of goods not in conformity with the contract because of their defectiveness [...], or whether a seller who has delivered defective goods cannot rely on Art 79 CISG at all [...]. An exemption pursuant to Art 79 CISG [...] is not applicable because, in any case, the defectiveness of the vine wax was not outside defendant's control. It is, therefore, responsible for the consequences of a delivery of goods not in conformity with the contract. The possibility of exemption under CISG Art 79 does not change the allocation of the contractual risk. According to the [CISG], the reason for the seller's liability is that he has agreed to provide the purchaser with goods that are in conformity with the contract. If the supplier's (or suppliers') breach of the contract is a general impediment within the meaning of CISG Art 79 at all, it is generally an impediment that the seller must avoid or overcome according to the content of the contract of sale. This follows the typical meaning of such a contract [...]. From the buyer's point of view, it makes no difference whether the seller produces the goods himself—with the consequence that the non-performance is generally in his actual control so that, as a rule, a dispensation pursuant to CISG Art 79(1) is generally excluded—or whether the seller obtains the goods from suppliers. Just as in the case of unspecified obligations, where the seller is liable for the timely delivery by his supplier [...], he is also responsible to see that his supplier delivers defect-free goods. In this respect, the [CISG] does not distinguish between an untimely delivery and a delivery of goods not in conformity with the contract. For both breaches of contract the same standard of liability applies. The appeal does not indicate that the parties agreed to a different allocation of risk at the formation of the contract, nor is this otherwise apparent. Pursuant to CISG Art 79, the seller's exemption from consequences of goods not in conformity with the contract can only be considered—if at all (see above)—when the non-conformity cannot be deemed to be within the seller's control. Because the seller has the risk of acquisition (as shown), he can only be exempted under CISG Art 79 (1) or (2) (even when the reasons for the defectiveness of the goods are—as here—within the control of his supplier or his sub-supplier) if the defectiveness is due to circumstances out of his own control and out of each of his suppliers' control. The appeal cannot show this. Insofar as the appeal points out that the manufacturer, in 1994, used an inappropriate raw material possibly imported from Hungary during the production of the delivered vine wax, this is not relevant with respect to CISG Art 79 because the manufacturer would be liable—and thus also plaintiff vis-à-vis defendant—for those product defects within its control.

b) For this reason, the basic responsibility of defendant for plaintiff's damages is not questioned by the appeal's argument that the damage would have occurred in the same way if defendant in 1994 had delivered the same vine wax to plaintiff as it had delivered in prior years and that was used by plaintiff without any damages instead of the newly developed vine wax, because all brands of vine wax produced by the manufacturer in that year had the same defect due to the defective raw materials used only in this year. That is so because defendant would also have been liable for plaintiff's damages in this hypothetical case. The

---

[315] Translation taken from CISG Pace (citations omitted).

liability under the [CISG] is [...] not based on the supplier's obligation to inspect the goods before delivery to its purchaser, which—according to the appeal—was not necessary in this case because the vine wax previously purchased had always been free of defects. That is so because the seller's culpability is not important due to the statutory allocation of risk and the lack of a different agreement between the parties concerning the allocation of risk, resulting in a guarantee [warranty] liability of the seller.

[...]

C 79-6

Hamburg Chamber of Commerce (Germany),
Partial Award of 21 March 1996,
CISG-online 187

[Facts][316]

A German buyer concluded two framework agreements with two Hong Kong companies (the sellers), concerning delivery of goods produced in the People's Republic of China. In the course of the business relationship the buyer ordered 10,000 units of product from one of the sellers. The latter asked for advance payment; later on it informed the buyer that its own Chinese supplier was undergoing serious financial and personal difficulties, and refused to deliver the goods unless the buyer paid all outstanding debts. The buyer refused. The seller brought an action before the Arbitral Court. The buyer declared the sales contract avoided and asked for damages deriving from breach of the individual sales contract in dispute and breach of the framework agreement.

[Judgment][317]

[...]

In particular, the claim for damages is not excluded under Art 79 CISG. According to Art 79(1) CISG, the seller is not liable for a failure to perform any of his obligations if he proves that the failure was due to an impediment beyond his control and that he could not reasonably be expected to have taken the impediment into account at the time of the conclusion of the contract, or to have avoided or overcome it or its consequences. The sub-supplier (the Chinese manufacturer) could only guarantee the continuation of its activity and thereby the supply of goods to the seller on the condition of the immediate availability of a considerable amount of cash. But this is not an 'impediment beyond the control' of the seller. It is true that the seller does not answer for the manufacturer or sub-supplier in the same measure as he does for a sub-contractor and his own staff under Art 79(2) CISG. Still, the financial straits of the manufacturer and its need for cash are not an unmanageable risk or a totally exceptional event, such as force majeure, economic impossibility or excessive onerousness. Rather, the risk related to the supply is to be borne by the seller, also if the circumstances become more onerous. Further, he must guarantee his financial capability to perform, an aspect which belongs typically to the sphere of responsibility of the debtor. The seller is not freed from his responsibility as to his financial capability to perform even where he loses

---

[316] Summary of facts taken from UNILEX.
[317] Translation taken from CISG Pace (citations omitted).

the necessary means because of subsequent, unforeseeable events. The same applies to the cash difficulties in the relationship with the Chinese sub-supplier, as a consequence of the withdrawal of [the sub-supplier's] State credit under pressure from the Government. Nor is it relevant whether the seller was surprised by the buyer's failure to pay the debts due under the previous deliveries, or whether the seller, who insofar as he has to submit the facts to substantiate his claim, complied with his duty to make enquiries in good time when the conclusion of the contract was being prepared. Only the apportionment of the risk in the contract is relevant here, which apportionment is made clear by the pre-payment agreement. Because of the agreement for pre-payment, the failure of the buyer to pay his previous debts is irrelevant also as far as the question of the cause of the buyer's failure to perform according to Art 80 CISG is concerned.

[…]

Questions

Q 79-11

On an examination of the wording of Article 79(2) CISG, would you say that Article 79(2) CISG makes it more difficult for the breaching party to be exempt than Article 79(1) CISG?

Q 79-12

Are suppliers covered by Article 79(2) CISG (see C 79-5)?

Q 79-13

It has been stated that a manufacturer does not fall under Article 79(2) CISG. How else could a seller's liability for its manufacturer be established? See C 79-6.

Q 79-14

Numerous decisions state that the party relying on Article 79 CISG bears the burden of proof. This is expressly laid down in the wording of Article 79(1) CISG: 'if he proves that the failure [to perform] was due to an impediment beyond his control'. Which general principle can be drawn from this provision?

Q 79-15

If one of the parties can successfully rely on Article 79 CISG, does this hinder the other party from exercising any right other than claiming damages, in particular, the right to claim performance?

VII. CISG Advisory Council

CISG Advisory Council Opinion No 7: Exemption of Liability for Damages under Article 79 of the CISG—Black Letter Rules:[318]

1. Article 79 exempts a party from liability for damages when that party has failed to perform any of its obligations, including the seller's obligation to deliver conforming goods.

2.1 If the non-performance or defective performance results from a third person's failure to perform, Article 79 sets forth different requirements for establishing an exemption, depending on the nature of the engagement of the third person with the contracting party.

2.2 Article 79(1) remains the controlling provision even if a contracting party has engaged a third person to perform the contract in whole or in part.

    (a) In general, the seller is not exempted under Article 79(1) when those within its sphere of risk fail to perform; for example, the seller's own staff or personnel and those engaged to provide the seller with raw materials or semi-manufactured goods. The same principle applies to the buyer in relation to the buyer's own staff or personnel and those engaged to perform the obligations of the buyer under the contract.

    (b) In exceptional circumstances, a contracting party may be exempted under Article 79(1) for the acts or omissions of a third person when the contracting party was not able to choose or control the third person.

2.3 Article 79(2) applies when a contracting party engages an independent third person to perform the contract in whole or in part. In such a case, the contracting party claiming an exemption must establish that the requirements set forth in Article 79(1) are satisfied both in its own regard and in regard to that third person.

3.1 A change of circumstances that could not reasonably be expected to have been taken into account, rendering performance excessively onerous ('hardship'), may qualify as an 'impediment' under Article 79(1). The language of Article 79 does not expressly equate the term 'impediment' with an event that makes performance absolutely impossible. Therefore, a party that finds itself in a situation of hardship may invoke hardship as an exemption from liability under Article 79.

3.2 In a situation of hardship under Article 79, the court or arbitral tribunal may provide further relief consistent with the CISG and the general principles on which it is based.

---

[318] Taken from www.cisgac.com.

Article 80 CISG

A party may not rely on a failure of the other party to perform, to the extent that such failure was caused by the first party's act or omission.

I. Overview

Article 80 CISG prevents a party from relying on the other party's breach of contract and from exercising the corresponding remedies if the breach was caused by an 'act or omission' of the first party. Articles 80 and 79 CISG form their own section dealing with exemptions.

Article 80 CISG has no specific forerunner in the ULIS. It has frequently been used as a tool for 'sorting out' the parties' rights when both sides have allegedly failed to perform their obligations.

II. Article 80 CISG in Detail

Article 80 CISG requires that the debtor's failure to perform be caused by the creditor's act or omission. Whether or not there was fault on the creditor's behalf is irrelevant.

As a legal consequence, to the extent that its act or omission has caused the debtor's failure to perform, the creditor loses the remedies it would otherwise have had, such as a claim for specific performance, payment of the purchase price, avoidance of the contract or reduction of the price. It will, furthermore, not be entitled to claim damages; to this extent, there is an overlap with Article 79 CISG.

C 80-1

Oberster Gerichtshof (Austria),
6 February 1996,
CISG-online 224[319]

For a summary of the facts see C 9-3 above.

[Judgment]

[...]

The lower courts decided that the increase of the quantity to be delivered (which was incidentally desired by the [sellers]) was agreed upon by phone on the afternoon of 19 December 1990. According to the factual findings, an agreement was also reached about the opening of a letter of credit. The deal between the parties, therefore, was concluded on the evening of 19 December 1990. In the aftermath, however, neither did the [buyer] open the letter of credit nor did the [sellers] deliver the sold goods, i.e., the liquid gas.

According to Art 54 CISG, the buyer has the obligation to pay the purchase price and to comply with such formalities as may be required under the contract or any laws and regulations to enable payment to be made. If, as in this case, the opening of a letter of credit was agreed upon, the buyer is obligated to make sure it is opened on time. This can only be assumed as being done when the [seller] has acquired the claim against the bank. Therefore, the agreement about a letter of credit requires the buyer to perform before the seller does. It is only after the letter of credit is opened that the buyer acquires the claim against the [seller] to perform as agreed upon [...]. According to the unanimous opinion of scholars [...], the opening of a letter of credit is part of the obligation to pay the purchase price with the consequence that the non-performance in this regard triggers the legal remedies of breach of contract (Art 61 *et seq.* CISG) and not just the remedies of an anticipatory breach (Arts 71 to 73 CISG [...]).

However, the letter of credit was not issued because the [sellers] did not inform the [buyer] of the place of loading despite their obligation to do so and their express confirmation in this regard (last telefax of 19 December 1990). Though Juergen S., even when on Christmas vacation, urged the [sellers] to release this information, the [sellers] did not even inform him of the place of loading at the beginning of January. As a consequence, the notice of the [buyer] in the telefax of 2 January 1990 can only mean that [buyer] obviously thought that the release of this information would happen on that very day, but that [buyer] could not take any measures anymore on that very day due to the little time left. The fact that the [buyer] did not fulfill its obligation—the advance performance by means of opening a letter of credit—until the beginning of January, is the [sellers'] fault, who did not name the place of loading despite their corresponding obligation, even though they had reason to know that the [buyer] would only issue the letter of credit after being informed of the place of loading. It is irrelevant whether the opening of a letter of credit would have been possible even without information about the place of loading, because the parties expressly agreed upon the naming of the place of loading by the [sellers]. Due to this agreement, the [sellers] had the primary duty to name the place of loading. Only after this act on the part of the [sellers], did the [buyer] have the

---

[319] Translation taken from CISG Pace (citations omitted).

obligation to issue the letter of credit. The non-issuance of the letter of credit, therefore, was caused by an omission of the [sellers], and—following Art 80 CISG—the latter cannot rely on the [buyer's] failure to open the letter of credit.

[...]

III. Comparison with Other Legal Provisions

Art 7.1.2 PICC 2010:

A party may not rely on the non-performance of the other party to the extent that such non-performance was caused by the first party's act or omission or by another event for which the first party bears the risk.

§ 254(1) BGB:[320]

(1) If fault on the aggrieved party's behalf has contributed to the occurrence of the loss, the duty to pay damages and the amount of damages depends on the circumstances, in particular on the extent to which the loss has been caused by one party or the other.

Art 44(1) OR:[321]

Where the injured party consented to the action which caused the loss or damage or circumstances attributable to him helped give rise to or compound the loss or damage or otherwise exacerbated the position of the party liable for it, the court may reduce the compensation due or even dispense with it entirely.

Questions

Q 80-1

Which rule does Article 80 CISG establish?

Q 80-2

Explain the scope of application of Articles 77 and 80 CISG, respectively.

---

[320] Author's translation.
[321] Translation taken from www.admin.ch/ch/e/rs/2/220.en.pdf.

Q 80-3

(a) Explain the differences between Article 79 and Article 80 CISG.
(b) Compare Article 80 CISG with the provisions from other legal systems. How do the latter differ from Article 80 CISG with regard to their scope of application?

Q 80-4

Under Article 80 CISG, the consequences where the debtor's failure to perform is caused by both parties are disputed. Is there a total or partial exclusion of remedies?

Q 80-5

How did the seller in C 80-1 cause the buyer's breach of contract?

Q 80-6

(a) Can you think of a situation where the debtor, instead of relying on Article 80 CISG, will be required to make an effort to overcome the disturbance caused by the creditor?
(b) On which general principle could such a duty of the debtor be based?

Q 80-7

When will the debtor, who was not able to fulfil one or several of its contractual duties due to an act or omission of the creditor, be entitled to remedies against the creditor?

Article 81 CISG

(1) Avoidance of the contract releases both parties from their obligations under it, subject to any damages which may be due. Avoidance does not affect any provision of the contract for the settlement of disputes or any other provision of the contract governing the rights and obligations of the parties consequent upon the avoidance of the contract.
(2) A party who has performed the contract either wholly or in part may claim restitution from the other party of whatever the first party supplied or paid under the contract. If both parties are bound to make restitution, they must do so concurrently.

I. Overview

Articles 81 to 84 CISG are combined in a separate section dealing with the effects of avoidance of the contract. This section governs only the legal *consequences* of avoidance of the contract; it does not provide the legal *basis* for the right to avoidance. Rather, the legal basis for the right to avoidance is Article 49 for the buyer and Article 64 for the seller; Articles 72 and 73 contain the right to avoid a part of the contract or the contract as a whole in case of anticipatory breach or in case the contract is an instalment agreement.

Articles 81 to 84 CISG provide for the legal consequences of contract avoidance with regard to contractual duties only. This has a double significance. First, the restriction to contractual duties means that extra-contractual liabilities based, for instance, on unjust enrichment, disgorgement of profits or tort law, are not affected by Articles 81 to 84 CISG. Whether and to what extent such non-contractual rights exist will, in principle, depend on the applicable national law. However, it must be borne in mind that Articles 81 to 84 must be applied autonomously and that their scope of application might be broader than that of any contractual restitution regime under national law. In order to determine whether, in addition to the rights conferred under Articles 81 to 84, national, non-contractual rights between the parties exist, the scope of application of Articles 81 to 84 CISG must be determined first. By doing so, regard must be had to the fact that the Convention aims at promoting uniformity in its application (Art 7(1)) and that such uniformity would be undermined if one could resort to supplementary national law and receive further benefits it would not receive under Articles 81 to 84 CISG.

Secondly, the fact that Articles 81 to 84 CISG deal only with contractual duties after contract avoidance means that these provisions do not deal with property law (see Art 4(b) CISG). That is, the situation *in rem* after having avoided the contract, notably the question of when title of the goods passes back to the seller, is subject to the applicable domestic law.

II. The Principle (Article 81(1) CISG)

Article 81(1) CISG, sentence 1, states that avoidance of the contract releases both parties from their contractual obligations. However, avoidance of the contract does not affect any claims for damages, provisions for the settlement of disputes or other provisions governing the parties' rights after avoidance of the contract (Art 81(1), sentence 2). As a matter of course, the avoidance of the contract mentioned in Article 81(1) CISG must be rightful and effective. That is, it must comply with the requirements of Articles 49, 64, 26 and 27 CISG.

A. Claims for Damages

Nowadays, it is almost undisputed that, after avoidance of the contract, the contract continues to exist during the time of contract liquidation. As a consequence of the fact that the contract is kept alive for as long as the contract has not been wound up, damages claims accrued prior to avoidance survive under the avoided contract. Furthermore, it may be that new damages claims arise as a consequence of the avoidance of the contract, for example, where the creditor makes a loss of profit because, due to the avoidance of the contract, it cannot resell, lease and so on the goods to third parties. Those damages can be claimed under the Convention by an analogous application of Articles 74 *et seq.*

B. Provisions for the Settlement of Disputes

According to Article 81(1) CISG, second sentence, provisions for the settlement of disputes are not affected by the avoidance of the contract. Such provisions for the settlement of disputes may be choice of jurisdiction clauses, but may also be agreements on extrajudicial settlement, such as arbitration clauses, clauses providing for mediation, conciliation or yet another mechanism of dispute resolution.

C. Other Provisions of the Contract

Contractual provisions governing the rights and obligations of the parties consequent upon the avoidance of the contract are not affected by the avoidance either. Whether a contract clause is meant to survive avoidance of the contract must be determined by interpreting the contract (Art 8(2), (3)). This will not always be easy: whereas, for example, confidentiality clauses will typically have to be regarded as having post-contractual effect (and often state so explicitly), the situation will be less clear with regard to other clauses. An exclusive agreement clause, for instance, is more difficult to interpret, as the time the exclusivity envisaged by the parties does not necessarily correspond to the end of their contractual relationship.

III. Duty to make Restitution (Article 81(2) CISG)

Article 81(2) CISG governs the situation where the contract or parts of it have already been performed. It states the parties' duty to make restitution of what they had received under the contract, be it goods, money or the supply of drafts, plans, drawings and so on. Restitution of what has been performed under the contract must take place concurrently.

The duty to make restitution raises several questions to which diverse solutions have been proposed. The controversial issues relate, in particular, to: where and when restitution of the goods and the price, respectively, must be made; who must bear the costs connected with restitution; and who bears the risk of damage to or loss of the goods between avoidance and redelivery. The questions cannot be further analysed here; to show the extent of the discussion, it should suffice to refer to the following case excerpt of 1999, which has been further developed by the Opinion of the CISG Advisory Council of 2008. The two excerpts deal with the question of where restitution must take place.

C 81-1

Oberster Gerichtshof (Austria),
29 June 1999,
CISG-online 483[322]

[Facts]

[...]

In the context of a longer business relationship, [seller], domiciled in Germany, delivered cut and drilled dividing wall panels to a building site in Vienna serviced by the domestic [buyer]. The condition 'ex factory' was agreed between the parties for all deliveries. In October 1992, non-formatted (i.e., neither cut, nor drilled) panels, manufactured for the [seller] by [the] manufacturer in Peiting, Germany, were delivered to the [buyer] instead of the cut and drilled panels ordered in the contract. Employees of the parties agreed over the telephone on

---

[322] Translation taken from CISG Pace (citations omitted).

the return of these panels by the [buyer]. The assertion of the [seller] that, according to the agreement, the return of the panels to the manufacturer would have to be undertaken by the [seller], remained unproven. On 29 October 1992, at the time of the delivery by the forwarder commissioned by the intervener, the manufacturer confirmed the receipt of the panels without reservation on the CMR consignment note, showing the manufacturer as the recipient. While unloading the panels on the following day, the manufacturer established that they were damaged. ...

[Judgment]

b) ... For breach of contract, the CISG allows the buyer to claim compensatory damages and provides several other alternative legal remedies, among them the right of avoidance of the contract under Art. 49 CISG. In the present case, the parties have validly and by mutual understanding (Art. 6 CISG) agreed on the avoidance of the sales contract. ...

According to the CISG, the contract is not entirely annulled by the avoidance, but rather it is 'changed' into a winding-up relationship ...

The CISG does not contain any provisions pertaining to the place of performance for restitution. Nevertheless, the gaps arising from the absence of relevant agreements within the framework of Art. 7(2) CISG can be bridged without recourse to national provisions ... The place of performance for the obligations concerning restitution should mirror the place of performance for the primary contractual obligations ... If, under Art. 31 CISG, the delivery obligations require the goods to be picked up at the seller's place of business (or as here, the manufacturer's), or if the seller is obliged to give the goods to a carrier for delivery, then, in the event of a consensual avoidance of the contract and in the absence of a different arrangement, the seller has to pick up the goods at the buyer's place of business or the buyer has to hand the goods over to a carrier for return delivery to the seller (or, as here, the manufacturer), respectively. Restitution is to be effected in these cases at the buyer's place of business ... Since in this case, the primary contractual performance was of a sale by delivery to a place other than the place of performance, with the risk passing to the German manufacturer, this arrangement for the passing of the risk must also reversibly apply for a consensual avoidance of the contract. Subsequent to the consensual avoidance of the contract, the passing of risk to the seller is effected with the handing over of the goods to be returned to the commissioned carrier at the place of business of the buyer. According to the agreement, the [buyer] had to send the panels back to the manufacturer. The [seller] also did not claim that the delivery of the panels to the intervener as a commissioned carrier was equal to a breach of contract. ...

CISG Advisory Council Opinion No 9: Consequences of Avoidance of the Contract:[323]

[...]

ee) Place of Restitution

3.12 The place of restitution is not dealt with expressly by the Convention but it is a matter governed by the Convention and so is to be determined by the general principles on which the Convention is based. Taking first redelivery of the goods, suppose that the contract of sale calls for delivery at the seller's premises. If it is the buyer who avoids the contract for the seller's unexempted non-performance, requiring the buyer to redeliver to the seller's premises

---

[323] Taken from www.cisgac.com.

would give rise to an additional damages liability of the seller under Article 74. Furthermore, nothing in Article 81 would allow the buyer to insist on reimbursement of these carriage costs before handing the goods over. Concurrence goes to the reversal of delivery and payment and not to damages. The avoidance of economic waste may be seen as a general principle underlying the Convention. A requirement of redelivery at the buyer's premises, even if the contract is avoided for the buyer's non-performance (see below), would allow for disposal of the goods in the local market and thus minimise the costs of the restitutionary process. In addition, redelivery at the buyer's premises avoids the complications of allocating risk in transit. It would also delay the process of restitution if the buyer had to hands over the goods at the seller's premises, thus adding further to the cost of restitution. Redelivery at the buyer's premises is therefore the general rule and is supported by cases where the seller is the non-performing party. [...]

3.13 Two exceptional cases should however be considered. If the contract calls for delivery of the goods at another place, then this place should be the place of redelivery. If the buyer acting reasonably has warehoused the goods at another place still, then the warehouse should be the place where the goods are to be redelivered, though any warehouse warrant or similar document that has to be produced to release the goods should be the subject of transfer at the buyer's premises.

3.14 In addition, if it is the seller who avoids the contract for the buyer's unexempted non-performance, it is less clear that redelivery should be required at the buyer's premises. If redelivery did take place there, the seller would have an action for damages against the buyer under Article 74 for any consequent costs of carriage. Nevertheless, the likely cause of a seller avoiding the contract is where the buyer fails to pay for the goods, in which case the seller would have a practical interest in taking an active position and expediting the redelivery process. This points to the efficacy of a clear rule in all cases, including cases where the contract is avoided for exempted non-performance, that redelivery should take place at the buyer's premises.

3.15 The place of repayment of the purchase price is also not dealt with expressly by the Convention. Treating the seller as the buyer of the redelivered goods, the price should be repayable at the original buyer's premises. This obligation of the seller should not be interpreted too literally since the means of payment and repayment also have to be considered. If payment under the contract of sale has been made by a bank transfer, repayment by the same method to a bank of the buyer's choice represents the most practical method of effecting restitution. Requiring restitution of the goods and the purchase price in different places is not as such inconsistent with the rule of concurrency of restitution, though exact concurrency may be hard to achieve in all cases where redelivery and repayment occur in different places.

...

A last point should be mentioned, that is, the question of whether countervailing claims can be set off under the CISG. The Convention is silent on the question. However, the fact that Art 81(2) calls for 'concurrent' restitution has been interpreted as to constitute a general principle (cf. Art 7(2) CISG) of the possibility to set off countervailing claims—but only if both claim and cross-claim arise out of the same contract. If the cross-claim arises out of another contract, it is preponderantly held that the question of whether it may be set off depends on the applicable domestic law (Art 7(2) *in fine*).

Questions

Q 81-1

(a)   Which general rule does Article 81 CISG establish consequent upon the avoidance of the contract?
(b)   How is the statement that avoidance does not entirely annul the contract to be understood? See C 81-1.

Q 81-2

What are the legal consequences if no effective avoidance is made?

Q 81-3

Most arbitration laws and institutional arbitration rules state that the arbitration agreement is to be regarded as an agreement separate from the contract and thus capable of remaining in force independently of the contract ('separability doctrine'). See, for example, Article 16(1) UNCITRAL Model Law on International Commercial Arbitration 1985 (amended in 2006): 'The arbitral tribunal may rule on its own jurisdiction, including any objections with respect to the existence or validity of the arbitration agreement. For that purpose, an arbitration clause which forms part of a contract shall be treated as an agreement independent of the other terms of the con-tract. A decision by the arbitral tribunal that the contract is null and void shall not entail *ipso jure* the invalidity of the arbitration clause.

Discuss whether, in light of this, it was necessary to mention in Article 81(1) CISG that dispute settlement clauses remain unaffected by the avoidance of the contract.

Q 81-4

What is, according to C 81-1 and the CISG Advisory Council, the place of making restitution of the goods and the price, respectively? Could there be other solutions?

Article 82 CISG

(1) The buyer loses the right to declare the contract avoided or to require the seller to deliver substitute goods if it is impossible for him to make restitution of the goods substantially in the condition in which he received them.

(2) The preceding paragraph does not apply:

    (a) if the impossibility of making restitution of the goods or of making restitution of the goods substantially in the condition in which the buyer received them is not due to his act or omission;

    (b) if the goods or part of the goods have perished or deteriorated as a result of the examination provided for in article 38; or

    (c) if the goods or part of the goods have been sold in the normal course of business or have been consumed or transformed by the buyer in the course of normal use before he discovered or ought to have discovered the lack of conformity.

I. Overview

Article 82 CISG governs the situation where the buyer cannot make restitution of the goods, at least not in substantially the same condition in which it took them over. The provision addresses the buyer because the problem of not being able to restitute what one has received arises only in connection with goods. The seller's duty, the reimbursement of money, is never deemed to be impossible.

Article 82 CISG is based on the Roman law principle of restitution in an unimpaired condition. In principle, the inability to make restitution of the goods in kind deprives the buyer of the right to avoid the contract (Art 82(1)). The same applies if the buyer wishes to exercise its right to require substitute goods (Art 46(2)).

However, Article 82(2) CISG provides three exceptions to this rule: the buyer may nonetheless avoid the contract if, (1) the impossibility of making restitution of the goods (substantially in the condition in which the buyer received them) is not due to its act or omission (subparagraph (a)); (2) the goods or part of the goods have perished or deteriorated as a result of examining the goods (subparagraph (b)); or (3) the goods or part of the goods have been sold in the normal course of business or have been consumed or transformed by the buyer in the course of normal use before it discovered or ought to have discovered the lack of conformity (subparagraph c)).

The exceptions provided for in Article 82(2) were vividly discussed at the Drafting Conference. In their present form, they restrict the principle of inadmissibility of avoidance where restitution is not possible considerably, particularly by subparagraph (c) of paragraph 2.

II. The Principle: No Avoidance where Restitution has become Impossible (Article 82(1) CISG)

Article 82(1) CISG establishes the principle that the inability to return the goods is a bar to avoidance.

Avoidance under Article 82(1) CISG is only barred where the impossibility of restitution *in natura* affects the goods as such. If the buyer is unable to return other benefits which it received under the contract, for example bonds and the like, Article 82(1) CISG is no obstacle to avoidance. 'Impossibility' under Article 82(1) CISG refers to an actual and objective impediment to restitution; economic obstacles such as substantial changes in the market value of the goods do not bar avoidance.

Article 82(1) CISG provides for a *de minimis* rule, pursuant to which insignificant changes in the condition of the goods are harmless. Such minor deficiencies must be compensated by way of damages. The decisive criterion is whether the seller can reasonably be expected to accept the returned goods. For an illustration of what 'the seller's reasonable expectation' means, see the excerpt below.

A 82-1

Text of Secretariat Commentary on Article 67 of the 1978 Draft

[Draft counterpart of CISG Article 82]

...

3. It is not necessary that the goods be in the identical condition in which they were received; they need be only in 'substantially' the same condition. Although the term 'substantially' is not defined, it indicates that the change in condition of the goods must be of sufficient importance that it would no longer be proper to require the seller to retake the goods as the equivalent of that which he had delivered to the buyer even though the seller had been in fundamental breach of the contract. ...

III. The Three Exceptions (Article 82(2) CISG)

Article 82(2) CISG significantly restricts the principle embodied in Article 82(1) CISG. Subparagraphs (a) and (b) provide that the buyer can still avoid the contract, even if the goods cannot be returned in an unimpaired condition, if loss or deterioration of the goods is due to a seller's breach of contract, but also where loss or damage is accidental or due to *force majeure*. For example, where the goods cannot be returned because of confiscation, which occurred due to the non-conformity of the goods, or where the buyer is not in possession of the goods because of the seller's delivery to the wrong place, the buyer maintains the right to declare the contract avoided.

Subparagraph (c) of Article 82(2) states that the risk of consummation or transformation of the goods in the normal course of use as well as the risk of resale of the goods within the normal course of business, is the seller's. However, there is a time limit. From the time at which it knew or ought to have known of the lack of conformity in the goods, the buyer can no longer rely on Article 82(2)(c) CISG. For an application of subparagraphs (b) and (c) of Article 82(2) CISG, see the following case abstracts.

C 82-1

Bundesgerichtshof (Germany),
25 June 1997,
CISG-online 277[324]

[Facts]

Plaintiff [seller], which trades in steel produced in South Korea, delivered to Defendant [buyer], whose place of business is in Switzerland, a total of 125.81 tons of stainless steel wire upon an order dated 7 February 1992, which was confirmed by the [seller] on 10 March 1992. It is in dispute between the parties whether the delivery took place in July or September 1992. Of the total purchase price, Deutsche Mark [DM] 366,174.51, the amount of DM 63,180 is still unpaid. The [buyer] notified the [seller] with 'notices of substandard material', dated 5 November 1992, and 6 April 1993, that specific, individually indicated quantities of the raw material could not be processed, and that it placed the substandard material at the [seller]'s disposal. At the same time, the [buyer] inquired about what should be done with these materials and also with the 'semi-processed materials' that was 'possibly' still in storage. In letters dated 2 December 1992, and 27 January 1993, the [seller] notified the [buyer] that, if the complaints [were] justified, the value of the material would be credited, and if further substandard material was found in the [buyer]'s stock, responsibility would also be taken if the complaint [was] justified. Both parties have obtained expert opinions regarding the suitability of the raw material, which, however, reached conflicting conclusions.

With its complaint, the [seller] demands that the [buyer] pay the outstanding purchase price plus interest. After the [buyer] had processed the extant raw material during the course of the litigation before the Court of First Instance at the end of 1995, it continued to pursue the avoidance of the contract in its brief dated 6 November 1995 only with regard to the substandard quantities indicated there. Alternatively, it declared a set-off against the claims for damages of DM 4,800, Swiss francs [Sfr] 2,850.50 and DM 75,578.53. ...

---

[324] Translation taken from CISG Pace (citations omitted).

[Judgment]

...

II. e) The avoidance of the contract is also not excluded according to CISG Art. 82(1) by the fact that the [buyer] cannot return the processed material in the same condition as it had received it. The [buyer] stated that, in order to determine which portion of the delivered raw material was still substandard, it had to process all of the raw material; the [seller] also stated that the defects claimed by the [buyer] were apparent in their entirety only in the course of the processing of the material. Thus, the material was altered under CISG Art. 38 due to the necessary processing for the investigation. But if the [buyer] keeps its right to declare the contract avoided even when the goods have perished or deteriorated by the investigation (CISG Art. 82(2)(b)), this rule must apply especially when—as the buyer claimed—the goods improved through the processing. The fact that the alteration of the goods took place only after the avoidance of the contract was declared, does not change anything with regard to the earlier avoidance of the contract. ...

IV. Comparison with Other Legal Provisions

Art 7.3.6 PICC 2010:[325]

(1) On termination of the contract to be performed at one time either party may claim restitution of whatever it has supplied under the contract, provided that such party concurrently makes restitution of whatever it has received under the contract.
(2) If restitution in kind is not possible or appropriate, an allowance has to be made in money whenever reasonable.
(3) (...)

Art 207 OR:

(1) Termination of the contract can also be claimed where the goods have perished in consequence of their defects or by accident.
(2) In such a case, the buyer has to return only what has remained from the goods.
(3) If the goods perished due to the buyer's fault, or if they were resold or altered, [the buyer] can only claim a reduction of the price.

Art 1647 CC:[326]

(1) Where the thing which had defects perishes because of its bad quality, the loss falls upon the seller who is liable to the buyer for restitution of the price and other compensations explained in the two preceding Articles [Articles 1645 and 1646].
(2) But a loss occasioned by a fortuitous event falls upon the buyer.

---

[325] See also the similar provision in Art. 9:309 PECL.
[326] Translation taken from www.legifrance.gouv.fr.

Questions

Q 82-1

(a) Which principle is embodied in Article 82(1) CISG?
(b) Compare Article 82(1) CISG with Article 7.3.6(1) and (2) PICC 2010, as well as with Article 207 OR and Article 1647 CC and describe the differences in relation to Article 82 CISG.

Q 82-2

How is the principle established in Article 82(1) CISG 'watered down'? See Article 82(2) CISG.

Q 82-3

(a) To what extent does Article 82(2) CISG provide for a particular risk allocation mechanism to govern the situation after the contract has been declared avoided?
(b) What is the idea underlying Article 82(2) CISG?

Q 82-4

(a) Why was the buyer allowed to declare the contract avoided in C 82-1?
(b) According to the court, does it matter at what point in time the alienation of the goods, consequent upon an examination within the meaning of Article 38 CISG, takes place?

Q 82-5

It has been disputed whether Article 82 CISG should apply only where it is the buyer who declares avoidance, or whether it should also apply where the contract is terminated by mutual agreement or (unilaterally) by the seller. What do you think? It will be helpful to consider which party should be protected by Article 82 CISG.

Article 83 CISG

A buyer who has lost the right to declare the contract avoided or to require the seller to deliver substitute goods in accordance with article 82 retains all other remedies under the contract and this Convention.

Article 83 CISG supplements the foregoing provision and is usually quoted in conjunction with it. It maintains the principle that the various remedies available under the CISG exist independently from each other. This affects, in the first instance, the right to damages and to a reduction of the purchase price.

There is an interplay between the various remedies; for example, a claim for damages will vary in amount depending on whether or not the contract was avoided.

Questions

Q 83-1

Which general rule of the Convention's remedies concept is affirmed in Article 83 CISG?

Q 83-2

Why will remedies other than damages and reduction of the purchase price be of only limited relevance in connection with Article 83 CISG?

Article 84 CISG

(1) If the seller is bound to refund the price, he must also pay interest on it, from the date on which the price was paid.
(2) The buyer must account to the seller for all benefits which he has derived from the goods or part of them:
    (a) if he must make restitution of the goods or part of them; or
    (b) if it is impossible for him to make restitution of all or part of the goods or to make restitution of all or part of the goods substantially in the condition in which he received them, but he has nevertheless declared the contract avoided or required the seller to deliver substitute goods.

I. Overview

Article 84 CISG comprises a twofold rule: paragraph (1) states the seller's duty to pay interest on the purchase price that it must refund, whereas paragraph (2) establishes the buyer's obligation to account for all benefits which it has derived from the goods. The purpose of the rule is to reinstate the parties in the economic position in which they were before exchanging performances.

Article 84(1) CISG must be read in conjunction with Article 78 CISG, which reflects the general rule that interest must be paid on sums that are in arrears. The parallel existence of Articles 78 and 84 CISG can only be explained historically: the predecessor of the Convention, the ULIS, provided for a duty to pay interest only where the *price* was to be refunded, but it did not provide for a *general* duty to pay interest, as it has been laid down in Article 78 CISG. During the drafting process of the CISG, Article 84 CISG had already been agreed on when, at the last minute, Article 78 CISG was included in the Convention. This is why the CISG contains two provisions dealing with the duty to pay interest, Articles 78 and 84(1) CISG. However, as will be shown in section II below, the two provisions serve different purposes, which leads to different solutions in the determination of the applicable interest rate.

Article 84(2) refers to the buyer's duty to repay any benefit derived from the goods. Subparagraph (a) refers to the case where restitution is possible, whereas subparagraph (b) relates to Article 82(2) CISG, which deals with cases in which the buyer may avoid the contract despite the fact that restitution of the goods has become impossible. Article 84(2) CISG makes it clear that the unwinding of a CISG contract aims at restitution of the goods or their surrogates *combined* with an equalisation of benefits.

It is undisputed that Article 84 CISG applies not only in case of unilateral avoidance of the contract but also where the contract has been terminated by mutual agreement.

II. Duty to Pay Interest (Article 84(1) CISG)

Article 84(1) CISG states that, if the price is to be paid back, the seller must pay interest on it from the date the price was paid.

The interest rate has not been determined. Various solutions have been proposed in case law and literature which cannot be described in detail here. In our opinion, the correct solution is found by considering the idea underlying Article 84 CISG: the provision bears a restitutionary character; none of the parties should draw a benefit from the fact that the contract has been avoided. In this regard, Article 84(1) establishes the fiction that the seller has invested the money in an interest-bearing account or has otherwise benefited from it. The seller must thus pay interest on the purchase price whether it actually benefited from it or not, in order to make restitution of the—actual or fictitious—benefit drawn from the money which was left at its disposition. Absent any proof to the contrary or absent any contractual agreement providing for another solution, it must further be assumed that the benefit-bearing investment of the purchase price took place at the seller's place of business. Thus, the standard rate for commercial investments at the seller's place of business should generally be applied.

While this solution has been followed in many judgments and awards, the ways to get there often differ. In this respect, compare C 84-1 and C 84-2.

C 84-1

Tribunal of International Commercial Arbitration
at the Russian Federation Chamber of
Commerce and Industry,
28 May 2004,
CISG-online 1513[327]

...

3.5 [Recovery of interest]

[...]

Based on [Articles 78 and 84(1)] of the CISG, the Tribunal considers that the claim of the buyer for recovery of the interest has legal foundation and is to be granted from the date of payment of the prepayment for the first instalment of the goods.

---

[327] Translation taken from CISG Pace.

However, the CISG does not regulate the interest rate to be used. Pursuant to art. 7(2) of the CISG, this issue is to be settled on the basis of the national substantive law applicable as the subsidiary statute. As was indicated above, the Tribunal regards the Egyptian substantive law as the applicable subsidiary law. According to the information available to the Tribunal from the foreign sources on the Egyptian substantive law regarding the amount of the annual interest rate in respect to pecuniary obligations, the debtor is obliged to pay to the creditor interest at the rate of 5 per cent. Therefore, the Tribunal concludes that the interest is to be calculated for the period indicated by the [Buyer] at the rate of 5 per cent.

Based on the above and following arts. 84(2) and 78 of the CISG and provisions of Egyptian substantive law applied to the dispute as the subsidiary statute, the Tribunal finds that [Buyer]'s claim for recovery of the interest is well-founded and is to be granted in the amount determined with due account of the rules of the Egyptian law. ...

C 84-2

Handelsgericht des Kantons Zürich (Switzerland),
5 February 1997,
CISG-online 327[328]

...

Upon contract avoidance and a thereby following duty of the seller is to refund the purchase price received beforehand or parts thereof, the seller has to pay interest on it from the date on which the price was paid (CISG Art. 84(1)). ... The interest rate is to be determined by the interest rate at the Seller's place of business, as the interest yielding investment of the money occurs there. In France, the going interest rate is at about ten percent. The [Buyer] only demands an interest rate of six percent. Because of no answer to the complaint the amount of interest rate is accepted as accurate. ...

III. Accounting for Benefits (Article 84(2) CISG)

Article 84(2) states the buyer's duty to make restitution of all benefits derived from the fact that the buyer had the goods in its possession. Subparagraph (a) deals with the situation in which the goods can be returned *in specie*; in this case, the buyer must return the goods as well as pay out the benefits to the seller. Subparagraph (b) rests on Article 82(2)(c) CISG. It governs the situation where the goods cannot or cannot wholly be restituted, but the buyer is nevertheless entitled to declare the contract avoided, be it because the goods were sold in the normal course of business, or because they were consumed or transformed in the course of normal use before the buyer discovered the non-conformity of the goods that entitled it to avoid the

---

[328] Translation taken from CISG Pace (citations omitted).

contract. This means that the compensation for the value of the goods is the surrogate that replaces the goods.

Under both subparagraph (a) and (b), a point of dispute has been whether the seller may also claim for benefits which the buyer could have drawn but, in fact, did not. See the Opinion of the Advisory Council in this respect:

CISG Advisory Council Opinion No 9: Consequences of avoidance of the contract:[329]

...

jj) Benefits Flowing from the Goods

3.28 The buyer's duty to account for benefits received under Article 84, unlike the seller's duty to pay interest, is based on actual benefits and not notional benefits. These benefits should also be net benefits, after the cost of using or enjoying the goods has been taken into account. There will be many cases where a buyer, despite delivery having occurred long before avoidance, will have received no measurable benefits. An example is where the goods have been sold on to a domestic sub-buyer who has eventually rejected them or who may yet reject them. Any money derived from that sub-buyer does not count as a benefit under the head contract of sale if it has to be returned to the sub-buyer, since Article 84 concerns only retained benefits. The burden of proof is on the seller to show that the buyer has obtained benefits. There may be difficult cases arising out of the supply of durable machines and similar goods that yield profits over a lengthy term. The calculation of benefits in such cases would require a close examination of the buyer's business and a calculation of its profit margin and its fixed and variable overhead. There are no decided cases quantifying benefits that the buyer must restore to the seller.

Questions

Q 84-1

What is the idea underlying Article 84 CISG?

Q 84-2

What is the relationship between Articles 84(1) and 78 CISG?

Q 84-3

What are the solutions adopted in case law concerning the determination of the applicable interest rate? Which solution is the most convincing?

---

[329] Taken from www.cisgac.com.

Q 84-4

Will the buyer be entitled to claim compensation of expenses that led to an increase in value of the goods? On which provision of the CISG could such a right be based? Consider, in particular, the situation:

(a) where the expenses were necessary to preserve the value of the goods,
(b) where the buyer incurred expenses which now turn out to have been in vain (such as installation of goods, instruction and training costs for the personnel),
(c) where the goods were sold and the buyer had expenses for advertising, transport, personnel and similar costs.

Article 85 CISG

If the buyer is in delay in taking delivery of the goods or, where payment of the price and delivery of the goods is to be made concurrently, if he fails to pay the price, and the seller is either in possession of the goods or otherwise able to control their disposition, the seller must take such steps as are reasonable in the circumstances to preserve them. He is entitled to retain them until he has been reimbursed his reasonable expenses by the buyer.

I. Overview

Articles 85 to 88 CISG are compiled in a separate section dealing with the preservation of goods. The duty to preserve the goods may arise if the buyer rejects them or does not take them over. Since, under those circumstances, it will often be unclear whether there is a breach of contract on behalf of one of the parties, the purpose of this section is to prevent a deterioration of the goods by imposing on either the seller or the buyer the duty to preserve and store the goods until the legal situation has been clarified.

Article 85 CISG defines the situations in which the seller will be bound to preserve the goods. Article 86 CISG states the corresponding duty of the buyer. Articles 87 and 88 CISG address both parties and govern details concerning the preservation and storage of the goods.

II. Operation of Article 85 CISG

Article 85, sentence 1 CISG establishes the seller's duty to undertake adequate steps to preserve the goods where the goods are either in its possession or the seller controls their disposition in some other way and the buyer does not take delivery on time. Article 85, sentence 1 CISG equates the situation where the buyer refuses to pay the purchase price and performance of the contract is to be made concurrently with a delay in taking delivery; furthermore, it is undisputed that Article 85, sentence 1 CISG also governs the case—at least in analogy—where the buyer expressly refuses to take delivery.

The provision is of practical significance since, in those situations, the risk will usually have passed to the buyer and, at the same time, the seller will generally be entitled to the purchase price (Art 62). Absent Article 85 CISG, the seller could be tempted to abandon the goods and simply insist on the purchase price.

The buyer's delay in taking delivery of the goods must be unjustified, that is, it must constitute a breach of Articles 53 and 60 CISG, to the effect that the risk has passed to the buyer.

The seller must be in possession of the goods or otherwise able to control their disposition. It will have control over the goods where, for example, a bill of lading has been issued 'order of seller'. However, whether or not title to the goods has passed is irrelevant. The only significant element is the passing of risk from the seller to the buyer.

If these requirements are met, the seller is bound to take such steps as are reasonable to preserve the goods. The measures that ought to be taken will depend on the circumstances of the individual case. Usually, the seller will have to store the goods and protect them against damage. Under certain circumstances, it will be obliged to resell them (see Art 88(2) CISG). Article 85, sentence 1 CISG adopts a lower standard than that of Article 79 CISG, in that the seller may refrain from taking steps, even if they are within its control, if such steps would cause unreasonable costs or are otherwise disproportionate.

The duty to preserve the goods ends at the time at which the buyer takes delivery or declares the contract avoided, or where the seller undertakes a resale (Art 88). The seller is entitled to withhold the goods until the buyer reimburses it for the costs of storage and preservation (Art 85, sentence 2).

Questions

Q 85-1

(a)   What is the function of Articles 85 to 88 CISG?
(b)   Which party do they address?
(c)   Which general rule is reflected in Article 85 CISG?

Q 85-2

What are the consequences if the seller who is bound to preserve the goods does not comply with its duty?

Q 85-3

Who bears the preservation costs under Article 85 CISG if the buyer's refusal to take delivery is justified?

Q 85-4

Does Article 85 CISG apply in the following situations where:

(a)   the seller has tendered conforming goods of which the buyer does not take delivery;
(b)   the buyer unequivocally refuses to take delivery of the goods because of their glaring non-conformity with the contract;

(c)   the seller has tendered properly and the buyer is willing to take delivery of the goods but unjustifiably refuses to pay the purchase price;

(d)   the seller avoids the contract because of an anticipatory breach on behalf of the buyer;

(e)   the seller has tendered and the buyer takes delivery of only part of the goods, because there is allegedly no larger storage room available.

Q 85-5

Under Article 85 CISG, does it matter who the owner of the goods is?

Q 85-6

Which factors set the benchmark for the adequacy of measures that the seller must take in order to preserve the goods?

Q 85-7

Could the seller base its claim for compensation for preservation and storage costs on Article 74 rather than Article 85, sentence 2 CISG? Would it make a difference? See, in particular, Article 79 CISG.

Q 85-8

The majority holds that the seller's right to retention under Article 85, sentence 2 CISG should extinguish where the buyer provides reasonable security. What other provisions of the CISG allow for the issuance of adequate assurance in order to prevent the seller from taking steps which will burden the buyer?

Article 86 CISG

(1) If the buyer has received the goods and intends to exercise any right under the contract or this Convention to reject them, he must take such steps to preserve them as are reasonable in the circumstances. He is entitled to retain them until he has been reimbursed his reasonable expenses by the seller.

(2) If goods dispatched to the buyer have been placed at his disposal at their destination and he exercises the right to reject them, he must take possession of them on behalf of the seller, provided that this can be done without payment of the price and without unreasonable inconvenience or unreasonable expense. This provision does not apply if the seller or a person authorized to take charge of the goods on his behalf is present at the destination. If the buyer takes possession of the goods under this paragraph, his rights and obligations are governed by the preceding paragraph.

I. Overview

Article 86 CISG imposes a duty to preserve the goods on the buyer who has received the goods but does not wish to retain them, or in the case where the goods have been placed at the buyer's disposal but the buyer has the right to reject the goods. Like under Article 85, sentence 2 CISG, the buyer who is bound to preserve the goods is entitled to reimbursement of its reasonable expenses (Art 86(1), sentence 2).

II. Buyer's Duty to Preserve the Goods (Article 86(1) CISG)

Article 86(1), sentence 1 CISG requires that the buyer has received the goods, that is it has taken them into its possession. Furthermore, the buyer must have the intention to reject the goods for justified reasons, be it because the prerequisites for an avoidance of the contract are met (Arts 49, 51(2), 72, 73); because it is entitled to substitute goods (Art 46(2)); because the goods were only delivered in parts or ahead of time (Art 52); or because it is entitled to reject the goods pursuant to Article 71(1), (3) CISG. If none of these requirements are met, the buyer's rejection of the goods is unjustified and Article 86 CISG does not apply. In fact, in such a case, it will be in the buyer's own interest to preserve the goods as it bears the risk of their deterioration or loss (see Art 69 CISG).

Where the buyer rightfully intends to reject the goods, it will have to take such steps as are reasonable in the circumstances in order to preserve them. The criteria are the same as in Article 85 CISG.

Article 86(1), sentence 2 CISG states the buyer's right to compensation for the reasonable costs arising from the preservation and storage of the goods.

III. Buyer's Duty to Take Possession of the Goods (Article 86(2) CISG)

Article 86(2) CISG governs the situation where the buyer has not yet taken over the goods but where the goods have been dispatched and placed at the buyer's disposal at the place delivery was to be made and the buyer declares that it will reject the goods. Here, the buyer is bound to take possession of the goods and preserve them on behalf of the seller, provided that it is reasonable for the buyer to do so. As Article 86(2), sentence 1 CISG states, these measures will be unreasonable if the buyer would first have to pay the purchase price. Furthermore, the buyer need not take possession of the goods if the seller or a person authorised to take charge of them on behalf of the seller is present at the destination (Art 86(2), sentence 2).

Where the requirements of Article 86(2) CISG are met, the buyer must take the steps necessary to preserve the goods to the extent that is reasonable in the circumstances (Art 86(2), sentence 3 CISG).

Questions

Q 86-1

(a)   Which criterion is decisive in determining whether a situation falls within Article 86(1) or within Article 86(2) CISG?
(b)   Where the buyer unjustifiably rejects the goods, Article 86 CISG does not apply. Will the buyer still have to take steps to preserve the goods?

Q 86-2

Should the buyer be obliged to take possession of the goods and resell them if this would cause considerable inconvenience but the goods are subject to rapid deterioration? Discuss.

Q 86-3

Under Article 86(2) CISG, the buyer must only take possession of the goods on behalf of the seller if, among other things, it can do so without having to pay the purchase price. Do you think that the buyer should be obliged to take possession of the goods under Article 86(2) in the case where the buyer has paid the price in advance?

Article 87 CISG

A party who is bound to take steps to preserve the goods may deposit them in a warehouse of a third person at the expense of the other party provided that the expense incurred is not unreasonable.

I. Overview

Article 87 CISG is a specification of Articles 85 and 86 CISG in that it expressly provides for the possibility of storing the goods in a warehouse of a third person at the expense of the other party, unless the expense incurred is unreasonable. The provision serves as a clarification and did not raise any discussion at the Drafting Conference.

II. Operation of Article 87 CISG

A. Requirements

As a prerequisite of Article 87 CISG, there must be a duty on one of the parties to preserve the good pursuant to Articles 85 and 86 CISG. That party may choose to store the goods in a warehouse, but it is not obliged to do so. The only restriction on storing the goods in a warehouse is that the storage costs are 'reasonable'.

B. Consequences

Depositing the goods in a warehouse has no effect on the allocation of risk. Whether or not the first party has to insure the goods will depend on the parties' agreement, any practices established or usages applying between the parties. As a general rule, there is no obligation to insure the goods when storing them in the warehouse.

By storing the goods in a warehouse, the party obliged to preserve the goods has not made restitution within the meaning of Articles 81 *et seq.* CISG. A general principle can be derived from this that, when unwinding the contract, performance is only made where the buyer hands the goods over within the meaning of Article 31 CISG.

Questions

Q 87-1

What are the consequences if the goods are not deposited in a warehouse?

Q 87-2

Article 87 CISG does not mention any obligation to notify the other party of the intention to deposit the goods in a warehouse or of the fact that the goods have been stored there. Having regard to the general principles of the Convention, do you think that such notification is necessary? If so, what should the consequences be if no such notification has been given?

Q 87-3

Can you think of a situation where, with a view to Articles 77, 85 and 86(1) CISG, the party that is bound to preserve the goods *ought* to deposit the goods in a warehouse?

Q 87-4

(a) Which law defines the relationship between the party that is obliged to preserve the goods and the owner of the storage facility?
(b) Does the CISG provide for any direct claims between the other party and the owner of the storage facility?

Q 87-5

What should be the legal consequences of unreasonably high storage costs? The wording of Article 87 CISG seems to suggest that the reasonableness of the storage costs is a precondition of the right to deposit the goods. But can the requirement that the storage costs be 'reasonable' also be understood in another way?

Article 88 CISG

(1) A party who is bound to preserve the goods in accordance with article 85 or 86 may sell them by any appropriate means if there has been an unreasonable delay by the other party in taking possession of the goods or in taking them back or in paying the price or the cost of preservation, provided that reasonable notice of the intention to sell has been given to the other party.

(2) If the goods are subject to rapid deterioration or their preservation would involve unreasonable expense, a party who is bound to preserve the goods in accordance with article 85 or 86 must take reasonable measures to sell them. To the extent possible he must give notice to the other party of his intention to sell.

(3) A party selling the goods has the right to retain out of the proceeds of sale an amount equal to the reasonable expenses of preserving the goods and of selling them. He must account to the other party for the balance.

I. Overview

Article 88 CISG deals with the right to a 'self-help sale' and the duty of an 'emergency sale'. The self-help sale is the *right* of the party that is bound to preserve the goods to resell them. It is dealt with in paragraph (1) of Article 88. The emergency sale is the *duty* to resell the goods if those goods are subject to rapid deterioration or cause unreasonable costs of preservation. It is governed by paragraph (2) of Article 88. The purpose of both the self-help and the emergency sale is to avoid exaggerated preservation costs and/or the deterioration of goods. Paragraph (3) of Article 88 CISG lays down the right of the party who undertook the resale to retain the costs of preserving and reselling the goods from the resale price.

II. Right to Resell the Goods (Article 88(1) CISG)

Article 88(1) CISG gives the party who is bound to preserve the goods pursuant to Articles 85 and 86 CISG the right to resell the goods and, thereby, to terminate the abeyance. It applies where the buyer delays in taking possession of the goods or paying the price (Art 85), where the seller delays in taking the goods back (Art 86), or where either of the parties does not pay the costs of the preservation of the goods (Arts 85, 86, 87). The right to resell also arises from the other party's refusal to perform a duty that it should render concurrently.

The delay must be unreasonable. Its unreasonableness will depend on the circumstances. Examples of an unreasonable delay would be accumulated preservation costs of a substantial amount, or difficulties in collecting these costs from the other party.

The party intending to resell the goods must give notice of its intention to the other party to enable it to avoid the resale by performing its outstanding obligations.

The resale can be made 'by any appropriate means'. The party making the resale could purchase the goods on its own account. Here, in particular, regard is to be had to the requirement that the resale price be reasonable. Even a resale at scrap value may be appropriate, especially if the goods were specifically tailored to the buyer's needs or if, for some other reason, the goods cannot be sold on the market, as long as the party reselling the goods can show that it made sufficient effort to obtain a reasonable price in the resale of the goods.

As to the resale at a scrap price, see the following case abstract. It deals also with the question of whether the failure to give notice affects the effectiveness of the self-help sale.

C 88-1

Watkins-Johnson Co & Watkins-Johnson Ltd v The Islamic Republic of Iran & Bank Saderat Iran, Iran/US Claims Tribunal, Award No 370, 28 July 1989, CISG-online 9[330]

[Facts]

(*Iran and Watkins-Johnson Ltd. entered into a contract, under which Watkins-Johnson was to manufacture, assemble, test and deliver electronic communications equipment and provide related services for the IBEX program. Watkins-Johnson Co. was Watkins-Johnson Ltd.'s sub-contractor in this project.*

The case was decided based on national law, which did not hinder the Tribunal from referring to Article 88 CISG. The seller retained the goods because the buyer kept refusing to pay the purchase price. The Tribunal held that Watkins-Johnson's right to sell undelivered equipment in mitigation of its damages was 'consistent with recognized international law of commercial contracts'.)

[Judgment]

The conditions of Article 88 of the United Nations Convention on Contracts for the International Sale of Goods (1980) are all satisfied in this Case: there was unreasonable delay by the buyer in paying the price and the seller gave reasonable notice of its intention to sell. Based on the evidence before it, the Tribunal is further convinced that Watkins-Johnson made a reasonable effort in selling the equipment. The invoices presented by Watkins-Johnson

---

[330] Abstract taken from UNILEX.

demonstrate sufficiently the effort to find buyers for the equipment all over the world. A substantial part of the equipment was sold, even though for less that the Contract price agreed with Iran. Watkins-Johnson explained to the Tribunal's satisfaction that much of the equipment was modified or designed according to the specifications of the Iranian Air Force and, therefore, difficult to sell to other customers.

[...]

Moreover, the Tribunal finds it credible that a part of the equipment could not be sold at all and was used for 'training' purposes or [was] 'scrapped'. [...]. There is also no reason to doubt that it was in Watkins-Johnson's own interest to sell as much equipment as possible at the best price. Under these circumstances, the evidence presented by Watkins-Johnson is sufficient to establish, prima facie, that it made its best effort to sell all the equipment. Nothing in the record gives rise to serious doubts in that regard.

While one could argue that Watkins-Johnson had a duty to give specific notice of its intention to 'scrap' equipment, the Tribunal finds that Iran cannot rely on the absence of such a specific notice in the circumstances of this Case. Iran never responded to Watkins-Johnson's notices of its intention to sell equipment. Neither did it attempt to pursue delivery in accordance with the previous agreements. Moreover, in view of the determination of the IBEX program, Iran's continued interest in such delivery must be doubted. Therefore, Iran cannot now rely on the argument that it should have been formally notified of Watkins-Johnson's intention to scrap equipment which could not be sold.

The Tribunal is persuaded, on the basis of the documentation submitted, that Watkins-Johnson sold equipment for a total of $ [...]. Objections by Iran to the documentation of sales and costs were not only received rather late in the proceedings, but also were not substantiated. They raise no serious doubts as to the conclusiveness of the evidence presented. Watkins-Johnson is entitled to deduct from the proceeds reasonable expenses incurred in carrying out the sales (See Uniform Commercial Code section 2-706; Article 88(3) of the UN Convention). It showed that it incurred $ [...] for the completion and modification of equipment, and an additional $ [...] in selling costs. The [sale] of equipment, thus, yielded net proceeds in the total amount of $ [...] which are credited to Iran. [...]

III. Duty to Resell the Goods (Article 88(2) CISG)

Pursuant to Article 88(2) CISG, the party who is bound to preserve the goods according to Articles 85 and 86 CISG has the duty to resell the goods if the goods are likely to deteriorate rapidly or if their preservation costs would be unreasonably high. The latter would be the case where the costs of storage and preservation exceed the value of the goods, or if they are higher than the difference between the original purchase price and the price obtainable in a resale. Rapid deterioration of the goods must generally be assumed where the goods are perishables and cannot be preserved through freezing (regard must be had to the costs of freezing—if those are unreasonably high, an emergency resale must be undertaken, even if the goods as such will not qualify as deteriorating rapidly). In case law, Article 88(2) has also been applied where, originally, the goods were not subject to 'rapid' deterioration but where long preservation had made them susceptible to rapid deterioration in the near future.

Unlike a self-help sale under Article 88(1), an emergency sale pursuant to paragraph (2) only requires a notification 'to the extent possible'. The criterion is whether the resale would be made impossible were prior notice to be given.

C 88-2

International Court of Commercial Arbitration Chamber of Commerce and Industry of the Russian Federation, Arbitral Award No 340/1999, 10 February 2000, CISG-online 1084[331]

[Facts]

This action was brought by [seller], a Pakistani company, against [buyer], a Russian company, in connection with failure to take delivery of the second lot of goods (*kind of goods unknown*) prepared for shipment under the contract concluded between the parties on 22 March 1995.

The [seller]'s claims included: Recovery of the price for the second lot of goods at the price of the contract, plus interest on that sum; recovery of the expenses incurred for warehouse storage of the second lot of the goods; and recovery of the cost of raw materials bought by the [seller] for the manufacture of the next lot of the goods.

The [buyer] objected to the claims upon which of the [seller] based its assertions, inter alia, on [buyer]'s breach of the contract conditions.

[Judgment]

[…] It should be noted that the [buyer], when receiving more than 10% of defective products in the first lot of goods, on the basis of clause 11 of the contract was entitled to refuse to take any further delivery of goods or performance of the contract prior to notifying the [seller]. However, the [buyer] has admitted during the hearings that she had not exercised those rights. Under such circumstances, the buyer pursuant to Article 60 CISG should have taken the delivery, including acceptance of the goods, and pursuant to Article 54 CISG, the buyer should have paid the price for the goods as required by the contract.

The buyer [stated] during the hearings that it had not refused to take [over] the second lot of the goods [...]. [...] The seller, in turn, based on buyer's failure to perform [the] contract provisions, had not shipped the second lot of the goods to the buyer and instead left them in his warehouse.

In connection with this it has to be mentioned that, in accordance with Article 77 CISG, the seller, as the party relying on a breach of contract, should have taken such measures as are reasonable in the circumstances to mitigate the loss resulting from the breach. Pursuant to Article 88 CISG, if the goods are subject to rapid deterioration or their preservation would involve unreasonable expenses, the party who is bound to preserve the goods (the seller in this case) must take reasonable measures to sell them. However, the seller has not provided

---

[331] Case taken from UNILEX.

any evidence of any measures taken to sell the goods or inability to make such a sale, and admitted during the hearings that, due to long preservation, a significant part of [the] goods was spoiled and the rest was given without payment to charity organizations. Resulting from this, the price of the goods manufactured by the seller cannot be imposed fully on the buyer. It should be also considered that from the price of the goods should be deducted expenses for insurance and transportation costs, which are components of the price of the goods to be shipped under the contract on the term "C.I.F. Russian port (St. Petersburg)".

Considering the aforesaid and taking into account that both parties had breached both the contractual provisions and the rules of applicable law, the claims of the seller as to recovery of the contract price of this lot of goods have to be granted in the amount proportional to 25% of the price. [...]

IV. Right to Retain Amount for Preservation and Resale Costs (Article 88(3) CISG)

Article 88(3) CISG states that the party undertaking the resale may deduct the reasonable costs for preservation and resale from the sum obtained in the resale. Those costs include commission fees and administrative expenses incidental to the sale. However, Article 88(3) does not provide for a general right to abate the proceeds of sale by retaining other amounts to which it might feel entitled under the contract, such as the outstanding purchase price or damages.

   A point of dispute is the place at which the proceeds of the resale must be paid to the other party. The majority holds that they are to be paid at the place where the goods were originally to be delivered (if Art 85 applies) or where restitution were to be made (if Art 86 applies). This is true, albeit with some modifications. In our opinion, the seller must pay the proceeds of the resale to the buyer at the seller's place of business (in analogy to Art 31(c) CISG), even if the contract originally provided for delivery of the goods in application of Article 31(a) or (b) CISG and thus at some other place than the seller's place of business. It would make little sense to require payment of the proceeds of resale at some port or other destination (see Art 31(a), (b)) at the moment the goods have been *replaced by an amount of money* (the sales proceeds).

   If it was the *buyer* who undertook the resale, it must be considered that the proceeds of the resale replace the goods which the buyer originally had to return to the seller (see Art 81(2) CISG). Thus, in principle, the buyer ought to pay the proceeds of the resale at the place where restitution was to take place. However, since the resale proceeds replace the goods, it would make little sense to apply the 'mirror rule' literally. The 'mirror rule' makes sense where goods are involved and the bearing of the risk must be determined. However, where performance consists entirely of money and, thus, risk determination is not an issue, strict compliance with the original place-of-delivery scheme is unnecessarily complicated. Thus, the place of repayment of the resale proceeds should always be the buyer's place of business, even if, in mirror-image application of Article 31, the place of restitution of the goods would have been some other place.

V. Comparison with Other Legal Provisions

§ 2-603 UCC:

(1) [...] [W]hen the seller has no agent or place of business at the market of rejection a merchant buyer is under a duty after rejection of goods in his possession or control to follow any reasonable instructions received from the seller with respect to the goods and in the absence of such instructions to make reasonable efforts to sell them for the seller's account if they are perishable or threaten to decline in value speedily. Instructions are not reasonable if on demand indemnity for expenses is not forthcoming.

(2) When the buyer sells goods under subsection (1), he is entitled to reimbursement from the seller or out of the proceeds for reasonable expenses of caring for and selling them, and if the expenses include no selling commission then to such commission as is usual in the trade or if there is none to a reasonable sum not exceeding ten per cent on the gross proceeds.

(3) In complying with this section the buyer is held only to good faith and good faith conduct hereunder is neither acceptance nor conversion nor the basis of an action for damages.

§ 2-604 UCC:

Subject to the provisions of the immediately preceding section on perishables if the seller gives no instructions within a reasonable time after notification of rejection the buyer may store the rejected goods for the seller's account or reship them to him or resell them for the seller's account with reimbursement as provided in the preceding section. Such action is not acceptance or conversion.

Questions

Q 88-1

(a) Distinguish Article 88(1) from Article 88(2) CISG.
(b) Compare Article 88 CISG with Sections 2-603(1) and 2-604 UCC. Does the UCC make the same distinction as paragraphs 1 and 2 of Article 88 CISG?

Q 88-2

(a) Which factors are relevant in determining whether a resale was made by appropriate means? Are there any particular formalities to be observed?
(b) Which criteria guided the court in C 88-1 in holding that the resale was appropriate? Can a general rule be formulated?
(c) What are the consequences of a resale that was not made by appropriate means?

Q 88-3

(a) When will the notice required by Article 88(1) CISG become effective? See also Article 27 CISG.
(b) What are the legal consequences if no such notice is given?
(c) Is it possible that, in exceptional cases, the fact that no notice was given will not harm the party who undertook the self-help sale? See C 88-1.

Q 88-4

What are the legal consequences if goods subject to rapid deterioration are not resold? See C 88-2.

Q 88-5

It is virtually undisputed that a rapid decrease of the economic value of the goods does not constitute a 'rapid deterioration' within the meaning of Article 88(2) CISG.

(a) Compare the situation under the Convention with Section 2-603(1) UCC. Are there any differences?
(b) Is a rapid decline in market value completely irrelevant under Article 88(2) CISG? Consider, in particular, the criterion of 'unreasonable preservation expenses' mentioned in Article 88(2) CISG.

Q 88-6

What criteria are taken into account by courts when deciding whether the preservation costs are 'unreasonably high'?

Answers to Sample Questions

Article 1 CISG

Q 1-1

When does the CISG apply according to Article 1(1) CISG?

The CISG applies either if the parties to a sales contract have their places of business in different Contracting States (Art 1(1)(a)) and they were aware of that at the time of conclusion of the contract (Art 1(2)), or if the rules of private international law of the forum lead to the application of the law of a Contracting State (Art 1(1)(b)).

Q 1-2

Which other provisions of the CISG complement Article 1(1) CISG?

Article 1(1) is complemented by Articles 91, 92, 94, 95, 99 and 100 CISG. Furthermore, Article 1 CISG must be read in conjunction with Articles 2 to 5.

Q 1-3

What is meant by an 'autonomous' or 'direct' definition of the Convention's sphere of application (Art 1(1)(a))?

The definition of the Convention's applicability in Article 1(1)(a) is autonomous because this provision does not refer to any rules of private international law.

Q 1-4

Why are Articles 92, 93, 99 and 100 CISG relevant in connection with Article 1(1)(a) CISG?

Article 99(2) defines the date from which a State becomes a Contracting State within the meaning of Article 1(1)(a). Article 100 specifies the intertemporal applicability of the CISG. Articles 92 and 93 allow a State to not be bound either with regard to certain of its territorial units (Art 93) or with regard to certain provisions of the CISG (Art 92).

Q 1-5

(a) What is meant by the requirement that the fact that the parties have their place of business in different States be 'objectively recognisable'?
(b) Which other provision is to be taken into account when assessing a party's place of business?

(a) According to Article 1(2) CISG, the diversity of places should be apparent either (1) from the contract; (2) from any dealings between the parties; or (3) from any information disclosed by the parties that they have their places of business in different States. The requirement of 'objective recognisability' enhances legal certainty and predictability of the applicable law.
(b) Article 10 CISG, which deals with the question of which out of several places of business is decisive and how cases in which a party's place of business cannot be established are dealt with.

Q 1-6

What is the purpose of Article 1(3) CISG?

Article 1(3) CISG states that the nationality of the parties, their civil or commercial character, as well as the civil or commercial character of the contract is not to be taken into account for determining the applicability of the Convention. Thus, Article 1(3) serves the purpose of defining 'internationality' and 'commercial transaction' for the purposes of the Convention.

Q 1-7

(a) Why did the CISG apply in C 1-1?
(b) Why was it important to decide at what point in time the contract was concluded?

(a) It applied through Article 1(1)(a). The court refers also to Article 1(1)(b) and states that the rules of private international law also lead to the application of the CISG; the reference to Article 1(1)(b) is actually redundant, as subparagraph (b) is subsidiary to subparagraph (a).
(b) According to Article 100(2), the CISG, by way of Article 1(1)(a), applies only to contracts concluded on or after the date when the CISG enters into force in the Contracting States. *In casu*, the CISG applied because the contract was concluded after the entry into force of the Convention in Italy and Ontario, respectively.

It is interesting to note that, in this respect, the court refers to whether the CISG was enacted in Ontario and not whether it had entered into force in Canada. In fact, Canada is a Contracting State whose territorial units have different systems of law. Canada has thus relied on Article 93 CISG and declared that, in a first step, the Convention would extend to Alberta, British Columbia, Manitoba, New Brunswick, Newfoundland and Labrador, Nova Scotia, Ontario, Prince Edward Island and the Northwest Territories. In a declaration received on 9 April 1992, Canada extended the application of the Convention to Quebec and Saskatchewan. In a notification received on 29 June 1992, Canada extended the application of the Convention to the Yukon Territory. In a notification received on 18 June 2003, Canada extended the application of the Convention to the Territory of Nunavut (see www.uncitral.org/uncitral/en/uncitral_texts/sale_goods/1980CISG_status.html).

Q 1-8

(a) Did the CISG apply to the distribution agreement in C 1-2? Why or why not?
(b) Why did the CISG govern the distribution agreement in C 1-3?
(c) Considering C 1-2 and C 1-3, can you develop a rule as to when the Convention could or should apply to a distribution agreement?

(a)   The distribution agreement was not governed by the CISG. The court accepted the parties' view that whether or not the CISG applied turned on whether the Distributor Agreement could be characterised as a contract for the sale of goods. This again was dependent on whether it contained definite terms for specified goods. The court stated that the only contract for a specified set of goods was the February 1996 amendment but that these goods were not the subject of the breach. Thus, the CISG did not apply.

(b)   The parties had chosen the CISG as the law applicable to their agreement. The Arbitrator therefore held that, to the extent the CISG provided rules that could be applied to the termination of a distribution agreement, the CISG was the law governing the dispute at hand.

(c)   If the parties have chosen the CISG as the law applicable to the distribution agreement, the CISG should apply to the extent its provisions are apt to govern the question at issue. In principle, the same holds true where the law applicable to the distribution agreement is determined objectively (absent a choice of law), even though, in such a case, the applicability test may be stricter. The question will be whether the agreement is sufficiently specific about the sales obligations of the parties, eg, by providing for warranties, the modalities of delivery and/or payment, or by specifying the determinability of the price.

Q 1-9

Why is the application rule in Article 1(1)(b) CISG called an 'indirect application mechanism'?

Because the Convention refers to the private international law of the forum which determines whether the Convention applies or not.

Q 1-10

Why does Article 95 CISG provide for the possibility of a reservation?

Article 1(1)(b) enlarges the sphere of application of the Convention. The purpose of Article 95 is to grant Contracting States who are not willing to accept this enlargement the possibility to declare that they will not be bound by that subparagraph.

Q 1-11

(a) In C 1-4, why did the CISG not apply through Article 1(1)(a)?
(b) Why did the CISG not apply through Article 1(1)(b)?

(a)   The CISG did not apply through Article 1(1)(a) because the contract was concluded between the buyers who had their place of business in Contracting States (Spain and Argentina) and the seller who was located in a non-Contracting State (UK). The fact that the contract was later transferred from the seller to a third party who had its place of business in a Contracting State did not change the fact that the CISG did not apply through its Article 1(1)(a) because the decisive point in time is the moment of the conclusion of the contract.

(b)   The CISG did not apply by way of Article 1(1)(b) because the claim was brought before a US District Court. The USA have made a reservation under Article 95 CISG, according to which they are not bound by Article 1(1)(b). Thus, the court did not examine further whether its conflict of laws rules would lead to the application of the law of a Contracting State.

Q 1-12

(a) In C 1-5, did the parties litigate before the court of a State which has made a reservation under Article 95 CISG?
(b) In this case why was the CISG not applicable through Article 1(1)(a)?
(c) The decision of the court to apply the CISG was criticised in A 1-1. Do you agree that Article 95 should be respected not only by the courts of the State which has made such a reservation, but rather every time the conflicts rule of the forum leads to the application of the law of a reservation State?
(d) Could the court have found out that the USA had made a reservation under Article 95 CISG? Where could it have looked it up?

(a)   No, they litigated before the court of a State which had not yet become a Contracting State to the CISG.

(b)   For Article 1(1)(a) to apply, the parties must have their place of business in a Contracting State at the moment of contract conclusion. In the case at hand, the parties had their respective places of business in Germany and Indiana, USA. At the time of the conclusion of the contract, the CISG had not yet entered into force in Germany.

(c)   The conflicts rule of the forum lead to the application of the law of Indiana. The court held that, pursuant to Article 1(1)(b), the CISG was applicable as the USA were a Contracting State. A 1-1 notes that the court in C 1-5 did not respect the reservation made by the USA under Article 95. In fact, prevailing case law and legal writing hold that a state which has made a declaration under Article 95 has stated that it will not consider the CISG as the indirectly applicable law for international sales contracts. Thus, if the private international law leads to the application of the law of a reservation State, the domestic law of that State should apply rather than the CISG.

A minority, however, holds that the reservation under Article 95 only applies where the dispute has been brought before the court of a reservation State. In other words, the reservation under Article 95 is held to operate as a forum rule, without hindering the application of the CISG in the case where the parties do not litigate in a reservation State and the conflicts rule of the forum leads to the law of the reservation State (*cf* C 1-5).

(d)   A list of the Contracting States that have made a reservation under Article 95 CISG can be found on the website of UNCITRAL: www.uncitral.org/uncitral/en/uncitral_texts/ sale_goods/1980CISG_status.html.

Q 1-13

Look at the following examples and decide whether the CISG is the applicable law, assuming that the parties have not made a choice of law:

(a)   *A Czech and a Brazilian party litigate before a Czech court; the lex fori leads to the application of Czech law.*

(b)   *A claim arising from a sales contract between a US and an Italian enterprise has been brought before a US court.*

(c)   *An English and a Chinese party litigate before a Swiss court; the lex fori leads to the application of the law of China.*

(d)   *A US buyer sues a Slovakian seller in a US court.*

(a)   Brazil is not yet a party to the CISG. The Czech Republic is a Contracting State which has made a reservation under Article 95 CISG. Thus, domestic Czech law applies rather than the CISG, which, absent a reservation, would have applied through Article 1(1)(b).

(b)   The USA and Italy are both Contracting States. Thus, the CISG applies through Article 1(1)(a), notwithstanding the fact that the USA have made a reservation under Article 95 CISG.

(c)   The UK has not enacted the CISG. China is a Contracting State which has made a reservation under Article 95 CISG. *In casu*, the constellation resembles that in C 1-5: according to the majority view (*cf* A 1-1), the CISG does not apply because the reservation under Article 95 is deemed to express the intention of the reservation State to never be bound to apply the CISG instead of domestic law if the dispute is not between parties from Contracting States (see Q 1-12(c)).

(d)   The CISG applies pursuant to Article 1(1)(a), notwithstanding the fact that both the USA and Slovakia are reservation States under Article 95 CISG.

Q 1-14

Describe the significant differences between the applicability of the PICC 2010, the PECL, and the CISG. Consider the legal status of the PICC 2010 and the PECL.

The PICC and the PECL are 'general principles of law' without being binding law. Unlike the CISG, neither the PICC nor the PECL are Conventions that can be enacted in Contracting States. They are mere private rules. Thus, they only apply if they have been chosen by the parties as the 'law' governing their contract (as to the extent in which the PICC/PECL may be chosen as the applicable 'law', see Q 1-16), or for the purpose of interpretation and gap-filling of the applicable law. As they do not qualify as binding 'law', they do not—and could not—provide for a unilateral conflicts rule like the one in Article 1 CISG.

Q 1-15

Compare the way in which 'international' is defined in the PICC 2010 and the CISG.

The PICC define 'international' broadly. As long as there is a cross-border element, the international character of the contract will be admitted. The CISG is more restrictive, as the international character of the contract must emanate from the diversity of the parties' places of business.

Q 1-16

Are the parties to an international sales contract able to choose the PICC 2010 or the PECL as the law applicable to their contract?

The question depends on the applicable choice of law rules. Many arbitration laws and arbitration rules allow for the choice of mere 'rules of law', such as the PICC or the PECL. However, according to most state court conflicts rules, the choice of the PICC, the PECL or other rules of law does not qualify as a 'real' choice of law, that is, the mandatory provisions of the otherwise applicable domestic law cannot be derogated from.

Article 2 CISG

Q 2-1

(a) Why have consumer contracts been excluded from the CISG?
(b) Why are consumer contracts sometimes treated differently from commercial contracts? See also Section 2-104(1) UCC and § 13 BGB.

(a) Consumer contracts have been excluded from the CISG in order to avoid an overlap or rivalry between the CISG and domestic consumer law.
(b) Merchants are deemed to be equal when doing business, whereas consumers are deemed having less knowledge about the goods they intend to buy. Thus, in a consumer contract, the merchant is deemed having an advantage compared to consumers and the law tries to even out this imbalance by increasing the protection of the consumer.

Q 2-2

(a) Do the PICC 2010 apply to consumer contracts?
(b) Do the PICC 2010 provide for a reservation similar to Article 2(a) CISG, second half-sentence?

(a) No, they apply to 'commercial contracts', under exclusion of consumer transactions.
(b) No. Indeed, such a reservation would not have been possible: since the PICC are mere 'general principles of law', they cannot derogate from the underlying mandatory domestic law.

Q 2-3

Why were sales by auction excluded from the Convention's sphere of application (Art 2(b) CISG)?

Sales by auction are often subject to mandatory rules of domestic law.

Q 2-4

(a) Why have sales of stocks, investment securities and negotiable instruments been excluded (Art 2(d) CISG)?
(b) Documentary sales are types of contract for the sale of goods in which possession of the goods is transferred from the seller to the buyer through delivery of a negotiable document of title issued by the carrier. They are governed by the CISG (see below Art 57 et seq.). Explain the difference between a documentary sale and a sale of stocks, negotiable instruments etc excluded under Article 2(d) CISG.

(a) Domestic mandatory rules cover this field as well.
(b) The difference refers to the object of the sale. In a documentary sale, the object of the sale (what is bought) are the goods, but those goods are represented by the negotiable document. In contrast, in a sale of stocks etc, the object of the sale are rights which, by its definition of the scope of application in Article 1(1), are not governed by the Convention.

Q 2-5

(a) Why is the sale of ships, vessels, aircrafts and hovercrafts not governed by the CISG (Art 2(e))?
(b) The sale of parts of those goods (motor, railing, furniture, etc) is governed by the Convention. Explain why.

(a) Those vehicles are usually registered under domestic law and thus considered immovable goods.
(b) Those parts of the vehicles are independent goods, as long as they have not been installed in the vehicle.

Article 3 CISG

Q 3-1

Which terms used in the CISG indicate that it was originally drafted for the sale of tangible goods?

The terms 'delivery', 'taking over' and 'passing of risk *in transitu*'.

Q 3-2

Why should the distinction between contracts for standard software and contracts for customised software be irrelevant to the question of whether the CISG applies? See A 3-1.

The sale of software should, in principle, be considered in the same way as any other sale involving intellectual property rights. As is the case with most goods, software may vary in terms of creativity, production costs or technology used. The differences in terms of personal investment, and whether or not the software is customer-tailored, should be irrelevant for the definition of 'goods' under the CISG.

Q 3-3

(a) How did the court in C 3-1 interpret the term 'substantial part' mentioned in Article 3(1) CISG?
(b) What were the criteria applied in C 3-2 and C 3-3 with regard to the interpretation of 'a substantial part'?
(c) Compare the results with CISG Advisory Council Opinion No 4: in which ways can 'substantial part' be understood? Which interpretation seems better to you? Give your reasons.

(a) It applied a purely economic test by comparing the value of the goods supplied by the buyer to the total value of the goods.
(b) In C 3-2, the court took into account the global value, function and importance of the tools offered by the buyer with regard to the end product. Similarly, in C 3-3, the court stated that: 'The quantitative balance does not constitute the sole requirement in respect to the question whether the supply of services is predominant. In addition, further components have to be taken into account in each case such as in particular the interest of the parties as regards the remaining performances.'
(c) According to the CISG Advisory Council, the question of whether the buyer supplied 'a substantial part' of the materials should primarily be assessed on an economic basis. However, a specific threshold in terms of a predetermined value-percentage should be rejected in favour of an overall assessment. Where it is impossible or inappropriate to use an economic value criterion, all relevant circumstances of the case should be taken into account. The courts in C 3-2

and C 3-3 seem to have interpreted the term 'substantial part' in a similar way.

Indeed, the economic value test should be the starting point, as it provides for a relatively clear and measurable basis. However, the CISG allows for taking into account 'subjective' considerations (*cf* Art 35(2)(b)). Thus, if it can be shown that, in the circumstances, the parties had attributed a special importance to the part of the material supplied by the buyer, or a considerably smaller one than would usually be expected, this should be taken into account in the assessment of 'a substantial part'.

Q 3-4

Could the parties agree on the applicability of the CISG to contracts which would normally be excluded pursuant to Article 3(1) CISG? Remember what has been stated above, Article 1 CISG, section I.

The CISG may apply even if the requirements of Article 3(1) are not fulfilled, that is, where the buyer supplies a substantial part of the material necessary for the production of the goods, but the parties have agreed on its application. Whether such a choice of law is valid is subject to the conflict of laws rules of the forum (see also below, Art 6).

Q 3-5

What factors are taken into account when determining whether the seller fulfils mere ancillary obligations of a sales contract or whether its duty is to perform a mixed contract which does not fall within the scope of the CISG in its entirety?

The main factor is the economic value of the different obligations. The subsidiary factor is the particular interest that the buyer has in an obligation.

Q 3-6

(a) *How does the* Oberlandesgericht München *in C 3-4 quantify the 'preponderant part'?*
(b) *Should such an approach, which is based on the economic value of the various performances, be followed?*
(c) *The Russian Tribunal in C 3-5 adopts a 'percentage' view to determine the 'preponderant part'. Is this approach any different from that adopted in C 3-4?*

(a) The court refers to the economic value of each obligation. It adds that the particular interest that the buyer may have in an obligation can be taken into account.
(b) Yes, it should be the starting point, as it gives a relatively quantifiable basis.
(c) Not really. The court in C 3-5 also states that 'an approximately identical value of the different obligations is sufficient to render the Convention applicable', which amounts to a 50% percentage value test.

Article 4 CISG

Q 4-1

Which law governs the issues which do not fall within the CISG's scope of application?

The law applicable in accordance with the private international law rules of the *lex fori/lex fori arbitri*.

Q 4-2

Are remedies for vitiated consent based on domestic law applicable in addition to the CISG?

The CISG only deals with the formation of the contract and the rights and obligations of the parties. However, to the extent that the mistake relates to the characteristic of the goods or to the creditworthiness or ability of the other party to perform the contract, its consequences should be governed by the provisions of the CISG explicitly dealing with those questions (Arts 35 *et seq*, Arts 45 *et seq*, Art 71), to the exclusion of domestic law. If the domestic law governing vitiated consent aims at remedying a wrong for which the CISG does not state any provision, as is, for example, the case with 'fraud', the domestic law remedy is concurrently applicable.

Q 4-3

Other uniform law does not show the same restriction in the scope of application. The PICC 2010, for example, also deal with the validity of contract, including mistake, fraud, threat and gross disparity.

(a) Why did the drafters of the CISG refrain from settling settling issues affecting the validity of the contract?

(b) Why are there no particular difficulties when dealing with those issues in the PICC 2010?

(a) The purpose of the CISG was to be accepted by as many countries as possible. It therefore had to broadly respect domestic rules embodying important social values on those points.

(b) Those principles are not ratified by a country, that is, they do not directly interfere with domestic provisions. When the parties decide to opt in for those principles, despite Article 3.1.4 PICC 2010, any mandatory rule of the law applicable under the private international law of the lex fori/lex fori arbitri will have priority.

Q 4-4

What might have been the reason for excluding the issue of ownership from the Convention's scope of application?

National laws on ownership and transfer of property differ considerably. Thus, agreement on those points seemed unlikely.

Q 4-5

When will domestic law pre-empt a right granted to a party to the contract by the CISG? See C 4-1.

It will be the case where domestic law grants property rights or other rights *in rem* in the goods sold under the CISG contract, such as a security interest in the goods. Thus, as the CISG only deals with the rights of the seller and the buyer, domestic law rules might indirectly interfere and prevent a party from claiming or exercising a right under the CISG.

Article 5 CISG

Q 5-1

(a) Why does the CISG not apply to damages for death or personal injury?
(b) In this respect, is it relevant whether the claims available under the applicable domestic law are non-contractual or contractual damages? In other words, is the CISG always pre-empted in case of damages claims for death or personal injury or only if the respective claim under the domestic law would be tort claim? See A 5-1.

(a)   The drafters of the CISG wished to ensure that 'complex' domestic product liability rules would not be displaced by the Convention.
(b)   The CISG is always pre-empted in such a case regardless of whether the claim for compensation of death or personal injury is contractual or extra-contractual.

Q 5-2

(a) Which law governs a claim for damages to property other than the goods sold which are due to the seller's breach of contract? See A 5-1.
(b) Can extra-contractual claims for which the applicable domestic law would provide in such a case be concurrently relied on? See A 5-1.

(a)   They are governed by the CISG.
(b)   The question is disputed. Basically, there are two positions: either the CISG governs the case exclusively; or, if the claim available under domestic law qualifies as a non-contractual claim (which is to be determined under the applicable domestic law), the buyer can avail itself both of Articles 74 et seq CISG and the domestic tort claim.

Q 5-3

If, because of the seller's breach of contract, the buyer is sued for personal injury caused to its customers by the defective product, does the buyer's claim for indemnity against the seller fall under the CISG?

A first view holds that the term 'any person' in Article 5 includes the buyer's customers and, therefore, that the buyer's recourse against the seller cannot be based on the CISG. According to a second view, the recourse claim is actually not triggered by death or personal injury but by economic loss consisting of that sum of money the buyer has to pay as compensation to its customers, and thus the CISG applies.

Article 6 CISG

Q 6-1

What options are available to the parties under Article 6 CISG?

The first principle embodied in Article 6 is the principle of party autonomy: the parties are free to choose the law applicable to their contract. Most legal systems recognise this principle. The second principle is the non-mandatory character of the CISG. All provisions are non-mandatory; the only exception is Article 12 CISG.

Q 6-2

(a) *Can you explain why the greatest controversy arises from a choice of law clause in which the parties agree on the application of the law of a Contracting State?*
(b) *How has the issue been decided in C 6-1 to C 6-3? Is it reasonable to assume that, in these cases, the parties opted out of the CISG?*
(c) *Draft a clause under which there is an effective opting-out of the CISG.*

(a) Such a choice is somewhat ambiguous and can be interpreted in different ways. One could argue that it amounts to an implied exclusion of the CISG, because otherwise the choice would have no practical meaning (*cf* C 6-1). One could, however, also argue that the choice of the law of a Contracting State identifies the national law to be used for filling gaps in the Convention and avoids the detour through private international law.

(b) In C 6-1, the majority of the Arbitral Tribunal adopted the view that the parties excluded the CISG by agreeing on Italian law. However, there was a dissenting opinion by one of the arbitrators. He took the position that was later also adopted in C 6-2, C 6-3, namely that the choice of the law of a Contracting State does not amount to a opting-out of the CISG. (For a recent decision, see *Bundesgerichtshof* (Germany), 11 May 2010, CISG-online 2125.) This latter view is preferable: the Convention, when adopted, becomes part of the law of the Contracting State. When the parties choose this State's law, the choice includes the Convention as the law governing international sales contracts, and matters not governed by the Convention are governed by the domestic law of that Contracting State. In other words, the choice of the law of a Contracting State is a derogation from Article 7(2) CISG in that the law applicable to matters not governed by the CISG will not be determined by the conflict of laws rules of the forum. Rather, by choosing the law of a Contracting State, the parties agree on the law which applies to CISG-external gaps.

(c)   The effectiveness of an opting-out clause is subject to the CISG and depends first and foremost on an unambiguous wording. Two examples are:
'The parties submit the present contract to the *domestic* law (or: "the Commercial and Civil Code") of State X.'
'The CISG does not apply to the present contract.'

Q 6-3

On what does it depend whether the parties are allowed to opt into the CISG?

It depends on the applicable private international law rules and the degree of party autonomy they grant.

Q 6-4

(a)   If the parties have excluded the CISG, which law will apply instead of the CISG:
*   — if the parties have chosen a particular law;*
*   — if the parties have not settled that question?*
(b)   Which law governs the question of whether the parties have effectively agreed on modifying a provision of the CISG?

(a)   In both cases, the question is governed by the private international law of the forum. In the first case, the parties' choice of law must comply with the formal and substantive requirements of the applicable private international law. In the second case, the law applicable to the contract will be determined objectively, for which most conflict of laws rely on the criterion of 'closest connection'.
(b)   The question is governed by the CISG, Article 11, Articles 14 *et seq.*, Article 29.

Q 6-5

(a)   Why is the reservation in Article 1.5 PICC 2010 extraordinary? Compare the legal status of the PICC.
(b)   Are there any provisions in the PICC 2010 which are of such a mandatory character?

(a)   It is extraordinary because those principles are, by definition, non-mandatory soft law. Thus, any mandatory character of a provision of the PICC must be understood as mere indication of the importance of that provision rather than as pretence of amounting to mandatory law in the sense domestic or international law use it.
(b)   The provisions of the PICC 2010 which are mandatory are normally expressly indicated as such, eg, Article 1.7 on good faith and fair dealing; the provisions of Chapter 3 on substantive validity (see Art 3.1.4); and Article 10.3(2) on limitation periods. Exceptionally, the mandatory character of a provision is only implicit and follows from the content and purpose of the provision itself (see, eg, Articles 1.8 and 7.1.6).

Article 7 CISG

Q 7-1

(a) How do major states, such as the USA, or state-like organisations, such as the EU, ensure that the common nucleus of their law is applied and interpreted uniformly?
(b) Is this possible in relation to the CISG?

(a) The decisions of courts of last instance, such as the US Supreme Court or the Court of Justice of the European Union, are binding the courts of lower instances, which ensures a uniform application of the law.
(b) Not at present. This would necessitate an extension of the mandate of UNCITRAL.

Q 7-2

Are CISG precedents binding?

No, they are not binding on foreign courts or on arbitral tribunals. However, foreign CISG precedents serve the purpose of a uniform interpretation of the CISG. Whether the decisions of a higher court are binding for lower courts within the same jurisdiction depends on the system of jurisdiction and the constitution of the courts in the respective country.

Q 7-3

When should case law and literature relating to law other than the CISG be considered?

They should be consulted only to the extent that certain terms or solutions of the CISG have clearly been influenced by this legal system.

Q 7-4

(a) What may cause difficulties when consulting foreign decisions? Consider language, accessibility etc.
(b) Can you explain what prompted the 'turn-around' with respect to quoting foreign CISG decisions?

(a) The fact that the case law is in an unknown language; that it may be unpublished or difficult to find for a foreigner; the quality of the foreign decision; and the different styles of domestic courts in rendering a decision which make it difficult to understand the facts and/or its content.
(b) The accessibility of case law thanks to various electronic databases (eg, www.cisg-online.ch) or the Digest and the translation of many cases into English (CISG Pace).

Q 7-5

Compare the UNCITRAL Digest to the Opinions of the Advisory Council. What are their similarities and differences?

The Digest is a synopsis of the relevant case law on each article of the CISG. It shows the evolution of case law, by highlighting common views and reporting divergent approaches. The CISG Advisory Council issues opinions relating to the interpretation and application of the Convention, in order to respond to the need to address some controversial and unresolved issues.

Q 7-6

(a) In which countries are legal texts published in more than one official language?
(b) Does the fact that there are six authentic texts of the CISG really cause major difficulties in the interpretation of the CISG?

(a) Most countries with more than one official language publish their legal texts in various languages, for instance, Belgium, Canada, Cyprus, India, Montenegro and Switzerland.
(b) Not really. Although a definitive interpretative approach under the CISG is yet to be developed, it is often emphasised in the literature, but also in the case law that a literal interpretation of the CISG is just one interpretative approach out of several. Thus, the various official CISG texts actually prevent a too literal (and too technical) interpretation in favour of an integrated purposive approach, which takes into account the CISG's international character, its underlying principles and its drafting history.

Q 7-7

(a) Explain the principle of good faith embodied in Article 7(1) CISG. Does this rule apply only to the interpretation of the provisions of the CISG, or should it also be applied in interpreting the contract and behaviour of the parties? See also C 7-1.
(b) What is the consequence of holding 'good faith' to be a rule for the interpretation of the CISG?
(c) Can you find provisions in the CISG which reflect the principle of good faith?
(d) Compare Article 7(1) CISG with similar provisions from other sets of rules. Which ones provide for a solution similar to that under the CISG; which ones are different?
(e) Why did the drafters of the CISG refrain from establishing a 'good faith' principle for interpreting the parties' contract or any of their statements?

(a) It is a principle which only relates to the interpretation of the Convention and cannot be applied directly to individual contracts or to the parties' behaviour.
(b) The consequence is that 'good faith' may influence the relationship between the parties only indirectly, in particular by limiting abuse by the parties and in the way the provisions of the Convention and its concepts are interpreted. Apart from that, 'good faith' under the CISG serves a gap-filling purpose which allows for reading ethical business standards into the Convention.

(c)   Manifestations of good faith as a standard of conduct can be found in Article 8 CISG (individual communications); Article 9 (usages and practices the parties have agreed on, including ethical business standards); Articles 16(2)(b), 29(2) and 80 (*venire contra factum proprium*); Article 40 (no right to rely on the lack of notice of non-conformity of the goods if seller could not have been unaware of the non-conformity); Articles 32(3) and 60(a) (duty to cooperate); Article 77 CISG (duty to mitigate damages).

(d)   All of the provisions depicted here use the principle of good faith for interpreting the parties' behaviour. The duty to act in good faith as a party is even embodied in the UCC (note that the common law of contract has generally been reluctant to adopt an implied duty of good faith).

(e)   Delegations with a common law background were against adopting a duty of good faith as a standard of conduct for the formation and performance of the contract, as the common law has hitherto in general rejected such a doctrine because of the vagueness of the term and because it might weaken existing contractual common law doctrines. On an international level, it could also have been feared that contractual parties may have different expectations and a different understanding of 'good faith', corresponding to their own ethical values. Stating 'good faith' as a tool of interpreting the Convention was the compromise achieved in the drafting process of the CISG.

Q 7-8

What is the rule established in Article 7(2) CISG?
Article 7(2) CISG addresses the question of gap-filling. Matters governed by the CISG but not expressly settled in it (internal gaps) are to be solved in conformity with the general principles on which the CISG is based, whereas matters which are not governed by the CISG are to be solved by having recourse to domestic law.

Q 7-9

(a)   *Does the court in C 7-5 consider the burden of proof to be a procedural question or a substantive law issue?*

(b)   *Why does the court come to the conclusion that the CISG contains rules on the burden of proof?*

(c)   *Is there a provision in the CISG which, through its wording, makes it clear who has to prove a certain fact?*

(a)   The burden of proof is considered to be a question of substantive law.

(b)   By considering that the Convention enshrines the general principle that the party who invokes a right or a fact bears the burden to prove it.

(c)   Article 79(1) CISG, for example, explicitly mentions burden of proof by stating that '[a] party is not liable for a failure to perform any of his obligations if he proves that the failure was due to an impediment beyond his control and that he could not reasonably be expected to have taken the impediment into account at the time of the conclusion of the contract or to have avoided or overcome it or its consequences'.

Q 7-10

(a)   What was the question to be decided in C 7-6 and C 7-7?
(b)   What was the holding of the respective courts?
(c)   What was different in C 7-6 and C 7-7 with regard to the legal question at issue? Might this explain the difference in the verdicts?
(d)   Which provision might constitute the basis for deriving a general principle of set-off?

(a)   The question was whether or not set-off—a matter not explicitly settled in the Convention—was governed by the CISG.
(b)   In C 7-6, the court held that the CISG could not govern set-off and that recourse should be made to domestic law in order to decide whether or not set-off was admissible in the case at hand. In C 7-7, the court found that the set-off was governed by the CISG.
(c)   In C 7-6, one of the claims resulted out of a contract not governed by the Convention, whereas in C 7-7, both claims arose out of the same contract. This might explain the different positions taken in the two decisions.
(d)   Articles 58(1) and 81(2) CISG (those two articles underlie the principle of concurrent performance) and Article 88(3) CISG (this article gives a right to set-off to the party who sold goods subject to rapid deterioration).

Q 7-11

(a)   Are there any questions which cannot be settled in accordance with the general principles underlying the Convention but must rather be answered under the applicable domestic law?
(b)   Which provision of the CISG would help answer this question?

(a)   Examples are: issues related to the transfer of ownership, the validity of the contract, assignment of claims, and transfer of the contract to a third party or agency.
(b)   Article 4 CISG, which delimitates the legal issues dealt with by the Convention.

Q 7-12

What difficulties do we encounter when deciding whether we can develop a general principle from a particular provision of the CISG?

As general principles are not labelled as such, and as their content, operation and effect are not expressly defined in the CISG, there is the risk of diverging solutions, not only with regard as to whether a general principle exists, but also as to its content, operation and effect.

Article 8 CISG

Q 8-1

(a) What is the purpose of Article 8 CISG?
(b) Explain the difference in scope between Articles 7 and 8 CISG.

(a)   It governs the interpretation of a party's statements and conduct as well as the interpretation of the contract.

(b)   Article 7 CISG deals with the interpretation and gap-filling of the Convention, whereas Article 8 CISG deals with the interpretation of the parties' statements and conduct.

Q 8-2

(a) How can Article 8(1) and (2) CISG be distinguished?
(b) Do the PICC 2010 make the same differentiation? See Articles 4.1, 4.2 PICC 2010.

(a)   Article 8(1) requires that the contract or a party's declarations and conduct be interpreted according to the subjective intent of that party, even if this intention differs from the literal wording of the declaration, or even if an objective view would lead to another understanding of the contract, declaration or conduct.

Article 8(2) is the default rule which applies if there is no sufficient evidence of any subjective intent. In such a case, the contract, declarations and conduct must be interpreted from an objective point of view, that is, in the way in which reasonable persons of the same kind as the parties would read and understand the statements in the same circumstances.

(b)   Yes. Here as well, the subjective or 'real intent' theory is stated as the primary rule and the 'objective theory' as the default rule.

Q 8-3

(a) In which legal systems are the Parol Evidence Rule and the Plain Meaning Rule rooted?
(b) What is the difference between the Parol Evidence Rule and the Plain Meaning Rule?

(a)   In common law legal systems.

(b)   The Plain Meaning Rule prevents a court from considering evidence external to an unambiguous piece of writing, whereas the purpose of the Parol Evidence Rule is to guarantee the integrity of written contracts, and it thus prevents the courts from admit external evidence, for instance a witness, who could contradict the written agreement.

Q 8-4

(a)   What was the legal question at issue in C 8-1?
(b)   What does the court state with regard to whether the Parol Evidence Rule applies under the CISG? On what considerations does it base its decision?

(a)   The question was whether the plaintiff-appellant, MCC, could rely on the non-conformity of the goods. It was established as a fact that MCC had not complied with the time-limits provided for in clause 4 of the sales conditions. But MCC argued that the parties never intended those sales conditions (printed on the reverse of the order form) to apply to the parties' agreements, and the evidence provided for this argument was an affidavit by MCC's president, Mr Monzon. The first and second instance, based on the Parol Evidence Rule, did not take the affidavit into consideration, and accordingly held that MCC was bound by clause 4 of the sales conditions. MCC appealed, and the Appellate Court had to decide whether the Parol Evidence Rule could be evoked under the CISG.

(b)   The court states that the Parol Evidence Rule is not a rule of evidence, and thus a procedural rule, but rather a substantive rule of law preventing the litigant from attempting to show 'the fact itself' which did not show in the written document. It is thus a rule of interpretation. Since the CISG governs the question of contract interpretation in its Article 8, the Parol Evidence Rule—as a domestic rule of interpretation—is superseded by Article 8 CISG.

Q 8-5

Explain the effect of a merger clause. See also C 8-2.

An effective merger clause bars extrinsic evidence which could supplement or contradict the written terms. In C 8-2, the parties had included such a merger clause in their contract. The effect of the merger clause was that the respective provisions of the CISG were derogated from and all questions explicitly addressed in the contract were controlled by the latter.

Q 8-6

How will a merger clause be interpreted under the CISG?

A Merger Clause will be interpreted in accordance with the interpretation rules of the Convention, in order to decide the meaning the parties wanted to give to such a clause that derogates from Article 8 CISG.

Q 8-7

The PICC 2010 specifically address merger clauses.

(a)   Can you explain why they deal with merger clauses, while the CISG does not?
(b)   How should a merger clause be interpreted under Article 2.1.17 PICC 2010? Compare this answer to the respective rule under the CISG.

(a)   The PICC were drafted more than 10 years after the CISG (and have since been revised), that is, at a time where the issue of merger clauses in relation to uniform substantive law (CISG) had been identified as a question which could potentially raise problems. The PICC thus settled the question explicitly.

(b)   The PICC expressly state the interpretation rule which has been developed under the CISG. That is, the merger clause as such has the effect that statements or agreements other than those embodied in the contract document containing the merger clause will be disregarded for the purpose of establishing the terms of the contract. However, in order to determine whether the parties wanted the clause to have a merger clause effect, all circumstances relevant to the case, including prior statements or agreements, are to be taken into account.

Article 9 CISG

Q 9-1

Which rules govern the question of whether a usage has been agreed on or a practice established?

The rules are those governing the formation of contract (Arts 8 and 14 *et seq* CISG).

Q 9-2

What is the hierarchy of legal norms applicable to a CISG contract? Rank the following legal sources:

— *provisions of the CISG;*
— *individually negotiated contract clauses;*
— *usages agreed upon by the parties or practices established between themselves (Art 9(1) CISG);*
— *widely known and regularly observed international trade usages (Art 9(2) CISG).*

The hierarchy of norms must be derived from the principle of party autonomy, as established in Article 6 CISG. Thus the hierarchy is as follows:

(1)   Individually negotiated contract clauses;
(2)   Usages agreed upon by the parties or practices established between themselves (Art 9(1) CISG);
(3)   Widely known and regularly observed international trade usages (Art 9(2) CISG);
(4)   Provisions of the CISG.

Q 9-3

(a)   Is it necessary for the usages agreed upon to be internationally accepted?
(b)   Why was the buyer in C 9-1 held to not have inspected the goods on time?
(c)   According to C 9-2, how many times must a particular practice have taken place in order to satisfy the requirement of an 'established practice' in Article 9(1) CISG?
(d)   How does the decision of the Oberster Gerichtshof in C 9-3 extend that rule?

(a)   No, the usages explicitly or impliedly agreed upon by the parties may also be merely regional or local usages or usages from another trade branch.

(b)   According to an international usage, to which the parties had explicitly agreed, the buyer had to inspect the goods and give notice of any non-conformities within 30 days after arrival of the goods at the port of destination. Thus, the 'reasonable time' for giving notice under Article 39 had been derogated from.

(c)   According to C 9-2, a 'long lasting contractual relationship' is required and a practice applied only in two contracts between the same parties is not sufficient proof of an 'established practice'.

(d)   It considers that usages and practices could be relevant even if they take place before the conclusion of the contract, with reference to the general conditions of sale, the prior correspondence and the draft of a framework agreement.

Q 9-4

Why did the Court in C 9-3 find that the parties had effectively concluded a contract?

The parties had not established any practice which would require a specific form of contract conclusion, neither was there an international usage within the meaning of Article 9(2) which would require contracts of sale in the oil industry to be in writing. Thus, the Court found that, in accordance with Articles 11, 14 *et seq.*, the contract had been effectively concluded.

Q 9-5

(a)   Under Article 9(2) CISG, must there be evidence that the parties positively agreed on a usage?
(b)   Compare Article 9(2) CISG with Article 1.9(2) PICC 2010. Do you see any differences?

(a)   No, Article 9(2) CISG only requires that the usage be widely known and regularly observed by parties in the trade branch concerned and that the parties ought to have known of the usage.

(b)   Article 1.9 PICC does not refer to the fact that the parties knew or ought to have known of the usage. The usage thus becomes part of the contract by the fact that it is widely known and regularly observed between parties in international trade concerned 'except where the application of such a usage would be unreasonable'.

Q 9-6

Can you find any examples of usages that, in cross-border sales, are widely known and regularly observed by parties in the trade concerned?

Examples are as follows:

(a)   In the wood industry: a usage according to which, inter alia, the buyer must give written notice of any non-conformity of the wood within 14 days after having taken delivery at the latest (*cf* C 9-4).

(b)   In the fish industry: a usage according to which Latin terms are used for designating the fish (Danish Maritime Commercial Court (Denmark), 31 January 2002, CISG-online 679).

(c)   In the steel plate industry: a usage according to which the seller must be given the opportunity to be present at the examination of the goods (Appellate Court of Helsinki (Finland), 29 January 1998, CISG-online 1302).

(d)   In certain Contracting States, independent of the trade concerned: a usage according to which the parties are bound by a so-called letter of confirmation by which the terms of an orally concluded contract are confirmed but, at the same time, slightly modified, if the addressee of the letter of confirmation remains silent upon receipt.

Q 9-7

(a)   In C 9-4, it was held that even merely local usages may be usages in the meaning of Article 9(2) CISG. According to that decision, when will that be the case?

(b)   Does the fact that domestic and even local usages may constitute usages within the meaning of Article 9(2) CISG comply with the wording of Article 9(2) CISG?

(a)   According to C 9-4, merely local usages may fulfil the requirements of Article 9(2) CISG if the parties had their place of business within the area of these usages, or if they continuously do business in this area for a considerable period of time.

(b)   Yes. Article 9(2) CISG expressly states that the usage should be widely known, and regularly observed, in international trade. This will be the case if a purely national usage is of international renown, but also where it is of geographically limited importance but the parties are located within the geographical area in which the usage is known and regularly adhered to.

Q 9-8

(a)   Why did the court in C 9-5 affirm that there was a usage within the meaning of Article 9(2) CISG with regard to the effects of a letter of confirmation?

(b)   Would the court have come to the same conclusion if the letter of confirmation had been sent from a German party to a party located in a country whose law does not provide for the same effect of such confirmation letter?

(c)   In light of this, can we ignore the parties' domestic law with respect to whether a merely local or regional usage is considered a usage within the meaning of Article 9(2) CISG?

(a)   The *Zivilgericht* affirms that there was such a usage within the meaning of Article 9(2) CISG because the domestic legal systems of both parties generally agree on the binding effect of a letter of confirmation.
(b)   No. If the scope of the usage is geographically limited and does not reach the other party's place of business, the usage is not a usage 'widely known in international trade' within the meaning of Article 9(2) CISG. Thus, the question of whether silence upon the receipt of a letter of confirmation amounts to acceptance of the terms of that letter must be solved on the basis of Articles 14 *et seq.* CISG. (As to the usage regarding the effect of a letter of confirmation *cf.* above, Q 9-6 (d)).
(c)   Not really. In order to know whether a usage is recognised by the majority of traders doing international business in the same field, regard must be had to the place of business of the parties and to whether usages exist at that place, including legal usages, which are usually observed in cross-border sales contracts between parties of the respective countries.

Article 10 CISG

Q 10-1

What is the significance of the 'place of business'?

The place of business is important for determining a number of questions, such as whether the Convention applies, where delivery or payment must be made, whether the risk has passed, and so on.

Q 10-2

(a)   *What difficulty arises from the fact that Article 10(a) CISG simultaneously relies on the closeness to the contract and its performance?*
(b)   *In case law, what have been the indicating factors for deciding which out of several places of business has the closest connection to the contract and its performance? See C 10-1.*

(a)   A contract may have been negotiated, concluded, modified etc at a place other than the place at which the contractual obligations are subsequently performed.
(b)   The centre of gravity of the contract is the relevant element. It mainly depends on the place where the person in charge of the contract (contract communication) is located and the place where the decisions regarding the contract are taken.

Q 10-3

Is the parties' nationality significant in answering the question of where their place of business is?

The nationality of the parties is irrelevant for the purposes of the CISG.

Article 11 CISG

Q 11-1

(a) Which principle is stated in Article 11 CISG?
(b) Compare Article 11 CISG with Article 1.2 PICC 2010.
(c) Compare the result with Section 2-201 UCC, Article 1341 CC. What are the differences?
(d) What is the effect of an unwritten contract that exceeds the indicated sum under the UCC? Is it invalid?

(a) The principle of the freedom of form.

(b) Both Article 11 CISG and Article 1.2 PICC use almost identical wording.

(c) Under French CC, sales contracts exceeding a certain value are subject to form requirements in order to be enforceable. A similar rule can be found in Section 2-201(1) UCC, even though its paragraph 3 provides for some important exceptions.

(d) The lack of writing does not render the contract invalid, it merely prevents its enforceability. However, according to Section 2-201(3), even a contract which does not live up to the form requirements is enforceable if the seller has already made substantial beginnings or commitments for the procurement of goods that are specifically manufactured for the buyer. An unwritten contract is also enforceable to the extent to which the other party admits in court that a contract of sale was made. Finally, it is enforceable, despite the lack of writing, with respect to goods of which the buyer has already taken delivery.

Q 11-2

(a) Can the parties to a CISG contract still agree that a certain form must be complied with?
(b) Is an implied modification or termination of the contract possible pursuant to Article 11 CISG? See also Article 29 CISG.

(a) Yes, they can derogate from Article 11 CISG and provide for specific form requirements (*cf* Art 6 CISG). However, the parties' arrangement will have no effect in those cases which are governed by Article 12 CISG and in which domestic form requirements prevail over Article 11 CISG.

(b) The CISG does not require that a modification or termination of the contract be in writing, but the parties can make a different agreement.

Q 11-3

According to Article 11, sentence 2 CISG, the existence of a contract may be proven by any means. Why was Article 11, sentence 2 CISG incorporated into the CISG?

This sentence prevents domestic procedural rules from undermining the principle of freedom from form requirements.

Article 12 CISG

Q 12-1

What was the reason for incorporating Articles 12 and 96 CISG into the CISG? See also above Article 1 CISG.

Articles 12 and 96 CISG were introduced after pressure from Eastern countries, especially the former Soviet Union, who had a rigid state control system applying to the validity of form of foreign trade contracts.

Q 12-2

Why did the court in C 12-1 adopt the view that domestic form requirements must only be observed if the international private law of the forum leads to the application of the law of the Reservation State?

The court held that where the CISG applies by virtue of Article 1(1)(a) but one of the Contracting States has made a reservation under Article 96, there is no general principle which would govern the question of whether a damages claim could be based on a contract which had been concluded orally. Thus, the court proceeded under the second alternative of Article 7(2) and applied its rules of international private law in order to determine which law governs the question of form requirements in the case at hand.

Article 13 CISG

Q 13-1

To which situations does Article 13 CISG refer?

It refers to situations in which the contract or other contractual statements must be in writing. The writing requirement may have been agreed on by the parties or it may be a practice established or a trade usage. A writing requirement may also exist by virtue of Article 12 CISG.

Q 13-2

What might be the reasons for subjecting a contract to written form?

Writing requirements serve several purposes. In international trade, they generally serve as a means of seriousness and of evidence.

Q 13-3

(a) How could Article 13 CISG be extended to include electronic communication data? In this respect, can the UNCITRAL Model Law on Electronic Commerce, the PICC 2010 and the UN Convention on the Use of Electronic Communications in International Contracts be of interpretive help?

(b) In the light of the purpose of writing requirements, should, for example, short text messages made by mobile telephones be on par with 'writing'?

(a) From Article 13 CISG, a general principle can be derived (Art 7(2)) that the Convention is amenable to the use of communication which is, from a functional perspective, equivalent to paper messages. It could also be argued that Article 13 CISG ought to be interpreted in the light of other international uniform instruments, such as those cited above.

According to the Advisory Council to the CISG, the functions of a paper message are the ability to save (retrieve) the message and to understand (perceive) it. Similarly, the UNCITRAL Model Law requires that the information contained in a data message be accessible so as to be usable for subsequent reference. The PICC even require that the data message be 'capable of being reproduced in tangible form' and of 'providing a readable record of the statement on both sides', respectively.

(b) Short text messages are retrievable and perceivable. They even are reproducible in tangible form with the aid of special PC programmes. SMS are thus included in the term 'writing'.

Article 14 CISG

Q 14-1

On what basis did the court in the Geneva Pharmaceuticals *case (C 14-1) hold that the offer was 'sufficiently definite'?*

Claimant's allegation of an industry custom, which was affirmed by one of the defendants.

Q 14-2

(a) What other instances can be held as being 'sufficiently definite' to constitute an offer under the CISG?

(b) What about under Section 2-204 UCC?

(a) Any communication, oral or written, in which the goods are identified and provision is made for determining the quantity and the price. For example, an offer for the sale of cars that mentions the brand and model, but expressly leave the 'detailed colour and equipment to be determined at a later stage', see CIETAC, 23 April 1997, CISG-online 1151.

(b)   The parties have showed an intention to make a contract and the terms are definite enough for a remedy to be determined.

Q 14-3

An offer will not be valid by virtue of Article 14 CISG alone. What matters under domestic law will also need to be taken into consideration in determining whether or not a valid offer has been made?

The ability to conclude a contract about the subject matter concerned; establishing the identity of the offeror, and the party to whom the offer is directed; and the long-term business relationship and practices established between the parties.

Q 14-4

(a)   Upon whose understanding do you think the court placed emphasis in C 14-2 and C 14-3, respectively—that of the buyer or that of the seller?
(b)   What was the reasoning behind this?
(c)   Which principle, present in both civil and common law domestic systems, does this approach reflect?

(a)   The buyer.
(b)   The buyer was in the position of offeree in both these cases. It was important that the buyer understood that its acceptance would lead to the conclusion of a contract. Consequently, it was the buyer's understanding that was relevant in determining whether an offer had been made.
(c)   The protection of the offeree from unwittingly entering into a contract.

Q 14-5

Why was a contract not concluded in the above case?

Because the course of dealing that had been established in the twenty prior transactions between the parties showed that the parties did not intend to be bound until they had achieved agreement on the final terms embodied in the contract documents.

Q 14-6

(a)   Did the Tribunal rely on Article 55 CISG in C 14-5?
(b)   Why or why not?

No, it did not rely on Article 55 CISG, because this was not a case where the price of goods needed to be determined outside the contract. Rather, the parties had agreed to agree on the price of the goods in the future, with the consequence that Article 55 was inapplicable.

Q 14-7

Would a clause whereby price will be determined at an agreed point of time in the future be sufficient to satisfy the requirements of Article 14 CISG?

Yes, because an agreed point in time in the future provides the means for determining the price. On that date, the parties will reach agreement on a price for the goods, with the consequence that the offer is sufficiently definite.

Q 14-8

(a)   Which phrase did the court cite as being 'sufficiently certain' in C 14-6 in holding that a valid offer had been made?
(b)   What does this case say about the relationship between Articles 14 and 55 CISG?

(a)   'a larger number of furs'
(b)   Articles 14 and 55 operate independently of one another. In C 14-6, the contract had been concluded with 'an at least determinable price', with the consequence that Article 55 did not need to be examined.

Q 14-9

(a)   Do you think the court made the correct judgment in C 14-7 with respect to the existence of an offer under Article 14(1) CISG?
(b)   What limitation did it place on the interpretation of Article 55 CISG?

(a)   No, the parties' intention demonstrated that they wished to conclude a contract and each offer fulfilled the requirements of Article 14(1), taking into account the billing customs for aircraft engines, whereby the engine price would have been billed to the aircraft manufacturer.
(b)   Article 55 CISG can only be applied where market prices exist.

Q 14-10

(a)   What principle, present in both civil and common law systems, is reflected in Article 14(2) CISG?
(b)   Does the wording of Article 14(2) CISG reflect more the common law or the civil law approach?

(a)   An offer to the world at large is not an offer to conclude a contract, but an *invitatio ad offerendum*, or invitation to treat.
(b)   Common law.

Q 14-11

According to the Bundesgerichtshof (C 14-8) and the Oberster Gerichtshof (C 14-9), what other provisions of the CISG should a court have reference to in determining whether standard terms have been incorporated into the contract?

Reference should be had to Article 8, in order to determine whether such terms have been reasonably incorporated into the contract.

Q 14-12

(a)   What is required of a party seeking to rely on standard terms to incorporate them into the contract?
(b)   How is this achieved?

(a)   The party seeking to incorporate standard terms must make them part of the offer.
(b)   The party seeking to incorporate standard terms must show its intention to include such terms was apparent to the recipient party. Further, the other party must receive the text of the standard terms.

Q 14-13

(a)   What role does the language of the standard terms play in determining whether or not they will be held to have been validly incorporated into the contract?
(b)   Do you think this is the correct approach? Why or why not?

(a)   Standard terms written in a foreign language may still be validly incorporated if they are referred to in the language of the contract. Whether or not they are will depend on the individual circumstances of the case, having regard to the length, intensity and economic importance of the business relationship between the parties, as well as the use of the language in their society. If standard terms are provided in an internationally common language, knowledge is presumed unless the recipient notifies the other party of its lack of understanding.
(b)   For English, this would appear to be a reasonable approach. However, if, having regard to the business relationship between the parties, it would be unreasonable to send terms in another language, even in English, they should not, without more, be deemed to have been incorporated into the contract.

Article 15 CISG

Q 15-1

In what way is the operation of Article 15 CISG relevant in light of modern forms of communication?

The notion of 'reaches' needs to be considered in the light of email and other electronic communication forms.

Q 15-2

What problems can you perceive associated with the 'receipt' of messages by electronic communication?

If there is a problem with the recipient's email account, it could reach the recipient but be unable to be read; if the recipient's server is down, messages may not reach the recipient.

Q 15-3

(a) More specifically, do you think the approach of the CISG Advisory Council to the term 'reaches' is appropriate in light of the modern problems associated with spam filters?
(b) Do you think the approach under Article 16 PRC CL is appropriate?

(a) Yes, if a message ends up in a spam folder, most email programs notify the recipient on a regular basis, so that the message still reaches the recipient. If a recipient does not receive a message identified as spam mail immediately, the circumstances of the case must dictate whether or not it was validly withdrawn.

(b) The same should apply under Article 16 PRC CL. In particular, where parties have been negotiating with one another, email addresses should be known and usually messages from known senders will usually not end up in spam filters. If they do, a message should inform the recipient that a message has entered the spam filter and the notification requirement should be satisfied.

Article 16 CISG

Q 16-1

Based on the above, do you think it is accurate to say that Article 16 CISG represents a compromise between the different legal systems? Why or why not?

Yes, it is appropriate to say that Article 16 CISG represents a compromise. The general revocability under common law systems is reflected in Article 16(1). Article 16(2) CISG takes the civil law approach into account, whereby offers are held to be irrevocable in certain circumstances.

Q 16-2

(a) Why is it sufficient to dispatch acceptance?
(b) When does acceptance become effective?

(a)   Because the offeree should not bear the risk of transmission of the acceptance. It is also important to fix a point in time from which the offer is binding.
(b)   Acceptance becomes effective, and a contract is concluded, when the acceptance reaches the offeror.

Q 16-3

In what way does Article 16(1) CISG apply to electronic communications? See CISG Advisory Council Opinion No 1 above. Consider also the problems associated with spam filters addressed in Q 15-3 above.

Article 16(1) CISG applies to electronic communications in that an offer can be revoked if the revocation enters the offeree's server before the offeree has dispatched an acceptance. If a revocation lands in the spam filter, it should still be deemed effective as it is the responsibility of the offeree to ensure that such messages reach it if it has agreed to receive messages in this way.

Q 16-4

How did the conclusion of the contract arise in the above case (C 16-1)? See also the discussion of Article 18(3) CISG.

The seller made a written offer and the buyer accepted by transferring an amount of money in accordance with the offer.

Q 16-5

Why was the seller not entitled to cancel its offer?

Because it stated in its offer that payment needed to be made by 25 June 2008. As such, the offer was irrevocable until this date.

Q 16-6

(a)   Can you reiterate the difference between Article 16(2)(b) CISG and the doctrine of promissory estoppel/detrimental reliance?
(b)   What would be the consequences of allowing the doctrine of promissory estoppel to pre-empt the CISG?

(a)   Under Article 16(2)(b), it is not explicitly stated that the offeree's reliance must have been foreseeable and detrimental; under the doctrine of promissory estoppel, reliance must have been foreseeable and to the offeree's detriment.
(b)   This would contradict one of the guiding principles of the CISG, which is for uniformity in interpretation, as the doctrine of promissory estoppel is not a universally accepted concept.

Article 17 CISG

Q 17-1

(a) What might be the cases in which Article 17 CISG may play a practical role?
(b) Explain the interplay between Article 19(1) (see Art 19 section II below) and Article 17 CISG.

(a) Cases in which one party claims an offer was rejected and the other party claims that the offer was accepted.
(b) Article 19(1) CISG applies where an offer purports to be an acceptance but contains additional or different terms such as to constitute a counter-offer. The relevance of Article 17 CISG is that the counter-offer under Article 19(1) is also a rejection of the initial offer.

Q 17-2

How could Article 17 CISG play a role in cases in which the offeree dispatches a rejection of the offer, but then decides that it does, in fact, want to accept?

In such cases, the offeree will need to send its acceptance by a means quicker than its rejection to ensure that the offer is not terminated by the rejection.

Q 17-3

Consider the approach of the CISG Advisory Council in light of the modern problems associated with spam filters addressed in Q 15-3 above.

Here again, if such a communication lands in the spam filter of the offeror, it is still effective if the offeror has agreed to receive communications in this way.

Article 18 CISG

Q 18-1

(a) Was acceptance found to have been made in the Frankfurt am Main *case (C 18-1)?*
(b) On which factors did the court base its decision?
(c) How does this compare with the position under your domestic legal system?

(a) No.
(b) The delivery of only 2,700 pairs of shoes constituted a material modification of the offer and not an acceptance.

(c)   Depending on legal system: same result or acceptance with respect to the 2,700 pairs only.

Q 18-2

(a)   Was there acceptance in the Saarbrücken *case (C 18-2)?*
(b)   If so, how was it given?

(a) and (b) Yes, the buyer's taking over of the goods indicated assent to the offer.

Q 18-3

(a)   Does the decision in the US Federal District Court case have implications for electronic commerce?
(b)   What kind of implications?
(c)   Is the position taken in this case in accordance with Article 13 UN Convention on the Use of Electronic Communications in International Contracts?

(a) and (b) Yes, if general conditions are attached to the email transmitting an offer, they will form part of the offer and the recipient will be held bound by them.

(c)   Yes. A general obligation exists that standard terms be made available to the recipient party. Here, the negotiation of a contract through electronic communication did not change this obligation, and the court found that attaching standard terms to the email made the terms available to the recipient.

Q 18-4

(a)   Was there acceptance by conduct in the US Court of International Trade case (C 18-4)?
(b)   What factors did the court take into account in reaching its decision?

(a)   No, there was not acceptance by conduct.
(b)   The court decided that regard should be had to the evidence of the parties concerning the arranging of the transactions, according to which there was nothing to suggest that production against the purchase orders should constitute acceptance where a contrary invoicing practice was in place.

Q 18-5

(a)   In the Arnhem case why did the court find that the seller's terms had not been incorporated into the contract?
(b)   What factors did the court indicate were relevant in making this determination?

(a) and (b) It was neither alleged nor proven that the buyer explicitly accepted the seller's general terms. As it was neither alleged nor proven that the parties had a steady business relationship, it cannot be assumed that the buyer accepted the seller's general terms tacitly or expressly.

Q 18-6

(a)   Is there a requirement in the electronic communications world that the offeror actually read the acceptance?
(b)   Why or why not?
(c)   What are the problems associated with this approach? Refer to Q 15-3 above.

(a)   No, acceptance is effective when it enters the offeror's server, regardless of whether it is ever actually read.
(b)   If the offeror has consented to receive communications in such a way, it bears the risk of their content.
(c)   If the acceptance remains unread (eg, because it lands in the spam filter), there is a risk that the offeror will conclude that its offer was not accepted. It may then conclude another contract with a different party or delay performance of the contract with the offeree.

Q 18-7

Explain how the 'oral offers' requirements for acceptance apply to electronic communications.

Oral offers must be accepted immediately even in the case of electronic communications (for example, skype).

Article 19 CISG

Q 19-1

(a)   Explain the mechanism of Article 19 CISG in the above case (C 19-1).
(b)   How would this case have been decided under your domestic legal system?
(c)   What are the similarities and differences between that system and the CISG?

(a)   The buyer's enquiry to the seller constituted an invitation to make offers. The seller then made an offer within the meaning of Article 14 CISG. The buyer then made a counter-offer within the meaning of Article 19 CISG because it ordered a different quantity and different goods. As this counter-offer was not accepted by the seller, no contract was concluded.
(b)   US, English and German law: same solution as under Article 19 CISG.
(c)   See section on domestic legal systems under section I B above.

Q 19-2

(a)   What factor did the court rely on in applying Article 19 CISG in the Baden-Baden
     case (C 19-2)?
(b)   How could a term appearing on an invoice become part of the bargain?
(c)   Did the court decide that this term was a material or an immaterial deviation?

(a)   The term contained on the invoice of the seller that complaints will be acknowledged
      only before the installation of the goods and that in any case goods may only be
      rejected up to 30 days from the date of the invoice.
(b) and (c) The seller's agent referred to the terms in the order confirmations. As
it was an immaterial change, it constituted an acceptance with the addition of the
change.

Q 19-3

(a)   What was the offer, and what was the acceptance, according to the court?
(b)   Do you agree with the finding of the court?
(c)   How would this have been decided under your national legal system?

(a)   The seller's reply to the buyer's offer was a new, or counter-offer. The buyer's reply
      to this new offer did not object to the change in terms and should be considered
      an unconditional acceptance under Article 8(2) CISG.
(b)   No—I find the difference between unwrapped and wrapped bacon to be an
      immaterially different term, although the result in this case would have been the
      same concerning the seller's avoidance.
(c)   English law: same result. US, German law: arguably immaterial, therefore seller's
      reply would have constituted an acceptance and not a counter-offer.

Q 19-4

*Why were the terms of the seller's confirmations of order not part of the contract
between the parties in the above case?*

The court held that the seller had accepted the buyer's general purchase conditions
by performance of the contract, and not by through sending its confirmation of
order. As the seller's jurisdictional clause is a material change under Article 19
CISG, but performance was made without discussing or asking for any modification, the buyer's and not the seller's jurisdictional clause became part of the
contract.

Q 19-5

*(a)   In the above case, did the court find that purchase order 55 constituted a counter-
     offer?*
(b)   What reasoning did it provide for its finding?

(a)   The court did not make a definitive finding on this issue, but stated that a reasonable argument could be made that a forum-selection clause would materially alter the offer under the CISG.

(b)   The reason given was that a forum-selection clause relates to the settlement of disputes, which is included in the non-exhaustive list in Article 19(3) CISG.

Q 19-6

Do you think a forum selection clause should fall within the scope of Article 19(3) CISG? Why or why not?

The general view is that it should fall within, for the reasons stated above. Since a forum selection clause will determine the seat of the dispute and a range of procedural issues associated with this, it should be considered material within the meaning of Article 19(3) CISG.

Q 19-7

Explain what is understood by the 'battle of the forms'.

The situation by which both parties send their standard terms and conditions in negotiating the conclusion of a contract, in an attempt to have their standard terms and conditions govern the contract ultimately concluded.

Q 19-8

What solutions are offered to the battle of the forms problem?

The 'knock-out rule', whereby only those terms that do not contradict each other are incorporated, with the remaining rules left to the applicable law.
The 'last shot rule', whereby the last set of standard terms communicated will govern the contract.

Q 19-9

What was the basis for the decision of the court in the above case (C 19-5)?

The court applied the knock-out rule.

Q 19-10

What approach, according to this case (C 19-5), is to be taken when considering and comparing standard forms?

The knock-out rule, by making a full appraisal of all relevant provisions.

Q 19-11

(a)   What is the approach to the problem of the battle of the forms under your domestic legal system?

(b)   What similarities or differences are there between your domestic legal system and the CISG?

(a)   Most legal systems use the knock-out rule.
(b)   Answer dependent on legal system; for teachers to assess on an individual basis.

Q 19-12

What additional requirements does this case (C 19-6) set out for the incorporation of standard terms?

That the standard terms be provided in the language of the contract.

Q 19-13

What do you think would have been the case if, even if the language of the contract was not German, the seller had been able to understand German?

If it was reasonable under Article 8 CISG to assume that the seller had received proper notice of the buyer's terms and could understand them, the court may have held that the buyer's terms were properly incorporated.

Q 19-14

Compare the case of the Amtsgericht Kehl *(C 19-4) with the case of the* Oberster Gerichtshof *(C 14-9).*

(a)   Which solution seems more correct to you?
(b)   Could the holding of the OGH (C 14-9) be applied to a battle of the forms situation?

(a)   *Amtsgericht Kehl* seems more correct, because it provides more certainty for parties to international sales contracts.
(b)   Yes.

Q 19-15

(a)   What role does the language of the negotiations play?
(b)   How is the battle of the forms resolved where the language of the negotiations and the language of the contract itself differ?

(a)   The language of negotiations will be an indicator of the language of the contract, which could have the consequence that understanding of terms in that language is implied.
(b)   Language of the negotiations could still be relevant if reasonable under Article 8 CISG and the individual circumstances of the case.

Article 20 CISG

Q 20-1

How could Article 20(1) CISG be applied to email communications? Refer to CISG Advisory Council Opinion No 1, the UNCITRAL Model Law on Electronic Commerce and the Draft Resolution II, and the UN Convention on the Use of Electronic Communications in International Contracts.

Article 20(1) CISG could apply to email communications whereby the period of time for acceptance of an offer begins to run from when the offeror presses 'send' on the email containing the acceptance. This would accord with the dispatch rule in the first sentence of Article 20(1). Alternatively, a period for acceptance could run from the moment the offer reaches the offeree, which in the context of email could mean when it enters the offeree's email account or when it becomes aware of it entering another email account. This would be in accordance with the second sentence of Article 20(1). The second alternative is preferable, both because email is a form of instantaneous communication and because the offer has entered the sphere of risk of the offeree and places the offeree in a position to give a reply.

Q 20-2

(a)   *Why are holidays included in the calculation? Consider the peculiarities of international trade accounted for in Article 20(2) CISG.*

(b)   *What is the meaning and purpose of the exception in Article 20(2) CISG?*

(a)   Holidays are included in the calculation to take account of the particularities of international sales, whereby different countries have different holidays.

(b)   The sense and purpose of the exception in Article 20(2) is to ensure that the offeror receives notice of acceptance, which would not necessarily be feasible if delivery was made on non-business days.

Article 21 CISG

Q 21-1

Can information be given to the offeree in the form of an electronic message under Article 21(1) CISG?

Yes, under the CISG Advisory Council opinion, 'oral' can include an electronically transmitted sound and notice can include email; this provides that the offeree has consented to receiving messages in this way.

Q 21-2

Can you think of the reason for the mechanism of Article 21(2) CISG, taking into account the requirements of international trade?

The offeree will often not be in a position to ascertain that its acceptance has arrived late and therefore is in a weaker position, with the consequence that the obligation is then on the offeror to communicate if it does not accept the late acceptance.

Q 21-3

In electronic communications, what would be a typical situation in which acceptance could be delayed?

If technical problems cause delay on either the offeree's or the offeror's server. If an acceptance lands in the spam filter, it may not be read in time.

Q 21-4

What are the 'dispatch' requirements under electronic communications? See also the ICC eTerms in Article 20 CISG above.

A notice of acceptance is not dispatched until it has left the offeree's server. Consequently, if the notice gets stuck before leaving the offeree's server, this is the responsibility of the offeree. According to the ICC eTerms, an electronic message is dispatched when it enters an information system outside the control of the sender. There is thus a definitional—if not practical—disparity in the understanding of 'dispatch' in the context of electronic communications.

Article 22 CISG

Q 22-1

(a) Give a practical example of how an acceptance may be validly withdrawn.
(b) How can an acceptance be validly withdrawn in the context of electronic communications?

(a) If the offeree sends an acceptance by post, it may call the offeror before the acceptance arrives to withdraw its acceptance.
(b) If the offeree sends an email accepting, but then immediately sends another email withdrawing the acceptance, this should be effective under Article 22 CISG. Alternatively, the offeree could call the offeror in an attempt to ensure that the offeror is informed of the withdrawal before it reads the email concerning the acceptance.

Article 23 CISG

Q 23-1

Where can you find references to the time of the conclusion of the contract in the CISG? See if you can find them all!

Articles 1(2), 10(a), 16(1), 31(b) and (c), 35(2)(b) and (3), 42(1), 55, 57(2), 68, 71(1), 73(3), 74, 79(1) and 100(2).

Q 23-2

What is the situation in legal systems applying the mailbox rule?

The situation is the same in that acceptance becoming effective and the contract being concluded coincide. However, this takes place upon the dispatch of acceptance by the offeree, and not at the time of receipt by the offeror.

Q 23-3

What is the practical difference between Article 23 CISG and Article 10 OR?

Under Article 23 CISG, a contract is concluded when the acceptance reaches the offeror. Under Article 10 OR, a contract comes into effect at the time the acceptance is presented for dispatch, which will usually be earlier than the point in time at which the acceptance reaches the offeror.

Q 23-4

How would the point in time at which acceptance by conduct becomes effective be determined under the CISG?

Under Article 18(3) CISG, acceptance by conduct will become effective at the point in time at which the act is performed.

Q 23-5

Using your references from the answer to Q 23-1, explain the significance of the time of the conclusion of the contract in the context of each provision.

Article 1(2): determining whether parties have their places of business in different states at time of conclusion of contract.
Article 10(a): determining a party's place of business at time of conclusion of contract.
Article 16(1): ability to revoke an offer before conclusion of contract.
Article 31(b) and (c): knowledge of location of goods and seller's place of business at time of conclusion of contract.

Article 35(2)(b) and (3): time of conclusion of contract for communicating particular purpose/awareness by buyer of lack of conformity.

Article 42(1): seller's knowledge of IP rights in goods at time of conclusion of contract.

Article 55: prices generally charged at time of conclusion of contract.

Article 57(2): seller to bear costs for change in place of business after conclusion of contract.

Article 68: transfer of risk of goods sold in transit at time of conclusion of contract.

Article 71(1): time for assessing anticipatory breach of contract conclusion of contract.

Article 73(3): purpose contemplated for deliveries at time of conclusion of contract.

Article 74: foreseeability of loss at time of conclusion of contract.

Article 79(1): foreseeability of impediment at time of conclusion of contract.

Article 100(2): applicability of Convention.

Article 24 CISG

Q 24-1

List all the provisions relevant for a communication 'reaching' a party?

Articles 15(1) and (2), 16(1), 17, 18(2), 20(1), 22, 47(2), 48(4), 63(2), 65(1) and (2), 79(4).

Q 24-2

(a) What is meant by an oral declaration?
(b) What is the situation when a declaration is received by an answering machine?
(c) Does an oral declaration need to be understood in order to be effective? Why or why not?

(a) An oral declaration is a verbal communication from one party to the other where both parties are present.

(b) An answering machine should not satisfy the requirement of an oral declaration because the communication is not *inter praesentes*. It would therefore fall under the rules for other forms of communication.

(c) Yes, an oral declaration does need to be understood, otherwise it does not 'reach' the recipient.

Q 24-3

What is the situation when the declaration arrives outside working hours?

If the declaration is an oral declaration made *inter praesentes*, then it does not matter that it is made outside working hours. If it is another form of communication, it should not be regarded as reaching the recipient until working hours commence.

Q 24-4

(a) What solution is proposed in the CISG Advisory Council Opinion No 1?
(b) What would argue against the application of this solution? Consider again the problems addressed in Q 15-3 above.

(a)   If the addressee has consented to receiving electronic messages in this way, the message reaches the addressee when it enters the addressee's server. Oral declarations include electronic sound in real time, so the *inter praesentes* consideration is reflected here.

(b)   Technical problems may result in emails not being read or electronically transmitted sound not being heard. A possible solution to this would be to impose an acknowledgement requirement when dealing with electronic communication—this could be implied as a practice of the parties under Article 9(1) CISG.

Article 25 CISG

Q 25-1

Why is Article 25 to be interpreted restrictively?

Because determination of a fundamental breach entitles the non-breaching party to declare avoidance of the contract, which, in light of the complexities involved in international sales, is the *ultima ratio* remedy and should only apply in limited circumstances.

Q 25-2

(a) According to the Polish case (C25-2), what should the court consider in determining whether a fundamental breach exists?
(b) Is the question of the existence of a substantial detriment relevant?

(a)   The circumstances of the contract and the expectations of the parties, under a full analysis of the text of the contract, any practices, usages, negotiations and all other relevant circumstances.

(b)   The existence of a substantial detriment must be assessed subjectively and not objectively.

Q 25-3

(a) How does foreseeability come into play?
(b) Who bears the burden of proof?

(a)   The breaching party must have been able to foresee that the consequence of the breach would be that the non-breaching party is substantially deprived of what it is entitled to expect under the contract. The foreseeability of the breach itself is not decisive.
(b)   The non-breaching party as the party asserting a fundamental breach.

Article 26 CISG

Q 26-1

Why do you think there is a requirement to give notice under Article 26 CISG?

In the international sales law context, *ipso facto* avoidance would be unsuitable, as the other party may not be in a position to become aware that the first party has avoided the contract. Moreover, as avoidance needs to be declared for a fundamental breach of contract, there may be uncertainty as to the characteristics of the breach.

Q 26-2

Can a declaration of avoidance be revoked after the notice has reached the other party?

No, under the general principles of this Part (Arts 15(2), 22), a notice of avoidance could only be revoked before the notice has reached the other party.

Article 27 CISG

Q 27-1

(a) What is the purpose of drawing a distinction between the effect of communications made pursuant to the offer/acceptance of a contract and other communications?
(b) What communications are covered by Article 27 CISG (give examples from the CISG)?

(a)   At the phase of concluding a contract, different considerations apply (such as a meeting of the minds about the content of the contract) than once a contract is already concluded and notifications are confined to issues concerning the execution of the contract.

(b)   Articles 39 (notice of lack of conformity), 43 (notice of third party right or claim), 46(3) (request for repair), 71(3) (notice of suspension of performance), 72(2) (notice of intention to avoid), 88(1), (2) (notice of intention to sell).

Not covered: Articles 47 (notice of non-performance), 48(2) (request to indicate acceptance of performance), (3) (notice of performance) (cf. 48(4) (request/notice not effective unless received by the buyer)), 63 (notice of non-performance), 65(2) (details of specification), 67(2) (notice of goods), 79(4) (notice of impediment).

Q 27-2

Which principle does Article 1.10 PICC 2010 follow?

The notification must reach the recipient.

Q 27-3

(a)   Look at the wording of Article 27 CISG. Are there any indications that would lead to the conclusion that oral communications do not fall within the ambit of Article 27 CISG?
(b)   If so, what could these be?

(a) and (b) Yes, it is questionable whether oral communications could be included in the phrase 'failure to arrive', as oral declarations require that they are not simply heard, but also understood.

Q 27-4

(a)   What does the party relying on Article 27 CISG have to prove?
(b)   How is proof to be provided?

(a)   That it dispatched the notice by means appropriate in the circumstances.
(b)   Receipt from post office, email copy, telephone memo etc.

Q 27-5

(a)   What are the 'means appropriate' in the circumstances?
(b)   What is appropriate from a language perspective?

(a)   The usual means for making communications taking account of practices established between the parties, distance, time of day etc.
(b)   The language of the notice should be the usual language of the contract.

Q 27-6

Does the issue of 'appropriate means' fall within the ambit of Article 27 CISG?

No, what constitutes appropriate means should be governed by Article 9 CISG. In any case, appropriate means is not defined in the CISG.

Q 27-7

What is the situation with respect to electronic means of communication and the e-commerce phenomenon?

It is clear that email is now an appropriate form of communication of notices where the parties concerned have agreed to receive messages by email. Under Article 27 CISG, an email message is effective when it leaves the information system of the sender. Proof of this can be obtained by a sent receipt.

Article 28 CISG

Q 28-1

(a)   What factor does the UCC focus on in order for a court to decide to award specific performance?
(b)   What could be the reason for this?

(a)   Uniqueness of the goods.
(b)   The reason for this could be that the plaintiff will not be able to obtain a reasonable substitute if specific performance is not granted. If the goods are not unique, then damages will usually be a sufficient remedy.

Q 28-2

Discuss those cases in which specific performance is necessary, and those in which it would not make sense.

Delivery of oil paintings, signed copies of books, goods having a value beyond their simple financial value (heirlooms). To the contrary, commodities and other interchangeable goods can be obtained elsewhere, so an order for specific performance would be impractical.

Q 28-3

What is the difference between the duty to perform a monetary obligation and the duty to perform a non-monetary obligation?

In respect of a monetary obligation, the remedy (damages) is effectively the same as requiring specific performance. With non-monetary obligations, requiring specific performance will entail a different act than claiming the remedy of damages.

Q 28-4

What is the difference between the duty to perform a monetary obligation and payment of damages?

In practice virtually nothing; however, performance of a monetary obligation is specific performance and damages is a remedy in kind.

Q 28-5

(a) For non-monetary obligations, what is the approach of Article 7.2.2 PICC 2010?
(b) Which legal system does the approach of Article 7.2.2 PICC 2010 reflect?

(a) The general principle is that specific performance is required, subject to logical exceptions.
(b) The provision generally reflects the common law approach.

Q 28-6

In what specific situations do you think Article 28 CISG generally applies?

Claims for specific performance concerning the delivery of (unique) goods; claims for repair or replacement of non-conforming goods.

Q 28-7

(a) What factor gave rise to the applicability of Article 28 CISG in the above case (C 28-1)?
(b) Is this reasonable in international sales contracts?

(a) A claim for performance under Article 46(1) CISG.
(b) Yes, reference was had to the UCC in determining whether or not there was a prima facie case for specific performance. The court found that a claimant need only allege the difficulty of a cover purchase to satisfy this. This is the intended application of Article 28 CISG.

Article 29 CISG

Q 29-1

Compare and contrast the wording of Article 29 CISG and Section 2-209 UCC. What similarities and differences can you find?

Article 29 CISG and Section 2-209 UCC contain similar general principles on the modification of contract, whereby consideration is not required. Both also uphold formal requirements, but allow an exception where modification in ignorance of formal requirements or other conduct may operate as a waiver of, or preclude reliance on, formal requirements. Under Article 29 CISG, reliance on formal requirements is precluded where the other party has relied on the conduct. Under the UCC, the waiver applies regardless and can only be retracted where the other party has not materially changed its position in reliance on such waiver. The UCC also contains a separate provision for the statute of frauds.

Q 29-2

(a) *What was the contentious factor in the above case (C 29-1)?*
(b) *What did the court conclude on this point?*

(a) There was dispute as to whether there was an agreement to cancel the contract because the buyer had acquiesced in the agreement on the cancellation of the original agreement.
(b) The court concluded that in combination with other circumstances, silence may be interpreted as the acceptance of an offer of cancellation, which was the case here because the buyer refrained from further performance of the contract and did not exercise any contractual remedies.

Q 29-3

(a) *What does this case say about the interaction between Article 29(1) and Article 19 CISG?*
(b) *What is the implication for Article 19(2) in the context of modifications to a contract?*
(c) *Do you think this is the correct approach?*

(a) In attempting to modify a contract, the same concerns apply as when making counter-offers under Article 19 CISG. As the attempt to modify in the present case concerned the settlement of disputes by way of a forum selection clause, it was to be regarded as a material change which required specific acceptance from the offeree in order to constitute a valid modification of the existing contract.
(b) If you take this line of reasoning to its logical conclusion, then the risk exists that immaterial modifications proposed after the conclusion of a contract could become part of an existing contract if the offeree does not object to them without undue delay.
(c) This cannot be the correct approach because it would go against the agreed terms between the parties at the time they concluded their contract. The interaction between these two provisions needs to be assessed on a case-by-case basis.

Q 29-4

(a) *Was there a valid modification in the above cases (C 29-3 and C 29-4)?*
(b) *If so, how did the modification come about?*
(c) *How can the differences in findings of the two courts be explained?*

(a) In C 29-3, there was a valid modification; in C 29-4, there was no valid modification.

(b)   In C 29-3, the modification came about by a representative of the buyer counter-signing the seller's general conditions of sale.
(c)   Counter-signing a document evidences assent to its content. Where a party does nothing, and indeed does not have authority to do anything, assent cannot be established.

Q 29-5

How did the court in Solae, LLC v Hershey Canada, Inc (C 29-3) distinguish the case from the Chateau Des Charmes Wines *case (C 29-2)?*

In *Chateau des Charmes Wine*, there was no conduct indicating assent to the change.

Q 29-6

What are the similarities and differences between a merger clause and a written modification clause?

A merger clause excludes any external information and provides that the written contract contains the entirety of the agreement between the parties. A written modification clause states that any modifications to the contract must be made in writing. They are similar to the extent that they both provide for the exclusivity of the written contract. However, the clauses have different purposes: a merger clause excludes extrinsic evidence, whereas a written modification clause allows subsequent modifications to be made in writing.

Q 29-7

(a)   What was the relevant fact in the above case (C 29-5)?
(b)   What part of Article 29 CISG did the arbitral tribunal rely on to reach its conclusion?

(a)   Whether the Respondent could have relied on an oral promise that the goods would be delivered before the expiry of the US import licenses.
(b)   Article 29(2) was relied on by the arbitral tribunal in holding that the Respondent could not rely on an oral promise that the goods would be delivered at a date different to the date set out in the contract.

Q 29-8

(a)   What impact does a course of dealing between the parties have on a written modification clause?
(b)   Can a written modification clause be overthrown by a usage of trade?

(a)   Parties may become bound by a particular course of dealing over a long-term relationship that may override a written modification clause within the meaning of Article 29(2) CISG.
(b)   No, the explicit terms of the written contract prevail over any usage of trade.

Q 29-9

(a) On what basis did the court in the Innsbruck *case come to the conclusion that the contract had been validly modified?*
(b) Why were the seller's objections invalid?

(a) The buyer's order form had been amended by the Austrian standard B 2110 form concerning the writing requirement for changes to the contract. As the parties' actions complied with the standard form requirements, the contract had been validly modified.
(b) The seller's objections were too late because they were not sent until six weeks later.

Article 30 CISG

Q 30-1

Compare and contrast the three delivery obligations under INCOTERMS® above. What is the significance of 'delivery' in each context for the obligations of the seller?

EXW constitutes the minimum delivery obligation of the seller, whereby it is required to make the goods available, but not to load them onto a particular form of transport.

Under FOB, the seller has to deliver the goods on board the ship nominated by the buyer or ensure that the goods are delivered in this way.

Under DAT; which is new to the INCOTERMS® 2010, the seller is required to unload the goods and make them available at the agreed terminal at their place of destination. This obligation is more onerous than under EXW or FOB and bears the risk of the goods during transport.

Q 30-2

(a) Outline the main differences in the documents required under CIF and those required under DDP.
(b) Are there any other documents that might be relevant? List any documents which may be relevant in an international sales contract.

(a) Under CIF; the seller must arrange cargo insurance and provide the buyer with the evidence of such insurance cover. In addition, the seller must hand over the usual transport document to the buyer. Under DDP, the delivery document is defined by cross-reference to the nature of delivery. The seller is also under an obligation to provide the buyer with any documents and information needed for the transport of goods to the final destination from the named place of destination.

(b)   Documents certifying origin, certificates for the clearance of customs, inspections etc. All documents that will enable the buyer to take over the goods at the agreed place.

Q 30-3

(a)   When does title pass to the buyer according to these domestic legal rules?
(b)   Which systems recognise a property transfer through the mere conclusion of a contract, and which require the actual handing over of the goods?
(c)   What system of property transfer does the US legal system apply?

(a), (b) and (c) Under English law, title passes at the time the contract is made with respect to specific goods, and at the time goods are unconditionally appropriated to the contract in the case of unascertained goods.

Under US law, title passes when the seller completes its delivery obligation. The extent of the delivery obligation depends on the provisions of the contract.

German law requires consensus and that the goods are handed over to the buyer.

Under French law, title passes on agreement.

Article 31 CISG

Q 31-1

(a)   When is delivery effected in cases of multiple carriers?
(b)   When is delivery effected in cases of transport by the seller's own employees?
(c)   When is delivery effected in handing goods over to a freight forwarder?

(a)   When the goods are handed over to the first carrier to be sent to the buyer.
(b)   If the seller still has control over the goods, carriage within the meaning of Article 31(a) CISG does not take place. In such circumstances, delivery is not effected until the goods leave the seller's sphere, usually by handing them over to the buyer at the place of destination.
(c)   Delivery is effected when the goods are handed over to the freight forwarder.

Q 31-2

Could delivery be effected in the case of non-conforming goods? Compare and contrast the CISG and the UCC in this respect.

Under the CISG, there is no requirement that the goods be conforming in order for delivery to be effected; any lack of conformity is dealt separately. Under the UCC, there is a requirement that the goods are conforming in order for delivery to be tendered.

Q 31-3

According to the above case (C 31-1), what situations are excluded from the scope of Article 31 CISG?

Situations where the seller has to deliver the goods to the buyer's place of business. In general, the seller only has an obligation to dispatch the goods; transport risks will be borne by the buyer.

Q 31-4

Article 31(b) CISG covers four different scenarios. Describe these.

Contracts for specific goods.
Contracts for unidentified goods to be drawn from a specific stock.
Contracts for unidentified goods to be manufactured.
Contracts for unidentified goods to be produced.

Q 31-5

Are goods in transit covered by Article 31(b) CISG?

No, goods in transit constitute a special delivery obligation not covered by Article 31(b). Arguably, if the location of such goods is known at the time of the conclusion of the contract, Article 31(b) could be used to establish the seller's obligation to place the goods at the buyer's disposal.

Q 31-6

What does 'placing the goods at the buyer's disposal' actually mean?

Making the goods available to the buyer in such a way that it does not need to do anything more to take over the goods. Implicit in this is the seller's agreement that the buyer take possession of the goods.

Q 31-7

Compare the above provisions of INCOTERMS® to the provisions of Article 31 CISG. What are the similarities and differences?

The EXW delivery obligation corresponds in substance to Article 31(c) CISG. The delivery obligation under CPT and CIP corresponds to Article 31(a) CISG. Under both CPT and CIP, the seller is obliged to clear the goods for export; this would act as a supplementary agreement to Article 31(a) CISG in practice.

Q 31-8

Compare and contrast Article 5(1) Brussels Convention with Article 5(1) Brussels Regulation.

The Brussels Regulation addresses the sale of goods as a separate, autonomous point to contracts generally, whereas the Brussels Convention does not make this distinction.

Q 31-9

How is the relationship between jurisdictional seat and place of performance resolved under Article 5(1) Brussels Convention and Article 31 CISG?

Under the Brussels Convention, the *lex causae* is decisive. Under Article 31 CISG, it is where the goods were handed over to a carrier or placed at the buyer's disposal.

Q 31-10

What actions are governed by Article 5(1) Brussels Regulation in the case of the sale of goods?

All actions concerning the sale of goods, including specific performance, damages and actions for the price.

Q 31-11

How does Article 5(1) Brussels Regulation define the place of performance for contracts involving the sale of goods?

It defines the place of performance autonomously, having regard to the facts of the case, using actual criteria, rather than legal criteria.

Q 31-12

(a) What do the above cases have to say regarding the interaction between Article 5(1) Brussels Convention, Article 5(1) Brussels Regulation and the CISG?
(b) Is this convincing?

(a) Where the CISG applies as the substantive law, the place of delivery will be the place where the goods are handed over to the buyer. Article 5(1) Brussels Regulation prevails over Article 31 CISG.
(b) I do not find this convincing because it ignores the legal agreement of the parties. It would be more congruent to determine the place of jurisdiction according to the same criteria and the place of performance under the substantive law.

Article 32 CISG

Q 32-1

Which circumstances require a notice of dispatch?

If the goods are not clearly identifiable to the buyer.

Q 32-2

Compare Article 32(1) CISG with the notice and delivery provisions of the FOB clause of INCOTERMS® (2010).

Both clauses make notice a requirement in order for the seller to have fulfilled its obligations. The provisions generally correspond.

Q 32-3

What consequences does the giving of notice have for the passing of the risk in the goods? See also the discussion on Article 67(2) CISG below.

Giving notice that the goods have been delivered transfers the risk in the goods from the seller to the buyer.

Q 32-4

How did the court interpret 'appropriate means of transportation' in the above case (C 32-1)?

The seller may choose a means of transportation as appears appropriate in the specific circumstances and necessary for the general terms for such transportation.

Article 33 CISG

Q 33-1

(a) What do you believe is the purpose of a provision like Article 33 in the CISG?
(b) For which of the buyer's rights is it significant?

(a) To ensure uniform interpretation and application of the seller's delivery obligations under the CISG.
(b) The right to claim specific performance or damages, avoid the contract, or set a *Nachfrist* for the performance of the seller's obligations.

Q 33-2

What kind of circumstances could give rise to a determination of the date by reference to the contractual terms?

Where there is a provision for delivery to be made '5 days after payment', or delivery is dependent on a specific event, such as a Trade Fair.

Q 33-3

Under which circumstances might the right to choose the date for delivery lie with the buyer?

If the buyer has to undertake certain steps in order to obtain the goods, for example, when the parties agree on EXW delivery. If it is agreed that delivery will be made on payment, and the buyer is able to choose when payment is to be made.

Q 33-4

Look at the following examples and state whether, in your opinion, each one falls within the ambit of Article 33(a) or Article 33(b) CISG:

(a) 'Wednesday after Easter';
(b) 'Within 10 days after Easter';
(c) 'At the latest 10 days after sight of sample'.

(a)   Article 33(a) CISG.
(b) and (c) Article 33(b) CISG.

Q 33-5

(a) Which aspects did the court consider relevant in assessing the 'reasonable time' in the above case (C 33-1)?
(b) How is this reconcilable with the general notion of 'reasonableness' under the CISG?

(a)   The proximity of Christmas and the fact that the goods concerned were seasonal fabrics, in which time is an important consideration.
(b)   What a reasonable person would have done in the situation is also acceptable here.

Q 33-6

(a) Do you agree with the provision that the court in C 33-2 relied on?
(b) Why or why not?
(c) Do you agree with the interpretation of the 'delivery date'?

(a) and (b) No, I would have thought that Article 33(b) CISG was the more appropriate provision to rely on because the seller agreed to deliver within April 1997. However, this period was uncertain since it was subject to a reservation by the seller, so perhaps Article 33(c) offered the best solution in the circumstances.

(c)   I disagree with the finding of the court that 15 March 1997 constituted the outside limit of the seller's delivery obligation. The buyer had already signed the seller's confirmation indicating April 1997 but reserving the date. Consequently, the buyer could not unilaterally modify this to 15 March 1997. Any assessment of Article 33(c) CISG should have started from the seller's statement of April 1997.

Q 33-7

What factors did the court consider in the above case (C 33-3) to determine whether or not a 'reasonable time' was complied with under Article 33(c) CISG?

The time required for the refurbishment of the loader and the fact that the buyer had indicated to the seller that it had no immediate need for the loader.

Article 34 CISG

Q 34-1

Which documents does Article 34 CISG relate to?

The documents required for the buyer to take possession of and exercise rights over the goods. Depending on the circumstances, these could include negotiable or non-negotiable documents for the carriage of the goods, import certificates, insurance policies and invoices.

Q 34-2

(a)   Do you think that trade usages could still be relevant in the context of Article 34 CISG?
(b)   Why or why not?

(a)   Yes, particularly internationally accepted trade usages such as INCOTERMS® if they have been made part of the contract.
(b)   They will establish whether there is an obligation to hand over documents at all and the associated details.

Q 34-3

Which documents were required to be delivered under the contract discussed in the above case (C 34-1)?

An airway bill and 'other documents' relating to the goods to enable the buyer to carry out customs formalities.

Q 34-4

(a)   Which trade sectors would generally displace the dispositive rule of the second sentence of Article 34 CISG?
(b)   Why?
(c)   Must this be done contractually, or is there another way?

(a) and (b) Commodity trade would generally displace the dispositive rule. In volatile markets, the goods will be on-sold immediately and the seller will have no chance to make a subsequent cure.
(c)   It could take place pursuant to an international trade usage.

Q 34-5

Is the inclusion of Article 34 in the CISG necessary at all? Why or why not?

No, it has merely a clarifying effect of obligations that would exist under the contract.

Q 34-6

Do you think the CISG is suited to deal with documentary sales? Why or why not?

Yes, because it provides an adequate structure of the parties' rights and obligations that still holds up under the peculiarities of documentary sales.

Article 35 CISG

Q 35-1

(a)   Compare Article 35 CISG to the national solutions set out above. Which do you think were influential in the drafting of Article 35 CISG?
(b)   What differences and/or problems can you perceive between the national solutions and the CISG?

(a)   Article 35 CISG is clearly based on common law principles. There is no distinction between *peius* and *aliud*. Rather, the distinction between ordinary purpose and particular purpose can be found in Article 35(2)(a) and (b) CISG. Furthermore, the requirements relating to packaging clearly have been influenced by § 2-314(2)(e) UCC.
(b)   Many legal systems still draw a subtle distinction between a so-called *peius* (inferior quality) and an *aliud* (different goods). Different rules apply to each category. Packaging is usually not dealt with under conformity of the goods, but is regarded as an additional duty also leading to a different liability scheme. The same holds true for defects in quantity which are regarded as partial non-delivery. There is a certain danger that national courts still hold on to these well-known domestic distinctions which would heavily undermine the unification purposes of the CISG.

Q 35-2

(a) What is the origin of § 434 BGB?
(b) Compare § 434 BGB and Article 35 CISG. Describe the similarities and differences.

(a)   § 434 BGB was modelled on Article 35 CISG.
(b)   Similarities: Basis for conformity is the contract, furthermore fitness for ordinary or particular purpose. No distinction between *peius* and *aliud*, nor between non-conformity and defects in quantity.

Differences: Packaging not mentioned in § 434 BGB. § 434(1), sentence 3 BGB is based on the EC Directive on Sale of Consumer Goods and Guarantees (1999/44/EC) and has no equivalent in Article 35 CISG.

Q 35-3

Compare the provisions of the PRC CL relating to the conformity of the goods with other domestic provisions and Articles 35 CISG. Explain the similarities and differences.

Similarities: Primary source for quality specifications is the contract. Packaging is also part of conformity.

Differences: If no quality specifications can be found in the contract, conformity is to be determined through gap filling according to Articles 61, 62(i) PRC CL. The hierarchy then is subsequent agreement, usage, state or industry standard, and only in the last resort customary standard or particular purpose.

Q 35-4

According to the case of the Swiss Bundesgericht *(C 35-1) above, what other provision/s of the CISG can be applied to determine what the contract actually required under Article 35(1) CISG?*

The parties' statements have to be interpreted under Article 8 CISG. Thereby, regard is to be had to the respective position of the parties. In the case at hand, relevance was given to what a professional buyer may expect under the contract.

Q 35-5

(a) What exactly was relied on to establish the lack of conformity under Article 35(1) CISG in the case of the Oberlandesgericht München *(C 35-2) above?*
(b) Under which 'head' (quantity, quality or description) of Article 35(1) CISG did the lack of conformity fall?

(a)   Buyer did not receive certificates of origin.
(b)   Quality required under the contract.

Q 35-6

What would be the consequences of considering delivery of an aliud *as non-delivery rather than as non-conforming delivery?*

Articles 38 and 39 CISG only apply in case of non-conforming delivery. Furthermore, the buyer could claim specific performance under Article 46(1) CISG without the restrictions contained in Article 46(2), (3) CISG.

Q 35-7

What common law approach shares similarities with the approach taken under Article 35(2)(a) CISG?

The warranty of merchantability (Sec 14(2) SGA: now satisfactory quality; § 2-314 UCC).

Q 35-8

List the differences between merchantable, average and reasonable quality.

Merchantable quality refers to the question of whether the goods are still marketable, even if only on an alternate market. Goods to have average quality in general must be better than simply merchantable. Reasonable quality mainly is focused on the expectations of the individual buyer.

Q 35-9

How did the tribunal in the Netherlands Arbitration case (C 35-4) try to reconcile the different approaches concerning fitness for ordinary purpose?

It did not use any of the well-known domestic legal concepts but instead tried to find a new term, namely that of reasonableness. This approach seems most appropriate because reasonableness itself is one of the general principles underlying the CISG.

Q 35-10

(a) *Which party's public law provisions was the court relying on in C 35-5 to determine whether there was a breach of contract?*
(b) *Why do you think this was the case?*
(c) *What are the exceptions?*

(a) Primarily the public law provisions of the seller's country.
(b) Because the seller could not know the public law provisions in the buyer's country.
(c) Same requirements in the seller's and in the buyer's country; public law requirements made known to the seller under Article 35(2)(b) CISG; seller should know due to particular circumstances of the case.

Q 35-11

The court did not take a position as to whether Article 35(2)(a) or Article 35(2)(b) CISG applies to public law provisions. Discuss this question.

In general, the approach through Article 35(2)(b) CISG seems to be appropriate. This approach allows taking into account the special circumstances of each case, eg the country where the goods are to be marketed or used, and the respective positions of the seller and buyer in their countries and in the international trade.

Q 35-12

(a)   What were the special circumstances which prima facie justified an exception of the general rule that the seller is not obliged to deliver goods in compliance with regulatory provisions or standards of the importing country that the court applied at hand?

(b)   What were the considerations the court found to outweigh these special circumstances?

(c)   How could these considerations be abstracted from the current case and be described in a more general way?

(a)   The seller advertised in Australia and had previously exported trucks to Australia.

(b)   The advertisement stated 'landed at Brisbane'. Furthermore, the seller recommended Australian contractors to assist the buyer with importation.

(c)   Under Article 35(2)(b) CISG one could deny that reliance on the seller's skill and judgement was reasonable.

Q 35-13

The court discusses the question of controlling public law requirements. Is this case (C 35-7) comparable to the New Zealand mussels case (C 35-5)?

The true issue in the Belgian pork case is whether a suspicion suffices for a finding of non-conformity. The public law requirements set for all European Community members was issued after delivery of the goods and thus could never be known by the seller.

Q 35-14

On what basis was it argued in the Medical Marketing *case (C 35-8) that the goods had to conform to public laws at the buyer's place of business?*

On the basis that the seller was or should have been aware of the GMP regulations by the FDA upon the conclusion of the contract. Unfortunately, the facts relied upon by the arbitral tribunal are not reiterated in the published decision.

Q 35-15

(a)   In a comparison of all three provisions (Art 35(2)(b) CISG, § 2-315 UCC and Sec 14(3) SGA), which condition/s for a finding of fitness for particular purpose is/are common to all of them?

(b)   How do they differ?

(a)   The seller must know or at least could not have been unaware of the particular purpose.
(b)   Under Section 14(3) SGA emphasis is put on the fact that the buyer expressly or impliedly makes known the particular purpose to the seller; under Article 35(2)(b) CISG, although it must be made known to the seller, this does not have to be done by the buyer itself; under Section 2-315 UCC it suffices that the seller has reason to know of the particular purpose. Furthermore, liability under SGA and CISG is excluded if the buyer could not reasonably rely on the seller's skill and judgement.

Q 35-16

In this respect, where the seller did not know of the particular purposes for the goods, but should in fact reasonably have known, can it still be held liable under the CISG?

Yes, it is enough if the seller has reason to know of the particular purpose. Whether it indeed has is a question of proof.

Q 35-17

What was the result of the seller's implicit knowledge in the Landgericht München *case (C 35-9)?*

It was partially liable under Article 35(2)(b) CISG.

Q 35-18

(a)   What were the circumstances in the Aargau *case (C 35-10) that might lead to the conclusion that the buyer did not rely on the seller's knowledge?*
(b)   Do you agree with the court's reasoning?

(a)   From the very beginning there were doubts about the seller's knowledge concerning the statics. The court, however, held that the seller should have pointed out its lack of expertise.
(b)   The court's reasoning seems doubtful as the question of statics remained open and the buyer rejected any additional charge for finding out the optimal fixation of the arches.

Q 35-19

What facts must the buyer prove if it wants to rely on Article 35(2)(b) CISG?

The buyer only has to show that the goods were not fit for the particular purpose. It does not have to show precisely the existence and the nature of the defect, ie why or how the goods are unfit.

Q 35-20

Are you aware of similar provisions under national laws?

This is a well-known source for defining conformity, see eg Section 2-313(1)(c) UCC, Section 15 SGA, Article 168 PRC CL.

Q 35-21

What was the effect of applying Article 35(2)(c) CISG in the Landgericht München *case (C 35-12)?*

In this case, the fact that there was a sample led to the consequence that the goods were conforming and the seller was not liable for the extreme noise emission.

Q 35-22

(a) *Which domestic sales laws also recognise a provision similar to Article 35(2)(d) CISG?*
(b) *How are defects in packaging dealt with under your domestic law?*

(a)   Section 2-314(2)(e) UCC, Article 156 PRC CL.
(b)   Under many domestic laws, packaging is regarded as being an additional duty arising from a sales contract. Defects in packaging do not trigger the remedies for non-conforming goods.

Q 35-23

(a) *What requirements did the packaging in the case above (C 35-13) have to live up to?*
(b) *Compare this case with the cases on public law requirements discussed above (C 35-5 to C 35-8).*

(a)   The public law requirements in the buyer's country which ask for labels on the sachets as to the composition of the contents and expiry date.
(b)   There is no discussion about whether the seller must know about the marketing regulations in the country of the buyer. The seller's knowledge of public law requirements or at least its duty to inform itself about them seem to be simply inferred from the fact that the seller knew that the goods would be marketed in France.

Q 35-24

Based on the analysis of the court's approach above (C 35-14), how can the buyer's state of knowledge be determined under Article 35(3) CISG?

For example by way of information by the seller or examination by the buyer before the conclusion of the contract.

Q 35-25

(a) *In the absence of rules under the CISG, how should we decide on matters concerning the burden of proof?*
(b) *Are there general principles from which we could derive an approach to burden of proof issues (see discussion on Art 7 CISG above)?*
(c) *Based on these general principles, how do you think burden of proof issues should be resolved under Article 35 CISG?*

(a)   Today it is generally acknowledged that burden of proof has to be ascertained under general principles of the CISG and not according to domestic law.

(b)   The rule is that the party who wants to assert a right has to prove all its preconditions. However, there are certain exceptions to this rule, eg where the very wording of a provision so indicates. Thus, for example, under Article 35(2) (b) CISG the buyer must prove that the particular purpose was made known to the seller; on the other hand the seller must prove that the buyer could not reasonably rely on its skill and judgement. Another principle is that the party who has (sole) access to evidence and is thus in a better position to prove certain facts also bears the burden of proof.

(c)   If the buyer takes possession of the goods, it has to prove that they were non-conforming at the time of delivery. However, if the buyer rejects the goods, the burden of proof for the conformity of the goods is on the seller.

Q 35-26

Compare the Swiss Bundesgericht *case (C 35-15) with the case of the German* Bundesgerichtshof, *8 March 1995, CISG-online 144 (detailed excerpt C 35-5). There, the court stated:*

> *After taking delivery without giving notice of the lack of conformity, the buyer must allege and prove that the goods do not conform with the contract and the seller does not have to allege and prove that they do conform with the contract. Contrary to [buyer's] contention at trial, she accepted the mussels by physically taking delivery (CISG Art 60(b)) at the place of destination in G.G., and she did not give notice of the lack of conformity of the goods at that time.*

How does this case approach the issue as to which party is to bear the burden of proof?

The German *Bundesgerichtshof* seems to suggest that the buyer only bears the burden of proof if the buyer has not given notice of the lack of conformity.

Q 35-27

How could the buyer have proven the non-conformity in this case (C 35-16)?

In this case, it was not proven that the rotten ribs were those delivered by the seller. It is purely a question of evidence whether the buyer can prove this fact.

Q 35-28

(a)   Why is it essential that the CISG pre-empts concurring domestic remedies?
(b)   What are the purposes of the law of contract and the law of torts?
(c)   How do you determine whether a claim is of tortious or contractual nature?

(a)   As there are substantial differences between the domestic legal systems in allowing such concurring domestic legal remedies, the uniformity achieved by the CISG would be undermined in a core area, namely liability for non-conformity of the goods.

(b)   The law of contracts seeks to protect expectations arising from the very agreement of the sales contract. The law of torts primarily aims at guaranteeing a basic safety standard in order to protect life, limb and property.

(c)   In a CISG contract, the CISG itself defines what is contractual and what is outside its sphere of application. Wherever concurring domestic remedies are only concerned with the non-conformity of the goods, such remedies are pre-empted by the CISG.

Article 36 CISG

Q 36-1

Discuss the cases in which Article 36(1) or (2) CISG could come into play.

Article 36(1) CISG clarifies that the seller is liable for any latent defect that exists *in nuce* at the time of the passing of the risk. Under Article 36(1) CISG the seller would also be liable if due to a defect in packaging that exists at the time of passing of risk, the goods themselves are damaged or destroyed after this point in time.

Article 36(2) CISG would apply in a case where the seller damages goods when taking back the containers they had been packed in or where due to unclear instruction to the carrier the goods are damaged in transit after risk of loss has passed.

Q 36-2

Describe and analyse the distinction between Article 36(1) and 36(2) CISG.

Whereas under Article 36(1) CISG the defect already exists at the time of the passing of the risk, under Article 36(2) CISG at this time no defect can be discerned.

Q 36-3

(a) Describe some of the usual guarantees that manufacturers give.
(b) How does the warranty of durability under Article 35(2) CISG relate to a guarantee in the sense of Article 36(2) CISG?

(a)   The seller may guarantee the goods for example for a certain period of time, such as two years or 5,000 working hours, or for a certain mileage, such as 20,000 km.

(b)   A guarantee in the sense of Article 36(2) CISG relating to durability facilitates the proof for the buyer that the goods are non-conforming if a defect is discovered within the time frame of the guarantee.

Article 37 CISG

Q 37-1

What are the consequences of the seller's right to cure under Article 37 CISG?

Up to the date for delivery provided for in the contract the seller may cure any non-conformity without some of the restrictions set forth in Article 48 CISG on the one hand and the buyer cannot resort to any remedies according to Article 45 *et seq* CISG on the other hand.

Q 37-2

What are the consequences of the buyer refusing to allow the seller to remedy the defects?

If the buyer refuses to allow the seller to cure the defects, this refusal may be the cause of the seller's breach of contract. According to the *ratio* of Article 80 CISG the buyer loses all rights except the right to request the delivery of missing goods.

Article 38/39 CISG

Q 38/39-1

Compare the domestic solutions and their practical consequences.

The issue of the duty to examine and notify reveals the respective attitude a legal system takes towards the interests of sellers and buyers. Where a strict examination/notice duty exists, the legal system clearly prefers the seller (in breach); where such a duty does not exist or is limited, buyers are in a much better position.

Q 38/39-2

Based on a comparison of the domestic law approaches above, can you specify which countries are referred to in each of the three approaches described in the CISG Advisory Council Opinion No 2?

Group 1: Germanic legal systems with Germany in the forefront.

Group 2: Under Section 35(1) SGA, the buyer loses the right to avoid the contract if it has accepted the goods. Thus indirectly it must give notice of any non-conformity if it does not want to accept the goods and be able to avoid the contract.

Group 3: USA Uniform Commercial Code as well as the modern codifications based on the CISG.

Q 38/39-3

How would you describe the approach of the Oberlandesgericht Karlsruhe *(C 38/39-1)?*

Requiring the buyer to give notice of the lack of conformity within 10 or 11 days after receipt at the latest reveals that the court relies on domestic preconceptions. Interpreting Article 38, 39 CISG in such a strict sense is a typical Germanic approach.

Q 38/39-4

Against what background must this decision be understood?

Against § 377 German HGB and its interpretation by German courts.

Q 38/39-5

How does the Landgericht Paderborn *case (C 38/39-2) determine the limits of examination?*

At least in the case of PVC plastic intended to manufacture rolling shutters, the buyer is not obliged to carry out a quantitative chemical analysis relating to the correct amount of titanium dioxide.

Q 38/39-6

According to the case of the Oberster Gerichtshof *(C 38/39-3), upon which circumstances will the scope of examination required depend?*

Details of examination may be agreed upon in the contract or they may be developed from the relevant usages of trade. In essence, the *Oberster Gerichtshof* seems to be quite strict as it requires that the examination must be thorough and professional and experts in the broadest sense must be called in.

Q 38/39-7

List all the circumstances that may be relevant in determining the buyer's duty to examine.

The nature of the goods; whether they are perishable or durable; the quantity of the goods; the packaging; whether the goods can be examined without destroying them; the position of the buyer; time and costs of examination; infrastructure at the place of examination; cultural differences.

Q 38/39-8

How was the method of examining the goods determined in the Russian Federation case (C 38/39-4)?

As the contract referred to the Technical Conditions, they were also regarded as setting the frame for the examination process, which in the case at hand provided for examination by a neutral control organisation.

Q 38/39-9

(a)   What prerequisites can you identify in Article 38(2) and (3) CISG?
(b)   What potential problems could arise in this context?

(a)   Article 38(2) CISG: the contract involves carriage of the goods
      Article 38(3) CISG: the goods are redirected in transit or redispatched and
      the seller knew or ought to have known of such a possibility at the time of the
      conclusion of the contract
(b)   Under Article 38(3) CISG, the question arises whether it suffices that the buyer
      is in the resale business in order to assume the seller's knowledge that the goods
      will be redirected or redispatched. In case of redispatch of the goods, it may be
      questionable whether the buyer in fact did not have a reasonable opportunity for
      examination before redispatching the goods.

Q 38/39-10

*(a)   Compare the above two cases (C 38/39-5 and C 38/39-6). Who undertook the
      examination in the first case?*
(b)   And in the second?
(c)   Was the examination binding on the buyer in both cases?

(a)   In the first case, examination was carried out by a third party on behalf of buyer's
      customers.
(b)   In the second case, the contract called for examination by a neutral inspection
      body, which was carried out after a joint examination by both parties.
(c)   In the first case, it was binding on the buyer as it was solely in the buyer's sphere
      of risk that carried out the examination. However, if the parties have agreed
      on a certain third party or jointly examined the goods, any inadequacies are at
      the risk of both parties and thus the examination is not binding on the buyer.

Q 38/39-11

*(a)   What reason did the court in the above case (C 38/39-7) give for a short calculation
      of the period of time for giving notice?*
*(b)   On a consideration of the requirements of international trade, can you think of any
      reasons as to why the court took this approach?*

(a)   The duty to give notice of non-conformity serves the purpose of clarifying the
      legal relationship between the parties.
(b)   Evidence must be secured; the seller may want to take recourse against its own
      supplier; the goods have to be transported back to the seller if the buyer avoids
      the contract.

Q 38/39-12

*What insight did the court in the above case (C 38/39-7) provide as to the development
of a general 'rule of thumb' for the calculation of a reasonable period of time under
Article 39 CISG?*

As the different legal systems take very different attitudes towards the calculation of the period for examination and giving notice, it is vital to distil a uniform approach in order to guarantee the uniform interpretation and application of the CISG. The *Bundesgerichtshof* indicates that this may be the so-called 'noble month' that had been previously suggested in scholarly writing.

Q 38/39-13

Does the Swiss court (C 38/39-9) share the view of the earlier German (BGH) case (C 38/39-7)?

The Swiss *Bundesgericht* approves of the application of the 'noble month'; it allows one week for examination and one month for giving notice.

Q 38/39-14

Does the Austrian court (C 38/39-10) share the view of the German and Swiss courts?

No. It considers 14 days to be an appropriate period.

Q 38/39-15

Does the court in the Austrian case (C 38/39-10) distinguish between the period for examination and that for giving notice?

The Austrian *Oberster Gerichtshof* rejects the 'noble month' approach. Instead it supports an overall two-week period, thus not distinguishing between the period for examination under Article 38 CISG and the period for giving notice under Article 39 CISG. It thus demonstrates a clear tendency towards a Germanic interpretation of the provisions of the CISG without having due regard to the necessity of a uniform interpretation.

Q 38/39-16

(a) How does the BGH in the 1999 case (C 38/39-8) calculate the period for examination of the goods; and for the period for giving notice?
(b) When did the period for giving notice commence in the 1999 case (C 38/39-8)? Compare this approach to the position of the earlier BGH case (C 38/39-7).

(a) The period for examination includes one week for the decision and initiation of necessary measures followed by two weeks for an expert's investigation. The regular period for giving notice is considered to be one month.
(b) The period for giving notice starts to run after the separate period for examination. Now the *BGH* is taking a clear stance in favour of the separate one-month period for giving notice.

Q 38/39-17

(a) Based on the above cases decided under the French legal system (C 38/39-11 and C 38/39-12), how would you characterise the approach of Article 39 CISG under the Roman law tradition?

(b)   Compare this approach to the approach of German and Austrian courts (C 38/39-7, C 38/39-8 and C 38/39-10).

(a)   French courts are rather generous and buyer-friendly in interpreting Articles 38 and 39 CISG which can easily be understood against their domestic background.

(b)   French courts are not only less rigid than the Austrian Supreme Court that requires to give notice within two weeks after delivery, but even more generous than the German Supreme Court. In the case C 38/39-11 notice was only given five weeks after the examination of the goods, ie not within the 'noble month'.

Q 38/39-18

(a)   What are the relevant criteria according to the court in Shuttle Packaging *(C 38/39-13) when determining the period of notice?*

(b)   How can the general approach of the US District Court be characterised and compared to the approaches of the other courts outlined above?

(a)   The court considers whether the goods were complicated, the different respective expertise of the parties, and delivery of the goods in instalments.

(b)   Again, this approach is more buyer-friendly than that of the Germanic Supreme Courts, emphasising that even requiring notice within a few weeks may not be adequate. Thus the American interpretation is much more in line with that of the French courts.

Q 38/39-19

Can you see any relationship between the cases cited above concerning the period for giving notice (C 38/39-7–13) and those concerning the specificity of notice (C 38/39-14–17)?

The requirement of specificity of the notice seems to be used as another mechanism to protect sellers (in breach). It is revealing that all case law on the question of specificity stems from courts from Germanic legal systems.

Q 38/39-20

According to the BGH *case of 3 November 1999 (C 38/39-16), what minimum requirements exist for the content of a notice?*

It was considered sufficient that the notice contained an explanation of the symptoms; an explanation of the underlying causes was not required.

Q 38/39-21

How would you describe the approach of the BGH *(C 38/39-15 and C 38/39-16)?*

As with the calculation of the period for giving notice, the *Bundesgerichtshof* in C 38/39-16 took a slightly more buyer-friendly approach to the question of specificity than in C 38/39-15. Thus, all in all there seems to be a move towards more buyer-friendliness under the CISG compared to domestic German sales law.

Q 38/39-22

(a) Summarise the arguments presented in the Bundesgericht *case (C 38/39-17) interpreting the specificity of notice requirement.*
(b) In light of the reasoning in section 4.3 of the Bundesgericht *case (C 38/39-17), would you have expected the outcome of this case?*

(a) The *Bundesgericht* emphasises the discrepancy between the unofficial German translation and the original versions of Article 39 CISG. It agrees with scholarly writing that the standard for specificity, especially in the age of electronic communication, should not be too strict, as the seller may ask what is wrong with the goods.
(b) No, instead of applying these principles the Swiss *Bundesgericht* seems to be quite strict.

Q 38/39-23

(a) What does the Frankfurt am Main *case (C 38/39-18) have to say about the form that notice of lack of conformity can, and should, be given in?*
(b) Who bears the burden of proof?
(c) How can notice be proven?

(a) There is no form requirement for the notice of lack of conformity. A complaint by telephone is sufficient although this may cause problems of proof. However, the parties may provide in their contract that notice has to be given in writing. If they do so, regard is to be had to Article 13 CISG under which 'writing' includes e-mail.
(b) The buyer bears the burden of proof for having given specific and timely notice. However, according to Article 27 CISG, the buyer must only prove that it dispatched the notice. The notice travels at the risk of the seller.
(c) This is a question of the law of evidence which is not covered by the CISG. It may be proven by documents, witnesses or party testimony.

Q 38/39-24

(a) Why would the application of a domestic one-year limitation period violate public international law?
(b) Which solutions exist to reconcile a short domestic limitation period with Article 39(2) CISG?

(a) If the domestic limitation period is less than two years, it would be possible that although under the CISG the buyer is still allowed to give notice of non-conformity and thus rely on all relevant CISG remedies, its claim would be time-barred under the domestic rules on limitation. Public international law prohibits the Member States from defeating a buyer's claim by applying a short limitation period whereas it could still rely on the non-conformity under Article 39(2) CISG.

(b)   The first possibility is to apply the general limitation period of domestic law instead of the short limitation period for remedies for non-conformity of the goods. In Switzerland this would be Article 127 OR, which provides for a general limitation period of 10 years. A second solution is to simply extend the domestic limitation period and to harmonise it with the two-year cut-off period of Article 39(2) CISG. Finally, a third option was taken by the German legislator upon implementing the CISG. The relevant statute provided that the then six-months limitation period only started to run with the giving of notice.

Q 38/39-25

Which reasons speak for applying Article 39 by way of analogy?

In the case of defective repair or replacement, as in the case of an initial delivery of non-conforming goods, the buyer may rely on all remedies. The interests of the seller in clarifying the legal relationship in this situation are comparable to the ones envisaged by Articles 38 and 39 CISG. This speaks for an application of these provisions by analogy.

Q 38/39-26

Compare CISG Advisory Council Opinion No 2 to the above case law.

The CISG Advisory Council Opinion No 2 emphasises the circumstances of the individual case and rejects any fixed period of time for giving notice. However, it clearly states that the period for examination on the one hand and that for giving notice on the other hand must be distinguished and kept separate.

Article 40 CISG

Q 40-1

(a)   According to this decision (C 40-1) what are the requirements for Article 40 CISG?
(b)   Under which circumstances would there be a disclosure?

(a)   In case law and scholarly writing there is much discussion about the standard upon which Article 40 CISG is based. There is agreement that 'could not have been unaware' is more than mere negligence. The arbitral award interprets Article 40 CISG in the way that there must be a 'conscious disregard of facts that meet the eyes'.

(b)   According to the arbitral award, mere information in the service manual did not amount to a disclosure of the non-conformity. Disclosure could only be assumed if the seller had brought the non-conformity to the attention of the buyer and informed the buyer of the risk resulting from the non-conformity.

Article 41 CISG

Q 41-1

Compile a list of possible rights or claims by third parties that may fall under Article 41 CISG.

Property, security interests of warehouse owners or carriers, rights to challenge a disposition under domestic insolvency law, public law encumbrances such as tax and public duties, measures taken to return cultural objects.

Q 41-2

(a) How did the court in the above case (C 41-1) expand the application of Article 41 CISG?
(b) What other Article of the CISG could be considered instead?

(a) The seller did not obtain an export clearance from its own supplier who had restricted the export of the goods. Thus, the seller was unable to deliver the goods.
(b) It could be questioned whether Article 41 CISG was rightly applied in this case. Rather, the seller breached its delivery obligation under Article 30 CISG.

Q 41-3

(a) How would the situation in which a mere claim is made be resolved under your domestic law where it turns out that the third party does not have a right over the goods?
(b) How would this situation be resolved under the CISG?

(a) Under many domestic legal systems, especially in civil law countries, the seller is only liable if the buyer loses possession of the goods because of the third party's right (so-called liability for eviction).
(b) Under the CISG it is sufficient if a third party asserts a claim against the buyer. Whether or not an underlying right actually exists is irrelevant.

Q 41-4

Some authors want to exclude 'frivolous' claims from the ambit of Article 41 CISG. Discuss this question.

There should be no distinction between 'frivolous' and 'non-frivolous' claims. First, the line drawn between the two is not clear. Even if a claim is 'frivolous', the seller is usually in a better position than the buyer to defeat such a claim without difficulty or great delay. By way of exception, the seller is not liable where the buyer and the third party are colluding.

Article 42 CISG

Q 42-1

Can you think of any reasons to differentiate between defects in title and encumbrances by intellectual property rights?

While the concept of third party property right is known to all legal systems, there are many different intellectual property rights in different legal systems. Furthermore, there is generally a territorial limitation to their scope of protection. Thus, the seller cannot be expected to guarantee worldwide freedom from intellectual property rights.

Q 42-2

What differences between the CISG and the US approach are apparent from the provision above (§ 2-312(3) UCC)?

Article 42 CISG provides a much more restricted protection against encumbrance with intellectual property rights as it contains a territorial restriction as well as the requirement of knowledge on the part of the seller.

Q 42-3

(a) In which way is the seller's liability under Article 42 CISG restricted?
(b) What is the reasoning behind the restrictions imposed by Article 42 CISG?

(a)   The primary restriction on the seller's liability is a territorial one. The seller is only liable for freedom from third party intellectual property rights in the State where the goods will be resold or otherwise used and only if this was contemplated by the parties at the time of the conclusion of the contract. If there is no such contemplation, freedom from intellectual property rights must only be guaranteed in the State of the buyer's place of business.

(b)   As explained above (Q 42-1), the seller cannot be held liable worldwide because some intellectual property right of some third party may always exist in some country. In essence, this restriction aims at drawing the line between the sphere of risk of the buyer and that of the seller.

Q 42-4

What is the reasoning behind this restriction imposed by Article 42 CISG?

Requiring knowledge on the part of the seller ensures that the seller cannot be held liable for claims that even an investigation may not reveal. This is primarily true for non-registered third party intellectual property rights.

Article 43 CISG

Q 43-1

Why do you think there is no parallel provision to Article 38 CISG with respect to third party rights and claims?

Examination is generally not possible or would not yield the necessary results.

Q 43-2

Describe the purpose of Article 43(1) CISG. How does it contribute to the seller's interests?

As in case of non-conformity of the goods, the notice requirement under Article 43 CISG aims at clarifying the legal relationship between the seller and the buyer. If any claim or assertion of a claim by a third party is brought against the buyer, it is in the interest of the seller to know about this fact in order to be able to bring a claim of its own against the third party without any further delay. This in turn may also indirectly benefit the buyer and is in line with good faith and fair dealing in international commerce.

Q 43-3

Compare and contrast Article 39(1) and Article 43(1) CISG. What similarities and differences can you find?

Article 39(1) CISG and Article 43(1) CISG are quite similar regarding the prerequisites for giving notice and the consequences for failure of giving notice. Article 39(2) CISG regarding the two-year cut-off period does not have a counterpart in Article 43 CISG. Instead, Article 43(2) CISG is similar to Article 40 CISG.

Article 44 CISG

Q 44-1

(a) What were the relevant considerations of the court in applying Article 44 CISG in the German case (C 44-1)?
(b) What criteria would you consider in this case?

(a) The nature of the buyer's business; a single trader, an artisan or a free professional might more readily rely on Article 44 CISG than a globally acting corporation.
(b) Buyer's place of business, customs in existence there, buyer's familiarity with requirements of giving notice, subjective factors such as illness or lack of

experience, organisational difficulties, communication of notice to the wrong representative of the seller, nature of the goods and of the non-conformity.

Q 44-2

What does the Russian Arbitration case (C 44-2) say generally about the interpretation of Article 44 CISG?

The tribunal relies on the standard of reasonableness.

Q 44-3

(a)   What was the factor relied upon in the ICC case (C 44-3) to establish excuse under Article 44 CISG?
(b)   Who bore the burden of proof and for which reasons?

(a)   The examination was carried out jointly by a neutral inspection body and the parties. The risk of non-discovery of the non-conformity should thus not be solely on the buyer.
(b)   The burden of proof lies with the buyer according to the general principle that the party that is trying to rely on facts favourable to it has to prove these facts.

Q 44-4

What is the relationship between Articles 40 and 44 CISG?

If the prerequisites of Article 40 CISG are fulfilled, the seller may not at all rely on the buyer's failure to give notice, ie the buyer has all remedies arising from the non-conformity. If the buyer has a reasonable excuse under Article 44 CISG, failure to give notice still results in the loss of the right to avoid the contract and to claim damages for loss of profit; the buyer, however, keeps its remedies for reduction of the price as well as the claim for damages for all losses except loss of profit. Thus, the buyer is better off if it can prove knowledge of the seller under Article 40 CISG.

Article 45 CISG

Q 45-1

What did the court decide in the above case (C 45-1)?

The tribunal emphasises that damages and avoidance are two distinct remedies for a breach of contract by the seller. Thus, the buyer may sue for damages and at the same time avoid the contract and claim restitution of the purchase price. A penalty clause or a contractually agreed penalty or liquidated damages clause may pre-empt a further claim for damages under Article 74 CISG, however, it does not preclude a claim for restitution under Article 81(2) CISG after avoidance of the contract.

Q 45-2

(a) What general principle of the CISG does Article 45(2) CISG embrace?
(b) Is this general principle also a feature of your own domestic law?

(a) Under the CISG there is no so-called election of remedies.
(b) As under common law damages are the primary remedy, there is no discussion of election of remedies. The amount that has been paid as purchase price forms part of the damages claim. As under common law the seller is liable for damages without fault, usually no problems arise. The situation is different under civil law. There, a damages claim by the buyer requires fault on the part of the seller. In the absence of fault, the buyer can only reclaim the purchase price after avoidance of the contract. However, historically, it has been held that once the contract has been avoided, damages can only be asked for in the amount of the reliance but not the expectation loss. As for granting expectation loss, there must be a (still valid) contract. Hence, in many civil law legal systems, the buyer must elect whether it wants to claim damages for expectation loss or recover the purchase price in conjunction with damages for reliance loss.

Article 46 CISG

Q 46-1

What is the crucial difference between § 439(1) BGB and Article 46(2) CISG?

Under Article 46(2) CISG, the buyer may only require delivery of substitute goods if the lack of conformity constitutes a fundamental breach of contract. This restriction is not found in § 439(1) BGB.

Q 46-2

What remedies could be inconsistent with the right to require performance?

Avoidance of the contract, reduction of the price, and damages for a substitute transaction.

Q 46-3

Consider the requirements of Article 28 CISG in light of Article 46(1) CISG. How does this represent a further limitation of Article 46(1) CISG?

Under Article 28 CISG, a court is only required to enter a judgment for specific performance, if it would do so under its own law in the case at hand. This poses a restriction on the possibility of the buyer to claim specific performance under Article 46(1) CISG.

Q 46-4

Can you outline the preconditions for requiring substitute delivery under Article 46(2) CISG?

Article 46(2) CISG requires that the non-conformity amounts to a fundamental breach and that the buyer requests the delivery of substitute goods at least within a reasonable time after giving notice of the non-conformity. The buyer may require the delivery of substitute goods not only if the contract calls for generic goods, but also in the case of a sale of specific goods where substitute goods exist that are economically equivalent to the goods sold.

Q 46-5

Why does Article 46(2) CISG restrict the buyer's right to substitute delivery?

Article 46(2) CISG envisages the situation where the goods are already in the buyer's hands. In this case, substitute delivery would call for a reshipment of the goods to the seller and thus cause the seller to incur considerable additional costs.

Q 46-6

How is a 'reasonable time' to be determined for the purposes of Article 46(2) CISG?

A 'reasonable time' under Article 46(2) CISG is determined by taking into account the nature of the goods and of the defect, the market conditions (especially price fluctuations), and the respective positions of the parties.

Q 46-7

Under what circumstances might a request for repair be regarded as unreasonable?

The buyer's interests in repair by the seller must be weighed against the seller's expenses. Thus, a request for repair can be regarded as unreasonable where the costs for repair are unreasonably high compared to the costs for substitute delivery or compared to the decrease in the value of the goods caused by the non-conformity; where the seller as a retailer does not have the necessary skills for repair; or where the costs for repair by the seller itself are unreasonably high compared to the costs of a repair by the buyer or a third person.

Q 46-8

If the buyer is able to repair the non-conforming goods itself, is the seller thereby totally relieved of its obligations?

No, the buyer may claim damages in the amount of the costs of the repair (see above C 46-1). It may be questionable whether the buyer may claim the costs for repair on an abstract level if it decides to refrain from actually remedying the defect. In any case, the costs of repair are indicative of the reduced value of the goods due to the non-conformity. Thus, they may be taken into account when calculating a reduction of the price under Article 50 CISG, or damages under Article 74 CISG.

Article 47 CISG

Q 47-1

Based on the outline above, what is the essential difference between the Germanic approach and the approach under Article 47(1) CISG?

Under Article 47(1) CISG, the buyer may fix an additional period of time. It does not have a duty to do so as it is generally the case under German law. Thus, under the CISG, the buyer may claim a reduction of the purchase price under Article 50 CISG or damages under Article 74 CISG without having set a *Nachfrist*. Furthermore, under German law, the buyer may avoid the contract if the additional period of time has lapsed without the seller having fulfilled its obligations. This is not a necessary consequence under the CISG (see Q 47-2).

Q 47-2

Explain the interaction between Article 47 CISG and the right to avoid under Article 49(1)(b) CISG.

According to Article 49(1)(b) CISG, the buyer may avoid the contract if the seller has not delivered the goods within the additional period of time set by the buyer. Thus, even if the original non-delivery did not amount to a fundamental breach, it can be rendered fundamental through the lapse of the additional period of time.

Q 47-3

What are the consequences of the buyer failing to set an additional period under Article 47(1) CISG?

If time is not of the essence and thus non-delivery by the seller in itself does not amount to a fundamental breach, the buyer may not avoid the contract before having set an additional period of time.

Q 47-4

What criteria should be used to determine whether the period of additional time was of a reasonable length?

What is a reasonable length has to be decided on a case-by-case basis. The following circumstances should be taken into account: the nature of the goods, the buyer's interest in timely delivery, the mode of delivery, the availability of transport, and the time needed by the seller to procure substitute goods.

Q 47-5

What are the consequences for the buyer of failing to set a 'reasonable' additional period of time?

If the additional period fixed by the buyer is too short to be reasonable, in principle it is ineffective; however, the buyer is bound during the unreasonably short period according to Article 47(2), sentence 1 CISG. Although the buyer may not avoid the contract after the lapse of the unreasonably short period, it may do so if the breach had been fundamental from the beginning or at least after a reasonable time.

Q 47-6

Describe the circumstances in which a buyer could avoid sitting out the additional period before having recourse to remedies.

If the seller during the additional period of time commits a fundamental breach of contract that in and of itself gives rise to avoidance of the contract, eg delivery of fundamentally non-conforming goods or repudiation of the contract.

Article 48 CISG

Q 48-1

Name some similarities and differences between Article 48 CISG and Article 7.1.4 PICC 2010.

Similarities: Both articles provide for the seller's right to cure after the date of performance. They both protect the interests of the aggrieved party. The costs of cure are to be borne by the non-performing party. If the non-performing party gives notice of cure, the aggrieved party may not resort to any remedy which is inconsistent with performance. The right to cure does not preclude the other party's right to damages.

Differences: Article 7.1.4 PICC 2010 is much more detailed than Article 48 CISG. Under Article 7.1.4 PICC 2010 the non-performing party must give notice of its intention to cure, whereas such a notice under Article 48(2) CISG is only relevant with regard to the buyer's ability to resort to a remedy which is inconsistent with performance. According to Article 7.1.4(2) PICC 2010, the right to cure is not precluded by a notice of termination by the aggrieved party; according to Article 48(1), sentence 1 CISG the right to cure is subject to Article 49 CISG, thus it cannot be exercised if buyer has already avoided the contract. Article 7.1.4(4) PICC 2010 explicitly mentions the aggrieved party's right to withhold performance pending cure. Although the CISG does not contain a similar provision, the right to withhold performance can be regarded as a general principle of the CISG.

Q 48-2

Do you agree with the position of the Handelsgericht Aargau *(C 48-1) that Article 48 CISG provides a legal remedy for the buyer granting it a right to cure?*

No, Article 48 CISG is only concerned with the seller's right to cure. The buyer's right to cure is contained in Article 46 CISG.

Q 48-3

(a)   *How did the court (C 48-1) judge the relationship between Articles 48(1) and 49(1)(a) CISG?*
(b)   *What other interpretations can you think of?*

(a)   In the court's view, as long as a defect can be cured, there is no fundamental breach that could give rise to a right of avoidance under Article 49(1)(a) CISG. Thus, in the end, Article 48(1) CISG prevails over Article 49(1)(a) CISG.
(b)   Some legal writers argue that the seller's right to cure under Article 48 CISG is excluded if there is a fundamental breach or at least if the buyer has avoided the contract according to Article 49(1)(a) CISG.

Q 48-4

Why do you think this is the case?

To protect the interests of the buyer.

Q 48-5

What criteria should be used to determine 'unreasonable delay and inconvenience'?

This depends upon the circumstances of the individual case. Criteria to be taken into account are the market situation, price fluctuations, previous attempts to cure, buyer's loss of trust in the seller, disruption of buyer's production, threatened actions for damages by buyer's customers, and buyer's need to have conforming goods at its disposal.

Q 48-6

(a)   *According to the court (C 48-2), what should the buyer have done in order to be able to avoid the contract?*
(b)   *Would the outcome be different under Article 48 CISG?*

(a) According to the standard terms the buyer had to declare its intention to avoid the contract, which still gave the seller the opportunity to cure within 15 working days after the receipt of the buyer's warning.

(b) If there were no standard terms, under Article 48 CISG, the seller's failure to perform within the period within which it had promised to cure certainly amounted to a fundamental breach of contract that gave the buyer the right to avoid the contract after 10 September 1993.

Article 49 CISG

Q 49-1

Compare the modern approaches regarding the circumstances under which avoidance of contract may take place. What are the similarities and differences?

Under § 323 BGB, unlike under the traditional civil law approach, no distinction is made between non-delivery and non-conformity of the goods. Avoidance is only possible if either there has been a fundamental breach (§ 323(2) BGB), in which case an additional period of time is not required, or after the lapse of a *Nachfrist* (§ 323(1) BGB). Article 49 CISG and Article 7.3.1 PICC 2010 share the same starting point. Avoidance primarily requires that the breach can be regarded as being fundamental. Only in case of non-delivery may the buyer avoid the contract after the lapse of an additional period of time (Art 49(1)(b) CISG, Art 7.3.1(3) PICC 2010). However, remarkable differences exist between the notions of fundamental breach under Article 25 CISG and Article 7.3.1(2) PICC 2010. Note that intentional or reckless non-performance is a decisive factor in determining the fundamentality of the breach under Article 7.3.1(2)(c) PICC 2010.

Q 49-2

What circumstances of the above case (C 49-1) did the court consider and how did it treat them when dealing with fundamental breach?

Primary regard was given to the express contractual stipulations. Absent such stipulations, the court considered whether or not the defect could be remedied, in the latter case, if the buyer can reasonably be expected to use the goods in a way other than originally intended. Finally, fraud on the part of the seller might be considered.

Q 49-3

What were the considerations concerning the fundamental breach in the above case (C 49-2)?

Although according to the court one could have found the breach to be fundamental due to the explicit stipulations in the contract, the fact that the buyer was able to process the goods differently or sell them in the normal course of business, if only with a price discount, militates against assuming a fundamental breach.

Q 49-4

Based on the above case (C 49-3), what will be decisive for a finding of fundamental breach in such cases?

It will be decisive whether there is another opportunity to process or resell the non-conforming goods in the ordinary course of business without an excessive burden for the buyer.

Q 49-5

In the absence of express stipulations as to the characteristics of the goods, what other factors will be relevant in determining whether a fundamental breach has occurred in a specific case? Give examples of fact patterns in which these might be relevant.

Some factors to be considered could be usages of trade, whether time to receive conforming goods is of the essence, and the position of the buyer.

Q 49-6

What were the considerations concerning the fundamental breach in C 49-4?

It appears that the court is satisfied to find a fundamental breach because the non-conformity leads to a certain decrease in value. Other considerations such as the ones found in C 49-2 and C 49-3 are not discussed. Thus, it seems that here the threshold for finding a fundamental breach is lower than in those cases.

Q 49-7

Discuss the findings that the Handelsgericht Aargau *(C 48-1) makes with respect to the interaction between the seller's right to cure and the buyer's right to avoid the contract.*

As long as cure is possible, the seller is willing to cure and the buyer can reasonably be expected to accept cure, the fundamentality of the breach of contract must be denied.

Q 49-8

(a) What approach does the court take in the above case (C 49-5) with regard to the issue of non-conforming documents?
(b) According to this case, in which circumstances will non-conformity of documents result in a fundamental breach of contract?

(a) Non-conforming documents are treated on an equal footing with cases of non-conformity of the goods.
(b) Non-conformity of the documents will lead to a fundamental breach of contract if remedying the defect is not possible—either by the seller or the buyer—and if the goods cannot be sold without conforming documents.

Q 49-9

How do the black letter rules compare with the analysis of the foregoing case law?

The black letter rules of the CISG Advisory Council Opinion No 5 reiterate the considerations found in the above case law. Special emphasis is put on the weight accorded to the time of performance, special circumstances in the commodity trade, as well as the buyer's right to withhold performance even if there is no fundamental breach.

Q 49-10

When will late delivery constitute a fundamental breach?

If timely delivery is of the essence.

Q 49-11

As a lawyer, how would you advise a buyer who comes to you and tells you that the seller has not delivered on time?

In many instances, it may not be clear whether a court or tribunal finds a breach to be fundamental. Thus, it is usually advisable for the buyer to set an additional period of time.

Q 49-12

How did the court interpret the requirements of Article 49(1)(b) CISG in the above case (C 49-7)?

Although the additional period of time set by the buyer may have been too short, the seller was deemed to have declared not to deliver within a reasonable period because it asked for a pre-payment of the purchase price which was not due under the contract. After the seller had sold the goods to a third party the buyer was later entitled to avoid the contract for fundamental breach as the seller could no longer perform; in this case, no additional period of time was necessary.

Q 49-13

(a) *Article 49(2) CISG calls for the buyer to declare the contract avoided within a 'reasonable time'. Why do you think this requirement was written into the CISG?*
(b) *When does the period of time for declaring avoidance start running?*
(c) *Is there a general period of time which is considered as reasonable?*

(a) This requirement exists in order to clarify the legal situation between the seller and the buyer as soon as possible in view of the necessity of unwinding the contract.

(b) For the point in time when the period starts to run, see the detailed rules in Article 49(2) CISG. In case of non-conformity of the goods, the decision in C 49-8 clarifies that the period only starts to run once the buyer is aware that the breach is fundamental, thus giving it the right to avoid the contract.

(c) In general, the circumstances of the case have to be considered, such as the nature of the goods, alternative markets, nature of the defect, position of the parties, and the need to obtain legal advice. The court in C 49-8 suggests a period of one to two months unless the circumstances call for an extended or reduced period.

Article 50 CISG

Q 50-1

What are the practical differences between the solution under the CISG and that under common law?

Different outcomes are only possible if the purchase price agreed upon was either lower or higher than the real value of the goods. If the purchase price equals the value of the goods, the results are the same. In many instances, where the market price cannot be ascertained by referring to listed market prices, it can be assumed that the purchase price constitutes the real value of the goods.

Q 50-2

Do you think Article 50 CISG also applies in the case of encumbrances with third party intellectual or industrial property rights? Why or why not?

The clear wording of Article 50 CISG militates against its application in case of encumbrances with third party intellectual property rights, although it can be argued that it would be economically reasonable to apply Article 50 CISG by analogy as Article 42 CISG is more similar to Article 35 CISG than to Article 41 CISG.

Q 50-3

How does the above case (C 50-1) explain the relationship between Article 49(1)(a) CISG and Article 50 CISG?

Unlike Article 205(3) OR (Swiss Law of Obligations) that explicitly excludes a price reduction to zero, the court in C 50-1 came to the conclusion that under the CISG, Article 49 CISG does not prevail over Article 50 CISG. Thus, a price reduction to zero under Article 50 CISG may be made if the prerequisites for avoidance are not given.

Q 50-4

If a fundamental breach is found to exist, what consequences does this have for any price reduction?

In many cases, where there is a fundamental breach the goods may be 'worthless' to the buyer. However, this does not mean that they are indeed completely worthless—if only they have a scrap value—so that a price reduction to zero could be claimed by the buyer.

Q 50-5

(a) What does this case (C 50-2) state as to the method to be used to calculate the reduction of the price under Article 50 CISG?
(b) Is this solution workable in practice?

(a)   The reduction in price is determined by a proportional calculation. The reduced price should bear the same proportion to the contract price as the value of the goods actually delivered bears to the value of conforming goods at the time of delivery.

(b)   This solution is workable in practice only if the true value of the goods at the time of the conclusion of the contract as well as the reduced value of the non-conforming goods can be determined.

Article 51 CISG

Q 51-1

According to the interpretation in this case (C 51-1), in which cases will avoidance for fundamental breach under Article 51(2) CISG be permissible?

Partial delivery may amount to a fundamental breach of contract, eg where no or no timely substitute transaction for missing goods by the buyer is possible.

Q 51-2

Consider the case of a defect in a component of a machine, which, although delivered separately, is necessary in order for the whole machine to function properly. Do you think such a case is subject to the provisions of Article 51 CISG, or rather to Article 49(1)(a) CISG?

As the machine including the component part should be considered as one item and not as separate goods, Article 49(1)(a) CISG should be applied.

Article 52 CISG

Q 52-1

Under which provision of the CISG could the buyer have a duty to take possession of the goods notwithstanding its right to refuse to take delivery under Article 52(1) and (2) CISG?

Under Article 86(2) CISG if the goods have been placed at the buyer's disposal at their destination and this does not cause unreasonable inconvenience or expense for the buyer.

Q 52-2

If the buyer accepts the seller's early delivery, is it thereby excluded from making any further claims due thereto? If not, what sort of claims could it assert?

The buyer may, for example, claim damages for additional storage costs.

Q 52-3

(a) Upon what basis was the buyer unable to reject the goods in the above case (C 52-1)?
(b) What other provision of the CISG could the court have relied upon regarding this issue?

(a) There was a contract clause allowing for a deviation of 10 per cent.
(b) Article 39 CISG, as the court stated that there was no adequate notice of non-conformity.

Q 52-4

What happens if the buyer does not reject the goods?

The buyer is deemed to have accepted the greater quantity of goods and has to pay the higher purchase price for the excess quantity at the contract rate.

Q 52-5

What happens if the buyer does reject the goods?

The buyer is not bound to pay the higher price. According to Article 86 CISG it is under a duty to preserve the goods as is reasonable in the circumstances.

Article 53 CISG

Q 53-1

Does Article 53 CISG allow any leeway to the parties to agree on specific rights and duties not mentioned in the provision?

Yes, the provision gives precedence to the contractual agreement between the parties.

Q 53-2

Does Article 53 CISG, by only mentioning the buyer's duty to pay the purchase price and take over the goods, treat a breach of these duties differently from other breaches of contract? See also Article 61 CISG.

No. Since these duties are the core duties of the buyer, however, this provision serves to clarify these obligations in the context of the remedies that can be sought for their breach under Article 61 CISG.

Q 53-3

(a) *According to the above case (C 53-1), should account be taken of any other agreements when determining the buyer's obligations?*
(b) *Why do you think this is the case?*

(a) No. The court found that the agreement the buyer was relying on had no relation to the case and the seller had no knowledge of the agreement. Therefore, the buyer cannot rely on an extrinsic agreement as an excuse for non-payment.
(b) Because the seller cannot be expected to know of, or be held responsible for, dealings that the buyer has with a third party that may impact on his payment to the seller. Only the contractual obligations between buyer and seller are decisive.

Q 53-4

(a) *Explain how the currency in which the price has to be paid is determined under the CISG.*
(b) *If the currency is to be determined according to Article 7(2) CISG, it is disputed whether the currency issue is to be resolved according to the general principles of the CISG or under the law applicable through the rules of private international law. Are there any provisions of the CISG which might establish a general principle as to the currency in which payment is to be made?*
(c) *How does the PICC 2010 answer the question as to the currency in which payment is to be made?*
(d) *Why does it not seem advisable to derive a general principle from Articles 31(c), 57(1)(a) CISG with a view to determining the applicable currency rate? Consider their importance from a practical point of view.*

(a)   Primarily, party agreement prevails (Art 6 CISG). In the absence of specific agreement, trade usages may play a role (Art 9(1) CISG) and, failing those, then Article 7(2) CISG applies.

(b)   Articles 30 to 33 CISG could be of assistance in deriving a general principle that the currency of the contract should be the currency of the place at which delivery of the goods is made. Article 57 CISG determines the place of payment, which would be an appropriate starting point to determine the currency.

(c)   The general rule is that the currency of the place of payment applies, except where another currency was expressed and that currency is not freely convertible or the parties have made a specific agreement in this regard.

(d)   In practice, these two places may be different, in which case it would not be sense to use them to dcrive a general principle concerning the applicable currency rate.

Article 54 CISG

Q 54-1

Explain the purpose and scope of Article 54 CISG.

The purpose of Article 54 CISG is to clarify that, in the absence of agreement to the contrary, it is the buyer's obligation to complete all formalities necessary for payment to be made under the contract. The costs of such formalities are to be borne by the buyer. Moreover, it is implicit in the reference to an 'obligation' that the buyer's failure to comply will result in the seller's entitlement to claim remedies.

Q 54-2

If the contract provides, for example, for the opening of a letter of credit and the buyer does not comply with its duty, what are the seller's remedies?

The seller can claim specific performance, damages, or, as in C 54-1, avoid the contract if the obligation is regarded as an essential term of the contract.

Q 54-3

(a)   Is the buyer's duty to take the steps necessary to enable the seller to be paid an 'obligation de résultat' or an 'obligation de moyen'?

(b)   What was the position of the Supreme Court of Queensland (C 54-1)?

(a)   It is an *obligation de résultat*.

(b)   The position of the Supreme Court of Queensland in C 54-1 was that this duty was an *obligation de résultat*. This should be the result generally. If the seller cannot make the buyer responsible for failing to successfully arrange the formalities for payment, this provision is devoid of legal relevance.

Furthermore, to hold otherwise would be to provide the buyer with a way to avoid one of its legal obligations, since it could claim it was not responsible for achieving a successful result. The application of Article 79 CISG remains unaffected.

Article 55 CISG

Q 55-1

(a) Under what circumstances does Article 55 CISG apply?
(b) According to the Czech Supreme Court case (C 55-1), what is the pre-requisite for Article 55?
(c) What does the Swiss case (C 55-2) say about the risk allocation under Article 55 CISG?

(a)   Where no price is determined or determinable from the contract.
(b)   Article 55 CISG is only applicable if a contract has been validly concluded.
(c)   Article 55 CISG is representative of a proper division of risk between seller and buyer concerning a price: the buyer is protected from paying too much and is also prevented from benefiting from a very advantageous price.

Q 55-2

(a) Divide the corresponding provisions from the other legal systems into two groups: a liberal group which allows for a contract where the contract price has not been determined, and a group representing a narrower interpretation.
(b) Where, on a scale of very strict to flexible provisions, would you place Article 55 CISG?

(a)   Liberal: Article 57 ULIS, Article 5.1.7(1) PICC 2010, Section 2-305(1) UCC, Article 1474 *Codice Civile*.
      Narrow: Article 1591 CC.
(b)   Article 55 CISG takes a liberal view.

Q 55-3

(a) Sometimes, courts or tribunals try to determine a missing price with a view to 'saving' the contract or rendering it effective. Under what circumstances will there definitely be no contract under the CISG, notwithstanding Article 55?
(b) In which of the provisions from other legal systems referred to above is this legal position made particularly clear?

(a)   If the other essential elements of Article 14 CISG are missing.
(b)   Under Article 1591 CC, the price has to be designated by the parties. If a price is not designated, there is no contract.

Q 55-4

(a)   How is the missing contract price to be determined under Article 55 CISG?
(b)   To what do the other legal provisions refer?
(c)   On the determination of the sales price, see, in particular, Article 57 ULIS. What changes have been made in Article 55 CISG? Is there another domestic sales law provision providing for a similar solution to Article 57 ULIS? Is there still a difference between Article 57 ULIS and that other domestic rule?
(d)   Do you regard Article 55 CISG as giving clear instructions on how to establish the missing purchase price? See Article 5.1.7 PICC 2010.

(a)   By reference to the price generally charged at the time of conclusion of the contract for such goods under comparable circumstances.

(b)   ULIS: price generally charged by seller.

PICC 2010: price generally charged for such goods under comparable circumstances, or reasonable price.

UCC: reasonable price at the time for delivery.

Codice Civile: price usually charged by the seller.

(c)   No longer price charged by seller, but price generally charged. Article 57 ULIS and Article 1474 *Codice Civile* both refer to price charged by seller. *Codice Civile* refers to the parties' intention and it is a presumption. There is no presumption and no reference to parties' intention in ULIS.

(d)   Yes, it sets out the circumstances of application and provides for clear reference points. In the absence of a price, one could have reference to PICC 2010 and imply a reasonable price in order to give effect to the parties' intentions.

Article 56 CISG

Q 56-1

What is the purpose of Article 56 CISG?

To provide a rule of interpretation for determining the contract price if the price is fixed according to weight without further specifications.

Q 56-2

To what extent is the rule stated in Article 56 CISG subsidiary?

The parties are free to agree specifically on how the price is to be calculated in such circumstances, or to apply their own or commercial usages.

Q 56-3

Compare Article 56 CISG to the other legal provisions set out above.

(a) Does Article 56 CISG reflect a rule generally acknowledged in commercial trade?

(b) What is the reason underlying Article 56 CISG?

(a) Yes, it would appear to reflect a generally acknowledged rule.

(b) To provide clarity in accordance with the circumstances if precise rules have not been agreed upon in this regard.

Article 57 CISG

Q 57-1

What does the above case (C 57-2) say about the interaction between Article 57 CISG and Article 5(1)(b) Brussels Regulation?

Article 57 CISG still determines the place of performance as the applicable substantive law with respect to the legal obligations of the parties. Article 5(1)(b) Brussels Regulation is relevant to the extent that a rule exists granting international jurisdiction to the courts at the place of performance. However, case law has held that Article 5(1)(b) Brussels Regulation is to be interpreted autonomously, with regard to where delivery actually took place and without recourse to the law applicable to the underlying contract.

Q 57-2

How does the CISG determine the place where payment of the purchase price is to be made?

It provides for two alternatives depending on whether the parties are to perform their obligations concurrently or separately.

Q 57-3

(a) To what extent is Article 57 CISG a subsidiary rule? See the corresponding provisions from the other legal systems.

(b) According to the INCOTERM® 'EXW' (Ex Works (insert named place)), the seller delivers when it places the goods at the disposal of the buyer at the seller's premises or another named place (ie works, factory, warehouse, etc). What does that mean in relation to where the buyer has to pay the purchase price?

(a) It is subsidiary to the extent that party agreement in divergence from Article 57 will prevail. This includes agreement on internationally recognised trade terms such as INCOTERMS®.

(b)   An agreement on INCOTERMS® constitutes a contrary agreement and prevails over Article 57 CISG. Consequently, the buyer will have to pay the purchase price in accordance with the EXW provision.

Q 57-4

(a)   How can we distinguish Article 57(1)(a) from Article 57(1)(b) CISG?
(b)   Why is Article 57(1)(b) CISG of higher practical importance than Article 57(1)(a)?

(a)   Article 57(1)(b) is the general rule when the parties are to perform their obligations concurrently. Article 57(1)(a) only applies when one of the parties has to perform in advance.
(b)   Because Article 57(1)(b) CISG constitutes the general scenario to be decided in practice; Article 57(1)(a) is the exception.

Q 57-5

What kind of documents are referred to in Article 57(1)(b) CISG? (See C 58-1).

Documents required to identify the goods and take possession of them, such as airways bills, documents of origin, customs documents etc. The phrase includes all documents required by the sales contract and by the law and rules applicable to the relevant delivery and payment arrangement.

Q 57-6

(a)   Does the CISG address the issue of where monetary obligations other than the purchase price are to be paid?
(b)   What possible solutions are there to this question?
(c)   Compare Article 57(1) CISG with the corresponding provisions of the PICC 2010, OR, and ABGB. To what extent do they differ from Article 57(1) CISG?

(a) and (b) No, but an implied rule arguably exists that applies Article 57(1) CISG to other monetary claims by analogy.

(c)   PICC 2010 provides a similar rule as does OR, but does not differentiate between different scenarios, and is therefore broader. ABGB differs because it clarifies that the buyer bears the risk and expense of paying at the creditor's domicile.

Q 57-7

Compare Article 57(1) CISG with the other legal provisions.

(a)   Is it commonly acknowledged that the purchase price is paid at the seller's place of business?
(b)   In particular, are there differences between Article 57(1) CISG, on the one hand, and the UCC and the French CC, on the other
   —   with regard to the structure of the corresponding provisions?
   —   in substance?

(a) Yes.
(b) Yes, the UCC provides only for the situation contemplated in Article 57(1)(b)—the result will usually be the same in practice. In the French CC, focus is placed on where the thing forming the object of the obligation is located. In the case of a payment obligation, this will mean where the money is at the time of payment. This could indeed lead to different consequences as to the place of payment, as the money will usually be with the buyer.

Q 57-8

If the seller's place of business changes after the conclusion of the contract, where is payment to be made:

(a) according to Article 57(2) CISG?
(b) according to the corresponding provisions of the BGB, ABGB, Codice Civile, and OR?
(c) In which cases is the place of payment the creditor's new domicile?
(d) In all other cases, where is the debtor to make payment? Are there any differences between the various provisions?

(a) At the seller's new place of business; seller bears additional expense.

(b), (c) and (d) BGB: at the seller's new place of business or domicile; seller bears additional expense and additional risk.
ABGB: at the seller's new place of business or domicile; seller bears additional expense and additional risk.
Codice Civile: buyer may elect to make payment at its own domicile if it informs the seller first.
OR: buyer may elect to make payment at its own domicile if the change of seller's domicile imposes a considerable burden on the buyer.

Q 57-9

What happens if there is not only a change in the seller's place of business, but a change in the person of the creditor itself?

(a) What did the court in C 57-2 decide?
(b) What other possibilities are there, according to A 57-1?

(a) Place of payment will be the place of the assignee.
(b) It could be decided according to the private international law rules governing assignment of the forum; no change, place of payment remains at the seller's place of business.

Article 58 CISG

Q 58-1

(a) Which principle does Article 58 CISG establish?
(b) Do you find a similar principle encapsulated in the provisions of the other legal systems set out above?

(a) That of concurrent performance of payment against delivery.
(b) Yes, all the legal systems set out embrace similar requirements.

Q 58-2

The time at which goods, or the documents controlling their disposition, are placed at the buyer's disposal, thereby making the buyer's payment due, depends on the type of contract. Define when the buyer must pay in the following situations:

(a) The goods are delivered at the seller's place of business.
(b) The goods are delivered at the buyer's place of business.

(a) At the time the goods are handed over to the buyer.
(b) Immediately.

Article 59 CISG

Q 59-1

Which principle is embodied in Article 59 CISG?

The obligation to pay the price exists without any need for the seller to request it.

Q 59-2

Why will the buyer, in practice, usually be notified by the seller that payment is due?

Because it will receive notice that the goods have been delivered or will receive an invoice indicating that the payment is due.

Article 60 CISG

Q 60-1

(a) What does the duty to take delivery, according to Article 60 CISG, consist of?
(b) Which general principle can be derived from Article 60 CISG?

(a) Reasonably enabling the seller to make delivery and taking over the goods by the buyer.
(b) A principle of reasonableness.

Q 60-2

(a) Is there a limitation on what steps the buyer is obliged to take in order to enable delivery of the goods?
(b) Is there a limit to the buyer's obligation to take over the goods?

(c)   In which provisions of the CISG do you find indications that the buyer's duty to take over the goods or documents is not infinite?

(a)   Yes, the buyer should facilitate everything necessary but cannot be held liable for, eg, actions of third parties required to enable delivery.

(b)   The buyer must do everything reasonable to take over the goods but does not have an obligation to take them over if they are non-conforming and such non-conformity would constitute a fundamental breach of contract, or if the goods are delivered early or in a larger quantity than agreed.

(c)   Articles 49(1)(a) and 52 CISG.

Q 60-3

What are the consequences of the buyer failing to comply with its duty as set out in Article 60 CISG?

The seller can claim specific performance, damages, and/or avoidance of the contract.

Q 60-4

Who bears the risk if the buyer refuses to take over the goods or documents

— *and has the right to do so?*
— *but is not entitled to do so?*

The seller bears the risk if the buyer is rightfully entitled to refuse the goods or documents. If the buyer wrongfully refuses to take over the goods or documents, it is the buyer's risk.

Q 60-5

(a)   Why did the arbitral tribunal find in C 60-1 that the buyer had breached its obligations?
(b)   Did the tribunal base its decision on Article 60(b) CISG?

(a)   The arbitral tribunal found that the buyer had not complied with its obligation to take prompt delivery of the goods by discharging the vessel and as a result, had to bear the costs and the additional demurrage costs caused by its delay.

(b)   The tribunal's finding was based on the contract and the INCOTERM® CFR, which it used to supplement the general obligation under Article 60(b) CISG.

Article 61 CISG

Q 61-1

Explain the operation of Article 61 CISG.

Article 61 CISG sets out the remedies that are available to the seller when the buyer does not perform any of its obligations under the contract or the CISG. It clarifies that the right to claim damages can be exercised concurrently with other remedies and that a court or arbitral cannot grant an extension of time for performance.

Q 61-2

(a)   What was the reason for including Article 61(3) CISG? See also Article 1184 CC.
(b)   Which situations does Article 61(3) CISG currently deal with?

(a)   It was included as a clarification to ensure uniformity of interpretation in light of differences in approach to this issue under domestic laws.
(b)   Predominantly situations under domestic bankruptcy and insolvency laws, where statutory extensions of time for performance of obligations may be granted.

Q 61-3

(a)   How did the US District Court in C 61-1 solve the conflict between Article 58(3) CISG and the US bankruptcy provisions?
(b)   Keeping Article 7 CISG in mind, could you visualise an approach different from the one the court took in this case?

(a)   It held in obiter that the US bankruptcy provisions would prevail over the CISG.
(b)   Yes, it would be in line with the uniformity of interpretation that the CISG could be held to prevail regardless of the provisions in local bankruptcy laws.

Article 62 CISG

Q 62-1

(a)   What kind of seller's rights does Article 62 CISG govern?
(b)   Which generic term do we generally use for those rights?

(a)   The seller's rights to require performance by the buyer of its obligations.
(b)   Specific performance of the contract.

Q 62–2

Why, from an international point of view, is Article 62 CISG not a self-evident provision?

Because some legal systems do not include a claim for the purchase price within the scope of claims for specific performance.

Q 62-3

In what way are the seller's rights to specific performance restricted?

If the seller has resorted to a remedy inconsistent with this requirement, for example, by declaring avoidance of the contract, and if the remedy of specific performance would not be granted under the domestic legal system at the seat of the proceedings.

Q 62-4

Why could it be doubted whether Article 28 CISG applies to the seller's rights for specific performance?

Because Article 28 CISG allows reference to domestic laws to determine whether or not a claim for specific performance is admissible.

Q 62-5

To which cases do the SGA and the UCC restrict the seller's price action?

SGA: Property in the goods has passed or the due date for payment has passed.
UCC: Price has become due and goods have been accepted or goods lost or damaged after the risk of loss has passed to the buyer. Where the risk of the goods still lies with the seller, the seller must have been unable to resell them at a reasonable price or shown that such effort will be unavailing.

Q 62-6

Which principle governs the seller's claim for the buyer to pay the purchase price under the PICC 2010?

The principle of specific performance of the contract.

Q 62-7

Can you find a provision under the CISG from which a general principle may be derived, possibly restricting the seller's claim to the purchase price?

The principle of concurrent performance embodied in Article 58 CISG, whereby the seller can only claim payment of the purchase price upon delivery of the goods.

Article 63 CISG

Q 63-1

In which cases will the seller proceed under Article 63 CISG?

Where it wishes to remain cautious about remedies if it is unsure that a breach is fundamental, or where it wants to 'transform' a non-fundamental breach into a fundamental one by awaiting an extension period.

Q 63-2

(a) In what circumstances of non-compliance by the buyer may the seller fix an additional period of time?

(b) In which cases does the expiration of an additional period, without action by the buyer, automatically amount to a fundamental breach of contract, thereby entitling the seller to avoid the contract?

(a)   Where the breach is non-fundamental, or where the breach is fundamental but the seller is still interested in upholding the contract.

(b)   If the buyer has not paid the purchase price or taken delivery of the goods.

Q 63-3

Consider situations where a period, in order to be reasonable, will be quite short, and others where it will be longer. On what will such reasonableness usually depend?

The circumstances of the case. If seasonal goods are involved, the period may be rather short; in other circumstances, a longer period may equally be regarded as reasonable.

Q 63-4

Why is it not sufficient to request performance 'soon' or 'promptly', but rather to indicate a specific period or date? See also Article 47 CISG above.

Because it is important that the seller give the buyer certainty concerning the period after which it may resort to other remedies, including avoidance of the contract.

Q 63-5

Is it possible to combine an additional period under Article 63(1) CISG with a declaration of avoidance in the event that the buyer fails to fulfil its contractual duties? See also C 63-1.

Yes, provided that the avoidance does not become effective until expiry of the additional period granted. In such cases, the seller should ensure that the additional period granted is reasonable, because failure to grant a reasonable period may result in any consequent avoidance being declared invalid.

Article 64 CISG

Q 64-1

In which cases is the seller entitled to avoid the contract?

Where the buyer has committed a fundamental breach or, where the buyer has not paid the price or taken delivery of the goods, after the expiration of an additional period of time, has still not performed these obligations or has indicated that it will not perform them.

Q 64-2

(a) Does the buyer's mere non-payment of the purchase price allow the seller to avoid the contract? See also C 64-1.

(b) Can a definite refusal to pay or take over the goods constitute a fundamental breach?

(c) Does the buyer's failure to take over the goods entitle the seller to avoid the contract? See C 64-2.

(a) Yes. However, a seller would be advised to act cautiously and set an additional period of time for performance in case a court later finds that non-payment did not amount to a fundamental breach of contract in and of itself.

(b) Yes, because then an additional period of time for performance is rendered pointless.

(c) It will depend on the circumstances. This will be the case where the seller sets an additional period of time and has informed the buyer that its failure to take over the goods within that period of time will result in it declaring avoidance of the contract.

Q 64-3

(a) Could the buyer's violation of obligations other than the ones mentioned in Article 64(1)(b) CISG constitute a fundamental breach of contract?

(b) If the seller has doubts as to whether such a breach amounts to a fundamental one, what can it do to clarify the situation?

(a) Yes, but subject to the requirements of Article 64(2) CISG.

(b) Set an additional period of time for performance by the buyer of its obligations.

Q 64-4

(a) What should a seller, who does not receive payment or whose goods are not taken over in time, do with a view to obtaining the right to avoid the contract?

(b) If the buyer does not comply with its duties other than to make payment and take over the goods, will an additional period of time (Art 63) automatically enable the seller to avoid the contract? Under which pre-conditions will the seller be entitled to terminate the contract? See also C 64-2.

(a) It should set an additional period of time for performance by the buyer of its obligations under the contract, after which the seller should declare to the buyer by notice avoidance of the contract.

(b) No, not automatically. Only where the seller does not have notice that performance has been made (in cases of late performance) or gives notice of avoidance within a reasonable time after the expiry of an additional period (other cases) will the seller be able to avoid the contract.

Q 64-5

(a) Which duties does the buyer's obligation to make payment include?
(b) How broadly should the scope of the duties connected to the obligation to take over the goods be construed?

(a) It includes the obligations set out in Article 54 CISG.
(b) All obligations under Article 60(a) CISG fall within the scope of this duty.

Q 64-6

(a) Why was the seller unable to rely on Article 64 in C 64-3 above?
(b) Do you think this is the correct approach?

(a) It was not able to rely of Article 64(1)(a) because the quantity not accepted by the buyer did not amount to a fundamental breach. It was not able to rely on Article 64(1)(b) CISG because the obligation breached by the buyer did not concern the taking of delivery but the ordering of goods.
(b) No, the court should have looked at Article 64(2) CISG with respect to breaches not falling under the 'taking of delivery', whereby the seller is still able to set an additional period for performance and declare avoidance within a reasonable time after the expiry of this period.

Q 64-7

What factors did the court look at to determine whether or not there was substantial detriment?

The circumstances of the case, including the percentage of goods not accepted in light of the entirety of the contract.

Q 64-8

How can Article 64(2)(a) and Article 64(2)(b) CISG be distinguished?

Article 64(2)(a) applies in respect of late performance, Article 64(2)(b) applies to all other cases of breach.

Q 64-9

Decide whether the seller can avoid or has justifiably avoided the contract in the following situations:

(a) Buyer has not paid timely, seller has fixed a reasonable additional period of time until yesterday and
   — *buyer has not made payment until today.* Yes
   — *buyer has made payment within the additional period granted and notified the seller thereof.* No.
   — *buyer paid this morning at 11 am. The seller has declared the contract avoided before this time this morning.* Yes.

— *buyer made payment yesterday and notified seller thereof; the money is transferred today, but prior to transfer the seller has declared avoidance.* No.

— *same situation as before, but buyer does not notify the seller of its having made payment.* No, payment was still made within the *Nachfrist*, so not 'late' within the meaning of Article 64(2)(a) CISG.

(b) Buyer has neither paid timely nor has taken over the goods within an additional period of time. Shortly after,
— *buyer pays, takes over the goods and notifies the seller thereof.*

No.

— *buyer pays but does not take over the goods.*

Yes.

— *buyer pays and takes over the goods, but is still in breach of another obligation which would allow it to avoid the contract.*

Depends on whether other obligation is fundamental in and of itself and whether it was already covered by the *Nachfrist* set.

Q 64-10

Since, generally, where the requirements of Article 64(1)(a) and (b) are met, the seller can freely choose whether it avoids the contract or claims specific performance of the contract, there might be a risk that it speculates to the detriment of the buyer by avoiding the contract at a date particularly favourable to it. For example, it could avoid the contract when the market price is particularly high and claim damages under Article 76(1) CISG. Is there a general principle under the CISG which obliges a party to keep the damage of the other party to a minimum?

Yes, Article 77 CISG imposes an obligation on the non-breaching party to mitigate the damage claimable.

Article 65 CISG

Q 65-1

(a) Why was Article 65 CISG disputed at the Drafting Conference?
(b) Which party's interests come to the fore?

(a)   Because it allows the seller to make its own specifications if the buyer fails to do so.
(b)   The seller's interest in performance of the contract.

Q 65-2

Even if there is little chance that the buyer will be prepared to execute the contract, why is it helpful for the seller to make a specification of the goods?

Because specifying the goods enables the seller to proceed with its performance under the contract and to assess the remedies that arise from the buyer's breach.

Article 66 CISG

Q 66-1

What are the consequences of the fact that the risk has passed to the buyer? See C 66-1 and 66-2 in this respect.

Once the risk has passed to the buyer, it must account for the full purchase price, although the goods have been lost or damaged, unless the loss or damage is due to an act or omission of the seller.

Q 66-2

How do we find out whether a contract term concerns the passing of risk? See also C 66-2.

It is a matter of interpretation under Article 8 CISG.

Q 66-3

Who bears the burden of proving whether the risk passed from the seller to the buyer?

The seller who has not received payment must, in order to claim the purchase price, prove that the risk had passed to the buyer at the time the goods were damaged or lost. The buyer who has paid the purchase price must, in order to claim restitution, prove that the risk was still on the seller when the damage or loss occurred.

Q 66-4

How will the rules on passing of risk established in INCOTERM® clauses be interpreted in a CISG contract?

Where a 'codified' trade practice has been developed around a particular trade term, as is the case with INCOTERMS®, Article 8(3) CISG calls for full incorporation of those standard interpretations into the contract.

Q 66-5

Give an example of a loss of or damage to the goods which is neither due to an act or omission of the seller nor to natural forces and which remains out of the sphere of influence of the buyer. See C 66-1 in this respect.

For example acts of State, such as new laws, decrees or orders. If the goods are damaged or destroyed due to such act, the buyer remains bound to pay the purchase price if the act of State entered into force after the risk has passed.

Q 66-6

Articles 66 to 69 CISG govern the question of when the risk passes under an effectively concluded sales contract. Can the parties provide that the risk passes even before the contract has been concluded? See C 66-2.

Yes, the parties can, for instance, agree that the risk of casual loss or damage passes prior to the sales contract. In C 66-2, the defendant had taken into custody a horse for a certain period of time with the option to buy the horse after the period had elapsed. The parties had agreed that the defendant would make a down payment which was due regardless of whether or not the sales contract would be concluded. Thus, the court held that the parties made an agreement on the passing of risk for the time the contract had not yet been finally binding.

Article 67 CISG

Q 67-1

Which situations are governed by Article 67 CISG?

Article 67 CISG governs the passing of risk in situations where the contract involves carriage of the goods. Article 67(1) sentence 1 addresses the common situation where the goods must be forwarded and no particular place has been determined, while Article 67(1) sentence 2 CISG deals with the exception where the seller is bound to hand over the goods at a particular place.

Q 67-2

Who is meant by 'carrier'—is it a third party, or personnel under the seller's control?

The word 'carrier' refers to a third person or legal entity that is independent from the seller. Risk should pass when the seller loses control over the goods, which is the case only where the seller hands over the goods to an independent third party (or directly to the buyer).

Q 67-3

Article 67(1), sentence 1 CISG is said to state a generally accepted international rule. Why is it reasonable to impose the risk on the buyer as soon as the goods are handed over to carriers?

A splitting of the risk is justified by the fact that, after arrival of the goods, the buyer is usually considered to be in a better position than the seller to establish any damage to the goods which has occurred as a result of the transport and to claim damages against the carrier.

Q 67-4

How can the parties derogate from Article 67 CISG?

The parties can incorporate an INCOTERM® clause or another trade term in their contract dealing with the passing of risk. They can also provide for an individual agreement with regard to the passing of risk.

Q 67-5

What considerations guided the court in C 67-2 in holding that 'franco domicile' also governed the question of when the risk passed?

It held that the clause could reasonably be understood as derogation from Article 31(a) because *'franco domicile'* implied that the buyer need not 'worry about transportation and insurance', because the seller had insured the goods and because, in previous dealings, the seller had often used its own transportation means. Thus, delivery was not made by handing over the goods to the first carrier but rather only once the goods were delivered to the buyer's premises. Accordingly, the risk did not pass with handing over the goods to the first carrier but only once the goods had reached the buyer's premises.

Q 67-6

With regard to Article 67(2) CISG, must the buyer have become the legal owner of the goods in order to say that the goods damaged or lost were 'the buyer's'?

The passing of risk must be dealt with separately from the passing of title. The latter is governed by the applicable domestic law.

Q 67-7

When does the risk pass in the following situations?

(a) Seller transports goods using its own equipment and personnel and delivers the goods at the agreed place of delivery.
(b) Seller initially transports goods and then hands them over to a third party who, after having carried them for a while, hands them over to another carrier.
(c) Seller is bound to hand the goods over to the first carrier at a particular place, but hands them over before the agreed place has been reached.
(d) Goods are handed over to the first carrier but have not yet been identified.

(a)   The risk passes at the moment of the delivery at the agreed place.
(b)   The risk passes when the seller hands over the goods to the first carrier (Art 67(1) CISG).

(c)   The risk only passes to the buyer once the goods are delivered at the agreed place and at the time due (Art 67(1) CISG).

(d)   The risk does not pass to the buyer until the goods have been clearly identified (Art 67(2) CISG).

Q 67-8

In which of the above situations is the burden of the risk split during transport?

The risk is split in situations (b), (c) and (d). In the situations (b) and (c), the risk passes to the buyer once the goods are properly handed over to the first carrier. In situation (d), the risk passes to the buyer while the goods are in possession of the carrier once they have been identified.

Q 67-9

Compare Article 67 CISG with domestic sales laws.

(a)   Are there any similarities between Article 67(1) CISG and Section 2-509 UCC?

(b)   What is the corresponding rule in the BGB?

(c)   Why is the BGB clearer than the CISG with respect to the passing of risk in the case of handing the goods over to a freight forwarder?

(a)   The provisions are similar in the situation where the seller is bound to hand over the goods to a carrier (Art 67(1), first sentence CISG; § 2-509(1)(a) UCC). However, the UCC does not deal specifically with the situation described in Article 67(1), second sentence CISG. What is dealt with in Section 2-509(1)(b) UCC is the situation where delivery must be made either at the buyer's premises or at a third place. In those cases, the risk passes once the buyer is able to take delivery.

(b)   § 447(1) BGB is similar to Article 67(1) CISG, first sentence.

(c)   The BGB gives more precise guidance as to who that third party designated to dispatch the goods is, by mentioning not only the 'carrier', but also the 'forwarder' or 'other person or body designated to dispatch the thing'.

Q 67-10

It has been stated that, under the CISG, although from a dogmatic view, the time of delivery and the time of passing of risk have been distinguished, in practice they will often coincide. This differs from French and Swiss law, which have settled the passing of risk in sales contracts differently.

(a)   To what extent do Swiss and French law provide for a similar rule on the passing of risk?

(b)   Which point in time is decisive as to whether the risk has passed to the buyer?

(c)   Which rules are more suited for modern international trade, the French and Swiss ones or those found in Article 67 CISG and the other sales laws? Discuss.

(d)   Under Swiss law, title to the goods will not pass until handing over the goods to the buyer. How does the CC settle the passing of title to goods? See Article 1138(1) CC.

(e)   In light of your answer to (c) above, do you see a rationale in French law for how it handles the passing of risk?

(f)   Which difficulty persists in Swiss law with regard to risk allocation between the buyer and the seller?

(a)   Under both Swiss and French law, the risk passes to the buyer at the time of the conclusion of the contract.

(b)   The decisive moment is the conclusion of the contract.

(c)   Linking the passing of risk to the moment of taking delivery is based on the idea that the party who possesses the goods is in a better position to control and protect the goods. Thus, the solution provided by French or Swiss law seems to excessively favour the position of the seller, especially in international trade, where the conclusion of the contract will not usually lead to a simultaneous taking of possession of the goods.

(d)   Under French law, title to the goods passes at the moment of the conclusion of the contract.

(e)   French law links the passing of risk to the passing of title to the goods. Since, with the conclusion of the contract, the buyer becomes the owner and beneficiary of the goods, it should, from that moment on, also bear the risk of their loss of or damage.

(f)   The moment of contract conclusion does not necessarily coincide with the taking of possession and the passing of title. Thus, although the buyer may not yet be in a position to control and protect the goods, according to Article 185(1) OR, it already bears the risk of loss of or damage to the goods.

Article 68 CISG

Q 68-1

As a general rule, when does the risk pass with regard to goods sold in transit?

It passes to the buyer from the time the contract of sale is concluded.

Q 68-2

What are the difficulties with the general rule?

Difficulties arise when damage or loss occurs during transport; it may indeed be quite difficult for the buyer to prove that the damage or loss occurred prior to the conclusion of the contract.

Q 68-3

What is the exception to the general rule?

According to Article 68 sentence 2 CISG, the risk it retroactively imposed on the buyer from the time the goods were handed over to the carrier if 'the circumstances so indicate'.

Q 68-4

Why is the exception of greater practical relevance than the general rule?

It is undisputed that the term 'if the circumstances so indicate' relates to the situation where an insurance contract has been concluded which covers all risks and where the buyer may directly claim from the insurer the amount insured. Such insurance is common in practice.

Q 68-5

To which documents do Article 68, sentence 2, and Article 58, respectively, refer? Decide whether the following documents represent documents within the meaning of Article 58, or Article 68, sentence 2, or both:

(a) bill of lading
(b) insurance policy insuring the goods in shipment;
(c) carriage contract document.

(a)   The documents mentioned in Article 58 CISG have to represent the goods, while the ones mentioned in Article 68 sentence 2 CISG only have to prove the carriage contract.
      The standard short form of a bill of lading is evidence of the contract of carriage of goods. A bill of lading can be a document of transfer if it is endorsed ('order bill of lading'). In that case, it is a document which falls within Article 58 as well as within Article 68 CISG.
(b)   The insurance policy is a contract with a third party, the insurer; it does not evidence either the contract of carriage or the title in the goods and is thus neither a document according to Article 58 nor pursuant to Article 68.
(c)   The carriage contract represents the goods within the meaning of Article 68 sentence 2 CISG but does not represent any title to the goods.

Article 69 CISG

Q 69-1

Article 69(1) also applies where the buyer is exempt under Article 79 CISG—can you explain why?

Under Article 79 CISG, the buyer will be exempt from paying damages if its failure to take delivery constitutes a breach of contract but is due to *force majeure*. But this does not change the fact that the risk of damage to or loss of the goods passes at the moment the buyer ought to take delivery (Art 69(1)).

Q 69-2

Analyse C 69-1:

(a) Where were the goods to be delivered?
(b) Did the question of whether delivery had been made become relevant for the question of whether the risk had passed to the buyer?
(c) Who bore the burden of proof as to whether the risk had passed?

(a) According to the facts, the goods were to be delivered to a warehouse in Hungary and stored there. The seller would then issue invoices to the buyer which the buyer would not pay before the furniture had been delivered at the buyer's premises. The court came to the conclusion that the place of delivery was the warehouse.

(b) Under the CISG, the passing of risk is linked to taking delivery of the goods, or to the moment delivery by the buyer should have been taken (see Art 69(1), (2)). Thus, the question of whether delivery had occurred was relevant for assessing whether the risk had passed. But it is not only the making but also the taking of delivery that is important: in the case at hand, the risk would have passed if the warehouse had been the place of delivery, if delivery had been due, and if the buyer had been notified or otherwise made aware of the fact that the goods had been placed at its disposal at the warehouse.

(c) The burden of proof is on the party that purports that the risk has passed. In the case at hand, the plaintiff, ie, the party to whom the seller had assigned its claims against the buyer, had to prove that the risk had passed to the buyer and that the goods were destroyed after the risk had passed.

Article 71 CISG

Q 71-1

What is the idea behind a right to withhold performance as stated in Article 71 CISG?

The idea is to emphasise the principle of concurrent performance, according to which a party should not be obliged to perform if it is sufficiently obvious that the promised counter-performance will not be rendered or not be conforming to the contract.

Q 71-2

See C 71-2 and Article 82 OR (Switzerland). Could the seller have withheld performance under Swiss law?

In C 71-2, it was not the buyer's execution of the main performance that was jeopardised, ie, the payment of the purchase price, but rather the protection of the seller's patent right and the confidentiality of its expertise. Article 71 CISG applied to this situation, first, because it allows for suspension of performance before the date performance by the debtor is due, and secondly, because it only requires that a 'substantial part' of the other party's performance be compromised. In contrast, Article 82 OR would not apply to this case: withholding performance is permitted only where the debtor's performance is already due, and even then, performance can only be withheld if the other party fails to tender its main obligations, ie, its counter-performance in the proper sense.

Q 71-3

(a) What are the differences between the two categories of suspension rights dealt with in paragraphs 1 and 2 of Article 71 CISG?
(b) Do the PICC 2010 provide for such a differentiation?
(c) Which of the two suspension rights mentioned in Article 71 CISG is dealt with in Section 2-705 UCC and Section 44 SGA?

(a)   The right to suspend performance in Article 71(1) is available to both seller and buyer and allows for the suspension of performance of a party's obligations if it becomes apparent that the other party will not perform a substantial part of its obligations. The right to prevent the handing over of the goods in Article 71(2) CISG is available to the seller only and allows the prevention of handing over of the goods to the buyer after they have been dispatched.

(b)   No, Article 7.3.4 PICC refers to the right to withhold performance, without making any further distinctions.

(c)   Both Section 2-705 UCC and Section 44 SGA deal with the seller's right to prevent the handing over of the goods, that is, with the situation which, under the Convention, is governed by Article 71(2).

Q 71-4

Is sluggish payment behaviour an indication of lack of creditworthiness within the meaning of Article 71(1)(a) CISG? See C 71-1.

According to the court, 'singular delayed payments or a sluggish mode of payment are normally not sufficient to show a serious loss of creditworthiness.' Thus, the 'buyer's default in payment of the deliveries from February and March 1993 [were] not sufficient to legitimise a right of suspension according to Art 71 CISG'.

Q 71-5

Article 71(3) CISG requires immediate notice of the conforming party's suspension of performance.

(a) What are possible consequences if the conforming party does not give the required notice? See C 71-3 on the one hand and C 71-4 on the other hand.
(b) Which of the two positions do you find more convincing?

(a)   According to the view expressed in C 71-3, the lack of notification allows the debtor to claim damages to cover its loss of profit resulting from the creditor's suspension of performance. In C 71-4, the arbitral tribunal held that the compensation of damages arising out of the suspension should be limited to the immediate and direct damage caused by the suspension.

(b) The position taken in C 71-3 extends the damages to the consequences of the lack of notification in the execution of the whole contract, whereas the position adopted in C 71-4 limits the damages to the immediate consequences of the suspension. The first view seems prohibitively strict and renders the self-help remedy of Article 71 virtually meaningless.

Q 71-6

As regards the time span within which adequate assurance must be given, are there any differences between the Convention and the corresponding provisions in the PICC 2010 and Section 2-609(4) UCC? Which arrangement do you find more appropriate to the needs of international commercial parties?

The Convention does not state any period of time within which adequate assurance must be furnished. The PICC require that it be provided 'within a reasonable time'. Section 2-609(4) UCC is more precise in stating that a failure to provide assurance within a reasonable time not exceeding 30 days constitutes a repudiation of the contract. The solution under the UCC is to be preferred over that of the CISG. Under Article 71(3), the creditor can take no action as long as a breach of contract is impending and no adequate assurance has been provided, whereas the solution of the UCC is clear-cut and does not put the creditor at the mercy of the debtor.

Article 72 CISG

Q 72-1

Things are more complicated both where the notice given is unreasonably short and where the assurance provided by the debtor is insufficient. Should these two cases really be treated in the same way as those where no notice or no assurance at all were provided?

There is no clear answer to those questions. However, based on the idea of a 'second chance' reflected in Article 48 CISG, it seems preferable to give the creditor the possibility to adjust the period fixed in the notice and make it conform to the 'reasonableness' requirement. Likewise, the debtor should have the opportunity to subsequently provide assurance which is 'adequate'.

Q 72-2

Distinguish Article 72 CISG from Articles 71, 49 and 64 CISG.

Articles 72 and 71 both operate in the run-up to performance. Whereas Article 72 allows for an avoidance of the contract, Article 71 provides for a preliminary remedy only. Articles 49 and 64, like Article 72, relate to a fundamental breach and provide for the right to avoid the contract. However, under Articles 49 and 64, the fundamental breach must have actually occurred, whereas Article 72 requires that there clearly will be a fundamental breach in the future.

Q 72-3

How must the requirement that an anticipatory fundamental breach be 'clear' be distinguished from the prerequisite in Article 71 CISG that it must 'become apparent' that one party will not perform a substantial part of its obligations?

It is virtually undisputed that Article 72 CISG requires a higher degree of probability than Article 71. This is implied already in the wording used in Articles 71 and 72, respectively; but, more importantly, it follows from the differences in purpose and legal consequences of Articles 71 and 72.

Q 72-4

(a) What is the purpose of the 'notice' requirement in Article 72(2) CISG?
(b) In which cases will a notice within the meaning of Article 72(2) CISG not be required? See also C 72-1.

(a)   To give the debtor the opportunity to provide adequate assurance and thus dispel doubts about its capacity or willingness to perform.
(b)   Article 72(3) CISG states that a notice is unnecessary if a party has declared its intention not to perform the contract. C 72-1 illustrates this: the declaration of a party not to meet the delivery deadline was regarded as a repudiation of the contract.

Q 72-53

(a) What are the consequences if no notice is given under Article 72(2) CISG?
(b) What happens if the debtor cannot furnish any adequate assurance?

(a)   Failure to give notice deprives the creditor of its right to declare the contract avoided. If such declaration of avoidance has been made without prior notification of the debtor, the creditor itself commits an anticipatory breach of contract within the meaning of Article 72(3) CISG.
(b)   The debtor unable to furnish adequate assurance cannot avert the avoidance of the contract by the creditor.

Q 72-6

(a) How does the UCC settle the conflict between renewed willingness on behalf of the debtor to perform and the creditor's already having resorted to a remedy incompatible with the debtor's performance of the contract?
(b) Has this question been solved under the CISG? What could be a reasonable solution?

(a)   The creditor may resort to any remedy for breach, even though it has notified the repudiating party that it would await the latter's performance.

(b)   The question has not been explicitly settled, but for the purpose of Article 72(2), it must be assumed that if the debtor does not furnish adequate assurance within a reasonable time, the creditor may avail itself of any remedy, including the one to avoid the contract.

Article 73 CISG

Q 73-1

How do you distinguish 'instalment contracts' and simple contracts, several separate agreements, respectively? See also Section 2-612(1) UCC.

Instalment contracts provide for the delivery of goods in separate lots. An instalment contract consists of at least two successive deliveries taking place at different moments in time and which must be severable from each other. It implies that the execution of performance lasts for some time. Those elements distinguish instalment contracts from simple contracts, in which the goods are delivered in one single delivery.

An instalment contract must also be distinguished from the case where several contracts have been concluded. An instalment contract forms a contractual unity for the parties, be it because the counter-performance consists of a single payment, or because all deliveries depend on one single order. Section 2-612(1) UCC gives predominance to an instalment contract even if the parties agreed to have one separated contract per delivery, as soon as the deliveries can be considered as a contractual unity. This is also the way case law under the CISG has dealt with the question: in case of doubt, a contract will be considered as an instalment contract.

Q 73-2

Differentiate between the three situations mentioned in Article 73(1) to (3) CISG and explain their interaction.

Article 73(1) CISG governs the situation where the failure of a party to perform only one of the instalments constitutes a fundamental breach of the contract, without jeopardising the others. Article 73(2) CISG governs the situation where the failure of a party to perform one of the instalments gives good grounds to conclude it will commit a fundamental breach with respect to future instalments. Article 73(3) CISG governs the situation where the failure of a party to perform one of the instalments makes other instalments unusable for the purposes initially contemplated by the parties. Those three situations address different parts of the instalment contract, respectively: the actual instalment (Art 73(1) CISG); future instalments (Art 73(2) CISG); and the whole instalment contract (Art 73(3) CISG).

Q 73-3

How do you distinguish Article 73 from Articles 71 and 72 CISG?

Articles 71 and 72 CISG are general rules applicable both to simple contracts involving one single delivery and to instalment contracts. As to their requirements and effects, see Articles 71 and Article 72 above.

Article 73 CISG specifically governs 'instalment contracts', as defined above in the answer to Q 73-1. Thus, Article 73 CISG provides for remedies tailored to contracts involving several subsequent deliveries of goods.

Q 73-4

(a) For which remedy does Article 73(1) CISG provide in case of fundamental breach in respect of a single instalment?
(b) Compare Article 73(1) CISG to Section 2-612(2) UCC with regard to requirements and available remedies.

(a) Article 73(1) provides for the right to avoid the contract with regard to a single defective instalment. The residual contract remains in force and has to be adjusted to the new situation.
(b) Section 2-612(2) UCC provides for a stricter solution than Article 73(1) CISG: avoidance with regard to the defective instalment is only possible if the seller fails to give adequate assurance of its cure, unless the non-conformity of the instalment substantially impairs the value of the whole contract.

Q 73-5

Article 73(2) CISG allows for an avoidance of the contract in respect of future instalments where there are 'good grounds' to conclude that a fundamental breach will occur with respect to future instalments. The question is whether this probability standard is higher or lower than the probability standard in Articles 71 and 72 CISG.

(a) See C 73-2: according to the tribunal, which of the three provisions provides for the lowest standard and which provides for the highest standard of prognosis?
(b) Note that the view adopted by the tribunal is a minority view. The majority in scholarly writing holds that the lowest probability standard applies in connection with Article 71 CISG and the highest under Article 72 CISG, with Article 73(2) somewhere in-between. Explain why this order has been suggested and why, in particular, Article 71 CISG is considered to provide for the lowest level of prognosis.

(a) The tribunal adopts the view that the lowest level of probability is required in Article 73(2) CISG and the highest in Article 72 CISG, whereas the degree of probability of Article 71 CISG is somewhere in-between.
(b) The level of probability depends on the kind of remedy. Article 72 requires the highest degree of probability because it deals with avoidance of the whole contract. Article 71 CISG deals with suspension of performance and thus with a preliminary remedy; it therefore requires the lowest degree of probability. Article 73(2) CISG allows for the avoidance of future instalments, which do not affect

the part of the contract that has already been performed. The level of probability required in Article 73(2) is thus placed in-between those required in Articles 71 and 72 CISG.

Q 73-6

(a) Give an example of a situation that would give rise to avoidance pursuant to Article 73(3) CISG.
(b) Do you find similar solutions within the UCC?

(a) Examples may be the supply of uniform materials for a specific building (cladding, roof, windows), of material necessary for a special production item of a specified size (important in textile or chemical industry), or the supply of a product for a specific group of customers according to their instructions.
(b) Section 2-612 UCC states a rule similar to Article 73(3) CISG.

Article 74 CISG

Q 74-1

Describe the damages concept of the CISG. In particular:

(a) what is the basic principle as to when a party will be entitled to damages?
(b) how is the no-fault rule attenuated?

(a) The CISG is based on the full compensation principle without any fault on the part of the breaching party. Any loss sustained is recoverable.
(b) By way of the foreseeability rule (Art 74, sentence 2 CISG) as well as Article 79 CISG and Article 80 CISG.

Q 74-2

Compare the CISG to PICC 2010:

(a) with regard to the possibility of combining damages with other remedies.
(b) with regard to the exemption rule. Do the PICC 2010 embody the same features of the damages concept as the CISG?

(a) Article 7.4.1 PICC 2010 explicitly mentions the possibility of combining damages with other remedies. In the CISG, this possibility can be found in Articles 45, 61 CISG.
(b) Again, Article 7.4.1 PICC 2010 explicitly mentions the possibility that non-performance may be excused; whereas under the CISG, Article 79 CISG has to be taken into consideration. There is no explicit reference in Article 74 CISG.

Q 74-3

Explain the distinction between the various types of losses as under the UCC.

'Direct loss' is the difference in value of the goods, which may be calculated either having regard to a concrete substitute transaction or to the market price. Furthermore, 'incidental damages' and 'consequential damages' can be distinguished.

Q 74-4

Are there any losses that can only be allocated to one of those categories with difficulty?

Pain and suffering.

Q 74-5

Why, in your opinion, does the CISG refrain from specifying particular types of losses?

Because domestic connotations differ considerably and the CISG aims to build up a neutral concept.

Q 74-6

(a) *Read C 74-1. Is it possible to accumulate various types of losses, for example, consequential and incidental damages?*
(b) *On which principle can the answer to (a) be based?*
(c) *Based on these principles, do you agree with the reasoning of the first instance as reported in C 74-1?*

(a) Yes, different losses may be compensated at the same time.
(b) The full compensation principle.
(c) Yes. The expenses for which damages were denied would have to be borne by Delchi even if the contract had been fully performed.

Q 74-7

(a) *What is the decisive criterion for determining whether or not losses are to be compensated?*
(b) *Can the aggrieved party claim damages for expenditure that would have occurred in any case?*
(c) *Can the aggrieved party claim damages for ongoing charges, such as renting localities, machinery and electricity bills?*
(d) *What would be the situation if the buyer had launched a broad advertising campaign for various goods, including, but not limited to, the goods that the seller failed to deliver properly?*

(a) Losses may be claimed as incidental damages when the expenditures became futile.

(b) In general, no.

(c) If the aggrieved party receives damages for lost profit, no recovery may be had.

(d) The loss would have to be attributed according to the percentage of defective goods.

Q 74-8

On what do the courts focus when deciding whether or not debt collection costs should be recoverable? See C 74-2 and C 74-3.

In general, costs for debt collection are regarded to be recoverable if they are reasonable.

Q 74-9

Is there any possibility of imposing attorneys' fees on the other party under Article 74 CISG? See C 74-4.

C 74-4 left the question open as to whether pre-trial attorneys' fees may be recoverable under Article 74 CISG. However, it seems preferable to also deal with pre-trial attorneys' fees under the applicable procedural laws.

Q 74-10

Read the decision of the Amtsgericht Alsfeld *in C 74-3, and answer the following questions.*

(a) Why was the aggrieved party denied its debt collection costs?

(b) Would it have been able to recover them if the lawyer who represented it in court was the same lawyer who had tried to collect the outstanding sum? Which law would have governed that claim?

(a) Relying on an Italian lawyer was seen as a breach of the duty to mitigate under Article 77 CISG.

(b) Compensation could be had under these circumstances according to the applicable procedural law.

Q 74-11

What does C 74-4 state on the question of whether the aggrieved party will be compensated for the costs of legal proceedings? In particular:

(a) which law governs the costs of legal proceedings?

(b) for what crucial reason did the court refuse to allow damages for legal expenses?

(c) why is it doubtful, according to C 74-4, that the USA would have signed the CISG if 'loss' was intended to include attorneys' fees?

(a)   The *lex fori*; the applicable procedural law.
(b)   There were two main reasons; the first relating to the procedural/substantive divide; the second being that only a winning claimant but not a winning defendant could recover legal costs under Article 74 CISG.
(c)   Because it would contradict the 'American rule', according to which each party bears its own legal costs.

Q 74-12

Do you see any practical difficulties resulting from extra-judicial legal costs being governed by the CISG?

The same reasoning as developed in C 74-4 regarding judicial legal costs equally applies to extra-judicial legal costs. Again, only the winning claimant but not the winning defendant may recover the costs as damages.

Q 74-13

Are losses caused by currency fluctuations to be compensated? See C 74-5.

Losses caused by currency devaluation are recoverable if the creditor converts the currencies immediately after receipt.

· Q 74-14

(a) Define 'loss of profit'.
(b) Under what circumstances does the differentiation between loss of profit and other damages become relevant?
(c) Why is lost profit usually more uncertain than other damages?

(a)   Any deprivation of gain that the aggrieved party would have been able to realise if the contract had been duly performed.
(b)   If the aggrieved party claims loss of profit, costs that it would have had to bear if the contract had been duly performed, may not be compensated for. Furthermore, under Article 44 CISG, loss of profit cannot be claimed even if the buyer has a reasonable excuse for failing to give the required notice.
(c)   Because it usually accrues in the future and thus has a speculative element.

Q 74-15

(a) Does Article 74 CISG state the standard of proof that the party claiming loss of profit must satisfy?
(b) Compare your answer to (a) with Article 7.4.3 PICC 2010. Are there, in practice, any differences to how the courts determine the level of proof under the CISG?

(a)   Article 74 CISG itself does not state a standard of proof. However, it is currently held that the standard of proof can be derived as a general principle under the CISG. The standard thus developed should be one of reasonable certainty.
(b)   The standard is the same.

Q 74-16

(a) *How did the Court of Appeals calculate* Delchi's *loss of profit in C 74-6, and on which rules did it base its calculation?*
(b) *The* Rotorex *case in C 74-6 deals, inter alia, with a so-called 'lost volume sale'. Can you explain what this means?*

(a) Claimant's lost profits were determined by calculating the hypothetical revenues less the hypothetical variable costs that would have been incurred.
(b) The seller would have been able to sell more as it had other customers and sufficient inventory and capacity.

Q 74-17

Article 74 allows for liabilities towards third parties to be compensated. What are the requirements for this compensation, and how are such damages to be limited?

The seller must be liable for breach of contract and the buyer's liability towards third parties must have been foreseeable.

Q 74-18

(a) *Is loss of reputation necessarily reflected in money?*
(b) *Does the CISG allow for (non-material) loss of goodwill? See C 74-7.*
(c) *Compare the solution under the CISG with the PICC 2010. Are there any differences?*

(a) The financial amount of loss of reputation may be hard to prove.
(b) In C 74-7, compensation for loss of goodwill was denied because it was not possible to calculate the exact losses resulting therefrom. However, this approach seems very Germanic. The CISG does not limit compensation to exactly measurable financial losses.
(c) According to Article 7.4.2(2) and Article 7.4.3(3) PICC 2010, non-pecuniary losses, which include loss of reputation, may be compensated for. Where the exact amount cannot be calculated, the determination is at the discretion of the court.

Q 74-19

(a) *Which level of proof did the court in C 74-7 apply for establishing loss of reputation?*
(b) *Why would it place an insurmountable burden on the aggrieved party if it were required to calculate the damages for loss of reputation exactly?*

(a) It required sufficiently substantiated submissions by way of the buyer's business papers.
(b) Loss of reputation could never be calculated exactly and thus there could never be compensation.

Q 74-20

In some legal systems, damages are awarded for the mere loss of a chance. For example, where a horse, as a result of delays in transport, arrives too late to run in a race, its owner may be able to recover a certain amount of the prize money if it can be established that the horse was the favourite to win.

(a) Does the CISG cover the loss of a chance?
(b) Why does Article 7.4.3(2) PICC 2010 explicitly mention loss of a chance?
(c) If loss of a chance were not included in Article 74 CISG, how could this conflict with other principles underlying the CISG?

(a) It does not explicitly mention the loss of a chance, but there is no reason why it should be excluded.
(b) The PICC were heavily influenced by French legal thinking. Under French law, loss of a chance has long been held recoverable.
(c) It would undermine the principle of full compensation.

Q 74-21

What is the underlying idea of the foreseeability test? See the English decision of Hadley v Baxendale.

Where liability does not depend on fault, the foreseeability operates to limit liability. There are slight differences between the different approaches. Whereas *Hadley v Baxendale* and the Restatement (Second), Contracts, talk about a 'probable' result of the breach and the Chinese Contract Law speaks of the 'likely loss', under Article 74 CISG a 'possible' consequence is sufficient.

Q 74-22

If one party—after the conclusion of the contract, but before committing the breach of contract—learns of circumstances which indicate a risk of extraordinary loss for the other party, is this relevant to the extent of the first party's liability? See C 74-8.

No, it is not. It is decisive whether the consequences were foreseeable at the time of the conclusion of the contract.

Q 74-23

(a) What kind of loss was at issue in C 74-8?
(b) How certain must the foreseeability of a loss be, according to C 74-8?

(a) Consequential loss.
(b) An objective standard—that of a reasonable person—is applied.

Q 74-24

Which party bears the burden of proving whether or not the loss was foreseeable?

The claimant bears the burden of proof that it sustained loss. The respondent has to prove that this loss was not foreseeable.

Q 74-25

(a) Is there a way to derogate from Articles 74 to 77 CISG? See C 74-8.
(b) What do we call such clauses, and what is their effect?
(c) What factors are relevant in determining the degree to which such a clause displaces the CISG provisions?
(d) Which law governs the question of whether such a contract clause is valid?
(e) If the limiting clause is found to be invalid, what law will displace it?

(a) Yes, according to Article 6 CISG, the parties may derogate from or vary the effect of any of the CISG's provisions.
(b) Exclusion or limitation of liability clauses. Depending on the clause, liability is excluded or limited.
(c) This is a question of interpretation.
(d) In general, this is a question of validity, which is governed by domestic law according to Article 4(a) CISG. However, general principles under the CISG can be developed on a comparative basis.
(e) The CISG.

Article 75 CISG

Q 75-1

(a) Which situations does Article 75 CISG govern?
(b) Was it necessary to establish Article 75 alongside Article 74 CISG?
(c) If the aggrieved party does not proceed under Article 75 CISG, is it deprived of any other remedies available under the CISG?

(a) According to the wording of Article 75 CISG, the contract must have been avoided and a concrete substitute transaction must have taken place.
(b) Under the principle of full compensation, a substitute transaction could be used to calculate damages for non-performance. Article 75 CISG offers an easy way to prove the non-performance loss.
(c) If no avoidance has taken place, damages may still be recovered under Article 74 CISG according to C 75-1. Furthermore, damages in the amount of a concrete substitute transaction may be asked for if the other party had seriously and finally refused to perform (see C 75-2). C 75-2 seems to leave the question open as to whether the damages claim can be based on Article 75 CISG or on Article 74 CISG. The decision emphasises that the substitute transaction prior to avoidance of the contract was reasonable, preventive and ultimately successful.

Q 75-2

(a) What factors are used to determine whether the cover transaction satisfies the 'reasonability test' in Article 75 CISG?

(b) On which other provision of the CISG can the requirement that the cover transaction be reasonable be based?

(a) Quality and amount of the goods, time of the substitute transaction.
(b) Article 77 CISG, the duty to mitigate damages.

Q 75-3

What is the consequence if there is a significant difference between the contract price and the price in the substitute transaction?

Depending on the circumstances this could lead to a reduction in damages because of the duty to mitigate damages under Article 77 CISG.

Q 75-4

(a) Is there a guideline as to what constitutes a reasonable time?
(b) When will the reasonable time begin to run? See C 75-4.

(a) In general, the reasonableness depends upon the circumstances of the case.
(b) The reasonable time begins to run at the time of the avoidance of the contract. Article 77 CISG may call for a cover transaction before performance would be due under the contract.

Q 75-5

(a) Compared to corresponding legal provisions from other legal systems, does Article 75 constitute a generally acknowledged rule?
(b) Do the domestic legal provisions also require a termination of the contract prior to the cover transaction?

(a) The rules laid down in Article 7.4.5 PICC 2010 and in the UCC are comparable. Other legal systems know similar rules.
(b) The domestic provisions reprinted here (UCC and OR) do not require a prior avoidance of the contract.

Article 76 CISG

Q 76-1

What is the idea underlying Article 76 CISG?

In cases where no substitute transaction can be pinpointed, Article 76 CISG provides for an abstract calculation of damages.

Q 76-2

(a) When is it possible to claim damages under Article 76 CISG without declaring avoidance of the contract according to C 76-1?

(b) If a calculation of damages under Article 76 CISG is not allowed, which calculation of damages will nonetheless be possible and on which provision will the claimant rely?

(c) Does the methodological order of the damages provisions indicate whether the CISG favours the method of concrete calculation of damages over the abstract method, or vice versa?

(a) In C 76-1 it was held that if the obligor unambiguously and definitely repudiates the contract, it would be a mere formality to require a separate declaration of avoidance. The obligee may rely on Article 76 CISG without prior declaration of avoidance as the seller's requiring an explicit declaration of avoidance would constitute a *venire contra factum proprium*.

(b) Damages may still be asked for under Article 74 CISG. Non-performance loss must be calculated based on the value of the goods which in turn can be assessed by the market price.

(c) Articles 74 to 76 CISG seem to prefer a concrete calculation as suggested by civil law legal systems.

Q 76-3

(a) It has been said that there is a danger inherent in the method of determining the point in time relevant for determination of the market price *(Art 76(1), sentence 1 CISG)*, in that the creditor speculatively delays avoidance of the contract. Explain this concern.

(b) Which tool does the CISG provide to counter such abuse?

(c) May the creditor be obliged to avoid the contract before the time of performance?

(a) As the market price is determined upon the time of avoidance of the contract, a creditor seeing the market rising may speculate at the expense of the debtor.

(b) Article 77 CISG (mitigation of damages).

(c) Following on from Article 77 CISG, a duty to avoid the contract before the time of performance may be imposed on the creditor in view of a market development detrimental to the debtor. However, it will extremely difficult to prove that the creditor actually foresaw such a development.

Q 76-4

(a) If the aggrieved party has undertaken a substitute transaction, is it still entitled to claim damages under Article 76 CISG? Consider, for example, the situation where the substitute transaction does not include all of the goods.

(b) Which difficulties will the respondent who wants to hinder the claimant from claiming *(higher)* damages under Article 76 CISG *(than it would be entitled to claim under Art 75)* encounter if claimant is a 'permanent market trader', that is it buys and sells those kinds of goods continuously?

(a) In general, if a substitute transaction has taken place, the creditor must calculate its damages according to Article 75 CISG. Where the substitute transaction does not include all of the goods, a calculation based partially on Article 75 CISG and partially on Article 76 CISG.

(b)   The obligor will not be able to prove which of the contracts amounts to a substitute transaction.

Q 76-5

(a)   Which criteria determine whether there is a current market price?
(b)   Who must prove the existence of a current market price?

(a)   Whether there is a market where the goods are usually traded. A market regularly exists for commodities and ready-made products.
(b)   The burden of proof is on the creditor.

Q 76-6

How will the damages be calculated if there is no market price for the goods in question, neither at the place of performance nor at the substitute place?

If there is a concrete substitute transaction, damages will be calculated according to Article 75 CISG. Under Article 74 CISG, the value of the goods must be estimated, whereby any development of related prices may be taken into account.

Q 76-7

Compare Article 76(2) CISG to the domestic law provisions.

(a)   Do the other provisions also allow for additional damages other than those representing the difference between the contract and the market price?
(b)   Do they require a termination of the contract prior to the abstract calculation of the difference between the contract and the market price?
(c)   Which other provision contains a similar rule as to the determination of the market price?

(a)   Yes, although in Article 191(3) and 215(2) OR this is not explicitly provided for.
(b)   Whereas Article 7.4.6 PICC 2010 like Article 76 CISG explicitly requires prior avoidance, neither the UCC nor the OR contains such a prerequisite.
(c)   Article 7.4.6 PICC 2010.

Article 77 CISG

Q 77-1

(a)   What concept underlies Article 77 CISG?
(b)   What are the legal consequences if the aggrieved party fails to take 'such measures'?
(c)   To what kind of remedies does Article 77 CISG apply?
(d)   Are there similar provisions in domestic sales laws?

(a)   Avoidable losses should not be compensated.
(b)   Exclusion or reduction of damages.

(c) According to its wording, systematic position, and drafting history, Article 77 CISG only applies to damages. However, Article 77 CISG must also have implications for other remedies. Hence, delaying avoidance of the contract for speculative reasons, although it does not exclude avoidance, may lead to a reduction in damages.

(d) All legal systems acknowledge the principle of the duty to mitigate damages.

Q 77-2

(a) *Specify the most important factors that a court must take into account in order to determine whether the aggrieved party acted in accordance with Article 77 CISG. See C 77-2.*

(b) *At what point in time are measures to mitigate damages to be taken? Consider seasonal goods, goods in a highly volatile market, non-perishable goods, the urgency in receiving the goods, etc.*

(c) *When will a cover transaction be necessary in order to comply with Article 77 CISG? See C 77-1.*

(d) *Is a party obliged to conclude a substitute transaction with the contract breacher?*

(a) The most important factors to consider are the certainty of the breach, possible time constraints, reasonableness, and the availability of substitute transactions.

(b) At the earliest point in time when it becomes clear that the contract is breached and loss will occur. The point in time may nevertheless vary. A speedier reaction is called for in the case of seasonal goods, goods in a volatile market or when the goods are urgently needed and loss is imminent than in cases of non-perishable goods.

(c) In general, it depends upon the circumstances of the case. The court in C 77-1 takes a very restrictive approach in upholding the performance principle. In contrast, the court in C 77-2 even required the buyer to contract for substitute goods with its direct competitor.

(d) If the breach has not entirely destroyed the trust between the parties, the aggrieved party may be obliged to contract with the breaching party. For example, if the seller refuses to perform at the contract price but offers the goods at a price still below the current market price.

Q 77-3

Decide whether the party complied with Article 77 CISG in the following cases:

(a) *Seller does not resell the goods as long as the buyer, which is the party in breach, could still claim performance of the contract.*

(b) *Seller does not resell goods which had been made on the buyer's instructions.*

(c) *Seller collects debts through an agent or a lawyer where the legal situation is not particularly complicated.*

(d) *Buyer fails to resell defective, rapidly deteriorating goods.*

(e) *Buyer uses its own buffer stocks of coal where the seller is late in delivery.*

(f) *Buyer fails to look for replacement goods in markets other than the local region.*

(g) *Buyer offers the goods delivered too late by the seller to its own buyer at a 10% discount.*

(h) Buyer fails to examine the shipments before mixing the shipments together.

(a) It depends on whether the seller is obliged to avoid the contract, See C 77-1 and Q 77-2 (c)).
(b) It depends on whether there is a market for the goods.
(c) If seller can be expected to collect the debts itself, employing an agent or lawyer constitutes a breach of the duty to mitigate damages under Article 77 CISG.
(d) It depends on whether the buyer is knowledgeable and has access to the respective market.
(e) In this case, buyer complied with its duty under Article 77 CISG.
(f) It depends on whether the buyer is knowledgeable and has access to markets other than the local region.
(g) Article 77 CISG is complied with if the buyer can thus prevent higher damages.
(h) In general, this is a question of Articles 38 and 39 CISG. In extreme circumstances, the duty to examine may form part of the duty to mitigate damages under Article 77 CISG.

Q 77-4

(a) To what extent will the aggrieved party's damages be reduced if it fails to comply with Article 77 CISG? See C 77-4.
(b) Who bears the burden of proof for compliance with the duty to mitigate damages?

(a) Reduction as far as the loss could be prevented by reasonable measures.
(b) The party breaching the contract bears the burden of proof that the other party violated its duty to mitigate damages.

Q 77-5

Can the party who incurred expenses in order to comply with Article 77 CISG be compensated for these expenses? See also Article 88(3) CISG. On which provision(s) would the creditor base its calculation?

The costs incurred in mitigating damages may be claimed as part of damages under Article 74 CISG.

Article 78 CISG

Q 78-1

Which duty does Article 78 CISG establish?

The general duty to pay interest.

Q 78-2

What follows from the fact that the CISG itself has a provision on interest?

Interest is a matter of substantive law and not one of procedural law as it has been perceived in many legal systems belonging to the Common Law.

Q 78-3

On which sums is interest to be paid?

On any sum of money that is due. This encompasses not only the purchase price but also damages, repayment after price reduction, reimbursement for expenses. For repayment of the purchase price after avoidance see Article 84(1) CISG.

Q 78-4

Why has the applicable interest rate not been settled in Article 78 CISG?

Because no agreement was possible at the diplomatic conference in 1980.

Q 78-5

(a) *When will the purchase price fall due? See Article 58 CISG.*
(b) *Has the question of the point in time at which other monetary obligations fall due been expressly settled in the CISG?*
(c) *Why will the debtor who is entitled to withhold its performance (Arts 71(1), 81(2), sentence 2 CISG) not be obliged to pay interest?*

(a) Primarily, this has to be decided based on the contract terms. If nothing is specified in the contract, Article 58 CISG stipulates that the purchase price is to be paid reciprocally in exchange with the goods.
(b) No, other monetary obligations become due as soon as they accrue.
(c) As long as there is a right to withhold performance, the sum is not yet due.

Q 78-6

Originally, a topic of dispute was whether a sum must have been made certain ('liqui-dated') in order to be interest-bearing. Can you explain why there used to be a controversy, due to this uncertainty, about whether or not interest could accrue? (It should be noted that, nowadays, the legal majority does not require a liquidated sum in order to incur interest.)

If the amount is uncertain, the debtor may be prevented from paying.

Q 78-7

Is compound interest possible under Article 78 CISG (See C 78-1)?

Article 78 CISG does not expressly prohibit compound interest. It is disputed in scholarly writing whether it may be granted or not.

Q 78-8

(a)   *Describe the different approaches in determining the applicable interest rate under the CISG.*
(b)   *What general principle of the CISG may be relied upon in determining the interest rate?*
(c)   *If this principle is applied, what effect does this have on the concrete interest rate?*
(d)   *Which interest rate is provided for in the PICC 2010 (Art 7.4.9(2))? Are there any problems in applying this rate?*
(e)   *What problems can you identify when relying on the subsidiary applicable domestic law?*
(f)   *Could there be a compromise between a truly uniform determination and reliance on the private international law/domestic law approach?*

(a)   Primarily, it is up to the parties to provide for an interest rate to be applied (C 78-1). As Article 78 CISG does not provide for an interest rate, there is a gap in the meaning of Article 7(2) CISG. The question is how this gap may be filled. One approach (C 78-2) is to determine the applicable interest rate autonomously in conformity with general principles underlying the CISG. Another possibility is to rely on the PICC (C 78-3). And finally, to resort to domestic law that is subsidiarily applicable by virtue of the rules of private international law (C 78-4).
(b)   The principle of full compensation (Art 74 CISG), see C 78-2.
(c)   There are two different sub-questions to this question. First, the place at which the interest is to be calculated has to be determined. In case of the purchase price, for example, this may be either the place of payment or the place of business of the seller. Having determined the relevant place, different interest rates might come into play. There may be a statutory interest rate, and there may be different interest rates for borrowers and investors.
(d)   Article 7.4.9(2) PICC 2010 provides for the average bank short-term lending rate to prime borrowers prevailing for the currency of payment at the place for payment. This rate fluctuates daily. Although it is possible to average a rate for the time passed until a judgment or award, it is not possible to foresee its development for the time after the award/judgment until effective payment.
(e)   This approach undermines uniform interpretation and application of the CISG. The rules of private international law usually lead to the law of the State of the place of business of the seller. Although this solution may be appropriate in relation to the purchase price where the seller is the creditor, it may not lead to just results in case of a damages claim of the buyer.
(f)   One might start from the general principle of full compensation under the CISG (Art 74 CISG) which may lead to the place of business of the creditor and then apply the (statutory) interest rate there. This solution on the one hand guarantees uniformity as to the place and certainty as well as foreseeability as to the rate on the other hand.

Q 78-9

Does the duty to pay interest on sums in arrears prejudice a claim for damages recoverable under Article 74 CISG? See C 78-5 and Article 7.4.9(3) PICC 2010.

No. Article 74 CISG is still applicable. However, Article 74 CISG is less favourable to the creditor than Article 78 CISG as under Article 74 CISG, the creditor must prove its loss and thereby reveal details of its business.

Q 78-10

(a) To the extent that interest is recoverable, does the aggrieved party have a choice between Article 74 and Article 78 CISG?
(b) In which situations will the creditor prefer to proceed under Article 74 CISG? When will Article 78 CISG provide the only suitable basis?

(a) Yes.
(b) If the loss suffered by the creditor exceeds the interest rate, it will proceed under Article 74 CISG. If loss cannot be proven or was not foreseeable for the debtor at the time of the conclusion of the contract (Art 74, sentence 2 CISG), Article 78 CISG will provide the only suitable basis. Furthermore, certain provisions of the CISG, for example, Article 77 CISG applies to damages only, but not to interest under Article 78 CISG.

Article 79 CISG

Q 79-1

(a) Which principle is laid down in Article 79 CISG?
(b) Describe the liability concept of the CISG, considering Articles 45, 61 and 79 CISG.
(c) Compare this liability concept to those found in domestic legal systems and the PICC 2010.

(a) Exemption from liability which is dealt with in domestic legal systems under *force majeure*, impossibility, frustration or impracticability.
(b) The CISG is based on the principle of strict liability without fault with the possibility of exceptional exemption.
(c) The original civil law approach is fault-based whereas the strict liability approach could be found in the common law legal systems. The modern approach advocated by the CISG has been followed by PICC as well as by the PRC contract law.

Q 79-2

To which contractual duties does Article 79 CISG apply?

It applies to all contractual duties, be they core duties or only additional duties. In principle, Article 79 CISG may also apply to seller's duty to deliver goods in conformity with the contract according to Article 35 CISG. However, those cases will be very rare.

Q 79-3

At which point in time must the impediment occur in order to fall under Article 79 CISG?

Usually, the impediment occurs after the conclusion of the contract. However, Article 79 CISG should also be applied to impediments that, without the knowledge of the parties, had already occurred before the conclusion of the contract, ie to cases of so-called initial impossibility. For example, it may be almost impossible in case of goods *in transitu* to determine whether the goods were lost before or after the conclusion of the contract.

Q 79-4

Describe the circumstances under which an impediment in the sense of Article 79 CISG can be found.

Exemption will often be considered in typical cases of so-called *force majeure*, eg natural phenomena and catastrophes, acts of war or terrorist attacks. It is disputed whether State interventions, such as export or import bans, may also lead to an impediment.

Q 79-5

Could the seller be exempted under Article 79 CISG if its supplier fails (see C 79-1)?

In general exemption will be very rare as the seller bears the procurement risk.

Q 79-6

Could the debtor be exempted under Article 79 CISG if it was already in breach of contract when the impediment occurred?

If the impediment occurred while the debtor was already in breach, causality between the impediment and the non-performance will usually be missing, as in this case the breach is the relevant cause for the non-performance and not the impediment.

Q 79-7

What obligations are imposed on the seller who is not able to deliver the goods as originally intended (see C 79-2)?

The seller is bound to overcome the consequences of the impediment. It has to find a commercially reasonable substitute.

Q 79-8

Compare the prerequisites in Article 79(1) CISG, Article 6.2.2 and 6.2.3 PICC 2010 and § 313 BGB.

Article 79(1) CISG does not explicitly mention hardship at all. However, the criteria under which an exemption may be claimed are quite similar to those mentioned in Article 6.2.2 PICC 2010. The same applies to the threshold laid down in § 313(1) BGB. Article 79(1) CISG as well as Article 6.2.2 PICC 2010 can be applied to cases where there was an initial imbalance between the obligations unknown to the parties. § 313(1) BGB, however, only applies to subsequent changes of circumstances.

Q 79-9

Compare C 79-3 and C 79-4.

(a) What provisions do they apply to cases of hardship?
(b) What is the relevant threshold beyond which hardship can be found?

(a) C 79-3 obviously applies Article 79 CISG. C 79-4 suggests that hardship is not covered by the CISG; instead, the court applies Article 6.2.2 and 6.2.3 PICC.
(b) Whereas C 79-3 denies hardship where the price had tripled, C 79-4 even accepts an increase of 70% as qualifying for hardship.

Q 79-10

What are the consequences of hardship under Article 79(1) CISG, Article 6.2.3 PICC 2010 and § 313(3) BGB?

Under Article 79(1) CISG, the sole consequence is an exemption of the non-performing party from liability for damages. There is no explicit duty to renegotiate. However, applying Article 77 CISG may well yield similar results by requiring the aggrieved party to deal with the contract breacher. Article 6.2.3 PICC 2010 provides for an explicit duty to renegotiate as well as the power of the court not only to avoid the contract but also to adapt it to the changed circumstances. § 313(3) BGB does not contain a duty to renegotiate but provides for adaptation and possible avoidance of the contract.

Q 79-11

On an examination of the wording of Article 79(2) CISG, would you say that Article 79(2) CISG makes it more difficult for the breaching party to be exempt than Article 79(1) CISG?

Yes, there must be a double exemption; first, it is necessary for the party itself to be exempt under Article 79(1) CISG and, secondly, the person engaged by the party would also have to be exempt.

Q 79-12

Are suppliers covered by Article 79(2) CISG (see C 79-5)?

In C 79-5, the question of whether suppliers fall under Article 79(2) CISG was not finally decided as the risk of non-conforming goods was deemed to lie in the sphere of the seller.

Q 79-13

It has been stated that a manufacturer does not fall under Article 79(2) CISG. How else could a seller's liability for its manufacturer be established? See C 79-6.

It is determined by whether the circumstances are within the sphere of risk of the seller and thus in the realm of Article 79(1) CISG.

Q 79-14

Numerous decisions state that the party relying on Article 79 CISG bears the burden of proof. This is expressly laid down in the wording of Article 79(1) CISG: 'if he proves that the failure [to perform] was due to an impediment beyond his control'. Which general principle can be drawn from this provision?

Each party bears the burden of proof for facts that are advantageous for its position.

Q 79-15

If one of the parties can successfully rely on Article 79 CISG, does this hinder the other party from exercising any right other than claiming damages, in particular, the right to claim performance?

According to Article 79(5) CISG, the exemption only relates to damages and not to other remedies. However, it would be contradictory if in case of an impediment beyond the control of the debtor, it could be sentenced to specific performance. If specific performance is not deemed to be excluded by Article 79 CISG, such a result must be achieved by relying on Article 28 CISG.

Article 80 CISG

Q 80-1

Which rule does Article 80 CISG establish?

Article 80 CISG lays down the principle that an aggrieved party may not rely on a failure of performance that was caused by itself.

Q 80-2

Explain the scope of application of Articles 77 and 80 CISG, respectively.

Article 80 CISG relates to situations where the debtor caused the breach itself; Article 77 CISG concerns cases in which the creditor failed to mitigate the loss after a breach which was solely caused by the debtor. In case where the creditor caused the failure of performance, under Article 80 CISG all remedies are excluded in contrast to Article 77 CISG which in principle only relates to damages.

Q 80-3

(a) Explain the differences between Article 79 and Article 80 CISG.
(b) Compare Article 80 CISG with the provisions from other legal systems. How do the latter differ from Article 80 CISG with regard to their scope of application?

(a) Under Article 79 CISG, the debtor is only exempted from the liability for damages, whereas—again—Article 80 CISG relates to the breach itself.
(b) PICC 2010 are comparable to the CISG; Article 7.1.2 PICC 2010 equals Article 80 CISG whereas the counterpart to Article 77 CISG can be found in Article 7.4.7 PICC 2010. In contrast to this approach, many civil law legal systems do not have a clear distinction but treat both situations under the same statutory rule.

Q 80-4

Under Article 80 CISG, the consequences where the debtor's failure to perform is caused by both parties are disputed. Is there a total or partial exclusion of remedies?

The clear wording of Article 80 CISG ('to the extent that') militates for a partial exclusion.

Q 80-5

How did the seller in the C 80-1 cause the buyer's breach of contract?

The buyer was not able to open the letter of credit because the seller did not name the port of shipment.

Q 80-6

(a) Can you think of a situation where the debtor, instead of relying on Article 80 CISG, will be required to make an effort to overcome the disturbance caused by the creditor?
(b) On which general principle could such a duty of the debtor be based?

(a) Where the debtor realises, for example, that information given by the creditor will necessarily lead to a breach of contract, it must inform the creditor accordingly.
(b) On the principle of good faith and fair dealing in international trade.

Q 80-7

When will the debtor, who was not able to fulfil one or several of its contractual duties due to an act or omission of the creditor, be entitled to remedies against the creditor?

If the causation of the debtor's failure to perform at the same time amounts to a breach of a (additional) duty of the creditor.

Article 81 CISG

Q 81-1

(a) Which general rule does Article 81 CISG establish consequent upon the avoidance of the contract?

(b) How is the statement that avoidance does not entirely annul the contract to be understood? See C 81-1.

(a) Article 81 CISG states that, upon declaration of avoidance, any unperformed original obligation is cancelled.

(b) Damages claims that may have existed prior to the avoidance of the contract or that arise in connection with it persist, as do dispute settlement clauses. As is shown in C 81-1, avoidance triggers also the obligation to make concurrent restitution of what had been supplied or paid under the contract. Accordingly, avoidance changes the contract into a winding-up relationship.

Q 81-2

What are the legal consequences if no effective avoidance is made?

If no effective avoidance is made, the contract continues to exist.

Q 81-3

Most arbitration laws and institutional arbitration rules state that the arbitration agreement is to be regarded as an agreement separate from the contract and thus capable of remaining in force independently of the contract ('separability doctrine'). Discuss whether, in light of this, it was necessary to mention in Article 81(1) CISG that dispute settlement clauses remain unaffected by the avoidance of the contract.

With regard to arbitration clauses, such a provision was probably not necessary. However, the term employed in Article 81(1) CISG is broad enough to encompass any dispute settlement arrangement and is therefore not superfluous.

Q 81-4

What is, according to C 81-1 and the CISG Advisory Council, the place of making restitution of the goods and the price, respectively? Could there be other solutions?

In C 81-1, the view was adopted that the place of performance for the obligations concerning restitution should mirror the place of performance for the primary contractual obligations. The Advisory Council holds that, as a principle, restitution of the goods and repayment of the purchase price should be made at the buyer's premises. Other solutions suggest relying on the applicable domestic law, because it would not be possible to infer from the definition of the seller's place of business as the place of performance whether it was intended to specify the principle of performance at the seller's place of business or rather the general principle of payment at the creditor's place of business, and that therefore gap-filling according to Article 7(2) should not be possible. It has also been argued that all restitutionary obligations should be fulfilled at the innocent party's place of business. This view is less persuasive, as the Convention does not support a 'punishing' of the party in breach.

Article 82 CISG

Q 82-1

(a) Which principle is embodied in Article 82(1) CISG?
(b) Compare Article 82(1) with Article 7.3.6(1) and (2) PICC 2010 as well as with Article 207 OR and Article 1647 CC and describe the differences in relation to Article 82 CISG.

(a) Article 82(1) CISG embodies the principle of restitution of the goods in an unimpaired condition.

(b) The provisions of the PICC and the CC do not bar the buyer from avoiding the contract where it is unable to return the goods. Article 207 OR is similar to the CISG but bars avoidance only where the buyer destroyed the goods or sold or transformed them.

Q 82-2

How is the principle established in Article 82(1) CISG 'watered down'? See Article 82(2) CISG.

Article 82(2) CISG enshrines three exceptions of great practical importance: for the purposes of determining the buyer's ability to declare the contract avoided, the seller bears the risk of loss or deterioration of the goods where those are due to the seller's breach of contract, but also where they are due to casualty or *force majeure*, or where the goods were consumed or transformed in the normal course of use or resold in the normal course of business.

Q 82-3

(a) To what extent does Article 82(2) CISG provide for a particular risk allocation mechanism to govern the situation after the contract has been declared avoided?
(b) What is the idea underlying Article 82(2) CISG?

(a) After avoidance of the contract, the seller bears the risk of (fortuitous) loss, deterioration, alteration or consummation of the goods although the seller has performed its obligation to deliver. Article 82(2) is thus deviating from the general rules on the passing of risk (Arts 67–69 CISG), according to which the buyer normally bears the risk once the goods have been delivered.

(b) The idea is to shift the risk of loss or deterioration of the goods that had passed to the buyer in conformity with Articles 67 to 69 CISG back to the seller; this is justified in those cases where the contract is avoided because of a breach of contract on behalf of the seller.

Q 82-4

(a) Why was the buyer allowed to declare the contract avoided in C 82-1?
(b) According to the court, does it matter at what point in time the alienation of the goods, consequent upon an examination within the meaning of Article 38 CISG, takes place?

(a) Because the goods deteriorated during their examination according to Article 38 CISG. The fact that the buyer processed the entirety of the goods did not bar the buyer from declaring avoidance because the defects in the goods became apparent only in the course of processing.
(b) No. The decisive point was the reason for which the goods were altered, that is, the fact that the goods were altered in order to comply with the examination duty of Article 38 CISG.

Q 82-5

It has been disputed whether Article 82 CISG should apply only where it is the buyer who declares avoidance, or whether it should also apply where the contract is terminated by mutual agreement or (unilaterally) by the seller. What do you think? It will be helpful to consider which party should be protected by Article 82 CISG.

Article 82 CISG is specially tailored to the case where the buyer is entitled to declare the contract avoided as a result of a breach of contract by the seller, with the consequence that risk of loss or deterioration of the goods is completely borne by the seller. Where it is the seller who has the right to terminate the contract, the application of Article 82 would mean that the seller would not be able to exercise its right to avoid whenever the goods had deteriorated or were lost. The application of Article 82 would thus 'punish' the seller although it is not the seller who is in breach of contract but rather the buyer. In order to avoid such an unreasonable result, Article 82 should be limited to the case where it is the buyer who declares avoidance.

In case of consensual avoidance, the application of Article 82 CISG should depend on the reasons for which the contract was mutually terminated, that is, it only should apply if it was the seller who gave reason to the mutual termination.

Article 83 CISG

Q 83-1

Which general rule of the Convention's remedies concept is affirmed in Article 83 CISG?

Article 83 CISG affirms the general rule that the various remedies available under the CISG exist independently from each other.

Q 83-2

Why will remedies other than damages and reduction of the purchase price be of only limited relevance in connection with Article 83 CISG?

Requiring repair will often not make sense: if the buyer was entitled to declare the contract avoided and is then barred from doing so because of Article 82(1), a remedy by repair will generally be 'unreasonable' within the meaning of Article 46(3) CISG. Also, the right of performance (Art 46(1)) will usually not be available because, in order for Articles 82 and 83 to apply, the buyer has already received the goods. The right to claim substitute delivery will not be available either because Article 82 bars not only the right to avoid but also the right of substitute delivery.

Article 84 CISG

Q 84-1

What is the idea underlying Article 84 CISG?

Article 84 aims at the equalisation of benefits subsequent upon the avoidance of the contract.

Q 84-2

What is the relationship between Articles 84(1) and 78 CISG?

Article 84(1) CISG absorbs the rule stated in Article 78 CISG that interest must be paid on unpaid sums. However, the purpose of the two provisions is different: Article 84(1) is of a restitutionary nature (see Q 84-1), whereas Article 78 aims to compensate for delayed payment. The distinction has an impact on the calculation of the interest rate (see Q 84-3).

Q 84-3

What are the solutions adopted in case law concerning the determination of the applicable interest rate? Which solution is the most convincing?

In C 84-2, the view was adopted that the interest rate should be determined in application of domestic law. In C 84-3, the court applied the interest rate at the seller's place of business 'as the interest yielding investment of the money occurs there'. Other approaches suggest the application of the interest rate at the buyer's place of business or the application of the interest rate of the state whose currency has been agreed on in the contract. Considering that Article 84(1) CISG is based on the idea that the seller must account for the benefits it has derived from receipt and use of the purchase price, it seems that a general principle can be formulated according to which the interest rate at the seller's place of business should be applied, because the seller's opportunity to use the money for which it might otherwise have had to take out a loan existed at its place of business. It therefore seems that the interest rate can be determined from within the Convention and that there is no need to resort to domestic law.

Q 84-4

Will the buyer be entitled to claim compensation of expenses that led to an increase in value of the goods? On which provision of the CISG could such a right be based? Consider, in particular, the situation:

— *where the expenses were necessary to preserve the value of the goods,*
— *where the buyer incurred expenses which now turn out to have been in vain (such as installation of goods, instruction and training costs for the personnel),*
— *where the goods were sold and the buyer had expenses for advertising, transport, personnel and similar costs.*

The question must be solved with a view to the purpose of Article 84(2): the parties should be reinstated in the economic status in which they were before the exchange of performances. Thus, expenditures necessary to preserve the goods should be compensated. The expenditures in the third scenario should, as a rule, also be compensated; otherwise, the seller would not only be reinstated in its original economic position but it would even benefit from the failed contract at the expense of the buyer. Finally, the loss in the second case should also be compensated, as those costs arose specifically in connection with the failed transaction.

Article 85 CISG

Q 85-1

(a) What is the function of Articles 85 to 88 CISG?
(b) Which party do they address?
(c) Which general rule is reflected in Article 85 CISG?

(a) To prevent a deterioration of the goods until the legal situation has been clarified.
(b) Article 85 CISG specifically addresses the seller; Article 86 specifically addresses the buyer; Articles 87 and 88 address both seller and buyer.
(c) In the situations in which Article 85 CISG applies, the risk has already passed to the buyer. Thus, the seller could be tempted to let the goods decay. This is exactly what Article 85 prohibits.

Q 85-2

What are the consequences if the seller who is bound to preserve the goods does not comply with its duty?

The seller may not claim damages for the deterioration of the goods, although the risk will usually have passed to the buyer.

The buyer will be entitled to damages according to Articles 45, 61, 74 *et seq* CISG. However, those damages might often be reduced in accordance with Article 77 CISG, because the buyer, by not taking delivery, will be also liable for the deterioration of the goods.

Q 85-3

Who bears the preservation costs under Article 85 CISG if the buyer's refusal to take delivery is justified?

In such a case, it is the seller who bears the preservation costs.

Q 85-4

Does Article 85 CISG apply in the following situations where:

(a) the seller has tendered conforming goods of which the buyer does not take delivery;

(a) Yes.

(b) the buyer unequivocally refuses to take delivery of the goods because of their glaring non-conformity with the contract;

(b) Yes.

(c) the seller has tendered properly and the buyer is willing to take delivery of the goods but unjustifiably refuses to pay the purchase price;

(c) Yes.

(d) the seller avoids the contract because of an anticipatory breach on behalf of the buyer;

(d) No, the seller is no longer under a duty to preserve the goods for the buyer (the risk has never passed to the buyer).

(e) the seller has tendered and the buyer takes delivery of only part of the goods, because there is allegedly no larger storage room available.

(e) Yes, for that part that has not been taken over.

Q 85-5

Under Article 85 CISG, does it matter who the owner of the goods is?

No, the only relevant question is whether the risk has passed to the buyer.

Q 85-6

Which factors set the benchmark for the adequacy of measures that the seller must take in order to preserve the goods?

The test is whether the measures are reasonable. The question should be solved with reference to objective standards and take into account all the concrete circumstances of the case as well as the interest of the buyer. However, the fact that the seller would have done otherwise in its own affairs should in general not be relevant.

Q 85-7

Could the seller base its claim for compensation for preservation and storage costs on Article 74 rather than Article 85, sentence 2 CISG? Would it make a difference? See, in particular, Article 79 CISG.

The seller could base its claim for compensation for preservation and storage costs on Article 74 rather than on Article 85, but then, Article 79 CISG would apply. That is, the buyer would be exempt from paying for the preservation and storage costs in cases of *force majeure*. Article 85 CISG has the purpose of 'objectifying' the compensation for preservation and storage costs, which corresponds to the buyer's bearing of the risk at that time.

Q 85-8

(a) The majority holds that the seller's right to retention under Article 85, sentence 2 CISG should extinguish where the buyer provides reasonable security. What other provisions of the CISG allow for the issuance of adequate assurance in order to prevent the seller from taking steps which will burden the buyer?

(a) Articles 71(3) and 72 (2) CISG expressly provide for the possibility of the debtor to furnish adequate assurance.

Article 86 CISG

Q 86-1

(a) Which criterion is decisive in determining whether a situation falls within Article 86(1) or within Article 86(2) CISG?
(b) Where the buyer unjustifiably rejects the goods, Article 86 CISG does not apply. Will the buyer still have to take steps to preserve the goods?

(a) If the buyer is already in possession of the goods, Article 86(1) CISG applies, otherwise Article 86(2) CISG applies.

(b)   In such a case, the Convention does not require the buyer to preserve the goods. However, as the buyer bears the risk of deterioration of the goods (*cf* Arts 67–69 CISG), it will take such steps in its own interest.

Q 86-2

Should the buyer be obliged to take possession of the goods and resell them if this would cause considerable inconvenience but the goods are subject to rapid deterioration? Discuss.

The question is controversial. In our view, the buyer should, in general, not be obliged to take possession and resell the goods, as this would unreasonably burden the buyer who then suffers not only 'considerable inconvenience' but also the risk inherent to the resale.

Q 86-3

Under Article 86(2) CISG, the buyer must only take possession of the goods on behalf of the seller if, among other things, it can do so without having to pay the purchase price. Do you think that it should be obliged to take possession of the goods where he has paid the price in advance?

Yes. Article 86(2) aims at avoiding further financial risk for the buyer. The question of whether it takes possession of the goods or not does not increase its risk, as the insecurity of return payment has been created beforehand, at the moment the buyer made the advance payment.

Article 87 CISG

Q 87-1

What are the consequences if the goods are not deposited in a warehouse?

There is no obligation to store the goods in a warehouse; a party who is bound to preserve the goods can do so by any means. Storage in a warehouse is just an option.

Q 87-2

Article 87 CISG does not mention any obligation to notify the other party of the intention to deposit the goods in a warehouse or of the fact that the goods have been stored there. Having regard to the general principles of the Convention, do you think that such notification is necessary? If so, what should the consequences be if no such notification has been given?

The storage of the goods by a party according to Article 87 CISG causes expenses that the other party will have to bear. Several provisions can be found in the CISG which require that, if one of the parties envisages taking steps that will deteriorate the other party's position, the first party must notify the other party of its intention, see, for example, Articles 71(3), 72(2). Furthermore, Article 77 provides for a duty to mitigate damages. Thus, it seems reasonable to argue that the other party should, in principle, be informed of the fact that the goods are stored in a warehouse in order to be able to react and minimise the costs. A failure to give notice should have the consequences provided for in Article 77, that is, the party depositing the goods in a warehouse might be refused full compensation of the storage costs.

Q 87-3

Can you think of a situation where, with a view to Articles 77, 85 and 86(1) CISG, the party that is bound to preserve the goods ought to deposit them in a warehouse?

The question is relevant where the party that is bound to preserve the goods is not able to reasonably preserve the goods itself. In such a case, not storing them in a warehouse will lead to a reduction of a possible damages claim (see Art 77 CISG).

Q 87-4

(a) Which law defines the relationship between the party that is obliged to preserve the goods and the owner of the storage facility?

(b) Does the CISG provide for any direct claims between the other party and the owner of the storage facility?

(a)   Domestic law applies.

(b)   No. The parties to the sales contract could agree on such a possibility in their contract. In order to be effective, such a direct claim ought to also be provided for in the contract between the depositing party and the depositary.

Q 87-5

What should be the legal consequences of unreasonably high storage costs? The wording of Article 87 CISG seems to suggest that the reasonableness of the storage costs is a precondition of the right to deposit the goods. But can the requirement that the storage costs be 'reasonable' also be understood in another way?

A party can always store the goods in a warehouse in order to preserve them without committing a breach of contract. Unreasonable costs would only have an impact on the claim for reimbursement: the party who stores the goods at unreasonable costs could not claim the whole storage costs; rather, its claim would be reduced to the amount that would have been reasonable with regard to the circumstances of the case.

Article 88 CISG

Q 88-1

(a) Distinguish Article 88(1) from Article 88(2) CISG.
(b) Compare Article 88 CISG with Sections 2-603(1) and 2-604 UCC. Does the UCC make the same distinction as paragraphs 1 and 2 of Article 88 CISG?

(a) Article 88(1) CISG embodies the right of the party that is bound to preserve the goods to resell them, whereas Article 88(2) CISG states the duty to resell the goods if those goods are subject to rapid deterioration or cause unreasonable costs of preservation.

(b) The distinction is slightly different: Section 2-603(1) UCC imposes the duty to sell the goods if they are perishable or threaten to decline in value speedily, whereas Article 88(2) CISG imposes the same duty in case of rapid deterioration or unreasonable costs of preservation. Unlike the UCC, which expressly requires a resale where the economic value of the goods may decline rapidly, the CISG does not require a resale in that case, and depreciation in the value of the goods is not included in the term 'deterioration' either.

Q 88-2

(a) Which factors are relevant in determining whether a resale was made by appropriate means? Are there any particular formalities to be observed?
(b) Which criteria guided the court in C 88-1 in holding that the resale was appropriate? Can a general rule be formulated?
(c) What are the consequences of a resale that was not made by appropriate means?

(a) The most important element is the reasonability of the resale price, which will depend on the circumstances. Even a very low resale price may be reasonable if the party reselling the goods can show that it made sufficient effort to obtain a reasonable price.
No particular formalities or special procedures must be observed.

(b) The behaviour of the buyer, who was obviously unwilling to take over the goods; the efforts undertaken by the seller to resell the goods; the difficulty in reselling goods that were specifically tailored to the buyer. Thus, a 'scrap' price was admissible.
As a general rule, it can be stated that, if the goods were catered to the specific needs of the buyer, the seller can resell them at a substantially lower price, as long as it is able to show that it made reasonable efforts to obtain the best price in the circumstances.

(c) It results in a liability for damages which could have been avoided, but the effectiveness of the resale as such is not affected.

Q 88-3

(a) When will the notice required by Article 88(1) CISG become effective? See also Article 27 CISG.

(b)   What are the legal consequences if no such notice is given?
(c)   Is it possible that, in exceptional cases, the fact that no notice was given will not harm the party who undertook the self-help sale? See C 88-1.

(a)   The notice is effective upon dispatch.
(b)   It results in a liability for damages which could have been avoided, but the effectiveness of the resale as such is not affected.
(c)   The purpose of the notice is to give the other party an opportunity to take measures to prevent the resale. Thus, failure to give notice does not trigger the consequences described in C 88-1 where the other party never answered previous communications and demonstrated by its conduct that it would not take delivery of the goods at all.

Q 88-4

What are the legal consequences if goods subject to rapid deterioration are not resold? See C 88-2.

The loss due to the deterioration of the goods cannot be imposed on the other party. In C 88-2, the seller who did not try hard enough to resell the goods could not claim the full damages arising out of the buyer's breach of contract.

Q 88-5

It is virtually undisputed that a rapid decrease of the economic value of the goods does not constitute a 'rapid deterioration' within the meaning of Article 88(2) CISG.

(a)   Compare the situation under the Convention with Section 2-603(1) UCC. Are there any differences?
(b)   Is a rapid decline in market value completely irrelevant under Article 88(2) CISG? Consider, in particular, the criterion of 'unreasonable preservation expenses' mentioned in Article 88(2) CISG.

(a)   Yes, see above Q 88-1(b).
(b)   A rapid decline in market value may lead to the preservation expenses for such goods becoming unreasonably high. Where the market price of the goods is worth less than the costs of preservation, an emergency sale of the goods within the meaning of Article 88(2) must be undertaken.

Q 88-6

What criteria are taken into account by courts when deciding whether the preservation costs are 'unreasonably high'?

The costs of storage and preservation are compared to the value of the goods. Where the costs exceed the value of the goods, a preservation of the goods is unreasonable. Their preservation is also unreasonable if the costs are higher than the difference between the original purchase price and the price obtainable in a resale.

Appendix

Text of the CISG

UNITED NATIONS CONVENTION ON CONTRACTS FOR THE INTERNATIONAL SALE OF GOODS (1980)

Preamble

THE STATES PARTIES TO THIS CONVENTION,

BEARING IN MIND the broad objectives in the resolutions adopted by the sixth special session of the General Assembly of the United Nations on the establishment of a New International Economic Order,

CONSIDERING that the development of international trade on the basis of equality and mutual benefit is an important element in promoting friendly relations among States,

BEING OF THE OPINION that the adoption of uniform rules which govern contracts for the international sale of goods and take into account the different social, economic and legal systems would contribute to the removal of legal barriers in international trade and promote the development of international trade,

HAVE DECREED as follows:

Part I

Sphere of Application and General Provisions

Chapter I

Sphere of Application

ARTICLE 1

(1) This Convention applies to contracts of sale of goods between parties whose places of business are in different States:
   (a) when the States are Contracting States; or

    (b) when the rules of private international law lead to the application of the law of a Contracting State.

(2) The fact that the parties have their places of business in different States is to be disregarded whenever this fact does not appear either from the contract or from any dealings between, or from information disclosed by, the parties at any time before or at the conclusion of the contract.

(3) Neither the nationality of the parties nor the civil or commercial character of the parties or of the contract is to be taken into consideration in determining the application of this Convention.

ARTICLE 2

This Convention does not apply to sales:

    (a) of goods bought for personal, family or household use, unless the seller, at any time before or at the conclusion of the contract, neither knew nor ought to have known that the goods were bought for any such use;

    (b) by auction;

    (c) on execution or otherwise by authority of law;

    (d) of stocks, shares, investment securities, negotiable instruments or money;

    (e) of ships, vessels, hovercraft or aircraft;

    (f) of electricity.

ARTICLE 3

(1) Contracts for the supply of goods to be manufactured or produced are to be considered sales unless the party who orders the goods undertakes to supply a substantial part of the materials necessary for such manufacture or production.

(2) This Convention does not apply to contracts in which the preponderant part of the obligations of the party who furnishes the goods consists in the supply of labour or other services.

ARTICLE 4

This Convention governs only the formation of the contract of sale and the rights and obligations of the seller and the buyer arising from such a contract. In particular, except as otherwise expressly provided in this Convention, it is not concerned with:

    (a) the validity of the contract or of any of its provisions or of any usage;

    (b) the effect which the contract may have on the property in the goods sold.

ARTICLE 5

This Convention does not apply to the liability of the seller for death or personal injury caused by the goods to any person.

ARTICLE 6

The parties may exclude the application of this Convention or, subject to article 12, derogate from or vary the effect of any of its provisions.

Chapter II

General Provisions

ARTICLE 7

(1) In the interpretation of this Convention, regard is to be had to its international character and to the need to promote uniformity in its application and the observance of good faith in international trade.
(2) Questions concerning matters governed by this Convention which are not expressly settled in it are to be settled in conformity with the general principles on which it is based or, in the absence of such principles, in conformity with the law applicable by virtue of the rules of private international law.

ARTICLE 8

(1) For the purposes of this Convention statements made by and other conduct of a party are to be interpreted according to his intent where the other party knew or could not have been unaware what that intent was.
(2) If the preceding paragraph is not applicable, statements made by and other conduct of a party are to be interpreted according to the understanding that a reasonable person of the same kind as the other party would have had in the same circumstances.
(3) In determining the intent of a party or the understanding a reasonable person would have had, due consideration is to be given to all relevant circumstances of the case including the negotiations, any practices which the parties have established between themselves, usages and any subsequent conduct of the parties.

ARTICLE 9

(1) The parties are bound by any usage to which they have agreed and by any practices which they have established between themselves.
(2) The parties are considered, unless otherwise agreed, to have impliedly made applicable to their contract or its formation a usage of which the parties knew or ought to have known and which in international trade is widely known to, and regularly observed by, parties to contracts of the type involved in the particular trade concerned.

ARTICLE 10

For the purposes of this Convention:

(a) if a party has more than one place of business, the place of business is that which has the closest relationship to the contract and its performance, having regard to the circumstances known to or contemplated by the parties at any time before or at the conclusion of the contract;
(b) if a party does not have a place of business, reference is to be made to his habitual residence.

ARTICLE 11

A contract of sale need not be concluded in or evidenced by writing and is not subject to any other requirement as to form. It may be proved by any means, including witnesses.

ARTICLE 12

Any provision of article 11, article 29 or Part II of this Convention that allows a contract of sale or its modification or termination by agreement or any offer, acceptance or other indication of intention to be made in any form other than in writing does not apply where any party has his place of business in a Contracting State which has made a declaration under article 96 of this Convention. The parties may not derogate from or vary the effect of this article.

ARTICLE 13

For the purposes of this Convention 'writing' includes telegram and telex.

Part II

Formation of the Contract

ARTICLE 14

(1) A proposal for concluding a contract addressed to one or more specific persons constitutes an offer if it is sufficiently definite and indicates the intention of the offeror to be bound in case of acceptance. A proposal is sufficiently definite if it indicates the goods and expressly or implicitly fixes or makes provision for determining the quantity and the price.

(2) A proposal other than one addressed to one or more specific persons is to be considered merely as an invitation to make offers, unless the contrary is clearly indicated by the person making the proposal.

ARTICLE 15

(1) An offer becomes effective when it reaches the offeree.

(2) An offer, even if it is irrevocable, may be withdrawn if the withdrawal reaches the offeree before or at the same time as the offer.

ARTICLE 16

(1) Until a contract is concluded an offer may be revoked if the revocation reaches the offeree before he has dispatched an acceptance.

(2) However, an offer cannot be revoked:
   (a) if it indicates, whether by stating a fixed time for acceptance or otherwise, that it is irrevocable; or
   (b) if it was reasonable for the offeree to rely on the offer as being irrevocable and the offeree has acted in reliance on the offer.

ARTICLE 17

An offer, even if it is irrevocable, is terminated when a rejection reaches the offeror.

ARTICLE 18

(1) A statement made by or other conduct of the offeree indicating assent to an offer is an acceptance. Silence or inactivity does not in itself amount to acceptance.

(2) An acceptance of an offer becomes effective at the moment the indication of assent reaches the offeror. An acceptance is not effective if the indication of assent does not reach the offeror within the time he has fixed or, if no time is fixed, within a reasonable time, due account being taken of the circumstances of the transaction, including the rapidity of the means of communication employed by the offeror. An oral offer must be accepted immediately unless the circumstances indicate otherwise.

(3) However, if, by virtue of the offer or as a result of practices which the parties have established between themselves or of usage, the offeree may indicate assent by performing an act, such as one relating to the dispatch of the goods or payment of the price, without notice to the offeror, the acceptance is effective at the moment the act is performed, provided that the act is performed within the period of time laid down in the preceding paragraph.

ARTICLE 19

(1) A reply to an offer which purports to be an acceptance but contains additions, limitations or other modifications is a rejection of the offer and constitutes a counter-offer.

(2) However, a reply to an offer which purports to be an acceptance but contains additional or different terms which do not materially alter the terms of the offer constitutes an acceptance, unless the offeror, without undue delay, objects orally to the discrepancy or dispatches a notice to that effect. If he does not so object, the terms of the contract are the terms of the offer with the modifications contained in the acceptance.

(3) Additional or different terms relating, among other things, to the price, payment, quality and quantity of the goods, place and time of delivery, extent of one party's liability to the other or the settlement of disputes are considered to alter the terms of the offer materially.

ARTICLE 20

(1) A period of time for acceptance fixed by the offeror in a telegram or a letter begins to run from the moment the telegram is handed in for dispatch or from the date shown on the letter or, if no such date is shown, from the date shown on the envelope. A period of time for acceptance fixed by the offeror by telephone, telex or other means of instantaneous communication, begins to run from the moment that the offer reaches the offeree.

(2) Official holidays or non-business days occurring during the period for acceptance are included in calculating the period. However, if a notice of acceptance cannot be delivered at the address of the offeror on the last day of the period because that day falls on an official holiday or a non-business day at the place of business of the offeror, the period is extended until the first business day which follows.

ARTICLE 21

(1) A late acceptance is nevertheless effective as an acceptance if without delay the offeror orally so informs the offeree or dispatches a notice to that effect.

(2) If a letter or other writing containing a late acceptance shows that it has been sent in such circumstances that if its transmission had been normal it would have reached the offeror in due time, the late acceptance is effective as an acceptance unless, without delay, the offeror orally informs the offeree that he considers his offer as having lapsed or dispatches a notice to that effect.

ARTICLE 22

An acceptance may be withdrawn if the withdrawal reaches the offeror before or at the same time as the acceptance would have become effective.

ARTICLE 23

A contract is concluded at the moment when an acceptance of an offer becomes effective in accordance with the provisions of this Convention.

ARTICLE 24

For the purposes of this Part of the Convention, an offer, declaration of acceptance or any other indication of intention 'reaches' the addressee when it is made orally to him or delivered by any other means to him personally, to his place of business or mailing address or, if he does not have a place of business or mailing address, to his habitual residence.

Part III

Sale of Goods

Chapter I

General Provisions

ARTICLE 25

A breach of contract committed by one of the parties is fundamental if it results in such detriment to the other party as substantially to deprive him of what he is entitled to expect under the contract, unless the party in breach did not foresee and a reasonable person of the same kind in the same circumstances would not have foreseen such a result.

ARTICLE 26

A declaration of avoidance of the contract is effective only if made by notice to the other party.

ARTICLE 27

Unless otherwise expressly provided in this Part of the Convention, if any notice, request or other communication is given or made by a party in accordance with this Part and by means appropriate in the circumstances, a delay or error in the transmission of the communication or its failure to arrive does not deprive that party of the right to rely on the communication.

ARTICLE 28

If, in accordance with the provisions of this Convention, one party is entitled to require performance of any obligation by the other party, a court is not bound to enter a judgment for specific performance unless the court would do so under its own law in respect of similar contracts of sale not governed by this Convention.

ARTICLE 29

(1) A contract may be modified or terminated by the mere agreement of the parties.
(2) A contract in writing which contains a provision requiring any modification or termination by agreement to be in writing may not be otherwise modified or terminated by agreement.

However, a party may be precluded by his conduct from asserting such a provision to the extent that the other party has relied on that conduct.

Chapter II

Obligations of the Seller

ARTICLE 30

The seller must deliver the goods, hand over any documents relating to them and transfer the property in the goods, as required by the contract and this Convention.

Section I. Delivery of the goods and handing over of documents

ARTICLE 31

If the seller is not bound to deliver the goods at any other particular place, his obligation to deliver consists:

    (a)   if the contract of sale involves carriage of the goods—in handing the goods over to the first carrier for transmission to the buyer;

    (b)   if, in cases not within the preceding subparagraph, the contract relates to specific goods, or unidentified goods to be drawn from a specific stock or to be manufactured or produced, and at the time of the conclusion of the contract the parties knew that the goods were at, or were to be manufactured or produced at, a particular place—in placing the goods at the buyer's disposal at that place;

    (c)   in other cases—in placing the goods at the buyer's disposal at the place where the seller had his place of business at the time of the conclusion of the contract.

ARTICLE 32

(1)   If the seller, in accordance with the contract or this Convention, hands the goods over to a carrier and if the goods are not clearly identified to the contract by markings on the goods, by shipping documents or otherwise, the seller must give the buyer notice of the consignment specifying the goods.

(2)   If the seller is bound to arrange for carriage of the goods, he must make such contracts as are necessary for carriage to the place fixed by means of transportation appropriate in the circumstances and according to the usual terms for such transportation.

(3)   If the seller is not bound to effect insurance in respect of the carriage of the goods, he must, at the buyer's request, provide him with all available information necessary to enable him to effect such insurance.

ARTICLE 33

The seller must deliver the goods:

    (a)   if a date is fixed by or determinable from the contract, on that date;

    (b)   if a period of time is fixed by or determinable from the contract, at any time within that period unless circumstances indicate that the buyer is to choose a date; or

    (c)   in any other case, within a reasonable time after the conclusion of the contract.

ARTICLE 34

If the seller is bound to hand over documents relating to the goods, he must hand them over at the time and place and in the form required by the contract. If the seller has handed over documents before that time, he may, up to that time, cure any lack of conformity in the documents, if the exercise of this right does not cause the buyer unreasonable inconvenience or unreasonable expense. However, the buyer retains any right to claim damages as provided for in this Convention.

Section II. Conformity of the goods and third party claims

ARTICLE 35

(1)   The seller must deliver goods which are of the quantity, quality and description required by the contract and which are contained or packaged in the manner required by the contract.

(2)   Except where the parties have agreed otherwise, the goods do not conform with the contract unless they:
  (a)   are fit for the purposes for which goods of the same description would ordinarily be used;
  (b)   are fit for any particular purpose expressly or impliedly made known to the seller at the time of the conclusion of the contract, except where the circumstances show that the buyer did not rely, or that it was unreasonable for him to rely, on the seller's skill and judgement;
  (c)   possess the qualities of goods which the seller has held out to the buyer as a sample or model;
  (d)   are contained or packaged in the manner usual for such goods or, where there is no such manner, in a manner adequate to preserve and protect the goods.

(3)   The seller is not liable under subparagraphs (a) to (d) of the preceding paragraph for any lack of conformity of the goods if at the time of the conclusion of the contract the buyer knew or could not have been unaware of such lack of conformity.

ARTICLE 36

(1)   The seller is liable in accordance with the contract and this Convention for any lack of conformity which exists at the time when the risk passes to the buyer, even though the lack of conformity becomes apparent only after that time.

(2)   The seller is also liable for any lack of conformity which occurs after the time indicated in the preceding paragraph and which is due to a breach of any of his obligations, including a breach of any guarantee that for a period of time the goods will remain fit for their ordinary purpose or for some particular purpose or will retain specified qualities or characteristics.

ARTICLE 37

If the seller has delivered goods before the date for delivery, he may, up to that date, deliver any missing part or make up any deficiency in the quantity of the goods delivered, or deliver goods in replacement of any non-conforming goods delivered or remedy any lack of conformity in the goods delivered, provided that the exercise of this right does not cause the buyer unreasonable inconvenience or unreasonable expense. However, the buyer retains any right to claim damages as provided for in this Convention.

ARTICLE 38

(1) The buyer must examine the goods, or cause them to be examined, within as short a period as is practicable in the circumstances.
(2) If the contract involves carriage of the goods, examination may be deferred until after the goods have arrived at their destination.
(3) If the goods are redirected in transit or redispatched by the buyer without a reasonable opportunity for examination by him and at the time of the conclusion of the contract the seller knew or ought to have known of the possibility of such redirection or redispatch, examination may be deferred until after the goods have arrived at the new destination.

ARTICLE 39

(1) The buyer loses the right to rely on a lack of conformity of the goods if he does not give notice to the seller specifying the nature of the lack of conformity within a reasonable time after he has discovered it or ought to have discovered it.
(2) In any event, the buyer loses the right to rely on a lack of conformity of the goods if he does not give the seller notice thereof at the latest within a period of two years from the date on which the goods were actually handed over to the buyer, unless this time-limit is inconsistent with a contractual period of guarantee.

ARTICLE 40

The seller is not entitled to rely on the provisions of articles 38 and 39 if the lack of conformity relates to facts of which he knew or could not have been unaware and which he did not disclose to the buyer.

ARTICLE 41

The seller must deliver goods which are free from any right or claim of a third party, unless the buyer agreed to take the goods subject to that right or claim. However, if such right or claim is based on industrial property or other intellectual property, the seller's obligation is governed by article 42.

ARTICLE 42

(1) The seller must deliver goods which are free from any right or claim of a third party based on industrial property or other intellectual property, of which at the time of the conclusion of the contract the seller knew or could not have been unaware, provided that the right or claim is based on industrial property or other intellectual property:
(a) under the law of the State where the goods will be resold or otherwise used, if it was contemplated by the parties at the time of the conclusion of the contract that the goods would be resold or otherwise used in that State; or
(b) in any other case, under the law of the State where the buyer has his place of business.
(2) The obligation of the seller under the preceding paragraph does not extend to cases where:
(a) at the time of the conclusion of the contract the buyer knew or could not have been unaware of the right or claim; or
(b) the right or claim results from the seller's compliance with technical drawings, designs, formulae or other such specifications furnished by the buyer.

ARTICLE 43

(1)   The buyer loses the right to rely on the provisions of article 41 or article 42 if he does not give notice to the seller specifying the nature of the right or claim of the third party within a reasonable time after he has become aware or ought to have become aware of the right or claim.

(2)   The seller is not entitled to rely on the provisions of the preceding paragraph if he knew of the right or claim of the third party and the nature of it.

ARTICLE 44

Notwithstanding the provisions of paragraph (1) of article 39 and paragraph (1) of article 43, the buyer may reduce the price in accordance with article 50 or claim damages, except for loss of profit, if he has a reasonable excuse for his failure to give the required notice.

Section III. Remedies for breach of contract by the seller

ARTICLE 45

(1)   If the seller fails to perform any of his obligations under the contract or this Convention, the buyer may:

    (a)   exercise the rights provided in articles 46 to 52;

    (b)   claim damages as provided in articles 74 to 77.

(2)   The buyer is not deprived of any right he may have to claim damages by exercising his right to other remedies.

(3)   No period of grace may be granted to the seller by a court or arbitral tribunal when the buyer resorts to a remedy for breach of contract.

ARTICLE 46

(1)   The buyer may require performance by the seller of his obligations unless the buyer has resorted to a remedy which is inconsistent with this requirement.

(2)   If the goods do not conform with the contract, the buyer may require delivery of substitute goods only if the lack of conformity constitutes a fundamental breach of contract and a request for substitute goods is made either in conjunction with notice given under article 39 or within a reasonable time thereafter.

(3)   If the goods do not conform with the contract, the buyer may require the seller to remedy the lack of conformity by repair, unless this is unreasonable having regard to all the circumstances. A request for repair must be made either in conjunction with notice given under article 39 or within a reasonable time thereafter.

ARTICLE 47

(1)   The buyer may fix an additional period of time of reasonable length for performance by the seller of his obligations.

(2)   Unless the buyer has received notice from the seller that he will not perform within the period so fixed, the buyer may not, during that period, resort to any remedy for breach of contract. However, the buyer is not deprived thereby of any right he may have to claim damages for delay in performance.

ARTICLE 48

(1)   Subject to article 49, the seller may, even after the date for delivery, remedy at his own expense any failure to perform his obligations, if he can do so without unreasonable

delay and without causing the buyer unreasonable inconvenience or uncertainty of reimbursement by the seller of expenses advanced by the buyer. However, the buyer retains any right to claim damages as provided for in this Convention.

(2) If the seller requests the buyer to make known whether he will accept performance and the buyer does not comply with the request within a reasonable time, the seller may perform within the time indicated in his request. The buyer may not, during that period of time, resort to any remedy which is inconsistent with performance by the seller.

(3) A notice by the seller that he will perform within a specified period of time is assumed to include a request, under the preceding paragraph, that the buyer make known his decision.

(4) A request or notice by the seller under paragraph (2) or (3) of this article is not effective unless received by the buyer.

ARTICLE 49

(1) The buyer may declare the contract avoided:
(a) if the failure by the seller to perform any of his obligations under the contract or this Convention amounts to a fundamental breach of contract; or
(b) in case of non-delivery, if the seller does not deliver the goods within the additional period of time fixed by the buyer in accordance with paragraph (1) of article 47 or declares that he will not deliver within the period so fixed.

(2) However, in cases where the seller has delivered the goods, the buyer loses the right to declare the contract avoided unless he does so:
(a) in respect of late delivery, within a reasonable time after he has become aware that delivery has been made;
(b) in respect of any breach other than late delivery, within a reasonable time:
(i)   after he knew or ought to have known of the breach;
(ii) after the expiration of any additional period of time fixed by the buyer in accordance with paragraph (1) of article 47, or after the seller has declared that he will not perform his obligations within such an additional period; or
(iii) after the expiration of any additional period of time indicated by the seller in accordance with paragraph (2) of article 48, or after the buyer has declared that he will not accept performance.

ARTICLE 50

If the goods do not conform with the contract and whether or not the price has already been paid, the buyer may reduce the price in the same proportion as the value that the goods actually delivered had at the time of the delivery bears to the value that conforming goods would have had at that time. However, if the seller remedies any failure to perform his obligations in accordance with article 37 or article 48 or if the buyer refuses to accept performance by the seller in accordance with those articles, the buyer may not reduce the price.

ARTICLE 51

(1) If the seller delivers only a part of the goods or if only a part of the goods delivered is in conformity with the contract, articles 46 to 50 apply in respect of the part which is missing or which does not conform.

(2) The buyer may declare the contract avoided in its entirety only if the failure to make delivery completely or in conformity with the contract amounts to a fundamental breach of the contract.

ARTICLE 52

(1) If the seller delivers the goods before the date fixed, the buyer may take delivery or refuse to take delivery.
(2) If the seller delivers a quantity of goods greater than that provided for in the contract, the buyer may take delivery or refuse to take delivery of the excess quantity. If the buyer takes delivery of all or part of the excess quantity, he must pay for it at the contract rate.

Chapter III

Obligations of the Buyer

ARTICLE 53

The buyer must pay the price for the goods and take delivery of them as required by the contract and this Convention.

Section I. Payment of the price

ARTICLE 54

The buyer's obligation to pay the price includes taking such steps and complying with such formalities as may be required under the contract or any laws and regulations to enable payment to be made.

ARTICLE 55

Where a contract has been validly concluded but does not expressly or implicitly fix or make provision for determining the price, the parties are considered, in the absence of any indication to the contrary, to have impliedly made reference to the price generally charged at the time of the conclusion of the contract for such goods sold under comparable circumstances in the trade concerned.

ARTICLE 56

If the price is fixed according to the weight of the goods, in case of doubt it is to be determined by the net weight.

ARTICLE 57

(1) If the buyer is not bound to pay the price at any other particular place, he must pay it to the seller:
   (a) at the seller's place of business; or
   (b) if the payment is to be made against the handing over of the goods or of documents, at the place where the handing over takes place.
(2) The seller must bear any increases in the expenses incidental to payment which is caused by a change in his place of business subsequent to the conclusion of the contract.

ARTICLE 58

(1) If the buyer is not bound to pay the price at any other specific time, he must pay it when the seller places either the goods or documents controlling their disposition at the buyer's disposal in accordance with the contract and this Convention. The seller may make such payment a condition for handing over the goods or documents.

(2) If the contract involves carriage of the goods, the seller may dispatch the goods on terms whereby the goods, or documents controlling their disposition, will not be handed over to the buyer except against payment of the price.

(3) The buyer is not bound to pay the price until he has had an opportunity to examine the goods, unless the procedures for delivery or payment agreed upon by the parties are inconsistent with his having such an opportunity.

ARTICLE 59

The buyer must pay the price on the date fixed by or determinable from the contract and this Convention without the need for any request or compliance with any formality on the part of the seller.

Section II. Taking delivery

ARTICLE 60

The buyer's obligation to take delivery consists:
   (a) in doing all the acts which could reasonably be expected of him in order to enable the seller to make delivery; and
   (b) in taking over the goods.

Section III. Remedies for breach of contract by the buyer

ARTICLE 61

(1) If the buyer fails to perform any of his obligations under the contract or this Convention, the seller may:
   (a) exercise the rights provided in articles 62 to 65;
   (b) claim damages as provided in articles 74 to 77.

(2) The seller is not deprived of any right he may have to claim damages by exercising his right to other remedies.

(3) No period of grace may be granted to the buyer by a court or arbitral tribunal when the seller resorts to a remedy for breach of contract.

ARTICLE 62

The seller may require the buyer to pay the price, take delivery or perform his other obligations, unless the seller has resorted to a remedy which is inconsistent with this requirement.

ARTICLE 63

(1) The seller may fix an additional period of time of reasonable length for performance by the buyer of his obligations.

(2) Unless the seller has received notice from the buyer that he will not perform within the period so fixed, the seller may not, during that period, resort to any remedy for breach of contract. However, the seller is not deprived thereby of any right he may have to claim damages for delay in performance.

ARTICLE 64

(1) The seller may declare the contract avoided:
   (a) if the failure by the buyer to perform any of his obligations under the contract or this Convention amounts to a fundamental breach of contract; or

(b) if the buyer does not, within the additional period of time fixed by the seller in accordance with paragraph (1) of article 63, perform his obligation to pay the price or take delivery of the goods, or if he declares that he will not do so within the period so fixed.

(2) However, in cases where the buyer has paid the price, the seller loses the right to declare the contract avoided unless he does so:

(a) in respect of late performance by the buyer, before the seller has become aware that performance has been rendered; or

(b) in respect of any breach other than late performance by the buyer, within a reasonable time:

(i) after the seller knew or ought to have known of the breach; or

(ii) after the expiration of any additional period of time fixed by the seller in accordance with paragraph (1) of article 63, or after the buyer has declared that he will not perform his obligations within such an additional period.

ARTICLE 65

(1) If under the contract the buyer is to specify the form, measurement or other features of the goods and he fails to make such specification either on the date agreed upon or within a reasonable time after receipt of a request from the seller, the seller may, without prejudice to any other rights he may have, make the specification himself in accordance with the requirements of the buyer that may be known to him.

(2) If the seller makes the specification himself, he must inform the buyer of the details thereof and must fix a reasonable time within which the buyer may make a different specification. If, after receipt of such a communication, the buyer fails to do so within the time so fixed, the specification made by the seller is binding.

Chapter IV

Passing of Risk

ARTICLE 66

Loss of or damage to the goods after the risk has passed to the buyer does not discharge him from his obligation to pay the price, unless the loss or damage is due to an act or omission of the seller.

ARTICLE 67

(1) If the contract of sale involves carriage of the goods and the seller is not bound to hand them over at a particular place, the risk passes to the buyer when the goods are handed over to the first carrier for transmission to the buyer in accordance with the contract of sale. If the seller is bound to hand the goods over to a carrier at a particular place, the risk does not pass to the buyer until the goods are handed over to the carrier at that place. The fact that the seller is authorized to retain documents controlling the disposition of the goods does not affect the passage of the risk.

(2) Nevertheless, the risk does not pass to the buyer until the goods are clearly identified to the contract, whether by markings on the goods, by shipping documents, by notice given to the buyer or otherwise.

ARTICLE 68

The risk in respect of goods sold in transit passes to the buyer from the time of the conclusion of the contract. However, if the circumstances so indicate, the risk is assumed by the buyer from the time the goods were handed over to the carrier who issued the documents embodying the contract of carriage. Nevertheless, if at the time of the conclusion of the contract of sale the seller knew or ought to have known that the goods had been lost or damaged and did not disclose this to the buyer, the loss or damage is at the risk of the seller.

ARTICLE 69

(1)   In cases not within articles 67 and 68, the risk passes to the buyer when he takes over the goods or, if he does not do so in due time, from the time when the goods are placed at his disposal and he commits a breach of contract by failing to take delivery.

(2)   However, if the buyer is bound to take over the goods at a place other than a place of business of the seller, the risk passes when delivery is due and the buyer is aware of the fact that the goods are placed at his disposal at that place.

(3)   If the contract relates to goods not then identified, the goods are considered not to be placed at the disposal of the buyer until they are clearly identified to the contract.

ARTICLE 70

If the seller has committed a fundamental breach of contract, articles 67, 68 and 69 do not impair the remedies available to the buyer on account of the breach.

Chapter V

Provisions Common to the Obligations of the Seller and of the Buyer

Section I. Anticipatory breach and instalment contracts

ARTICLE 71

(1)   A party may suspend the performance of his obligations if, after the conclusion of the contract, it becomes apparent that the other party will not perform a substantial part of his obligations as a result of:
   (a)   a serious deficiency in his ability to perform or in his creditworthiness; or
   (b)   his conduct in preparing to perform or in performing the contract.

(2)   If the seller has already dispatched the goods before the grounds described in the preceding paragraph become evident, he may prevent the handing over of the goods to the buyer even though the buyer holds a document which entitles him to obtain them. The present paragraph relates only to the rights in the goods as between the buyer and the seller.

(3)   A party suspending performance, whether before or after dispatch of the goods, must immediately give notice of the suspension to the other party and must continue with performance if the other party provides adequate assurance of his performance.

ARTICLE 72

(1)   If prior to the date for performance of the contract it is clear that one of the parties will commit a fundamental breach of contract, the other party may declare the contract avoided.

(2) If time allows, the party intending to declare the contract avoided must give reasonable notice to the other party in order to permit him to provide adequate assurance of his performance.
(3) The requirements of the preceding paragraph do not apply if the other party has declared that he will not perform his obligations.

ARTICLE 73

(1) In the case of a contract for delivery of goods by instalments, if the failure of one party to perform any of his obligations in respect of any instalment constitutes a fundamental breach of contract with respect to that instalment, the other party may declare the contract avoided with respect to that instalment.
(2) If one party's failure to perform any of his obligations in respect of any instalment gives the other party good grounds to conclude that a fundamental breach of contract will occur with respect to future instalments, he may declare the contract avoided for the future, provided that he does so within a reasonable time.
(3) A buyer who declares the contract avoided in respect of any delivery may, at the same time, declare it avoided in respect of deliveries already made or of future deliveries if, by reason of their interdependence, those deliveries could not be used for the purpose contemplated by the parties at the time of the conclusion of the contract.

Section II. Damages

ARTICLE 74

Damages for breach of contract by one party consist of a sum equal to the loss, including loss of profit, suffered by the other party as a consequence of the breach. Such damages may not exceed the loss which the party in breach foresaw or ought to have foreseen at the time of the conclusion of the contract, in the light of the facts and matters of which he then knew or ought to have known, as a possible consequence of the breach of contract.

ARTICLE 75

If the contract is avoided and if, in a reasonable manner and within a reasonable time after avoidance, the buyer has bought goods in replacement or the seller has resold the goods, the party claiming damages may recover the difference between the contract price and the price in the substitute transaction as well as any further damages recoverable under article 74.

ARTICLE 76

(1) If the contract is avoided and there is a current price for the goods, the party claiming damages may, if he has not made a purchase or resale under article 75, recover the difference between the price fixed by the contract and the current price at the time of avoidance as well as any further damages recoverable under article 74. If, however, the party claiming damages has avoided the contract after taking over the goods, the current price at the time of such taking over shall be applied instead of the current price at the time of avoidance.
(2) For the purposes of the preceding paragraph, the current price is the price prevailing at the place where delivery of the goods should have been made or, if there is no current price at that place, the price at such other place as serves as a reasonable substitute, making due allowance for differences in the cost of transporting the goods.

ARTICLE 77

A party who relies on a breach of contract must take such measures as are reasonable in the circumstances to mitigate the loss, including loss of profit, resulting from the breach. If he fails to take such measures, the party in breach may claim a reduction in the damages in the amount by which the loss should have been mitigated.

Section III. Interest

ARTICLE 78

If a party fails to pay the price or any other sum that is in arrears, the other party is entitled to interest on it, without prejudice to any claim for damages recoverable under article 74.

Section IV. Exemptions

ARTICLE 79

(1) A party is not liable for a failure to perform any of his obligations if he proves that the failure was due to an impediment beyond his control and that he could not reasonably be expected to have taken the impediment into account at the time of the conclusion of the contract or to have avoided or overcome it or its consequences.

(2) If the party's failure is due to the failure by a third person whom he has engaged to perform the whole or a part of the contract, that party is exempt from liability only if:

    (a)   he is exempt under the preceding paragraph; and

    (b)   the person whom he has so engaged would be so exempt if the provisions of that paragraph were applied to him.

(3) The exemption provided by this article has effect for the period during which the impediment exists.

(4) The party who fails to perform must give notice to the other party of the impediment and its effect on his ability to perform. If the notice is not received by the other party within a reasonable time after the party who fails to perform knew or ought to have known of the impediment, he is liable for damages resulting from such non-receipt.

(5) Nothing in this article prevents either party from exercising any right other than to claim damages under this Convention.

ARTICLE 80

A party may not rely on a failure of the other party to perform, to the extent that such failure was caused by the first party's act or omission.

Section V. Effects of avoidance

ARTICLE 81

(1) Avoidance of the contract releases both parties from their obligations under it, subject to any damages which may be due. Avoidance does not affect any provision of the contract for the settlement of disputes or any other provision of the contract governing the rights and obligations of the parties consequent upon the avoidance of the contract.

(2)   A party who has performed the contract either wholly or in part may claim restitution from the other party of whatever the first party has supplied or paid under the contract. If both parties are bound to make restitution, they must do so concurrently.

ARTICLE 82

(1)   The buyer loses the right to declare the contract avoided or to require the seller to deliver substitute goods if it is impossible for him to make restitution of the goods substantially in the condition in which he received them.
(2)   The preceding paragraph does not apply:
   (a)   if the impossibility of making restitution of the goods or of making restitution of the goods substantially in the condition in which the buyer received them is not due to his act or omission;
   (b)   if the goods or part of the goods have perished or deteriorated as a result of the examination provided for in article 38; or
   (c)   if the goods or part of the goods have been sold in the normal course of business or have been consumed or transformed by the buyer in the course of normal use before he discovered or ought to have discovered the lack of conformity.

ARTICLE 83

A buyer who has lost the right to declare the contract avoided or to require the seller to deliver substitute goods in accordance with article 82 retains all other remedies under the contract and this Convention.

ARTICLE 84

(1)   If the seller is bound to refund the price, he must also pay interest on it, from the date on which the price was paid.
(2)   The buyer must account to the seller for all benefits which he has derived from the goods or part of them:
   (a)   if he must make restitution of the goods or part of them; or
   (b)   if it is impossible for him to make restitution of all or part of the goods or to make restitution of all or part of the goods substantially in the condition in which he received them, but he has nevertheless declared the contract avoided or required the seller to deliver substitute goods.

Section VI. Preservation of the goods

ARTICLE 85

If the buyer is in delay in taking delivery of the goods or, where payment of the price and delivery of the goods are to be made concurrently, if he fails to pay the price, and the seller is either in possession of the goods or otherwise able to control their disposition, the seller must take such steps as are reasonable in the circumstances to preserve them. He is entitled to retain them until he has been reimbursed his reasonable expenses by the buyer.

ARTICLE 86

(1)   If the buyer has received the goods and intends to exercise any right under the contract or this Convention to reject them, he must take such steps to preserve them as are reasonable in the circumstances. He is entitled to retain them until he has been reimbursed his reasonable expenses by the seller.

(2) If goods dispatched to the buyer have been placed at his disposal at their destination and he exercises the right to reject them, he must take possession of them on behalf of the seller, provided that this can be done without payment of the price and without unreasonable inconvenience or unreasonable expense. This provision does not apply if the seller or a person authorized to take charge of the goods on his behalf is present at the destination. If the buyer takes possession of the goods under this paragraph, his rights and obligations are governed by the preceding paragraph.

ARTICLE 87

A party who is bound to take steps to preserve the goods may deposit them in a warehouse of a third person at the expense of the other party provided that the expense incurred is not unreasonable.

ARTICLE 88

(1) A party who is bound to preserve the goods in accordance with article 85 or 86 may sell them by any appropriate means if there has been an unreasonable delay by the other party in taking possession of the goods or in taking them back or in paying the price or the cost of preservation, provided that reasonable notice of the intention to sell has been given to the other party.

(2) If the goods are subject to rapid deterioration or their preservation would involve unreasonable expense, a party who is bound to preserve the goods in accordance with article 85 or 86 must take reasonable measures to sell them. To the extent possible he must give notice to the other party of his intention to sell.

(3) A party selling the goods has the right to retain out of the proceeds of sale an amount equal to the reasonable expenses of preserving the goods and of selling them. He must account to the other party for the balance.

Part IV

Final Provisions

ARTICLE 89

The Secretary-General of the United Nations is hereby designated as the depositary for this Convention.

ARTICLE 90

This Convention does not prevail over any international agreement which has already been or may be entered into and which contains provisions concerning the matters governed by this Convention, provided that the parties have their places of business in States parties to such agreement.

ARTICLE 91

(1) This Convention is open for signature at the concluding meeting of the United Nations Conference on Contracts for the International Sale of Goods and will remain open for signature by all States at the Headquarters of the United Nations, New York until 30 September 1981.

(2) This Convention is subject to ratification, acceptance or approval by the signatory States.

(3) This Convention is open for accession by all States which are not signatory States as from the date it is open for signature.
(4) Instruments of ratification, acceptance, approval and accession are to be deposited with the Secretary-General of the United Nations.

ARTICLE 92

(1) A Contracting State may declare at the time of signature, ratification, acceptance, approval or accession that it will not be bound by Part II of this Convention or that it will not be bound by Part III of this Convention.
(2) A Contracting State which makes a declaration in accordance with the preceding paragraph in respect of Part II or Part III of this Convention is not to be considered a Contracting State within paragraph (1) of article 1 of this Convention in respect of matters governed by the Part to which the declaration applies.

ARTICLE 93

(1) If a Contracting State has two or more territorial units in which, according to its constitution, different systems of law are applicable in relation to the matters dealt with in this Convention, it may, at the time of signature, ratification, acceptance, approval or accession, declare that this Convention is to extend to all its territorial units or only to one or more of them, and may amend its declaration by submitting another declaration at any time.
(2) These declarations are to be notified to the depositary and are to state expressly the territorial units to which the Convention extends.
(3) If, by virtue of a declaration under this article, this Convention extends to one or more but not all of the territorial units of a Contracting State, and if the place of business of a party is located in that State, this place of business, for the purposes of this Convention, is considered not to be in a Contracting State, unless it is in a territorial unit to which the Convention extends.
(4) If a Contracting State makes no declaration under paragraph (1) of this article, the Convention is to extend to all territorial units of that State.

ARTICLE 94

(1) Two or more Contracting States which have the same or closely related legal rules on matters governed by this Convention may at any time declare that the Convention is not to apply to contracts of sale or to their formation where the parties have their places of business in those States. Such declarations may be made jointly or by reciprocal unilateral declarations.
(2) A Contracting State which has the same or closely related legal rules on matters governed by this Convention as one or more non-Contracting States may at any time declare that the Convention is not to apply to contracts of sale or to their formation where the parties have their places of business in those States.
(3) If a State which is the object of a declaration under the preceding paragraph subsequently becomes a Contracting State, the declaration made will, as from the date on which the Convention enters into force in respect of the new Contracting State, have the effect of a declaration made under paragraph (1), provided that the new Contracting State joins in such declaration or makes a reciprocal unilateral declaration.

ARTICLE 95

Any State may declare at the time of the deposit of its instrument of ratification, acceptance, approval or accession that it will not be bound by subparagraph (1)(b) of article 1 of this Convention.

ARTICLE 96

A Contracting State whose legislation requires contracts of sale to be concluded in or evidenced by writing may at any time make a declaration in accordance with article 12 that any provision of article 11, article 29, or Part II of this Convention, that allows a contract of sale or its modification or termination by agreement or any offer, acceptance, or other indication of intention to be made in any form other than in writing, does not apply where any party has his place of business in that State.

ARTICLE 97

(1) Declarations made under this Convention at the time of signature are subject to confirmation upon ratification, acceptance or approval.

(2) Declarations and confirmations of declarations are to be in writing and be formally notified to the depositary.

(3) A declaration takes effect simultaneously with the entry into force of this Convention in respect of the State concerned. However, a declaration of which the depositary receives formal notification after such entry into force takes effect on the first day of the month following the expiration of six months after the date of its receipt by the depositary. Reciprocal unilateral declarations under article 94 take effect on the first day of the month following the expiration of six months after the receipt of the latest declaration by the depositary.

(4) Any State which makes a declaration under this Convention may withdraw it at any time by a formal notification in writing addressed to the depositary. Such withdrawal is to take effect on the first day of the month following the expiration of six months after the date of the receipt of the notification by the depositary.

(5) A withdrawal of a declaration made under article 94 renders inoperative, as from the date on which the withdrawal takes effect, any reciprocal declaration made by another State under that article.

ARTICLE 98

No reservations are permitted except those expressly authorized in this Convention.

ARTICLE 99

(1) This Convention enters into force, subject to the provisions of paragraph (6) of this article, on the first day of the month following the expiration of twelve months after the date of deposit of the tenth instrument of ratification, acceptance, approval or accession, including an instrument which contains a declaration made under article 92.

(2) When a State ratifies, accepts, approves or accedes to this Convention after the deposit of the tenth instrument of ratification, acceptance, approval or accession, this Convention, with the exception of the Part excluded, enters into force in respect of that State, subject to the provisions of paragraph (6) of this article, on the first day of the month following the expiration of twelve months after the date of the deposit of its instrument of ratification, acceptance, approval or accession.

(3) A State which ratifies, accepts, approves or accedes to this Convention and is a party to either or both the Convention relating to a Uniform Law on the Formation of Contracts for the International Sale of Goods done at The Hague on 1 July 1964 (1964 Hague Formation Convention) and the Convention relating to a Uniform Law on the International Sale of Goods done at The Hague on 1 July 1964 (1964 Hague Sales Convention) shall at the same time denounce, as the case may be, either or both the 1964

Hague Sales Convention and the 1964 Hague Formation Convention by notifying the Government of the Netherlands to that effect.

(4)   A State party to the 1964 Hague Sales Convention which ratifies, accepts, approves or accedes to the present Convention and declares or has declared under article 52 that it will not be bound by Part II of this Convention shall at the time of ratification, acceptance, approval or accession denounce the 1964 Hague Sales Convention by notifying the Government of the Netherlands to that effect.

(5)   A State party to the 1964 Hague Formation Convention which ratifies, accepts, approves or accedes to the present Convention and declares or has declared under article 92 that it will not be bound by Part III of this Convention shall at the time of ratification, acceptance, approval or accession denounce the 1964 Hague Formation Convention by notifying the Government of the Netherlands to that effect.

(6)   For the purpose of this article, ratifications, acceptances, approvals and accessions in respect of this Convention by States parties to the 1964 Hague Formation Convention or to the 1964 Hague Sales Convention shall not be effective until such denunciations as may be required on the part of those States in respect of the latter two Conventions have themselves become effective. The depositary of this Convention shall consult with the Government of the Netherlands, as the depositary of the 1964 Conventions, so as to ensure necessary co-ordination in this respect.

ARTICLE 100

(1)   This Convention applies to the formation of a contract only when the proposal for concluding the contract is made on or after the date when the Convention enters into force in respect of the Contracting States referred to in subparagraph (1)(a) or the Contracting State referred to in subparagraph (1)(b) of article 1.

(2)   This Convention applies only to contracts concluded on or after the date when the Convention enters into force in respect of the Contracting States referred to in subparagraph (1)(a) or the Contracting State referred to in subparagraph (1)(b) of article 1.

ARTICLE 101

(1)   A Contracting State may denounce this Convention, or Part II or Part III of the Convention, by a formal notification in writing addressed to the depositary.

(2)   The denunciation takes effect on the first day of the month following the expiration of twelve months after the notification is received by the depositary. Where a longer period for the denunciation to take effect is specified in the notification, the denunciation takes effect upon the expiration of such longer period after the notification is received by the depositary.

DONE at Vienna, this day of eleventh day of April, one thousand nine hundred and eighty, in a single original, of which the Arabic, Chinese, English, French, Russian and Spanish texts are equally authentic.

IN WITNESS WHEREOF the undersigned plenipotentiaries, being duly authorized by their respective Governments, have signed this Convention.